Economic Lives

Economic Lives

HOW CULTURE SHAPES THE ECONOMY

Viviana A. Zelizer

PRINCETON UNIVERSITY PRESS

PRINCETON & OXFORD

Copyright © 2011 by Princeton University Press
Published by Princeton University Press, 41 William Street, Princeton, New Jersey 08540
In the United Kingdom: Princeton University Press, 6 Oxford Street,
Woodstock, Oxfordshire OX20 1TW
press.princeton.edu

All Rights Reserved

Library of Congress Cataloging-in-Publication Data

Zelizer, Viviana A. Rotman.
Economic lives : how culture shapes the economy / Viviana A. Zelizer.
p. cm.
Includes index.
ISBN 978-0-691-13936-4 (cloth : alk. paper)
1. Economics—Sociological aspects.
2. Social values.   I. Title.
HM548.Z42 2011
306.3—dc22   2010006027

British Library Cataloging-in-Publication Data is available

This book has been composed in Adobe Garamond.
Printed on acid-free paper. ∞

Printed in the United States of America

1 3 5 7 9 10 8 6 4 2

For Edgardo and Leandro Rotman

MIS QUERIDOS HERMANOS

CONTENTS

What explains our everyday economic actions? How and why do we spend, misspend, save, invest, or gamble away our monies? Do women and men treat money differently? Why is it, for instance, that women are more likely to allocate the household's money to children, as compared to men's allocation of similar resources? What accounts for the fact that even among the most loving couples, partners often conceal or misrepresent their earnings or expenditures?

All of us regularly confront a whole range of such puzzling economic dilemmas. Many of them involve our most intimate ties: should we help our adult child with his or her finances, and if so, for how much and how long? How and for whom should we spend the tax rebate or income tax refund? When should we write our wills? How can we manage the care of an aging parent without losing our jobs? What do we owe our uninsured mother-in-law who needs expensive medical treatment? Does the sibling who cares for our parent have a greater right to that parent's inheritance?

Our responses are not always consistent. Why, for instance, do people often react with disgust or discomfort at efforts to set a monetary value on human life, yet embrace life insurance and multiple other legal arrangements for compensating with cash the injury or loss of life? For less daunting quandaries, think of routine gift-giving dilemmas: when, for instance, are gifts of cash appropriate and when are they tacky? When does offering a gift certificate offend the recipient?

The search is on for superior explanations of these and many other features of our economic lives. Impatient with standard accounts of economic action as inexorably driven by calculating self-interest, in the past few decades scholars from a range of disciplines have proposed sparkling new understandings of economic activity. Turning away from abstract theories and plunging into the messiness of actual economic practices, sociologists, anthropologists, psychologists, and others are slowly but surely revolutionizing how we understand life's commerce. From different perspectives, these scholars expose a rigid concept of "homo economicus" as a rusty, old-fashioned notion ready for retirement. Even some economists, while fully embracing rational choice models, have broadened their vision to provide often surprising and instructive explanations for the economics of everyday life.

The serious political implications of the challenge to standard economics became clear in 2008. The financial debacle that jolted the world painfully dramatized the need for new macroeconomic paradigms. The crisis not only upset economic institutions and practices but radically undermined prevalent understandings of how the economy works. The fantasy that real contemporary capitalist systems have perfectly free markets and that these can produce the best of all possible economic worlds crumbled along with the speculative, unregulated market policies and products it had spawned. Even the staunchest free-market advocate, Alan Greenspan, former chairman of the Federal Reserve, famously conceded in October 2008 before the House Committee on Oversight and Government Reform that he had "found a flaw" in his free-market ideology.

Indeed, in 2009, the newly elected Obama administration paid close attention to the strategic alternative insights of behavioral economists such as Richard Thaler. Thaler and Cass R. Sunstein's best-selling *Nudge* (2008), along with George A. Akerlof and Robert Shiller's equally influential *Animal Spirits* (2009), further expanded the public debunking of neoclassical orthodoxy. In July 2009, even the *Economist*'s cover proclaimed, "Modern Economic Theory: Where It Went Wrong—and How the Crisis Is Changing It."

Farther away from the political and best-selling limelight, sociologists have been making their own crucial inroads into alternative visions of economic life. Note the difference. Inspired by Daniel Kahneman's revolutionary behavioral paradigm, some economics-based rebels typically challenge standard notions of individual rationality by documenting people's unpredictable and often irrational decisions. Sociologists move away from such psychological diagnoses, focusing instead on the cultural and structural grounding of individual economic preferences. While personal choice and incentives may explain a great deal of economic behavior, our relations to others become the centerpiece of sociological accounts.

Our economic actions, sociologists insist, remain mysterious or may even appear to be irrational until we understand that they exist within dense webs of meaningful relationships. When we spend, save, invest, give, loan, share, or donate, it matters who we are doing it with, for whom, when, and what the meaning of those transactions convey to others. Monies we spend or refuse to spend, for instance, often signal which relations matter to us. Economic action, therefore, does not revolve around just our own individual selves but our relational selves as well. One cannot predict behavior from individual preferences alone, because people are constantly negotiating those preferences in their interactions with others.

As a result, when we replace theories of individual rationality with theories of individual irrationality, we just introduce a different kind of problem. We need to probe further into those social relations that frequently help us decipher and explain seemingly irrational preferences. Instead of irrationality, we discover variable forms and definitions of what constitutes both rationality and self-interest. Such variation often hinges on the social interactions in which economic action involves us. What determines, for instance, the kind of social relations that people establish for different sorts of economic transactions, such as buying a used car or renting an apartment? Conversely, how do the kinds of social relations already existing among the parties to an economic action affect its character and outcome? When buying a house, what difference does it make if buyer and seller are kin, friends, or strangers connected by a real estate agent? In each case, how and what we define as rational action will vary significantly.

With a focus on such socially based questions and drawing from a range of theoretical frameworks, in the past thirty years or so sociologists have created a set of important alternative explanations of economic activity. Relying on an increasingly broad spectrum of methods, from sophisticated network analyses to rich ethnographic observation, economic sociologists offer revealing accounts of how economic organizations and activities actually work.

This book does not embark on a full survey of the academic specialty called economic sociology. But if you follow it from chapter to chapter, you will discover a shadow history of that field. As later sections of the book detail, when my scholarly career began, economic sociology was a very small field that divided its attention between broad sketches of the social contexts in which different sorts of economic systems developed and narrower analyses of constraints placed by social structure on such economic activities as finding jobs.

My own research in the cultural history of economic practices took place in an entirely different intellectual world from that of early economic sociology. But, as the book's chapters document, gradually the field expanded its range as my own analyses gained from increasing interaction with those of other economic sociologists—at first mainly critical, but eventually collaborative. This volume gathers a set of papers that document my path for the past thirty years within the developing field of economic sociology. The essays represent my efforts to explore selected features of everyday economic behavior and thus propose a distinctive approach to thinking about our economic lives.

Any republication of papers drawn from the length and breadth of a scholarly lifetime makes two strong claims and one weak claim. The first strong assertion declares that the papers have retained a significant share of their original value despite the passage of time and the accumulation of other scholars' work on the same subjects. The second contends that the ensemble of papers adds value to the simple sum of individual contributions. The third, weaker, claim concerns the reader's convenience: having all the papers available in one compact volume will facilitate getting hold of publications that would otherwise take a substantial effort to track down. Simply producing this volume commits me to all three claims. I have tried to add extra value and convenience, however, by preparing brief background essays introducing the entire collection as well as its smaller clusters of essays.

Published over the course of thirty years of work on the social side of economic life, the articles in this book inevitably overlap to some extent. At least in my case, dogged pursuit of such questions as how people attach monetary values to goods that are not routinely available in commodity markets means that similar questions come up repeatedly, sometimes with identical answers from one iteration to the next. In compensation, the essays as a whole identify an evolution of theory, method, and materials for the explanation of economic processes, from an early concern to place them firmly within their cultural and historical settings to a more recent effort to describe and explain how people negotiate solutions to the knotty problem of reconciling economic activities with the demands and conflicts of delicate interpersonal relations. However well you think the book's chapters attack these issues, at a minimum the volume as a whole shows why they are worth addressing and how they require close observation of small-scale economic life.

Of course, institutions and people helped me along the way. A John Simon Guggenheim Fellowship, a visiting appointment at the Russell Sage Foundation, and another visiting appointment at the Institute for Advanced Study gave me precious respite from teaching and administration. My service on the advisory committee of the Paris School of Economics has opened the organizational life of professional economics to me as never before, just as my collaboration with Avinash Dixit in organizing Princeton University's workshops on economics and sociology has involved me in creating intellectual and personal links between the two communities. My unexpected election as first chair of the American Sociological Association's Section on Economic Sociology in 2001 offered me an unprecedented opportunity to bring together previously disparate currents within the field. Less formally, expanding contacts with western European scholars (especially in Paris), have brought me into fruitful interchanges with kindred spirits across the Atlantic. More recently, I have begun similar conversations with researchers in Argentina and Brazil.

Over the years during which I wrote this volume's essays, generous colleagues, friends, and family—too many to list—have earned my gratitude with advice, criticism, information, and encouragement. Sadly, some of those dear collaborators are no longer here, but their memory continues to inspire and guide me. Whole cohorts of talented Princeton graduate students have also given me the benefit of their insights, while my colleagues at Princeton have offered support and provided models of academic excellence.

As I prepared the new essays in this book, several friends and colleagues gifted me with their time and caring effort, helping me to clarify ideas and correct misconceptions. I am grateful to Nina Bandelj, Paul DiMaggio, Avinash Dixit, Alice Goffman, Alexandra Kalev, and Michael Katz. Martha Ertman, Mark Momjian, and Carol Sanger offered their expert advice on legal materials. Pierre Kremp provided valuable research assistance. I thank also Ronald Burt and an anonymous reviewer for their excellent suggestions on an earlier draft of the volume. The magical Chuck Tilly beamed his enthusiasm and support as I began this project. Sophia and Nathan Zelizer brightened the path.

Once again, Princeton University Press has been a marvelous home for my book. Beth Clevenger oversaw the project with great care, Victoria Hansard managed copyright requests, and Pamela Schnitter created the lovely cover design. Beth Gianfagna contributed once more her graceful editing of the text. For more than twenty years, it has been my good fortune to have Peter Dougherty, the press's extraordinary director, as my editor and friend. Ever since he arrived there, Peter has been a crucial contributor to the dissemination and promotion of economic sociology.

Il Mulino has published an overlapping Italian language collection of my papers. I thank Carlo Trigilia and Roberta Sassatelli for proposing the translation of my work to Il Mulino.

Economic Lives

The Lives behind Economic Lives

When I started my academic journey during the 1970s, I never imagined that I would arrive at the center of a field called economic sociology. This collection of papers from across that journey—so far!—traces the intersection of three initially separate paths: the development of one scholar's theoretical and empirical concerns; the transformation of a once-marginal intellectual field into a flourishing enterprise; and the opening of new conversations between two established but long-alienated disciplines: economics and sociology. This triple perspective has a deep disadvantage and a strong advantage. On the negative side, it suggests a false claim that I accomplished the syntheses and new discoveries on my own. On the positive side, it provides a privileged observation post for inspection of how intellectual enterprises change through interaction among their discipline-bound participants.

Here's another way of looking at the book. The pages you have before you trace an intellectual journey through the obscure borderlands of culture and the economy. Although the chapters draw mainly on evidence from the United States since about 1850, they address issues of concern to anyone anywhere who wants to clarify how shared understandings and interpersonal relations infuse and shape the ostensibly impersonal worlds of production, consumption, distribution, and asset transfers: When new forms of economic activity arise, how do ordinary people integrate them into their existing webs of meaning and solidarity? (For example, do people treat electronic currency differently from hard cash?) How do markets and interpersonal networks shape each other? (Is it true, as commonly believed, for example, that marketization drains personal relations of their strength, warmth, and meaning?) Once they are trying to describe and explain the economic lives of households or of children's friendships, how must analysts modify standard economic models based on firms and production markets? (Should we assume, for example, that efficiency matters less to the viability of economic activity outside of firms and production markets?) Each chapter in the book addresses such questions by rejecting narrow economic reductionism but without fleeing to the opposite extreme—construction of a fantasy world consisting entirely of beliefs and sentiments.

This introduction contains three main sections: a review of my personal itinerary through the study of economic phenomena; a sketch of how the field of economic sociology took shape from the 1980s onward, including my place within it; and reflections on current relations between the disciplines of economics and sociology.

At the start of my long effort to make sense of intersections among economic activities, small-scale interpersonal relations, and shared culture, I supposed that the central challenge was to show how slowly moving and humanly motivated shifts in culture—in shared understandings and their representations in symbols and practices—generated changes in ordinary people's treatments of social dilemmas such as the adoption of life insurance in the face of sacred prohibitions on the monetary evaluation of human life. That conception belonged part and parcel to a major current of historical sociology as practiced back then. We might call it the analysis of culture in social history. That approach offered a welcome alternative to the rational materialism that then constituted its chief rival within social history.

As with most beginners in a professional field, my graduate school mentors provided the platform from which my intellectual career began. Three sociologists and a historian stand out among the stellar figures who were teaching at Columbia University during the 1970s. Historical sociologist Sigmund Diamond (who had in fact received a Ph.D. in history), analyst of changes in American wealth and power, revealed a vision of historical evidence as a basis of sociological interpretation. Historically and theoretically ambitious Bernard Barber, whose specific work centered on the sociology of natural science but proliferated into general analyses of social structure, showed enormous sympathy for my fumbling efforts to make theoretical sense of historical evidence. Historian of medicine and the criminal system David Rothman integrated me into a group of fledgling scholars who were learning the delights and perils of social history. Although he stood at a greater distance from my particular work, the always wise Robert K. Merton repeatedly intervened to help me sharpen my arguments and connect them more firmly to relevant strands of social theory.

These early influences imposed a cost that only later became a benefit. I remember all too painfully an early interview for a job in a university sociology department during which my interrogators asked pointedly how my social historical research qualified as sociology at all. Fortunately, the boom in collaboration between American history and social science that was occurring during the 1970s in the work of such diverse scholars as Michael Katz and Herbert Gutman provided a partial justification for my own style of work. It also differentiated my efforts from the other great enterprise then under way in historical sociology: the comparative-historical study of large structures and big processes in the vein of Immanuel Wallerstein and Theda Skocpol. Thus, unexpectedly, my work found a temporary home within sociology.

Of course, later intellectual interchanges also shaped my thinking. From the late 1980s, work in new institutional settings expanded the range of my intellectual relations. A delightful year at the Russell Sage Foundation brought me into contact with a spirited, diverse group of specialists in various economic processes; among other things, it initiated a long-term dialogue with fellow Russell Sager Charles Tilly, who constantly urged me to expand my theoretical range. A move from Barnard College to Princeton University intensified my exchanges with Paul DiMaggio and Alejandro Portes, while adding more frequent conversations with Michael Katz at the nearby University of Pennsylvania. About the same time, Richard Swedberg and Neil Smelser helped me find my place in economic sociology by mapping me into their own influential systematizations of the field. At Princeton, a marvelous crop of graduate students likewise stimulated me to extend the range of my own thinking.

In retrospect, I now see that the cultural social history with which I began greatly underplayed two problems that eventually occupied the center of my work: how interpersonal negotiations actually transform both available culture and personal relations, and how negotiated interpersonal relations shape the accomplishment of concrete economic activity. Among other things, then, this book chronicles a transformation of my personal approach to the analysis of social processes.

Almost unconsciously, that shift of theoretical perspectives induced alterations in my methods and materials. My earlier work generally assembled and connected two bodies of evidence: observations of changes in widely shared conceptions of some social phenomenon—the value of human life, the character of money, and so on—and partly independent observations of changes in social practices, such as the creation of particularized monies matched to different sorts of social relations.

Increasingly, however, my methods and materials shifted toward two other foci: (1) examination of how people accomplished apparently similar economic work, such as provision of personal care and maintenance of households, in different social settings, and (2) close scrutiny of disputes that arise in the course of negotiating economic relations, notably including legal cases that simultaneously dramatize the issues of everyday social relations and clarify how different social milieus deal with similar dilemmas. As a result, the long-term inspiration of social history transmuted into a concern for locating contemporary economic processes within their social contexts.

Starting in the 1990s, my increased interest in the legal treatment of economic processes brought me into valuable conversations with legal scholars, especially with participants in the so-called New Chicago School critique of the prevailing law and economics approach, such as Dan Kahan, Lawrence Lessig, and Cass Sunstein. Gradually, the dialogue extended to feminist legal scholars involved in vigorously contesting standard approaches to commodification for, among other things, failing to acknowledge women's unpaid economic contributions.

Rather than following the nuances and uncertainties of my intellectual itinerary, let me schematize by breaking my successive inquiries into big chunks. Over the roughly thirty years that these problems have preoccupied me, my work on them has fallen into six clusters: (1) valuation of human lives, (2) the social meaning of money, (3) intimate economies, (4) the economy of care, (5) circuits of commerce, and (6) critiques and syntheses.

I first approached the valuation of human lives with a historical analysis of how Americans came to accept life insurance as a prudent investment in the future rather than an obscene wager on human mortality; my book *Morals and Markets* (1979) summarized that analysis. I complemented this study with a similarly historical analysis of how Americans shifted from treating children as economic assets to considering them as priceless; the book *Pricing the Priceless Child* (1985) reported that line of work most extensively.

Second, my analysis of the social meaning of money centered on a similarly historical treatment of the ways that ordinary Americans responded to their government's imposition of uniform legal tender by creating a wide variety of "special monies" that they used to mark off different activities and social relations from each other; *The Social Meaning of Money* (1994) reported that inquiry. These studies of valuation and money also produced some useful offshoots, notably synthetic essays on children's economic lives and consumption by both adults and children.

My third field of interest, intimate economies, introduced a less historical but more synthetic survey of intersections between economic activity and intimate relations in four areas: households, erotically linked couples, the provision of personal care, and legal disputes arising from those relations. *The Purchase of Intimacy* (2005) proposes what I call a "connected lives" approach for investigating and explaining multiple forms of mingling between economic transactions and intimate ties. Although it did reach back occasionally to nineteenth-century practices and legal disputes, the book broke the mold of cultural social history that had shaped most of my previous work. The work on intimacy continues to have ramifications, in analyses of corporate ethical codes or the impact of intimacy on the performance of economic organizations, for example.

A fourth cluster of analyses stemming from the work on intimacy dealt with the economy of personal care—the provision of welfare-enhancing personal attention ranging from professional health services to household labor. This cluster took my research farther into the distinction between paid and unpaid forms of economic interaction.

I call the fifth cluster circuits of commerce, the exploration of how people create distinctive, bounded arrangements of social relations that sustain economic activity in ways that the standard terms of firms, hierarchies, and markets do not grasp, for example, in such arrangements as migrant remittances, rotating credit and savings associations, and local monies.

Finally, a sixth set of studies consists of more general essays, mostly critical, concerning the interplay of economic activity and social life, especially as pursued by economic sociologists in Europe and the United States; these analyses appear here together for the first time within the same book. This volume, then, offers samples of all six lines of work.

The remainder of this introduction reviews economic sociology's development as seen from my perspective and provides a snapshot of current relations between the disciplines of economics and sociology.

ECONOMIC SOCIOLOGY

My grounding in the social-historical study of culture, interpersonal relations, and economic activity prepared for a peculiar encounter between my work and the distinctive subdiscipline called economic sociology. Unexpectedly, that encounter swept me into some of economic sociology's central debates. My entry occurred through deep suspicion of three common modes of thought concerning economic processes. I eventually labeled those perspectives "separate spheres," "hostile worlds," and "nothing-but." Separate-spheres doctrines posited two distinct arenas of social life, one oriented toward rational effectiveness, the other toward sentiment and solidarity. Left to itself, according to the doctrines, each sphere operated more or less harmoniously. But the hostile-worlds model predicted mutual contamination if the two spheres intersected closely: the penetration of rational calculation into the sphere of sentiment would disrupt solidarity, just as the penetration of sentiment into the sphere of rationality would disrupt efficiency.

As alternatives to these paired doctrines, other scholars proposed an array of nothing-but characterizations for socially informed economic activity: nothing but rationally organized markets, nothing but power, nothing but culture. My work on the valuation of lives and on monetary practices forced me to recognize the inadequacies of all these views. I therefore first discovered economic sociology with surprise and some dismay—not least because then almost no women numbered among economic sociology's practitioners. Little did I then think that it would become the site of my work to come.

To be sure, the sociological study of economic processes has a long lineage. Karl Marx, Max Weber, and Emile Durkheim led the way. In the United States during the 1950s, Talcott Parsons and Neil Smelser set out to synthesize economic and sociological approaches, but their efforts failed to galvanize a new specialty. What is now called the "new economic sociology" took off in the 1980s. As the chapter "Pasts and Futures of Economic Sociology" points out, in its early stages, economic sociologists remained closely attached to mainstream economics. Specialists concentrated on two activities: extending economic analysis into areas economists ignored and identifying social contexts that facilitated or constrained economic action.

Most notably, the concept of embeddedness became economic sociology's icon; in its simplest versions, embeddedness described the way that price setting, asset transfers, and other standard economic activities (presumed to operate internally according to the precepts of neoclassical economics) responded to their location within varied social settings. These insights launched a broad program of inquiry. But they also perpetuated the fallacies of nothing-but economic reductionism on one side and of separate spheres on the other. Nothing-but extension views promoted an understanding of all economic processes as conforming to the thin models of mainstream economics. In contrast, context theorists maintained the distinction between a world of social life and a distinct world of economic activity, instead of integrating them.

Gradually, however, criticism of these deficiencies accumulated. In the process, economic sociologists began formulating a variety of alternatives to extension and context approaches. In recent analyses, they have moved from straightforward network conceptions of interpersonal ties to an emphasis on the variable quality, intensity, meaning, and consequences of relational ties among economic actors. They have also moved away from the simple exportation of economic models to areas outside of firms and markets to a critical examination of the distinctive economic forms that arise in such settings as households, informal economies, consumption markets, the care economy, microcredits, migrant remittances, and gift transactions.

In Europe, economic sociology's path differs from the U.S. trajectory for two main reasons. First, the economics to which Europeans are responding is quite different in emphasis, reflecting more of an institutional, historical, and comparative background than U.S. economics. Second, economic sociology connects more closely with reform and applied programs in Europe than it does in the United States. My work with the Economic Sociology section of the American Sociological Association has led me to recognize the tense but potentially very fruitful dialogue Americans are carrying on along the same line. Despite starting out as a specialist in the American economy, within the section of the ASA, I found myself increasingly connecting European and American work in this vein. (It helps that I grew up bilingual in Spanish and French.)

My extensive contacts with European sociologists and economists, especially in the Paris region, have revealed a world of scholarship in which many people are trying to make strong connections among moral theories of the economy, ideas of social change, and public policy. French economists and sociologists have moved toward the formulation of truly alternative, socially based description and explanation of economic activity. Denying any intrinsic division between sociology and economics, for example, in 2005 economist André Orléan issued a stirring call for what we can name alternative accounts of economic activity in general.

As I pointed out earlier, I did not start out as a self-defined economic sociologist. In a sense, I just backed into the field. For years I worked mainly on changes in American social life, with special attention to how economic processes affected it. My first three books dealt with the development of life insurance, the valuation of children, and people's uses of money. I thought of myself as a historical sociologist, but not in the grand style of comparing empires, whole economies, and industrial revolutions. Then scholars who clearly belonged to economic sociology, such as Pierre Bourdieu, Harrison White, and Richard Swedberg, began using my work and treating it as a challenge to conventional economic thinking.

Surprised but pleased, I gladly joined debates about how economic processes work. By the time I published *The Purchase of Intimacy* in 2005, I was both teaching my own version of economic sociology and contributing regularly to symposia on the subject—especially when organizers wanted to show how economic analysts could treat culture and small-scale interpersonal relations effectively. The same effort found me integrating gender differences and relations into economic analysis far more extensively than other economic sociologists had previously done. My students then drew me farther into the study of economic organizations and transnational economic processes. That placed me in the middle of discussions about the proper pursuit of economic sociology.

Authors of books that are still in print can gain insight into their intellectual locations by consulting a dramatic feature presented on line by the bookseller Amazon.com. The Web site amaznode.com compiles Amazon's own sales for a network-style visual presentation of what *other* books people who bought a given book also bought.[1] When last consulted, amaznode displayed the commercial connections of *Pricing the Priceless Child* (*PTPC*), *The Social Meaning of Money* (*SMM*), and *The Purchase of Intimacy* (*POI*). The network graph tells a story of its own. *PTPC* links to more recent economic sociology, but it connects most closely with books on the history of childhood and nineteenth-century American history. *SMM* locates closer to standard economic sociology, but it clusters especially with books (including mass-audience books) on markets, economic life at large, and connections between law and markets. *POI*, finally, lies in the very middle of current economic sociology but also—and more surprisingly—makes connection with work on network analysis. We could hardly ask for a more graphic depiction of the initially quite separate but eventually convergent development of my analyses and those of economic sociology in general.

ECONOMICS AND SOCIOLOGY

Despite the advances of economic sociology during recent decades, the intellectual relationship between the disciplines of economics and sociology remains enormously lopsided.[2] Economists intermittently draw on material assembled by sociologists (for example, concerning the economics of migration) to document their own discipline-based arguments. But nothing like the relatively free flow of ideas that currently runs between sociology and political science links economics to sociology. On their side, sociologists who study economic processes all too easily accept the problem-setting of standard economics rather than intervening in ways that place new analytical problems on the economics agenda.

Economic sociologists' almost obsessive commitment to their one-sided dialogue with economists has mixed effects. On one side, it opens a channel of communication through which good, new ideas can flow fruitfully in both directions. Within my own university, I have helped organize colloquia from which both the economists and the sociologists have visibly benefited. On the negative side, let me signal one pernicious effect: a strong tendency to concentrate on the same economic sites—notably capitalist firms and production markets—that have largely captured mainstream economists' attention. This weakness encourages economic sociologists to ignore households, informal economies, and trust networks (or relegate them to the economic periphery, treated as quasi-economies).[3]

Yet a halting dialogue between economics and sociology is developing. As it happens, the recent successes of behavioral economics, game theory, feminist economics, organizational economics, institutional economics, and household dynamics have all produced welcome openings for dialogue between the disciplines. Some economists have begun to look seriously at culture and social relations. Take just three prominent examples.

First is economist Robert Gibbons's 2005 article, "What Is Economic Sociology and Should Any Economists Care?" Gibbons answers yes to his rhetorical question, reporting that his own interest began "when I recognized that some sociologists were working with independent and dependent variables that were barely mentioned in the economics literature, but seemed potentially quite important." Gibbons calls for a "Pareto-improving dialogue between the appropriate margins of economics and sociology."

Second, Luigi Guiso, Paola Sapienza, and Luigi Zingales in their 2006 paper also answer a resounding yes to their own query: "Does Culture Affect Economic Outcomes?" Although they do not cite economic sociologists (with the exception of rightly praising Paul DiMaggio's work), they treat culture—by which they mean collective beliefs, identities, and preferences—seriously, not as outcome but as an independent causal factor. They conclude that "importing cultural elements will make economic discourse richer, better able to capture the nuances of the real world, and ultimately more useful."

Finally, George A. Akerlof's 2007 presidential address to the American Economic Association emphatically called for recognizing norms as the "missing motivation in macroeconomics" and outlined specific ways of incorporating those norms into economists' analyses. While remaining faithful to economics' focus on individual preferences and motivation, Akerlof broke crucial new grounds for dialogue between economists and sociologists (see also Akerlof and Kranton 2010).

However, if they want to have a serious impact on economics, economic sociologists cannot simply wait for bright-eyed economists to notice what they are doing. Economists pay serious attention when analysts make direct and cogent bids to revise existing economic analyses. Notice the great difference in impact by three bodies of relevant, innovative work that have grown up over the past twenty years: game theory, behavioral economics, and economic sociology itself. Game theory for all practical purposes has become an integral part of economic theory. Every economics student learns it. Game theory has made it perfectly legitimate to set up analyses of economic choice situations not as individual cognitive decision making but as a form of social interaction. It is a success story for a research framework that at one point was alien to neoclassical economics.

Behavioral economics, despite its remarkable success, still remains at a halfway point. It may well follow game theory, but there is still a question whether it will fundamentally modify mainline economic theory or remain a critical, dissident movement within economics. In a review of advances in behavioral economics, Wolfgang Pesendorfer (2006) notes that behavioral economics "remains a discipline that is organized around the failures of standard economics." This "symbiotic relationship with standard economics," he notes, "works well as long as small changes to standard assumptions are made." Despite the Nobel Prize in economics shared by Vernon Smith and Daniel Kahneman, we have yet to see the microfoundations of standard economics transformed in the manner that behavioral economists claim they should be.

Conclusion

In my opinion, economics has paid a stiff price for its current scope and precision. It has, on the whole, located its central causes in the decisions of largely autonomous individuals who operate within constraints set by well-defined resources and institutions. Even game theory, after all, generally features individuals who make choices individually with no more than anticipation of how other parties will make their own autonomous choices. Such an approach has the virtue of parsimony. But it almost entirely neglects the incremental negotiation of shared understandings and interpersonal relations that lies at the center of alternative, more sociological, analyses of economic processes.

Sociologists, to be sure, pay the opposite price: a potpourri of theories and observations so various that a researcher can rarely be sure that a new finding actually fits with or contradicts previously accumulated understandings of the economic process at hand. It is even worse than that, because economic sociologists so regularly specialize in one structure or process at a time, some dealing with households, some with migration, some with firms, some with the exchange of particular commodities. As a consequence, intellectual accumulation proceeds slowly and uncertainly. Gradually, I have come to see my own work partly as a rescue operation: helping other students of economic processes recognize similar forms of interpersonal negotiation and cultural accumulation in a wide range of settings, whether or not they belong to the traditional subject matter of economics.

Yet I see hope. Economic sociology certainly has some of the same potential as game theory or behavioral economics, but it has remained far outside of economists' main conversation. So far, it attracts only dissidents within economics. It is certainly not something that economics students routinely learn about. Economic sociologists face an interesting choice: plunge into the core models of economics in the wake of game theory and behavioral economics, or continue their current business in hope that friendly economists will do the importing for them.

The first choice means deploying the concepts, models, mathematics, and econometrics that have become economists' stock in trade. As economist Dan Silverman (2006) points out about the thus far incomplete success of behavioral economics, it typically involves identifying processes that standard economic models must treat as anomalies, rewriting relevant economic models so they account for the anomalies, and establishing the empirical validity of the revised models. It may also mean reducing the dialogue with the rest of sociology. But the second option means remaining peripheral to the exciting current transformations of economics. Given my own limited knowledge of technical economics and my preference for direct observation of economic interactions, of course, I hope that some of each—both integration of economic sociology into economic theory and sociological inquiry into economic processes—will continue for the foreseeable future.

It will not be easy, if only because the exemplary cases of game theory and behavioral economics involve modification, but not elimination, of economic models' deep individualism. It will take great theoretical, technical, and even rhetorical finesse to make interpersonal processes, including culture, genuine foci of economic analysis. How will sociologists rewrite economic models so that they incorporate the culturally drenched dynamics of organizations, households, institutions, and interpersonal ties?

Evidence that a rapprochement is possible in principle, however, comes from a fourth innovative field: the new institutional economics. Researchers in this field have absorbed the findings from behavioral economics about the departure of actual behavior from traditional economic rationality and selfishness, and used the framework of game theory with varying degrees of formality. Starting with Douglass North's distinction between the rules of the game and the play of the game, through Oliver Williamson's analysis of opportunism based on Thomas Schelling's concept of credibility, to the formal models of constitutions developed by Daron Acemoglu and James Robinson, this work has elucidated how institutions influence the form and outcome of economic transactions, most notably property and contracts. This has profoundly changed and enriched our understanding of firms, industries, and markets, as well as the historical processes of economic growth and development. Institutional economists have plenty in common with institutional and economic sociologists: awareness of organizational processes, concerns about contract enforcement, openness to culture, and more. Although I hope we can continue the dialogue about small-scale economic processes and microfoundations, we also have an opportunity for an innovative economics-sociology alliance on the large scale.

By no means does the book before you synthesize contemporary thinking in economics and economic sociology. Far from it: the book's chapters trace an itinerary into and through economic sociology with only side glances at parallel developments within economics. But they do, I think, raise issues about which economists could benefit from studying more extensively. Most centrally, the book examines how connected people incorporate available culture and interpersonal relations into their daily negotiation of economic activity. In doing so, all of us incessantly reshape the economy at the small scale and the large. That is why I have called this book *Economic Lives*.

NOTES

1. I thank Kieran Healy for alerting me to the site (http://amaznode.fladdict .net) and making a presentation based on it in his paper "The Performativity of Networks," at the American Sociological Association annual meetings, August 2007.

2. The following two sections are drawn from "Interview: Viviana Zelizer Answers Ten Questions about Economic Sociology," *European Economic Sociology Newsletter* 8 (July 2007): 41–45.

3. To be sure, there are exceptions on both sides, as a number of economists and economic sociologists have contributed important work to those areas.

REFERENCES

Akerlof, George A. 2007. "The Missing Motivation in Macroeconomics." *American Economic Review* 97 (March): 5–36.

———, and Rachel Kranton. 2010. *Identity Economics: How Our Identities Shape Our Work, Wages, and Well-Being.* Princeton, N.J.: Princeton University Press.

Gibbons, Robert. 2005. "What Is Economic Sociology and Should Any Econo-
    mists Care?" *Journal of Economic Perspectives* 19 (Winter): 3–7.
Guiso, Luigi, Paola Sapienza, and Luigi Zingales. 2006. "Does Culture Affect
    Economic Outcomes?" *Journal of Economic Perspectives* 20 (Spring): 23–48.
Orléan, André. 2005. "La sociologie économique et la question de l'unité des sci-
    ences sociales." *L'Année sociologique* 55:279–305.
Pesendorfer, Wolfgang. 2006. "Behavioral Economics Comes of Age: A Review
    Essay in Behavioral Economics." *Journal of Economic Literature* 44 (Septem-
    ber): 712–21.
Silverman, Dan. 2006. Review of *The Law and Economics of Irrational Behavior*,
    edited by Francesco Parisi and Vernon L. Smith. *Journal of Economic Litera-
    ture* 44:728–31.

PART ONE

Valuation of Human Lives

Pricing life raises daunting questions: How can we establish monetary equivalents for human existence? Should we? Are all lives worth the same, or are some more valuable than others? Who decides? Is giving money to compensate for death proper recognition of a serious loss, or is it a morally corrupting practice? Is accepting payment evidence of a recipient's greediness or a legitimate way to seek justice? Who is entitled to receive money for the death of others? Which others?

After the terrorist attacks of September 11, 2001, Kenneth Feinberg, appointed by Congress as special master of the Victim Compensation Fund, faced such troublesome issues. As he recounts in his book, *What Is Life Worth?*, "I realized what a huge responsibility I confronted, putting price tags on lost loved ones' lives. . . . It was not just about the money, about providing bereaved families with a cash lifeline. It was about compensating for a catastrophic emotional loss—trying to fill the hole in a family's life with money" (2005, xxi, xxiii). Yet he managed to successfully apportion almost $7 billion to settle 2,900 claims for death and 4,400 claims for personal injury. It was an arduous process. Feinberg repeatedly faced deep hostility from outraged survivors offended by what they perceived as pitifully inadequate awards. At the same time, indignant critics accused him of cheapening human life with his crass economic ledgers.

A few 9/11 survivors opted out of the fund. Michelle and Clifton Cottom, for instance, sued the airlines instead. Their eleven-year-old daughter Asia died on American Airlines flight 77 when hijackers crashed the plane into the Pentagon. She was heading to Los Angeles on a school trip. Because Feinberg's compensation scheme used lost economic value as its main standard, survivors of victims with low or no earning potential received significantly less compensation than high earners. Michelle Cottom sued the airlines because she found the victim compensation calculations unfair and offensive. As she put it in a *New York Times* interview, "To me, it just smelled of dishonesty. How do you justify, O.K., an 11-year-old is worth $2, but because you're the pilot of the plane, that's worth $2 million?" (Hartocollis 2007).

Other tragedies brought their own dilemmas on pricing life and death. The Iraq War, for example, raised the issue of compensation for the death of U.S. service members but also for Iraqi civilians killed. In 2005, partly as a result of embarrassing comparisons to the much higher 9/11 awards, the so-called death gratuity for survivors of military personnel killed in combat operations was increased from $12,000 to $100,000. Although a welcome relief for most families, some women, as one Navy widow put it, "feel like they were paid off for their husband's life" (Foderaro 2008).

Compensating for Iraqi civilian casualties created its own complexities. Legal scholar John Fabian Witt suggests that "American-style damages payments are fast becoming one of the ways the twenty-first-century U.S. military attempts to win the hearts and minds of civilians in war zones" (Witt 2008, 1456). Besides damages paid through the Foreign Claims Act, the United States offers condolence or "solatia" payments to Iraqis killed or injured by U.S. armed forces. According to Department of Defense estimates, between 2003 and 2006, the United States distributed about $30 million in such payments to Iraqi as well as Afghan civilians. Individual awards, however, remain paltry. After an American missile killed his brother, sister, wife, and six children, Said Abbas Ahmed received $6,000 compensation. According to a *New York Times* report, he complained, "This war of yours costs billions . . . are we not worth more than a few thousand?" (Gettleman 2004).

What is striking about all these cases is that the solutions typically rely on some formula built on economic value: so much money to compensate for a given death. Yet they all repeatedly raise questions of justice and fairness. Is the compensation fair? For whom? What defines fairness? Who defines it? Pricing lives thus sets up a problem for economic analysis. No straightforward price-setting market exists for valuation of human life—and therefore for the loss of life—the way a price-setting market values gold or other commodities. No magical calculator yields a neat ranking of human lives.

We find three frequent responses to the dilemmas posed by pricing life: cost-benefit accounting, a moral justice ledger, and separate-spheres/hostile-worlds purism. Cost-benefit analysts provide efficient calculations gauging life's value by its past and future economic potential. Here life is treated as another commodity. Feinberg's compensation awards, for instance, used lost economic value as their main standard, not only computing the victim's likely future earnings but also estimating the market price of lost services. In the same way, government agencies routinely assign monetary values to human lives that may be saved by a particular piece of legislation. For that purpose, agencies calculate the value of a statistical life based on people's willingness to pay in order to avoid specific risks.

Impatient with the emotional neutrality of cost-benefit estimates, moral justice advocates add outrage to the ledger. In cases of wrongful death they not only seek compensation from the perpetrators but also demand retribution. As Charles Tilly eloquently explains in his *Credit and Blame*, justice-seekers "become indignant if authorities assign too light a penalty, or say that no one was to blame. They ask for justice in something like the old *lex talionis*: an eye for an eye, a tooth for a tooth, tit for tat" (2008, 94). That's why juries frequently award enormous settlements for the loss of life, including compensation for survivors' pain and suffering.

In sharp contrast, separate-spheres/hostile-worlds critics decry any economic valuation of life as an unseemly profanation of the sacred. In this view, life is priceless; it should therefore be kept apart from any market calculation. Otherwise, the logic of the market will inevitably swallow up and soil life's preciousness. Such concern places survivors who claim compensation for the death of loved ones in a morally uncomfortable spot. Indeed, in the case of 9/11 payments, critics often accused victims' families of distasteful greed. Most outrageously, in 2007 conservative author Ann Coulter sparked a controversy when she described a group of 9/11 widows who backed the Democratic Party as the millionaire "witches of East Brunswick" enjoying their newfound celebrity, adding: "I've never seen people enjoying their husbands' deaths so much." Chastising these women turned into millionaires by compensation funds, Coulter blamed them for "reveling in their status as celebrities and stalked by grief-arazzis" (Coulter 2007, 112).[1] Because they accepted money from their husbands' death, Coulter accused the widows of being mercenary.

The essays in this section go beyond these standard responses to pricing life. While all three approaches introduce crucial considerations, they ultimately fall short of explaining what exactly is going on. Treating the valuation of life as an ordinary market transaction will not do: it denies the specific meanings of that transaction and occults the process by which people arrive at appropriate compensation. Seeking moral justice is certainly a vital element in some forms of economic calculations of life's worth, but it surely does not exhaust the process. Segregating life from market contamination fails as well. In fact, in less extreme cases than terrorist attacks and contentious wars, people are constantly attaching economic value to human lives and making strong claims based on those values—most notably when they take out a life insurance policy, but also in cases of medical malpractice, wrongful death settlements, or compensation for on-the-job injuries.

I came to the study of pricing life indirectly. Having moved from Buenos Aires to the United States in a series of adventures with unanticipated consequences, I became fascinated with three related questions: (1) How do people manage uncertainties? (2) How is it that so much human action ends up producing effects different from those that people intended? (3) How do people nevertheless seem to live relatively orderly lives? As I struggled to find a way to turn these questions into a doctoral dissertation, my father, an Argentine lawyer and book lover, sent me a copy of a small 1924 French legal treatise, L'aléas dans le contrat, a fascinating philosophical discussion of gambling and insurance contracts as rational mechanisms to deal with fortuitous events.

That's how I started reading about life insurance and soon discovered that beneath its dull veneer, insurance raised fascinating questions about the valuation of life and death. Why did Americans at first resist this formidable economic institution? How did the industry go from a stigmatized gamble on human life to a widely praised arrangement to secure a family's future?

What did the case of life insurance reveal about the construction of new markets, especially those trading in sacred products? More generally, how do shared meanings and social relations inform people's economic activities?

I published my first article on life insurance in a 1978 issue of the *American Journal of Sociology*. Based on extensive analysis of historical documents, I show how the industry, initially shunned as a sacrilegious enterprise, was later adopted as a new form of contemporary death ritual. Pricing life became part of an American's "good death." Insurance thus provided a revealing test case of how morals and markets mingle in practice.

Although the article as well as the subsequent dissertation and book were well received, at least one major sociologist expressed concern about my excursion into economic territory. In a friendly letter he sent me in March 1979 (a couple of months before his death), Talcott Parsons, whom I had met during a year he spent at Rutgers University, worried about my article's argument concerning the greater legitimacy of economic definitions of death. That notion could, in Parsons's view, be confused with those promulgated by economic ideologists such as Gary Becker, against which he was on a "warpath." "I like your approach so much," Parsons wrote, "I would hate to have it identified with the kind of position these people are putting forward" (personal communication).

The next two chapters extend the analysis of how economic value gets constructed by tackling the valuation of children's lives. An obscure footnote in a 1900 insurance history book provided the catalyst for "The Price and Value of Children." The note referred to a little-known controversy surrounding the sale of low-cost children's insurance at the turn of the century. Between 1870 and 1930, as child labor laws removed most children from the labor market, the economic valuation of young lives turned into a problematic and sensitive task. If children were economically worthless but emotionally priceless, how could insurance companies determine the economic loss created by a child's death? What explains the fact that they did so with remarkable success? How could poor parents justify taking a policy on their child's life?

The article documents how the child insurance market was shaped by the changing economic and sentimental valuation of children. Child policies did not sell as an opportunistic contrivance for cashing in on a child's death but at first as a way of providing the "sacred" child with a proper burial, and later as a prudent investment in his or her future education. Intrigued by the paradoxes involved in the economic valuation of children, I expanded my analysis into a book, *Pricing the Priceless Child*, published in 1985.

"From Baby Farms to Baby M" is a further extension of these issues. It examines the impact of children's changing economic and sentimental value on turn-of-the-twentieth-century baby markets, including profound transformations in the sale and exchange value of "priceless" children in foster care and adoption. Why is it that today's infertile parents eagerly offer thousands of dollars to obtain a baby, but in the late nineteenth century unwanted babies found no buyers? The essay then traces the late-twentieth-century emergence of a controversial surrogacy market.

"The Priceless Child Revisited" closes this section with a view of what is happening to children in our own times. It examines children's current economic value with a different slant. While the earlier study focused on the emergence of new cultural conceptions defining children's productive activities, here I lay out a framework for understanding two other persistent questions: (1) When and why does thinking about children's productive activities make us uncomfortable? (2) In what ways do children generate immediate economic value but also contribute to their own financial, human, social, and cultural capital as well as that of their families and communities? Drawing mostly from household carework and immigrant enterprises, the chapter focuses on children's economic practices.

In different ways, the papers in this section provide an account of the valuation of human life as a historically contingent, socially organized, deeply meaningful process. They trace the particular kinds of cultural work involved in organizing markets that deal in sacred products. People certainly worry about the pricing of life and whether economic considerations violate moral precepts. That is why widows at first rejected life insurance benefits as unseemly "blood money" and why turn-of-the-century parents insuring their children were often suspected of mercenary intent. So, too, must surrogate mothers protect themselves against accusations of reprehensible greediness for "renting" out their bodies. As we will see later, similar concerns arise in other markets for human goods, such as blood, organs, or eggs. At the same time, these essays contest what I call "boundless market" models that assume the inevitable commodification of any good introduced into the market. Instead, what results is the emergence of multiple markets, differentially shaped by shared understandings and varying social relations.

Notes

1. See also "Plugging New Book in Latest Solo *Today* Appearance, Coulter Attacked Liberals, 9-11 Widows," Media Matters for America, http://mediamatters .org/research/200606060006 (accessed June 7, 2009).

References

Coulter, Ann. 2007. *Godless: The Church of Liberalism.* New York: Three Rivers Press.
Feinberg, Kenneth R. 2005. *What Is Life Worth?* New York: Public Affairs.

Foderaro, Lisa W. 2008. "Military Kin Struggle with Loss and a Windfall." *New York Times*, March 22.

Gettleman, Jeffrey. 2004. "For Iraqis in Harm's Way, $5,000 and 'I'm Sorry.'" *New York Times*, March 17.

Hartocollis, Anemona. 2007. "Little-Noticed 9/11 Lawsuits Will Go to Trial." *New York Times*, September 24.

Tilly, Charles. 2008. *Credit and Blame*. Princeton, N.J.: Princeton University Press.

Witt, John Fabian. 2008. "Form and Substance in the Law of Counterinsurgency Damages." *Loyola Law Review* 41:1455–81.

1

Human Values and the Market

The Case of Life Insurance and Death in

Nineteenth-Century America

For Durkheim and Simmel, one of the most significant alterations in the moral values of modern society has been the sacralization of the human being, his emergence as the "holy of holies" (Wallwork 1972, 145; Simmel 1900). In his *Philosophie des Geldes* (1900), Simmel traces the transition from a belief system that condoned the monetary evaluation of life to the Judeo-Christian conception of the absolute value of man, a conception that sets life above financial considerations. The early utilitarian criterion was reflected in social arrangements, such as slavery, marriage by purchase, and the *wergeld* or blood money. The rise of individualism was the determining factor in the transition. "The tendency of money to strive after ever-growing indifference and mere quantitative significance coincides with the ever-growing differentiation of men . . . and thus money becomes less and less adequate to personal values" (Altmann 1903, 58).[1] For Simmel, money the equalizer became money the profaner. Considered *sub specie pecuniae*, the uniqueness and dignity of human life vanished.

Only small fragments of Simmel's penetrating analysis of personal and monetary values have been translated, and, with a few exceptions, this work has been ignored in the sociological literature.[2] There has been much generalizing about the "cash nexus" but, strangely, very little work on the area. The problem of establishing monetary equivalences for such things as death, life, human organs, and generally ritualized items or behavior considered sacred and, therefore, beyond the pale of monetary definition is as intriguing as it is understudied. Perhaps the absorption of many social scientists with "market" models and the notion of economic man led them and others to disregard certain complexities in the interaction between the market and human values.[3] Market exchange, although perfectly compatible with the modern values of efficiency and equality, conflicts with human values that defy its impersonal, rational, and economizing influence. Titmuss's imaginative cross-national comparison of voluntary and commercial systems of providing human blood for transfusions stands as a lone effort to consider this conflict in depth. His study suggests that commercial systems of distributing blood are not only less efficient than voluntary blood donation but also, and more important, morally unacceptable and dangerous to the social order. Transform blood into a commercial commodity, argues Titmuss, and soon it will become "morally acceptable for a myriad of other human activities and relationships also to exchange for dollars and pounds" (1971, 198).[4] Dissatisfied with the consequences of market exchange, Titmuss is persuaded that only reciprocal or gift forms of exchange are suitable for certain items or activities: among others, blood transfusions, organ transplants, foster care, and participation in medical experimentation. His resistance to the laws of the marketplace is not unique. In his early writings, Marx was already concerned with the dehumanizing impact of money. In *The Economic and Philosophic Manuscripts*, Marx deplored the fact that in bourgeois society human life is easily reduced to a mere salable commodity; he pointed to prostitution and the sale of persons that flourished in his time as ultimate examples of this degrading process (1964, 151).[5] Similarly, Blau, despite his predominantly "market" model of social behavior, states that "by supplying goods that moral standards define as invaluable for a price in the market, individuals prostitute themselves and destroy the central value of what they have to offer" (1967, 63). Using love and salvation as examples, Blau suggests that pricing intangible spiritual benefits inevitably leaves some unwholesome by-product; not love but prostitution, not spiritual blessing but simony.[6] The marketing of human organs presents a similar dilemma. Significantly, while organ donations have become more common, organ sales are still rare.[7] Parsons, Fox, and Lidz note that "regardless of how scientific the setting in which this transaction occurs may be, or how secularized the beliefs of those who take part in it, deep religious elements . . . are at least latently present in the transplant situation" (1973, 46). Likewise, even after the repeal of most prohibitions against the sale of corpses, the majority of medical schools still obtain corpses and cadavers through individual donations and unclaimed bodies from the morgue. People refuse to sell their bodies for "ethical, religious or sentimental reasons" ("Tax Consequences of Transfers of Bodily Parts," 1973, 862–63). The law itself remains ambivalent. While the Uniform Anatomical Gift Act permits the gift of one's body or organs after death, "the state of the law on anatomical sales remains in a flux" (ibid., 854).

This paper uses data concerning the diffusion of life insurance in nineteenth-century America as a testing ground to explore the larger theoretical problem of establishing monetary equivalences for sacred things. My hypothesis is that cultural resistance to including certain items in the social order—namely, those related to human life, death, and emotions—into a market-type of exchange introduces structural sources of strain and ambivalence into their marketing. Life insurance raises the issue in its sharpest terms by posing the question of how one establishes a fixed-dollar amount for any individual death.

Life insurance was part of a general movement to rationalize and formalize the management of death that began in the early part of the nineteenth century. In the eighteenth century, the widow and her orphans were assisted by their neighbors and relatives as well as by mutual aid groups that ministered to the economic hardships of the bereaved. In the nineteenth century, the financial protection of American families became a purchasable commodity. Trust companies, like life insurance companies, replaced more informal systems with professional management (White 1955). The funeral was another "family and neighborhood" affair that became a business. Previously, the physical care and disposal of the dead had been provided mostly by neighbors and relatives, but in the nineteenth century it became a financially rewarded occupational specialty (Bowman 1959; Habenstein and Lamers 1955). The process of formalization extended to the drafting of wills. The largely informal, generalized provisions drafted by a man shortly before his death turned into a highly structured system of estate planning in the nineteenth century (Friedman 1964).

The new institutions were primarily concerned with death as a major financial episode. Their business was to make people plan and discuss death in monetary terms. Life insurance defined itself as "the capitalization of affection. . . . Tears are nothing but salt water, to preserve a fresh grief. Insurance is business, genuine, old-fashioned sixteen-ounce precaution" (Phelps 1895, 12–13). Its avowed goal was to encourage men to "make their own death the basis of commercial action" (Beecher 1870). This was no simple enterprise. Putting death on the market offended a system of values that upheld the sanctity of human life and its incommensurability. It defied a powerful normative pattern: the division between the nonmarketable and the marketable, or between the sacred and the profane. Durkheim has written, "The mind irresistibly refuses to allow the two [sacred and profane] . . . to be confounded or even merely to be put into contact with each other . . ." (1965, 55). Sacred things are distinguished by the fact that men will not treat them in a calculating, utilitarian manner.

I will argue that resistance to life insurance in this country during the earlier part of the nineteenth century was largely the result of a value system that condemned the materialistic assessment of death, and of the power of magical beliefs and superstitions that viewed with apprehension any commercial pacts dependent on death for their fulfillment. By the latter part of the nineteenth century, the economic definition of the value of death became finally more acceptable, legitimating the life insurance enterprise. However, the data suggest that the monetary evaluation of death did not desacralize it; far from "profaning" life and death, money became ritualized by its association with them. Life insurance took on symbolic values quite distinct from its utilitarian function, emerging as a new form of ritual with which to face death and a processing of the dead by those kin left behind.

The present study is based on a qualitative analysis of historical documentary sources. The attempt was made to include an extensive and diversified set of different kinds of data. Among the primary sources consulted were advertising booklets published by life insurance companies, insurance journals and magazines, early treatises and textbooks on insurance, and life insurance agents' manuals and their memoirs. Although these sources represent predominantly the life insurance industry and not its customers, they provide important indicators of public opinion. For instance, the most prevalent objections against life insurance were repeatedly discussed and carefully answered by contemporary advertising copy. Primary sources outside the life insurance industry were consulted as well, among them nineteenth-century business periodicals and general magazines, widows' and marriage manuals, booklets written by critics of life insurance, and a series of government documents.

A BRIEF BACKGROUND

The first life insurance organizations in the United States were formed during the latter years of the eighteenth century to assuage the economic distress of the widows and orphans of low-paid Presbyterian and Episcopalian ministers. The idea soon appealed to the secular community, and by the early decades of the nineteenth century several companies had optimistically undertaken the business of insuring life. Legislatures were encouraging; special charters for the organization of the new companies were granted rapidly and eagerly by many states. Life insurance seemed the perfect solution to the increasing economic destitution of widows and orphans. The public, however, did not respond. Surprised and dismayed by their failure, many pioneering companies withdrew altogether or else turned to other businesses to compensate for their losses in life insurance. The contrasting success of savings banks and trust companies, as well as the prosperity of fire and marine insurance companies, attests to the fact that there was sufficient disposable income among the population at the beginning of the nineteenth century. In addition, the early companies offered a solid economic organization; no life insurance company failed before the 1850s. Epidemics and high mortality rates did not affect their stability; actuarial knowledge was sufficient to calculate adequate premium rates. Americans were offered sound policies that they needed and could well afford. They did not, however, want them.

After the 1840s there was a drastic reversal of trends, and life insurance began its fantastic history of financial success, becoming firmly established in the 1870s. Its sudden prosperity has puzzled insurance historians as much as the initial failure of the industry. The new companies were offering the same product; neither rates nor conditions of life insurance policies were significantly improved. Most analysts point to America's stage of economic growth as the major clue to the acceptance of life insurance. The great economic expansion that began in the 1840s and reached its peak in the 1860s explains the boom of life insurance at that time. The increased urbanization of midcentury America is also upheld as an explanation. Urban dependence on daily wages has been particularly linked to the growing acceptance of life insurance. Indeed, the acceleration of urbanization coincided in many states with the growth of life insurance. The percentage of people living in urban areas doubled between 1840 and 1860, with the greatest increase occurring in New York and Philadelphia, two cities in leading insurance states. The first life insurance companies were all organized in such heavily populated cities as New York, Philadelphia, Boston, and Baltimore.[8]

Other insurance historians, notably Stalson (1969), argue that the "rags-to-riches" transformation of life insurance in midcentury can be attributed unequivocally to the adoption of aggressive marketing techniques. Pioneer American life insurance companies used no agents, limiting themselves to passive marketing tactics such as discreet announcement advertisements. In the 1840s, the new companies introduced person-to-person solicitation by thousands of active, high-pressure salesmen who went into the homes and offices of prospective customers. Marketing systems, however, do not develop in a sociological vacuum. Their structure and characteristics are deeply interrelated with such other variables as customers' social and cultural backgrounds. The struggles and victories of life insurance have remained enigmatic and misunderstood because existing interpretations systematically overlook the noneconomic factors involved in its acceptance and adoption. Indeed, economists and economic historians monopolize the field, while sociologists for the most part have ignored it.[9]

In the first place, the development of the insurance industry reflects the struggle between fundamentalist and modernistic religious outlooks that worked itself out in the nineteenth century. Contrasting theological perspectives divided the clergy into opposing groups; there were those who denounced life insurance to their congregations as a secular and sacrilegious device that competed against God in caring for the welfare of widows and orphans. Others, more attuned to the entrepreneurial spirit, supported the industry. The cultural incompatibility of life insurance with literalist and fundamentalist beliefs hindered its development during the first part of the century. In opposition, the emerging liberal theology tended to legitimate the enterprise. Religious liberals supported insurance programs for practical considerations as well. Congregations that had been unwilling to raise the meager salaries of their underpaid pastors and ministers were most easily persuaded to pay the relatively small premiums to insure the lives of the clergymen.

Changing ideologies of risk and speculation also influenced the development of life insurance. Many practices considered to be deviant speculative ventures by a traditional economic morality were redeemed and transformed into legitimate, even noble investments by a different entrepreneurial ethos. Much of the opposition to life insurance resulted from the apparently speculative nature of the enterprise; the insured were seen as "betting" with their lives against the company. The instant wealth reaped by a widow who cashed her policy seemed suspiciously similar to the proceeds of a winning lottery ticket. Traditionalists upheld savings banks as a more honorable economic institution than life insurance because money was accumulated gradually and soberly. After the 1870s, as the notions of economic risk and rational speculation grew progressively more acceptable, the slower methods of achieving wealth lost some of their luster, and life insurance gained prominence and moral respectability.

The emergence of life insurance is also clearly tied to functional changes in the family system that resulted from urbanization. The urban family could no longer rely on informal, personal social arrangements in times of crisis. The care of widows and orphans, previously the responsibility of the community, became the obligation of the nuclear family with the assistance of formal, impersonal, bureaucratic mechanisms and paid professionals. Life insurance was the institutional response to the uncertain social and economic situation of a new commercial middle class without property and dependent exclusively on the money income of the father. Nineteenth-century writings clearly reflect the prevalent fear among businessmen of failure and downward mobility, if not for themselves, for their children.[10]

Finally, changing attitudes toward death made a major impact on the development of life insurance. Life insurance clashed with a value system that rejected any monetary evaluation of human life. However, by the latter part of the nineteenth century, a growing awareness of the economic value of death legitimated the life insurance business.

PROFANE MONEY

The resistance to evaluating human beings in monetary terms is among the major cultural factors either ignored by life insurance analysts or else dismissed in their historical accounts as a curious but certainly peripheral issue. Yet its centrality in Western culture is hardly disputable. Cultural aversion to treating life and death as commercial items is reflected in legal attempts to safeguard them from economic valuation. Roman law had early established the doctrine: *Liberum corpus nullam recipit aestimationem* (the life of a free man can have no monetary estimate) (Goupil 1905, 32–33).[11] Successorial contracts were considered "*stipulationes odiosae*" and "*contra bonos mores*" because they surrounded death with financial considerations. Roman tradition was perpetuated in many countries, particularly in France, where the Civil Code ruled that "only things belonging to commerce can be the subject of a contract" (Pascan 1907, 2). Declaring that a man's life "cannot be the subject of commercial speculation," French jurists prohibited any contract on the lives of persons, such as life insurance, trusts, and successorial contracts. Wills, sufficiently surrounded by religious symbolism to remain untainted by commercial aspirations, remained the only legitimate vehicle to dispose of property after death (Goupil 1905, 139).

In the United States, the utilitarian treatment of human lives poses similar problems. American law protects human life from commerce, declaring that the human body is not property and may not be "bargained for, bartered or sold" (Schultz 1930, 5). Many social arrangements, regardless of their economic efficiency, have been condemned as offensive to the sacred qualities of life. Life insurance became the first large-scale enterprise in America to base its entire organization on the accurate estimate of the price of death. It was necessary to know the cost of death in order to establish adequate policy benefits and determine premiums. The economic evaluation of human life was a delicate matter that met with stubborn resistance. Particularly, although not exclusively, during the first half of the nineteenth century, life insurance was felt to be sacrilegious because its ultimate function was to compensate the loss of a father and a husband with a check to his widow and orphans. Critics objected that this turned man's sacred life into an "article of merchandise" (Albree 1870, 18). They asked, "Has a man the right to make the continuance of his life the basis of a bargain? Is it not turning a very solemn thing into a mere commercial transaction?" (Beecher 1870). Mennonites, who went to the extreme of excommunicating any member who insured his life, cited similar reasons: "It is equivalent to merchandising in human life; it is putting a monetary price on human life which is considered unscriptural since man is the 'temple of the Holy Ghost'" (*Mennonite Encyclopedia* 1957, 343). Life insurance benefits, however profitable, became "dirty money" (Knapp 1851).

MAGICAL MONEY

Whal notes the "remarkable paradox of an almost universal recourse to magic and irrationality" to handle death even among the most firm believers in science and the scientific method (1959, 17). But while examples of the relationship of magic to death in less-developed cultures are easily found (see Malinowski 1954, Habenstein and Lamers 1955; L. Simmons 1945, Blauner 1966), little is known about contemporary magic rituals. For instance, few people make plans for their own death, largely because of magical fears that to do so will hasten it. Most wills are drafted shortly before death (Dunham 1963). Likewise, people rarely prearrange their own funerals, despite the evidence that this reduces expenses considerably (M. Simmons 1975).

Its commercial intimacy with death made life insurance vulnerable to objections based on magical reasoning. A New York Life Insurance Company newsletter (1869, 3) referred to the "secret fear" many customers were reluctant to confess: "the mysterious connection between insuring life and losing life." The lists compiled by insurance companies in an effort to respond to criticism quoted their customers' apprehensions about insuring their lives: "I have a dread of it, a superstition that I may die the sooner" (*United States Insurance Gazette*, November 1859, 19). Responding to the popular suspicion that life insurance would "hasten the event about which it calculates," Jencks urged the necessity to "disabuse the public mind of such nonsense" (1843, 111). However, as late as the 1870s, "the old feeling that by taking out an insurance policy we do somehow challenge an interview with the 'king of terrors' still reigns in full force in many circles" (*Duty and Prejudice* 1870, 3).

Insurance publications were forced to reply to these superstitious fears. They reassured their customers that "life insurance cannot affect the fact of one's death at an appointed time" (ibid., 3). Sometimes they answered one magical fear with another, suggesting that not to insure was "inviting the vengeance of Providence" (Pompilly 1869). The audience for much of this literature was women. It is one of the paradoxes in the history of life insurance that women, intended to be the chief beneficiaries of the new system, became instead its most stubborn enemies. An Equitable Life Assurance booklet quoted wives' most prevalent objections: "Every cent of it would seem to me to be the price of your life. . . . It would make me miserable to think that I were to receive money by your death. . . . It seems to me that if [you] were to take a policy [you] would be brought home dead the next day" (1867, 3).

Thus, as a result of its commercial involvement with death, life insurance was forced to grapple with magic and superstition, issues supposedly remote from the kind of rational economic organization it represented.

SACRED MONEY

Until the late nineteenth century, life insurance shunned economic terminology, surrounding itself with religious symbolism and advertising more its moral value than its monetary benefits. Life insurance was marketed as an altruistic, self-denying gift rather than as a profitable investment. Most life insurance writers of this period denied the economic implications of their enterprise: "The term life insurance is a misnomer . . . it implies a value put on human life. But that is not our province. We recognize that life is intrinsically sacred and immeasurable, that it stands socially, morally, and religiously above all possible evaluation" (Holwig 1856, 4).

Later in the nineteenth century, the economic value of human life finally became a less embarrassing topic in insurance circles. The *United States Insurance Gazette* could suggest, "The life of every man has a value; not merely a moral value weighed in the scale of social affection and family ties but a value which may be measured in money" (May 1868, 2).[12] Rev. Henry Ward Beecher urged men to make their death "the basis of commercial action" (1870, 2). The process of introducing the economic value of human life culminated in 1924 when the concept was formally presented at the annual convention of life underwriters: "The most important new development in economic thought will be the recognition of the economic value of human life. . . . I confidently believe that the time is not far distant when . . . we shall apply to the economic organization, management and conservation of life values the same scientific treatment that we now use in connection with property" (Huebner 1924, 18).

Death was redefined by the new economic terminology as "all events ending the human life earning capacity" (Huebner 1959, 22). It was neatly categorized into premature death, casket death, living death (disability), and economic death (retirement). From this perspective, disease was the "depreciation of life values" (Dublin and Lotka 1930, 112) and premature death an unnecessary waste of money. In 1930, Dublin and Lotka developed the first estimate of capital values of males as a function of their age. By establishing differential financial values for lives, they also set a new criterion for stratifying them. Exceptional lives were those that made the greatest contributions, while substandard lives burdened their communities with financial loss (ibid., 80–82). It is claimed that the rational-utilitarian approach to death typified by life insurance has deritualized and secularized death (Vernon 1970; Gorer 1965). Death, however, is not tamed easily. Keener observers deny the hypothesis of deritualization and see instead the secularization of religious ritual (Faunce and Fulton 1957; Pine and Phillips 1970; Blauner 1966). This "metamorphosis of the sacred" (Brown 1959, 253) does not exempt ritual but changes its nature. The dead can be mourned in very different ways. Paradoxically, money that corrupts can also redeem: dollars can substitute for prayers.

Brown criticizes traditional sociology for perpetuating a secular and rational image of money without paying due attention to its symbolic and sacred functions (1959, 239–48). There is a dual relationship between money and death, actual or symbolic. While establishing an exact monetary equivalence for human life represents a profanation of the sacred, the symbolic, unrestrained use of money may contribute to the sanctification of death.

Durkheim briefly dwells on the sacred qualities of money: "Economic value is a sort of power of efficacy and we know the religious origins of the idea of power. Also richness confers mana, therefore it has it. Hence, it is seen that the idea of economic value and of religious value are not without connection" (1965, 466). The widespread practice of spending large sums of money at times of death testifies to the existence of a powerful and legitimate symbolic association between money and death. Expensive funerals are held without regard to the financial position of the deceased (Dunham 1963). Accusing fingers point routinely at the undertakers, blaming unreasonable expenses on their exorbitant prices (Mitford 1963; Harmer 1963). Historical evidence, however, shows that high expenditures at the time of death preceded the rise of the professional undertaker in the nineteenth century. Habenstein and Lamers describe the "wanton lavishness" of eighteenth-century funerals, when gloves, scarves, and all kinds of expensive gifts were distributed (1955, 203). The symbolic ties between money and death are also revealed by the norm that proscribes bargaining at times of death (M. Simmons 1975). Comparison shopping for funerals is strictly taboo, even though it reduces costs. Similarly, in the case of life insurance, "to count our pennies is tempting the Gods to blast us" (Gollin 1969, 210). Parsons and Lidz suggest that spending large sums of money may be an attempt to affect "the ultimate well being, or even the salvation of the deceased soul" (1967, 156).

When it comes to death, money transcends its exchange value and incorporates symbolic meanings. The dual relationship between money and death—actual as well as symbolic—is essential to the understanding of the development of life insurance. Sacrilegious because it equated cash with life, life insurance became on the other hand a legitimate vehicle for the symbolic use of money at the time of death. I will briefly examine three different aspects of the ritualization of life insurance: its emergence as a secular ritual, as an additional requirement for a "good death," and as a form of immortality.

LIFE INSURANCE AS RITUAL

Funeral expenditures have been defined as a secular ritual (Pine and Phillips 1970, 138; Bowman 1959, 118).[13] The evidence suggests that life insurance became another one. Curiously, its critics and not its proponents have been particularly sensitive to the ritualistic overtones of life insurance. Among others, Welsh claims that life insurance is a way of coming to terms with death not only financially but also emotionally and religiously (1963, 1576).

The view of life insurance as ritual can be substantiated with firmer evidence. From the 1830s to the 1870s, life insurance companies explicitly justified their enterprise and based their sales appeal on the quasi-religious nature of their product. Far more than an investment, life insurance was a "protective shield" over the dying, and a consolation "next to that of religion itself" (Holwig 1886, 22). The noneconomic functions of a policy were extensive: "It can alleviate the pangs of the bereaved, cheer the heart of the widow and dry the orphans' tears. Yes, it will shed the halo of glory around the memory of him who has been gathered to the bosom of his Father and God" (Franklin 1860, 34).

Life Insurance and the "Good Death"

Most societies have some conception of what constitutes an appropriate death, whether than means dying on a battlefield or while working at a desk. A "triumphant" death in pre–Civil War America meant a holy death; it involved spiritual transportation and the "triumph" of the faith (Saum 1975). Religiosity and moral generosity alone, however, soon became dysfunctional to a changed social context. In the eighteenth and early nineteenth centuries, widows and orphans had generally inherited sufficient land to live on and support themselves. Urbanization changed this, making families exclusively dependent on the father's wage. If he did not assume responsibility for the economic welfare of his wife and children after his death, society would have to support them. The principle of testamentary freedom in American law exempted men from any legal obligation to their children after death. Moral suasion, therefore, had to substitute for legal coercion. It was crucial to instill in men a norm of personal financial responsibility toward their families that did not stop with death. More and more a good death meant a wise and generous economic provision for dependents. A man was judged posthumously by his financial foresight as much as by his spiritual qualities. Only the careless father left "naught behind him but the memory of honest, earnest work and the hopeless wish that love ones . . . might somehow find their needed shelter from poverty . . ." (*Insurance Journal*, October 1882, 313). Diamond (1955) and Goody (1962) point out how attitudes toward death and the dead serve as efficient mechanisms for controlling the behavior of the living. Newspaper obituaries or clergymen's eulogies, for instance, remind the living what behavior is sanctioned by a particular social system. The public reformulation of social norms after a man's death reaffirms their value for the living. Life insurance writings referred to the new standards of dying in America: "The necessity that exists for every head of family to make proper provision for the sustenance of those dear to him after his death, is freely acknowledged and there is no contingency whereby a man stand excused from making such a provision" (*Life Insurance*, journal of the Manhattan Life Insurance Co., 1852, 19).

As an efficient mechanism to ensure the economic provision of dependents, life insurance gradually came to be counted among the duties of a good and responsible father. As one midcentury advocate of life insurance put it, the man who dies insured and "with soul sanctified by the deed, wings his way up to the realms of the just, and is gone where the good husbands and the good fathers go" (Knapp 1851, 226). Economic standards were endorsed by religious leaders such as Rev. Henry Ward Beecher, who pointed out, "Once the question was: can a Christian man rightfully seek Life Assurance? That day is passed. Now the question is: can a Christian man justify himself in neglecting such a duty?" (1870). The new criteria for a "good death" emerge from this excerpt from a sermon delivered in the 1880s:

> I call to your attention Paul's comparison. Here is one man who through neglect fails to support his family while he lives or after he dies. Here is another who abhors the Scriptures and rejects God. . . . Paul says that a man who neglects to care for his household is more obnoxious than a man who rejects the Scriptures. . . . When men think of their death they are apt to think of it only in connection with their spiritual welfare. . . . It is meanly selfish for you to be so absorbed in heaven . . . that you forget what is to become of your wife and children after you are dead. . . . It is a mean thing for you to go up to Heaven while they go into the poor-house. (T. DeWitt Talmage, quoted in Hull 1964, 240)

LIFE INSURANCE AND ECONOMIC IMMORTALITY

Theological concern with personal immortality was replaced in the nineteenth century by a growing concern with posterity and the social forms of immortality. Carl Becker (1932) points out that as early as the eighteenth century, European *philosophes* replaced the Christian promise of immortality in the afterworld with the belief that good men would live in the memory of future generations. This shift was reflected in the changing nature of wills. Earlier wills were concerned primarily with the spiritual salvation of the dying. The testator regulated all the details of his burial, assuring his chances of salvation by donations to the poor who would pray for his soul and by funding hundreds or thousands of masses and religious services in his honor, often in perpetuity (Vovelle 1974). After the mid-eighteenth century, wills were no longer concerned with matters of personal salvation; they became lay instruments for the distribution of property among descendants. Vovelle attributes the change in wills to the "de-Christianization" and deritualization of attitudes toward death in the mid-eighteenth century. It is likely, however, that the new format of wills was less the reflection of a loss of religious belief than an indicator of a new set of ideas and beliefs about immortality.[14] Feifel describes the transition in America: "When we gave up the old ideas of personal immortality through an afterlife we created the idea of social immortality. It meant that I could not live on but I would live on [*sic*] my children" (1974, 34). The Puritan concern with individual salvation was pushed aside by the new emphasis on posterity. Men became preoccupied less with their souls and more with leaving an estate for their heirs. The concern with social immortality interacted with structural pressures generated by new economic conditions and the process of urbanization. The multiplication of people with no more capital than their personal incomes made the economic future of their children painfully precarious. The premature death of the breadwinner spelled economic disaster to his widow and orphans. The new institutions that specialized in the economic consequences of death, such as life insurance and trusts, responded to that economic plight by serving the practical needs of dependents. However, they went beyond mere functionality by also symbolizing a form of economic immortality.

The appeal of life insurance as a pathway to immortality was early recognized by the insurance companies, which used it very explicitly to attract their customers. Life insurance was described as "the unseen hand of the provident father reaching forth from the grave and still nourishing his offspring and keeping together the group" (United States Life Insurance Co. booklet, 1850, 5). The idea of rewards and punishments after death also served to reinforce the father's responsibility for his widow and orphans. Goody suggests that the belief in afterworld retribution, like other supernatural beliefs, reinforces the system of social control over the living by placing it beyond human questioning (1962, 375–78). The uninsured could anticipate an uneasy afterlife. The dead also assumed a more active role than in the past; there was a shift from "service to serving" (Goody 1975, 4). They were no longer the passive recipients of their survivors' prayers; it was soon recognized that "the desire to outlive life in active beneficence is the common motive to which [life insurance] appeals" (Tyng 1881, 4).

CONCLUSION

My concern in this paper goes beyond a historical narrative of life insurance. Using previously unanalyzed aspects of that history, I explore the more general problem of establishing monetary equivalents for relations or processes that are defined as being beyond material concerns, a problem of long-standing interest in sociological thought. With life insurance, man and money, the sacred and the profane, were thrown together; the value of man became measurable by money. The purely quantitative conception of human beings was acceptable in primitive society where only the gods belonged to the sacred sphere while men remained part of the profane world. The growth of individualism resulted in a new respect for the infinite worth of human personality, displacing the earlier utilitarianism with an absolute valuation of human beings. In an increasingly industrialized market economy dominated by the "cash nexus," human life and human feelings were culturally segregated into their separate, incommensurable realm. Life insurance threatened the sanctity of life by pricing it. In the earlier part of the nineteenth century, the American public was not ready to commercialize death. Life insurance was rejected as a sacrilegious enterprise.

The task of converting human life and death into commodities is highly complex, creating inescapable sources of structural ambivalence in any enterprise that deals commercially with such sacred "products." Business demands profits for survival, yet profits alone remain a justification too base for an institution of its kind. I suggest that one solution, in the case of life insurance, was its "sacralization"; the transformation of the monetary evaluation of death into a ritual. Death yielded to the capitalist ethos—but not without compelling the latter to disguise its materialist mission in spiritual garb. For instance, life insurance assumed the role of a secular ritual and introduced new notions of immortality that emphasized remembrance through money. A "good death" was no longer defined only on moral grounds; the inclusion of a life policy made financial foresight another prerequisite. One finds, in addition to religious legitimation, attempts at moral and social legitimation of the industry. The public was assured that marketing death served the lofty social purpose of combating poverty, thereby reducing crime. At the individual level, there were moral rewards for the selfless and altruistic insurance buyer.

This religious, moral, and social legitimation was also true of American business in general until the 1870s. Sanford (1958) refers to the "psychic" factor of moral justification that distinguished America's industrial pioneers from their European counterparts. American industry was not justified by profits alone but as an agency of moral and spiritual uplift. Business was seen to serve God, character, and culture.[15] But if profit alone was an unacceptable motivation for most commercial enterprises, it was a particularly unseemly justification for a business, like life insurance, that dealt with human life and death. Indeed, by the latter part of the nineteenth century, when American business felt sufficiently confident to seek no other justification than the wealth it produced, life insurance still retained part of its religious camouflage. Even some of the most hard-bitten business leaders of the industry slipped into sentimentalism in speaking of life insurance as a "conviction first and then a business" (Kingsley 1911, 13).

I do not suggest that ingenious sales pitches alone were responsible for the adoption of life insurance. Its newly acquired legitimate status by the latter part of the nineteenth century was the result of profound economic, social, and cultural changes in America. Marketing techniques, however, can be useful indirect indicators of cultural values. In the case of life insurance, its earlier moralistic appeal reflected the powerful ideological resistance to commercializing death. As the economic definition of death became finally more acceptable by the latter part of the nineteenth century, life insurance could afford a more direct, businesslike approach to death without, however, fully discarding its ritualistic appeal. The pivotal role of the life insurance agent further confirms the cultural struggle of the industry. Life insurance sales began to improve in the 1840s when companies introduced personal solicitation. In sharp contrast to life policies, marine and fire insurance sold with only minor participation of agents. Customers who would not insure their lives unless pursued sought voluntarily the protection of their homes and ships. The distinctive role of the agent in life insurance was not simply an ingenious marketing device. It was a response to powerful client resistance. From the data available, it is safe to hypothesize that the adoption of life insurance would have been much slower and far less successful without the agency system. Persuasive and persistent personal solicitation alone could break through the ideological and superstitious barriers against insuring life.[16] Indeed, historical evidence clearly attests to the failure of all experiments to sell life insurance directly in this country and abroad.[17] The agent was indispensable. His role, however, was ambiguous. The dilemma of marketing life was again evident in the ambivalent role definition of agents. Death could not be pushed and promoted as a common ware. Official rhetoric urged agents to remain above materialistic concerns, performing their task with the spiritual devotion of a missionary. The rewards, however, went to the successful salesman who solicited the most policies.

Other "businessmen" of death are caught in the same structural ambivalence as life insurance. To undertakers, as to life insurance salesmen, death is a money-making business. As "businessmen" of death they are differentiated from the "professionals" of death, physicians and clergymen, whose connection to death is made legitimate by their service orientation.[18] Parsons (1949) and Merton (1975) distinguish between individual motivational patterns and the institutional structures of business and the professions. Regardless of the individual motivations of the practitioners—their greed or beneficence—professions institutionalize altruism while businesses institutionalize self-interest. Particularly when it comes to death, to save and to heal is holier than to sell. The powerful normative stigma of the utilitarian association of money with death results in a negative evaluation of those involved in making money out of death. In sum, marketing death is what Hughes has instructively called "dirty work" (1958, 49–52). As with life insurers, undertakers attempt to legitimate their business by transforming it into a sacred ritual. Warner describes the tendency on the part of the undertaker "to borrow the ritual and sacred symbols of the minister . . . to provide an outward cover for what he is and does. His place of business is not a factory or an office but a 'chapel' or a 'home'" (1959, 317).

This paper has shown that the "profanation" of the sacred, such as making money out of death, creates sources of strain and ambivalence in its practitioners that can be assuaged but not resolved by "sacralizing" the profanation. This hypothesis would be enriched by further investigation of the marketing of other similarly "sacred" products such as human organs or even the recently expanding business of mercenary mothers and their "black-market" babies, in which human life is routinely handled as a commodity to be exchanged, as Titmuss feared, for "dollars and pounds."

NOTES

Viviana A. Zelizer, "Human Values and the Market: The Case of Life Insurance and Death in Nineteenth-Century America," *American Journal of Sociology* 84 (November 1978): 591–610. Reprinted with permission.

1. Parsons and Lidz (1967, 163) also attach the conception of the sanctity of life to the stress on individualism.

2. For English versions of some portions of the book, see Becker 1959; Altmann 1903; Levine 1971; Lawrence 1976; and Etzkorn 1968.

3. On the "absolutization" of the market as an analytical tool for social analysis in most social science disciplines, and for a discussion of the types and functions of different forms of economic and social exchange, see Barber 1974.

4. According to a recent report, the nation appears to be shifting toward almost total reliance on volunteer, nonpaid donors (*New York Times*, June 19, 1977).

5. See also the *Manifesto of the Communist Party* (Marx 1971, 11). Above all, money for Marx (1964, 165–69) destroys individuality by enabling its possessor to achieve objects and qualities that bear no connection to individual talents or capacities.

6. Cooley formulated another, different perspective on the "moral problem" created by the fact that "pecuniary values fail to express the higher life of society." Although he accepted the fact that human values such as love, beauty, and righteousness were not traditional market commodities, Cooley rejected the permanent segregation of pecuniary values into a special, inferior province of life. His alternative was the enhancement of monetary evaluation; precisely by encouraging "the translation into it of the higher values . . . the principle that everything has its price should be rather enlarged than restricted" (1913, 202–3).

7. A recent policy-oriented analysis of organ transplants concludes that "if the body is to be made available to others for personal or societal research, it must be a gift" (Veatch 1976, 269).

8. On the impact of economic growth and urbanization on the development of life insurance, see, among others, Buley 1967; North and Davis 1971; and Mannes 1932.

9. There are a few exceptions. See, e.g., Riley 1963. An entire issue of the *American Behavioral Scientist* (May 1963) was devoted to social research and life insurance. Two doctoral dissertations have been written on the life insurance agent (Taylor 1958; Bain 1959).

10. On the fear of failure among nineteenth-century businessmen, see Katz 1975. For a fuller explanation of the cultural and sociostructural factors involved in the adoption of life insurance, see Zelizer 1979.

11. Only slaves were considered to have pecuniary value. This explains why countries that forbade life insurance in principle allowed the insurance of slaves. Their lack of human value justified economic equivalences without presenting serious moral difficulties (Reboul 1909, 23).

12. The greater acceptance of the economic value of a man's life did not include women. The *Insurance Monitor*, among others, was outspoken against insuring wives for the benefit of husbands: "The husband who can deliberately set a money value upon his wife, is so far destitute not only of affection for her, but of respect for himself. . . . To him she is but a chattel . . ." ("The Insurable Value of a Wife" [September 1870], 712d). The insurance of children was similarly opposed by many individuals and organizations who objected to the economic evaluation of a child's life. In the 1870s, industrial insurance companies began insuring the poor. For the first time children under ten years of age were insured on a regular basis. There were at least seventy legislative attempts in various states to prohibit it as being against public policy and the public interest. The *Boston Evening Transcript* reflected their prevalent feeling that "no manly man and no womanly woman should be ready to say that their infants have pecuniary value" (March 14, 1895).

13. Ariès (1975) sees the contemporary American funeral rite as a compromise between deritualization and traditional forms of mourning. Group therapy and family reunions have also been suggested as secular rituals (Patterson 1975).

14. Ariès's interpretation of Vovelle's data may have some bearing on this hypothesis. Ariès uses the rise of the family and of new family relationships based on feelings and affection in the mid-eighteenth century to explain the change in wills. The dying person no longer used legal means to regulate the rituals of his burial because he now trusted his family to remember him voluntarily (1974, 64–65). The growing importance of family ties may have encouraged religious belief in posterity and social forms of immortality.

15. The accumulation of great fortunes was justified by the ultimate social and philanthropic purposes to which the money was put (Diamond 1955, 13–15). On this subject, see also Hofstadter 1963, 251.

16. For the impact of personal influence on the diffusion of innovations, see Rogers and Shoemaker 1971; on marketing, see Katz and Lazarsfeld 1955.

17. Savings bank life insurance, e.g., which has offered low-price quality policies since 1907, has never been very successful. Interestingly, one of the few commercial failures of the Sears Roebuck catalogue business was an attempt in the 1930s to sell life insurance directly.

18. Parsons (1951, 445) suggests that even medical students need certain rites to justify their association to death, such as the ritualistic dissection of cadavers in the early stages of medical training.

References

Albree, George. 1870. *The Evils of Life Insurance*. Pittsburgh: Bakewell and Mathers.

Altmann, S. P. 1903. "Simmel's Philosophy of Money." *American Journal of Sociology* 9 (July): 46–68.

Ariès, Philippe. 1974. *Western Attitudes toward Death*. Baltimore: Johns Hopkins University Press.

———. 1975. "The Reversal of Death: Changes in Attitudes toward Death in Western Society." In *Death in America*, edited by David E. Stannard, 134–58. Philadelphia: University of Pennsylvania Press.

Bain, Robert K. 1959. "The Process of Professionalization: Life Insurance Selling." Ph.D. diss., University of Chicago.

Barber, Bernard. 1974. "The Absolutization of the Market: Some Notes on How We Got from There to Here." Paper read at the conference on Markets and Morals, Battelle Institute, Seattle.

Becker, Carl. 1932. *The Heavenly City of Eighteenth-Century Philosophers*. New Haven, Conn.: Yale University Press.

Becker, Howard. 1959. "On Simmel's Philosophy of Money." In *Georg Simmel*, edited by Kurt H. Wolff, 216–32. Columbus: Ohio State University Press.

Beecher, Henry Ward. 1870. *Truth in a Nutshell*. New York: Equitable Life Assurance Co.

Blau, Peter M. 1967. *Exchange and Power in Social Life*. New York: Wiley.

Blauner, Robert. 1966. "Death and Social Structure." *Psychiatry* 29 (November): 378–94.

Bowman, Leroy. 1959. *The American Funeral*. Washington, D.C.: Public Affairs Press.

Brown, Norman O. 1959. *Life against Death*. Middletown, Conn.: Wesleyan University Press.

Buley, R. Carlyle. 1967. *The Equitable Life Assurance Society of the United States*. New York: Appleton-Century-Crofts.

Cooley, Charles H. 1913. "The Sphere of Pecuniary Valuation." *American Journal of Sociology* 19 (September): 188–203.

Diamond, Sigmund. 1955. *The Reputation of the American Businessman*. Cambridge, Mass.: Harvard University Press.

Dublin, Louis I., and Alfred J. Lotka. 1930. *The Money Value of Man*. New York: Ronald.

Dunham, Allison. 1963. "The Method, Process and Frequency of Wealth Transmission at Death." *University of Chicago Law Review* 30 (Winter): 241–85.

Durkheim, Emile. 1965. *The Elementary Forms of the Religious Life*. New York: Free Press.

Duty and Prejudice. 1870. New York: J. H. and C. M. Goodsell.

Etzkorn. Peter. 1968. *Georg Simmel: Conflict in Modern Culture and Other Essays*. New York: Teachers College Press.

Faunce, William A., and Robert L. Fulton. 1957. "The Sociology of Death: A Neglected Area of Research." *Social Forces* 36 (October): 205–9.

Feifel, Herman. 1974. "Attitudes towards Death Grow More Realistic." *New York Times*, July 21.

Franklin, Morris. 1860. "Proceedings from the First Annual Session of the Convention of Life Insurance Underwriters." *American Life Assurance Magazine* 1 (January): 34–39.

Friedman, Lawrence M. 1964. "Patterns of Testation in the 19th Century: A Study of Essex County (New Jersey) Wills." *American Journal of Legal History* 8 (January): 34–53.

Gollin, James. 1969. *Pay Now, Die Later.* New York: Penguin.

Goody, Jack. 1962. *Death, Property and the Ancestors.* Stanford, Calif.: Stanford University Press.

———. 1975. "Death and the Interpretation of Culture: A Bibliographic Overview." In *Death in America*, edited by David E. Stannard, 1–8. Philadelphia: University of Pennsylvania Press.

Gorer, Geoffrey. 1965. *Death, Grief and Mourning in Contemporary Britain.* London: Cresset Press.

Goupil, René. 1905. *De la considération de la mort des personnes dans les actes juridiques.* Caen: University of Caen.

Habenstein, Robert, and William M. Lamers. 1955. *The History of American Funeral Directing.* Milwaukee: Bulfin Printers.

Harmer, Ruth. 1963. *The High Cost of Dying.* New York: Crowell.

Hofstadter, Richard. 1963. *Anti-Intellectualism in American Life.* New York: Vintage.

Holwig, David. 1886. *The Science of Life Assurance.* Boston: Provident Life and Trust Co.

Huebner, S. S. 1924. *Proceedings of the 35th Annual Convention of the National Association of Life Underwriters.* New York: National Association of Life Underwriters.

———. 1959. *The Economics of Life Insurance.* New York: Crofts.

Hughes, Everett Cherrington. 1958. *Men and Their Work.* Glencoe, Ill.: Free Press.

Hull, Roger. 1964. "Immortality through Premiums." *Christian Century* 81 (February): 239–40.

Jencks, T. R. 1843. "Life Insurance in the United States." *Hunt's Merchants' Magazine* 8 (February): 109–30.

Katz, Elihu, and Paul F. Lazarsfeld. 1955. *Personal Influence.* Glencoe, Ill.: Free Press.

Katz, Michael B. 1975. *The People of Hamilton.* Cambridge, Mass.: Harvard University Press.

Kingsley, Darwin P. 1911. *Militant Life Insurance.* New York: New York Life Insurance Co.

Knapp, Moses L. 1851. *Lectures on the Science of Life Insurance.* Philadelphia: E. J. Jones and Co.

Lawrence, P. A. 1976. *Georg Simmel: Sociologist and European.* New York: Harper and Row.

Levine, Donald, ed. 1971. *Georg Simmel on Individuality and Social Forms.* Chicago: University of Chicago Press.

Malinowski, Bronislaw. 1954. *Magic, Science, and Religion*. New York: Doubleday.

Mannes, Alfred. 1932. "Principles and History of Insurance." In *International Encyclopedia of the Social Sciences*, 8:30–47. New York: Macmillan.

Marx, Karl. 1964. *The Economic and Philosophic Manuscripts of 1844*. New York: International Publishers.

———. 1971. *Manifesto of the Communist Party*. New York: International Publishers.

Mennonite Encyclopedia, The. 1957. Scottdale, Pa.: Mennonite Publishing House.

Merton, Robert K. 1975. "The Uses of Institutionalized Altruism." In *Seminar Reports*, vol. 3, no. 6. New York: Columbia University.

Mitford, Jessica. 1963. *The American Way of Death*. Greenwich, Conn.: Fawcett.

North, Douglass C., and Lance E. Davis. 1971. *Institutional Change and American Economic Growth*. Cambridge: Cambridge University Press.

Parsons, Talcott. 1949. "The Professions and the Social Structure." In *Essays in Sociological Theory*, 34–49. Glencoe, Ill.: Free Press.

———. 1951. *The Social System*. Glencoe, Ill.: Free Press.

Parsons, Talcott, Renee C. Fox, and Victor Lidz. 1973. "The Gift of Life and Its Reciprocation." In *Death in American Experience*, edited by Arien Mack, 1–49. New York: Schocken.

Parsons, Talcott, and Victor Lidz. 1967. "Death in American Society." In *Essays in Self-Destruction*, edited by Edwin S. Shneidman, 133–40. New York: Science House.

Pascan, Michel. 1907. *Les pactes sur succession future*. Paris: University of Paris.

Patterson, Raul R. 1975. "Children and Ritual of the Mortuary." In *Grief and the Meaning of the Funeral*, edited by Otto S. Margolis, 86–99. New York: MAS Information Corp.

Phelps, James T. 1895. *Life Insurance Sayings*. Cambridge, Mass.: Riverside Press.

Pine, Vanderlyn R., and Derek L. Phillips. 1970. "The Cost of Dying: A Sociological Analysis of Expenditures." *Social Problems* 17 (Winter): 131–39.

Pompilly, Judah T. 1869. *Watchman! What of the Night? or Rejected Blessings for Wives and Mothers*. New York: English and Rumsey.

Reboul, Edmond. 1909. *Du droit des enfants bénéficiaires d'une assurance sur la vie contracteé par leur père*. Paris: Librairie Nouvelle de Droit.

Riley, John W. 1963. "Basic Social Research and the Institution of Life Insurance." *American Behavioral Scientist* 6 (May): 6–9.

Rogers, Everett M., and F. Floyd Shoemaker. 1971. *Communications of Innovations*. New York: Free Press.

Sanford, Charles L. 1958. "The Intellectual Origins and New-Worldliness of American Industry." *Journal of Economic History* 18, no. 1:1–15.

Saum, Lewis O. 1975. "Death in the Popular Mind of Pre–Civil War America." In *Death in America*, edited by David E. Stannard, 30–48. Philadelphia: University of Pennsylvania Press.

Schultz, Oscar T. 1930. *The Law of the Dead Human Body*. Chicago: American Medical Association.

Simmel, Georg. 1900. *Philosophie des Geldes*. Leipzig: Duncker and Humblot.

Simmons, Leo W. 1945. *The Role of the Aged in Primitive Society*. New Haven, Conn.: Yale University Press.

Simmons, Marilyn G. 1975. "Funeral Practices and Public Awareness." *Human Ecology Forum* 5 (Winter): 9–13.

Stalson, Owen J. 1969. *Marketing Life Insurance*. Bryn Mawr, Pa.: McCahan Foundation.

"Tax Consequences of Transfers of Bodily Parts." 1973. *Columbia Law Review* 73 (April): 842–65.

Taylor, Miller Lee. 1958. "The Life Insurance Man: A Sociological Analysis of the Occupation." Ph.D. diss., Louisiana State University.

Titmuss, Richard M. 1971. *The Gift Relationship*. New York: Vintage.

Tyng, Stephen H. 1881. "Life Insurance Does Assure." *Harper's Monthly Magazine* 62 (April): 754–63.

Veatch, Robert M. 1976. *Death, Dying and the Biological Revolution*. New Haven, Conn.: Yale University Press.

Vernon, Glenn. 1970. *The Sociology of Death*. New York: Ronald.

Vovelle, Michel. 1974. *Piété baroque et déchristianisation en Provence au XVIII siècle*. Paris: Plon.

Wallwork, Ernest. 1972. *Durkheim: Morality and Milieu*. Cambridge, Mass.: Harvard University Press.

Warner, Lloyd W. 1959. *The Living and the Dead: A Study of the Symbolic Life of Americans*. New Haven, Conn.: Yale University Press.

Welsh, Alexander. 1963. "The Religion of Life Insurance." *Christian Century* 80 (December 11): 1541–43, 1574–76.

Whal, Charles W. 1959. "The Fear of Death." In *The Meaning of Death*, edited by Herman Feifel, 16–29. New York: McGraw-Hill.

White, Gerald T. 1955. *A History of the Massachusetts Hospital Life Insurance Company*. Cambridge, Mass.: Harvard University Press.

Zelizer, Viviana A. 1979. *Morals and Markets: The Development of Life Insurance in the United States*. New York: Columbia University Press.

2

The Price and Value of Children

The Case of Children's

Insurance in the United States

On March 14, 1895, the *Boston Evening Transcript* stated: "No manly man and no womanly woman should be ready to say that their infants have pecuniary value." The paper was attacking the widespread contemporary practice of insuring children. For three cents a week, for instance, a one-year-old child could be insured for $10, a ten-year-old for $33. To this day, the concept of making money out of the life or death of a child seems mercenary and morally repugnant to most people. Yet a major national survey sponsored by the American Council of Life Insurance in 1976 reveals that 57 percent of all American children under fifteen have some kind of life insurance coverage. Surprisingly, children's insurance has been largely ignored in the voluminous life insurance literature. Despite its commercial success, it remains mostly unadvertised and unpublicized, and it is difficult to obtain information on the subject.

The development of children's insurance offers the possibility of probing into the complex relationship between human values and the market. The single most profound and extensive analysis of this issue is found in Simmel's *Philosophy of Money* (1978), where he traces the historical dichotomization of money and personal values. Simmel attributes this polarization to a dual process that transformed both the value of a person and the value of money. While an earlier, relativist concept of human life legitimated its quantification, Christianity sacralized and absolutized human existence, setting life above financial considerations. Paradoxically, the growing inadequacy of money is also a consequence of its success. The "sacred dignity" of primitive money disappears in modern society as money expands into the "colourless and indifferent" equivalent of everything and anything. Money's successful leveling of all qualitative distinctions into quantitative measurement clashes with a powerful "ideal of distinction" that stresses the uniqueness of human values (Simmel 1978, 365–66, 389).

Thus, Simmel posits a radical contradiction and a necessary tension between money and human values in modern society, which limit or at least obstruct the expansion of the market into all areas of exchange. His arguments may be examined with empirical data. In my previous work, based on the development of adult life insurance, I analyzed the powerful cultural resistance in the earlier part of the nineteenth century against profaning the sanctity of human life and death with commercial considerations. Gradually, the capitalization of the value of adult life and the monetary indemnification of that value became acceptable. However, the monetary evaluation of death did not desacralize it. Far from "profaning" life and death, money became ritualized by its association with them. Life insurance took on symbolic values quite distinct from its utilitarian function, emerging as a new form of ritual with which to face death (Zelizer 1978, 1979).

Ironically, as men's lives became more and more entangled with market considerations, children's lives were gradually severed from market ties. The radical transformation in the value of children that began in the twentieth-century United States—specifically, the emergence of the economically "worthless" but emotionally "priceless" child—offers another empirical possibility of examining the interaction between the market and personal values. The case of adult life insurance suggests that commercialization of those aspects of the social order, such as life and death, that are defined as above financial relationships involves cultural as well as economic processes. Similarly, exclusion from the market—as in the case of children—implies changes in values, not only in social structure.[1]

This paper will argue that the removal of children from the "cash nexus" at the turn of the past century was part of a cultural process of sacralization of children's lives. I use the term "sacralization" in the sense of objects being invested with moral and religious meaning. While in the nineteenth century the market value of children was culturally acceptable, the new normative ideal of the child as an exclusively emotional and moral asset precluded instrumental or fiscal considerations. The primacy of children's qualitative, intrinsic value was affirmed by forsaking any immediate quantitative money value. Historical data on the controversial development of children's insurance between 1875 and the early decades of the twentieth century are analyzed as a specific measure of the radical transformation in the cultural meaning of childhood.

THE PRICE AND VALUE OF CHILDREN: LIMITATIONS OF EXISTING INTERPRETATIONS

It is now a documented fact that a major shift in the value of children took place at the turn of the past century: from "object of utility" to object of sentiment and from producer asset to consumer good. Economically, a child today is worthless to his or her parents. He is also expensive. The total cost of raising a child—combining both direct maintenance costs and indirect opportunity costs—was estimated to average between $100,000 and $140,000 in 1980 (Espenshade 1980). In return for such expenses, a child is expected to provide love, smiles, and emotional satisfaction but no money. In fact, the contemporary parent-child relationship in America can be considered a prototype of a non-market-exchange relationship. Parents cannot even expect significant public support for their expenses. While in all other major industrial countries a system of family allowances grants children at least partial monetary value, in America income-transfer programs remain inadequate and mostly restricted to female-headed, single-parent households below a certain income level. The actual value of a $750 tax deduction for each dependent child is determined by the family's tax bracket. For low-income families, the deduction is minimal (Keniston 1977; Kamerman and Kahn 1978).

In sharp contrast to our conceptions of the value of children, the birth of a child in eighteenth-century rural America was welcomed as the arrival of a future laborer and as security for parents later in life. By the mid-nineteenth century, however, the construction of the economically worthless child was completed among the urban middle class. Fiscal rewards were postponed as concern shifted to children's education as the determinant of future marketplace worth. Yet the economic value of the working-class child increased. Rapid industrialization after the 1860s introduced new occupations for children, and according to the 1870 census about one out of every eight children was employed. Child labor laws, compulsory education, and strict legal regulation of "baby farming" gradually destroyed the class lag. By the early decades of the twentieth century, lower-class children joined their middle-class counterparts in the new nonproductive world of childhood. Its new sanctity and emotional value made a child's life industrially taboo. To make profit out of children, declared Felix Adler in 1905, was to "touch profanely a sacred thing" (quoted in Brenmer 1971, 653).[2]

Although the shift in children's value is indisputable, Kett notes that "precise characterization of this change has remained elusive" (1978, S196). Its sociological import has never been systematically explored. Research on the value of children has been dominated by demographers, and more recently by psychologists and economists, all similarly concerned with parental motivation for childbearing and its relation to fertility patterns (Easterlin 1969; Schultz 1973; Hoffman and Hoffman 1973; Becker 1976; Sawhill 1977; Arnold et al. 1975).[3] Although these studies are significant contributions to the understanding of children's value, they remain limited by a primarily individualistic and utilitarian framework and by an ahistorical perspective. Microeconomic theorists, for instance, conclude that shifts in children's value are dictated by market shifts in price. Accordingly, children became consumption goods when they ceased to be profitable as economic investment goods. Value preferences "are assumed not to change substantially over time, nor to be very different between wealthy and poor persons, or even between persons in different societies and cultures" (Becker 1976, 5).

American historians, on the other hand, seem to be more intrigued with the social creation of adolescence than the changing status of younger, pre-adolescent children (Kett 1977; Katz and Davey 1978; Elder 1980). Existing historical interpretations are psychologically oriented (DeMause 1974) or else focus mostly on the impact of structural change. The success of indus-trial capitalism at the turn of the past century is assigned primary responsi-bility for putting children out of work and into schools to satisfy the growing demand for a skilled, educated labor force (Minge-Kalman 1978). Huber suggests that the new economic system also triggered a conflict of interest between age groups (1976). In an agrarian economy, as in early stages of industrialization, the labor of "little work people" was a welcome alternative that freed men for agriculture (*Niles' Register*, June 7, 1817, 226). By the turn of the century a cheap juvenile labor force threatened to depress adult male wages.

Changes in the family also are linked with the shift in children's value. Increasing differentiation between economic production and home trans-formed the basis of family cohesion. As instrumental ties weakened, the emo-tional value of all family members—including children—gained new saliency (Smelser and Halpern 1978; Hareven 1977; Zaretsky 1976). In addition, the specialization of women into efficient full-time motherhood, while in reality restricted to the middle class, nevertheless made the widespread labor of children awkward (Rothman 1978; Degler 1980).

Demographic theories contend that the new emotional value of children is best explained by falling birth and mortality rates in the twentieth century. In two landmark studies of childhood in Europe and England, respectively, Ariès (1962) and Stone (1977) suggest that in periods of high mortality par-ents protect themselves against the emotional pain of a child's death by re-maining affectively aloof. From this perspective it is "folly to invest too much emotional capital in such ephemeral beings" (Stone 1977, 105). A similar cost-benefit accounting explains why falling birth rates and smaller family size increase the emotional value of each individual child. The economic equation of longevity or scarcity with value remains highly speculative. For instance, Demos submits that in seventeenth-century Plymouth, Massachu-setts, a high death rate may have encouraged a special concern for and ten-derness toward infants (1978; see also Slater 1977).

With some important exceptions (Smelser and Halpern 1978; Greven 1977; Wells 1978; Boli-Bennett and Meyer 1978), the independent impact of cultural variables redefining the value of children in the United States has received much less attention in the literature.[4] This paper will focus on the cultural dimension, namely, the sacralization of children.

MARKETING CHILDREN'S INSURANCE:
A BRIEF BACKGROUND

Ordinary life insurance companies, which had operated in the United States since the latter part of the eighteenth century, had confined their business to husbands and fathers of middle-class families. In 1875, for the first time, John F. Dryden of the Prudential Life Insurance Company began insuring the lives of children under ten. It was part of industrial insurance, a major marketing innovation aimed at the rapidly expanding working-class population. Besides accepting the insurance of children and women, industrial life policies were available in small units—the average face value of a policy was about $100.[5] Industrial agents went into the homes of prospective buyers, usually insuring their lives without medical examination and collecting premiums weekly on a house-to-house basis. They were effective. In four months, 1,000 lives had been insured in Newark, New Jersey, including 329 children under ten. After one year of operation, Prudential had received about $14,000 in premiums. In 1879, two more companies, Metropolitan Life and John Hancock, began selling industrial insurance. Perhaps because premiums were as low as five or ten cents per week, the business grew beyond all expectations. By 1895, $268 million of insurance was in force, and Prudential alone had received over $33 million in premiums. The company now employed ten thousand agents (Dryden 1895, 22; Huebner 1921, 276).

As a crucial component of that prosperity, children's insurance became firmly established; one and a half million children were insured in 1896. The greatest growth of the business took place between 1882 and 1902; at the end of that period over three million children were insured (Hoffman 1903, 4). It was also during those years that the trouble started. Between 1889 and 1902, there were at least eighty legislative attempts across the country to prohibit or restrict the insurance of children's lives as being against public policy and the public interest. In 1884, as sales multiplied, the legislative battle began when Governor Benjamin Butler of Massachusetts included in his address to the legislature the first official suggestion to prohibit the insurance of children. In 1889, Governor Beaver of Pennsylvania revived the attack in his annual message to the legislature, and a bill was introduced to make the insurance of children unlawful in the state. Although the bill was defeated, the antagonism persisted and additional bills were presented—and rejected—in Pennsylvania in 1897, 1903, and 1907. This relentless attack on the industry that insured children was nationwide. Every few years bills were introduced in New York, Ohio, Illinois, Massachusetts, Wisconsin, and thirteen other states. In Colorado the opposition was finally successful: in 1893 the insurance of children was declared illegal in that state.

Insuring children was expensive to the parents. Although premiums were low, so were benefits. The industry had to guard itself against the higher mortality of the class insured and particularly of children. Costs were also increased by the need to subsidize an army of industrial agents in their weekly door-to-door collections. Industrial policies had little or no surrender value to their owners, and the lapse rate was extremely high. The battle against children's insurance, however, had little to do with these economic issues. It was a moral crusade by child savers on behalf of poor children. An examination of the arguments and rationales used by the equally relentless opposition and defense in their testimonies to state legislatures, in the press, and other publications reveals a struggle over the changing value of the lower-class child.

THE OPPOSITION: CHILD SAVERS VERSUS CHILD INSURERS

In 1874, only one year before the child-insuring business started, upper- and middle-class groups organized the New York Society for the Prevention of Cruelty to Children, the first and one of the leading institutions of a national child-saving movement. The almost twin births were more than an unrelated coincidence. In different ways, both organizations became involved in the changing status of the lower-class child. The primary goal of child savers, pursued through a wide variety of programs, was to enforce a new respect for the sanctity of poor children's lives, creating for them a special nonproductive world.[6] To many child savers, child insurers were the enemy. The insurance of poor children stood as an offensive symbol of the prevalent materialistic orientation toward childhood; they opposed it as a form of commercial exploitation even more sordid than most, since it speculated on a child's death.

To its detractors, "child-insurance companies"—as they dubbed the industrial insurance business collectively—had "child-blood" on their hands (Waugh 1890, 59). Newspapers across the nation carried sensational articles on the dangers of making a child's death profitable. The *Trenton True American*, for instance, suggested that children's insurance be declared invalid as a "dangerous incentive to murder": "It is not only the inducement which inhuman parents . . . find in insurance on their children to ill-treat them or put them out of the way, but it is the tendency to cause them to neglect their children in their sickness and . . . the demoralizing effect produced by parents speculating on the lives of their children" (March 26, 1878). Even within the insurance community some leaders warned that one "should shrink with horror from the ungodly speculation" (Wright 1873, 65).

The genealogy of the business did little to dispel fears. Children's insurance began as outright bets among sixteenth-century European businessmen on the birth and lives of boys and girls (Huizinga 1970, 73; de Roover 1945, 196). The evidence suggests that in England the insurance of children by burial clubs, which started in the 1830s and 1840s, was often a sordid affair. In *Past and Present*, Carlyle relates an 1840 case of a mother and father arraigned and found guilty of poisoning three of their children to collect insurance money from a burial society. He adds, "The official authorities . . . hint that perhaps the case is not solitary, that perhaps you had better not probe farther into that department of things" (1918, 4–5). Until the 1870s, government regulation in England was weak and seldom enforced. Baby farmers, for whom the death of one of their children was already a pecuniary gain, made it doubly profitable by insuring the children they "adopted," often in more than one company. A case of this "unspeakable trade partnership between the insurance touter and the ghoulish baby farmer" was presented before the Royal Commission on Insurance in 1875; a child had been insured for the benefit of his guardian in eight societies for a total of thirty pounds. During another investigation that same year, a Manchester lawyer testified that already in the 1840s "it was publicly said in the town that the children had been purposely killed [for insurance money]; it was a regular trade" (Campbell 1902, 283). Comparative data from France reveal similar accusations against child insurance for dangerously raising the price of children above their emotional value. Anecdotes circulated of mercenary *nourrices* and heartless parents grieving over the recovery of a sick child because it meant the loss of insurance benefits. Indeed, sales booklets popular in both France and Belgium enticed customers quite candidly with the potential profits to be gained from a dying child. One popular pamphlet, for example, included a conversation between two working-class fathers with one outdoing the other in marveling over how much money they had received from the insurance company after the death of one of their children (Goupil 1905, 101; François 1906, 10; Quiquet 1906).

The available evidence is not conclusive enough to prove beyond doubt that child insurance and child murder were related. However, taking into account the high rates of infanticide in England as in Europe in the eighteenth and early nineteenth centuries, the relationship seems likely. If the death of a child, particularly an unwanted child, was a lesser event, the possibility of making money out of it could well become a tempting incentive.[7]

Until the 1880s the opposition to child insurance in the United States remained sporadic and unorganized. But in 1893 the national American Humane Society for the Prevention of Cruelty to Animals and Children passed a resolution that "the practice of insuring the lives of children under 10 years of age, under any pretext, is against public policy." Member organizations were urged to secure prohibitive legislation making it a criminal offense to insure "or in any way offer a reward upon the death of a child" (Read 1895, 19–20). The legislative battle was on. The fiercest fight took place in 1895, when the Massachusetts Society for the Prevention of Cruelty to Children introduced a bill to the legislature to prohibit the insurance of children under ten. For weeks the opposition and the defense argued their cases, making sensational front-page news with their alarming statistics and emotional pleas. Clergymen, physicians, judges, and politicians took the stand to denounce the "diabolical" practice of insuring children. Concerned citizens urged legislators to stop "the traffic in the lives of children" and the "merciless temptation of making young death a profitable event" (McKenzie 1895, 28; James 1947, 122). Charity workers presented heartrending accounts of families in extreme poverty whose sick children, often dying of starvation, received no care but whose insurance premiums were paid regularly. Insurance companies were accused of joining with mercenary parents to "feather [their] own nest at the cost of blood and tears and deaths of human beings" (Read 1895, 4). Charles C. Read, a vociferous critic, instructed legislators: "I do not know whether you have seen the building of the Metropolitan Company in New York. . . . Go up . . . to the directors' room where the floor is soft with velvet carpets and the room is finished in rich red mahogany . . . and there you will find these gentlemen who think what a beautiful thing this child insurance is. . . ." From every block of marble of that magnificent place peered "the hungry eyes of some starving child." Agents were also attacked as an unscrupulous "band of sharpers": "the more they hustle, the more they make" (Read 1895, 39, 51; Fiske 1895, 4). English agents, often imported by American companies for their experienced background, were even suspected of "baby-baiting," paying parents for the death of an uninsured child to attract new customers. Benjamin Waugh, president of the English Society for the Prevention of Cruelty to Children, quoted alleged admissions of agents that "we bait our hook with a dead child" or "I am glad of a funeral, I look out for one. . . . I get business by funerals" (1890, 54). On October 15, 1895, the *New York Times* joined the ranks of outspoken critics, its columns exposing the child insurance business as an unconscionable "temptation to inhuman crimes" and insurance agents as "pests of society" (23).

The moral condemnation of children's insurance, however, went beyond the arguments of possible child neglect or murder. For many child savers, it was not the danger of death but the profanation of the child's life that was at stake. They decried parents "ready to traffic in their offspring as if they were horses or goats" (*Insurance Monitor*, February 1881). To them, the insured child was but another version of the working child, one earning through its death what the other earned by its labor. In both cases, the sanctity of a child's life was polluted by monetary considerations. Critics asked: "Can any reflecting citizen . . . justify himself in assisting . . . the unnatural practice of child-insurance? . . . It is certainly not too much to claim that there should be no bargaining or trafficking in our Commonwealth under our auspices, in infant life, which has been held sacred" (letter by Chas. F. Donnelly, in Read 1895, 28). Insurance agents were despised for making the death of a child a matter of economics, a routine business transaction by which, as the English put it, "you change the child for the pound" (Waugh 1890, 41). Regardless of individual motivation, the necessarily commercial involvement of agents with the life and death of little children was defined as morally deviant.

Despite its dramatic impact, the evidence against children's insurance was weak and unconvincing. In fact, the striking feature of the legislative hearings was not the cases of neglect but the intensity of the accusers' fears, based on unquestioned certainty that lower-class parents could be so cheaply bribed into destroying their children. In their moral outrage, and following the often distorted perceptions of middle-class observers, child savers assumed that the economic ties between working-class parent and child could easily become mercenary ones. If they were willing to profit from the labor of their children, parents would be equally willing to profit from their death. "Until fathers and mothers cease to be brutal and drunken," warned anxious critics, "it is not safe to put them in the way of such temptation as this child insurance" (Savage 1895, 28).[8]

After six weeks of heated debate, the Massachusetts bill to prohibit the insurance of children was defeated 149 to 23. With the exception of Colorado, all other states similarly endorsed the business. In some ways, the outcome was not surprising. It is true that powerful economic interests were at stake; the death of children had become big business not only for the insurance companies but for undertakers as well. Commercial insurance also saved cities, churches, and taxpayers money previously spent in subsidizing pauper burials. Yet the success of children's insurance cannot be reduced to the clever manipulations of capitalist entrepreneurs at the expense of poor people. The basis for its appeal among the working class is a clue to the changing value of their children.

THE DEFENSE: CHILD INSURERS AS CHILD SAVERS

As a recent insurance writer avows, the purpose of insurance on children has always been "somewhat dubious" (Vogel 1969, 60). Legally, life insurance is justified only by the existence of an insurable interest, a reasonable expectation of gain or advantage in the continued life of another person, and no interest in his death. Against objections that child insurance was an illegal wager, nineteenth-century American courts ruled that the right of parents to the services and earnings of minor children gave them an insurable interest in their lives. Judicial approval thus rested entirely in the pecuniary bond between parent and child. In *Mitchell v. Union Life* the judge declared: "A father, as such, has no insurable interest resulting merely from that relation in the life of a child. . . . But the insurance in the present case was effected by a father upon the life of a minor son. . . . The father is entitled to the earnings of his minor child, and may maintain action for their recovery. . . . He has a pecuniary interest in the life of a minor child which the law will protect and enforce" (45 Maine 105 [1858]).[9] In the late nineteenth century, the monetary value of even very young lower-class children, many of whom started working before they were ten, made their insurance legitimate. Walford's influential *Insurance Cyclopedia* explained: "Regarding the practice [of insuring children] it may find some defense in the manufacturing districts where every parent has an interest in the prospective earnings of his child" (1871). Insurance companies reminded state legislatures: "The industrial classes have the moral and legal right to insure their children, for it is well known that these children contribute to the support of their families at very early ages. . . . There is a just and reasonable expectation of advantage or benefit from the continuance of their lives and it logically follows that a proper justification inheres in the parents to protect that benefit" (statement by the representative of Prudential Life Insurance Company at the 1893 hearings before the Insurance Committee of the Colorado legislature, in Hoffman 1900, 198–99).

The vice-president of Prudential Insurance Company explained that for identical premiums, eight- or nine-year-olds received higher benefits than one- or two-year-old children partly because "at the older ages, to speak in a commercial and what may seem a heartless way, there gets to be more of a money value in the life of the child" (Dryden 1895, 16). This economic appraisal of a parent's interest in his child's survival was not confined to the insurance business. Similarly, compensation for the wrongful death or injury of small children was settled by estimating the actual or prospective loss of earnings of a child from the time of death through his minority, deducting expenses for food and education. In one 1856 case, Hetty Downie, seven years old, was killed by the railroad cars of the New York and Harlem River Company. The court awarded her mother $1,300 on the basis that "the damages are to be assessed by the jury with reference to the pecuniary injuries sustained. . . . This is not actual present loss which the death produces . . . but prospective losses also" (*Oldfield v. New York, etc. R. Co.*, 14 N.Y. 310).[10]

But while the law routinely recognized the monetary value of children, the insurance business did not press the issue outside the courts. Instead, insurance leaders themselves adopted their opponents' child-saving rhetoric, stressing the priceless emotional value of children above their cash value. Children's insurance was sold as a symbolic concern for the dying child; it was never marketed as insurance for the working child. This industry approach split child-saving organizations. While some members attacked insurance as a mercenary business, many others enthusiastically welcomed it as a new partner in the defense of childhood. In Massachusetts, for instance, the main spokesman for the opposition was Charles C. Read, attorney of the Massachusetts Society for the Prevention of Cruelty to Children, and yet John Long, vice-president of the same organization, represented insurers. Refuting accusations that "I am opposing the cause of little children," Long insisted that in pleading for their insurance, he was pleading for their welfare (1895, 1). Charges of neglect for the sake of insurance money were found to be unsubstantiated. Insurance commissioners from every state attested to the fact that no specific cases of abuse, cruelty, or murder of children for insurance money had ever been reported (*Extracts from Official Reports, . . . 1880–1901*). In an open letter to the *Philadelphia Evening Bulletin* (December 12, 1894), J. Lewis Crew, secretary of the Philadelphia Society for the Prevention of Cruelty to Children, confirmed the irreproachable record of the industry. In its periodic investigations the society had found no criminal uses of insurance even by baby farmers. Children were insured as "a token of love and affection" and not for profit. In hearings across the nation, leaders of child-welfare organizations, lawyers, politicians, policemen, and physicians testified in favor of the industry, while many clergymen praised it as a "grand blessing" (Long 1895, 14, 35).

Ultimately, the debate over child insurance was a debate on the value of poor children, a public assessment of their emotional versus their economic worth. The director of the Philadelphia Organized Charities called it a "gross libel" to say that "parents in the laboring classes deliberately make away with their offspring for the sake of securing . . . thirty or forty dollars," noting that "among the poorer classes, parents are very fond of their children" (*Child Insurance as Regarded by Anti-Cruelty and by Charity Societies* 1897). Attacking bills against insurance as discriminatory class legislation, insurance supporters rejected the "repugnant idea . . . that the poorer classes . . . do not have that natural affection for their offspring," insisting at every opportunity that "the natural love of parent . . . beats as strongly under the coarser vest as under the costliest" (report from the Insurance Commission of Wisconsin, June 1, 1904, in *Child Insurance in the Legislatures* 1909, 4; *Weekly Underwriter*, July 24, 1880). After working among the poor, a Boston minister concluded that "children insured are loved the most" (Long 1895, 35).

Sympathetic child savers saw child insurance as a symbolic recognition of the emerging sacred value of poor children's lives. It was not the hope of ready cash but the desire for a proper mourning ritual that prompted poor parents to invest their meager funds in premiums. The press noted: "Thousands of children are assured . . . and this is regarded in the light of a burial fund, to secure for the child in case of its death a decent Christian burial" (*Spectator*, March 13, 1890). Defending children's insurance as a "grand institution for the poor," Jacob Huack, a Denver shoemaker, wrote to Colorado legislators in 1893: "I lost a child which never was insured, and do you know

where that poor thing is buried? Away out in the prairie in a place called
Potter's Field and there, among unknown men and women, lies that child of
mine. It makes my heart ache. . . . I take it as a personal insult when I hear
people say that the poor would kill their little ones for a few pieces of silver"
(Hoffman 1900, 279).[11]

Although child savers admitted that "for a parent to speculate a profit from
the death of his offspring is repugnant to the natural feelings," they held that
"a provision by insurance for the cost of sacred decencies to the relics and
memory of the dead [children] is worthy and legitimate" (Fiske 1895, 24).
Defending the "sentiment of respect for the body of a child" as a Christian
sentiment, supporters elevated buying insurance to an act of piety: "If death
should come into the family they want the household to be protected from
harsh and profane influence and they want . . . a decent burial" (Fiske 1898,
12; *Bulletin of the Bureau of Labor* 1906, 613–14).

Social historians have suggested that concern with the death and proper
burial of little children is a telling indicator of their changing value. Although
parents in colonial America were never indifferent to the death of their children, studies detect a certain aloofness and emotional detachment from the
child in the seventeenth and eighteenth centuries. Young death was lamented
but passively accepted (Stannard 1977; Walzer 1974; Illick 1974). In her perceptive analysis of American culture, Ann Douglas suggests that a change
took place in the nineteenth century between 1820 and 1875. She describes
the "magnification" of mourning during that period, specifically, the surge of
concern among the middle class with the sorrow of a child's untimely death.
The emotional pain of the bereaved father and mother became the subject of
countless stories and poems. Mourners' manuals instructed parents how to
cope with the tragedy of a "vacant cradle," while elaborate coffins were designed for the "small household saints" (Douglas 1978, 243, 246, 251). The
acceptance of children's insurance suggests that after 1875 lower-class parents
adopted middle-class standards of mourning young children.

Insurance historians at the time were convinced that this new concern
with children's burial was inspired by the excessive mortality in industrial
areas during the 1870s. All demographic records indicate, however, that
it was precisely during that period that children's mortality rates began a
dramatic decline.[12] Mortality records of insurance companies, based on the
lives of their lower-class customers, show that the reduction cut across class
lines. By 1896 the mortality of poor children had decreased to the extent
that companies were willing to raise benefits without significantly increasing
premiums. Insurance officials were quick to congratulate themselves for the
demographic improvements, suggesting that their business lifted the poor to
"a higher plane of life" (Dryden 1895, 6). Insured children had in fact lower
mortality rates than the uninsured at comparable age levels. For example,
between 1897 and 1901 the expected mortality for American children one to

two years old was 46.6 per thousand, but mortality for children of that age insured by Prudential was only 31.6 per thousand. For ages five to nine the expected mortality during those years was 5.2 per thousand nationally but only 4.4 for those insured by Prudential (Hoffman 1903, 23; Jones 1894). Insurance companies did not require any medical examination for children, so the lower mortality was not a result of selected lives.

Since the concern with children's deaths was not due to rising mortality rates, the alternative demographic explanation is that children were mourned more deeply as they began to live longer. It is difficult, however, to determine precise causal links between changing mortality rates and emotional attachment to children. Unidimensional explanations, perhaps theoretically satisfying, seldom capture the complexity of real social change. The surge of concern about the death of poor children in the late nineteenth century, which became the main sales appeal of the insurance business, was determined by the interaction of many variables, from demography to changes in the economic and occupational structures, and even by the marketing techniques of undertakers and life insurance agents who "sold" parents on giving their children a proper burial. It is my argument that one important variable was the cultural redefinition of the value of children. As children's lives became economically worthless but emotionally priceless, their deaths became a social problem.[13]

CONCLUSIONS: FROM A PROPER BURIAL TO A PROPER EDUCATION

The struggle over children's insurance reflects the transformation of lower-class childhood that began in the latter part of the nineteenth century. The business was caught in the transition. To its opponents, children's insurance was an extension of the old utilitarian view of childhood. Yet child insurers had an economic interest, if not a moral one, in the goals of the child-saving movement. The new respect for the sanctity of children's lives was good for business. Insurance companies became active partners in the effort to prolong young lives; they distributed free booklets instructing parents on proper care of their children and even sent visiting nurses to tend the sick or to assist new mothers.[14] The union of child savers and child insurers was formalized in the Child Welfare Conference of 1909, at which the president of Metropolitan Life, a guest speaker, called it "one of the anomalies of both insurance history and of child welfare history, that . . . since the introduction of industrial insurance . . . well-meaning men and women have taken occasion to condemn the insurance of children" (Frankel 1909, 1).

The business continued its expansion, and by 1928, 37.4 percent of all policies issued by the three largest insurance companies were for children. Postwar sales increased beyond all expectations; in 1945, $10 billion worth of life insurance was in force for children under fifteen. By 1950 the total was $17 billion (Thornton 1940, 68; Scoins 1953, 122). The changing value of children's lives, however, transformed the legal foundations of the business after the 1920s. The strictly pecuniary standard of insurable interest became progressively inadequate to measure the worth of the economically worthless child. Already in the 1880s courts began recognizing the validity of ties of love and affection as a measure of the child's value. In a landmark decision, the judge in *Warnock v. Davis* declared: "It is not necessary that the expectation of advantage or benefit should be always capable of pecuniary estimation; for a parent has an insurable interest in the life of his child. . . . The natural affection in cases of this kind is considered as more powerful—as operating more efficaciously—to protect the life of the insured than any other consideration" (104 U.S. 775). Legal criteria used for recovery in the wrongful death of children shifted in the same direction, from estimating the economic loss of a child's earnings to weighing the loss of its love and companionship. In the twentieth century, courts rejected the "child-labor" standards and the "bloodless bookkeeping imposed upon our juries by the savage exploitations of the last century" (*Wycko v. Gnodtke*, 361 Mich. 331 [1960]; 72 Misc. 2d 332). It was recognized that only in exceptional cases, such as child actors (Shirley Temple, for example, was insured for $600,000 at the age of nine in 1936), did parents lose money when they lost a child. Indeed, sustaining the legal fiction of pecuniary loss would lead to the awkward conclusion that the average child had a negative worth and its death was a benefit for parents.

Other reasons for insuring children also emerged. Rituals for the dying child became less necessary as lower-class children began living longer. Instead, there were new pressures to subsidize the living unproductive child. By the 1930s, a family of moderate means with an average income of $2,500 a year needed an average of $7,766 to raise a child to age eighteen (Dublin and Lotka 1930, 55). The marketing approach of insurance companies mirrored the new status of children as expensive consumer items; policies were now sold as "nest eggs" for children. Endowments that matured by the age of sixteen or twenty-one, creating funds for an education or a dowry, became the most popular policies. As it moved from burial coverage to education fund, children's insurance gradually became also a middle-class type of investment. While nineteenth-century insured children came from working-class families, today 74 percent of children in households with incomes of $20,000–$24,999 have some form of life insurance, compared with only 37 percent in households with incomes below $6,000 (*Families and Their Life Insurance* 1940, 61; Gregg 1964, 105; *The 1949 Buyer* 1950).[15]

The success of children's insurance cannot be understood simply in economic terms. Even insurance experts agree that funds for a child's education can be more profitably accumulated through investments other than a life policy. Mehr considers that arguments to sell life insurance for children are "more effective in making the sale than in solving the buyer's problems" (1977, 118). The 1974 *Consumers Union Report on Life Insurance* reports that children's insurance is irrational in economic terms. From the start, customers have been drawn by the symbolic appeal of a policy, a token of respect for the dead child in the late nineteenth century and one of love for the living child in the twentieth century. Agents' manuals and insurance-selling booklets recognize the noneconomic appeal. One booklet admits: "There are few tangible advantages for you in buying life insurance on your son. . . . You would be buying life insurance to pay him back his love, his trust, his respect, his confidence, you would be paying back for all those wonderful unforgettable moments that only a little boy can share with his father." A 1951 manual instructs agents that the market for children's insurance is "as wide and as deep as the love of parents and grandparents for their children and grandchildren." Insurance advertisements have gradually hushed all reference to dying children and infant burials (*Give Your Son a Hand* 1958; Gravengaard 1951; Willard 1979).

This analysis of the history of children's insurance in the United States serves as an indicator of broader changes in the value of children's lives, specifically the emergence of the economically worthless but emotionally priceless child. The expulsion of children from the market at the turn of the past century, although clearly shaped by materialist concerns, ultimately exceeded a mere economic calculus. A shift in values redefined normative conceptions of childhood in America. As the emotional and moral uniqueness of children was stressed, pragmatic pecuniary equations of their value became increasingly inadequate. The new "sacred" child had to be kept off the market, useless but loving. The study of additional problem areas—as, for example, child labor, foster care, baby sales, and compensation for wrongful death and birth—will permit a better understanding of the complex relationship between the human and market values of children's lives.

Notes

Viviana A. Zelizer, "The Price and Value of Children: The Case of Children's Insurance," *American Journal of Sociology* 86 (March 1981): 1036–56. Reprinted with permission. A modified version of this article appears as a chapter in Viviana A. Zelizer, *Pricing the Priceless Child: The Changing Social Value of Children* (New York: Basic Books, 1985).

1. Economists and sociologists have expressed concern over the negative social, economic, and even moral consequences of a limitless expansion of the market (see, e.g., Titmuss 1971; Blau 1967; Hirsch 1978). There is little analysis, however, of specific processes by which activities, relations, or products are excluded from or introduced into the market sector.

2. Class differences in the value of children have not disappeared completely; the economic worth of a child is still a concern in rural areas and sometimes among the urban lower class. The National Child Labor Committee estimates that at least three hundred thousand migrant children are at work. A recent study suggests, however, that even parents of economically productive children are reluctant to discuss their children as if they were commercial goods (Arnold et al. 1975, 43).

3. Indeed, since the 1930s, the study of children has been excessively psychological in orientation. The sociology of childhood remains mostly an undeveloped specialty. Significantly, while the first edition of the *International Encyclopedia of the Social Sciences* (1930) included some twelve essays on social aspects of dependent childhood, the new *Encyclopedia* (1968) has only two listings under child: child development and child psychiatry.

4. In his explanation of changing family types in England (1500–1800), Stone (1977) relies primarily on a cultural explanation, contending that the rise of "affective individualism" was the determining factor.

5. These policies were primarily burial insurance. Before Prudential, urban working-class families joined friendly societies and mutual aid groups. The unsound financial methods used by these associations, however, resulted in frequent failures and little assistance for bereaved families. In addition, any assistance was for the adult dead; few arrangements existed for the death of poor children.

6. On the different programs of the child-saving movement, see Brenmer 1972 and Platt 1974.

7. On infanticide, see McKeown 1977; Langer 1972; DeMause 1974. On the mercenary orientation of French wet nurses, see Shorter 1975 and Donzelot 1979.

8. Waugh (1890) claimed that at least a thousand children were murdered every year in England for insurance money. He insisted that insurance benefits be paid directly and only to undertakers, to stop parents who otherwise chose a "little funeral" for the sake of the "big drink."

9. See also *Loomis v. Eagle Life Co.* (6 Gray 396 [1856]). Although these landmark cases concerned minors over fourteen, they served as legal precedent for insuring younger children. The expectation of assistance in old age was another argument legitimating parents' insurable interest in their child's life (15 Hun 74 [1878]).

10. The monetary value of children was already recognized legally in colonial times; see Speiser 1975 and *The Value of Children* (1882).

11. Unlike regular adult life insurance, which was rejected by customers in its early stages, children's insurance was opposed by middle-class critics but not by actual or potential buyers. Policyholders testified in defense of the business and signed petitions demanding the right to insure their children. The Boston Typographical Union sent a resolution to the 1895 Massachusetts hearing that "the passage of such a law . . . limiting the age of children [for insurance] would be a detriment to the interests of all working men and a reflection upon their intelligence."

12. Vinovskis suggests that death rates remained stable between 1800 and 1860 (1972). Yasuba argues that death rates increased in the decades before the Civil War, particularly among urban children under ten years of age (1962). Both agree,

however, that mortality rates decreased significantly in the latter part of the nineteenth century. According to Gore, the mortality for children aged five to nine in cities fell from 14.1 per thousand in 1850–54 to 5.9 per thousand in 1895–1900 (1904). In Massachusetts, the death rate in 1865 of children aged five to nine was 9.6 per thousand. By 1900 it had decreased to 5.3 per thousand (*Historical Statistics* 1960, 30).

13. Ariès (1962) too stresses the cultural hypothesis, pointing out that the surge of sensitivity toward the value of children's lives between the thirteenth and seventeenth centuries in Europe preceded by more than a century any reduction in mortality. He attributes the change to the cultural impact of Christianity and its discovery that the child's soul is immortal.

14. Companies did not insure babies in their first year of life until the 1920s, when their mortality began to decrease significantly. Black children were not insured until 1881 and even then received lower benefits than white children. The discrimination was explained as a "commercial matter," namely, the higher mortality rate among blacks (Dryden 1895, 30).

15. While available records do not suggest major sex differences in the insurance of children by industrial companies in the early period, after the 1920s middle-class parents insured their sons much more often than their daughters (Vogel 1969).

References

Ariès, Philippe. 1962. *Centuries of Childhood*. New York: Vintage.

Arnold, Fred, Rodolfo A. Bulatao, Chalio Buripakdi, Betty Jamie Chung, James T. Fawcett, Toshio Irritani, S. J. Lee, and Tson-Shien Wu. 1975. *The Value of Children*. Honolulu: East-West Population Institute.

Becker, Gary. 1976. *The Economic Approach to Human Behavior*. Chicago: University of Chicago Press.

Berelson, Bernard. 1972. "The Value of Children: A Taxonomical Essay." In *The Population Council Annual Report*, 17–27. New York: Population Council.

Blau, Peter. 1967. *Exchange and Power in Social Life*. New York: Wiley.

Boli-Bennett, John, and John W. Meyer. 1978. "Ideology of Childhood and the State." *American Sociological Review* 43 (December): 797–812.

Brenmer, Robert H. 1971. *Children and Youth in America*. Cambridge, Mass.: Harvard University Press.

———. 1972. *From the Depths*. New York: New York University Press.

Campbell, Alexander Colin. 1902. *Insurance and Crime*. New York: Putnam's.

Carlyle, Thomas. 1918. *Past and Present*. New York: Scribner's.

Child Insurance as Regarded by Anti-Cruelty and by Charity Societies. 1897. Pamphlet on file at Metropolitan Life Insurance Co., New York.

Child Insurance in the Legislatures. 1909. Pamphlet on file at Metropolitan Life Insurance Co., New York.

Consumers Union Report on Life Insurance. 1974. New York: Bantam.

Degler, Carl. 1980. *At Odds: Women and the Family in America from the Revolution to the Present*. New York: Oxford University Press.

DeMause, Lloyd. 1974. "The Evolution of Childhood." In *The History of Child-hood*, edited by Lloyd DeMause, 1–76. New York: Harper and Row.

Demos, John. 1978. "Infancy and Childhood in the Plymouth Colony." In *The American Family in Social-Historical Perspective*, edited by Michael Gordon, 157–65. New York: St. Martin's.

de Roover, Florence Edler. 1945. "Early Examples of Marine Insurance." *Journal of Economic History* 5 (May): 172–97.

Donzelot, Jacques. 1979. *The Policing of Families*. New York: Random House.

Douglas, Ann. 1978. *The Feminization of American Culture*. New York: Avon.

Dryden, John F. 1895. "Industrial Insurance Is Family Insurance, of Which Infantile Insurance Is an Essential Part: Is It against Public Policy?" Testimony presented before the Committee on Insurance of the Massachusetts Legislature, March. On file at Metropolitan Life Insurance Co., New York.

Dublin, Louis I., and Alfred J. Lotka. 1930. *The Money Value of a Man*. New York: Ronald.

Easterlin, Richard A. 1969. "Towards a Socioeconomic Theory of Fertility: A Survey of Recent Research on Economic Factors in American Fertility." In *Fertility and Family Planning: A World View*, edited by S. J. Behrman et al., 127–56. Ann Arbor: University of Michigan Press.

Elder, G. H., Jr. 1980. "Adolescence in Historical Perspective." In *Handbook of Adolescent Psychology*, edited by Joseph Adelson, 3–46. New York: Wiley.

Espenshade, Thomas J. 1980. "Raising a Child Can Now Cost $85,000." *Intercom* 8 (September): 1, 10–12.

Extracts from Official Reports of State Commissioners and Superintendents of Insurance between 1880–1901. Pamphlet on file at Metropolitan Life Insurance Co., New York.

"Families and Their Life Insurance: A Study of 2134 Massachusetts Families and Their Life Insurance Policies." 1940. Prepared for the Temporary National Economic Committee, 76th Cong., 3d sess. Washington, D.C.: Government Printing Office.

Fiske, Haley. 1895. "The Insurance of Children." Testimony presented before the Committee on Insurance of the Massachusetts Legislature, March 20 and 21. On file at Metropolitan Life Insurance Co., New York.

———. 1898. "Industrial Insurance." *Charities Review* 8 (March): 1–17.

François, L. 1906. "L'Assurance populaire en particulier l'assurance des enfants." In *Reports, Memoirs and Proceedings of the Fifth International Congress of Actuaries*, edited by Alfred Manes, 1–13. Berlin: Mittler.

Frankel, Lee K. 1909. "Industrial Insurance and Its Relation to Child Welfare." In *Child Welfare Conference, Proceedings*, 1–14. On file at Metropolitan Life Insurance Co., New York.

Give Your Son a Hand. 1958. Sales booklet on file at Metropolitan Life Insurance Co., New York.

Gore, John K. 1904. "On the Improvement in Longevity in the United States during the Nineteenth Century." In *Proceedings of the Fourth International Congress of Actuaries*, 30–54. New York: Actuarial Society of America.

Goupil, René. 1905. "De la consideration de la mort des personnes dans les actes juridiques." Ph.D. diss., University of Caen.

Gravengaard, H. P. 1951. *Juvenile Insurance*. Cincinnati: Diamond Life Bulletins.

Gregg, David W. 1964. *Life and Health Insurance Handbook*. Homewood, Ill.: Irwin.

Greven, Philip. 1977. *The Protestant Temperament*. New York: Signet.

Hareven, Tamara K. 1977. "Family Time and Historical Time." *Daedalus* 106 (Spring): 57–70.

Hirsch, Fred. 1978. *Social Limits to Growth*. Cambridge, Mass.: Harvard University Press.

Historical Statistics of the United States: Colonial Times to 1957. 1960. Washington, D.C.: Bureau of the Census.

Hoffman, Frederick H. 1900. *History of the Prudential Life Insurance Company*. Newark, N.J.: Prudential Press.

———. 1903. *Life Insurance for Children*. Newark, N.J.: Prudential Press.

Hoffman, Lois Wladis, and Martin L. Hoffman. 1973. "The Value of Children to Parents." In *Psychological Perspectives on Population*, edited by James T. Fawcett, 19–76. New York: Basic Books.

Huber, Joan. 1976. "Toward a Sociotechnological Theory of the Women's Movement." *Social Problems* 23 (April): 371–88.

Huebner, Solomon S. 1921. *Life Insurance*. New York: Appleton.

Huizinga, Johan. 1970. *Homo Ludens*. New York: Harper and Row.

Illick, Joseph E. 1974. "Child-Rearing in Seventeenth-Century England and America." In *The History of Childhood*, edited by Lloyd DeMause, 303–50. New York: Harper and Row.

James, Marquis. 1947. *The Metropolitan Life*. New York: Viking.

Jones, Hugh. 1894. "The Perils and Protection of Infant Life." *Journal of the Royal Statistical Society* 57:1–98.

Kagan, Jerome. 1977. "The Child in the Family." *Daedalus* 106 (Spring): 33–56.

Kamerman, Sheila, and Alfred J. Kahn, eds. 1978. *Family Policy*. New York: Columbia University Press.

Katz, Michael B., and Ian E. Davey. 1978. "Youth and Industrialization in a Canadian City." In *Turning Points*, edited by John Demos and Sarane Spence Boocock, S81–S119. Chicago: University of Chicago Press.

Keniston, Kenneth, and Carnegie Council on Children. 1977. *All Our Children*. New York: Harcourt Brace Jovanovich.

Kett, Joseph F. 1977. *Rites of Passage*. New York: Basic Books.

———. 1978. "Curing the Disease of Precocity." In *Turning Points*, edited by John Demos and Sarane Spence Boocock, S183–S211. Chicago: University of Chicago Press.

Langer, William L. 1972. "Checks on Population Growth: 1750–1850." *Scientific American* 226:93–99.

Long, John. 1895. "The Insurance of Children." Testimony presented before the Committee on Insurance of the Massachusetts Legislature, April 4. On file at Metropolitan Life Insurance Co., New York.

McKenzie, Alexander. 1895. Letter from First Church in Cambridge to Metropolitan Life Insurance Co., March 16. On file at Metropolitan Life Insurance Co., New York.

McKeown, Thomas. 1977. *The Modern Rise of Population*. New York: Academic Press.

Mehr, Robert I. 1977. *Life Insurance*. Dallas: Business Publications.

Minge-Kalman, Wanda. 1978. "The Industrial Revolution and the European Family: The Institutionalization of 'Childhood' as a Market for Family Labor." *Comparative Studies in Society and History* 20 (September): 454–68.

The 1949 Buyer. 1950. Hartford, Conn.: Life Insurance Agency Management Association.

Platt, Anthony. 1974. *The Child Savers*. Chicago: University of Chicago Press.

Quiquet, Albert. 1906. "L'assurance des enfants en France." In *Reports, Memoirs and Proceedings of the Fifth International Congress of Actuaries*, edited by Alfred Manes, 85–95. Berlin: Mittler.

Read, Charles Coolidge. 1895. "The Insurance of Children." Testimony presented before the Committee on Insurance of the Massachusetts Legislature, April 4. On file at Metropolitan Life Insurance Co., New York.

Rothman, Sheila. 1978. *Woman's Proper Place*. New York: Basic Books.

Savage, M. J. 1895. Testimony presented before the Committee on Insurance of the Massachusetts Legislature, March 29. On file at Metropolitan Insurance Co., New York.

Sawhill, Isabel V. 1977. "Economic Perspectives on the Family." *Daedalus* 106 (Spring): 115–26.

Schultz, Theodore W. 1973. "The Value of Children: An Economic Perspective." *Journal of Political Economy* 81 (March/April): 2–13.

Scoins, W. H. 1953. "Juvenile Insurance." In *Report of the Sixty-seventh Annual Meeting of the National Fraternal Congress of America*, 119–28. Madison, Wis.: National Fraternal Congress.

Shorter, Edward. 1975. *The Making of the Modern Family*. New York: Basic Books.

Simmel, Georg. 1978. *The Philosophy of Money*. Translated by Tom Bottomore and David Frisby. London: Routledge and Kegan Paul.

Slater, Peter G. 1977. *Children in the New England Mind*. Hamden, Conn.: Shoe String.

Smelser, Neil J., and Sydney Halpern. 1978. "The Historical Triangulation of Family, Economy, and Education." In *Turning Points*, edited by John Demos and Sarane Spence Boocock, S288–S315. Chicago: University of Chicago Press.

Speiser, Stuart M. 1975. *Recovery for Wrongful Death*. New York: Lawyers Cooperative Publishing Co.

Stannard, David E. 1977. *The Puritan Way of Death*. New York: Oxford University Press.

Stone, Lawrence. 1977. *The Family, Sex and Marriage in England 1500–1800*. New York: Harper and Row.

Thornton, Walter E. 1940. "Juvenile Insurance." In *Abstract of the Proceedings of the Fiftieth Annual Meeting of the Association of Life Insurance Medical Directors of America*, 26:29–58. New York: Press of Recording and Statistical Corp.

Titmuss, Richard M. 1971. *The Gift Relationship*. New York: Vintage.

"The Value of Children." 1882. *Central Law Journal* 15 (July–December): 286–88.

Vinovskis, Maris. 1972. "Mortality Rates and Trends in Massachusetts before 1860." *Journal of Economic History* 32:184–213.

Vogel, Julius. 1969. "Juvenile Insurance." In *Proceedings of the Home Office Life Underwriters Association*, 59–83. Hartford, Conn.: Home Office Life Underwriters Association.

Walford, Cornelius. 1871. *Insurance Cyclopedia*. London: Layton.

Walzer, John F. 1974. "A Period of Ambivalence: Eighteenth-Century American Childhood." In *The History of Childhood*, edited by Lloyd DeMause, 351–82. New York: Harper and Row.

Waugh, Benjamin. 1890. "Child-Life Insurance." *Contemporary Review* 58 (July): 40–63.

Wells, Robert. 1978. "Family History and Demographic Transition." In *The American Family in Social-Historical Perspective*, edited by Michael Gordon, 516–32. New York: St. Martin's.

Willard, William L. 1979. *Juvenile Insurance Today*. Indianapolis: Research and Review Service of America.

Wright, Elizur. 1873. *Politics and Mysteries of Life Insurance*. Boston: Lee and Shepard.

Yasuba, Yasukichi. 1962. *Birth Rates of the White Population in the United States, 1800–1860*. Baltimore: Johns Hopkins University Press.

Young Lives and Life Insurance. 1964. Sales booklet on file at Metropolitan Life Insurance Co., New York.

Zaretsky, Eli. 1976. *Capitalism, the Family, and Personal Life*. New York: Harper and Row.

Zelizer, Viviana A. 1978. "Human Values and the Market: The Case of Life Insurance and Death in 19th-Century America." *American Journal of Sociology* 84 (November): 591–610.

———. 1979. *Morals and Markets: The Development of Life Insurance in the United States*. New York: Columbia University Press.

3

From Baby Farms to Baby M

The Baby M deal would astonish any nineteenth-century baby trader. Not because of inflation in baby prices and not even because of Baby M's unusual mode of conception. The amazing fact, from a nineteenth-century perspective, is that Baby M has such eager and paying customers. For in the 1870s, there was no such market for babies. The only profitable undertaking was, as the *New York Times* described it in 1873, the "business of getting rid of other people's [unwelcome] babies." For about $10, baby farmers took in these generally illegitimate children. With babies' high rates of mortality, the turnover was quick, and business brisk. Indeed, one report estimated that a "tradeswoman in tiny lives" could make as much as $10,000 a year.

Selling babies, on the other hand, was a rare and largely unprofitable transaction: often no more than a twenty-five-cent deal. In an 1890 case, an agent of the New York Society for the Prevention of Cruelty to Children pretended interest in obtaining a two-week-old baby. The baby farmer demanded two dollars but quickly settled for half. "She . . . urged [the agent] to take the infant at once and at his own price." It was, unquestionably, a buyer's market.

Yet, by the 1920s and 1930s, "baby-hungry" couples were eagerly paying $1,000 or more to purchase an infant. As a 1939 article in *Collier's* put it: "It's [a] bonanza . . . there's gold in selling babies." The trade slogan of one baby seller in Chicago was "It's cheaper and easier to buy a baby . . . than to have one of your own." Today, the going rate for a healthy white infant in the black market is up to $50,000. "Special-order" Baby M cost the Sterns $25,000 plus the now surely steep legal fees. And this is just a down payment. It will take at least an additional $150,000 to provide Baby M with the first eighteen years of a proper upper-middle-class upbringing.

Lost in the emotional immediacy of the Baby M dispute are two more general and fundamental issues that underlie the surrogacy controversy. First, what explains our bullish baby market? Why were late-nineteenth-century mothers forced to pay baby farmers to get rid of a baby they did not want or could not afford, while today a Mrs. Whitehead is paid to produce a baby for others? Is it just a matter of the scarcity of babies? Second, what, precisely, defines the legitimacy or illegitimacy of baby markets? Are surrogacy fees necessarily a degrading payment or "dirty money"? Then, are adoption fees, foster care payments, and "gray" baby markets also "dirty money"?

I argue that the socially and morally problematic nature of the surrogacy baby market is not primarily, as Richard Neuhaus suggests, that sacred items are "placed in a contract and sealed by money," nor even that surrogacy is rigged against poor women (Neuhaus 1988, 9). More significantly, surrogacy unequivocally reveals our discriminatory valuation of children. Babies are made on "special order" because children already available on the adoption market are not "good" enough—too old, too sick, or of the wrong skin color. In this respect, surrogacy is only a technical innovation. In fact, it is just the latest stage of a very special adoption market that began in the 1920s.

CREATION OF A BABY MARKET

The creation of a market for babies in the 1920s was not the result of clever promotion and only partly a consequence of an increasing shortage of infants. The startling appreciation in babies' monetary worth was intimately tied to the profound cultural transformation in children's economic and sentimental value between the 1870s and 1930s; specifically, the emergence of the economically worthless but emotionally priceless child.

In eighteenth-century rural America the birth of a child was welcomed as the arrival of a future laborer and as security for parents later in life. By the mid-nineteenth century, the construction of the economically worthless child was completed among the urban middle class. It took longer among working-class families, which, even in the late nineteenth century, depended on the wages of older children and the household assistance of younger ones. Child labor laws and compulsory education gradually destroyed the class lag. By the 1930s, lower-class children joined their middle-class counterparts in a new nonproductive world of childhood, a world in which the sanctity and emotional value of a child made child labor taboo.

The "exchange" value of children changed accordingly. Nineteenth-century foster families took in useful children expecting them to help out with farm chores and household tasks. It was considered a fair bargain. After all, if children worked for their own parents, why not work for surrogate caretakers? Not surprisingly, the premium was for children older than ten, old enough to be useful. In this context, babies were "unmarketable," and hard to place except in foundling asylums or on commercial baby farms.

The redefinition of children's value at the turn of the century challenged established instrumental assumptions. If child labor was no longer legitimate, a working home was an anachronism. If children were priceless, it was obnoxious to profit from their misfortune. Thus, baby farming was singled out as a uniquely mercenary "traffic in children." Child-welfare workers actively sought to replace instrumental parenting of any kind with a new approach to adoption more suitable for the economically "useless" sacred child. Parents were urged by *Children's Home Finder* in 1897 not to take a child "for what you can get out of him, but, rather, for what you can put into him." By the 1920s and 1930s, a new consensus was reached. The only legitimate rewards of adoption were emotional—as the *New York Times* put it, "an enlargement of happiness to be got in no other way" (October 25, 1926). As one grateful adoptive father told a *Good Housekeeping* reporter in 1927, "Talk about children owing their parents anything! We'll never be able to pay what we owe that baby."

Sentimental adoption created an unprecedented demand for children under three, especially for infants. In 1910, the press already discussed the new appeal of babies, with *Cosmopolitan* warning, "there are not enough babies to go around." The Home-Finding Committee of the Spence Nursery, an agency organized for the placement of infants, was surprised to discover that, "instead of our having to seek these homes, they have sought us, and so great is the demand for babies that we cannot begin to meet it." By 1937, infant adoption was being touted as the latest American fad. *Pictorial Review* noted: "The baby market is booming. . . . The clamor is for babies, more babies. . . . We behold an amazing phenomenon: a country-wide scramble on the part of childless couples to adopt a child." Ironically, while the economically useless nineteenth-century baby had to be protected because it was unwanted, the priceless twentieth-century baby, "needs protection as ever before . . . [because] too many hands are snatching it."

The priceless child was judged by new criteria; its physical appeal and personality charms replaced earlier economic yardsticks. After talking to several directors of orphan asylums, the *New York Times* concluded that "every baby who expects to be adopted . . . ought to make it a point to be born with blue eyes. . . . The brown-eyed, black-eyed, or grey-eyed girl or boy may be just as pretty . . . but it is hard to make benevolent auxiliaries of the stork believe so" (January 17, 1909). The greatest demand was for little girls. Soon after launching its popular Child-Rescue Campaign in 1907, promoting foster home care, the *Delineator* commented that requests for boys were half that for girls: "a two-year old, blue-eyed, golden haired little girl with curls, that is the order that everybody leaves. It cannot be filled fast enough."

The gender and age preferences of twentieth-century adoptive parents were clearly linked to the cultural revolution in fostering. The earlier need for a useful child put a premium on strong, older children, preferably male; the later search for a child to love led to babies and, particularly, pretty little girls. It was not the innate smiling expertise of females, but established cultural assumptions of women's superior emotional talents that made girls so uniquely attractive for sentimental adoption.

PRICING THE PRICELESS CHILD

The sentimentalization of adoption had an unanticipated and paradoxical effect. By creating a demand for babies, it also stimulated a new kind of baby market. While nineteenth-century mothers had paid baby farmers to accept their unwanted baby, twentieth-century adoptive parents were willing to pay to obtain an infant. "Baby traffickers" thus found an additional line of business; making money not only from the surrender of babies, but doubling their profits by then selling them to their new customers. As a result, the value of a priceless child became increasingly monetized and commercialized. Ironically, the new market price for babies was set exclusively by their noneconomic, sentimental appeal.

By 1922, the dramatic findings of "A Baby a Day Given Away," a study conducted by the New York State Charities Aid Association, put commercialized adoption directly in the national public spotlight. The six-month investigation of newspaper advertisements offering and requesting children for adoption revealed an "indiscriminate exchange of children." An average of a baby a day was being disposed of in New York, "as casually as one would give away a kitten," many sold at "bargain-counter" prices. It was not a peculiar New York arrangement. In the classified advertisement column of almost any Boston newspaper, noted Ida Parker in *Fit and Proper?* in 1927, "together with items relating to automobiles, animals, amusements . . . may often be found the child offered for adoption."

Three years later, the notorious prosecution of a New York baby farmer shocked the nation, further raising the visibility of commercial child placement. Helen Augusta Geisen-Volk was charged and indicted for child substitution and for starving infants to death. The young wife of a well-to-do manufacturer added fuel to the scandal by publicly confessing that, unknown to her husband, Mrs. Geisen-Volk had sold her an infant for $75. None of the crimes committed by Geisen-Volk were new to the baby-farming business; similar accusations were made as early as the 1870s. More unusual were the severity of the reaction and the degree of public interest in the case.

Commercial child placement emerged as a significant social problem in the 1920s in large part because it violated new professional standards in adoption. Without proper supervision by a licensed child-placing agency, adoption could be dangerous both for children and their adoptive parents. Selling children undermined not only professional adoption; it also betrayed the new standards of sentimental adoption. It was a sacrilege to price a priceless child. Worse than a criminal, Mrs. Geisen-Volk was indicted by the judge as a "fiend incarnate." As a probation officer told *New York Times* reporters, "the woman . . . has no maternal affections. . . . [Babies] to her . . . are articles of merchandise to be bartered or exchanged. The defendant represents a revolting anomaly in human-kind" (July 23, 1925).

Harshly denounced as an "iniquitous traffic in human life" and a "countrywide shame" by the national media, the black market in babies flourished in the 1930s and 1940s. As demand for adoptable children grew, the booming traffic in infants reached a new stage. It was now a seller's market. Therefore, the mother of an unwanted child no longer needed to pay to dispose of her baby. Instead, entrepreneurial brokers approached her, offering to pay medical and hospital expenses and often a bonus in exchange for her baby. Even in independent placements arranged without profit, it became common practice to pay the hospital and medical expenses of the natural mother.

In 1955 a congressional investigation conducted by Senator Estes Kefauver officially pronounced baby selling a national social problem. The price tag of a black-market baby climbed, from an estimated $1,000 in the 1930s to $5,000 in the late 1940s. By 1951 some babies sold for as much as $10,000. The rising money value of infants was partly determined by a reduced supply. As the dramatic decline in the national birthrate, which began early in the nineteenth century, continued into the 1930s, fewer babies were available for adoption. Contemporary observers also suggested that the increased demand for babies was partly the result of higher rates of infertility among American couples. Growing concern with the preservation of the family unit further contributed to the baby shortage. After 1911, the mothers' pension movement allowed widows, and in some cases deserted wives or mothers, to keep their children. Reformers also encouraged unmarried mothers to keep their babies. As a result, the supply of adoptable infants shrank, and the waiting lists of adoption agencies grew longer. Unwilling to wait two or more years for a child, parents turned to the black market.

Scarcity alone does not determine value. A reduced supply raised the price of babies only because there was a growing number of enthusiastic buyers for white, healthy babies. The market capitalized on, but did not create, the infatuation with priceless babies. In sharp contrast, older children found few customers. Deprived of their former labor value, they were excluded from the new emotional market. Therefore, while the agencies' waiting list for babies had the names of hundreds of impatient parents, it was virtually impossible to find homes for children older than six, who had become both economically and sentimentally useless. Handicapped and minority children were also excluded from the adoption market.

PAYING FOR BABIES: A SPECIAL CURRENCY

The sentimentalization of adoption in the twentieth century, thus, led paradoxically to a greater commercialization and monetization of child life. As the market for child labor disappeared; a market price developed for children's new sentimental value. Childless couples were now willing to pay thousands of dollars to obtain a child's love, smiles, and emotional satisfactions. In 1975, a second congressional hearing on black-market practices estimated that more than five thousand babies were sold each year in the United States, some for as much as $25,000. Sellers retained bargaining leverage. As one black-market lawyer told a prospective customer, "Take it or leave it. I have five other couples." The capitalization of children's value extended into legitimate child placement. Reversing a long-standing policy, many agencies in the 1940s introduced adoption fees.

Today, surrogacy arrangements introduce a new "custom-made" market for children. Fees are paid not just to obtain someone else's baby but to produce a brand new one. For some economists, this further monetization of child life makes sense. Indeed, Landes and Posner, in the *Journal of Legal Studies*, advocate the outright legalization of baby selling as the best solution to the baby shortage. An undiluted price system, they argue, would match adoptive parents with adoptable children more efficiently than agencies. Landes and Posner dismiss "moral outrage" or "symbolic" objections against baby sales as antiquated and impractical (1978, 324–25).

Yet moral objections to baby payments cannot be easily appeased. For many, the exchange of children should be regulated only by altruism, never for profit. Indeed, money is what makes surrogacy particularly unsavory. Without payment, surrogacy can be an innovative act of altruism: making babies as a gift for childless couples. But $10,000 turns the giver into a salaried agent and the baby into commercial chattel. From this perspective, surrogate parenthood can be legitimized simply by making it unprofitable. For instance, last May in Michigan, a sixteen-member national panel of doctors, lawyers, and clergymen convened by state senator Connie Binsfield to discuss legislation covering reproductive technologies recommended that surrogate parenthood not be outlawed, but that the "production of babies for money, or a fee beyond reasonable expenses" be banned. Similarly, in Nebraska, a bill proposed by state senator Ernest Chambers of Omaha, would accept the legality of surrogate relationships, but would declare that any commercial surrogate contract could not be enforced through the state's judicial system. Surrogate babies, declared Chambers in the *New York Times* "become commodities like corn or wheat, things which can be purchased in the futures market."

Are surrogacy fees necessarily degrading? Does it only take a payment to transform a baby into a commodity? Ironically, both supporters and opponents of baby selling answer affirmatively; thus equally accepting the inevitable power of money. They only differ in their evaluation of the process: economists welcome the rationalization of baby exchanges while antimarket ideologists bemoan the monetization of child life. All agree that once money is exchanged, the sale of children is qualitatively indistinct from the sale of cars. After all, in both cases, the payoff is identical cold cash.

This is a narrow view of money. Money does serve as the key instrument of the modern economic market, transforming objects or even emotions and the value of life into quantifiable, objective sums. But money also exists outside of the sphere of the market, profoundly shaped by culture and social structure. Despite the physical anonymity of dollar bills, not all dollars are equal. We routinely assign different meanings and uses to particular monies. A paycheck, for instance, is "marked" as a different kind of money than a lottery winning. The money we obtain as compensation for an accident is not quite the same as the royalties from a book. A gift of money from a friend is distinct from our employer's Christmas bonus or a grandparent's Christmas check. Different monies are used differently: for instance, a wife's pin money was traditionally reserved for special purchases such as clothing or vacations and kept apart from the "real" money earned by her husband. Different uses can transform the meaning of money. What if Mrs. Whitehead, for instance, had intended to use her $10,000 as a donation to an infertility clinic? That would certainly mark the money differently than if she planned to use it for a Florida weekend, or simply for groceries. Such distinctions are not imposed by rational economic guidelines, but emerge from our cultural and social context.

Baby payments are a special category of money; shaped by the cultural definition of children as priceless. We also distinguish between legitimate and illegitimate baby purchases. Black-market sales, for example, are unacceptable because they treat children in the same impersonal, economizing manner used for less sacred commercial products. Yet a different kind of market exists that is, in most cases, legal and compatible with sentimental adoption. In this gray market, placements are arranged without profit by parents, friends, relatives, doctors, and lawyers. Within this context, professional fees for legal or medical services are acceptable. Justifying such payments during the 1975 congressional hearings on black-market practices, the executive director of the Child Welfare League of America explained, "Money exchanges hands, but it is only to pay for actual costs. There is no thought of profit." Thus, while the black market is defined as a degrading economic arrangement; a modified, legitimate market exists for the exchange of children.

Adoption fees are another category of "special money." Until the 1940s, agencies only accepted "gratitude donations" from adoptive parents. The Children's Home Society of Virginia, for instance, according to the 1941 *Child Welfare League of America Bulletin*, told parents "that a gift from them in such an amount as they choose will be gratefully received, but that it must be made as a gift and not as payment for services." The society's directors refused to even discuss any definite sum with foster families. The boundary between adoption and purchase was preserved by defining the money as an elective gift and a symbol of gratitude, not a price.

The shift from donations to fees was, therefore, a sensitive matter. Yet the system was accepted. How was the adoption fee distinguished from a purchase price? In large measure, the differentiation hinged on defining the payment as compensation for professional services, not in exchange for a child. A fee was also legitimized as a symbolic payment; a material expression of gratitude. Adoption fees were usually portrayed as a psychological crutch for parents, rather than a commercial device for agencies; for example, from the May 1947 *Child Welfare League of America Bulletin*: "For any human being to be in the position of asking another . . . for a child . . . is to admit inadequacy. . . . Payment of the fee may ease some of the discomfort arising from this deeply humiliating experience." Parents' voluntary contributions of additional monies to the agency, beyond the stipulated fee, further reinforced the boundary between the adoption fees and a purchasing price. Their elective gift of money served as a symbolic reminder that adopting a child is not an ordinary business deal.

The uniqueness of payments involving children is also apparent in their "rental." For example, at the beginning of the century, wet nurses employed by the foundling asylums were often accused of regarding their infant boarders simply as a source of income. Yet, while these "pay babies" were indeed a source of much needed income, it was defined as a very special payment. A Russell Sage report in 1914 remarked that "renting" out a baby to these poor New York women was often more a sentimental event than a business deal.

Similarly, when boarding homes for older children were first introduced at the turn of the century, boarding fees were defined as "dirty money," tempting foster parents into taking children for profit. This ambivalence over paid parenting was persistent. For instance, periodic efforts to raise board payments by defining the foster mother as an employee of the agency met with resistance and ultimately failure. In the 1940s, a special committee from the Washington Council of Social Agencies urged payment of a service fee to foster parents in return for their contributions over and above the physical care and maintenance of the child. But the service fee was opposed because it transformed mothering into a marketable job.

"SPECIAL-ORDER" BABIES

Adequate monetary incentive seems to have an effect on the number of foster homes available and even on the success of fostering. Yet foster parents—most of whom are recruited from lower-middle-class or working-class families—remain uneasy about asking for payment. They often find ways to transcend the instrumental parenting contract. In many cases, for instance, foster parents use their own funds for a foster child's incidental expenses: extra clothing, transportation, allowance, toys, or parties.

The gray market, adoption fees, and board payments illustrate some of the cultural contours of baby payments. Pricing the priceless child is a unique commercial venture; child "rental" and child sales are profoundly constrained by twentieth-century conceptions of children. The money involved is partly payment, but it can also be a symbolic expression of sentimental concern.

Surrogacy fees are the latest addition to this inventory of special monies. They remain in a definitional limbo. For opponents of surrogacy, surrogacy fees are no different than black-market price tags, unsuitable to measure the value of a child's life. Some see it as a perverse form of pin money for housewives; paying extra expenses by making a baby. But there is a moral arrogance as well as sociological blindness in the absolutist indictment of surrogacy payments. This money can indeed be "dirty" cash, used to entice poor women into renting their wombs for the rich. It can even be used by the surrogate to blackmail childless couples.

Is that how surrogate mothers define their payment? Most do acknowledge that they would not have entered the arrangement without compensation. Some seem to perceive it as an ordinary wage: "We wanted money to pay some bills and take a vacation," explained one housewife. But surrogates clearly mark the special quality of this money, sometimes refusing even to define it as a payment in exchange for a baby. A mother who was paid $10,000 and delivered twins was quoted by the *New York Times* as saying, "Believe me, . . . there are easier ways to make ten thousand dollars that involve a lot less time and a lot less pain" (Peterson 1987).

The fee is defined by many surrogates as the childless couple's expression of gratitude for their special gift of a baby. Indeed, a study of 125 surrogate mothers found that while 89 percent of the women said they would require a fee for their service, in no case was money the only reason for "baby-making." One woman who had had an abortion now wanted, according to *Psychology Today* in 2007, "to give the gift of a live baby to a loving couple." Others simply liked being pregnant. Surrogates are well aware of the vulnerable boundary between a noble payment and a mercenary fee. Some mark the special quality of the surrogacy fee by allocating the money to particularly unselfish expenses. Mrs. Whitehead, for instance, intended to use the $10,000 toward a college education for her two other children. As another surrogate mother explained in the *New York Times*: "If the money was just for me I'd feel as if I'd sold her [the baby], and it would be dirty money" (Peterson 1987).

Distinguishing between monies by differential uses occurs with other kinds of special payments. For instance, in cases of compensation for the accidental death of a young child, plaintiffs often ritualize the monetary award by donating it to charity, safety organizations, or scholarships for needy children. Baby payments, much as "death" money, are different from ordinary cash. We need to understand better the meaning of surrogacy fees. How does the father define this money? What about the baby brokers? How do their fees differ from the payment to the mother? How is a "just" surrogacy fee determined? Dr. Richard Levin, the head of Kentucky's Surrogate Parenting Associates explains that he has a "moral problem with paying a surrogate mother too much—as with one woman who . . . wanted $100,000—or not enough" (quoted in Keane and Breo 1981). But what makes $10,000 accept-able? Would a small token fee be defined as more appropriate? Or would an extraordinarily large sum—comparable to some wrongful-death settlements in child death cases—be a more dignified quantity?

The moralistic indictment of surrogacy fees obscures the complex reality of such payments. The involvement of money does not necessarily convert all exchanges into ordinary sales. The surrogate payment may be a venal and dehumanizing payoff, but it can also symbolize an acceptable reward. Thus, with proper regulation, money does not necessarily pollute the surrogacy baby market. The class bias in surrogacy arrangements, which is the focus of Neuhaus's argument, is a potentially more damaging feature of the surro-gacy market. Poor women, traditionally the wet nurses and baby minders of the rich, would now also become their baby makers. Subsidized surrogacies, much like subsidized adoptions, however, could make the benefits of surro-gacy available to poor, infertile women. That would only equalize the buyers. It is improbable, although not impossible, that affluent women would serve as surrogates.

In the cases of surrogacy, the inequities between parents are less funda-mental than the explicit discrimination between children. Surrogacy is not just a sentimental search for any child to love but the deliberate manufacture of a particular, suitable child. As one observer has pointed out, the advertise-ments to hire a surrogate do not follow any affirmative action plan. This "help-wanted" ad specifies: "English background," "Northern European," "white," "Caucasian." The desired product is a white infant, with no physi-cal or mental handicaps. In the 1920s rush to adopt babies, some wealthy Americans had their English-rose, golden-haired baby girls imported from London. Today, they can be made in America. They even carry the genetic insurance provided by the adoptive father's sperm.

Surrogacy further marks the distinction between priceless, desirable chil-dren and "unsuitable" children that was established earlier in the century. While babies are made to order, the National Committee for Adoption esti-mates that a minimum of thirty-six thousand hard-to-place children, some because they are sick, some disturbed, others because they are black, and still others because they are too old, cannot find an adoptive home. Surrogacy contracts often make the concern with quality-control quite explicit. Some contracts include provisions for amniocentesis and obligatory abortion if the results are not agreeable to the genetic father. But what if, despite all precau-tions, a child is born defective? Would Baby M be disputed with equal pas-sion if she were not a cute, healthy baby—the ultimate priceless child?

Private adoption of unwanted children cannot be mandated by the state. Neither should the search for a child—even through surrogate arrange-ments—be outlawed by the state, although it must be closely regulated and officially supervised. But we need to collectively recognize the curious and even cruel limits to our sentimentalization of childhood. We must invest emotionally and financially in finding ways to nurture—either in family groups or collective arrangements—those children who need care but are not infants, not white, or not healthy enough. The shortage of such care is as severe as the shortage of cute and healthy white babies.

NOTE

Viviana A. Zelizer, "From Baby Farms to Baby M," *Society* 25 (March/April 1988): 23–28. Reprinted with permission. This essay draws from chapter 6, "From Baby Farms to Black-Market Babies: The Changing Market for Children," in Viviana A. Zelizer, *Pricing the Priceless Child: The Changing Social Value of Children* (New York: Basic Books, 1985).

REFERENCES

Keane, Noel P., and Dennis L. Breo. 1981. *The Surrogate Mother.* New York: Dodd Mead.

Landes, Elizabeth M., and Richard A. Posner. 1978. "The Economics of the Baby Shortage." *Journal of Legal Studies* 7 (June): 323–48.

Neuhaus, Richard John. 1988. "Renting Women, Buying Babies and Class Struggles." *Society* 25 (March/April): 8–10.

Peterson, Iver. 1987. "Surrogate Mothers Vent Feelings of Doubt and Joy." *New York Times*, March 2.

4

The Priceless Child Revisited

American novelist Frederic Tuten recalls scenes from his New York childhood during World War II:

> She was a thin woman without much fantasy. In her dress, I mean. Black from head to toe, in the Sicilian manner. She was a Sicilian, in fact, and she was my grandmother. She spoke little, and to my humiliation—I wanted to be like the other American kids in the Bronx—in Sicilian. And then, too, we were at the tail end of the war with Italy. So that in the street and other public places I answered her in English to distance myself.
>
> Not that my Sicilian was great. But at 8 or 9 I managed to tell her what she wanted to know about my world at school and to conduct her from butcher to grocer to order for her and to check the scales when she thought they were tipping high. . . . I also, and more importantly, served as her translator for the American news on the radio, and for the American movies.

Tuten also remembers reading to his grandmother, Francesca LePare Scelfo. "Not in the conventional way of translating word for word my childhood books," but instead, he says, "by telling her—with my own editing and inventions—the stories in my reading" (Tuten 2002). A half-century ago, a Bronx boy was contributing a crucial form of work to his Sicilian-origin family.

Move forward half a century. In Tucumán, Argentina, in 2002, twelve-year-old Manuel Cruz was engaged in a very different kind of work for his family. In the midst of the Argentine economic crisis, Manuel worked as a *cartonero*, literally a cardboard gatherer, but in fact also a collector and seller of paper, bottles, plastic, aluminum cans, and a variety of other items for recycling. After returning from school, Manuel went out with Ana, his mother, and Maria, his grandmother. They trudged off to collect materials, working from 7 p.m. to 2 a.m. five days a week. On weekends, Manuel earned extra money watching cars and helping out in the Tucumán Lawn Tennis Club.

At the same time, Manuel was putting in one of the finest performances in his elementary school, recognized as the leading student as well as winning second place in the province's Mathematics Olympics. Interviewed by the national magazine *Gente*, this "little hero," as the reporter called him, explained why he had not told his classmates about his work: "I used to be embarrassed, but today I am proud. It's an honest job that allows me to feed my family. . . . Although to tell the truth, I don't much like what I do. . . . What everyone should understand here is that the only way to get out of poverty is studying. That is why I won't stop until I become an architect" (Quiroga 2002). Meanwhile, Manuel was helping to support his five younger siblings, Maria, Marcos, David, Pamela, and Rodrigo, at a time of widespread unemployment, poverty, and hunger.

The Bronx, New York, in 1943 and Tucumán, Argentina, in 2002: children of both places worked hard. But what they did, for whom, in whose company, and for what compensation they worked varied dramatically not only from place to place and time to time but also from family to family. Frederic Tuten gave his grandmother a distinctive sort of care—linguistic care—at home, just as he served as her intermediary with the anglophone world. Manuel Cruz split his great energy between schoolwork, gathering of refuse, and weekend jobs for the present benefit of his large family and the future benefit of his own career.

Widely held views about childhood mark an intense moral difference between the two experiences. Translating for a grandmother generally strikes observers as an appropriate and commendable childhood activity, but the *cartonero*'s night work looks like cruel exploitation. The young *cartonero* was indeed running risks: older *cartoneros* often attacked Manuel and stole his merchandise, while state authorities pursued his mother for allowing him to work. Still, the intense moral differentiation is puzzling. After all, both children are equally involved in virtuous activities, assisting their families while going to school. In fact, Manuel Cruz's efforts outshine Frederic Tuten's. Yet the two experiences look starkly different.

We cannot explain this differential evaluation if we only look at what a particular child—in this case Frederic or Manuel—is doing. Why not? Because the meaning and consequences of children's work depend on the social setting in which that work occurs. To understand what is going on, to explain puzzling variations, we need to look closely at the web of social relations in which these children's efforts take place.

Why is that so hard to do? What hinders understanding of the social processes occurring in these two cases? Analyses of children's work face two significant obstacles, both of them much more general misconceptions about intersections between the worlds of morality and economic activity. We might call the two misconceptions "hostile worlds" and "market work."

The widespread, potent idea of *hostile worlds* imagines social existence as falling into two distinct spheres, one of rationality and self-interest, the other of sentiment and solidarity. Let them mix, goes the argument, and two forms of corruption result: the entry of sentiment and solidarity into the rational arena causes cronyism and inefficiency, while the entry of self-interest into the sentimental arena weakens solidarity, empathy, and mutual respect. In a children's version, many observers fear that exposing tender youth to marketplace logic destroys virtuous childhood while introducing unreliable economic actors into the world of serious business. According to this logic, erecting a staunch boundary between childhood and adulthood defends against corruption in both directions.

But the hostile-worlds theory fails to explain what actually happens in the course of economic activity. In fact, close studies of routine social life uniformly contradict the idea that the mingling of economic transactions with personal relations necessarily produces corruption in either direction (Zelizer 2002a).

The *market work* doctrine holds that only work receiving monetary compensation qualifies as genuine. Housework, barter, volunteering, pro bono service, unpaid caring, family enterprises, and most efforts by children fall into the zone of non-work. If this doctrine seems implausible to students of childhood, it nevertheless affects a wide range of thought and practice. Notice, for example, that national income accounting generally neglects such efforts and that Western courts assessing damages for wrongful death or injury regularly value women's unpaid contributions at much less than similar efforts performed for wages. In this view, *cartonero* Manuel Cruz's midnight collecting may have qualified as work, but neither his stellar school performances nor Frederic Tuten's translations for his Sicilian grandmother meet the test.

Like the notion of hostile worlds, such an idea obscures more than it explains. Let us adopt a more generous and analytically useful conception of work: as any effort that produces transferable use value (Tilly and Tilly 1998). The definition sacrifices the neatness of market value as the measure of all work, but gains instantly by identifying similar efforts that differ mainly by the social settings in which they occur. Thus we immediately recognize similarities and differences between maid service and housework, professional nursing and family health care, paid clerical work and the study of bookkeeping.

For further clarification, we should introduce a rough distinction between two sorts of work: first, effort that immediately produces transferable goods and services; second, effort that adds to existing capital, and thus contributes to future production of goods and services. Following Pierre Bourdieu (1990), we can pay attention to several different sorts of capital: the *physical* capital that serves production directly, the *financial* capital that provides fungible claims to means of production, the *human* capital that informs an individual's or a group's capacity to produce, the *social* capital that facilitates individuals' and groups' interpersonal connections to productive resources, and the *cultural* capital that gives individuals or groups access to exclusive social settings. Obviously children play important parts both in immediate production of goods and services and in the accumulation of physical, financial, human, social, and cultural capital.

To this insight, this chapter adds the observation that the meaning, organization, contribution, and compensation of children's work in these regards vary systematically and dramatically from one social setting to another. Let us try to identify the principles of that variation. Here is how the overall argument runs:

- Children's work divides between immediate production of transferable use value and production of material, financial, human, social, and cultural capital. For example, children often work directly in household economic enterprises, but in so doing they acquire skills and social connections that will later serve them in enterprises of their own.
- Some of the capital production remains with the child itself for later transfer, but some of it immediately increases the capital of social relations and groups in which children participate, notably that of their families and households. For example, a child's stellar school performance enhances not only the child's own future, but also the standing of his or her family.
- Permissible and forbidden forms of children's work vary strikingly with the social relations to which they are attached. For example, many parents require their children to weed the family flower garden, but any teacher who required his pupils to weed his own family's garden would risk losing his job.
- Within each social relation, more precisely, participants and third parties promote proper matching of meanings, monetary media, and economic transactions, including the transactions we call work or production. For example, over a wide range of Western households, parents can reasonably tie allowances to their children's household work, but could not possibly hire outside children to do the same work for the same rewards.
- Participants also mark the boundaries between different social relations with labels, symbolic representations, and moral injunctions. For example, almost every household makes a sharp distinction between the rights and obligations of children that belong to their household and those of children who count as temporary visitors.
- Within those limits, however, children and other persons involved in their work incessantly negotiate the precise matching of meanings, media, and transactions. For example, children across the world bargain with their parents about what clothing, toys, or forms of entertainment they can and cannot buy.

For the sake of brevity, the chapter will not take up each of these points separately, but instead illustrate the main arguments, drawing from two main settings: household carework and immigrant enterprises. Both settings reveal an impressive variety of children's labor and illustrate the crucial contributions that children make to the maintenance of adult-run enterprises.

CAREWORK

Does personal care—sustained attention that enhances individual welfare—qualify as work? In recent years, feminist critics, focusing exclusively on women's invisible caring labor—including housework, attending to children, the sick, and the elderly in their families—have insisted that it does. In many cases, their arguments have changed legislation, establishing that in cases of lost personal attention, the loss deserved legally enforced compensation. Acknowledging children's carework, however, turns out to be even more challenging than recognizing their mothers' efforts. Children, after all, are not supposed to be carers but recipients of care.

Yet, as a number of researchers have recently shown us, children involve themselves in a great deal of caring work, ranging from babysitting their siblings to attending a sick grandparent. The kinds of caring work children engage in vary dramatically with social relations; for example, children provide very different kinds of caring services to neighbors and to siblings. The various caring efforts vary also in their moral legitimacy. Like adults, children mark very strong boundaries between what they define as appropriate and inappropriate relations for carework. For instance, a child who regularly cooks for or takes an ailing grandparent to the bathroom would not ordinarily do the same for a neighbor. Both adults and children typically mark such boundaries with invocations of hostile worlds, noting the dangers of providing intimate services to the wrong people. Children, and adults, also distinguish carework from other types of child work, such as housework or wage work. What is more, children's paid carework, such as babysitting for other families, differs practically and symbolically from unpaid help around the house.

Children's carework matters. It extends to such crucial activities as making sure that ailing family members receive their medicine, and thus at times involves children in collaboration with health-care professionals and social workers. In the course of such work, children not only produce goods and services directly, but also accumulate capital—for example the human capital gained by knowledge of medical treatment and the social capital gained with links to health-care workers. In addition, children's individual accumulation of capital commonly enhances the store of capital available to the household as a whole. By connecting households with powerful outside institutions, children's mediation sometimes greatly affects the family's social position. Immigrant families, for example, often depend on their native-born children to establish a wide range of connections between the household's adults and the alien environment. Counterintuitively, this means that a household lacking children will in certain circumstances accumulate less capital than those with children.

Children's caring efforts take a wide variety of forms, each corresponding to a different bundle of social relations. In her ethnographic account of pickup time at an elementary school in a mixed-income, ethnically diverse area of Oakdale, California, Barrie Thorne reports:

> The pick-up scene offers glimpses of children actively constructing and negotiating everyday life, including divisions of labor within and extending beyond households. Kids take responsibility for locating younger siblings and getting them home; they organize themselves into groups to head for after-school destinations; they make phone calls to check up on adults who are late; they carry messages between school and home. In addition, kids sometimes help out on adult job sites—for example, by sorting dry cleaning at an uncle's store or by helping a mother clear tables in a restaurant. Children also contribute to housework. (Thorne 2001, 364)

Ask the Children, Ellen Galinsky's national survey of a representative sample of more than one thousand U.S. children in grades 3 through 12, offers some revealing glimpses into the variety of children's carework. The survey, supplemented with interviews, found children saying they "take care" of their parents by finding strategies for reducing parents' stress and fatigue. One twelve-year-old girl reported using humor to help out her mother: "I try and make her feel better. My friend can make people laugh so easy. And so usually I'm like, 'Chris, my mom feels kind of bad right now—you wanna come over and cheer her up?' and in just at least five minutes my mom is laughing so hard" (Galinsky 1999, 240). Some of the children complained about their caring duties, feeling, says Galinsky, that "their parents had become their children and that they were parenting them" (Galinsky 1999, 240).

In a reversal of perspectives, Galinsky thus shows that children responded to their parents' work in interesting, unexpected ways. While most experts and parents worry that parents are not spending enough time with their children, children fretted less about the time deficit. They did worry a great deal about their parents, but mostly about the quality of their interchanges when parents were under a great deal of stress. Indeed, Galinsky points out, children often play detective, gathering "mood clues" from their parents. One child told about calling her parents at work "to get a reading on how they are feeling so she can determine whether she should clean up the house before they come home" (Galinsky 1999, xvii). The scope, variety, intensity, and value of children's caring labor clearly have not received the attention they deserve.

With precisely that deficit in mind, British advocates have coined the term "young carers" to designate children who make crucial contributions to other people's welfare. Child carers attend to ill or disabled family members, typically their parents, but also siblings or grandparents. In the United Kingdom the 1995 Carers' (Recognition and Services) Act acknowledged these children's work, by adding children under age eighteen to the category of private, informal carers entitled to social services.[1] However, Richard Olsen points out that current definitions of child caring perpetuate dubious distinctions between qualifying and nonqualifying forms of children's carework. They single out caring in some relations to the exclusion of similar work in a wide range of others. For example, as Olsen points out:

> We see young carers defined not simply by the type and quantity of tasks that they do, but also by the fact that their activity is directed towards the "care" of a "dependent" disabled person. The eldest child in a large family, contributing significantly to the care of infant siblings, is typically excluded from the definition of a young carer, whilst a sibling of a disabled child, performing largely the same tasks (nappy changing, keeping an eye on, and so on), is included. Similarly a child of a disabled single parent who finds herself doing most of the housework, cooking, cleaning, and so on, is, typically, included in the definition of a young carer, whilst a child having significant housework duties in a so-called "normal" family is excluded. (Olsen 2000, 391)

As Olsen says, such restrictive labels do not quite recognize how widespread children's caring labor is, and how much its acceptability or unacceptability depends not on the character of the child's effort but on the social context in which it occurs (on children's carework, see also Becker et al. 1998; Boulding 1980; Robson and Ansell 2000). Children actually provide a surprising range of services to their families.

CHILDREN AS LINGUISTIC MEDIATORS

Consider the impact of children's linguistic skills for their immigrant parents. Even young children educated and brought up in the receiving country often have far greater skills in the new country's language than their parents (see, for example, Portes and Hao 2002). In one crucial way, this reverses the usual skill distribution within the household. Studying Mexican immigrant households in Los Angeles, California, Abel Valenzuela (1999) recognized that these families typically faced urgent problems with respect to social and cultural capital. They knew little of how U.S. institutions—schools, workplaces, churches, unions, courts, and banks—functioned. Of more immediate importance, they often lacked the English-language skills to negotiate with such institutions.

Children became their parents' indispensable allies. In sixty-eight interviews, including forty-four adult heads of immigrant households and twenty-four of their now-grown children, Valenzuela drew from their recollections of past interactions. He found that children occupied three key household roles. They served first as their parents' and siblings' *tutors*, translating, interpreting, and teaching. Besides straightforward translation of television news or government documents, the children mediated delicate transactions between their parents and physicians, teachers, bank officials, and other authorities. Children's second role was as *advocate*, intervening on behalf of their parents in complex or controversial interactions; for instance, when a public official or salesperson misunderstood or became impatient with their parents or siblings. Finally, Valenzuela identified children's role as *surrogate parents*, performing household tasks, such as cooking, cleaning, and caring for their younger siblings.

Valenzuela's interviews revealed a strong gender pattern; daughters assisted their parents with financial, employment, legal, and political transactions more often than their brothers did. Regardless of gender, furthermore, Valenzuela found that older children "often took the lead role in assisting younger siblings with what is usually done in the household by the mother, such as feeding and caring for younger siblings, getting the brothers and sisters dressed for school, transporting them to and from school, and babysitting" (Valenzuela 1999, 728). Thus, second-generation Mexican children, especially girls, contributed serious work to their immigrant households. Although several forms of caring entered the mix, children's language skills made them essential within households and for households' links with outside institutions.

Following up the Valenzuela study, Marjorie Faulstich Orellana, Lisa Dorner, and Lucila Pulido (Orellana et al. 2003a) went directly to observation of young children (see also Orellana et al. 2003b). They studied bilingual fifth- and sixth-grade children of Mexican and Central American immigrants in four communities—one in central Los Angeles, California; two in Chicago, Illinois; and a fourth in Engleville, Illinois. Drawing on extensive interviews, participant observation in children's homes and classrooms, and audiotaped data, Orellana and her collaborators closely documented the remarkable range of parental reliance on their children's linguistic skills. Children, they report, intervened as translators in seven different domains:

- *Educational*, for example, translate at parent-teacher conferences for themselves and/or siblings, cousins, friends; call schools to report their own or siblings' absences.

- *Medical/Health*, for example, translate at doctors' and dentists' offices during family visits; interpret instructions for medicine, vitamins, other health-care products.
- *Commercial*, for example, shop for or with parents; complete refund transactions, settle disputes and check for mistakes in sales transactions.
- *Cultural/Entertainment*, for example, go to movies; translate plot and dialogue; read and translate stories, self-help guides, song lyrics, instructional manuals.
- *Legal/State*, for example, call an insurance company regarding car damage, car accidents; obtain welfare or social security by accompanying parents to office, answering questions.
- *Financial/Employment*, for example, cash or deposit checks at the bank or currency exchange, help parents fill out applications for work or for unemployment benefits.
- *Housing/Residential*, for example, translate between parents and landlords; talk to managers regarding things broken in apartment.

Children experienced most of these linguistic encounters as no more than daily routines of family life. Some of their interventions, however, not only demanded skill but also produced considerable stress. Skill and stress coincided most often when the children mediated between their parents and formidable outsiders. Take just two examples, one from the medical arena, another from the commercial:

When I was about 8–9 years old we went to the doctor because my baby brother was 1 month or so. He had to go for a check-up and a doctor told [asked] my mom if she was going to give my baby brother milk from he[r] breast, but I did not know what breast meant. So I told the doctor if she could explain what breast meant. She was nice and kind and said yes of course. She touched her breast and [I] told my mom what the doctor was saying. As far as I can remember this was the scariest translating thing I [had] ever done. I did not translate things that much this week but I did work long time ago translating stuff. Well, I felt so nervous to translate for the doctor because I thought I would not be able to understand the big words doctors use. (Jasmine, in Orellana et al. 2003a, 516)

My mother has never gone to Jewels or Dominick's by herself. She has always gone with someone who can translate for her. I often and still order her cheese and ham from the deli. I recall a miscommunication situation that made my mother upset and made me feel very embarrassed. I was about 7 years old. My mother and I were at Jewels. My mother told me to stand in line while she shopped for other items and

order a pound of American cheese from the deli. After about fifteen
minutes of waiting my turn, the woman behind the counter asked
for my order and I told her I wanted a pound of cheese. The woman
then said, "American, Italian, Swiss . . ." I thought she was asking for
my nationality. I responded saying "Mexican." In a frustrated tone of
voice, she told me that they did not have any Mexican cheese. (Beatríz,
in Orellana et al. 2003a, 519)

In these circumstances, children of immigrants assume serious responsibility for their parents' and their household's welfare. In the process, they
are not only performing fundamental services but adding to their family's
capital. Orellana et al. (2003a) note that children's knowledge of English
and U.S. cultural practices enhance their families' household production.
Nevertheless, as Orellana and her collaborators warn, these children sometimes resist and negotiate their obligations, while parents sometimes impose
them as family duties (see also Fernández-Kelly 2002, 198; Menjívar 2000,
chap. 7). No one should therefore take the crucial contributions of children
as mediators to be evidence of their untrammeled power.

CHILDREN IN IMMIGRANT ENTERPRISES

As we saw with Valenzuela, linguistic services are by no means the only assistance that immigrant parents receive from their children. In a different
study of Mexican and Central American immigrants in the Pico Union area
of central Los Angeles, Orellana observed children involved in a variety of
daily work, including "running errands; caring for siblings; cleaning; doing
the laundry; taking siblings to school, the library, and other appointments;
helping siblings with homework; . . . answering and making phone calls."
She also reports children's involvement in wage labor: "selling food, clothes,
or other merchandise alongside adult street vendors; helping their parents to
clean houses, care for children, or mow lawns; cleaning tables in a *pupuseria*
(a Salvadoran restaurant); sweeping the floors of a beauty salon" (Orellana
2001, 374–75; see also Orellana et al. 2001). Especially notable was the extent to which children served their families by caring for younger children.

Similarly, in immigrant family-run businesses, children often deploy not
only their linguistic skills but their efforts in helping operate the family's
shop or small business. Miri Song's (1999) study of Chinese take-away shops
in Britain closely documents children's vital labor contributions (see also
Sun-Hee Park 2002). Interviewing forty-two grown children (mostly in their
early to mid-twenties) in twenty-five Chinese families inhabiting the southeast of England, Song found—with some variation from family to family
as well as by age and gender—that by age seven or eight most of them had

begun helping out their parents. Young children started by assisting with simple kitchen tasks such as washing dishes or peeling prawns and potatoes. They gradually took up more public duties, dealing with customers' orders at the front counter, working evenings, after school, or during weekends.

Not that children simply complied with their parents' directions. Some children, Song reports, remember resisting the labor routines, while others reported collaboration among brothers and sisters, for example, in setting up their own work schedules with the shop. Nevertheless, for the most part, children did not remember their business involvement as distinctive training, but rather as a "natural" part of growing up in a family enterprise. For instance, when Song asked one of them, "How did you start helping out in the shop? Did your parents ask you?," she responded: "Well, we were just there. It wasn't even like 'Come and help us.' We were naturally there. We went there to eat" (Song 1999, 53). In fact, they mark the boundary between what they did and regular wage employment by calling their own efforts "helping out." Accordingly, they treated the payments they received from their parents not as standard wages but as a perk, or a bonus, a symbol of appreciation for their labor. Some of the children, on the other hand, resented parents' payments as bribes for unwelcome work demands.

As we saw with Mexican and Central American immigrants in the United States, Song found her British-Chinese respondents involved not only with shop work, but also with domestic work and caring labor. Linguistic services also figured prominently in these children's lives. Song reports how children served as translators and intermediaries for their Chinese parents who spoke, read, or wrote little or no English. One of her interviewees, Wong, explained how crucial language skills became in ordinary shop transactions, such as taking customers' orders:

> The moment you have, "Can I have the chicken chow mein, but I don't want some bean sprouts, and I want extra onions," then you know, that's exactly the scenario. I just want to show you how it [his parents' communication with customers] breaks down. To say "chicken chow mein" that's fine, no problem, but as soon as you say more. . . . That's the sort of thing they'll [his parents] have problems with. (Song 1999, 54)

Immigrant enterprises frequently rely on children not only for productive labor and mediation with outside authorities, but also for linguistic mediation between their owners and clients.

Household caring work and immigrant enterprises amply illustrate the themes with which I began: the division between children's immediate production of goods or services and their contributions to individual or family capital; the distinction of acceptable and unacceptable forms of children's work, dependent less on the basis of that work's intrinsic quality than on the social relations within which it occurs; the variable matching of work and compensation to those social relations; the further negotiation of meanings, compensation, and working conditions within the limits set by existing social relations; and finally, the substantial contributions children make to household production and capital accumulation.

CHILDREN'S WORK RECONSIDERED

Obviously I could pursue the same themes through a wide range of other children's work, not all of it as desirable as the cases I have examined. Child soldiers, child prostitutes, child thieves, child entertainers, child athletes, child volunteers, child speculators, child merchants, child factory workers, homeless children, and children in home production all deserve attention for the ways they and the adults around them organize their lives. So do schoolchildren's efforts both inside and outside of school.[2] Nor have I followed up the fascinating complexities of children's contributions to personal and family capital. But at least the variety of children's activities encountered in household caring and immigrant enterprises should alert us to the fine differentiation of children's work according to its social context, and to the sense in which it consists not of solitary effort but of energetic social interaction.

Recognition of children's work as varying systematically by social context produces a valuable clarification of debates over proper and improper efforts by children. The very same child effort, we have seen, qualifies as acceptable or unacceptable depending on whether it produces benefits for participants in the social interactions the effort involves, who it produces those benefits for, and with what consequences for the children themselves.[3] As a result, any moral or policy position that imposes wholesale classifications of effort alone on children's work misses crucial distinctions, for example, between helping parents in a shop and doing similar work for outsiders.

To be sure, some forms of effort so uniformly damage children and others that we can condemn them from the start; we can no doubt forbid child military service, child prostitution, child involvement in the distribution of hard drugs, and children's mine labor without worrying much about the social relations that lead children into those activities. But beyond that extreme we cannot effectively weigh goods and evils of children's work without serious consideration of the social relations within which the work occurs. Whether the same sort of effort constitutes exploitation or valuable experience depends heavily on the social context. Moralists and policymakers will do well to take that insight from close studies of children's work into account.

The study of children's work thus brings out valuable parallels with economic sociology as it has been developing over the past few decades. Once a relatively sharp division of labor between economics and sociology developed during the twentieth century, sociologists who cared about economic processes generally left the close analysis of production, distribution, consumption, and capital formation to economists while studying the prerequisites and consequences of economic change or variation. Starting in the 1970s, however, economic sociologists began to analyze economic processes more directly, either by extending economic models to sites economists themselves had not studied closely (for example, schools, churches, and voluntary associations) or by showing how social contexts affected economic processes (for example, how interpersonal networks shape labor markets).

More recently, economic sociologists have dared increasingly to propose alternative explanations of economic processes: the formation of markets, the management of risky transactions, the interaction of firms, and so on. In that alternative economic sociology, the analysis of differentiated interpersonal ties, their variable meanings, and their shaping of economic transactions has become a major preoccupation. Without fanfare, this chapter's treatment of children's work has drawn heavily on insights from economic sociology (Smelser and Swedberg 1994; Swedberg and Granovetter 2001; Swedberg 2003; Zelizer 2001).

Twenty years ago Basic Books published my *Pricing the Priceless Child*. That 1985 book documented a shift in American practices: during the nineteenth century, on the whole, American moralists and families alike valued children for their useful contributions, while by the century's end a shift occurred, toward a conception of children as priceless, with rejections of children's paid employment, increasing emphasis on children's unpaid work as moral training, adoption of insurance on children's lives as an educational investment rather than a practical necessity, growing awards for children's wrongful death, and proliferating restrictions on payments for adopted babies. Reading me now, some readers may think I am repudiating that earlier book. I am not. It is true that I have actually learned something during the last two decades (see Zelizer 2002b). I have gone much farther in pursuit of questions that *The Priceless Child* barely sketched: how people manage the mingling of monetary transactions with morally charged social relations, how boundaries between proper and improper economic transactions arise, how people negotiate and enforce those boundaries, what happens when legislatures, lawyers, judges, and juries get involved in setting prices for different sorts of social relations and transactions. Nevertheless, my 1985 book clearly distinguished between the powerful representations of children that affected social practices, on one side, and the fact that children continued to do a wide range of productive work, on the other.

The chief change in my perspective since then recognizes how representations and practices interact. The two sides do not simply struggle with each other as illusion and reality or ideology and praxis. Instead, their interaction illustrates an extremely general social process. In this process, representations and practices combine to establish social boundaries between different kinds of social relations. As people erect and enforce such boundaries, they generate three simultaneous effects: First, the boundaries separate social relations whose distinction matters greatly for routine social life. Second, they reinforce the proper matching of meanings, monetary media, and economic transactions within each social relation thus distinguished. Finally, they define the rights and obligations of third parties with respect to each sort of social relation.

This view of children's work challenges the doctrines of hostile worlds and market work. It challenges all hostile-worlds' notions by establishing that children's value-producing efforts repeatedly mingle economic transactions with intimate personal relations, yet the mingling does not corrupt. It causes neither the relaxation of means–end rationality that supposedly stems from the entry of personal relations into the economic sphere nor the crippling of interpersonal solidarity that supposedly follows from the entry of economic rationality into personal relations. My view of children's economic efforts challenges market work doctrines by emphasizing how much genuine adding of value occurs in efforts that take place outside of wage-mediated markets as conventionally defined. The dual challenge holds across a wide variety of economic activity: not just children's work, but also household production, the informal economy, and much more. In a wide variety of settings, one finds economic actors drawing boundaries, establishing rights and obligations within those boundaries, and matching social relations with meanings, media, and permissible economic transactions.

Children's work—widespread but camouflaged—conforms to these patterns. It takes place within differentiated social ties, acquiring different meanings and consequences depending on those ties. The productive child engages in social interactions that are every bit as complex as those pursued by adults.

NOTES

Viviana A. Zelizer, "The Priceless Child Revisited," in *Studies in Modern Childhood: Society, Agency and Culture*, edited by Jens Qvortrup, 184–200. London: Palgrave, 2005. Reprinted with permission of Palgrave Macmillan.

1. See http://www.hmso.gov.uk/acts/acts1995/Ukpga_19950012_en_1.htm.
2. Examples of recent work on this subject are Alexander 1991; Bachman 2000; Blagbrough and Glynn 1999; Bock and Sellen 2002; Cohen 2001; Goodwin-Gill and Cohn 1994; Kenny 2002; Krueger 2002; Kruse and Mahoney 1998; Lavalette 1999; Lee and Kramer 2002; Levison 2000; Lewis 2001; Mayall 2002; Nieuwenhuys

1996; Qvortrup 1995; Sereny 1984; Solberg 1994; Strom 2003; Woodhead 1999; Wuthnow 1995.

3. For an intriguing variant on these themes, notice that a considerable movement against doing schoolwork at home after school arose in the United States between 1897 and 1941; see Gill and Schlossman 1996, 2000.

REFERENCES

Alexander, S.J.G. 1991. "A Fairer Hand: Why Courts Must Recognize the Value of a Child's Companionship." *Thomas M. Cooley Law Review* 8:273.

Bachman, S. L. 2000. "A New Economics of Child Labor: Searching for Answers behind the Headlines." *Journal of International Affairs*, 53:545–72.

Becker, S., J. Aldridge, and C. Dearden. 1998. *Young Carers and Their Families*. Oxford: Blackwell Science.

Blagbrough, J., and E. Glynn. 1999. "Child Domestic Workers: Characteristics of the Modern Slave and Approaches to Ending Such Exploitation." *Childhood* 6:51–56.

Bock, J., and D. W. Sellen, eds. 2002. "Special Issue: Childhood and the Evolution of the Human Life Course." *Human Nature* 13:153–325.

Boulding, E. 1980. "The Nurture of Adults by Children in Family Settings." In *Research in the Interweave of Social Roles: Women and Men*, edited by Helena Lopata, 1:167–89. Greenwich, Conn.: JAI.

Bourdieu, P. 1990. *The Logic of Practice*. Stanford, Calif.: Stanford University Press.

Cohen, R. 2001. "Children's Contribution to Household Labour in Three Sociocultural Contexts: A Southern Indian Village, a Norwegian Town and a Canadian City." *International Journal of Comparative Sociology* 42:353–67.

Fernández-Kelly, P. 2002. "Ethnic Transitions: Nicaraguans in the United States." In *Transnational America: The Fading of Borders in the Western Hemisphere*, edited by B. Ostendorf, 177–203. Heidelberg: C. Winter.

Galinsky, E. 1999. *Ask the Children*. New York: Morrow.

Gill, B., and S. Schlossman. 1996. "'A Sin against Childhood': Progressive Education and the Crusade to Abolish Homework, 1897–1941." *American Journal of Education*, 105:27–66.

———. 2000. "The Lost Cause of Homework Reform." *American Journal of Education* 109:27–62.

Goodwin-Gill, G. S., and I. Cohn. 1994. *Child Soldiers*. Oxford: Oxford University Press.

Kenny, M. L. 2002. "Orators and Outcasts, Wanderers and Workers: Street Children in Brazil." In *Symbolic Childhood*, edited by D. T. Cook, 37–63. New York: Peter Lang.

Krueger, A. B. 2002. "Putting Development Dollars to Use, South of the Border." *New York Times*, May 2.

Kruse, D., and D. Mahony. 1998. "Illegal Child Labor in the United States: Prevalence and Characteristics." Working Paper 6479, National Bureau of Economic Research, Cambridge, Mass.

Lavalette, M., ed. 1999. *A Thing of the Past? Child Labour in Britain in the Nineteenth and Twentieth Centuries.* London: Palgrave.

Lee, R., and K. L. Kramer. 2002. "Children's Economic Roles in the Maya Family Life Cycle: Cain, Caldwell, and Chayanov Revisited." *Population and Development Review* 28:475–99.

Levison, D. 2000. "Children as Economic Agents." *Feminist Economics* 6:125–34.

Lewis, M. 2001. "Jonathan Lebed's Extracurricular Activities." *New York Times Magazine*, February 25.

Mayall, B. 2002. *Towards a Sociology for Childhood.* Buckingham: Open University Press.

Menjívar, C. 2000. *Fragmented Ties: Salvadoran Immigrant Networks in America.* Berkeley: University of California Press.

Nieuwenhuys, O. 1996. "The Paradox of Child Labor and Anthropology." *Annual Review of Anthropology* 25:237–51.

Olsen, R. 2000. "Families under the Microscope: Parallels between the Young Carers Debate of the 1990s and the Transformation of Childhood in the Late Nineteenth Century." *Children and Society* 14:384–94.

Orellana, M. F. 2001. "The Work Kids Do: Mexican and Central American Immigrant Children's Contributions to Households and Schools in California." *Harvard Educational Review* 71:366–89.

Orellana, M. F., L. Dorner, and L. Pulido. 2003a. "Accessing Assets: Immigrant Youth's Work as Family Translators or 'Para-phrasers.'" *Social Problems* 50:505–24.

Orellana, M. F., J. Reynolds, L. Dorner, and M. Meza. 2003b. "In Other Words: Translating or 'Para-phrasing' as a Family Literacy Practice in Immigrant Households." *Reading Research Quarterly* 38:12–34.

Orellana, M. F., B. Thorne, A. Chee, and W.S.E. Lam. 2001. "Transnational Childhoods: the Participation of Children in Processes of Family Migration." *Social Problems* 48:572–91.

Portes, A., and L. Hao. 2002. "The Price of Uniformity: Language, Family and Personality Adjustment in the Immigrant Second Generation." *Ethnic and Racial Studies* 25:889–912.

Quiroga, C. 2002. "Infancia Cartonera." *Gente*, October 22.

Qvortrup, J. 1995. "From Useful to Useful: The Historical Continuity of Children's Constructive Participation." *Sociological Studies of Children* 7:49–76.

Robson, E., and N. Ansell. 2000. "Young Carers in Southern Africa: Exploring Stories from Zimbabwean Secondary School Students." In *Children's Geographies*, edited by S. L. Holloway and G. Valentine, 174–93. London: Routledge.

Sereny, G. 1984. *The Invisible Children: Child Prostitution in America, West Germany and Great Britain.* London: Andre Deutsch.

Smelser, N. J., and R. Swedberg. 1994. "The Sociological Perspective on the Economy." In *The Handbook of Economic Sociology*, edited by N. Smelser and R. Swedberg, 3–26. New York: Russell Sage Foundation; Princeton, N.J.: Princeton University Press.

Solberg, A. 1994. *Negotiating Childhood.* Stockholm: Nordplan.

Song, M. 1999. *Helping Out: Children's Labor in Ethnic Businesses.* Philadelphia: Temple University Press.

Strom, S. 2003. "A Lesson Plan about Generosity." *New York Times*, March 21.

Sun-Hee Park, L. 2002. "Asian Immigrant Entrepreneurial Children." In *Contemporary Asian American Communities: Intersections and Divergences*, edited by L.T. Vo and R. Bonus, 161–74. Philadelphia: Temple University Press.

Swedberg, R. 2003. *Principles of Economic Sociology*. Princeton, N.J.: Princeton University Press.

Swedberg, R., and M. Granovetter, eds. 2001. *The Sociology of Economic Life*. 2nd ed. Boulder, Colo.: Westview.

Thorne, B. 2001. "Pick-up Time at Oakdale Elementary School: Work and Family from the Vantage Points of Children." In *Working Families: The Transformation of the American Home*, edited by R. Hertz and N. L. Marshall, 354–76. Berkeley: University of California Press.

Tilly, C., and C. Tilly. 1998. *Work under Capitalism*. Boulder, Colo.: Westview.

Tuten, F. 2002. "Still Replying to Grandma's Persistent, 'And Then.'" *New York Times*, October 21.

Valenzuela, A., Jr. 1999. "Gender Roles and Settlement Activities among Children and Their Immigrant Families." *American Behavioral Scientist* 42:720–42.

Woodhead, M. 1999. "Combating Child Labor: Listen to What the Children Say." *Childhood* 6:27–49.

Wuthnow, R. 1995. *Learning to Care*. New York: Oxford University Press.

Zelizer, V. A. 1985. *Pricing the Priceless Child: The Changing Social Value of Children*. New York: Basic Books.

———. 2001. "Economic Sociology." In *International Encyclopedia of the Social and Behavioral Sciences*, edited by N. J. Smelser and P. B. Baltes, 6:4, 128–31. Amsterdam: Elsevier.

———. 2002a. "Intimate Transactions." In *The New Economic Sociology: Developments in an Emerging Field*, edited by M. F. Guillén, R. Collins, P. England, and M. Meyer, 274–300. New York: Russell Sage Foundation.

———. 2002b. "Kids and Commerce." *Childhood* 4 (November): 375–96.

PART TWO

The Social Meaning of Money

When governments pump money into an economy to stave off recession, their economists ordinarily assume that as long as it reaches the same population of consumers, it little matters whether they package the payment as a wage rise, a tax credit, or a one-time grant of cash. Recipients' practices, however implicit, generally show that they disagree. Where the money comes from, in what form, and how, strongly affects how people actually use it.

A 2002 study of Wisconsin low-income households established, for example, that the families receiving checks for income tax refunds and earned income tax credits distinguished sharply between that money and their routine income. Instead of mingling their monies, they spent the new income on such items as accumulated debt, consumer durables, and aid to their kin (Romich and Weisner 2002, 383).

In a parallel way, researchers have recurrently found that welfare payments made to mothers are more likely to go for children's needs than if the money comes to a male head of household. What is going on here? This sort of behavior challenges the widely held view of how money works. In a time-honored conception, money is a seamlessly fungible medium in which each unit is identical to each other unit. Thus, what are apparently separate stores of money are actually completely interchangeable. Furthermore, this theory also presumes that precisely because of this impersonal fungibility, money transforms the social relations it touches, converting them willy-nilly into objects of the market. For this very reason, moralists fear that commercialization of goods and services previously not available in markets—a mother's attention to her child, the transplant of human organs, or spiritual counseling—will contaminate the quality of such goods and services. All of these views make a more fundamental assumption: that money ultimately refers back to a single standard, most often identified with government-backed legal tender.

The chapters in this section strongly counter this prevalent line of thought. As an alternative, these articles argue that people employ money as a means of creating, transforming, and differentiating their social relations. Instead of a single, fungible money that reduces social relations to a thin common denominator, they show us the integration of differentiated monies into the whole range of interpersonal ties. As a consequence, people are constantly creating new monies, and they do so by segregating different streams of legal tender into funds for distinct activities and relations. For example, people regularly distinguish between relations that are short-term or long-term, intimate or impersonal, and broad or narrow in the range of shared activities they encompass. People also mark moral boundaries among categories of money: consider the variable meanings of "dirty" money, "easy" money, or "blood" money. People often "launder" dubious earnings by making donations to charity or other morally cleansing destinations.

One major set of practices that people repeatedly adopt is the earmarking of currency so that its proper destination becomes obvious and compelling. Earmarking consists both of symbolic distinctions and of practices ranging from the keeping of cash in separate containers to the decoration of legal tender so that it becomes a personalized gift. Earmarking techniques fall into three broad categories:

1. Personal behavior that treats otherwise identical media (for example, two $100 bank notes) as distinctly different, depending on their destination or their source.
2. The creation of tokens, coupons, scrip, chits, food stamps, affinity credit cards, frequent flier miles, money orders, vouchers, or gift certificates, which represent diverse monetary transactions.
3. Transforming cigarettes, postage stamps, subway tokens, poker chips, baseball cards, or other objects into monetary media, once again differentiated by social use.

Behavioral economists have made a parallel observation with their ingenious model of mental accounts, in which different media and economic activities occupy distinctive positions within a cognitive space (for a review of the mental accounting literature, see Soman and Ahn, 2010). People label, for instance, windfall income much differently than a bonus or an inheritance, even when the sums involved are identical. However, economists have commonly ignored the strong relationships between the categories of mental accounting and the practices that signify distinctions between proper and improper uses of the monies in question. Earmarking integrates practices and cognitive categories.

Those practices, moreover, derive not only from mental distinctions or cognitive maps but are deeply grounded in our social relations and shared meaning systems. In fact, cognitively established categories remain mysterious unless we understand that they usually both emerge from and construct our distinctive relations to others. They become means of relational work. When we earmark money for our child's college fund, for example, we are affirming our parental relationship to that child. On the other hand, by gambling the money away we would seriously undermine that connection—unless the gambling was a means to obtain monies for some morally justifiable goal, such as subsidizing another child's emergency surgery. George Akerlof has proposed that mental accounting explanations of people's consumption practices should consider causal effects of decision makers' norms about "how money *should* be spent" (2007, 17). In this valuable model, however, norms remain principles internalized by individuals, a crucial "missing motivation" that nonetheless does not include in a systematic way norms' relational grounding. What still is missing, therefore, are social relations. Norms as well as mental accounts and practices are continuously affirmed, challenged, and transformed by our relations to others.

As the chapters in this section also suggest, my work on the social meaning of money grew out of my initial concern with the valuation of human lives rather than from general ideas about the nature of money. However, work on processes such as earmarking and the creation of special monies inevitably raised more general questions about how money works. That happened in two different ways: First, the analysis of social meaning required me to think more directly about correct and incorrect conceptions of monetary transactions. Second, my own heterodox views brought me into dialogue, sometimes contentious, with advocates of a more universal, transparent, and fungible understanding of money. In the course of such dialogues, I arrived at a clearer distinction among three components of money wherever it appears: accounting systems, media representing those accounting systems, and practices that govern people's use of accounting systems and media. In all three regards, my most distinctive contribution was no doubt to identify the great extent to which accounting systems, media, and practices vary with, respond to, and inform people's negotiation of interpersonal relations.

Fortunately, a number of economists and economic sociologists found this alternative view of money liberating. For example, economist André Orléan, reviewing a French translation of *The Social Meaning of Money*, remarked: "Zelizer refuses to think of money's presence in terms of its being a power that, regardless of the context in which it occurs, inevitably leads to the logic of rational exchange" (2007, 1,429).

The first published statement of this alternative view of money appeared in a 1989 issue of the *American Journal of Sociology*. The article concentrates on household money and its differentiation into separate pools, depending on its source, intended use, and relational context. This article retains its affinity with my earlier work by concentrating on U.S. historical experience.

The second essay takes up a very different line. It responds to a partly justified complaint from two economic analysts that my conception of money as represented by *The Social Meaning of Money* neglected general theories of money in favor of emphasizing the constant reintroduction of particularity into monetary transactions. My reply concedes that I avoided any attempt to construct a general theory of money or even to connect my account critically with either Marxist or neoclassical analyses of money in general. However, it also points out that the arguments and evidence in my work do challenge the universalism of dominant approaches to money.

"Payments and Social Ties" extends the analysis of earmarking by emphasizing the distinctions between three categories of monetary payments: gifts, entitlements, and compensation. It documents two points that matter significantly for this book's general themes. First, payers and recipients attach great importance to both the form and meaning of the payment and even grow indignant if confusion among types of payment arises. Second, a reciprocal relationship exists between the form of payment and the relationship at hand: the treatment of a payment as compensation already defines the relationship as different from one where a gift is appropriate, and different relations demand different forms of payment.

"Money, Power, and Sex" develops this line of argument by looking more particularly at sexually tinged relationships, a subject that will come up again in the next section. It builds on a two-dimensional classification of sexual relationships dependent on their duration (brief or durable) and their breadth (narrow or broad). It adds a new and interesting complication: that the organizational setting in which a sexually tinged relationship occurs significantly affects its meaning, its appropriate economic transaction, and the efforts of third parties to control or suppress them.

The chapters in this section, then, move us from questions of valuation to close analysis of how monetary practices enter into and help define interpersonal relations.

REFERENCES

Akerlof, George A. 2007. "The Missing Motivation in Macroeconomics." *American Economic Review* 97 (March): 5–36.

Orléan, André. 2007. Review of *La signification sociale de l'argent*, by Viviana Zelizer. *Annales: Histoire, Sciences Sociales* 62 (November–December): 1428–31.

Romich, Jennifer L., and Thomas S. Weisner. 2002. "How Families View and Use the Earned Income Tax Credit: Advance Payment versus Lump-Sum Delivery." In *Making Work Pay: The Earned Income Tax Credit and Its Impact on America's Families*, edited by Bruce D. Meyer and Douglas Holtz-Eakin, 366–91. New York: Russell Sage Foundation.

Soman, Dilip, and Hee-Kyung Ahn. 2010. "Mental Accounting and Individual Welfare." In *Perspectives on Framing*, edited by G. Keren. London: Psychology Press/Taylor and Francis.

5

The Social Meaning of Money

"Special Monies"

In Rossel Island, a small, traditional community in the southwestern Pacific, the gender of money was tangibly identified—separate lower-value coins were reserved exclusively for women. And in Yap, one of the Caroline Islands in the west Pacific, mussel shells strung on strings served as women's money, while men monopolized the more desirable large stones (Baric 1964, 422–23; Sumner [1906] 1940, 140). In contrast to the money in these primitive societies, modern money seems starkly homogeneous and surely genderless. Yet, camouflaged by the physical anonymity of our dollar bills, modern money is also routinely differentiated, not just by varying quantities but also by its special diverse qualities. We assign different meanings and designate separate uses for particular kinds of monies. For instance, a housewife's pin money or her allowance is treated differently from a wage or a salary, and each surely differs from a child's allowance. Or a lottery winning is marked as a different kind of money from an ordinary paycheck. The money we obtain as compensation for an accident is not quite the same as the royalties from a book. Not all dollars are equal.

But while there is an extensive literature dealing with primitive currency, the sociological bibliography on money remains remarkably sparse. Money is ignored, Randall Collins has suggested, "as if it were not sociological enough" (1979, 190).[1] Significantly, the *International Encyclopedia of the Social Sciences* devotes over thirty pages to money but not one to its social characteristics. There are essays on the economic effect of money, on quantity theory, on velocity of circulation, and on monetary reform but nothing on money as a "*réalité sociale*," using Simiand's apt term (1934). As a result, money remains confined primarily to the economists' intellectual domain; its noneconomic aspects have not been systematically explored.

The dominant utilitarian understanding of money is hardly surprising. It is a by-product of what Bernard Barber (1977) has called the "absolutization of the market": the illusory yet pervasive assumption that market exchange is free from cultural or social constraints.[2] And money, as the most material representation of market exchange, seems eminently exempt from extraeconomic influences. To be sure, Veblen ([1899] 1953) alerted us to the social meaning of what money buys, and others have significantly furthered the social, cultural, and historical analysis of consumerism (see, e.g., Parsons and Smelser 1956; Rainwater 1974; Sahlins 1976; Douglas and Isherwood 1979; Horowitz 1985; Schudson 1984; Appadurai 1986; Miller 1987). But the "freedom" of money itself is not directly challenged.

My article will argue that the utilitarian approach to money is a theoretical and empirical straitjacket. Money belongs to the market, but not exclusively so. And while money is indeed an objective means of rational calculation, it is not only that. I turn first to the traditional interpretation of money, that is, as "market money," and then propose an alternative model of "special monies" that incorporates the social and symbolic significance of money. In the third part of the article, I present a historical case study of domestic money as one example of a special money. I will argue that domestic money—which includes wife's money, husband's money, and children's money—is a special category of money in the modern world. Its meanings, uses, allocation, and even quantity are partly determined by considerations of economic efficiency, but domestic money is equally shaped by changing cultural conceptions of money and of family life as well as by power relationships, age, and gender. And while in certain respects domestic money transcends social class differences, I will show how class profoundly marks not only its quantity but its quality.

More specifically, my discussion will focus on the changing meaning of married women's money between the 1870s and 1930s, showing how this money, whether given by the husband or earned in the household or in the labor market, was marked as a different form of currency from an ordinary dollar. It was obtained in special ways, used for designated purposes, and even had a special vocabulary: allowance, pin money, "egg money," "butter money," spending money, pocket money, gift, or "dole," but seldom wage, salary, paycheck, or profit.

Market Money: A Utilitarian Approach to Money

To be sure, money occupies a central place in classic interpretations of the development of the modern world. But what kind of place? For Simmel and Weber, money was a key instrument in the rationalization of social life. On purely technical grounds, the possibility of money accounting was essential for the development of rational economic markets. As "the most abstract and 'impersonal' element that exists in human life," as Weber defined it, money became "the most 'perfect' means of economic calculation" ([1946] 1971, 331; [1922] 1978, 86). It transformed the world, observed Simmel, into an "arithmetic problem" ([1908] 1950, 412).

Presumably, the fundamental and revolutionary power of money came from its complete indifference to values. Money was perceived as the prototype of an instrumental, calculating approach; in Simmel's words, money was "the purest reification of means" ([1900] 1978, 211). It was also the symbol of what, in his *Philosophy of Money*, Simmel identified as a major tendency of modern life—the reduction of quality to quantity: "which achieves its highest and uniquely perfect representation in money" (1978, 280). Unlike any other known substance or product, money was the absolute negation of quality. Only money, argued Simmel, "is free from any quality and exclusively determined by quantity." And therefore, only with money, "we do not ask what and how, but how much" (1978, 279, 259).

That "uncompromising objectivity" allowed money to function as the "technically perfect" medium of modern economic exchange. Free from subjective restrictions, indifferent to "particular interests, origins, or relations," money's liquidity and divisibility were infinite, making it "absolutely interchangeable" (1978, 373, 128, 441). The very essence of money, claimed Simmel, was its "unconditional interchangeability, the internal uniformity that makes each piece exchangeable for another." Money thus served as the fitting neutral intermediary of a rational, impersonal market, "expressing the economic relations between objects . . . in abstract quantitative terms, without itself entering into those relations" (1978, 427, 125).

Noneconomic restrictions in the use of money were unequivocally dismissed by Simmel as residual atavisms: "The inhibiting notion that certain amounts of money may be 'stained with blood' or be under a curse are sentimentalities that lose their significance completely with the growing indifference of money" (1978, 441). As money became nothing but "mere money," its freedom was apparently unassailable and its uses unlimited. Thus, for Simmel, money's "purely negative quality" guaranteed its unbounded flexibility and indiscriminate intrusiveness. With money, all qualitative distinctions between objects were equally convertible into an arithmetically calculable "system of numbers" (1978, 444).

This quantification of quality was perceived to be a morally dangerous alchemy. In his early essay "The Power of Money in Bourgeois Society," Marx had warned that the transformational powers of money subverted reality: "confounding and compounding . . . all natural and human qualities . . . [money] serves to exchange every property for every other, even contradictory, property and object: it is the fraternization of impossibilities" ([1844] 1964, 169). As the "god among commodities" (Marx [1858–59] 1973, 221), money emerged as the ultimate objectifier, obliterating all subjective connection between objects and individuals and debasing personal relations into calculative instrumental ties.

Indeed, money fetishism, argued Marx in the *Grundrisse* (1973, 222) and in *Capital* ([1867] 1984, 96), was the most "glaring" form of commodity fetishism. The "perverted" process by which social relations between individuals were transmuted into material relations between things peaked with money (Marx [1858] 1972, 49). For other commodities might retain their more "natural" value or "use value" and therefore some distinctive quality.

But as pure exchange value, money necessarily assumed an "unmeaning" form, which in turn neutralized all possible qualitative distinctions between commodities (Marx 1984, 103). In their money form, noted Marx, "all commodities look alike" (1984, 111). And more incongruously still, money turned even intangible objects devoid of utility—such as conscience or honor—into ordinary commodities. Thus the priceless itself surrendered to price. "Not even the bones of saints . . . are *extra commercium hominum* able to withstand the alchemy" (Marx 1984, 132, 105).

For Marx, money was thus an irresistible and "radical leveler," invading all areas of social life (1984, 132). By homogenizing all qualitative distinctions into an abstract quantity, money allowed the "equation of the incompatible" (Marx 1973, 163). Echoing Marx's vocabulary half a century later, Simmel dubbed money a "frightful leveler," perverting the uniqueness of personal and social values: "With its colorlessness and indifference . . . [money] hollows out the core of things . . . their specific value, and their incomparability" (1950, 414). And in his essay "Religious Rejections of the World," Weber noted a fundamental antagonism between a rational money economy and a "religious ethic of brotherliness" (1971, 331).

In an essay published in 1913 in the *American Journal of Sociology*, Cooley submitted a dissenting argument in defense of the dollar. While acknowledging the extension of the cash nexus in modern society, Cooley refused to see money as a necessary antagonist of nonpecuniary values. Instead, sounding much like the eighteenth-century advocates of what Hirschman (1986) calls the "*doux commerce*" thesis of the market as a moralizing agent, Cooley argued that "the principle that everything has a price should be enlarged rather than restricted. . . . [P]ecuniary values are members of the same general system as the moral and aesthetic values, and it is their function to put the latter upon the market" (1913, 202). Progress, concluded Cooley, lay not in depreciating monetary valuation but in assuring the moral regulation of money: "The dollar is to be reformed rather than suppressed" (1913, 203). But Cooley's outlook was exceptional. For most contemporary observers, the dollar was an invulnerable transformer, not a morally reformable currency.

The prevailing classic interpretation of money thus absolutized a model of market money, shaped by the following five underlying assumptions:

1. The functions and characteristics of money are defined strictly in economic terms. Money, maintained Simmel, was the "incarnation and purest expression of the concept of economic value" (1978, 101). As a qualityless, absolutely homogeneous, infinitely divisible, liquid object, money is a matchless tool for market exchange.

2. All monies are the same in modern society. What Simmel called money's "qualitatively communistic character" (1978, 440) aborts any distinctions between types of money. Differences can exist in the quantity of money but not in its meaning. Thus, there is only one kind of money—market money.

3. A sharp dichotomy is established between money and nonpecuniary values. Money in modern society is defined as essentially profane and utilitarian in contrast to noninstrumental values. Money is qualitatively neutral; personal, social, and sacred values are qualitatively distinct, unexchangeable, and indivisible.

4. Monetary concerns are seen as constantly enlarging, quantifying, and often corrupting all areas of life. As an abstract medium of exchange, money has not only the freedom but also the power to draw an increasing number of goods and services into the web of the market. Money is thus the vehicle for an inevitable commodification of society. As Simmel put it, money "intervenes in the totality of existential interests and imposes itself upon them. . . . [It] has the power to lay down forms and directions for contents to which [it is] indifferent . . ." (1978, 442).

5. The power of money to transform nonpecuniary values is unquestioned, while the reciprocal transformation of money by values is seldom conceptualized or else is explicitly rejected. Unfettered by "objective or ethical considerations," money, insisted Simmel, was exempt from extraeconomic "directives [or] obstacles" (1978, 441).[3]

In this context, to speak about the distinctive "quality" of modern money seems anachronistic. After all, how can money have special meanings if its very essence is the absolute homogenization and objectivization of qualitative distinctions?

A link, an interdependence, is missing from the traditional approach to money. Impressed by the fungible, impersonal characteristics of money, traditional social thinkers emphasized its instrumental rationality and apparently unlimited capacity to transform products, relationships, and sometimes even emotions into an abstract and objective numerical equivalent. But money is neither culturally neutral nor morally invulnerable. It may well "corrupt" values into numbers, but values and sentiment reciprocally corrupt money by investing it with moral, social, and religious meaning. We need to examine more carefully how cultural and social structural factors influence the uses, meaning, and even quantity of money. What is the relationship of money as a medium of exchange and measure of utility to money as a symbol of social value?

SPECIAL MONIES: EXPLORING THE QUALITY OF MODERN MONEY

Significantly, even when the symbolic dimension of modern money has been recognized, the analysis stops short of fully transcending the utilitarian framework. Parsons, for instance, explicitly and forcefully called for a "sociology of money" that would treat money as one of the various generalized symbolic media of social interchange, along with political power, influence, and value commitments (1971a, 241; 1971b, 26–27). In contrast to Marx's definition of money as the "material representative of wealth" (1973, 222), in Parsons's media theory money was a shared symbolic language; not a commodity but a signifier, devoid of use value. Yet Parsons restricts the symbolism of money to the economic sphere. Money, Parsons contends, is the "symbolic 'embodiment' of economic value, of what economists in a technical sense call 'utility'" (1967, 358). Consequently, the symbolic meaning of money outside the market, money's cultural and social significance beyond utility, remains uncharted in Parsons's media theory.

Anthropologists provide some intriguing insights into the extraeconomic, symbolic meaning of money but only with regard to primitive money. For instance, ethnographic studies show that, in certain primitive communities, money attains special qualities and distinct values independent of quantity. How much money is less important than *which* money. Multiple currencies, or "special-purpose" money, to use Karl Polanyi's term (1957, 264–66), have sometimes coexisted in one and the same village, each currency having a specified, restricted use (for purchase of only certain goods or services), special modes of allocation and forms of exchange (see, e.g., Bohannan 1959), and, sometimes, designated users. Certain currencies, for instance, may be limited to specified social classes or else assigned by gender (see Einzig 1966).

Special monies are often morally or ritually ranked: certain kinds of money may be good for obtaining food but not for purchasing a wife; other monies are appropriate only for funeral gifts or marriage gifts or as blood money; still other monies serve exclusively for paying damages for adultery or insults, for burial with the dead, or for magical rites. In this context, the "wrong" quality or lesser-quality money, even in large quantities, is useless or degraded. This qualitative categorization of monies was also noted by Thomas and Znaniecki in their analysis of the traditional Polish peasant culture: "A sum received from selling a cow is qualitatively different from a sum received as a dowry, and both are different from a sum earned outside" ([1918–20] 1958, 164–65). Different monies were used differently and even kept separately. Indeed, Thomas and Znaniecki remarked that a peasant who set a sum aside for a designated purpose, and then needed some money for a different expense, would prefer to borrow it "even under very difficult conditions, rather than touch that sum" (1958, 166).

These special monies, which Mary Douglas (1967) has perceptively identified as a sort of primitive coupon system, control exchange by rationing and restricting the use and allocation of currency. In the process, money sometimes performs economic functions by serving as a medium of exchange, but it also functions as a social and sacred "marker," used to acquire or amend status or to celebrate ritual events. The point is that primitive money is transformable, from fungible to nonfungible, from profane to sacred.

But what about modern money? Has modernization indeed stripped money of its cultural meaning, establishing, as Simmel saw it, an "unconditional identity of money with sum"? (1978, 276). Economic development, suggested Thomas and Znaniecki, "tends to abolish all [the] distinctions and . . . make money more and more fluid" (1958, 65). Influenced by economic models, most interpretations thus establish a sharp dichotomy between primitive, restricted "special-purpose" money and modern "all-purpose" money, which, as a single currency unburdened by ritual or social controls, can function effectively as a universal medium of exchange. Curiously, when it comes to modern money, even anthropologists seem to surrender their formidable analytical tools. For instance, more than twenty years ago, Mary Douglas, in an important essay, suggested that modern money may not be as unrestricted and "free" after all. Her evidence, however, is puzzlingly limited. Modern money, argues Douglas, is controlled and rationed in two situations: in international exchange and at the purely individual personal levels, where "many of us try to primitivize our money . . . by placing restrictions at the source, by earmarking monetary instruments of certain kinds for certain purposes, by only allowing ourselves or our wives certain limited freedoms in the disposal of money." "Money from different sources," observes Douglas, "is sometimes personalized and attracts distinctive feelings which dictate the character of its spending" (1967, 139).

Surely, these restraints, which, as Douglas notes, "resemble strangely . . . restraints on the use of some primitive monies" (1967, 119–20), are more than purely individual "quirks" or a "clumsy attempt to control the all too liquid state of money," as she suggests (138, 140). Yet Douglas, who significantly advances a cultural theory of consumption, does not go far enough with the cultural analysis of money (Douglas and Isherwood 1979). Likewise, Thomas Crump refers to the existence of what he calls "bounded sub-systems" in modern societies (1981, 125–30): separate spheres of exchange with special currencies. But his focus is on economic distinctions between types of monies, such as the simultaneous yet separate use of a national and a foreign currency (usually the dollar) by a country, the selective use of specie versus "scriptural" money for certain goods and services, or the separate economy of credit cards versus cash payments, and includes even the chips used by a poker school as a separate form of currency (see also Melitz 1970).

Economic psychologists have recently challenged the purely rationalistic economic definition of modern money, particularly the idea of fungibility, by suggesting the concept of "mental accounting": the ways individuals distinguish between kinds of money. For instance, they treat a windfall income much differently from a bonus or an inheritance, even when the sums involved are identical (see, e.g., Thaler 1985; Kahneman and Tversky 1982; for an excellent review and analysis of the psychological literature on money, see Lea, Tarpy, and Webley 1987, 319–42).

But mental accounting cannot be fully understood without a model of "sociological accounting." Modern money is marked by more than individual whim or the different material form of currencies. As François Simiand, one of Durkheim's students, argued (1934), the extraeconomic, social basis of money remains as powerful in modern economic systems as it was in primitive and ancient societies.[4] Indeed, Simiand warned against an orthodox rationalist approach that mistakenly ignores the persistent symbolic, sacred, and even magical significance of modern money.

My general theoretical purpose, then, is to apply the concept of special money to the modern world and examine in what ways culture and social structure mark modern money by introducing controls, restrictions, and distinctions that are as influential as the rationing of primitive money. Special money in the modern world may not be as easily or visibly identifiable as the shells, coins, brass rods, or stones of primitive communities, but its invisible boundaries emerge from sets of formal and informal rules that regulate its uses, allocation, sources, and quantity. How else, for instance, do we distinguish a bribe from a tribute or a donation, a wage from an honorarium, or an allowance from a salary? How do we identify ransom, bonuses, tips, damages, or premiums? True, there are quantitative differences among these various payments. But, surely, the special vocabulary conveys much more than diverse amounts. Detached from its qualitative differences, the world of money becomes undecipherable.

The model of special monies thus challenges the traditional utilitarian model of market money by introducing different fundamental assumptions in the understanding of money:

1. While money does serve as a key rational tool of the modern economic market, it also exists outside the sphere of the market and is profoundly shaped by cultural and social structural factors.

2. There are a plurality of different kinds of monies; each special money is shaped by a particular set of cultural and social factors and is thus qualitatively distinct. Market money does not escape extraeconomic influences but is in fact one type of special money, subject to particular social and cultural influences.

3. The classic economic inventory of money's functions and attributes, based on the assumption of a single general-purpose type of money, is thus unsuitably narrow. By focusing exclusively on money as a market phenomenon, it fails to capture the very complex range of characteristics of money as a nonmarket medium. A different, more inclusive coding is necessary, for certain monies can be indivisible (or divisible but not in mathematically predictable portions), nonfungible, nonportable, deeply subjective, and therefore qualitatively heterogeneous.

4. The assumed dichotomy between a utilitarian money and nonpecuniary values is false, for money under certain circumstances may be as singular and unexchangeable as the most personal or unique object.

5. Given the assumptions above, the alleged freedom and unchecked power of money become untenable assumptions. Culture and social structure set inevitable limits to the monetization process by introducing profound controls and restrictions on the flow and liquidity of money. Extraeconomic factors systematically constrain and shape (a) the *uses* of money—earmarking, for instance, certain monies for specified uses; (b) the *users* of money, designating different people to handle specified monies; (c) the *allocation* system of each particular money; (d) the *control* of different monies; and (e) the *sources* of money, linking different sources to specified uses.

Even the quantity of money is regulated by more than rational market calculation. For instance, in *The Philosophy of Money*, Simmel suggests that money in "extraordinarily great quantities" can circumvent its "empty quantitative" nature: it becomes "imbued with that 'super-additum,' with fantastic possibilities that transcend the definiteness of numbers" (1978, 273, 406). The apparent objectivity of numbers, however, is escaped not only by large fortunes. Small sums of money can attain similar distinction. For example, in civil law countries that permit monetary compensation for the grief of losing a child in an accident, legal scholars advocate the "*franc symbolique*" (Mazeaud, Mazeaud, and Tunc 1957). A token sum of money is perceived as the only dignified equivalent for such a purely emotional loss. Thus, determining a proper amount often involves not only an instrumental calculus but a cultural or social accounting. (For an example of the connection between quantity of money and its social and symbolic meaning, see Geertz 1973, 425–42.)

Even identical quantities of money do not "add" up in the same way. A $1,000 paycheck is not the same money as $1,000 stolen from a bank or $1,000 borrowed from a friend. And certain monies remain indivisible—an inheritance, for instance, or a wedding gift of money intended for the purchase of a particular kind of object. The latter is a qualitative unit that should not be spent partly for a gift and partly for groceries.

Exploring the quality of special monies does not deny money's quantifiable and instrumental characteristics but moves beyond them, suggesting very different theoretical and empirical questions from those derived from a purely economic model of market money. Domestic money raises some of those questions. What kind of money circulates within the family? How is it allocated, and how is it used? How do changing social and power relationships between family members affect the meaning of the domestic dollar?

In terms of data, studying money in the family is entering largely uncharted territory. Although money is the major source of husband-wife disagreements and often a sore point between parents and children, curiously, we know less about money matters than about family violence or even marital sex.[5] Not only are families reluctant to disclose their private financial lives to strangers; husbands, wives, and children often lie, deceive, or simply conceal information from each other as well. Perhaps more fundamentally still, the model of what Sen (1983) calls the "glued-together family" has meant that questions about how money is divided between family members are seldom even asked. Once money enters the family, it is assumed to be somehow equitably distributed among family members, serving to maximize their collective welfare. How much money each person gets, how he or she obtains it, from whom and for what, are rarely considered. And yet, as Michael Young suggested more than thirty years ago, the distribution of money among family members is often as lopsided and arbitrary as the distribution of national income among families. Therefore, argues Young, we should stop assuming that "some members of a family cannot be rich while others are poor" (1952, 305; see also Hartmann 1981; Wong 1984; Delphy and Leonard 1986).

The period between 1870 and 1930 provides some unusual glimpses into this traditionally secret world of family money. As the consumer society was being established, Americans wrote about and studied money matters in an unprecedented manner. Household-budget studies richly documented how the working class and lower middle class spent their money. And in anonymous, "confessional" articles published in popular magazines, middle-class Americans disclosed their own domestic budgets, transforming the spending of money into a public issue. In that same period, as Daniel Horowitz (1985) has shown, social critics and social scientists presented their versions of the "morality of spending," discussing with passion and in detail the usually dreaded noneconomic contours of a commoditized American society. Thus, at the turn of the century, the renegotiation of the domestic economy broke through the usually closed doors of individual households and entered the public discourse.

I now turn to an analysis of the changing meanings, allocation systems, and uses of married women's money between 1870 and the 1930s, showing how definitional disputes over this category of domestic money, while partly a rational response to a new economic environment, were also deeply shaped by extraeconomic, social, and cultural factors. The battle over the purse strings was regulated by notions of family life and by the gender and social class of its participants.[6]

The Domestic "Fiscal Problem": 1870–1930

During the late nineteenth century, the domestic "fiscal problem" went public, as an appealing news story in magazines and newspapers, in poignant letters to the editor and advice columns, and as the topic of conferences in women's clubs. By 1928, one observer concluded that "[m]ore quarrels between husband and wife have been started by the mention of money than by chorus girls, blond waitresses, dancing men with sleek hair, [or] traveling men" (Kelland 1928, 12). Indeed, the battle over the purse strings often ended in court. Between 1880 and 1920, money quarrels increasingly became a ground for divorce among affluent as well as poor couples (May 1980, 137; Lynd and Lynd 1956, 126). And domestic money raised legal issues even in unbroken marriages. Did a wife have a right to an allowance? If she saved money from her housekeeping expenses, was that money hers? Was a wife a thief if she "stole" money from her husband's trousers? Could a wife pledge her husband's credit at any store? There was also the matter of women's earnings. When was a woman's dollar legally her own? Slowly, but steadily, court decisions began to overturn the common-law dictum that a wife's earnings belonged to her husband.

Why did domestic money become such a controversial currency at the turn of the century? Certainly money conflicts between family members had existed earlier. For instance, in her study of New York working-class women, Stansell tells of one—albeit extreme—1811 case in which a husband beat his common-law wife to death after she took four shillings from his pockets (1986, 29). Yet these disputes remained private, rarely entering the public discourse as a major issue of collective concern (Stansell, personal communication). A consensus of sorts existed about the proper regulation of family income, and it varied by class. Among middle- and upper-class households, money matters seem to have been established largely as the husband's business. In her landmark *Treatise on Domestic Economy*, Catharine Beecher noted how, particularly among businessmen, a family's expenses were "so much more under the control of the man than of the woman" (1841, 176). Likewise, Mary Ryan's study of family life in early-nineteenth-century Oneida County, New York, found men in charge of money matters (1984, 33; see also Norton 1979, 145; Cowan 1983, 81–82). After all, the nineteenth-century "cult of domesticity" established home life as an alternative to the dominance of the market: its guardian, the "true" Victorian woman, was a specialist in affect, not finances (Welter 1966; Cott 1977). A woman might handle the housekeeping expenses, but "serious money" was a man's currency. Working-class households, on the other hand, managed their limited and often uncertain incomes by appointing wives the family's cashier. Husbands and children handed their paychecks over to the wives, who were expected to administer the collective income skillfully. Most of these monies, to be sure, were limited to housekeeping expenses.

But at the turn of the century, a rise in real income and the increasing monetization of the American economy forced a reevaluation of family finances. Making more money and spending it required not only skillful bookkeeping; it also raised a new set of confusing and often controversial noneconomic quandaries. How should money be allocated in the family? How much money should a wife receive and for which expenses? Was an allowance a "good" mechanism of allocation for wives? What about children's allowances; should they be given one, or was it their duty to earn it through household chores? Should husbands hand over all their salaries to their wives, or how much could they keep for themselves?

Proper uses of money also baffled novice consumers: What did it mean to spend money well? How, for instance, should a family's extra income be used? How much should be saved, how much given to charity, how much for vacations, how much for clothing? And, most important, how was it to be determined how much each member of the family was entitled to spend? As the amount of disposable income increased and as the consumer economy and culture became more firmly established, family money was increasingly differentiated into husband's money, wife's money, and children's money.

This new "tightened competition for the family income," as Robert Lynd described it, was to a certain extent a "fixed" dispute, for the various competitors started with culturally assigned "handicaps" (1932, 90). Indeed, turn-of-the-century wives, even those married to wealthy men, often found themselves without a dollar of their own. As Lucy Salmon, professor of history at Vassar College, explained in 1909, "Men are still for the most part those whose wages are paid in hard cash, who have a bank account and carry a cash-book, and who therefore consider that they have the right to decide in regard to the way the money they earn shall be spent" (889).

The relative poverty of married women became increasingly untenable. For the twentieth-century version of the nineteenth-century moral guardian was expected to serve as the household's purchasing agent and budget expert. To be sure, the frugality and financial wisdom of wives had been a concern in the eighteenth century as well (Beecher 1841, 175–86; Jensen 1986, 119–28). But the expansion of the consumer economy made proper spending skills a dominant and visible parameter of domestic expertise. The "good housekeeper" was responsible "for the care of her husband's money, and she must expend it wisely" (*New York Times*, December 23, 1900, 10). After all, as one exemplary housewife explained in the same article, "a man does not understand the regulation of the household and its expenses."

But "Mrs. Consumer" 's, (Frederick 1929) increased financial role and responsibility came without a salary and most often without even a fixed and dependable income. Women were thus caught in the strange predicament of being cashless money managers expected to spend properly but denied control over money. The success of the home-economics movement, which urged women to run their homes like a business, further intensified the contradiction in women's economic lives.

Women's stratagems to extract some cash from their unforthcoming husbands were the subject of jokes and a staple of late-nineteenth-century vaudeville routines. But the domestic fiscal problem turned serious, forcing a difficult and controversial reevaluation of women's household money as well as of their earned income.

A DOLLAR OF HER OWN: DEFINING WOMEN'S HOUSEHOLD MONEY

American women, even those whose husbands could afford it, never had a legal claim to any portion of domestic money. As long as spouses lived together, the author of a 1935 *Law Review* article explained, "the wife's right to support is not a right to any definite thing or to any definite amount. . . . Whether the wife will get much or little is not a matter of her legal right but is a matter for the husband to decide" (Crozier 1935, 33).[7] As a result, the allocation of domestic money depended on unofficial rules and informal negotiation. At the turn of the century, married women—the majority of whom depended on their husbands' paychecks or incomes—obtained their cash in a variety of forms or special monies.

Upper- and middle-class wives received an irregular dole or, more rarely, a regular allowance from their husbands for housekeeping expenses, including household goods and clothing. Sometimes women relied almost entirely on "invisible" dollars, crediting their expenses and rarely handling cash at all. Working-class wives, on the other hand, were given their husbands' paychecks and were expected to administer and distribute the family money.

These official monies, however, were supervised and even, in the case of working-class women, ultimately owned and controlled by the husbands. Sometimes, husbands openly took over all monetary transactions. In a letter to the advice column of *Woman's Home Companion* in 1905, a thirty-year-old woman complained that John, her husband, although "liberal in a way . . . keeps the pocketbook himself, buys the provisions, prefers to purchase the dry-goods, the shoes, the gloves . . . and does not see that I need any money when he gets whatever I want" (Sangster 1905, 32).

Even if a woman managed to save some money from her housekeeping expenses, the law ultimately considered that money as her husband's property. For instance, in 1914, when Charles Montgomery sued his wife, Emma, for the $618.12 she had saved from the household expenses during their twenty-five years of marriage, Justice Blackman of the Supreme Court, Brooklyn, ruled for the husband, arguing "that no matter how careful and prudent has been the wife, if the money . . . belonged to the husband it is still his property, unless the evidence shows that it was a gift to his wife" (*New York Times*, Dec. 16, 1914, 22). Thus, a wife's channels to additional cash were limited to a variety of persuasion techniques: asking, cajoling, downright begging, or even practicing sexual blackmail.

If these techniques failed, there was also a repertoire of underground financial strategies, ranging from home pocket picking to padding bills. In 1890, an article in the *Forum* denounced the "amount of deceit, fraud, and double dealing which grow out of the administration of the family finances." Just to obtain "a few dollars they can call their own," women routinely engaged in systematic domestic fraud: some "get their milliners to send in a bill for forty dollars, instead of thirty, the real price, in order to take the extra ten to themselves . . . [others] overtax their tired eyes and exhausted bodies by taking in sewing without their husband's knowledge; and . . . farmers' wives . . . smuggle apples and eggs into town" (Ives 1890, 106, 111).

Other methods were even riskier. In 1905, Joseph Schultz was taken to the police court of Buffalo by Mrs. Schultz. It seems that Mr. Schultz, determined to stop his wife's nocturnal thefts of the change left in his trousers, set a small rattrap in the trouser pocket. About 2:00 a.m. the trap was sprung, and next morning the husband was taken to court. *Bench and Bar*, a New York legal journal, reported with some satisfaction that the judge turned down the wife's complaint and upheld the right of husbands to maintain rattraps for the protection of their small change (3 *Bench and Bar* 6). In another case, Theresa Marabella, forty years old, was sentenced to four months in a county jail for stealing $10 from the trousers of Frank Marabella, a laborer and her husband. She had spent the money on a trip to New York (*New York Times*, July 14, 1921).

But "stolen" dollars were not taken only by the wives of poor men. Indeed, one observer was persuaded that "the money skeletons in the closets of some nominally rich women may be as gruesome as are those in the closets of the nominally poor" (Salmon 1909, 889). While poor women rifled their husbands' trousers looking for some change, the affluent cashless wife used a variety of fraudulent techniques. Mrs. Gray, a grandmother married for twenty years but without any money "she could call her own," "adopted a systematic policy of deceit and fraud toward her husband. . . . When she wants to give a little money to help buy a stove for a poor family, or to assist some sick or starving creature to pay his rent, she tells her husband that the flour is out, or that the sugar is low, and so gets the needful amount." Thus, paradoxically, this "strict church member," who never told a falsehood, "cheats and deceives" the man "she has solemnly sworn to love and obey" (Ives 1890, 110).

There were other ways to "circumvent the holder of the purse" (Salmon 1909, 889). Women bargained with dressmakers, milliners, and shopkeepers to add extra items to their bills so that, when the bill was paid, "the rich man's wife may get a rake-off and possess a few dollars" (Peattie 1911, 466). In search of cash, some women even turned to their servants, selling them their old furniture (O'Hagan 1909). A Japanese visitor to the United States in the 1910s was shocked to hear from "men and women of all classes, from newspapers, novels, lecturers, and once even from the pulpit . . . allusions to amusing stories of women secreting money in odd places, coaxing it from their husbands, . . . or saving it secretly for some private purpose" (Sugimoto [1926] 1936, 176).[8]

As the consumer economy multiplied the number and attractiveness of goods—many of them targeted at a female audience—the demand intensified for a more definite and regular housekeeping income for the wife and increasingly for her "private purse," a free sum of unaccounted money to spend for the home, for entertainment, or on clothes, cosmetics, perfumes, or gifts. (On the sales strategies of department stores, 1890–1940, aimed at an almost entirely female middle-class clientele, see Benson 1986; on the commercialization of the beauty industry in the early twentieth century, see Banner 1983, 202–25.)

DOLE VERSUS ALLOWANCE: THE ALLOWANCE AS A SOLUTION

The traditional doling-out method of supplying women with money came under attack by the late nineteenth century in a battle that continued during the first three decades of the twentieth century. Anonymous letters to the editors of women's magazines conveyed the money troubles of housewives. "What Should Margaret Do?" asked one woman whose husband in 1909 gave her only $50 a month (from his $300 salary) to run the house, pay all bills, and clothe herself and a baby girl. When she asked for more, "John . . . gets very angry and accuses her of being dissatisfied . . . [and tells her] she is always wanting something" (*Good Housekeeping* 1909, 50).

Condemning a system that forced women to play the "mendicant before a husband," the well-known and widely syndicated columnist Dorothy Dix remarked on the irony of a man who "will trust [a] wife with his honor, his health, his name, his children, but he will not trust her with money" (1914, 408–9). The availability of credit was no solution, since it was simply another form of gift money supervised by the husband. Indeed, observers noted the "anomalous" situation in which men willingly paid "large bills . . . [of] wives and daughters" yet were unwilling "to trust them with the smallest amount of ready money" (Salmon 1909, 889). The rich wife, remarked the widely read writer and theologian Hugh Black, could order "anything from countless stores where they had a charge account. . . ." But often, "she could not give ten cents to a beggar" (1921, 58).

A better system was needed to assure women, as one commentator put it, "the divine right . . . to the pay envelope" ("Family Pocketbook" 1910, 15). Even the courts occasionally agreed, refusing to treat domestic stealing as real theft. In a 1908 case of a wife charged with robbing her husband of small change, Judge Furlong of a Brooklyn court supported the "thief," declaring that "a wife has a perfect right to go through her husband's pockets at night and take his money if he fails to provide for her properly" (15 *Bench and Bar* 10).

But what was a proper money income for wives? For some, the best solution for "penniless wives" was a dowry for every daughter (Messinger et al. 1890). Wives seemed to prefer a regular weekly or monthly allowance. A 1910 *Good Housekeeping* survey of 300 wives found that 120 supported the allowance system ("Family Pocketbook"). By 1915, according to *Harper's Weekly*, some young brides, "of the ultra-modern type," required the promise of an allowance "before vowing to love, honor and obey" ("Adventures in Economic Independence," 610).

Women's magazines increasingly endorsed the allowance in their articles and even in their fiction. In "Her Weight in Gold," for instance, a short story that appeared in the *Saturday Evening Post* in 1926, Mrs. Jondough, the wealthy female protagonist, declared "that all the gowns and diamond pins in the world were not compensation for even a tiny personal allowance of her very own" (Child 1926, 125). That same year, the Women's Freedom League of St. Louis went further, sponsoring a bill that would make a dress allowance for wives legally compulsory (*New York Times*, Oct. 11). Home-economics experts were in agreement. Mary W. Abel, an editor of the *Journal of Home Economics*, assailed the dole system, arguing that "to achieve the best results in the spending of the family money, the mother should have such control of the income as will ensure her efficiency as manager and buyer" (1921, 69). Even Emily Post certified the allowance with her stamp of approval (1928, 110).

Still, converting female currency from dole to allowance was not easily achieved. A 1928 survey of 200 upper-class men and women found that, while 73 used the allowance system, 66 still relied on the "old-fashioned system of husbands taking charge of all money, paying all bills and doling out funds to the wife as she asks for them" (Hamilton and MacGowan 1928) (the remainder had a more progressive joint bank account or an undefined arrangement).[9] Husbands, it seems, were less enthusiastic than their wives about the allowance. As Dix pointed out: "One question that is fought out in a battle that lasts from the altar to the grave, in most families, is the question of an allowance for the wife. She yearns for it. The man is determined that she shall not have it . . ." (1914, 409). As late as 1938, when the *Ladies' Home Journal* conducted a major national survey on "What Do the Women of America Think about Money?" and asked, "Should a wife have a regular housekeeping allowance?" they found that 88 percent of female respondents answered affirmatively, regardless of marital status or geographical location. And 91 percent of younger women (under thirty) were for it. Yet only 48 percent of the wives actually received an allowance (Pringle 1938, 102).

Husbands resisted the allowance because it officially carved out a separate portion of their income and made it "hers," thereby increasing a woman's financial control. But the allowance created an additional sort of confusion. What kind of money was it? If the allowance was no longer supposed to be a dole or gift, neither could it become real money or a wage. Indeed, supporters of the allowance were careful to distinguish it from a wage. "To the man who says, 'But I cannot pay my wife like a servant,'" recommended a writer in the *Forum*, "the answer must be 'Certainly not. She is a partner and as such is entitled to a share in the dividends'" (Ives 1890, 113).

If the allowance was difficult to define, it was also hard to regulate. Since it was not a payment, the actual amount of money involved could not depend on the performance of wifely duties. While usually it was expected to be "proportioned to the earnings of her husband," in practice, as a *New York Times* editorial pointed out, it remained a "delicate question," often creating a "sharp difference of opinion about [its] size" (*New York Times*, January 30, 1923). The uses of the allowance remained unclear as well. Was it exclusively for the household? Who "owned" the surplus, if there was one? Did it cover women's personal needs?

THE ALLOWANCE VERSUS A JOINT ACCOUNT: THE ALLOWANCE AS A "BAD" MONEY

In February 1925, Reverend Howard Melish, rector of the Holy Trinity Church of Brooklyn, addressing the New York Women's City Club on the importance of a wife's economic independence, related an anecdote that backfired. "Yesterday," Melish told his audience, "I asked an old lady . . . what her idea was of a happy marriage. Without an instant's hesitation she replied 'An allowance.'" The next day, in an editorial entitled "They Want More Than That," the *New York Times* expressed the new critical view on allowances: "Admitting . . . the equality of service rendered by wife and husband in . . . the family unit, why should the one rather than the other have an 'allowance' and . . . why should the 'allowance' be determined by the husband and be granted as a favor?" Allowances, concluded the editorial, "are for inferiors from superiors" and therefore an inappropriate currency for the modern woman (*New York Times*, March 2 and 3).

In the 1920s, even as popular support for allowances intensified, there was also a growing criticism of the allowance system from those who saw it as an inequitable and even degrading form of domestic money. Christine Frederick proclaimed it a "relic of some past time when women were supposed to be too inexperienced to handle money" (1919, 269). Frederick, a leader of the popular household-efficiency movement, rejected the allowance as an "unbusinesslike" scheme that undermined the modern goal of running the home as rationally as a factory or an office. The "anti-allowance" advocates supported a democratic "joint control of the purse" (Kyrk 1933, 182–83). The new, improved domestic money was to be shared, thus minimizing gender as well as age inequality. Families were urged to "hold a periodic council around a table, with frank and courteous discussion of its ways and means, and with due consideration of how, and how much, each member can contribute in work, in money, in cooperation, toward . . . this whole business of the home." The father and mother would act as a board of directors, allocating money according to the diverse needs (Winter 1925, 185; Friend 1930, 112). The new financial system would also include a specified sum for personal expenses for each family member, to be considered as a budgetary entitlement and not as a gift.

But how many couples actually adopted the new domestic dollar? *Harper's* 1928 study "Marriage and Money" found that, of 200 respondents, only 54 had what the magazine described as the more "feminist" financial arrangement: a joint bank account or common purse (Hamilton and MacGowan 1928, 440). In 1929, in *Middletown*, the Lynds reported that most couples depended on "all manner of provisional, more or less bickering" financial arrangements (1956, 127n24). And some two decades later, *Crestwood Heights*, studying suburban life, discovered that, despite democratic norms dictating cooperative spending of the husband's income, "the wife does not know, even roughly, how much her husband earns." Wives still had to "manipulate their household allowances" to obtain "unreported" personal funds (Seeley, Sim, and Loosley 1956, 184–85). Yet, even though the actual finances of housewives did not significantly improve, it is clear that, by 1930, the symbolic meaning of a wife's allowance was changing from a sign of independence and domestic control to a form of financial submissiveness.

A Husband's Allowance: Domestic Money in the Working Class

Domestic money was defined not only by gender but also by the social class of the household. The working-class wife, suggested one home-economics textbook, could well be envied by wealthier women. While the latter seldom have "ready money in hand," the wife of a workingman often "determines the . . . financial policy of the family and has control of the necessary funds" (Abel 1921, 5). Indeed, in her 1917 study, Mary Simkhovitch found that as a family's income increased, "the proportion controlled by the wife diminishes till often she becomes simply a beneficiary of the husband." Paradoxically, class—in most ethnic groups—seemed to reverse the gender power structure of domestic money. In her 1910 study, *Homestead*, Margaret Byington discovered that the men "are inclined to trust all financial matters to their wives." On payday, workmen turned over their wages to the wife, asking "no questions as to what it goes for" (1910, 108).[10]

In working-class families, the allowance was usually for husbands and children, not wives. Louise More's (1907) analysis of wage earner's budgets found that an allowance for "spending-money" was made in 108 of the 200 families she investigated: 94 men received all or part of the amount given, and in 29 families one or two children had an allowance. In most cases, it seems to have been the wife who "doles out spending money according to the needs and the earnings of each" (True 1914, 48). Leslie Tentler's study of working-class women from 1900 to 1930 concludes that this financial arrangement of working-class families granted a great deal of economic power to wives, making the home their "fief" (1982, 177). Indeed, to contemporary middle-class observers, it appeared that husbands "who accept a daily dole from their purse-keeping wives are usually subject beings" (*New York Times*, January 30, 1923).

But these studies and observations may have idealized and thus overestimated the economic clout of working-class wives. To be sure, administering the family income involved women actively in domestic finances, allowing them a degree of managerial control. What remains unclear, however, is their actual discretionary power.[11] In the first place, money management in families with limited money incomes was an arduous task. Although working-class standards of living improved at the turn of the century, family budget studies show the precariousness and uncertainty of their financial lives. Husbands' and children's wages went almost exclusively for food, clothing, shelter, and insurance. And being the cashier put a heavy burden of responsibility on wives: household money troubles could be conveniently blamed (by family members as well as outsiders) on female mismanagement rather than on a tight budget or an irregular labor market (Horowitz 1985, 60).

More important, as soon as there was any surplus income, a wife's apparent grip on the purse strings quickly loosened. While the ideal good husband was indeed expected to turn over all his wages intact to his wife, receiving one or two dollars a week for his personal use, many did not. Studies of New York's West Side conducted in 1914 found that while "there is a current belief that the American workingman turns his wages over to his wife on Saturday night and allows her to apportion all expenditures," in fact how much the wife received from the husband's wages and what he kept back "depends on the personal adjustment between them and not on a recognized rule" (Anthony 1914, 135–36). Evidence on precisely how the money was allocated is very limited. But the West Side study suggests that the outcome was usually rigged in favor of the husband. As one Italian wife explained: "Of course they don't give all they make. They're men and you never know their ways" (Odencrantz 1919, 176). A study of unskilled Chicago wage earners in 1924 found that, when asked about their husbands' weekly earnings, over two-thirds of the wives gave lesser amounts than the actual earnings found on the payroll. The investigator concluded that the man "may not give his entire earnings to his wife, but may simply give her the amount he thinks she should spend for the family" (Houghteling 1927, 37).

Thus, the idealized view of a solidary family economy coordinated and controlled by the wife concealed competing internal claims for money. The husband's pay envelope was not always intact on arrival. Neither were the children's. Tantalized by the attractions of a consumer culture, children increasingly withheld or manipulated their earnings. David Nasaw found that, in the early part of this century, wage-earning children "who were obedient in every other regard did what they had to to preserve some part of their earnings for themselves. They lied, they cheated, they hid away their nickels and dimes, they doctored their pay envelopes" (1985, 131–32; see also Zelizer 1987, 97–112). While working girls were more likely than their brothers to hand their wages over intact, not all of them did. Italian working girls on the New York West Side told investigators how easy it was to "knock down" a paycheck when they made overtime: "Whatever you make is written outside in pencil. . . . That's easy to fix—you have only to rub it out, put on whatever it usually is, and pocket the change" (True 1914, 49; on the increased individualization of children's income, especially after the 1920s, see Smith 1985; Ewen 1985).

Even the portion of money that the wife did receive and control was limited to housekeeping money. As with wealthier women, the working-class wife had no right and much less access to a personal fund. Pocket money for personal expenses was a male prerogative or a working child's right. The working-class husband's allowance was thus a very different kind of money from the allowance of middle-class wives. Although partly allocated for useful expenses, food or clothing or transportation, it was also a legitimate fund for personal pleasures. Indeed, Kathy Peiss's (1986) study of leisure among working-class women in turn-of-the-century New York clearly shows that while men could afford to pay for their amusements, drinking in saloons, attending movies and the theater, or buying tobacco, their wives had no money left for personal recreation. Thus, women's money retained a collective identity, while men's and children's money was differentiated and individualized.[12]

As home-economics experts began to encourage joint control of the domestic dollar, the working-class allowance system lost its legitimacy. Studies of English working-class families suggest that there was a shift to the middle-class system of housekeeping allowances for wives (Oren 1973, 115; Stearns 1972, 116; Pahl 1980, 332–33). Limited data make it difficult to determine whether the same was true for the United States. In the 1920s, when the Lynds studied Muncie, Indiana, they reported that it was rare for a husband to turn over his paycheck and allow his wife control over the household economy (1956, 127n24; see also Friend 1930, 108). But class differences seem to have persisted; by 1938, according to the *Ladies' Home Journal* national survey on money, only 38 percent of women in income groups under $1,500 received an allowance, compared with 62 percent of those in groups over $1,500 (Pringle 1938, 102).

PIN MONEY VERSUS REAL MONEY: DEFINING WOMEN'S EARNINGS

What happened when women's money did not come from their husbands' paychecks? When women worked for nonrelatives, whether at home or for wages, the boundary between that income and real money was still preserved, only in different ways. In the working class, for instance, a married woman's income, usually earned by caring for boarders, taking in sewing or laundry, or, among farm families, by selling butter, eggs, or poultry, did not have the same visibility as her husband's paycheck (Jensen 1980; Ulrich 1983, 45–47; Morawska 1985, 134–35). As her labor was part of a woman's traditional repertoire of domestic tasks, the money she made was merged into the family's housekeeping money and usually spent on home and family, for clothing or food. Legally, in fact, until the early decades of the twentieth century, those domestic earnings belonged to the husband. And the courts staunchly opposed converting a wife's money into her tangible property.[13] In a growing number of personal injury cases, where the law had to decide whether the husband or the wife was entitled to recover for a woman's inability to work, as well as in claims brought up by creditors, the courts insisted on distinguishing between the domestic dollar and an earned wage. If a wife worked at home, even if her labor was performed for strangers, caring for a boarder or nursing a neighbor, that money was not a real earning and therefore belonged to her husband. Ironically but significantly, in some states a wife's domestic earnings could become her property but only as her husband's gift (Thornton 1900; Rodgers 1902; Warren 1925).

Thus, earned domestic money, much like the allowance, retained a separate identity as a gift, not as real money. Money earned by married women in the labor force was also special and different. It even had its own name. The term "pin money," which in seventeenth-century England had meant a separate, independent income for a wife's personal use—and was included as a formal clause in upper-class marriage contracts—lost its elitist British origins in turn-of-the-century America and now meant the supplementary household income earned by wives (Stone 1977, 244; Gore 1834). Still it was treated as a more frivolous, less serious earning than the husband's. As a 1903 article in *Harper's Bazaar* aptly remarked: "No man works for pin-money. The very idea makes one smile" (Leonard 1903, 1060).

The boundary between women's earned income and the husband's salary was also marked by their differential uses. John Modell, for instance, suggests that among late-nineteenth-century, native-born American families, "all dollars were not equal" and women's income (as well as children's) was spent differently and less freely than the husbands' (1978, 225). Among farm families, women's egg money and butter money were distinguished from husbands' wheat money or corn money (Thornton 1900, 188; Atkeson 1929).[14] Jensen (1980) suggests that there existed a dual economy, with women and children providing for living expenses while husbands paid for mortgages and new machinery (see also Whitehead 1984, 112). For middle-class women, discreet forms of earning pin money at home (making preserves, pickles, or pound cake; knitting shawls or sweaters; or raising poultry or Angora cats) were approved, but, again, only for certain types of expenses: charity, for example, or "a daughter's lessons in music or art" (Sangster 1905, 32).

In the 1920s and 1930s, as more married women entered the labor force, their earnings, regardless of the sums involved, were still defined as pin money, categorized as supplementary income, used for the family's extra expenses, or earmarked by more affluent couples as discretionary, "fun" money. For instance, one women told an *Outlook* reporter that she reserved her income exclusively for buying clothes. Another explained: "We blow my money on extra trips abroad, antiques, anything extravagant." Others used their salary to pay the maid's wages and saved the rest (Smith 1928, 500). A story in the *Saturday Evening Post*, four years later, reported on the persistent "wife-keeps-all-theory" of wives' earnings. Couples in which the wife was employed were asked what her money was used for: "Keeps it all for herself . . . saves it, spends it, just as she likes," was a common response. "The important thing [is] . . . she mustn't help her husband out" (Ray 1932, 48).

CONCLUSION

Domestic money is thus a very special kind of currency. It would be difficult to understand its changing meanings, allocation, and uses in the United States between the 1870s and the 1930s without an awareness of the new cultural "code" and accompanying social changes. In the case of married women, their money was routinely set apart from real money by a complex mixture of ideas about family life, by a changing gender power structure, and by social class. Normative expectations of the family as a special noncommercial sphere made any overt form of market intrusion in domestic affairs not only distasteful but a direct threat to family solidarity. Thus, regardless of its sources, once money had entered the household, its allocation, calculation, and uses were subject to a set of domestic rules distinct from the rules of the market. Family money was nonfungible; social barriers prevented its conversion into ordinary wages.

But family culture did not affect its members equally. Thus, gender introduced a further type of nonmarket distinction in the domestic flow of funds: a wife's money was not the same kind of money as her husband's. When a wife did not earn wages, gender shaped many things.

1. *The allocation of her money.* In the hierarchically structured family, husbands gave wives part of their income. To obtain additional money, wives were restricted to asking and cajoling or else stealing.

2. *The timing of this allocation.* It either had no prescribed timing (dole method), so that to obtain money a wife had to ask each time, or it followed a weekly or monthly pattern (allowance).

3. *The uses of her money.* Wives' money meant housekeeping money, a necessary allotment restricted to family expenses and excluding personal spending money. Pocket money was a budgetary expectation for husbands and children, but not for wives. Ironically, it appears that even shoplifting by married women was often collectivity oriented, as women stole from department stores "ribbons or laces to adorn the babies' clothes . . . or often little gifts for [their husbands]" ("Husband Who Makes His Wife a Thief" 1915).

4. *The quantity of her money.* Wives usually received small sums of money. The amount of an allowance was not determined by the efficiency or even the quantity of a wife's domestic contributions but by prevalent beliefs of what was a proper amount. Therefore, a larger paycheck for the husband need not translate into a raise in the housekeeping allowance. On the basis of gender economics, it might in fact simply increase a husband's personal money (Oren 1973, 110; Land 1977).

Changes in gender roles and family structure influenced the meaning and methods of allocation of married women's money. The traditional dole or "asking" method became, as women's consumer role expanded, not only inefficient but also inappropriate in increasingly egalitarian marriages. The allowance, praised as a more equitable method of allocation in the early part of the century, was in turn condemned by home-efficiency experts of the 1920s and 1930s as an unsatisfactory payment for modern wives. The joint account emerged as the new cultural ideal. (For some recent changes in the allocation system of domestic money, see Blumstein and Schwartz 1985; Hertz 1986; Treas 1989.)

What about the uses of married women's money? In contrast to the variability of allocation methods, the earmarking of a wife's housekeeping income for collective consumption remained remarkably persistent. Despite the increasing individualization of consumption patterns and the encouragement by home-economics experts to allot personal funds for each family member in the domestic budget, personal spending money for wives was still obtained by subterfuge or spent with guilt. (For some recent evidence of the enduring division between wives' collective money and husbands' personal spending money, see Wilson 1987.)

Gender marked women's money even when their income was earned. Women's wages were still earmarked as separate and treated differently. A wife's pin money, regardless of its quantity, and even when it brought the family a needed income, remained a less fundamental kind of money than her husband's wages. It was either collectivized or trivialized, merged into the housekeeping fund and thus undifferentiated from collective income or else treated as a supplementary earning designated either for family expenses (a child's education or a vacation) or for frivolous purposes (clothing or jewelry). (For contemporary evidence on restricted uses of wives' earnings, see Hood 1983, 62.) The trivialization of women's earnings extended beyond the private domestic economy. For the opponents of women's labor, pin money was a socially irresponsible currency, a luxury income that threatened the wages of the real provider (see Kessler-Harris 1982, 100–101). Thus, despite strong statistical evidence that pin money was often in fact a "family coupling pin, the only means of holding the family together and of making ends meet," women's earnings were systematically stigmatized as "money for trinkets and trifles" (Anderson 1929, 921).

But the circulation of domestic money was not shaped by gender alone. Social class added a further set of social restrictions on the liquidity of money. The middle-class method of allocating household money was reversed in the working class, where wives handed out allowances instead of receiving them. The working-class wife's managerial power was thus greater than that of her middle-class counterpart, although her discretionary power may not have differed significantly.

Domestic money thus shows the limits of a purely instrumental, rationalized model of market money, which conceals qualitative distinctions among kinds of money in the modern world.[15] Domestic money is a special money, not just a medium of economic exchange but a meaningful, socially constructed currency, shaped by the domestic sphere where it circulates and by the gender and social class of its domestic "money handlers." Age also marks domestic money. In fact, between the 1870s and 1930s, children's money was the subject of much controversy within families and among educational experts. The allowance emerged as the proper money income for children. But it had a different meaning, method of allocation, and uses from the allowances of middle-class wives or working-class men. Closely supervised by parents, it was defined primarily as educational money, teaching children proper social and moral values, as well as consumer skills (see Zelizer 1987).

The cultural and social "life" of domestic money also challenges the allegedly irrevocable dominance of the "cash nexus" in the modern world. To be sure, Marx and Engels ([1848] 1971, 11) were partly correct when they accused the bourgeoisie of reducing family relations "to a mere money relation." Money concerns did increasingly permeate the American household. In fact, in the 1920s, some observers ironically predicted that the national enthusiasm for rationalized housekeeping and budget making would turn "Home, Sweet Home" into "Home, Solvent Home," with "Ma and Pa a couple of cash registers, and the kiddies little adding machines" (Phillips 1924, 64). Yet, such nightmare visions of a commercialized world failed to capture the complexity and reciprocal aspects of the phenomenon of monetization. Money came into American homes, but it was transformed in the process, as it became part of the structure of social relations and the meaning system of the family.

The case of domestic money is only one example, an empirical indicator of a complex social economy that remains hidden in the dominant economic paradigm of a single, qualityless, and rationalizing market money. This article attempts to lay some of the preliminary groundwork for a richer, alternative sociological model of special monies, one that argues for a plurality of qualitatively distinct kinds of money in the modern world, with each special money shaped by different networks of social relations and varying systems of meanings. No money, including market money, escapes such extraeconomic influences. For instance, at the turn of the century, not only the domestic dollar but other kinds of monies created different yet equally significant cultural and social dilemmas for American society. "Charitable money" raised questions about the proper uses and allocation of money as a gift among strangers or between kin, whether in the form of charity, wills, "ritual" gifts (for weddings, birthdays, bar mitzvahs, and Christmas), or even tipping, while "sacred money" provoked discussions about the moral quality of money: Under what conditions did money acquire sacred religious or moral value, and when did it become dirty money, defined as collectively or individually demeaning? Or consider the definitional problems of "institutional money." How should money be allocated, regulated, and defined in the separate social world of a prison, a mental asylum, or an orphanage?

But an inventory of monies, however revealing, provides only a descriptive catalog. To develop a social theory of money, we must then explain the sources and patterns of variation among special monies, exploring how various structures of social relations and cultural values shape and constrain the qualitative life of different monies by (a) earmarking specified uses of money, (b) regulating modes of allocation, (c) designating proper users, and (d) assigning special symbolic meanings. The concept of multiple monies thus raises fundamental questions about the characteristics of social and cultural boundaries, such as: (1) What are the origins of boundaries between monies? What, for instance, are the differences between special monies imposed by a central authority (as in a prison) and monies defined through social interaction (as in the family)? (2) How do the social statuses of transactors affect the formation of special monies? (3) What determines the relative rigidity or permeability of boundaries between special monies? (4) What are the patterns of conversions between special monies? (5) Is there a moral ranking between special monies, as has been suggested for primitive monies (see Bohannan 1959)? (6) When and how do boundaries between special monies break down?

Developing a sociological model of multiple monies is part of a broader challenge to neoclassical economic theory. It offers an alternative approach not only to the study of money but to all other aspects of economic life, including the market (see Zelizer 1988). As I show in this article, economic processes of exchange and consumption are one special category of social relations, much as is kinship or religion. Thus, economic phenomena such as money, although partly autonomous, are interdependent with historically variable systems of meanings and structures of social relations.

Notes

Viviana A. Zelizer, "The Social Meaning of Money: 'Special Monies,'" *American Journal of Sociology* 95 (September 1989): 342–77. Reprinted with permission.

1. For some exceptions, see Turner 1986; Smelt 1980; and Cheal 1988. To be sure, sociologists have recognized the symbolic and social meanings of money in various empirical settings but only in an ad hoc, nonsystematic way. Goffman (1961) remarked on the absence of any framework for understanding differences and similarities between coercive, economic, and social payments.

2. Granovetter (1985) chides sociologists for implicitly accepting the economists' assumptions that market processes are invulnerable to social influences and therefore unsuitable objects of sociological study. On recent theoretical and empirical advances of the "new economic sociology," see Swedberg 1987. While Granovetter focuses on structural constraints of markets, Sahlins (1976) presents a powerful cultural critique of market determinism. For a provocative, historically grounded alternative to "market culture" and utilitarian conceptions of money, see Reddy (1984, 1987). Brown (1959) offers a psychoanalytical critique of the rational model of money.

3. In fact, the only recognized limit to the commodification process is the preservation—albeit precarious—of selected items outside the cash nexus. This "singularization" of certain goods, as Igor Kopytoff (1986) describes it, does not, however, seem to include money. Instead, culture "marks" certain items as special and unexchangeable precisely by depriving them of a price tag (see Radin 1987). Within this framework, money acts as a "contaminator" of market values, immune to extraeconomic values and thus incapable of being itself marked as singular, unique, or unexchangeable.

4. Sorokin (1943) made the same argument in his brilliant analysis of the persistence of qualitative distinctions in modern conceptions of time and space. Taussig (1980), an anthropologist, deals with the social meaning of modern money but within the particular context of a South American peasant culture's being transformed by capitalist modes of production. The peasants construct magical rituals

that mark modern money as "dirty money": an evil currency obtained in illicit ways and restricted in its uses. Taussig interprets these morally stigmatized monies as part of the peasants' resistance to the commodification of their world. From this perspective, however, real modern money in a fully commoditized society would presumably lose such qualitative distinctions and thus attain moral indifference.

5. There is a body of literature that deals with the relationship between gender, class, money, and the distribution of family power (see, e.g., Blood and Wolfe 1965; Komarovsky 1961, 1967; Safilios-Rothschild 1970; Rubin 1976; Ostrander 1984; Blumstein and Schwartz 1985; Hertz 1986; Mirowsky 1985). Interestingly, much of this literature retains an instrumental framework by usually focusing on the market meaning of money and its effects on domestic power relationships. Contemporaneous and historical studies of English households provide a rich source of data on intrafamily accounting systems (see, e.g., Ross 1982; Oren 1973; Stearns 1972; Wilson 1987; Pahl 1980; Whitehead 1984; Ayers and Lambertz 1986). (For France, see Sullerot 1966; for French and English working-class households, see Tilly and Scott 1978.) Gullestad (1984) provides some wonderful data on working-class mothers in urban Norway, and Luxton (1980) does the same for Canada.

6. This article is based on a qualitative analysis of an extensive and diversified set of documentary sources. Among the primary sources consulted were (1) household-budget studies; (2) women's magazines, including feature articles, letters to the editor, fiction, advice columns, and occasional survey data; (3) newspapers, including news articles, editorials, and letters to the editor (mostly from the *New York Times*); (4) legal records, including court cases, law review articles, laws and regulations, and legal casebooks; (5) home-economics literature, including leading textbooks on home management, popular household manuals, and the *Journal of Home Economics*; (6) a foreigner's memoirs; (7) etiquette manuals; (8) social workers' investigations of working-class communities and reports on the conditions of working women, such as Russell Sage's West Side Studies; and (9) selected government documents such as the U.S. Department of Labor reports on the conditions of working women and children. To be sure, as with many such qualitative historical data, the precise representativeness of the documentary materials cannot be established. However, the reliability of the data is strengthened by corroborating the findings with very different and independent types of documentary evidence. For instance, a few magazines' surveys of readers or other audiences are used, despite their being methodologically weak by modern standards, but only as an additional, albeit imperfect, illustration of trends in the allocation and uses of family money. Thus, the changes in the domestic economy described here are not based simply on one set of data but are amply confirmed by the different primary sources. In addition, a rich set of secondary sources has been consulted, including recent studies on the rise of the consumer culture, the history of leisure, and the literature on family history and women's history that includes discussions of families' changing economic strategies.

7. The concept of a family wage—a salary that would support a male wage earner and his dependent family—further increased married women's dependence on their husband's wages. The doctrine of necessaries, however, provided wives with some legal recourse by making a husband directly responsible to a merchant

for the purchases made by his wife. Yet even this entitlement to pledge a husband's credit was restricted. Necessaries were so ambiguously defined that merchants were reluctant to risk extending credit to a wife for goods that might not be considered necessaries. Moreover, a husband was entitled to determine where necessaries should be purchased and could terminate a wife's authority to pledge his credit by demonstrating that he had provided the necessaries or a sufficient allowance to obtain them (see Weitzman 1981; Salmon 1986; Clark 1968). The law, in fact, was explicitly concerned with protecting husbands from the "mad" expenditures of extravagant wives (see, e.g., *Ryan v. Wanamaker* 116 Misc. 91; 190 N.Y.S. 250 [1921]; *Saks et al. v. Huddleston* 36 F. [2d] 537 [1929]; and W.A.S. 1922).

8. In her best-selling autobiography, Sugimoto (1936) recalled her puzzlement at this strange American custom that departed so radically from the Japanese arrangement, where, regardless of class, wives controlled the purse strings. I thank Sarane Boocock for this reference.

9. As described in *Harper's Monthly Magazine*, this survey of financial arrangements was part of a larger study of different aspects of married life conducted under the auspices of the Bureau of Social Hygiene. Using a prepared set of questions, the survey takers interviewed two hundred respondents individually over a period of two years.

10. The available evidence suggests that different ethnic groups operated with similar domestic financial arrangements (see, e.g., True 1914; Di Leonardo 1984; Bodnar 1987; research material from Morawska 1985, and personal communication). Lamphere (1986), however, suggests possible ethnic variations. Further research should better illuminate the effect of ethnicity on domestic money.

11. Determining the effect of a particular intrahousehold financial arrangement on the relative power of family members is a difficult task. Not only can power be measured in a number of ways, but all the dimensions of monetary power within the family—whether consuming, saving, investing, or managing—have very special meanings that are culturally and socially constructed. More research is needed to define and understand the relative degree of power of the "cashier" working-class wife.

12. If a working-class wife needed more money, her options were limited. With little access to credit accounts, she often turned to pawnbrokers and moneylenders (see Ross 1982, 590; Tebbutt 1983; Ayers and Lambertz 1986, 203–4). Sometimes women relied on their younger children for extra cash. During a government investigation of industrial home work conducted in 1918 ("Industrial Home Work of Children" 1924, 22), one mother explained that her little boy helped her wire rosary beads at home because she needed "some money of her own." Another mother needed false teeth and "thought the children might just as well help to buy them."

13. Starting in the mid-nineteenth century, Married Women's Property Acts granted wives the right to own and control their property but focused primarily on inherited property; married women's rights to their earnings were excluded by the acts and were incorporated only slowly and with much resistance by amendments or in later statutes (see Edwards 1893; Rodgers 1902; Warren 1925; Crozier 1935, 37–41; Shammas, Salmon, and Dahlin 1987, 88–89, 96–97, 163).

14. The relative importance of gender vs. the source of income in distinguishing between the two kinds of money remains unclear. For instance, Thomas and

Znaniecki suggested that the qualitative difference between the money a peasant got from selling a cow and the money his wife obtained from selling eggs and milk was not marked by gender but by the "different sort of value" represented by each type of money: the cow was property, while eggs and milk were income. Each type of money was set aside for different types of expenses ([1918–20] 1958, 165). However, since, within the peasant economy, property belonged to a "higher economic class" than income, it is clear that gender did intervene in the social marking of the two monies; lower-value money was assigned to women.

15. Ironically, Max Weber's own family of origin provided evidence against his rational conception of money. According to Marianne Weber, Weber's father "was typical of the husbands of the time [1860s] . . . who needed to determine by themselves how the family income was to be used and left their wives and children in the dark as to how high the income was" (1975, 141). Helene, Weber's mother, had no housekeeping allowance, "nor a special fund for her personal needs." I thank Marta Giel for this reference.

REFERENCES

Abel, Mary W. 1921. *Successful Family Life on Moderate Income*. Philadelphia: Lippincott.

"Adventures in Economic Independence." 1915. *Harper's Weekly* 61:610.

Anderson, Mary. 1929. *United States Daily*, September 23. Cited in editorial, *Journal of Home Economics* 21 (December): 920–22.

Anthony, Katherine. 1914. *Mothers Who Must Earn*. New York: Survey.

Appadurai, Arjun, ed. 1986. *The Social Life of Things*. Cambridge: Cambridge University Press.

Atkeson, Mary M. 1929. "Women in Farm Life and Rural Economy." *Annals of the American Academy of Political and Social Science* 143:188–94.

Ayers, Pat, and Jan Lambertz. 1986. "Marriage Relations, Money and Domestic Violence in Working-Class Liverpool, 1919–39." In *Labour and Love*, edited by Jane Lewis, 195–219. Oxford: Blackwell.

Banner, Lois W. 1983. *American Beauty*. Chicago: University of Chicago Press.

Barber, Bernard. 1977. "The Absolutization of the Market: Some Notes on How We Got from There to Here." In *Markets and Morals*, edited by G. Dworkin, G. Bermant, and P. Brown, 15–31. Washington, D.C.: Hemisphere.

Baric, Lorraine. 1964. "Some Aspects of Credit, Saving and Investment in a Non-Monetary Economy (Rossel Island)." In *Capital, Saving and Credit in Peasant Societies*, edited by Raymond Firth and B. S. Yamey, 35–42. Chicago: Aldine.

Beecher, Catharine E. 1841. *A Treatise on Domestic Economy*. Boston: Marsh, Capen, Lyon and Webb.

Benson, Susan Porter. 1986. *Counter Cultures*. Champaign: University of Illinois Press.

Black, Hugh. 1921. "Money and Marriage." *Delineator* 98:58.

Blood, Robert O., Jr., and Donald M. Wolfe. 1965. *Husbands and Wives*. New York: Free Press.

Blumstein, Philip, and Pepper Schwartz. 1985. *American Couples*. New York: Pocket.

Bodnar, John. 1987. *The Transplanted*. Bloomington: Indiana University Press.

Bohannan, Paul. 1959. "The Impact of Money on an African Subsistence Economy." *Journal of Economic History* 19:491–503.

Brown, Norman O. 1959. *Life against Death*. Middletown, Conn.: Wesleyan University Press.

Byington, Margaret F. 1910. *Homestead*. New York: Charities Publication Committee.

Cheal, David. 1988. *The Gift Economy*. London: Routledge and Kegan Paul.

Child, Maude Parker. 1926. "Her Weight in Gold." *Saturday Evening Post* 198:125.

Clark, Homer H., Jr. 1968. *The Law of Domestic Relations in the United States*. St. Paul, Minn.: West.

Collins, Randall. 1979. Review of *The Bankers*, by Martin Mayer. *American Journal of Sociology* 85:190–94.

Cooley, Charles H. 1913. "The Sphere of Pecuniary Valuation." *American Journal of Sociology* 19:188–203.

Cott, Nancy F. 1977. *The Bonds of Womanhood*. New Haven, Conn.: Yale University Press.

Cowan, Ruth S. 1983. *More Work for Mother*. New York: Basic Books.

Crozier, Blanche. 1935. "Marital Support." *Boston University Law Review* 15:33.

Crump, Thomas. 1981. *The Phenomenon of Money*. London: Routledge and Kegan Paul.

Delphy, Christine, and Diana Leonard. 1986. "Class Analysis, Gender Analysis and the Family." In *Gender and Stratification*, edited by Rosemary Crompton and Michael Mann, 57–73. Oxford: Polity.

Di Leonardo, Micaela. 1984. *The Varieties of Ethnic Experience*. Ithaca, N.Y.: Cornell University Press.

Dix, Dorothy. 1914. "Woman and Her Money." *Good Housekeeping* 58:408–9.

Douglas, Mary. 1967. "Primitive Rationing." In *Themes in Economic Anthropology*, edited by Raymond Firth, 119–45. London: Tavistock.

Douglas, Mary, and Baron Isherwood. 1979. *The World of Goods*. New York: Norton.

Edwards, Percy. 1893. "Is the Husband Entitled to His Wife's Earnings?" *Canadian Law Times* 13:159–76.

Einzig, Paul. 1966. *Primitive Money*. Oxford: Pergamon.

Ewen, Elizabeth. 1985. *Immigrant Women in the Land of Dollars*. New York: Monthly Review.

"Family Pocketbook." 1910. *Good Housekeeping* 51:9–15.

Frederick, Christine. 1919. *Household Engineering*. Chicago: American School of Home Economics.

———. 1929. *Selling Mrs. Consumer*. New York: Business Bourse.

Friend, Mata R. 1930. *Earning and Spending Family Income*. New York: Appleton.

Geertz, Clifford. 1973. "Deep Play: Notes on the Balinese Cockfight." In *The Interpretation of Cultures*, edited by Clifford Geertz, 412–53. New York: Basic Books.

Goffman, Erving. 1961. *Asylums*. Garden City, N.Y.: Anchor.

Gore, Catherine. 1834. *Pin-Money*. Boston: Allen and Ticknor.

Granovetter, Mark. 1985. "Economic Action and Social Structure: The Problem of Embeddedness." *American Journal of Sociology* 91:481–510.

Gullestad, Marianne. 1984. *Kitchen-Table Society*. New York: Columbia University Press.

Hamilton, G. V., and Kenneth MacGowan. 1928. "Marriage and Money." *Harper's Monthly* 157:434–44.

Hartmann, Heidi I. 1981. "The Family as the Locus of Gender, Class, and Political Struggle: The Example of Housework." *Signs* 6:366–94.

Hertz, Rosanna. 1986. *More Equal Than Others*. Berkeley and Los Angeles: University of California Press.

Hirschman, Albert O. 1986. *Rival Views of Market Society*. New York: Viking.

Hood, Jane. 1983. *Becoming a Two-Job Family*. New York: Praeger.

Horowitz, Daniel. 1985. *The Morality of Spending*. Baltimore: Johns Hopkins University Press.

Houghteling, Leila. 1927. *Income and Standard of Living of Unskilled Laborers in Chicago*. Chicago: University of Chicago Press.

"Husband Who Makes His Wife a Thief." 1915. *Ladies' Home Journal* 32:16.

"Industrial Home Work of Children." 1924. Washington, D.C.: U.S. Department of Labor, Children's Bureau Publication no. 100.

Ives, Alice. 1890. "The Domestic Purse Strings." *Forum* 10:106–14.

Jensen, Joan M. 1980. "Cloth, Butter and Boarders: Women's Household Production for the Market." *Review of Radical Political Economics* 12:14–24.

———. 1986. *Loosening the Bonds*. New Haven, Conn.: Yale University Press.

Kahneman, Daniel, and Amos Tversky. 1982. "The Psychology of Preferences." *Scientific American* 246:160–73.

Kelland, Clarence Budington. 1928. "Wives Are Either Tightwads or Spendthrifts." *American Magazine* 106:12, 104–10.

Kessler-Harris, Alice. 1982. *Out to Work*. New York: Oxford University Press.

Komarovsky, Mirra. 1961. "Class Differences in Family Decision-Making on Expenditures." In *Household Decision-Making*, vol. 4. of *Consumer Behavior*, edited by Nelson N. Foote, 255–65. New York: New York University Press.

———. 1967. *Blue-Collar Marriage*. New York: Vintage.

Kopytoff, Igor. 1986. "The Cultural Biography of Things: Commoditization as Process." In *The Social Life of Things*, edited by Arjun Appadurai, 64–91. Cambridge: Cambridge University Press.

Kyrk, Hazel. 1933. *Economic Problems of the Family*. New York: Harper.

Lamphere, Louise. 1986. "From Working Daughters to Working Mothers: Production and Reproduction in an Industrial Community." *American Ethnologist* 13:118–30.

Land, Hilary. 1977. "Inequalities in Large Families: More of the Same or Different?" In *Equalities and Inequalities in Family Life*, edited by Robert Chester and John Peel, 163–76. New York: Academic.

Lea, Stephen E. G., Roger Tarpy, and Paul Webley. 1987. *The Individual in the Economy*. New York: Cambridge University Press.

Leonard, Priscilla. 1903. "Pin Money versus Moral Obligations." *Harper's Bazaar* 37:1,060.

Letters to the Editor. *Good Housekeeping* 51 (February 1910): 245.

Leupp, Frances E. 1909. "The Cooperative Family." *Atlantic Monthly* 104: 762–67.

Luxton, Meg. 1980. *More Than a Labour of Love*. Toronto: Women's Press.

Lynd, Robert S. 1932. "Family Members as Consumers." *Annals of the American Academy of Political and Social Science* 160:86–93.

Lynd, Robert S., and Helen Merrell Lynd. 1956. *Middletown*. New York: Harcourt Brace.

Marx, Karl. [1844] 1964. "The Power of Money in Bourgeois Society." In *The Economic and Philosophic Manuscripts of 1844*. New York: International.

———. [1858] 1972. *A Contribution to the Critique of Political Economy*, edited by Maurice Dobb. New York: International.

———. [1858–59] 1973. *Grundrisse*. New York: Vintage.

———. [1867] 1984. *Capital*, vol. 1. Edited by Friedrich Engels. New York: International.

Marx, Karl, and Friedrich Engels. [1848] 1971. *The Communist Manifesto*. New York: International.

May, Elaine Tyler. 1980. *Great Expectations*. Chicago: University of Chicago Press.

Mazeaud, Henri, Léon Mazeaud, and André Tunc. 1957. *Traité théorique et pratique de la responsabilité civile delictuelle et contractuelle*. 5th ed. Paris: Editions Montchrestien.

Melitz, Jacques. 1970. "The Polanyi School of Anthropology on Money: An Economist's View." *American Anthropologist* 72:1020–40.

Messinger, C. S., et al. 1890. "Shall Our Daughters Have Dowries?" *North American Review* 151:746–69.

Miller, Daniel. 1987. *Material Culture and Mass Consumption*. Oxford: Blackwell.

Mirowsky, John. 1985. "Depression and Marital Power: An Equity Model." *American Journal of Sociology* 91:557–92.

Modell, John. 1978. "Patterns of Consumption, Acculturation and Family Income: Strategies in Late Nineteenth-Century America." In *Family and Population in Nineteenth-Century America*, edited by Tamara K. Hareven and Maris A. Vinovskis, 206–40. Princeton, N.J.: Princeton University Press.

Morawska, Ewa. 1985. *For Bread with Butter*. Cambridge: Cambridge University Press.

More, Louise Bolard. 1907. *Wage-Earners' Budgets*. New York: Holt.

Nasaw, David. 1985. *Children of the City*. New York: Anchor.

Norton, Mary Beth. 1979. "Eighteenth-Century American Women in Peace and War." In *A Heritage of Her Own*, edited by Nancy F. Cott and Elizabeth H. Pleck, 136–61. New York: Simon and Schuster.

Odencrantz, Louise C. 1919. *Italian Women in Industry*. New York: Russell Sage.

O'Hagan, Anne. 1909. "The Little Foxes." *Good Housekeeping* 49:369–74.

Oren, Laura. 1973. "The Welfare of Women in Laboring Families: England, 1860–1950." *Feminist Studies* 1:107–23.

Ostrander, Susan A. 1984. *Women of the Upper Class*. Philadelphia: Temple University Press.

Pahl, Jan. 1980. "Patterns of Money Management within Marriage." *Journal of Social Policy* 9:313–35.

Parsons, Talcott. 1967. "On the Concept of Influence." In *Sociological Theory and Modern Society*, 355–82. New York: Free Press.

———. 1971a. "Higher Education as a Theoretical Focus." In *Institutions and Social Exchange*, edited by Herman Turk and Richard L. Simpson. New York: Bobbs-Merrill.

————. 1971b. "Levels of Organization and the Mediation of Social Interaction." In *Institutions and Social Exchange*, edited by Herman Turk and Richard L. Simpson. New York: Bobbs-Merrill.

Parsons, Talcott, and Neil J. Smelser. 1956. *Economy and Society*. New York: Free Press.

Peattie, Elia W. 1911. "Your Wife's Pocketbook." *Delineator* 77:466.

Peiss, Kathy. 1986. *Cheap Amusements*. Philadelphia: Temple University Press.

Phillips, H. I. 1924. "My Adventures as a Bold, Bad Budgeteer." *American Magazine* 97:64.

Polanyi, Karl. 1957. "The Economy as an Instituted Process." In *Trade and Market in the Early Empires*, edited by Karl Polanyi, Conrad M. Arensberg, and Harry W. Pearson, 243–70. Glencoe, Ill.: Free Press.

Post, Emily. 1928. "Kelland Doesn't Know What He Is Talking About." *American Magazine* 106:110.

Pringle, Henry F. 1938. "What Do the Women of America Think about Money?" *Ladies' Home Journal* 55:102.

Radin, Margaret. 1987. "Market Inalienability." *Harvard Law Review* 100: 1849–1937.

Rainwater, Lee. 1974. *What Money Buys*. New York: Basic Books.

Ray, Mary Beynon. 1932. "It's Not Always the Woman Who Pays." *Saturday Evening Post* 205:15, 48–49.

Reddy, William. 1984. *The Rise of Market Culture: The Textile Trade and French Society, 1750–1900*. Cambridge: Cambridge University Press.

————. 1987. *Money and Liberty in Modern Europe*. New York: Cambridge University Press.

Rodgers, Helen Z. M. 1902. "Married Women's Earnings." *Albany Law Journal* 64:384.

Ross, Ellen. 1982. " 'Fierce Questions and Taunts': Married Life in Working Class London, 1870–1914." *Feminist Studies* 8:576–602.

Rubin, Lillian B. 1976. *Worlds of Pain*. New York: Basic.

Ryan, Mary P. 1984. *Cradle of the Middle Class*. New York: Cambridge University Press.

Safilios-Rothschild, Constantina. 1970. "The Study of Family Power Structure." *Journal of Marriage and the Family* 32:539–52.

Sahlins, Marshall. 1976. *Culture and Practical Reason*. Chicago: University of Chicago Press.

Salmon, Lucy M. 1909. "The Economics of Spending." *Outlook* 91:884–90.

Salmon, Marylynn. 1986. *Women and the Law of Property*. Chapel Hill: University of North Carolina Press.

Sangster, Margaret E. 1905. "Shall Wives Earn Money?" *Woman's Home Companion* 32:32.

Schudson, Michael. 1984. *Advertising, the Uneasy Persuasion*. New York: Basic Books.

Seeley, John R., R. Alexander Sim, and Elizabeth W. Loosley. 1956. *Crestwood Heights*. New York: Wiley.

Sen, Amartya. 1983. "Economics and the Family." *Asian Development Review* 1: 14–26.

Shammas, Carole, Marylynn Salmon, and Michel Dahlin. 1987. *Inheritance in America*. New Brunswick, N.J.: Rutgers University Press.

Simiand, François. 1934. "La monnaie, réalité sociale." *Annales Sociologiques*, ser. D, pp. 1–86.

Simkhovitch, Mary K. 1917. *The City Worker's World in America*. New York: Macmillan.

Simmel, Georg. [1900] 1978. *The Philosophy of Money*. Translated by Tom Bottomore and David Frisby. London: Routledge and Kegan Paul.

———. [1908] 1950. *The Sociology of Georg Simmel*. Edited by Kurt H. Wolf. Glencoe, Ill.: Free Press.

Smelt, Simon. 1980. "Money's Place in Society." *British Journal of Sociology* 31: 205–23.

Smith, Helena Huntington. 1928. "Husbands, Wives, and Pocketbooks." *Outlook*, p. 500.

Smith, Judith E. 1985. *Family Connections*. Albany: State University of New York Press.

Sorokin, Pitirim A. 1943. *Sociocultural Causality, Space, Time*. Durham, N.C.: Duke University Press.

Stansell, Christine. 1986. *City of Women*. New York: Knopf.

Stearns, Peter N. 1972. "Working-Class Women in Britain, 1890–1914." In *Suffer and Be Still*, edited by Martha Vicinus, 100–120. Bloomington: Indiana University Press.

Stone, Lawrence. 1977. *The Family, Sex and Marriage*. New York: Harper and Row.

Sugimoto, Etsu Inagaki. [1926] 1936. *A Daughter of the Samurai*. Garden City, N.Y.: Doubleday.

Sullerot, Evelyne. 1966. "Les femmes et l'argent." *Janus* 10:33–39.

Sumner, William Graham. [1906] 1940. *Folkways*. New York: Mentor.

Swedberg, Richard. 1987. "Economic Sociology: Past and Present." *Theory and Society* 16:169–213.

Taussig, Michael. 1980. *The Devil and Commodity Fetishism in South America*. Chapel Hill: University of North Carolina Press.

Tebbutt, Melanie. 1983. *Making Ends Meet: Pawnbroking and Working-Class Credit*. New York: St. Martin's.

Tentler, Leslie W. 1982. *Wage-Earning Women*. New York: Oxford University Press.

Thaler, Richard. 1985. "Mental Accounting and Consumer Choice." *Marketing Science* 4 (Summer).

Thomas, W. I., and Florian Znaniecki. [1918–20] 1958. *The Polish Peasant in Europe and America*. New York: Dover.

Thornton, W. W. 1900. "Personal Services Rendered by Wife to Husband under Contract." *Central Law Journal* 183.

Tilly, Louise A., and Joan W. Scott. 1978. *Women, Work, and Family*. New York: Holt, Rinehart and Winston.

Treas, Judith. 1989. "Money in the Bank: Transaction Costs and the Economic Organization of Marriage." *American Sociological Review* 58:723–34.

True, Ruth S. 1914. *The Neglected Girl*. New York: Survey.

Turner, Byran S. 1986. "Simmel, Rationalisation and the Sociology of Money." *Sociological Review* 34:93–114.

Ulrich, Laurel Thatcher. 1983. *Good Wives*. New York: Oxford University Press.

Veblen, Thorstein. [1899] 1953. *The Theory of the Leisure Class*. New York: Mentor.

Warren, Joseph. 1925. "Husband's Right to Wife's Services." *Harvard Law Review* 38:421.

W.A.S. 1922. "Charge It to My Husband." *Law Notes* 26:26–28.

Weber, Marianne. 1975. *Max Weber: A Biography*. New York: Wiley.

Weber, Max. [1922] 1978. *Economy and Society*. Edited by Guenther Roth and Claus Wittich. Berkeley: University of California Press.

———. [1946] 1971. "Religious Rejections of the World and Their Directions." In *From Max Weber: Essays in Sociology*, edited by H. H. Gerth and C. Wright Mills, 323–59. New York: Oxford University Press.

Weitzman, Lenore J. 1981. *The Marriage Contract*. New York: Free Press.

Welter, Barbara. 1966. "The Cult of True Womanhood: 1820–1860." *American Quarterly* 18:151–74.

Whitehead, Ann. 1984. "'I'm Hungry, Mum.'" In *Of Marriage and the Market*, edited by Kate Young, Carol Wolkowitz, and Roslyn McCullagh, 93–116. London: Routledge and Kegan Paul.

Wilson, Gail. 1987. *Money in the Family*. Brookfield, Vt.: Gower.

Winter, Alice Ames. 1925. "The Family Purse." *Ladies' Home Journal* 42:185.

Wong, Diana. 1984. "The Limits of Using the Household as a Unit of Analysis." In *Households and the World-Economy*, edited by Joan Smith, Immanuel Wallerstein, and Hans-Dieter Evans, 56–63. Beverly Hills, Calif.: Sage.

Young, Michael. 1952. "Distribution of Income within the Family." *British Journal of Sociology* 3:305–21.

Zelizer, Viviana. 1987. *Pricing the Priceless Child: The Changing Social Value of Children*. New York: Basic Books.

———. 1988. "Beyond the Polemics on the Market: Establishing a Theoretical and Empirical Agenda." *Sociological Forum* 3 (Fall): 614–34.

6

Fine Tuning the Zelizer View

Neoclassical economics has come under increasing siege. In the past decade or so, critics from a wide spectrum of disciplines (sociology, political science, psychology, law, management studies, international relations, economics), and from both sides of the Atlantic, have grown bolder in their complaints against mainstream economic theorizing (varied examples include Ben-Ner and Putterman 1998; Bloch 1994; Callon 1998; Zelizer 1998; Smelser and Swedberg 1994; Steiner 1999). In their provocative paper in this issue, "Markets and Money in Social Theory: What Role for Economics?," Fine and Lapavitsas (2000) join these critics with their own strongly argued alternative: Marxist political economy.

In their attempt to rebut standard economic reasoning, Fine and Lapavitsas welcome me as an ally who properly "stands up against the sociologically blind thrust of mainstream economics" (359). But first they propose to give my anemic theoretical bloodstream a hearty Marxist transfusion. To be more precise, they are willing to incorporate my critique of neoclassical economics and my empirical work, but not the theoretical basis for either one. In turn, I welcome their project to draw a different, interesting theory of markets and money from Marx's writing. However, Fine and Lapavitsas's theoretical enthusiasm for a political economy framework blinds them to the emergence of newer theoretical possibilities over the last decade or so. Let me therefore respond to their statement in two parts: first, reacting to specific criticisms of my view; and second, outlining alternative ways of explaining markets and monetary transactions.

Fine and Lapavitsas's most negative claims concerning my work cluster around five issues:

1. Failure to define money and markets adequately
2. An atheoretical, inductive research strategy
3. Exaggeration of heterogeneity in money and markets
4. Concentration on exceptional circumstances rather than standard economic processes
5. Neglect of available general theories, especially Marxist political economy

First, the matter of definitions: "Zelizer," Fine and Lapavitsas complain, "seems to approve of a highly flexible notion of the market" (361). "Given the absence of a clear definition of money," they argue, "Zelizer treats money ahistorically and asocially and offers no economic theory of money itself" (376). Failure to provide such definitions of the market and of money, they claim, makes my arguments poor in "analytical rigour and clarity" (361).

True, none of the writings Fine and Lapavitsas cite contains an extensive formal definition of money and markets. However, when it comes to markets, the passages just adjacent to those they do cite clearly point toward a distinctive conception of markets as sets of social relations in which actors transfer goods and services while establishing price-quantity-quality schedules that govern those transfers. Clearly, such a definition leads to recognition that the kinds of social relations and the kinds of transfers differentiate markets from each other.

When it comes to money, Fine and Lapavitsas confuse disapproval of my conception with absence of any definition at all. After all, *The Social Meaning of Money* says emphatically: "Social monies certainly include officially issued coins and bills, but they also include all objects that have recognized, regularized exchange value in one social setting or another" (1994, 21). Such a definition is expansive. Yet it points to a range of related social phenomena. The fuller definition of money flowing from the various writings they cite runs like this:

> Money is an abstraction that observers make from social interactions. It is a matter of degree; to the extent that interactions transfer rights to goods and services by means of tokens that could also serve transfers of other such rights, we can call those tokens money. The more generalizable across social locations, varieties of goods and services, interaction partners, types of rights, and physical forms of the token itself is that capacity to facilitate transfer of rights, the more readily people recognize the token involved as monetary. International currencies, nationally issued legal tenders, electronic monies, bank accounts, and other highly liquid tokens of transferable rights represent one extreme of a continuum running from such generalized forms to the narrowly limited circuits of such other monies as credits in baby-sitting pools, casino chips, or investment diamonds.

In haste to offer their competing view, Fine and Lapavitsas ignore the presence of definitions and arguments of which they disapprove.

When it comes to research strategy, Fine and Lapavitsas—while politely acknowledging the value of my "detailed and sophisticated case studies" (379)—dismiss the theoretical value of what is "primarily an empirically based" analysis (378). Two views of the relation between theory and evidence contend here. Confident that they already possess a coherent general theory, Fine and Lapavitsas proceed deductively, seeking to apply their theory to available facts. Less confident that we already know everything we need to know, I prefer to work back and forth between theory and evidence. Readers will have to judge which strategy works better.

Fine and Lapavitsas find equally disturbing my emphasis on heterogeneity, in particular my apparent disregard for money's "homogenizing influence" (372). They concede that "it is the dual nature of monetization that must always be emphasized—universal and homogenized money creates scope for expressing relations that are socially and culturally specific" (372). Yet money's socially bound variations, within Fine and Lapavitsas's framework, are feeble attempts to counter universalizing tendencies. "The broader aspects and meaning of social relations that are expressed through money," Fine and Lapavitsas tell us, "find themselves trapped within the featurelessness of universal exchangeability" (367). Here they resuscitate the very claims for money's universalizing force my research has repeatedly challenged.

In sum, Fine and Lapavitsas insist both on a universal money and on the causal priority of money's utter fungibility. "There is one money,'" they assert, "even though it assumes different forms" (377). My model of socially variable currencies, they argue, gets the causal sequence backward: "We argue instead that, precisely because it possesses a homogeneous aspect, money can fluidly express a variety of social relations" (360). Money's universality, however, means that "it is incapable of projecting refined differentiation among these relations" (368).

This model of "impoverished" (368) social differentiation does indeed lie at the heart of our disagreement. In sharp contrast, I argue that every currency attaches to a circuit of exchange and every circuit of exchange includes a concrete set of meaningful social relations. At the extreme, to be sure, we do find quite general monies. Electronic currencies, for example, do transcend social location, multiply interaction partners, activate a variety of rights, and cover a broad array of goods and services. Even they, however, attach to the small minority of humans who connect with the Internet. Territorial currencies do, indeed, facilitate national coherence. Even the dollar and the euro, nevertheless, divide as much as they unify.

A wide variety of monies, furthermore, attach to smaller circuits. Take the example of the growing local currency movements in, among other places, the United States, Britain, Australia, Canada, and Japan (see Gilbert and Helleiner 1999; Hart 2000). Local currencies are only one instance of differentiation. Consider as well frequent-flier credits, telephone cards, transit cards, food stamps, and the new digital monies privately issued by credit card companies and banks. In all these cases, the currency in question connects a well-defined network of participants and excludes many others.[1]

All monies are actually dual: they serve both general and local circuits. Indeed, this duality applies to all economic transactions. Seen from the top, economic transactions connect with broad, national symbolic meanings and institutions. Seen from the bottom, however, economic transactions are highly differentiated, personalized, and local, meaningful to particular relations. No contradiction therefore exists between uniformity and diversity: they are simply two different aspects of the same transaction. Just as people speak English in a recognizably grammatical way at the same time that they pour individual and personal content into their conversations, economic actors simultaneously adopt universalizing modes and particularizing markers.

What about market homogeneity? Here again Fine and Lapavitsas complain that my emphasis on "non-economic differentiation between markets" leads me to ignore "what economic content they have in common" (362). As with money, they contend that it is the market's "general properties" that "allow for heterogeneity across individual products" (373). Here we disagree dramatically. Along with such authors as Harrison White, I claim that, except for common properties that are true by definition, markets vary systematically in the way they set prices, in the relations among producers, and in the kinds of transactions that connect producers and consumers (White 1988). Indeed, Fine and Lapavitsas implicitly concede this when they complain about my concentration on final consumption markets (373). By their own showing, consumer markets, labor markets, and producers' goods markets operate in distinctive ways. Within such broad categories, further differentiation occurs according to locality, cultural milieu, legal setting, and, yes, type of commodity. Far from being "ahistorical and asocial" (372) this perspective necessarily situates markets in their historical and social context.

Fine and Lapavitsas's fourth major complaint turns to the allegedly "extremely unusual" (373) character of my research sites. It is certainly true that, in order to make my points, I chose market sites strategically. Those sites ranged from life insurance to markets for children to households and welfare economies. By Fine and Lapavitsas's own principles, however, all markets should share economic properties, so that hardly seems a valid objection. Despite those principles, furthermore, by insisting on the distinction between my research sites and the "mainstream of economic life" (375), Fine and Lapavitsas reinforce the common prejudice that serious economic life takes place only within the worlds of firms and corporations. As economist Julie Nelson points out, "the issues that end up on the nonmarket, 'social' side of the divide tend to be considered less central or important than those on the market, 'economic' side. . . . [S]urely something important is lost when this separation is pursued unchecked" (1998, 33).

In any case, let us look at my strategy. Why, for example, examine household or welfare economies? I deliberately chose areas where corrupting effects of money and market penetration should, in principle, be most devastating. Given prevailing "hostile-worlds" theories that consider any contact between personal ties and money as inevitably commodifying, households and welfare economies should be especially vulnerable. Instead, I demonstrated the social vigor of such economies as people use money and market transactions in the course of creating and maintaining meaningful social relations.

Fine and Lapavitsas's fifth and final complaint, however, is probably their most heartfelt. Considering its availability, why did I ignore the resources of Marxist theory as an answer to the questions I was raising? In particular, they lament my "analytical neglect of the nature of the commodity" (373), along with disregard for any discussion of "capital not only as the most developed source of commodity production but also in its detailed functioning" (373). Fine and Lapavitsas stress this point so strongly that in a number of their criticisms the only weakness in my analysis they actually identify is my failure to adopt their point of view. Note their claim that "Zelizer is negligent of economics" (372). They should have said negligent of *Marxist* economics. "It is significant," they declare, "that her focus is upon the amorphous market rather than the nature of the commodity as use value and value. Furthermore, she neglects (exchange) value and is preoccupied with use value." This boils down to a complaint that I have neglected their preferred interpretation.

By doing so, they contend, I offer no serious challenge to neoclassical dominance. "It is arguable," they conclude, "that such a strategy [mine] to defend sociology against the incursions of mainstream economics is already proving ineffectual" (379). Only Marxist political economy, it seems, will do the job.

Ultimately, Fine and Lapavitsas assume that there are only two possibilities in analyzing economic life: either one accepts neoclassical economics as a valid account of economic processes, or one turns to the only viable alternative: conventional Marxist political economy. However, they ignore the fact that, in the large space between those two, a variety of institutional, relational, and neo-Marxist alternatives have started to emerge.

Within economic sociology, two important positions lie outside both neoclassical economics and conventional Marxist political economy. One of them specifies and analyzes contexts within which well-known economic activities go on. A *context* approach identifies features of social organization that work as facilitators of or constraints on economic action. This position is intent on revamping economists' portrayals of individual and collective decision making—for example, by specifying conditions other than short-term gain that influence decisions. Advocates of context often speak of the "embeddedness" of economic phenomena in social processes, and often refer to interpersonal networks when they do so.

Another school of thought takes greater risks by attempting to develop alternative models drawing on ideas about culture, institutions, networks, and organizational processes. In the *alternative* perspective, sociologists propose competing accounts of economic transactions. Rather than expanding the economic approach or complementing it, one prominent view argues that, in all areas of economic life, people are creating, maintaining, symbolizing, and transforming meaningful social relations. My own work follows such a line. Necessarily this body of thought is more fragmentary and experimental, but it includes highly promising attempts at synthesis.

A full survey of alternatives would include, among others, the efforts of Mitchell Abolafia (1996), Wayne Baker (1987), Bernard Barber (1995), Jens Beckert (1996), Richard Biernacki (1995), Pierre Bourdieu (1997), Ronald Burt (1998), Nicole Woolsey Biggart (1989), Michel Callon (1998), Bruce Carruthers (1996), Randall Collins (1997), Paul DiMaggio and Hugh Louch (1998), Frank Dobbin (1995), Nigel Dodd (1994), Wendy Espeland (1998), Neil Fligstein (1996), Mark Granovetter ([1974] 1995), Mauro Guillen (2000), Geoffrey Ingham (1996), Calvin Morrill (1995), Jan Pahl (1999), Alejandro Portes (1995), Charles Smith (1989), Supriya Singh (1997), Arthur Stinchcombe (1983), Chris Tilly and Charles Tilly (1998), Bruce Western (1997), Robert Wuthnow (1996), and David Stark (1990). As it happens, a number of these authors draw on insights of Marxist political economy. Instead of deducing money and markets from established Marxist theory, however, these searchers for alternatives stand out for their insistence on confronting existing theory with carefully assembled evidence about the actual operation of money and markets. I gladly join their search for superior general explanations of economic processes.

NOTES

Viviana A. Zelizer, "Fine Tuning the Zelizer View," *Economy and Society* 29 (August 2000): 383–89. Reprinted with permission.

1. What is more, the rapid disintegration of the ruble as the money of account in the former Soviet Union demonstrates the complexity and fragility of the social infrastructure supporting any particular general currency (Woodruff 1999).

REFERENCES

Abolafia, M. Y. 1996. *Making Markets*. Cambridge, Mass.: Harvard University Press.
Baker, W. 1987. "What Is Money? A Social Structural Interpretation." In *Intercorporate Relations*, edited by M. S. Mizruchi and M. Schwartz, 109–44. Cambridge: Cambridge University Press.
Barber, B. 1995. "All Economies Are 'Embedded': The Career of a Concept, and Beyond." *Social Research* 62:387–413.
Beckert, J. 1996. "What Is Sociological about Economic Sociology? Uncertainty and the Embeddedness of Economic Action." *Theory and Society* 25/26:803–40.

Ben-Ner, A., and L. Putterman, eds. 1998. *Economics, Values, and Organization.* New York: Cambridge University Press.

Biernacki, Richard. 1995. *The Fabrication of Labor.* Berkeley: University of California Press.

Biggart, N. W. 1989. *Charismatic Capitalism: Direct Selling Organizations in America.* Chicago: University of Chicago Press.

Bloch, M., ed. 1994. "Les usages de l'argent." *Terrain* 23:5–10.

Bourdieu, P. 1997. "Le champ économique." *Actes de la Recherche en Sciences Sociales* 119:48–66.

Burt, R. S. 1998. "The Gender of Social Capital." *Rationality and Society* 10:5–46.

Callon, M., ed. 1998. *The Laws of the Markets.* Oxford: Blackwell.

Carruthers, B. 1996. *City of Capital: Politics and Markets in the English Financial Revolution.* Princeton, N.J.: Princeton University Press.

Collins, R. 1997. "Religious Economy and the Emergence of Capitalism in Japan." *American Sociological Review* 62:843–65.

DiMaggio, P., and H. Louch. 1998. "Socially Embedded Consumer Transactions: For What Kinds of Purchases Do People Most Often Use Networks?" *American Sociological Review* 63:619–37.

Dobbin, F. 1995. *Forging Industrial Policy: The United States, Britain and France in the Railway Age.* Cambridge: Cambridge University Press.

Dodd, N. 1994. *The Sociology of Money.* New York: Continuum.

Espeland, W. 1998. *The Struggle for Water.* Chicago: University of Chicago Press.

Fine, B., and C. Lapavitsas. 2000. "Markets and Money in Social Theory: What Role for Economics?" *Economy and Society* 29 (August): 357–82.

Fligstein, N. 1996. "Markets as Politics: A Political-Cultural Approach to Market Politics." *American Sociological Review* 61:656–73.

Gilbert, E., and E. Helleiner, eds. 1999. *Nation-States and Money: The Past, Present and Future of National Currencies.* London: Routledge.

Granovetter, M. [1974] 1995. *Getting a Job: A Study of Contacts and Careers.* Chicago: University of Chicago Press.

Guillen, M. F. 2000. "Diversity in Globalization: Organizational Change in Argentina, South Korea and Spain." *Occasional Papers,* School of Social Science, Institute for Advanced Study, Princeton, N.J.

Hart, K. 2000. *The Memory Bank: Money in an Unequal World.* London: Profile Books.

Ingham, G. 1996. "The 'New Economic Sociology.' " *Work, Employment and Society* 10:549–64.

Morrill, C. 1995. *The Executive Way: Conflict Management in Corporations.* Chicago: University of Chicago Press.

Nelson, J. A. 1998. "Labour, Gender and the Economic/Social Divide." *International Labour Review* 137:33–46.

Pahl, J. 1999. *Invisible Money: Family Finances in the Electronic Economy.* Bristol: Policy Press.

Portes, A., ed. 1995. *The Economic Sociology of Immigration.* New York: Russell Sage Foundation.

Singh, S. 1997. *Marriage Money: The Social Shaping of Money in Marriage and Banking.* St. Leonards, Australia: Allen and Unwin.

Smelser, N. J., and R. Swedberg, eds. 1994. *The Handbook of Economic Sociology*. New York: Russell Sage Foundation/Princeton, N.J.: Princeton University Press.

Smith, C. W. 1989. *Auctions: The Social Construction of Value*. New York: Free Press.

Stark, D. 1990. "Work, Worth, and Justice in a Socialist Mixed Economy." *Working Papers on Central and Eastern Europe*, no. 5. Center for European Studies, Harvard University.

Steiner, P. 1999. *La sociologie économique*. Paris: La Découverte.

Stinchcombe, A. L. 1983. *Economic Sociology*. New York: Academic Press.

Tilly, C., and C. Tilly. 1998. *Work under Capitalism*. Boulder, Colo.: Westview.

Western, B. 1997. *Between Class and Market: Postwar Unionization in the Capitalist Democracies*. Princeton, N.J.: Princeton University Press.

White, H. C. 1988. "Varieties of Markets." In *Social Structure: A Network Approach*, edited by B. Wellman and S. D. Berkowitz. New York: Cambridge University Press.

Woodruff, D. 1999. *Money Unmade: Barter and the Fate of Russian Capitalism*. Ithaca, N.Y.: Cornell University Press.

Wuthnow, R. 1996. *Poor Richard's Principle*. Princeton, N.J.: Princeton University Press.

Zelizer, V. 1994. *The Social Meaning of Money*. New York: Basic Books.

———, ed. 1998. Special issue on "Changing Forms of Payment." *American Behavioral Scientist* 41.

7

Payments and Social Ties

Suppose for a moment that this is the year 2096. Let's take a look at American families: although by now money often takes postelectronic forms unfamiliar to the twentieth-century, in the "traditional" home, "housewives" and "househusbands" receive monthly stipulated sums of money as salaries from their wage-earning spouses. Salaries are renegotiated yearly; fines are imposed for sloppy cleaning, incompetent cooking, careless child care, or indifferent lovemaking. Midyear raises or cash prizes are awarded for exceptional performance. An arbitration board solves domestic financial disputes. In other forms of households, spouses have separate accounts, distribute domestic and emotional tasks equally, and pay cash for the performance of any extra chores and activities: from housekeeping to child care to sexual relations. In all households, children have a piecework scale for their various domestic responsibilities. Good report cards bring a bonus, and bad grades a deduction. As they enter college, children sign a contract to repay all their parents' expenses within a stipulated number of years after graduation.

Now let's take a look at a successful business, likewise in the year 2096. As a matter of right, all workers receive a basic minimum of housing, food, and health care. Workers do not receive regular payment for time, effort, or qualifications. Bosses decide when, how, and in what quantity they make payments to their workers, and workers receive them as gifts; paychecks arrive sometimes at week's end, other times monthly. Owners reward exceptional performance with a gift certificate or by taking the worker out to dinner and a movie. Odd—perhaps—but not a fantastic script. There is, after all, nothing new or abhorrent about the types of monetary transfers I have just described; people do pay for sexual services, parents do pay children for certain tasks, and people often do give money in arbitrary ways. What makes the script odd, uncomfortable, or amusing is the mismatch between the social relations involved and the forms of monetary transfers. In these hypothetical cases, what seemed strange about the household was that all payments took the form of compensation. What was strange about the business was that all payments took the form of entitlements or gifts.

To see more clearly what is at issue, we need to distinguish among three possible ways of organizing monetary payments of any kind: as *compensation* (direct exchange), as *entitlement* (the right to a share), and as *gift* (one person's voluntary bestowal on another). Money as compensation implies an equal exchange of values and a certain distance, contingency, bargaining, and accountability among the parties. Money as an entitlement implies strong

claims to power and autonomy by the recipient. Money as a gift implies subordination and arbitrariness. All three forms of payment define the quality
of social relations between the parties. On the whole, entitlements and gifts
imply a more durable social relation between them than does compensation.

People care deeply about making such distinctions; the wrong transfers
challenge, confuse, or violate the definition of particular social relations.
Within the contemporary family, a monetary compensation system does not
fit the expected intimacy of domestic relations, while a gift system of payment
in the business world muddles the presumably impersonal working relations
between employer and employee. To be sure, people do play with variance
in these regards: some families tie allowances to children's performance of
specific tasks, thus inserting compensation into household relations; while
some business firms offer unscheduled gifts to highly prized employees, thus
inserting the gift relation into presumably businesslike interactions. Distinctions appear furthermore within each category: in the zone of gifts, tips
differ from wedding presents; within compensation, a coin slapped down
for a newspaper differs from an executive's annual salary with its perquisites and benefits; in the range of entitlements, Social Security checks differ
from alimony. Nevertheless, on the whole, different kinds of organizations
concentrate on one category of payment: compensation, entitlement, or
gift. Large discrepancies in these regards almost always cause organizational
troubles. For another example, consider the teacher-student relation: look at
the trouble Cornell's professor of psychology James Maas got into last year,
for among other things, spending money on gifts for his favorite women
students, like the $2,000 blue cocktail dress or the $500 camera. His explanation? Such students were "part of my family" (*New York Times*, Mar. 23,
1995). For some of the students, however, such gifts defined the relation as
unwanted sexual courtship.

In my recent work, I have been looking at this deliberate, persistent, and
often contested differentiation of monies, mapping out a complex social
economy far different from the gray world of modernity predicted by classical social thinkers: a world where money would homogenize, flatten out
social life, transforming diverse social relations into uniform, impersonal
exchanges. This paper forms a bridge between work I have already reported
and an inquiry I am just undertaking. Let me first summarize my previous
work and then turn to a new, different set of questions. After earlier investigations of life insurance (Zelizer 1979) and the value of children (Zelizer
1985), my most recent book examined changes in the public and private
uses of money in the United States between the 1870s and 1930s, focusing
on domestic transactions, the bestowing of gifts, and charity. In this period,
the modern consumer society turned the spending of money not only into
a central economic practice but into a dynamic, complex cultural and social
activity (Zelizer 1994). To be sure, money concerns increasingly permeated
the American household and gift exchanges, but they did not, as anticipated,

reduce every household, or every gift transfer into an impersonal transfer, blunting personal, social, and moral distinctiveness.

When I began work on the cultural context of life insurance twenty years ago, this seemed a peculiar topic. Few people were working on such subjects. Since then, I have become much less lonely. As the recent *Handbook of Economic Sociology* (Smelser and Swedberg, 1994) illustrates, a wide variety of scholars—including economists, anthropologists, historians, jurists, sociologists, and literary analysts—are now taking seriously the interplay between social context and economic transactions. Within the narrower range of monetary payments less work has been done, but even here a number of analysts are now exploring money as a socially contingent phenomenon (for examples since 1994, see Bloch 1994; Dodd 1994; Guyer 1995; Mizruchi and Stearns 1994; Shell 1995; Wuthnow 1994).

My own research shows how at each step in money's advance, people have reshaped their commercial transactions, introduced new distinctions, invented their own special forms of currency, earmarked money in ways that baffle market theorists, incorporated money into personalized webs of friendship, family relations, interactions with authorities, and forays through shops and businesses. More specifically, as money entered the household, gift exchanges, and charitable donations, individuals and organizations invented an extensive array of currencies, ranging from housekeeping allowances, pin money, spending money, to money gifts, gift certificates, remittances, tips, penny provident savings, mother's pensions, and food stamps. People sorted ostensibly homogeneous legal tender into distinct categories, and they created other currencies that lacked backing from the state. They marked distinct categories of social relations, furthermore, by means of distinct forms of monetary transfers. This, I claim, is how money works: in order to make sense of their complex and often chaotic social ties, people constantly innovate and differentiate currencies, bringing different meanings to their various exchanges. Thus, a multiplicity of socially meaningful currencies replaces the standard model of a single, neutral, depersonalizing legal tender.

Within households, families carefully, and sometimes passionately, differentiated and segregated their monies; they set food money apart from rent money, school money, or charity money; funds for burial, wedding, Christmas, or recreation also became distinct currencies. Wives, husbands, and children did not always agree on earmarking arrangements; family members struggled over how to define, allocate, and regulate their monies. A wife's money, for instance, differed fundamentally from her husband's or her child's, not only in quantity but in how it was obtained, how often, and how it was used, even where it was kept. Disputes were not always settled cordially: women, men, and children often lied, stole, or deceived each other in order to protect their separate currencies. Families thus constructed distinct forms of monies, shaped by a powerful domestic culture and by changing social relations between husbands and wives, parents and children. They also varied by class: middle- and working-class domestic dollars were not exact equivalents.

Families, intimate friends, and businesses likewise reshaped money into its supposedly most alien form: a sentimental gift, expressing care and affection. It mattered who gave gift money and who received it, when it was given, how it was offered and how spent. Defying all notions of money as neutral, impersonal, and fungible, gift money circulated as a meaningful, deeply subjective, nonfungible currency, closely regulated by social conventions. At Christmas, weddings, christenings, or other ritual and secular events, cash turned into a dignified, welcome gift almost unrecognizable as market money and clearly distinguished from other domestic currencies.

When authorities intervened in the earmarking of monies, a different category of currencies emerged. Concerned with ostensibly incompetent consumers, a number of institutions and organizations in the early twentieth century intervened in the earmarking systems of dependent populations. In the case of the poor, public and private welfare authorities became deeply involved in constructing charitable currencies designed to teach their clients the proper uses of money. Thus, ironically, in the early 1900s, just as the American state—after much effort—had finally achieved a significant degree of standardization and monopolization in the physical forms of legal tender, people were furiously differentiating, earmarking, and even inventing new forms of monies. The range of social relationships involving monetary transfers, moreover, had multiplied, which meant that the number of distinctions people made by the form, manner, and meaning of transfers likewise multiplied.

Why did I choose to focus on domestic transactions, gift exchanges, and charity? Because these are three areas that might seem most vulnerable to the dollar's rationalization. Here, of all places, the standardizing effects of state money should have been found. Contrary to prevailing theories of monetization, however, in each area, people innovated and differentiated monies as they managed their complex and changing social relations. But what does this tell us about market transactions? Does this analysis work to understand compensation systems? In a review of my *Social Meaning of Money*, economist Julie Nelson (1995) chides me for not going further in my challenge to traditional understandings of money. By focusing on family, friendship, and charity, she argues, I properly defend the traditional realms of sociology from economistic accounts. Why not go further into economic turf: exploring the differentiation and earmarking of the allegedly most colorless monies exchanged as compensation, in market transactions?

Nelson is both wrong and right: she is wrong to suggest that the areas of household, gift, and charity are any less theoretically problematic than strictly market transactions; after all, generations of theorists have argued that these areas of personal solidarities are especially vulnerable zones; in-deed, they had to be defended against monetary incursions. Nevertheless, Nelson is certainly right that the major challenge for us now is to take on what appear to be transparent, instantaneous, and therefore socially neu-tral monetary transfers. Unlike gifts or entitlements, the monetary exchange involved in compensation appears less constrained by social ties; after the transfer between payer and payee ends, it seems, the transaction vanishes. "Unlike the regulation of speech or the practice of medicine," compensation law, affirms one expert, "does not usually implicate deep and controversial social values. The means of payment are colorless instruments that serve a rather narrow economic purpose" (Rubin and Cooter 1994, 39).

Despite the formidable accumulation of new evidence, old-line assump-tions and misunderstandings about market transactions persist in two forms. First, many analysts suppose that markets and money necessarily overcome and dry up all social ties. Note, for instance, what George Ritzer concludes from his recent study of the credit card industry: "We live in a society that is undergoing increasing rationalization. . . . Being in itself rationalized, the credit card is playing a crucial role in fostering the expansion of rationaliza-tion and, with it, the dehumanization of our lives" (1995, 177). In one of 1994's distinguished lectures, the speaker warned once again that "the market is intruding into realms of time, space, emotions, language, ideas, and activ-ity previously reserved for civil society," and in the process, "market rational-ity supplants other moralities and changes social practices" (Persell 1994, 643, 648). Policymakers' promotion of free-market liberalization in both capitalist and postsocialist economies have only exacerbated fears of political analysts that calculating market relations would undermine the solidarities that sustain democracy.

Second, although institutionally alert economists recognize that payment systems and social relations interact, most professional analysts of payment still take an individualistic approach, missing the profound grounding of payments in social ties and their shared understandings. They suppose either that a manager chooses payment systems exclusively for the incentives they offer for greater, higher quality individual effort, or that individual work-ers respond to payment systems by maximizing their monetary returns, or both. How do systems of compensation actually work? Every analyst of in-dustrial organization recognizes differences among modes of payment such as straight salary, salary plus commission, piece rate, or bonus. As Aage Sorensen's (1994) useful synthesis of standard thinking about systems of com-pensation shows, the literature on payment systems divides between analy-sis from employers' perspectives and from workers' perspectives. From the employers' perspective, the literature looks at variation in payment systems as incentive structures, techniques for manipulating motivation. From the workers' perspective, a less abundant literature portrays payment systems as opportunity structures: in Trond Petersen's (1992) version, for instance, variation in payment types within department stores establishes a hierarchy of jobs and returns from work.

Analysts have generally lacked sensitivity to a third dimension of payments as definers of symbolic meanings and social relations. Let's be clear: those who pay certainly adopt modes of payment to obtain different sorts of efforts from recipients, and recipients are concerned with obtaining greater rewards. But pure efficiency explanations of payment systems, as effective performance measures or reward structures, fail to account for the creation, changing acceptability, and diversity of arrangements for compensation. Even strategically initiated contracts acquire moral force, such that people feel wronged, demeaned, or cheated when payers violate them—as ideas of the just wage or a fair day's work illustrate. Remember the distinctions among gift, compensation, and entitlement: such analysts as Sorensen and Petersen treat different systems of payment for work as if they were all essentially exchanges, thus neglecting their components of gift and entitlement.[1]

If extrapolation from my findings on domestic transfers, money gifts, and charitable exchanges makes sense, within the world of compensation we should actually find that organizations and people introduce distinctions and differentiations serving to create and maintain significantly different sets of social relations; they correspond to distinct social ties and their meanings. For example, we should find that within a university department not only different quantities of pay, but distinct forms of payment, mark the relations of the department chair to secretaries, janitors, student assistants, and colleagues. The payment relation, furthermore, involves interaction, adaptation, and bargaining rather than a one-time decision by an optimizing payer. Wage payment by the hour, for instance, implies a distinctly different sort of relation between employer and worker than does an annual salary, not to mention different modes of negotiation over modes of payment.

I am now investigating payment systems in two very different settings in twentieth-century America, putting today's varied forms of compensation in historical perspective. The two settings are the sexual economy (for example, payments for sex work or other sex-related transactions including alimony, dating, or compensation for loss of consortium in damage cases) and large bureaucratized organizations (for example, offices, factories, schools, prisons). I chose this comparison for a number of reasons; first, the prevailing types of payments differ in each setting, and second, most observers assume that the sexual economy teems with moral controversy while bureaucracies have routinized them out of existence. My study affirms the variation in payment forms within the two sectors but challenges the flat contrast between a technical world and an emotional world.

Within large bureaucracies, I am further examining both routine, continuous forms of compensation for work and intermittent, discretionary, contingent payments. The kinds of payment systems under investigation include (a) payment strategies, such as profit sharing, day wages, monthly salaries, payment by the hour, piecework task work; (b) the whole range of employee benefits, from health care to vacations; (c) such contrasting media of payment as scrip, truck, electronic credits, stock options, checks, cash; (d) bonuses, prizes, commissions, tips, seasonal gifts to service providers. Of course, such distinctions between types of payments apply to the sexual economy as well, but on the whole, contingent, intermittent, discretionary payments occupy much of the sexual economy while routinized, continuous payments occupy a larger portion of bureaucratized economies. Thus my chief comparisons concern (a) discretionary payments in the sexual economy, (b) discretionary payments in bureaucracies, and (c) routinized payments in bureaucracies. To illustrate this line of inquiry, let me focus on two cases from the discretionary side: one in the category of intermittent forms of payment within large organizations, and a second from the sexual economy. In my recent book, I treated these cases in a preliminary way, and I am now examining them in greater depth.

Let us first look at the case of the Christmas bonus. Notice the work of differentiation and contest. At the turn of this century, employers began substituting the traditional nineteenth-century Christmas offerings to employees—turkeys, watches, candy, or gold coins—with a cash bonus. As early as 1902, J. P. Morgan and Company had apparently broken the record by giving each of its employees a full-year's salary as a Christmas present. Gifts of cash were increasingly standardized, calculated as a percentage of the wage. Most employers, however, continued to want to treat the bonus as a discretionary gift; after all, this custom of "remembering the workers" served them well to oversee and regulate workers' productivity as well as assuring their loyalty. Significantly, while some companies offered a bonus to every employee, others made the Christmas present contingent on length of service or a worker's efficiency record. Or on a worker's proper disposition of the bonus; for Christmas 1914, a large Minneapolis flour-milling company reportedly gave each of its employees a $25 check to be deposited at a savings bank, the gift-check being valueless otherwise.

But the similarity to other forms of compensation invited recipients to treat the bonus as an entitlement, pressing for a definition of the additional income as a right. The personalization of a business gift from employer to employee was hard to sustain when the bestowal was standardized and expected. By the 1950s, the Christmas bonus officially lost its status as a gift: when one firm announced a reduction in its annual Christmas bonus as a way to make up for the expense of introducing a costly new retirement plan, the employees' union tried to negotiate the holiday bonus. After the company refused any bargaining, the union appealed to the National Labor Relations Board. The board ruled that the Christmas bonus could no longer be considered an employer's discretionary gift but an expected and negotiable component of a workers' wage. While a dissenting board member protested that a "genuine Christmas gift has no place at the bargaining table" (Niles-Bement-Pond Company and Amalgamated Local No. 405, International Union, United Automobile, Aircraft & Agricultural Implement Workers of America, C.I.O., 1952), it was generally agreed that the bonus was no longer a present but a separate category of payment from the regular paycheck. The patron-client, parent-child, benefactor-beneficiary component of the employer-employee relationship, it follows, was diminishing.

The Christmas bonus illustrates the complexities of instituting discretionary payments. At issue was not only the amount and character of the payment but also the appropriate social relations between employer and employee. Not only bonuses, but also commissions, prizes, expense accounts, company cars, frequent flier miles, health benefits, and even the key to executive washrooms become contested but crucial, contingent, discretionary payments defining relations among people within contemporary firms. They announce, and to some extent determine, which pairs of workers are equal or unequal, close or distant, solidary or competitive. One could of course examine the same kind of differentiation and contest at the boundary separating routine payments for work, or gifts and entitlements, in firms from morally contested payments; the annals of office affairs and sexual harassment overflow with stories of this kind.

Let us go straight into the territory of sex payments. Speaking of the period after World War I, Leo Rosten, chronicler of American immigrant and working-class life, recalled a Saturday night tour of three New York taxi-dance ballrooms and his encounters with the women who made their living by dancing with paying customers (Mona, Jean, Honey, and others). At Seventh Avenue's Honeymoon Lane Danceland, Mona led him to the dance floor letting "her body, all marshmallow, flow against mine . . . and murmured . . . a voluptuous 'Mmmm-mmh!' " After dancing for a moment "approaching ecstasy," a buzzer loudly "honked"; Mona quickly "disengaged her clutch" instructing him to get more dance tickets. When Rosten protested that he thought his ticket was for a whole dance, Mona announced that "a dance is every time the buzzer buzzes." Which was every minute. After Rosten promptly returned with ten more tickets, Mona was once again "warm and yielding in my arms—until the buzzer finished its tenth pecuniary decree." Jean later explained that the dancers kept half of the price of their tickets, plus "you have to add the presents . . . like nice lingerie, a bracelet, a purse, a piece of jewelry, maybe an evening gown." Or sometimes cash. At the Majestic Danceland, Honey told Rosten about a St. Louis real estate dealer who dated her: once "he leaned over in the cab he was taking me to some scrumptious Chinese food in, and without one single word he leaned over and kissed me—nothing rough or forcing, just a real sweet little kiss. Then he handed me ten dollars without a peep" (1970, 289–91, 297).

With taxi-dancers, noted Paul Cressey in his more systematic account of Chicago dance-halls in the 1920s, the date—"a conventionally accepted means for young people to get acquainted"—acquired "a suggestion of immorality." Yet taxi-dancers were not prostitutes but committed to an "intermediate" occupation (1932, 36, 84). In the form of dance tickets, taxi-dance halls even had their own currency that marked the particular sexual economy of patron and dancer. Taxi-dance girls were not prostitutes, yet they exchanged sexual services for money. What defines this sexual economy? How does it differ from prostitution, or from other sexual transfers? What distinguishes different forms of sexual payments: how do dance tickets, for instance, differ from cash, or from a gift of jewelry?

The same process of earmarking and differentiation that took place elsewhere also took place in the sexual economy. Cressey, for instance, observed five distinct relationships between dancer and client, each with its own rules of payment, not only the standard dance payment but also "free dances" for more "favored suitors"; "mistress" arrangements, an "alliance" in which for a few months a man paid for the dancer's rent or groceries; the "plural alliance," where the girl "enters an understanding by which she agrees to be faithful to a certain three or four men," who through "separate arrangements" meet her "financial requirements" of rent, groceries, or clothes; and the "overnight date," which "quickly take[s] on the character of clandestine prostitution" (1932, 50, 48–49).

In the early twentieth century, as middle-class and working-class courtship was being transformed by the new dating rituals of the young and as money increasingly entered the social relations of men and women, the differentiation of courtship currencies from the same legal tender used in other sexual transfers, including prostitution but also domestic payments and gifts, became a complex and delicate task. Consider treating, a popular turn-of-the-century working-class arrangement by which women received financial help, gifts—including clothing or even a vacation trip—and access to entertainment from men in exchange for a variety of sexual favors, from flirting to sexual intercourse. While many such transfers were paid by a woman's fiancé or her "steady," some women reportedly accepted treats from casual acquaintances as well. Yet the transfer remained within the realm of courtship gifts. In general, only a stipulated cash payment at the time of sexual relations marked a woman's activities as prostitution. Brothels, meanwhile, created their own special currencies, such as brass tokens, for the payment of prostitutes. They came closest to making payments a matter of bureaucratic routine.

The sexual economy was not limited to the heterosexual world. George Chauncey's study of New York's late-nineteenth-century gay subculture documents the differentiation of homosexual ties; from the working-class "fairies" to "queers," "trade," and "gays." Each group, he notes, "had a specific connotation and signified specific subjectivities" (1994, 14). Their monetary transfers surely varied as well.

How should one approach the analysis of sexual economies? Traditional market models simply assume that sexual payments are no different than any other market transfer—impersonal, anonymous, qualitatively indifferent—missing, therefore, the variation and personalization I have been discussing. Although the evidence is limited, it is known that prostitutes themselves differentiate their income: by type of activity or by customer. A study of the Oslo prostitution market in the 1980s, for instance, found a "divided economy" among many of the women; welfare money, health benefits, or other legal income were carefully budgeted, spent for the "straight life," paying rent and bills. Prostitution money, on the other hand, was quickly squandered on going out, on drugs, alcohol, and clothes. Paradoxically, the study notes, the women "sweat over, add up, and budget the legal money though the ends will never meet, while simultaneously thousands of crowns can be spent on 'going out.'" Dirty money, it seems, "burns a hole in your pocket and has to be used quickly" (Hoigard and Finstad, 1992, 49).

A seventeen-year-old prostitute from Copacabana, Brazil, reports Robert Coles in *The Moral Life of Children*, told him how some of the money she got "I want to throw it into a garbage can, or I want to send it out to be washed and dried and folded and returned to me in a plastic bag that says 'clean.'" Often, she continued, "I take [this dirty money] to the nuns. I tell them to give it to the kids who are the worst . . . living in the streets and sleeping in alleys . . . " (1986, 176–77). That same girl had a daytime job as a hairdresser and made similar distinctions among her customers' tips: tips from nasty customers "I put in a separate place in my wallet. I don't let the money touch some of the other money I make" (Coles 1986, 75). Thus, in the sexual economy, we find that payments can work to create and maintain distinctions that matter morally, sentimentally, and personally.

What is at issue in such cases as the Christmas bonus or sexual payments? In *The Social Meaning of Money*, I argued that (a) people maintain strong distinctions among entitlements, gifts, and payments, considering each to define different kinds of social relations and meaning systems; (b) as social, technical, and economic conditions changed, people devised new means for marking these old distinctions, for example, by inventing ways of labeling some monies as gifts, other monies as wages, (c) massive monetization and bureaucratization deeply altered the forms of monetary transfers but without reducing the pressure or the struggles among parties for the proper definition of the monies involved. For instance, within the welfare system, policymakers, care givers, and clients struggled over payments in cash versus in-kind, as well as over the proper use of relief money—in short, over whether welfare monies were entitlements, gifts, or payments for good behavior.

My work in progress follows up these insights by comparing two rather different economic sectors—industrial, commercial, and bureaucratic work on one side, the sexual economy on the other—seeking to document and explain differing forms of payment within and between them. Industrial, commercial, and bureaucratic work had already significantly monetized in the United States by 1900, but payments came increasingly under the control of rationalized administrations, both governmental and nongovernmental. The sexual economy underwent little bureaucratization, but differentiated and monetized enormously. Comparison between the two, therefore, provides a great opportunity to examine the effects of monetization as well as bureaucratization. The comparison raises an important set of specific problems: How do contrasting systems of payment come into being? To what extent do different forms of routine payment mark distinctive forms of social relations within workplaces? Do discretionary forms of payments such as bonuses, prizes, and tips define their own categories of relations among the parties? In these regards, what differences and similarities appear between the sexual economy and the world of industrial, commercial, and bureaucratic work?

Morally controversial payments enrich the inquiry by raising two problems: one, do the same principles of demarcation appear in morally sensitive areas as in the ostensibly bureaucratized zone of payment for work; and second, what makes certain kinds of payments morally controversial? In general, forms of payment that generate controversy are valuable both because the controversy indicates that people really care about them and because the controversy generates evidence. That is why in addition to moral controversies, I am examining disputes over types of payment in the world of work. It could turn out, of course, that moral controversies will appear frequently in the bureaucratized world of work with some of the same intensity as in the sexual economy. Certainly, miners and truckers have risked their lives in struggles over forms of payment. Whatever my findings, the comparison will deepen our understanding of what is at issue—historically and today as well—in the transformation of American systems of payment.

People might say that this process of differentiation in payment systems I am documenting belongs to the archives along with paper currency, that it is merely a transitional phase, that in the long run the rationality of money aided by new techniques of communication are bound to win out. Two examples disprove that view: take first the case of electronic money; that is, the creation of currencies by means of computers. This process has already begun and will surely expand in years to come. However, despite first impressions that electronic money creates an absolutely impersonal and uniform medium, we in fact already have signs that it will facilitate a wild multiplication of differentiations. As a recent *Business Week* commentary on the future of money noted: "There will be new forms of smart money and payment systems that can only be done online. . . . Digital money . . . moves through a multiplicity of networks instead of the current bank system. It comes in lots of guises, is created by a lot of individual parties" (1995, 70, 67). In the future, for instance, e-money may be issued privately by institutions other than banks. Because electronic money is software, notes *Business Week*, it could be programmed for restricted purposes, to be spent only on designated purchases: "a business could have an electronic version of petty cash to be used for supplies at an Office Depot— but not a beer at the local tavern. Or parents could wire to a college student E-money that is designated for rent or books" (1995, 70). My own work suggests that this is a highly probable outcome.

In the realm of credit cards, we again encounter the illusion of depersonalization and standardization. What could be thinner, more transient, and more routinized than the card-mediated transfer of money from buyer to seller? In reality, such devices as affinity cards—issued by a given community or organization and having proceeds earmarked for that group—prove just the opposite. The Rainbow Card, for example, recently introduced by Visa, the Travelers Bank, and Subaru, with the endorsement of Martina Navratilova, is earmarked for gay and lesbian communities. The Unity Visa Card, issued by the Boston Bank of Commerce, aims at the African American community (these two cards stand out from most affinity cards by distributing their benefits not to a specific organization such as the Sierra Club or the Elvis Presley Memorial Foundation but rather to a socially defined collectivity; *Wall Street Journal* 1995). Even in the apparently monotone world of credit cards, we discover the flourishing of many melodies, of multiple tones marking different qualities of social relations.

Analyzing the complex social life of payments is not just recollection of the past but talks to the future of payments. For more than a century, observers of monetization have predicted that money would produce gray uniformity and impersonality. But a close examination of today's money reveals that people are differentiating just as energetically and ingeniously as ever.

Notes

Viviana A. Zelizer, "Payments and Social Ties," *Sociological Forum* 11 (September 1996): 481–95. Reprinted with permission. In keeping with the bridge this paper makes between past and present work, I have adapted a substantial section of the text from various parts of *The Social Meaning of Money* (1994). The paper was first presented at a session organized by Eviatar Zerubavel on "Lumping and Splitting," at the 1995 annual meetings of the Eastern Sociological Association.

1. Even George A. Akerlof's (1982) provocative discussion of employment as a "partial gift exchange" reduces the payment to a market exchange without specifying the content of the relation between employer and worker.

REFERENCES

Akerlof, George A. 1982. "Labor Contracts as Partial Gift Exchange." *Quarterly Journal of Economics* 97:543–69.

Bloch, Maurice, ed. 1994. "Les usages de l'argent." *Terrain* 23.

Business Week. 1995. "The Future of Money." June 12:66–78.

Chauncey, George. 1994. *Gay New York*. New York: Basic Books.

Coles, Robert. 1986. *The Moral Life of Children*. Boston: Atlantic Monthly Press.

Cressey, Paul G. 1932. *The Taxi-Dance Hall*. Chicago: University of Chicago Press.

Dodd, Nigel. 1994. *The Sociology of Money*. New York: Continuum.

Guyer, Jane I., ed. 1995. *Money Matters*. Portsmouth, N.H.: Heinemann.

Hoigard, Cecilie, and Liv Finstad. 1992. *Backstreets: Prostitution, Money and Love*. Cambridge: Polity Press.

Mizruchi, Mark S., and Linda Brewster Stearns. 1994. "Money, Banking, and Financial Markets." In *The Handbook of Economic Sociology*, edited by Neil Smelser and Richard Swedberg, 313–41. Princeton, N.J.: Princeton University Press; New York: Russell Sage Foundation.

Nelson, Julie. 1995. Review of *The Social Meaning of Money*, by Viviana A. Zelizer. *Contemporary Sociology* 24:382–84.

New York Times. 1995. "Harassment Case Tarnishes Cornell Star's Luster." March 23.

"Niles-Bement-Pond Company and Amalgamated Local No. 405, International Union, United Automobile, Aircraft and Agricultural Implement Workers of America, C.I.O. (November 29, 1951)." 1952. In *Decisions and Orders of the National Labor Relations Board*, 97:172. Washington, D.C.: United States Government Printing Office.

Persell, Caroline Hodges. 1994. "Robin M. Williams Lecture, 1994: Taking Society Seriously." *Sociological Forum* 9:641–57.

Petersen, Trond. 1992. "Payment Systems and the Structure of Inequality." *American Journal of Sociology* 98:67–104.

Ritzer, George. 1995. *Expressing America*. Thousand Oaks, Calif.: Pine Forge Press.

Rosten, Leo. 1970. *People I Have Loved, Known, or Admired*. New York: McGraw-Hill.

Rubin, Edward L., and Robert Cooter. 1994. *The Payment System: Cases, Materials and Issues*. St. Paul, Minn.: West Publishing Co.

Shell, Marc. 1995. *Art and Money*. Chicago: University of Chicago Press.

Smelser, Neil J., and Richard Swedberg, eds. 1994. *The Handbook of Economic Sociology*. Princeton, N.J.: Princeton University Press; New York: Russell Sage Foundation.

Sorensen, Aage B. 1994. "Firms, wages, and incentives." In Neil J. Smelser and Richard Swedberg (eds.), *The Handbook of Economic Sociology*: 504–528. Princeton, NJ: Princeton University Press; New York: Russell Sage Foundation.

Wall Street Journal. 1995. "New Credit Cards Base Appeals on Sexual Orientation and Race." November 6.

Wuthnow, Robert. 1994. *God and Mammon in America*. New York: Free Press.

Zelizer, Viviana A. 1979. *Morals and Markets: The Development of Life Insurance in the United States*. New York: Columbia University Press.

———. 1985. *Pricing the Priceless Child: The Changing Social Value of Children*. New York: Basic Books.

———. 1994. *The Social Meaning of Money*. New York: Basic Books.

8

Money, Power, and Sex

During the late 1990s, John Bowe, Marisa Bowe, Sabin Streeter, and their collaborators were interviewing Americans about their work. Following the model of Studs Terkel, their book, *Gig: Americans Talk about Their Jobs*, reports how people in a wide range of occupations feel about what they do for a living. Among them is stripper Sara Maxwell. At twenty-two, Maxwell moved to San Francisco after graduating from a small Virginia college and strip-danced for men at a club called Lusty Lady. The most lucrative part of her work involved erotic performances without physical contact in a private booth occupied by one man at a time. Maxwell noted how her work experience affected her relationships to men in general:

> Every guy I saw walking down the street turned into a customer in my eyes. Even my boyfriend exhibited customerlike qualities. He'd say something like, "You need to brush your hair." And I'd hear it as, "Brush your hair for me." With the implication being, in my mind, that he wanted to have some fun. And of course, he would also ask for sex, which further demoted him to the role of customer. (Bowe et al. 2000, 368)

Similarly, any time one of her male friends, intrigued by her occupation, expressed an interest in watching her work: "I told them that if I saw them there, we really couldn't be good friends anymore, because then they'd turn into customers" (ibid.). For Maxwell, the bridge from sex work to intimate relations crossed a very rocky stream. On one side, she engaged in sexual performances for pay, while on the other side, she tried to keep all suggestions of commercial payment out of her sexual relations.

During the same period when the authors of *Gig* were conducting their interviews on Americans' jobs, Gloria González-López began relevant interviews of her own. She examined, however, very different combinations of money, power, and sex. González-López talked with immigrant Mexican women and men living in Los Angeles about their intimate lives. Among other things, she found that Mexican wives who earned independent incomes in the United States reported changed sexual relations with their husbands.

For example, forty-three-year-old Azalea, an apartment manager, reported that when she and her husband first arrived from Mexico City, her spouse was the main provider. At that time, he forced her to have sex with him whether she wanted it or not. When González-López asked Azalea what she would now tell her husband if he pressured her to have sex, Azalea said emphatically, "I tell him 'no' because I support myself. If he supported me and he gave me all the things that I need, then perhaps one might have to do what they [men] tell you. But since here, all we women work, we support ourselves and we help our parents" (González-López 2005, 190).

Life in Los Angeles, however did not abolish moral concerns on the part of Mexican husbands and wives. Thirty-four-year-old Victoria, a traditional full-time housewife, described sexual relations with her husband as a *compromiso moral*: a moral obligation, in which she exchanged sexual favors for her husband's material support (ibid., 198). Meanwhile a number of Mexican men described their companions' economic bargaining over sexual intercourse as *chantaje*: blackmail (ibid., 283n2). Both husbands and wives recognized how delicate was the mingling of economic exchange with sexual activity. Both worried about the uneasy triangulation of money, power, and sex.

The *Yale Journal of Law and Feminism* "Sex for Sale" symposium identified many instances of uneasy matching between sexual intimacy and commercial transactions. My own contribution is not to multiply examples but to fit those particular sorts of difficulties into a more general pattern of negotiation between intimacy and economic activity. Let me stress four points:

1. The widespread belief that money corrupts intimacy blocks our ability to describe and explain how money, power, and sex actually interact.
2. The opposite belief—that sex operates like an ordinary market commodity—serves description and explanation no better.
3. The intersection of sex, money, and power does indeed generate confusion and conflict, but that is precisely because participants are simultaneously negotiating delicate, consequential, interpersonal relations and marking differences between those relations and others with which they could easily and dangerously be confused.
4. In everyday social life, people deal with these difficulties with a set of practices we can call "good matches."

At first glance, Sara Maxwell's experience and the Mexican immigrants' reports confirm the first belief: that commodification inevitably corrupts sexual intimacy. We should, however, be skeptical about any such absolute formulation. We should think instead about some of the complexities into which the mingling of sexual relations and economic activity leads us.

How to Misunderstand Money, Power, and Sex

Even scholars who study intimate relations and economic activity often become confused about these issues. When it comes to the mingling of intimacy (both sexual and otherwise) with economic transactions we find widespread misconceptions blocking analyses of how intimate relations and economic transactions actually mingle. Most notably, many observers assume that any mixing of intimate personal ties with economic transactions inevitably corrupts intimacy, and that invasion of commercial activities by intimate relations corrupts those activities as well.

Where do these concerns come from? They draw from two complementary, but partly independent misunderstandings. We can call them "separate spheres" and "hostile worlds." Separate spheres notions identify two distinct domains of social life that operate according to different principles: rationality, efficiency, and planning on one side; solidarity, sentiment, and impulse on the other. Economic activity belongs to the first sphere, sexual relations to the second.

Hostile-worlds beliefs say that when such separate spheres come into contact they contaminate each other. Their mixing, goes the argument, corrupts both; invasion of the sentimental world by instrumental rationality depletes that world, while introduction of sentiment into rational transactions produces inefficiency, favoritism, and cronyism. In this account, a sharp divide exists—and should exist—between intimate relations and economic transactions, since any contact between the two spheres contaminates both of them.

Separate-spheres and hostile-worlds ideas appear in social science, where generations of analysts have deplored what they saw as the erosion of authenticity and intimacy by an encroaching market. Outside of social science, the same themes frequently resound in moral discourse, when people explain bad behavior as a consequence of greed and call money the root of all evil.

In American law, the doctrines of separate spheres and hostile worlds show up in new versions. Courts, for example, regularly rule that economic transactions between spouses must count as free gifts rather than quid pro quo exchanges—at least until the moment of divorce (Zelizer 2005, 284–85; Williams 2005, 115–20; Siegel 1994). But practices based on separate spheres and hostile worlds figure in everyday life as well. Sexually intimate couples, for example, ordinarily take great care to signal (both to others and to each other) that they are not simply exchanging sex for economic rewards.

The notion that marketing intimacy corrupts it reappears across a wide range of intimate relations. In a 2005 *New York Times* column, for example, David Brooks laments the increasing use of separate checking accounts by married couples. He worries that husbands and wives are forgetting the distinction "between the individualistic ethos of the market and the communal ethos of the home." As a result, Brooks warns, "a union based on love can easily turn into a merger based on self-interest, where the main criterion becomes: Am I getting a good return on my investment?" (2005, A19).

Social scientists who are rightly suspicious of those widely held ideas have often replied, "nothing-but." They assert that intimate settings are nothing but special sorts of economies, nothing but arenas of power, or nothing but expressions of an underlying culture. The most common version says hostile worlds thinkers are wrong because the whole world is nothing but a single, big economy: there are markets everywhere. This includes families and intimate relations. In this nothing-but view, love, sex, and personal care are in fact commodities like all the rest (Becker 1996, 148–55; Posner 1992). As descriptions and explanations, theories of separate spheres, hostile worlds, and nothing-but fail badly. Actual studies of concrete social settings, from corporations to households, do not uncover separate spheres, segregated hostile worlds, markets everywhere, or any of the other nothing-buts.

The surprising thing about such views is their failure to recognize how regularly intimate relations coexist with economic transactions without apparent damage to either one: couples buy engagement rings; parents pay nannies or child-care workers to mind their children; adoptive parents pay lawyers and agencies to obtain babies; divorced spouses pay or receive alimony and child support payments; parents give their children allowances, subsidize their college educations, help them with their first mortgage, and offer them substantial bequests in their wills. Friends and relatives send gifts of money as wedding presents, and friends loan each other money. Immigrants dispatch hard-earned money as remittances to family back home.

Indeed, people who maintain intimate relations with each other regularly pool money, make joint purchases, invest shared funds, organize inheritances, and negotiate divisions of household work. Yet such relations are in no way similar to stock exchanges or retail markets.

In contrast to hostile-worlds and nothing-but arguments, I propose an alternative explanation for the mingling of economic transactions with intimate relations: good matches. Good matches replies to both that economic activity and intimacy do intersect all the time, do not behave like minimarkets, but only work well when people make good matches between the two. By a good match I do not mean that you and I would approve of the bargain or that the match is equal and just. Instead, I mean that the match is viable: it gets the economic work of the relationship done and sustains the relationship. A set of economic transactions that would reinforce a husband-wife bond, for example, could ruin a relationship between boss and secretary. Relations matter so much that people work hard to match them with appropriate forms of economic activity and clear markers of those relations' character.

Good matches between intimate relations and economic transactions are interesting to watch. Seen close up, they depend heavily on negotiation between the partners, such as husband-wife, boss-secretary, doctor-patient, or call girl–customer. Matching practices also vary significantly from one class, ethnic, or cultural setting to another.

Still, three main features stand out in good matches:

1. The economic transactions distinguish the relationship from others that it might be confused with, and which might damage the

relationship itself. An example is confusion between a prostitute's fee and the economic contributions of occasional lovers.

2. Good matches demonstrate and enact agreements between the partners in a relationship. They share an understanding of what that relationship is. For example, wealthy courting couples, in which each person can easily afford to pay for all their joint expenses, usually work out an understanding of what constitutes an equitable share of the costs. When going on a vacation, for instance, who pays for the hotel, or the restaurants, or for travel?

3. Good matches identify the relationship clearly to any third party that is involved. An example is which third party pays for what in an engagement or wedding party: the ring, the dress, the dinner, the band.

In any particular situation, obviously, good matches depend on the stock of meanings, markers, and practices actually available in the local milieu. Beyond cultural particularism, however, one can identify some regularities that apply very widely.

INTIMACY: NARROW OR BROAD, DURABLE OR FLEETING

Think of intimate relations as varying along two dimensions: breadth and duration. A narrow relationship involves only one or a few shared practices, including economic practices. A broad relationship involves a wide range of practices, including economic practices. Speaking of relations that involve sexual intimacy, we might place prostitution at the narrow end and membership in a promiscuous community at the broad end.

Intimate relations also range in duration from almost instantaneous to very long term. At the fleeting end of this dimension we might find college students' one-night "hook-ups"; at the durable end, stable marriages. So far as I can tell, broad but short-term relations are either rare or nonexistent. Yet a relationship can remain narrow over a long period, as is the case of some sexual liaisons. Or it can be both broad and durable, as in many forms of cohabitation. Duration does not necessarily produce broadening of an intimate relationship. Breadth, however, requires duration.

Why do breadth and duration matter? A relationship that involves a wide range of activities, including economic activities, poses greater problems of management than a narrow one; performance or malfeasance in one regard has repercussions across other shared activities. A long-term relationship, whether broad or narrow, casts shadows of both past and future on current interactions; both the relationship's accumulated meanings and the parties' stakes in its future affect what happens today. Although breadth and duration by no means guarantee harmony and happiness, they make the ramifications of current interactions much more extensive.

For my purposes, the implications are clear. A wide variety of interpersonal relationships combine sexual and economic activity. Where the relations are narrow and short term, we tend to call them sex work (Stinchcombe 1994). Where they are broad and long term, we tend to call them households. Participants in these different relations take care to distinguish them from other relations with which they might easily and hurtfully be confused, share definitions of the relation, recognize practical implications of their shared definitions, and identify their relationship clearly to relevant third parties.

Our conceptual space thus identifies four quite different kinds of relationships: narrow and brief, narrow and durable, broad and brief, broad and durable. Let us look closely at concrete examples drawn from three of these four types: narrow and brief, narrow and durable, broad and durable.

In the narrow, brief type, we find people working hard to produce good matches. Here we see sex workers who earn their living from the sale of explicitly sexual services, including telephone and cybersex, production of pornography, live sex shows, erotic massage, escort services, and a wide variety of prostitution. One might imagine that a single relationship underlies this diverse range of occupations: a short-term quid pro quo exchange of sex for money. But that would be wrong.

Contrary to the hostile-worlds line that whores will do anything for a buck, in fact both providers and consumers of sex work make impressively fine distinctions among its many varieties. Sex workers care about differentiating what they do from the activities of other sex workers as well as from their nonprofessional sexual relations. To take just one example, listen to how Heart, a phone sex operator, describes her job:

> We're not like those streetwalkers—crawling down the street in the middle of the night. . . . We work in an office. I never touch a cock. I can't get a single disease. I can't get attacked. I'm not a prostitute. I can sit here, read a magazine and just moan occasionally . . . and still get paid. (Rich and Guidroz 2000, 35, 43; see also Flowers 1998)

Sex workers do not simply distinguish the sexual service itself, but who their clients are, their relationship to them, its duration and breadth, the amount and forms of payment, and the overall meaning of their work. Indeed the monetary payment itself signals the form of the relationship to both provider and consumer. Annie Sprinkle,[1] an erotic masseuse interviewed by Wendy Chapkis in the early 1990s, reflected on how money mattered in her relations to clients:

> The money is important. And it's not because we are desperate for it, like we're on drugs and need the money, 'cause we aren't, or that we are

money hungry. . . . But somehow when the money is there we can have a fabulous time with these people, really give and be loving and totally be of service. And if the money isn't there, forget it, don't want you in the same room with me. It's so weird. . . . What is it that the money provides? Maybe it's just a clear exchange, especially when you are with someone that you don't like that much, somehow if they give to you, you can give to them. You've been compensated in a clear, clean way. I mean I can actually like a person if they pay me that I wouldn't if they didn't. It's amazing. (Quoted in Chapkis 1997, 92)

Not only the form of payment but also the location, dress, personal style, and practices of the service provider identify the special properties of the relationships between sex workers and their clients. Street walkers, for example, differentiate sharply among clients, their relationship to them, sexual acts they will or will not perform, forms of payment, and locations of work. In all these cases, of course, one or both of the partners sometimes seek to broaden or lengthen the relationship involved. At that point further distinctions come into play. Sex workers live in a world of highly differentiated and well-marked social ties.[2]

Long but Narrow Sexual Relations

Some sexual relations, however, maintain their narrow character but last a long time. The most obvious examples are kept women and kept men. Although such relationships almost always cover a wider range of economic activity than the sex work I have just been describing, in general the parties focus their relationship on sexual activity.

Consider the case of Deborah Vandevelde and Thomas Colucci, a fifty-three-year-old wealthy Long Island businessman, married with two teenage children. In 1999, smitten by Vandevelde's beauty, Colucci showered her with gifts and set her up in a couple of Manhattan apartments. They signed a contract by which Colucci paid her as if she were an employee of one of his businesses. Two years later, however, after he suspected that Vandevelde was seeing another man, Colucci stopped paying the rent and all other expenses.

At that point, Vandevelde sued Colucci in a $3.5 million breach-of-contract suit. Vandevelde asserted that while their relationship lasted, Colucci "enjoyed unrestricted sex . . . while promising her financial security" (Maull 2002). On October 1, 2002, the *New York Post* ran a story on the case under a characteristically sassy headline: *Mistress: More Sugar, Daddy* (Gregorian 2002). Meanwhile, in an affidavit filed in Manhattan State Supreme Court, Colucci argued that since their contract was an agreement to facilitate adultery, it was illegal (Maull 2002; Peterson 2002).

The judge in this case, Manhattan State Supreme Court Justice Leland DeGrasse, struck a delicate balance between commercial and moral considerations. First, he separated Vandevelde's breach of contract suit from a different suit for unpaid rent by the owners of the building in which Vandevelde lived. In the latter case, he ruled against Colucci, ordering him to pay more than $50,000 in back rent (Peterson 2002).

Many legal cases deal with this sort of delicate interplay between business and pleasure. Other longer-term but narrow sexual relations raise many of the same moral and legal questions. For a different perspective, we might consider the relationship between a woman and her gynecologist or a man and his urologist. Although some might wonder whether these qualify as sexual, the parallels and differences with other long-term narrow relations are revealing.

In the case of gynecologists, practitioners take great care to limit their relationship with patients to the strictly professional. Consider the elaborate efforts to assure that the vaginal inspection, certainly a sexually connected event, remains within proper boundaries. James Henslin and Mae Biggs (1971) offer a detailed description of the vaginal exam, identifying the extent to which physicians and nurses depersonalize the situation, thus keeping it as far removed as possible from other similar sexual situations with which it could be confused.[3]

The gynecologists' official code of ethics, furthermore, forbids any confusion by barring interactions that others might construe as sexually improper. Among the code's guidelines are the following:

- Sexual contact or a romantic relationship between a physician and a current patient is always unethical. . . .
- Examinations should be performed with only the necessary amount of physical contact required to obtain data for diagnosis and treatment. . . .
- Physicians should avoid sexual innuendo and sexually provocative remarks. . . .
- It is important for physicians to self-monitor for any early indications that the barrier between normal sexual feelings and inappropriate behavior is not being maintained. These indicators might include special scheduling, seeing a patient outside of normal office hours or outside the office, driving a patient home, or making sexually explicit comments about patients. (American College of Obstetricians and Gynecologists 2004, 102–3)

Thus, long-term but narrow sexually tinged relations exist and, like sex work, have their own distinct properties. No doubt it is already obvious that the two differ significantly from durable, broad relations involving sexual activity. Long-term cohabitation—straight, gay, or lesbian—provides the prime example. Here we find couples engaged in a multitude of economic transactions without which their households would not survive.

Contradicting hostile-worlds visions of households as exclusive domains of sentiment and solidarity in which any intrusion of economic calculation threatens intimacy, household members routinely share in production, consumption, distribution, and transfers of assets. Living together necessarily produces shared economic problems, opportunities, rights, and obligations for everyone who takes part. Once a household contains more than a couple, things get more complicated: Relations to third parties such as children, careworkers, or aging parents start influencing household dynamics significantly. Inside complex households, relational work never ends.

Households differ from other sites of economic activity, however, in three crucial regards. First, continuous cohabitation creates more extensive mutual knowledge, influence, rights, and obligations than usually develop in other economic settings. Second, negotiations within households take place with a longer future in view and with greater consequences for long-term reciprocity than characteristically occur within other economic settings. Third, in American law, economic transactions within households occupy a substantially different position from those that take place among households, between households and other economic units, or entirely outside of households (Zelizer 2005).

Sexual relations connect strongly with most households' other interactions. Meg Luxton offers a surprising insight into these links. In her 1980 study of three generations of working-class housewives from a mining town in northern Manitoba, Luxton documented the women's extensive and intensive domestic labor, which included washing, ironing, vacuuming, dusting, tidying up, planning meals, cooking, baking, sewing, budgeting, shopping, and caring for children. In this traditional setting, where women worked hard at home while men brought in the cash, sex often turned into a bargaining chip. As one woman reported: "When I want something for the house, like a new washing machine or something, then I just make love like crazy for a while and then stop. Then I tell him what I want and say that if he wants more loving he has to buy it" (Luxton 1980).

From Canadians in northern Manitoba to Mexicans in southern California, then, a range of studies documents the interplay between sexual relations and household economic activity.

Kenneth Feinberg, the lawyer who administered the United States government's 9/11 fund, had to recognize that interplay indirectly. Although at first he tried to base awards to survivors of 9/11 victims exclusively on loss of the victims' financial contributions, he soon found himself considering the economic value of unpaid domestic labor and of companionship. That involved him in deciding which sorts of survivors from broken couples did and did not qualify for compensation, and what losses those survivors had actually sustained. Feinberg reached his limit, however, when a bereaved husband essentially requested funds to hire prostitutes as replacements for his lost wife's sexual services. Feinberg reported the man's request: "I don't want to sound gross, but there is something else that I pay for, or can pay for. You can figure that out. . . . [T]here are other services that could be replaced, but we're not going to go into that either" (Feinberg 2005).

At that point, even the cool-headed, generous Feinberg drew a hostile-worlds line and rejected his request.

Sex In-Between

In the space defined by duration and breadth, intermediate cases exist. Some relations involve broader ranges of economic activity and greater duration than sex work but far less of either than cohabiting households. In *Making Ends Meet*, their landmark study of how low-income and welfare single mothers survive financially, Kathryn Edin and Laura Lein provide unusual glimpses into how these women carve out a whole range of economic ties to the men in their lives.

Edin and Lein make three observations of great consequence for this paper's topic: first, that relationships to men played a significant part in the household finances of these mothers; second, that the women made strong distinctions among their various relationships to men who are or have been their sexual partners; and third, that they developed distinct systems of payment and obligations corresponding to these different relationships. In field observations and interviews of almost four hundred mothers, Edin and Lein identified a whole system of categories distinguishing the women's different relationships to men, from absent fathers to live-in boyfriends to prostitution, with other distinctions in between.

Perhaps the most remarkable are the ties to live-in boyfriends: These men—not legally married to the mother and usually not the father of any of her children—are expected to contribute regular amounts of cash and in-kind goods. In addition to weekly cash outlays of $20 or $30 for incidentals, for instance, one Chicago mother's boyfriend helped pay her phone bill and pay for her furniture; he also bought gifts for her children. In return for their contributions, boyfriends get a place to stay, sexual companionship, some meals, and the opportunity to "play Daddy" for the women's children (Edin and Lein 1997, 155).

The arrangement is clear: boyfriends who do not pay, mothers repeatedly told Edin and Lein, "can't stay" (ibid.). Occasionally the boundaries between "serial boyfriends" and prostitution blurred: one mother explained, for instance, that her reliance on boyfriends "isn't for love, and it isn't just for money. I guess I'd call it social prostitution" (Edin and Lein 1997, 157). Nevertheless, most mothers set clear distinguishing markers between real prostitution and their relationship to a boyfriend. "Turning tricks" or "street walking" meant one-night stands without a long-term relationship to the man; they involved short-term cash in exchange for short-term sex (ibid.). To each form of sexual relationship corresponded a somewhat different set of monetary transfers.

In a follow-up study with Maria Kefalas of 162 low-income single mothers, Edin further demonstrated that the women insisted on regular financial contributions from their longer-term male companions. Edin and Kefalas found, furthermore, that a large number of couples' blowups resulted precisely from the incompatibility of the men's economic performances with their household privileges and demands (Edin and Kefalas 2005).

The comparison of long-term cohabiting households with the more fleeting households described by Edin, Lein, and Kefalas yields an unexpected bonus. It shows us that the matches are by no means automatic consequences of cultural understandings or coercion but emerge from incessant bargaining among household members, especially sexually related couples. The bargains involve exercises of power.

GOOD, BAD, AND UNCERTAIN MATCHES

Not that all matches work, or that any economic transaction is compatible with any sexual relation. On the contrary, people work hard to negotiate the right match between economy and sexual intimacy, looking for economic arrangements that confirm their understandings of what the relation is about, and that sustain those relations. Is this person a gold digger or a real lover? Does this sexual relation involve caring or exploitation? When is it acceptable for a man to give a sex worker gifts instead of cash? And what does it mean for a sex worker to turn down a customer's fee? When a courting couple becomes sexually involved, how should they manage their entertainment expenses? When relations go sour, furthermore, people start begrudging their economic contributions, to the detriment of those relations. Sometimes they end up in court.

In the last analysis, the matching of sex, money, and power turns out to have common properties with a wide variety of interpersonal relations that involve economic activity. In everyday social life and in legal proceedings as well, people undertake serious efforts to match forms of economic activity effectively with relevant social relations, and to distinguish those relations from others with which they might easily and hurtfully be confused. The matching process always involves some exercise of power by the immediate parties to the relationship, and sometimes by third parties. Yes, managing the intersection of sex, money, and power presents serious problems. But they are problems we and other people solve every day. Far from being taboo, that intersection belongs to life itself.

Notes

Viviana A. Zelizer, "Money, Power, and Sex," *Yale Journal of Law and Feminism* 18 (2006): 303ff. Reprinted with permission.

1. The articulate Annie Sprinkle is of course far more than an ordinary sex worker. Successively prostitute, porn star, performance artist, sex expert, and activist, she is the author of at least four books, including *Dr. Sprinkle's Spectacular Sex*, not to mention Web sites, DVDs, and sexually related products.

2. See, for example, Brewis and Linstead 2000; Frank 2002; Hill 1993; Kempadoo 2004; Meckel 1995; Wilson 2004; Bernstein 1999, 2005; Hausbeck and Brents 2000; Lever and Dolnick 2000; Massey and Hope 2005; Murphy and Venkatesh 2006; Sanchez 1997; Trautner 2005. On sexual payments among men, see, for example, Aggleton 1999; Boag 2003; Chauncey 1994; Humphreys 1970; Moodie with Ndatshe 1994; Chauncey 1985; Reiss 1961; Sanchez 1997.

3. For a critique of this analysis, see Kapsalis 1997.

References

Aggleton, Peter, ed. 1999. *Men Who Sell Sex: International Perspectives on Male Prostitution and HIV/AIDS*. Philadelphia: Temple University Press.

American College of Obstetricians and Gynecologists. 2004. *Ethics in Obstetrics and Gynecology*. 2d ed. Washington, D.C.: American College of Obstetricians and Gynecologists.

Becker, Gary. 1996. *Accounting for Tastes*. Cambridge, Mass.: Harvard University Press.

Bernstein, Elizabeth. 1999. "What's Wrong with Prostitution? What's Right with Sex Work? Comparing Markets in Female Sexual Labor." 10 *Hastings Women's L.J.* 91.

———. 2005. "Desire, Demand, and the Commerce of Sex." In *Regulating Sex: The Politics of Intimacy and Identity*, edited by Elizabeth Bernstein and Laurie Shaffner. New York: Routledge.

Boag, Peter. 2003. *Same-Sex Affairs: Constructing and Controlling Homosexuality in the Pacific Northwest*. Berkeley: University of California Press.

Bowe, John, Marisa Bowe, and Sabin Streeter, eds. 2000. *Gig: Americans Talk about Their Jobs at the Turn of the Millennium*. New York: Crown Publishers.

Brewis, Joanna, and Stephen Linstead. 2000. *Sex, Work and Sex Work: Eroticizing Organization*. London: Routledge.

Brooks, David. 2005. Editorial, "To Have and to Hold, for Richer for Poorer." *New York Times*, March 1.

Chauncey, George. 1985. "Christian Brotherhood or Sexual Perversion? Homosexual Identities and the Construction of Sexual Boundaries in the World War One Era." 19 *J. Soc. Hist.* 189.

———. 1994. *Gay New York: Gender, Urban Culture, and the Makings of the Gay Male World, 1890–1940*. New York: Basic Books.

Edin, Kathryn, and Maria Kefalas. 2005. *Promises I Can Keep: Why Poor Women Put Motherhood before Marriage*. Berkeley: University of California Press.

Edin, Kathryn, and Laura Lein. 1997. *Making Ends Meet: How Single Mothers Survive Welfare and Low-Wage Work*. New York: Russell Sage Foundation.

Feinberg, Kenneth R. 2005. *What Is Life Worth? The Unprecedented Effort to Compensate the Victims of 9/11*. New York: Public Affairs.

Flowers, Amy. 1998. *The Fantasy Factory: An Insider's View of the Phone Sex Industry*. Philadelphia: University of Pennsylvania Press.

Frank, Katharine. 2002. *G-Strings and Sympathy: Strip Club Regulars and Male Desire*. Durham, N.C.: Duke University Press.

González-López, Gloria. 2005. *Erotic Journeys: Mexican Immigrants and Their Sex Lives*. Berkeley: University of California Press.

Gregorian, Dareh. 2002. "Mistress: More Sugar, Daddy." *New York Post*, October 1.

Hausbeck, Kathryn, and Barbara G. Brents. 2000. "Inside Nevada's Brothel Industry." In *Sex For Sale: Prostitution, Pornography, and the Sex Industry*, edited by Ronald Weitzer. New York: Routledge.

Henslin, James M., and Mae A. Biggs. 1971. "Dramaturgical Desexualization: The Sociology of the Vaginal Examination." In *Studies in the Sociology of Sex*, edited by James M. Henslin. New York, Appleton-Century-Crofts.

Hill, Marilynn Wood. 1993. *Their Sisters' Keepers: Prostitution in New York City, 1830–1870*. Berkeley: University of California Press.

Humphreys, Laud. 1970. *Tearoom Trade: Impersonal Sex in Public Places*. Chicago: Aldine.

Kapsalis, Terri. 1997. *Public Privates: Performing Gynecology from Both Ends of the Speculum*. Durham, N.C.: Duke University Press.

Kempadoo, Kamala. 2004. *Sexing the Caribbean: Gender, Race and Sexual Labor*. New York: Routledge.

Lever, Janet, and Deanna Dolnick. 2000. "Clients and Call Girls: Seeking Sex and Intimacy." In *Sex For Sale: Prostitution, Pornography, and the Sex Industry*, edited by Ronald Weitzer. New York: Routledge.

Massey, Joseph E., and Trina L. Hope. 2005. "A Personal Dance: Emotional Labor, Fleeting Relationships, and Social Power in a Strip Bar." In *Together Alone: Personal Relationships in Public Places*, edited by Calvin Morrill et al. Berkeley: University of California Press.

Maull, Samuel. 2002. "Businessman Must Pay Ex-Girlfriend's Rent." Associated Press, September 26.

Meckel, Mary V. 1995. *A Sociological Analysis of the California Taxi-Dancer: The Hidden Halls*. Lewiston N.Y.: Edwin Mellen Press.

Moodie, T. Dunbar, with Vivienne Ndatshe. 1994. *Going for Gold: Men, Mines, and Migration*. Berkeley: University of California Press.

Murphy, Alexandra K., and Sudhir Alladi Venkatesh. 2006. "Vice Careers: The Changing Contours of Sex Work in New York City." 29 *Qualitative Soc.*

Peterson, Helen. 2002. "True Love or Just Lust?" *New York Daily News*, September 27.

Posner, Richard. 1992. *Sex and Reason*. Cambridge, Mass.: Harvard University Press.

Reiss, Albert J., Jr. 1961. "The Social Integration of Queers and Peers." 9 *Soc. Probs.* 102.

Rich, Grant Jewell, and Kathleen Guidroz. 2000. "Smart Girls Who Like Sex: Telephone Sex Workers." In *Sex for Sale: Prostitution, Pornography, and the Sex Industry*, edited by Ronald Weitzer. New York: Routledge.

Sanchez, Lisa E. 1997. "Boundaries of Legitimacy: Sex, Violence, Citizenship, and Community in a Local Sexual Economy." 22 *Law & Soc. Inquiry* 543.

Siegel, Reva B. 1994. "The Modernization of Marital Status Law: Adjudicating Wives' Rights to Earnings, 1860–1930." 82 *GEO. L.J.* 2,127.

Stinchcombe, Arthur L. 1994. "Prostitution, Kinship, and Illegitimate Work." 23 *Contemp. Soc.* 856.

Trautner, Mary Nell. 2005. "Doing Gender, Doing Class: The Performance of Sexuality in Exotic Dance Clubs." *Gender and Society* 19:771–88.

Williams, Joan. 2005. *Unbending Gender: Why Family and Work Conflict and What to Do about It*. Oxford: Oxford University Press.

Wilson, Ara. 2004. *The Intimate Economies of Bangkok: Tomboys, Tycoons, and Avon Ladies in the Global City*. Berkeley: University of California Press.

Zelizer, Viviana A. 2005. *The Purchase of Intimacy*. Princeton, N.J.: Princeton University Press.

PART THREE

Intimate Economies

When divorcing couples negotiate their troubles in court, intimate economies go public. Legal reckoning of a household's work and finances turns routine transactions into openly contested exchanges. Consider the divorce case of *deCastro v. deCastro*, 616 N.E.2d 52 (Mass. 1993). At issue was the wife's claim to an equitable share of the couple's marital property. Jean, a schoolteacher, and Edson, a corporate employee, had married in 1963. Jean left her job to raise the couple's three children, while Edson launched a successful business venture, fully subsidized by the couple's joint savings. In 1980, Edson left Jean for another woman but still continued to visit the marital home and pay the family's expenses. Jean meanwhile returned to work as a school librarian, contributing her entire salary to the household.

After Jean filed for divorce, Edson contested the judge's decision to split his corporation's stock equally between the parties. By then the deCastros had accumulated significant wealth, including eight cars, their own airplane, and a boat. Edson contended that his "genius" in the computer industry and "super-contribution" to the joint estate entitled him to a greater portion of the assets. On appeal, the judge's initial decision was affirmed. The appellate court disparaged Edson's argument as an outdated and illegitimate "resurrection of the discarded idea that the wage earner is entitled to most if not all the benefits of the paid work." In its decision, the court referred back to the judge's detailed itemization of Jean's nonfinancial yet equally exceptional household contributions. Among other duties, the judge stated:

> The wife assumed ninety percent of the responsibility for the physical and mental needs of the children. She was responsible for all cooking and care of the interior of the house, and for the maintenance of her car . . . for entertaining both her family and the husband's, and for purchasing gifts. The wife transported the children to school, athletic events, dancing school, music lessons and other events. . . . [She purchased] the children's clothing, the food, and any household necessities, and managed the money for these and other expenses. She attended ninety percent of the athletic events, parent-teacher conferences . . . accompanied the children on college tours. . . . [She] was also responsible for the religious and moral upbringing of the children.

Divorce transforms the character of a couple's relationship and in so doing redefines their earlier economic exchanges. In *deCastro*, a wife's ordinary household tasks become legal evidence of her valuable contribution to the marital partnership, and thus implicitly acquire economic value. As spouses become "exes," legal principle and everyday practice combine to create a new kind of intimate economy. Divorce in fact generates its own distinct monies—alimony and child support—as well as special guidelines on how those monies should be transferred from one former spouse to the other and to any children involved. As a result, divorce leads to new kinds of disputes over domestic monies and changing strategies for negotiating rights over economic resources.

The study of intimate economies brings us into the world of households and their breakup as well as various forms of sexually tinged relationships. As some of the chapters in the earlier sections of this book show, my work on life insurance and money had already touched on some features of intimate economic life. After finishing those projects, I saw clearly that there was much more to do on how people connected money—and more generally economic activity—with their varying social relations, especially intimate ties. That became the project of my next book, *The Purchase of Intimacy* (2005).

As with the pricing of life, the economics of intimacy poses a set of delicate and often uncomfortable questions. How should we value economic exchanges with our intimates? Will not intimacy be spoiled if it is subjected to any form of economic calculation? More specifically, what sorts of monetary exchanges are appropriate for sexual partners? How should husbands and wives or unmarried cohabitants talk about and manage household work and monies? Is housework exclusively a labor of love, or does it count as "real" work? What about kids? What sorts of household work should children be doing, and should they receive any compensation? In many of these quandaries, as exemplified by *deCastro*, issues of gender loom large. That case also shows how the law sets forth its own answers to such questions: despite her husband's protestation, both courts agreed, for instance, that Jean's household activities held significant economic value.

As the essays in this section point out, standard responses to such debates fall mainly into the two categories that I call separate-spheres/hostile-worlds and nothing-but economic arguments. Intimacy is certainly an area that separate-spheres/hostile-worlds proponents have been especially keen to protect from economic activity. Critics, moralists, and social scientists at large have frequently thought not only that money corrupts, but more generally that economic rationality and the sentiments attached to intimate relations rest on fundamentally contradictory principles. To mix both, they argue, brings trouble. It is not only that economic considerations taint intimate relations, but in this view the reverse is also true: the introduction of sentiment and intimate connections threatens rational economic transactions.

Unfettered by such concerns, proponents of nothing-but economic accounts comfortably approach intimacy as another field of economic rationality. Indeed, some analysts contend that self-conscious revamping of households as rational economic organizations would improve their efficiency and rectify unjust inequalities. Other scholars offer provocative interpretations of hostile-worlds practices as efficiency-driven strategies for keeping intimate interactions segregated from explicit cost-benefit accounting. In his book *The Household*, legal scholar Robert C. Ellickson, for instance, argues that a couple's reliance on gift exchange instead of formal contracting as a mechanism for managing their everyday interactions greatly lowers transaction costs. "Participants who are confident that their spontaneous reciprocal exchanges will be mutually advantageous," Ellickson suggests, "can avoid the hassle of negotiating, interpreting, and enforcing explicit terms of trade" (2008, 104–5). Moreover, Ellickson notes, gift exchange has the advantage of being "money-free," which in his view further increases its effectiveness: "Intimates," he writes, "typically have a strong aversion to engaging in monetized transactions with one another" (2008, 105).

The four chapters in this section advance a very different explanation of intimate economies, which I call "connected lives." Intimacy and economic transactions, I argue, do not stand at two opposing corners like hostile pugilists. Instead, people constantly mingle their most intimate relations with economic activities, including monetary payments; households, for instance, are hotbeds of economic interaction. Instead of menacing alien intrusions, economic transactions repeatedly serve to create, define, sustain, and challenge our multiple intimate relations.

Nothing-but economic arguments do recognize that economic activity plays a significant role in intimate relations. However, by relying on universal principles of explanation, they fail to capture or explain the widely observed variations in combinations of economic transactions and intimate relations. This section's chapters explore such variation, showing how in their everyday life people put intense effort into finding the right match between their various intimate ties and specific kinds of economic transactions, including distinct forms of monetary payments. It is not, as Ellickson and others have suggested, that intimates necessarily avoid monetary transactions; instead, what they worry about is the wrong kind of payment. They fret, for example, over distinctions among payments as compensation, entitlements, or gifts. When you handed me that hundred dollar bill, were you paying me for my services, giving me my weekly allowance, or displaying your generosity?

In this context, separate-spheres/hostile-worlds everyday discourse can be understood as one kind of differentiating strategy. That is why we often find people invoking hostile-worlds doctrines to establish or maintain boundaries between intimate relations that could be easily confused. They say, "I'm not a hired maid; I'm a mother to your kid," "I'm not a whore; I'm your date," "You are not my lover; you're my lawyer," "This is friendship, not business," to protect valued relationships from others that seem bad or inappropriate.

While this blinds participants to the actual economic activity going on, the rhetoric asserts valued relational distinctions.

To be sure, the intersection of intimate relations and economic transactions do not make our "connected lives" easy, nor does the mingling always work out for the best. People sometimes cheat, hurt, disappoint, and fail their intimate partners. The discussion of sexually tinged relationships in the previous section already pointed to some of the complex variations in the matching of sexual intimacy and economic transactions.

Writing about intimate economies engaged me in unexpected dialogues. Both in the United States and abroad I spoke about my work to a varied range of audiences in law schools, business schools, seminars for the children of exceptionally wealthy families, international children's rights experts, and careworkers, as well as to a wide variety of social scientists and media outlets. In February 2006, at a conference on "Sex for Sale" at the Yale Law School, I even found myself on a panel with activists fighting prostitution and sex trafficking, an award-winning sex educator and pornographer, and a celebrity porn star and producer, along with legal scholars and other social scientists. Again unexpectedly, my arguments on the sexual economy have linked me with HIV experts and other analysts concerned with adolescent sexual practices in rural Malawi, practices that involve regular exchanges of sex for money and other material gifts, and yet remain distinct from prostitution (see, e.g., Poulin 2006). In 2009, a Spanish translation of *The Purchase of Intimacy* (2005) as *La negociación de la intimidad* (Fondo de Cultura Económica) took me to my hometown of Buenos Aires for my first professional appearance there. In yet another pleasantly surprising turn, the book met with much interest from the local media. And it started a valuable conversation with an energetic group of Argentine scholars studying economic activity with innovative approaches.

"The Purchase of Intimacy" was my first attempt to think about the problems of intimate economies. I prepared the paper for a session on commodification at the 1997 annual meetings of the American Anthropological Association during a year spent at the Institute for Advanced Study. What began as a detour from another project (studying corporate compensation systems) turned into a prolonged exploration of intimate payments that culminated in the book that bears the same title. The article concentrates on sexually tinged economic transactions, proposing a new explanation for the entanglement of sexual relations and economic concerns. Far from protecting their sexual intimacy from economic concerns, I show how people regularly mark the specific character of their various sexual relations—courtship, marriage, prostitution—with money or other economic transfers. The essay also raises the issue of what happens when the law gets hold of intimate relations: how do judges, juries, and legal scholars deal with the intersections between intimacy and economic activity? That analysis suggests a sort of shadow play where legal decisions and everyday practices influence each other while maintaining significant differences.

After *The Purchase of Intimacy* had already been published, I prepared "Do Markets Poison Intimacy?" for a more general audience. By then, my analysis of intimate economies had expanded from its earlier focus on sexual transactions to include a wide array of intimate connections, including households and caring relations, as well as close interactions with professionals, such as lawyers or psychotherapists. The article offers a framework for thinking about the variable connections between different kinds of intimate relations and various kinds of economic activities.

"Kids and Commerce" shifts the focus to children. As with "The Priceless Child Revisited," this chapter documents children's deep involvement in a variety of economic transactions, including production, but also consumption and distribution. While hostile-worlds theories insist that children's innocence should be protected from the ravages of the market, in reality children have active economic lives of a particular kind. The essay differentiates exploitative child labor from children's routine economic activities.

"Intimacy in Economic Organizations" reverses the emphasis of the earlier chapters, moving away from the analysis of economic transactions in intimate relations to studying intimacy within economic organizations. Just as some analysts have feared the commodification of intimacy, others worry about "intimization," the improper intrusion of intimacy in what are supposed to be efficiency-driven, impersonal organizations. The article asks why people worry so much about the presence of intimacy in organizations and reviews the evidence on its actual effects.

Overall, these four essays propose new approaches to the study of intimate economies. Similar concerns emerge with the provision of personal care, to be discussed in the next section.

References

Ellickson, Robert C. 2008. *The Household: Informal Order around the Hearth*. Princeton, N.J.: Princeton University Press.

Poulin, Michelle. 2006. "Giving and Getting: Money Exchange in Intimate Partnerships among Youth in Southern Malawi." In *Bridging Disciplines, Spanning the World: Approaches to Inequality, Identity, and Institutions*, edited by Rachel Beatty Riedl, Sada Askartova, and Kristine Mitchell. Princeton Institute for International and Regional Studies, Monograph Series 4. Princeton, N.J.: PIIRS.

9

Do Markets Poison Intimacy?

Myth: Economic activity corrupts intimate relations, and intimate relations make economic activity inefficient. Fact: People constantly mingle intimacy and economic activity without corruption.

In March 2005, a remarkable case stirred the courts and press of Florida before becoming a national cause célèbre. After years of struggle out of the limelight, Theresa Schiavo's husband and her close kin engaged in a furious public battle over whether to maintain the brain-damaged woman's life support. At stake was not only her life, but also who had the right to decide what sort of care she should receive.

Fifteen years earlier, Terry Schiavo had collapsed, never to regain consciousness. Before that, her parents, Mary and Bob Schindler, had helped the young couple financially with moving expenses and housing, and providing other forms of support. After Terry's collapse, they shared grueling daily care-giving tasks with her husband, Michael. But the sharing stopped and the fighting began in 1993. At that point, Michael won a million-dollar medical malpractice suit, which included $750,000 in economic damages for Terry—held in a trust fund—and $300,000 for Michael, for loss of his wife's companionship. The Schindlers claimed that they had equal rights both to decisions about Terry's care and to compensation for the care they provided.

The Schiavo case eventually became a national legal and political struggle over the "right to life." Long before that, however, the parties were fighting over who had the right to provide care, the right to decide the type of care, and the right to receive compensation for that care.

Both participants and commentators often explain such struggles by saying that the intrusion of economic motives into intimate social relations corrupts those relations. Where intimate relations appear in corporations and other economic organizations, observers often draw a mirror-image moral: mix intimacy with economic rationality, and you get inefficiency, favoritism, and failure. As I discuss in my book *The Purchase of Intimacy*, both ideas are wrong, yet both point to the difficulty of finding the right match between intimacy and economic activity.

MONEY AND INTIMACY

Surprisingly similar issues arose in cases of compensation for victims of 9/11 and their survivors. Take the case of fifty-year-old Patricia McAneney, who worked at an insurance company on the ninety-fourth floor of One World Trade Center. She died in the 9/11 disaster. McAneney and her partner, Margaret Cruz, had lived together for almost twenty years. In response to 9/11, New York agencies recognized such domestic partnerships; New York's crime victim board, the Red Cross, and other organizations awarded Cruz $80,000. The federal fund, in contrast, generally appointed a spouse or relative as the victim's single official representative. In McAneney's case, her brother James claimed and received compensation for his sister's death. Cruz bitterly contested the Victim Compensation Fund's award to James.

Cruz submitted her own statement to Kenneth Feinberg, who administered the 9/11 Compensation Fund, detailing the couple's relationship. As a result, Feinberg doubled the original award on behalf of McAneney to about half a million dollars, basing his new estimate on a two-person household. But the fund still paid the additional money to James, as his sister's official representative. James refused to release any of the money to Cruz. At that point, Cruz filed a lawsuit against James, claiming that at least $253,000 of the award belonged to her. James rejected that claim, saying that under New York State law, Cruz had no rights to any of his sister's property: the two women had no legally recognizable bond, they had never registered as domestic partners, and Patricia had died without leaving a will.

Cruz replied that "her status as the domestic partner of the victim is authenticated by the fact that they lived together since 1985; that they recently occupied the same house in Pomona, NY; that they both paid the mortgage and shared basic household expenses; that they shared joint credit cards and joint AAA membership; and they owned a joint mutual fund, naming each other as the beneficiaries of their respective life insurance policies" (*New York Law Journal* 2004, 2).

New York Supreme Court Justice Yvonne Lewis supported Cruz's claim. She turned down James McAneney's request to dismiss Cruz's motion and ruled that Cruz was indeed entitled to at least a portion of the award. The justice explained that "in light of the plaintiff's relationship with the deceased, it would seem equitable that she should receive a portion of any 9/11 fund" (Eaton 2004; Leonard 2004). Her loving, caring relationship to McAneney gave her legal rights at least equal to brother James's kinship claims.

The Schiavo and Cruz cases both raised questions of just compensation for lost love and care. At first glance, a third recent headline case looks very different. Early in 2005, high-flying Boeing chief executive Harry

Stonecipher lost his job when the board of directors learned he was having an affair with a divorced female executive whose career he had allegedly favored. After an anonymous informant disclosed evidence of the affair, including some racy e-mails, the board decided that the sixty-eight-year-old Stonecipher, long married and with grown children, had violated an internal code of ethics that he himself had instituted by involving himself romantically with a fellow employee. Days after Stonecipher's dismissal made front-page headlines, and a month after their fiftieth wedding anniversary, his wife, Joan, filed for divorce. She listed her occupation as housewife and demanded a "fair and reasonable" sum from her husband. She too asked just compensation for lost love and care. In Boeing's view, love and care had no place in a profit-making company.

What lesson might we draw from the three cases? Looking at them together, many people would apply a simple formula: market + intimacy = trouble. Money poisons intimate relations, goes the reasoning, and intimate relations undercut the rational efficiency of economic activity.

Such reasoning ignores a fundamental fact: in everyday life, people constantly mingle intimacy and all sorts of economic activity—production, consumption, distribution, and transfers of assets. Intimate relations between spouses, between lovers, between parents and children, and even between doctors and patients depend on joint economic activity. No loving household would last long without regular inputs of economic effort. What's more, family firms and mom-and-pop stores often thrive despite the everyday mingling of intimacy and economic activity. Something is wrong with the conventional reasoning.

BAD IDEAS

Common misconceptions block our understanding of how intimate relations and economic transactions actually mingle. Many observers assume that any mixing of intimate personal ties with economic transactions inevitably corrupts intimacy and that invasion of commercial activities by intimate relations corrupts those activities as well. Commentators on all three cases made one assumption or the other, or both. Claimants for 9/11 compensation, for example, repeatedly defended themselves by declaring that they were not in it for the money. They were fending off accusations of corruption.

Such concerns draw from two complementary but partly independent misunderstandings. We can call them "separate spheres" and "hostile worlds." The notion of separate spheres identifies two distinct domains of social life that operate according to different principles: rationality, efficiency, and planning on one side, and solidarity, sentiment, and impulse on the other.

Hostile-worlds beliefs say that when separate spheres come into contact, they contaminate each other. Their mixing, goes the argument, corrupts both; invasion of the sentimental world by instrumental rationality desiccates that world, while introduction of sentiment into rational transactions produces inefficiency, favoritism, and cronyism. In this account, a sharp divide exists—and should exist—between intimate relations and economic transactions, since any contact between the two contaminates both of them.

Ideas concerning separate spheres and hostile worlds appear in social science, where generations of analysts have deplored what they see as the erosion of authenticity and intimacy by an encroaching market. Outside of social science, the same themes frequently appear in moral discourse when people explain bad behavior as a consequence of greed and call money the root of all evil. In American law, the doctrines of separate spheres and hostile worlds show up in ever new versions. Courts, for example, regularly rule that economic transactions between spouses must count as free gifts rather than quid-pro-quo exchanges—at least until the moment of divorce.

Practices based on separate spheres and hostile worlds figure in everyday life as well. Sexually intimate couples, for example, ordinarily take great care to signal (to others and to each other) that they are not simply exchanging sex for economic rewards. The notion that the active marketing of intimacy corrupts it reappears across a wide range of intimate relations. In a recent *New York Times* column, for example, David Brooks laments the increasing use of separate checking accounts by married couples. He worries that husbands and wives are forgetting the distinction "between the individualistic ethos of the market and the communal ethos of the home." As a result, Brooks (2005) warns, "a union based on love can easily turn into a merger based on self-interest, where the main criterion becomes: Am I getting a good return on my investment?" The Boeing board that fired Stonecipher expressed the opposite concern: that office romance undermines a company's economic rationality and therefore its viability.

SEX WITH PROFESSIONALS

American courts implement their own version of these scruples by regulating intimate relations between professionals and their clients or patients. Courts ask if and when a lawyer's concern for his client or a therapist's empathy with her patient crosses the boundary into improper and therefore illegal intimacy. That is what happened to Jerry Berg, a Wichita, Kansas, divorce lawyer.

In 1997 the Kansas Board for Discipline of Attorneys convened to consider Berg's professional conduct. In separate complaints, six of Berg's female clients accused him of improper sexual behavior. After considering the evidence, the panel recommended disbarment. Although Kansas does not specifically ban attorney-client sexual relations, the board condemned "exploitation of the attorney-client relationship to the detriment of the client" (re Berg, 955 P.2d 1240).

In one of the six complaints, R. M. reported consulting Berg about her divorce in August 1993, after her first lawyer had made no progress with her case. Berg and R. M. had first met during her parents' divorce some three or four years earlier. Berg had discussed with the then fourteen- or fifteen-year-old R. M. her alcohol- and drug-addiction problems. R. M., "stressed, confused, suicidal and seeing a counselor," now worried about losing custody of her one-year-old child to her husband, as well as ensuring his child-support payments. On October 14, 1993, the night before her divorce became final, R. M. went to Berg's office between 6 and 7 p.m. to sign a property settlement agreement. Although she was below the drinking age, Berg invited her out, ordering several alcoholic drinks, including one called "Sex on the Beach." After discussing sexual matters, they returned to his office to sign further papers.

It was then, R. M. testified, that Berg "grabbed" and kissed her, and she performed oral sex on him. Although acknowledging that the sex was not forced, she reported being scared and worried that if she resisted, Berg would not represent her in court the next day. After the divorce was granted, R. M. endorsed an income tax refund as payment to Berg. Although she was still short by $200, Berg marked it "paid in full." R. M. testified: "I felt like a whore because I felt like I had paid for my services the night before." Berg did not send her any further bills.

Their sexual relationship continued, as R. M. still consulted Berg on other legal matters. It ended abruptly on June 14, 1994, when Berg, seeking consolation after losing an important case, visited R. M. at her apartment. Recovering from a miscarriage, she refused to have sex, but he insisted. Two days later, R. M. sent Berg a letter terminating his services as her attorney. Until then, R. M. stated, she considered Berg to be her lawyer.

In his defense, Berg contended that his sexual relations with R. M. did not start until October 15, 1993, after her divorce settlement. At that point, in his view, she was no longer his client. If the attorney-client relationship did not exist, Berg argued, the sexual relationship was legitimate. To bolster his defense, Berg brought in a psychologist who had been treating him as a sexaholic. Berg also stated he had been attending weekly Sexaholics Anonymous, Bible study, and Promise Keepers meetings, and finally that he was reconciling with his wife.

Berg appealed his disbarment. On March 6, 1998, however, the Supreme Court of Kansas concurred with the Board of Discipline's decision to disbar Berg. Among other issues, the court determined that R. M. continued to be Berg's client through June 16, 1994. In any case, the court declared, "It is no more persuasive to attempt to justify one's conduct by arguing a scenario of scarcely letting the ink on the divorce decree become dry, extracting all available funds from the client (an income tax refund), and then writing off the balance of the bill with the stroke of a pen and immediately beginning to seduce with alcoholic drinks an under the drinking age and vulnerable client." The discipline panel and the Kansas Supreme Court finally decided to treat Berg as a lawyer who had abused his relationship with a client.

NOTHING BUT . . . ?

Courts also worry about corruption in the reverse direction. They defend the intimate sphere from the market's encroachment. The 1993 case of *Borelli v. Borelli* made this clear (12 Cal. App.4th 647, 16 Cal. Rptr. 2d 16). Hildegard Borelli and Michael Borelli married in 1980. Three years later, as Michael's health began to falter, he went to the hospital repeatedly with heart trouble. In 1988, after he suffered a stroke, Michael's doctors recommended round-the-clock institutional care. But Michael resisted; instead, he promised his wife that if she cared for him at home, at his death he would leave her a large share of his estate. He did not keep the promise. The following year, after Michael's death, Hildegard discovered he had bequeathed the bulk of his estate to his daughter by an earlier marriage. Her legal appeals for enforcement of the marital promise failed.

In a 1993 decision, the California Court of Appeals turned down Hildegard's claims. The decision became notorious among feminist legal scholars. Condemning the Borellis' "sickbed bargaining," the court ruled that, as Michael's wife, Hildegard owed him nursing care free of charge and therefore had no right to ask for compensation of her efforts. A dissenting judge vigorously disagreed with the implication that Hildegard "had a preexisting . . . nondelegable duty to clean the bedpans herself." This judge commented that in this day and age spouses should have every right to contract with each other for services and their compensation. After all, Hildegard could easily have hired commercial help for the day-to-day drudgery of caring for an invalid, but responded to her husband's promise by doing it herself.

The court's majority rejected that view: "The dissent maintains that mores have changed to the point that spouses can be treated just like any other parties haggling at arm's length. Whether or not the modern marriage has become like a business . . . it continues to be defined by statute as a personal relationship of mutual support. . . . Thus, even if few things are left that cannot command a price, marital support remains one of them."

Are the judgments by Brooks and Boeing and in *Berg* and *Borelli* right? How might we reply to the advocates of separate spheres and hostile worlds? Social scientists who are rightly suspicious of those widely held ideas have often replied, "Nothing but"—that is, intimate settings are nothing but special sorts of economies, nothing but arenas of power, or nothing but expressions of an underlying culture.

The most common version says hostile-worlds thinkers are wrong because the whole world is nothing but a single, big economy. This includes families and intimate relations. In this "nothing-but" view, love, sex, and personal care are in fact commodities like all the rest. Look, for instance, at a book titled *The Family CFO: The Couple's Business Plan for Love and Money*. When asked by a reporter, "What should most couples do first to get their finances organized?" Christine Larson, one of the authors, answered, "Accept the idea that your family is a small business. You have goals. You have limited resources and unlimited desires. You generate revenue. You make investments. You have assets and liabilities. So if you start treating it like a business and using business tools and terms . . . then you can put all that emotional energy into your goals and your dreams" (Greenwood 2004). In short, accept the fact that families are nothing but special kinds of businesses. Other nothing-but arguments treat families as nothing but expressions of culture or nothing but arenas for power struggle.

INTIMATE ECONOMIES

As descriptions and explanations, theories of separate spheres, hostile worlds, and nothing-but fail badly. Actual studies of concrete social settings, from corporations to households, do not uncover separate spheres, segregated hostile worlds, universal markets, or any of the other nothing-buts.

The surprising thing about such views is their failure to recognize how regularly intimate relations coexist with economic transactions: couples buy engagement rings; parents pay nannies or child-care workers to attend to their children; adoptive parents pay lawyers and agencies to obtain babies; divorced spouses pay or receive alimony and child-support payments; parents give their children allowances, subsidize their college educations, help them with their first mortgages, and leave them substantial bequests. Friends and relatives send gifts of money as wedding presents, and friends lend each other money. Immigrants send hard-earned money to kinfolk back home. Indeed, people in intimate relations regularly pool money, make joint purchases, invest shared funds, organize inheritances, and negotiate divisions of household work. Yet such relations are in no way similar to stock exchanges or retail markets.

Does this mean that people who talk about separate spheres, hostile worlds, or nothing-but are speaking nonsense? No, the mingling of intimacy and economic activity does pose problems for social scientists, moralists, lawyers, and ordinary people alike. People who adopt these doctrines and practices are trying seriously to distinguish relations that differ greatly from each other and cause trouble when confused. It really matters whether a relationship between a woman and a man is mother-son, wife-husband, prostitute-client, doctor-patient, boss-worker, or something else. But that is the point: relationships differ. People defend the differences by drawing boundaries between relationships, assigning distinct meanings and practices to different relationships, and matching economic transactions to each relationship.

We all use economic activity to create, maintain, and renegotiate important ties, especially intimate ties, to other people. Loving households are constantly negotiating the right combinations of their various economic activities and their intimate relations; indeed, they often support those intimate ties with economic activity, for example, by buying an expensive house that will encourage sociability among all family members. People devote intense effort and worry to achieving the right match. For instance, when a wife's income equals or surpasses her husband's, how much more time should the man devote to household chores or child care? How should household monies be divided and used? What sorts of aid—financial or otherwise—do married couples owe their aging parents? Under what conditions are parents obligated to pay their children's college tuition? Should parents reward their kids' good grades with higher allowances? All these questions and more call for the right match between economic activity and intimate relations.

Even if they give lip service to the separate-spheres and hostile-worlds arguments, as a practical matter people regularly recognize the matching process. One woman replied, in a letter to the *New York Times*, to David Brooks's lament by commenting that "no great love is lost because a woman learns how to balance her own checkbook. My husband and I have been blessed with all the warm fuzzy things that a 54-year-old marriage can offer. And I submit that we may owe our continuing loving relationship, at least in part, to the fact that we have separate checking accounts."

Not that any economic transaction is compatible with any intimate relation. On the contrary, people work hard to find economic arrangements that both confirm their sense of what the relation is about and sustain it. Is this person a gold digger or an intimate friend? Is this a caring relation or exploitation? When should care be paid for? Why is it all right to pay a babysitter but not to pay a sister? Or when is it proper to pay your own child to work as a babysitter for a younger child? And when relations go sour, people start begrudging their economic contributions, to the detriment of those relations.

Kenneth Feinberg faced questions like these in a floodlit arena. As master of the 9/11 Victim Compensation Fund, he doled out $7 billion to survivors of the 2001 attacks—on average, more than $2 million for each person who died and $400,000 for each person injured. He did the job without pay, but he still took bitter criticism from two opposing sides. On one, survivors complained that the amounts he set demeaned the true value of the lost lives. On the other, outsiders complained that he was pandering to the greed of relatives who had, after all, survived, and was in any case cheapening life by assigning it monetary value.

From the start, Feinberg faced the problem of matching economic activity to intimacy. He varied awards according to how large a loss survivors had sustained. Feinberg's awards used lost economic value as their main standard, not only computing the victim's likely future earnings but also estimating the market price of lost services. Feinberg then augmented awards based on further information about personal hardship and relationship to the victim. He also had to decide which survivors deserved compensation for the loss: did the claim of an unmarried partner, a fiancé, or an estranged spouse trump the claim of a parent or sibling? In addition to computing the market value of lost lives, Feinberg found himself judging the meaning and quality of intimate relations.

On a very public stage, Feinberg was directing a somber, fateful version of a classic drama: given that we live in a world of money and cannot sustain our lives without it, how can we possibly decide who owes what to whom? Are some relations so priceless that we should keep money out of them? Some of Feinberg's critics, he tells us, said yes: he was turning sacred relations into market transactions. "Family after family," writes Feinberg, "accused me of devaluing the life of a husband or daughter, of failing to recognize the victim's true worth, of engaging in a cold-hearted calculation of dollars and cents when I should be focusing on the uniqueness and human qualities of the deceased." Seven grief-stricken families out of the thousands that were eligible for compensation actually refused to apply.

But many of his claimants declared, just as emphatically, that it was "not about the money." As one husband angrily reminded Feinberg, "This is not a business you're talking about, Mr. Feinberg. You're talking about my wife." Claimants asked for public recognition of their losses. Payments for the financial security, personal attention, and love that had vanished with the terrorist attack seemed just compensation.

Were the critics right? As we have seen, many people think that money is the root of all evil, that it contaminates the relations it touches, and that we can only hold on to moral values by rigidly separating the sphere of economic necessity from the sphere of authentic social being. But in fact people constantly integrate money into their intimate social lives without damaging them. Money honestly gained and well spent sustains families, friendships, and faiths.

NOTE

Viviana A. Zelizer, "Do Markets Poison Intimacy?" *Contexts* 5 (Spring 2006): 33–38. Reprinted with permission.

RECOMMENDED RESOURCES

Brooks, David. 2005. Editorial, "To Have and to Hold, for Richer for Poorer." *New York Times*, March 1.

Crittenden, Ann. 2001. *The Price of Motherhood: Why the Most Important Job in the World Is Still the Least Valued*. New York: Metropolitan Books. The case for fairer legal, economic, and political treatment of mothers.

Eaton, Leslie. 2004. "In Nation's Courtrooms, Wounds from 9/11 Attacks Persist." *New York Times*, September 9.

Ertman, Martha M., and Joan C. Williams, eds. 2005. *Rethinking Commodification: Cases and Readings in Law and Culture*. New York: New York University Press. The definitive collection of cases, opinions, and analyses of commodification as it confronts the law.

Feinberg, Kenneth R. 2005. *What Is Life Worth?* New York: Public Affairs. The master of 9/11 compensation tells how he did his work.

Greenwood, Katherine Federici. 2004. "Love and Money." *Princeton Alumni Weekly*, February 25.

Hochschild, Arlie Russell. 2003. *The Commercialization of Intimate Life: Notes from Home and Work*. Berkeley: University of California Press. A well-informed but worried look at the social consequences of commercialization.

Leonard, Arthur S. 2004. "Lesbian Partner Wins in 9/11 Fund Suit." *Downtown Express* 17 (July 16–22). http://www.downtownexpress.com/de_62/lesbianpartnerwins.html (accessed November 6, 2004).

New York Law Journal. 2004. "Domestic Partner's Suit to Win Portion of 9/11 Fund Award Goes Forward." *New York Law Journal*, online ed., July 16, 1–7.

Zelizer, Viviana A. 2005. *The Purchase of Intimacy*. Princeton, N.J.: Princeton University Press. Extended discussion of this article's themes, with comparisons of everyday and legal arenas.

10

The Purchase of Intimacy

In *Making Ends Meet* (1997), their important study of how low-income and welfare single mothers survive financially, Kathryn Edin and Laura Lein make three observations of great consequence for this paper's topic; first, that relationships to men played a significant part in the household finances of these mothers; second, that the women made strong distinctions among their various relationships to men who are or have been their sexual partners; and third, that they developed distinct systems of payment and obligations corresponding to these different relationships. In field observations and interviews of almost four hundred mothers, Edin and Lein identified a whole system of categories distinguishing the women's different relationships to men: from absent fathers to live-in boyfriends to customers for prostitution, with other distinctions in between.

Perhaps the most remarkable are the ties to live-in boyfriends. These men—not legally married to the mother and usually not the father of any of her children—are expected to contribute regular amounts of cash and in-kind goods. In addition to weekly cash outlays of $20 or $30 for incidentals, for instance, one Chicago mother's boyfriend helped pay for her furniture, phone bill, and gifts for her children. In return for their contributions, boyfriends get a place to stay, sexual companionship, some meals, and the opportunity to "play Daddy" for the women's children. The arrangement is clear: boyfriends who do not pay, mothers repeatedly told Edin and Lein, "can't stay." Occasionally the boundaries between "serial boyfriends" and prostitution blurred: one mother explained, for instance, that her reliance on boyfriends "isn't for love, and it isn't just for money. I guess I'd call it social prostitution" (1997, 157). Nevertheless, most mothers set clear distinguishing markers between real prostitution and their relationship to a boyfriend. "Turning tricks" or "street walking" meant one-night stands without a long-term relationship to the man; they involved short-term cash in exchange for short-term sex. To each form of relationship corresponded a somewhat different set of monetary transfers.

Contrary to widespread belief, furthermore, it was not the money involved that determined the relationship's quality, but the relationship that defined the appropriateness of one sort of payment or another. These observations lead directly to this paper's topic—the purchase of intimacy. I mean purchase in two senses: first, the frequent accusation that people use money to buy intimate relations and, second, the grip of intimacy on the forms and meaning of payments. Focusing on the intersection of monetary transfers and erotically tinged relations, the paper identifies parallels between analytic problems faced by social-scientific and legal treatments of economic processes. In both fields, analysts who assume that intimate relations and monetary transactions are utterly incompatible have difficulty recognizing the subtle ways in which people actually match their monetary transfers to their various social relations, including intimate ties.

Here is this paper's basic question: Under what conditions, how, and with what consequences do people combine monetary transfers with intimate relationships? That question has elicited three competing answers:

1. *Hostile worlds.* Such a profound contradiction exists between intimate social relations and monetary transfers that any contact between the two spheres inevitably leads to moral contamination and degradation.
2. *Nothing-but.* Intimate relations involving monetary transfers are (a) nothing but another rationally conducted exchange, indistinguishable from equivalent price-making markets; (b) nothing but another expression of prevailing cultural values; or (c) nothing but coercion.
3. *Differentiated ties.* Intimate relations involving monetary transfers include a variety of social relations, each marked by a distinctive pattern of payment.

The first two views have frequently misled analysts of intimacy. This paper urges the third view as a more viable alternative. In this context, I argue first that people routinely differentiate meaningful social relations; among other markers, they use different payment systems to create, define, affirm, challenge, or overturn such distinctions. When people struggle over payments, of course, they often quarrel over the amount of money due, but it is impressive how often they argue over the form of payment and its appropriateness for the relation in question. They argue, for example, over distinctions between payments as compensation, entitlements, or gifts.[1]

Second, I argue that such distinctions apply to intimate social relations, including those having a sexual component. People regularly differentiate forms of monetary transfers in correspondence with their definitions of the sort of relationship that obtains between the parties. They adopt symbols, rituals, practices, and physically distinguishable forms of money to mark distinct social relations.

Third, I show that when payments within intimate relations become matters of legal dispute, lawyers and judges apply their own differentiating categories, which also turn out to be relational. Fourth, I explore how this application of categories leads to a problem of translation, as participants in disputes go from categories of everyday life to legal classifications and back.

All four principles illustrate the meaningful, relational, deeply social character of distinctions between payment systems, including payment systems in intimate relationships. This paper draws its examples almost exclusively from erotically tinged relations in order to sharpen the issues. However, its arguments should apply to intimate relations more generally. They should apply to relations between parents and children, siblings, close friends, and more.

After a brief discussion of payment practices and intimacy, the paper reviews social-scientific treatments of these relationships. It then turns to the legal arena, comparing a few landmark legal cases that raise crucial questions about the relationship between intimate ties and monetary payments. The paper closes with an overview of recent attempts to deal with this problem by legal scholars and other critics.

Payment Practices and Intimacy

The intersection of money and intimacy provides a remarkable opportunity to examine how people carry on relational work. Robert Darnton puts it this way: "As carnal knowledge works its way into cultural patterns, it supplies endless material for thought, especially when it appears in narratives—dirty jokes, male braggadocio, female gossip, bawdy songs, and erotic novels. In all these forms, sex is not simply a subject but also a tool used to pry the top off things and explore their inner works. It does for ordinary people what logic does for philosophers: it helps make sense of things" (1994, 65).

As a matter of practical observation, social scientists have frequently been attentive to connections between economic practices and intimate social relations. Anthropologists have long documented such sexually connected financial arrangements as bride-price and dowry; economists have often analyzed marriage as an economic institution; and sociologists have repeatedly tangled over such questions as whether the monetary income of spouses affects their relative power.

It is not just the single mothers interviewed by Edin and Lein who use payment systems to mark their sexual relations. Across a wide range of periods and cultures, we find people distinguishing meaningfully different social ties—including sexual ones—by contrasting modes of payment. For instance, as they analyze marriage disputes in two South African Tswana chiefdoms, Comaroff and Roberts (1981, chap. 5; see also Comaroff 1980) distinguish three types of payment. They include a gift offered in the early stages of a relationship by a man's guardian and close kin to his selected future spouse; compensatory payments for seduction; and bride wealth. Each payment symbolizes a different kind of relationship between sexual partners. As Comaroff and Roberts show, bride-wealth transfers, or *bogadi*, do not mark the onset of conjugal bonds; in fact, the payment is typically delayed until much later in a couple's life, sometimes when their own children begin to marry. Bride wealth, however, serves to distinguish sexual relations within marriage from concubinage or short-term liaisons, thereby establishing rights to marital property, inheritance, and the jural status of children.

As they portray the fluid, ambiguous, and contested character of marital payments, Comaroff and Roberts subtly convey how the status of each payment is subject to negotiation between all parties; negotiation matches a definition of the payment to a definition of the relationship. The matching process emerges clearly as tribal dispute-settlement agencies adjudicate domestic quarrels.

Consider the case of Ramasu and Maggie, as reported by Comaroff and Roberts (1981, 153–54). When Ramasu, who was living with another woman, met Maggie (who had two children from another man), he promised her marriage, and she joined his homestead, along with his first wife. Maggie bore Ramasu two children, but the relationship soured, and Maggie left. Subsequently, she complained to the tribal chief that she had been promised marriage, and that Ramasu accepted her older children as his own, but that he had later neglected her while his first wife treated her as a servant. Ramasu responded that Maggie had never been his legal wife, but a concubine hired to serve as his wife's servant. If a wife, Maggie was entitled to substantial compensation; if a concubine, she could expect only moderate restitution. Despite a recognized promise of bride wealth, the tribal chief declared Maggie to be a servant involved in a casual relationship. Ramasu was ordered to pay a moderate sum, the standard fine for impregnating an unmarried girl. That judgment matched monetary payment to a defined relationship.

Shifting to the very different world of Brazilian *travestis*, we find another system of sexually tinged relations corresponding to distinct forms of payment. Travestis are men who not only adopt female clothing and names but develop feminine bodies by injecting silicone and ingesting female hormones. Still, travestis identify themselves as male homosexuals, not as women. In a study of these transgendered prostitutes in the Brazilian city of Salvador, anthropologist Don Kulick maps out the painstaking ways in which the men differentiate between their surprisingly varied erotic liaisons. In that milieu, travestis distinguish at least four relationships, each involving a different mode of payment as well as a set of distinct sexual practices: (1) *maridos*, or boyfriends; travestis provide money, meals, gifts of all kinds, and drugs to their usually handsome, unemployed, heterosexual, live-in boyfriends. "Gift giving by a travesti to a male" Kulick observes, "marks a relationship and signals to others that a relationship is under way" (1998, 109). Despite the unilateral flow of money from travesti to boyfriend, Kulick further notes, boyfriends are not equivalent with pimps; (2) *boyzinhos*, or adolescent boys; travestis offer these boys beer and/or some marijuana in exchange for sex, and afterwards give them cash to buy a snack or more marijuana; (3) *vícios* (vices), or attractive males; travestis have sex with vícios for free because they find the men attractive; and (4) *clientes*, or clients; these men pay travestis for their sexual services. These relationships, unlike the others, are fair game for theft or trickery.

Distinctions of this kind are not features of exotic cultures alone. In the twentieth-century United States people have regularly responded to changing forms of sexual relations by making new distinctions in payments. Take, for instance, the multiplication of courtship rituals at the turn of the century. Participants and observers distinguished new forms, called "treating" and "dating," from other varieties of courtship. *Treating* was a popular arrangement by which working-class young women obtained financial help, gifts, and access to entertainment from a fiancé or a "steady," but also from casual acquaintances, in exchange for a variety of sexual favors, from flirting to intercourse. People distinguished treating from the much more sexually restricted relationship of middle-class dating, but also from the sexually explicit bargain of prostitution.

As long as she did not accept cash payment from men at the time of sexual relations, the so-called treating (or "charity") girl did not become a prostitute. Surveying the practice of treating in New York City between 1900 and 1932, Elizabeth Clement reports how "the young women exchange sexual favors for dinner and the night's expenses, or more tangibly for stockings, shoes, and other consumer goods" (1998, 68). These women, Clement declares, used treating "to gain entry into the expensive world of urban amusements and to distinguish themselves from the prostitutes who lived and worked in the bars alongside them." To keep treating distinct from prostitution, furthermore, the women used the language of "gifts" and "presents" rather than payment. As Clement puts it: "Not only did they not accept cash, but they did not really exchange services for material goods. Instead, they received presents from their friends" (1998, 120).

Further distinctions separated relations pairing men with taxi dancers, long-term mistresses, and a variety of prostitutes. What is more, another system of distinctions applied to erotically charged relationships between men. In all these cases, what is generally striking is the concern of people to distinguish kinds of intimate relations and to devise systems of monetary transfers that support those distinctions.[2] Although in the extreme, the narrow exchange of sexual services for money does indeed occur, even within the world of prostitution we find differentiation, as prostitutes distinguish their income by type of activity or customer.[3]

Monetary transfers and erotic relationships, then, have actually coexisted and shaped each other for centuries. Every population that uses money at all adopts some set of distinctions between erotic relations; most populations mark those distinctions not with payment versus nonpayment, but with distinctive forms of monetary transfers. As Clifford Geertz has shown

(1973, 434), in some circumstances the presence of money can even deepen the significance of social relations. The question then is not whether money and erotic relations can coexist but what forms of monetary transfer attach to particular varieties of erotic relations. The problem therefore is not the availability of evidence but its interpretation.

SOCIAL SCIENCE CONFRONTS INTIMACY

Existing social-scientific approaches have difficulty accounting for the intertwining of monetary transfers with intimate relationships. Two different but equally problematic intellectual extremes—hostile worlds and nothing-but analyses—have hindered the treatment of these economic processes.

In a normative version, the hostile-worlds view places rigid moral boundaries between market and intimate domains. It condemns any intersection of money and intimacy, including sexual intimacy, as dangerously corrupting. Love and sex, Michael Walzer tells us, belong prominently among those spheres of life where monetary exchanges are "blocked, banned, resented, conventionally deplored" (1983, 97). In the context of our "shared morality and sensibility," Walzer explains, "men and women marry for money, but this is not a 'marriage of true minds.' Sex is for sale, but the sale does not make for 'a meaningful relationship'" (1983, 103). Or, as Fred Hirsch more pungently warns: "orgasm as a consumer's right rather rules it out as an ethereal experience" (1976, 101). This view springs from widespread popular concerns. As Murray Davis puts it:

> Sex for money . . . muddles the distinction between our society's sexual system and its economic system. Every transaction between prostitute and customer is an overlap point at which each social system exchanges characteristics: sex becomes commercialized while commerce becomes sexualized. Our society's attempt to avoid this cross-system contamination helps explain why it forbids us to sell our bodies but not our time, energy, thought, and behavior—even though most people identify with the latter at least as much as with the former. (1983, 274n9)

The normative view overflows into description and explanation. Social scientists continue to describe intimate relations as a world apart from the economy. They continue to explain that supposed segregation as a consequence of functional incompatibility.

Social scientists themselves carry symbolic representations of money as rationalizing, flattening, transparent, fungible, and ultimately corrupting; they also carry representations of erotic relations as sentimental, broad, singular, and profoundly vulnerable. On the one hand, they see money as the means of self-interested rational economic transactions. On the other, they see erotic relations as the means for mutuality and emotional fulfillment. Social scientists therefore conclude that any entry of money into erotic relationships transforms them into instrumental transactions; love gives way to prostitution. Even social-science students of family and gender relations often talk about emotion work, caring work, feeding work, volunteer work, or kin work as wide-ranging activities, yet sex work for them almost exclusively designates prostitution.[4] Prostitution, in this context, implies suppression of affect and intimacy.

Here the lines between normative, descriptive, and analytic treatments often blur. The hostile-worlds view builds its rhetorical power from social thinkers' long-standing concern with the broader commodification effects of an ever-expanding modern market. Take as just one instance of a recognizable trope Roger Friedland's lament that "the unparalleled hegemony and global expansiveness of the market have steadily reduced that sacred subject to an economic man, whose right to life is reduced to a set of rights to own, to buy and sell, to offer oneself in the marketplace. As the logic of the market penetrates into every domain of familial and community life, the territory of value independent of price shrinks" (1999, 18).[5]

In fact, the hypothesized contamination runs in both directions: according to the hostile-worlds view, sex can also contaminate rational economic behavior. Workplaces, as James Woods has shown, are typically constructed as asexual spheres where sexuality looms as "an external threat to an organization . . . something that must be regulated, prohibited, or otherwise held at the company gates" (1993, 33). What Woods calls the "asexual imperative" goes beyond protecting vulnerable workers, typically women, from sexual harassment. It supports organizational prohibitions against the use of sexuality to determine matters of workers' pay, promotion, or dismissal. One of the worst aspersions one can make against a rising company official is that he or she slept his or her way to the top. Corruption thus runs in both directions.[6]

Nothing-but analyses contradict the hostile-worlds views. Nothing-but ideas come in three varieties; one arguing that intimate relations are nothing but exchange relations of a special sort; another arguing that intimate relations are nothing but straightforward expressions of general values or ideological scripts, regardless of what economic connection they may entail; a third arguing that intimate relations are nothing but the outcome of coercive structures.

In social science as a whole, economic interpretations have provided the most coherent and powerful challenge to other views. In that category we have Richard Posner, who in the tradition of Gary Becker (1996) claims the equivalence of all transfers as quid-pro-quo exchanges. Take away any cultural camouflage, such nothing-but theorists maintain, and we will find that intimate transfers—be they of sex, babies, or blood—operate according to principles identical with transfers of stock shares or used cars. Consider how Posner—champion of the influential "law and economics" paradigm and a pioneer in its extension to the analysis of sexuality—draws parallels between prostitution and marriage:

> In describing prostitution as a substitute for marriage in a society that has a surplus of bachelors, I may seem to be overlooking a fundamental difference: the "mercenary" character of the prostitute's relationship with her customer. The difference is not fundamental. In a long-term relationship such as marriage, the participants can compensate each other for services performed by performing reciprocal services, so they need not bother with pricing each service, keeping books of account, and so forth. But in a spot-market relationship such as a transaction with a prostitute, arranging for reciprocal services is difficult. It is more efficient for the customer to pay in a medium that the prostitute can use to purchase services from others. ([1992] 1997, 131)

Posner argues, in short, that markets provide efficient solutions, and efficient solutions exhaust the legal problems posed by intimacy. Less common economic reductionisms treat sexual relations as another form of labor or consumption.[7]

Nothing-but cultural theorists, in contrast, replace efficiency, rationality, and exchange with meaning, discourse, and symbolism. In its extreme position this view sees cultural representations as determining both the character of sexual activity and the place of economic transfers. Take for instance Noah Zatz's analysis of the prostitution exchange as "a site of powerful sexual pluralism, capable of contesting hegemonic constructions of sexuality that at first seem far removed: the movement from anatomical sex to sexuality to identity and the maintenance of the public/private distinction through the isolation of sexuality and intimacy from productive work and commercial exchange" (1997, 306). While giving some nods to institutional features on his way to this conclusion, Zatz argues that prostitution has no necessary connection to genitalia or to sexual gratification: "constructivist theories of sexuality need to consider," he tells us, "both that sexuality may be nongenital and that genitalia may be nonsexual" (1997, 281).[8]

A third influential nothing-but analysis holds that intimate relations are nothing but the result of coercive, and more specifically patriarchal, power structures. Kathleen Barry's analysis of the "prostitution of sexuality," for instance, derives women's sexual subordination from "gender relations of sexual power" (1995, 78). Commercialized sex, as in prostitution, from this perspective is no different from unpaid sex in rape, dating, or marriage. The problem here is not commodification but men's coercion of women.

Common interpretations of the intersection between money and erotically tinged relations thus range from the moral concerns of hostile-worlds theorists to the pragmatism of nothing-but economistic views, the constructivism of nothing-but culturalists, and the political critique of nothing-but power analysts. In the case of hostile-worlds arguments, the spheres of monetary transfers and intimacy remain both morally unbridgeable and practically antagonistic; in the case of nothing-but views, only one sphere matters.

These two extreme arguments differ radically with respect to commensurability. Incommensurability is at the core of the hostile-worlds paradigm, while for nothing-but analyses, everything is commensurable once we recognize the basis of commensuration: market, culture, or power. Neither accepts degrees of commensurability.[9] The extremes miss the existence of differentiated ties—the many ways in which monetary transfers coexist with intimate relations. To be more precise, people incessantly match different forms of payment to their various intimate relations. What is more, they take great care to mark boundaries between social relations and their corresponding forms of payments.

This is serious work. It is serious precisely because different forms of payment signify differences in the character of the social relations currently operating. To label a payment as a gift (tip, bribe, charity, expression of esteem) rather than an entitlement (pension, allowance, rightful share of gains) or compensation (wages, salary, bonus, commission) is to make claims about the relationship between payer and payee. Negotiation, then, runs in both directions: from definition of social ties to selection of appropriate payments, from forms of payment to accepted definitions of ties.[10]

As we saw earlier in the discussion of payment practices, this differentiation and matching of payments to intimate ties has important consequences for participants in erotically tinged relations. That is why participants worry greatly about ambiguities between closely connected but different ties and relations: recall the treating girl's insistence on a different form of payment than a prostitute, or the travestis' distinct payment systems for boyfriends, clients, and boyzinhos.

As a way of clarifying the interconnections between monetary payments and intimate ties, let us examine legal cases in which financial conflicts intersect with sexually tinged relations. Legal controversy offers a privileged site to observe disputes of principle and interpretation carried out in the open. It also constitutes a parallel world in which the evidence concerning routine social relations converts into interpretations of individual intentions and responsibilities. How, then, does American law treat the coexistence of erotically tinged ties and financial transfers?

SEX IN LAW

By and large, the rhetoric of American law follows the hostile-worlds view; that is one reason why Posner's statement of an opposite view caused such stir among legal theorists. Just as courts resist the assignment of monetary value to spouses' domestic work, American law shies away from any monetary payment that can be construed as direct compensation for sexual services.[11] Nevertheless, in a number of legal cases, sexual and monetary exchanges do in fact coincide. At times, litigants, attorneys, judges, and juries explicitly negotiate matches between payments and erotically charged social relations.

Indeed, the courts single out for different forms of monetary compensation a wide variety of sexually tinged relations distinct from prostitution. These cases differ significantly from each other: for example, actions for criminal conversation and alienation of affections, tort of seduction, breach-of-promise suits, premarital contracts, alimony, testamentary rights, and life insurance benefits for concubines.[12] Thus, despite the specter of prostitution as the end point of any commodification in sexual relations, in practice courts and judges have not maintained a simple dichotomy of legitimate, nonmonetary sexual relations versus illegal monetized prostitution.

For instance, as Lea VanderVelde shows in her extensive analysis of the nineteenth-century tort of seduction, fathers received monetary damages for sexual injury to their daughters. In such cases, courts were indeed concerned with the commodification of sexual relations. "Nineteenth century tort law," VanderVelde tells us, "rejected the notion of compensating victims for those batteries that also assumed the character of moral wrongs" (1996, 852). This partly accounts for the courts' refusal to award money damages to victims in cases of rape. Yet they allowed compensation for the injury a daughter's seduction inflicted on her father's material welfare or honor. While earlier cases focused on the injuries caused by pregnancy, after midcentury courts addressed directly the damages created by a daughter's loss of sexual chastity. Thus, as VanderVelde notes, "despite the common law's aversion to redress for emotional harm, these cases show that nineteenth century courts were, in fact, quite receptive to fathers' arguments about affronts to their parental feelings" (1996, 888). Ironically, the courts' receptivity to paternal injury led to extraordinarily high monetary awards: "the noncommodifiability of the moral wrong of sex appears to have militated movement in the opposite direction. No award of damages seemed too high to compensate a father for the injury to his feelings" (1996, 889).

Similarly, Rebecca Tushnet has offered a telling analysis of changing legal treatments for breach-of-promise suits and anti–heart balm legislation— the latter being laws inhibiting compensation for injury to feelings. While nineteenth-century breach-of-promise cases centered on monetary compensation for the financial injuries of a broken engagement, including the loss of virginity, by the early twentieth century, courts increasingly awarded damages for emotional hardship. After the 1930s, anti–heart balm legislation was designed to eliminate such market considerations from intimate relations. Tushnet (1998, 2,615) notes how "when anticommodification rhetoric became the dominant language used to describe love, courts and commentators lost the ability to explore the subtler connections between love and material necessity." In summing up the currently dominant theory of conditional gifts in cases of broken engagements, Tushnet remarks how, in fact,

> [t]he theory accepts that people can make legally enforceable and mon-
> etarily measurable deals about marriage and thus involves courts in
> personal relationships in a way that cuts against the ideals of heartbalm
> reformers. The theory recognizes, however implicitly, that marriage in-
> tertwines material and emotional relations, just as the [engagement]
> ring functions as a symbol of the material support husbands are sup-
> posed to give wives. (1998, 2,604)

Notice four features of these cases; first, courts, despite their concern with commodification, do set monetary values—even if implicitly—on intimate relations, including sexual relations; second, the values set depend significantly on the kind of social relations between the parties involved as well as the parties' relations to other persons; third, legal categories and categories of routine social life often do not coincide, posing a problem of translation between the two; and fourth, in all these cases, we find interpreters hesitating uneasily between the extremes of nothing-but and hostile-world interpretations.

Let us concentrate on three exemplary cases—taken from tax law, contract law, and tort law—where sexual relations intersect with monetary payments. Among a wide variety of cases that qualify, I have chosen these three because they stand out for the sharpness of the central dispute and the variety of the principles at issue.

In all three cases I review variation with respect to both everyday social distinctions and legal distinctions. On the nonlegal side we have a mistress-patron relation, a cohabiting couple, and a husband-wife; on the legal side we have respectively a tax case, a contract case, and a tort case. For purposes of exposition I have chosen cases that vary in time period and that involve payments from men to women.[13]

Consider first the 1991 textbook tax case of *United States v. Harris* (942 F.2d 1125 [7th Cir. 1991]). David Kritzik, a wealthy widower, "partial to the company of young women," had over the course of several years given Leigh Ann Conley and Lynnette Harris, twin sisters, more than half a million dollars, in kind and cash: in fact, he regularly left a check at his office, which Conley picked up every week to ten days, either from Kritzik himself or from his secretary.

The case raises the issue of the taxability of transfers of money to a mistress in long-term relationships.[14] Were those transfers gifts or compensation? If gifts, Kritzik had to pay gift tax on the money; if compensation, the sisters had to pay income tax. The United States claimed that the money was compensation. As part of its evidence, the government argued that the form of transfer, the regular check, was that of an employee picking up regular wages. Harris and Conley were convicted of evading income tax obligations and sent to jail. After Kritzik's death, however, the case was appealed. Although the government insisted that the form of monetary transfer identified it as compensation, the appeal pointed out that it could just as easily have been an entitlement: "This form of payment . . . could be that of a dependent picking up regular support checks" (1991, 1,129).

The court finally agreed that it was a gift. Invoking legal precedent, the appellants' counsel successfully argued that "a person is entitled to treat cash and property received from a lover as gifts, as long as the relationship consists of something more than specific payments for specific sessions of sex" (1991, 1,136). A number of Kritzik's letters to Harris were shown as evidence of his continuing affection and trust, such as "I love giving things to you and to see you happy and enjoying them" (1991, 1,130).

What was appellants' counsel doing? The appeal demonstrated that distinctions between categories of payment, in this case between a gift and compensation hinge on the type of relationship between the parties involved: lover-mistress versus patron-prostitute. Of course, if Kritzik and Harris had been husband and wife, rather than lover and mistress, their transfers of money would have been tax-free domestic transactions.

The second case comes closer to a conventional domestic arrangement. A 1924 Supreme Court of Vermont decision concerns a contract-for-services dispute (*Stewart v. Waterman*, 123 A. 524 [1924]). In April 1899, the defendant, Joseph E. Waterman, then a forty-eight-year-old widower with four children, hired the plaintiff, twenty-four-year-old Mina Stewart, as his housekeeper. Five months later their relationship, as the court records, "had become intimate." By October, the couple, after a trip to Walden to visit her brother, decided to pose publicly as husband and wife. But in 1909, Mina, unhappy that Joseph no longer agreed to pay her wages, left him. She returned only after Joseph promised to deed her his house as compensation and gave her $100 for past services and labor—for which she signed a receipt. The financial disagreements, however, persisted, and in 1921 Mina left again. This time her erotic involvement with a boarder apparently led Joseph to throw her out. Unappeased by a $100 savings bank book and other valuables (for which Joseph had her sign a receipt "in full settlement for all labor for 23 years"), Mina sued Joseph to recover for her household services between April 1899 and October 1921.

How did the jury assess the legitimacy of Mina's case? By first determining her relationship to Joseph. Were the pair lover-mistress, husband-wife, or master-servant? If exclusively lover-mistress or husband-wife, Mina had no claims. Court instructions were emphatic: "if the services for which compensation is claimed were incidental to the meretricious relationship existing between the parties [and] . . . therefore tainted by the illegal consideration, there can be no recovery." The court's reasoning ran thus: "a woman who knowingly and voluntarily lives in illicit relations with a man cannot recover on an implied contract for services rendered him during such relationship," for the "relationship as of husband and wife [is] negative [to] that of master and servant." Also, such cohabitation constituted a "violation of principles of morality and chastity, and so against public policy" (1924, 526).

Joseph testified that indeed after their October visit to Walden, "their relations changed—that thereafter they were living together as husband and wife, and that the . . . services were performed as part of, and incident to, such illicit relation" (1924, 527). Mina herself had declared that she considered herself Joseph's "honest wife." But was she still partly his housekeeper? The court instructed the jury to establish whether the earlier service contract was independent from the couple's lover-mistress "illicit intercourse" and thus "not infected by the illegality of the relation" (1924, 526). If so, as Joseph's housekeeper, Mina could recover. Finding sufficient evidence that the original master-servant tie endured—including testimonies of the couple's repeated conversations about wages and the receipts for Joseph's two $100 payments to Mina—the jury supported Mina's suit.

Notice that the jury's decision did not depend on what a hidden observer would have seen Joseph and Mina do together sexually or otherwise, but on the court's definition of their relationship; in fact, the court explicitly acknowledged that "the services rendered by plaintiff were of the same character before and after the October arrangement." Suppose, moreover, that Mina had been tricked by Joseph into believing they were legally married: as his putative wife, deceived into an illicit arrangement, she might have recovered for services rendered to her supposed husband. Defined as a different relationship, the court would have treated the payment accordingly.[15] As in the Kritzik case, the court in *Stewart v. Waterman* was trying to decide the nature of the couple's relationship as it decided the proper legal treatment.

Let us turn now to a third case to see how contestation over a relationship's rights and obligations also takes place with legally married couples. We go to a Texas Court of Civil Appeals 1898 tort case involving loss of consortium (*City of Dallas v. Jones*, 54 S.W. 606 [1898]). After Mrs. Jones was severely injured by falling into a sidewalk hole on a Dallas street, her husband, James Jones, sued the city for damages including not only the cost of medical care but the loss of "the comfort and services and society" formerly provided by his now disabled wife. More specifically, Jones claimed damages for the loss of his wife's sexual services, testifying that "his wife could not stand sexual connection, and that, as it caused her pain, he did not enjoy it" (1898, 607).

The attending doctor confirmed that Mrs. Jones's injuries, "would be apt to not only cause conjugal relations to be unpleasant to the wife, but such relations would be injurious to her physically" (1898, 608). After a sequence of appeals, the court ruled that "evidence of damages by reason of the injury preventing intercourse is admissible in action by husband for injury to wife"

(1898, 606), and a jury award of $5,000 was upheld. Without any apparent moral discomfort, this turn-of-the-century Texas court priced conjugal sex.[16] In sharp contrast to the contract case, if the Joneses had not been married, Mr. Jones would not have collected. In fact, if he had been Mrs. Jones's lover, pimp, or sexual client, the court would have rejected his claim as utterly immoral.

Courts must thus reconcile four issues: first, a particular body of law—tax, contract, or tort; second, the presence of transfers of money; third, the interdependence of those payments with sexual relations; fourth, the proper definition of the relationship between the parties. Despite the courts' great reluctance in the contract case to countenance coexistence of sexual relations and monetary payment—with the phrase *meretricious sex* conveying the law's deep disapproval—tax cases show some courts identifying the underlying rationale for particular sexual payments without making moral judgments. Cases concerning recovery for loss of consortium go even further, showing us other courts that explicitly and deliberately set prices for sexual services while declaring both prices and services legitimate.

Of course, three hand-picked cases cannot identify trends or systematic variation in how Americans courts have dealt with the intersections of monetary transfers and intimate relations. They suffice, however, to establish that significant bodies of legal practice actually recognize principles of matching between the two. What have we learned? Despite a hostile-worlds rhetoric, courts in practice do their work by matching payments to different sets of intimate relations, including sexual ones. Nothing-but accounts cannot adequately explain what is going on; these are not simply market transactions, cultural constructions, or exercises in patriarchal power. They represent continuously negotiated correspondences between differentiated social ties and forms of payment.

PROBLEMS OF TRANSLATION

This relational work is obscured, however, by legal doctrines and practices that translate issues of social relations into matters of individual intention. This process poses a problem of translation. Let me clarify the problem. We have seen in these three cases the generation of problems by events taking place in ordinary social relations involving sexual ties—a man maintaining his mistresses, a cohabiting couple bickering over money, a spouse injured in an accident—which, for different reasons and through different paths, reach the courts. At that point lawyers, judges, and juries translate them into the available legal categories and idioms of tax, contract, and tort law. Notice what happens: Kritzik, Harris and Conley, Mina and Joseph, and the Joneses all have their own definitions of their relations, conflicts, and hardships—

their own conceptions of justice or injustice—but these must conform to existing legal criteria. Those criteria, as we have seen, are remarkably diverse, depending on the particular legal rubric under which courts and lawyers place a dispute. Indeed, in the case of Joseph and Mina, the court pressed Joseph to explain the wording of his receipt "for all the labor for 23 years," and asked, "And you owed her for it, didn't you?" In response, Joseph declared, "I owed her whatever balance she says if she had been a true woman to me—the wife I considered she was." Joseph and Mina accept that husbands owe their faithful wives payment for domestic services including sexual services, but as we saw earlier, the court would not tolerate any such reading of husband-wife obligations. Mina's victory was as housekeeper, not wife.

Some legal scholars have recognized this translation problem. For example, Felstiner, Abel, and Sarat report that courts "may transform the content of disputes because the substantive norms they apply differ from rules of custom or ordinary morality, and their unique procedural norms may narrow issues and circumscribe evidence" (1980–81, 647).[17] Actually the translation problem is double, not only from routine social life into legal discourse, but also from social interaction to individual behavior. Courts and juries must translate the interactions between the parties into statements of individual intent, thereby establishing the various parties' legal responsibilities. As Felstiner, Abel, and Sarat point out, "Courts may transform disputes by individualizing remedies" (1980–81, 648). Thus, in *Stewart v. Waterman*, the jury had to decipher whether Mina and Joseph intended their relationship to be conjugal or contractual. In *United States v. Harris*, the decision, following the landmark case of *Commissioner v. Duberstein*, 363 U.S. 278, 285 (1960)—which made a donor's intent the "critical consideration" in deciding whether a money transfer is a gift or income—hinged on Kritzik's motives. Indeed, earlier testimony by Harris—one of the twin sisters—that described her relation to Kritzik as a "job" and "just making a living" was disregarded.

Considering the way intentions and awareness emerge and alter in the course of routine social interaction, identifying individual intentions poses extremely complicated problems for courts and juries. In fact, some legal theorists have attempted to introduce social relations directly into legal decisions by means of what they call "relational" interests (see, e.g., Green 1934, 1936; Prosser 1971, 873).

More generally, the relationship between real life and legal categories of payments raises intriguing problems, as different linguistic codes, indeed different discourses, are used in each domain. Shifting from one to the other involves a process analogous to what linguistic anthropologists identify as code switching. Different codes index different social identities and relations between speakers, but they also frame the issue—such as payments—differently. The analogy to translation applies here as well. Ordinary knowledge and its coding are translated into the codes of expert knowledge, and vice versa. As with all translations, the key question is how, despite substantial differences in code, content, and context, actors are able to conceive of the two as somehow "the same," so that both types of discussion—lay and expert—are culturally linked and have important social effects on each other.[18]

Negotiation between legal proceedings and other arenas of social life, then, involves a double translation problem: between a legal world of specialized categories and the continually negotiated categories of social life outside the courtroom, and between legal conceptions of individual intent and social processes of interpersonal interaction (see also Rotman 1995).

RECONSIDERING THE SEXUAL ECONOMY

The translation problem becomes crucial as we find a number of scholars attempting to interpret and reshape legal practices involving the conjunction of monetary payments and intimate relations, including sexual ties. The ambivalence and fluctuation of American law with respect to the monetary valuation of sexual relations exemplify the contradiction between a hostile-worlds rhetoric and the reality of social differentiation. Impatient with such contradictions, a number of critics and theorists have recently challenged the two-spheres model. With Posner, we already saw one attempt to get rid of a hostile-worlds view by replacing it with a nothing-but economic alternative.

Others, as we have seen, have attempted a reduction of monetized sexual relations to pure expressions of culture or of coercion. But those options do not satisfy other theorists seeking some kind of middle ground, not only to explain the coexistence of sexual relations and monetary transfers but to improve its legal regulation. Nor will a little bit of each—a bit of economics, a dollop of culture, and a soupçon of coercion—produce a satisfactory synthesis.

Existing proposals range from only modest modifications of the hostile-worlds approach to its radical rejection. Let's proceed from minor revisions to major challenges. Take for instance philosopher Elizabeth Anderson. At first reading, Anderson's arguments cling closely to a hostile-worlds view, where intimate and market relationships occupy polar normative spaces. "Personal goods," Anderson argues, "are undermined when market norms govern their circulation" (1993, 152). More specifically, commodifying sexual relations "destroys the kind of reciprocity required to realize human sexuality as a shared good" (1993, 154). We see Anderson delicately addressing the need to renegotiate gender power relations without making them into marketlike contracts. She endorses, for instance, marriage contracts designed to equalize couples' equality "provided that the spirit of a market transaction . . . does not dominate their interactions" (1993, 157). A critical task for modern societies, therefore, "is to reap the advantages of the market while keeping its activities confined to the goods proper to it" (1993, 167).

Along the way, however, Anderson qualifies her hostile-worlds diagnosis by opening up the possibility of morally differentiated market practices. For instance, while declaring herself strongly against legalization of prostitution, she allows that under circumstances of dire economic deprivation, impoverished women should have the right to sell their sexual services. Invoking the possible scenario of professional sex therapy designed to free people from "perverse, patriarchal forms of sexuality," Anderson acknowledges that some commercial sexual services might have "a legitimate place in a just civil society" (1993, 156). Thus, Anderson envisages the use of legal means to maintain the boundaries between hostile worlds.

Anderson therefore leaves us with a theoretical dilemma: are markets inherently incompatible with intimacy, or do some forms of market transactions correspond to different forms of intimacy? Facing the same dilemma, legal philosopher Margaret Radin breaks with Anderson by offering a bold critique of hostile worlds analyses. Dismissing both Walzer-style "compartmentalization" of spheres, as well as Posner-like "universal commodification" theories, in her *Contested Commodities* we see Radin justifying a body of law that would regulate and distinguish the zone she calls incomplete commodification—where "the values of personhood and community pervasively interact with the market and alter many things from their pure free-market form" (1996, 114). As Radin states clearly, this zone includes instances of commodified sexual relations; in her model, "payment in exchange for sexual intercourse" along with "payment in exchange for relinquishing a child for adoption" are "nodal cases of contested commodification" (1996, 131).

Sexual relations, she argues, "may have both market and nonmarket aspects: relationships may be entered into and sustained partly for economic reasons and partly for the interpersonal sharing that is part of our ideal of human flourishing" (1996, 134). However, despite her insistence on the interaction of culture and law and her well-taken objections to what she calls the "domino" theory of commodification, Radin implies that "complete commodification" would occur with monetization in the absence of institutional—especially legal—protections. In the case of prostitution, for instance, while she advocates the decriminalization of the sale of sexual services, she also insists that "in order to check the domino effect," the law should prohibit "the free-market entrepreneurship" that would tag along with decriminalization and "could operate to create an organized market in sexual services." Different forms of regulation—including a ban on advertising—are necessary, she concludes, "if we accept that extensive permeation of our discourse by commodification-talk would alter sexuality in a way that we are unwilling to countenance" (1996, 135–36). While Radin comes much closer than Anderson to rejecting the hostile-worlds dichotomy, in the last instance she hesitates.[19]

Like Radin, legal theorist Cass Sunstein is trying to find a superior analytic position somewhere between hostile-worlds and nothing-but conceptions. Searching for ways out of the economic reductionism dominant in legal scholarship, Sunstein and other proponents of what Lawrence Lessig (1998) calls the "New Chicago School" of law are paying close attention to social meanings and norms (see also Lessig 1995, 1996).

More specifically, in his *Free Markets and Social Justice*, Sunstein insists that "we should agree that social norms play a part in determining choices, that people's choices are a function of their particular social role; and that the social or expressive meaning of acts is an ingredient in choice" (1997, 36). He notes that economics "at least as it is used in the conventional economic analysis of law—often works with tools that, while illuminating, may be crude or lead to important errors," and he challenges economistic accounts of human motivation and valuation (1997, 4). In particular, sharply critical of "monistic" legal theories of value, Sunstein makes a compelling argument for the multiplicity and incommensurability of human values, such as the distinction between instrumental and intrinsic values attached to goods or activities.

When it comes to the economic valuation of intimacy, including sexual relations, Sunstein's notion of norm-determined incommensurability marks a sharp cultural divide between financial and sexual exchanges: "If someone asks an attractive person (or a spouse) for sexual relations in return for cash," the offer would be insulting, as it reflects "an improper conception of what the relationship is" (1997, 75). As he explains:

> The objection to commodification should be seen as a special case of the general problem of diverse kinds of valuation. The claim is that we ought not to trade . . . sexuality or reproductive capacities on markets because economic valuation of these "things" is inconsistent with and may even undermine their appropriate kind (not level) of valuation. (1997, 76)

Yet Sunstein opens a significant wedge in his analysis. While on the one hand endorsing the view that some kinds of transactions, including sexual ones, are utterly incompatible with the market, hence with monetary transfers, he also acknowledges that markets and monetary transfers can accommodate multiple systems of valuation. Markets, Sunstein points out, "are filled with agreements to transfer goods that are not valued simply for use. People . . . buy human care for their children. . . . They purchase pets for whom they feel affection or even love." Therefore,

> the objection to the use of markets in certain areas must depend on the view that markets will have adverse effects on existing kinds of valua-

tion, and it is not a simple matter to show when and why this will be the case. For all these reasons, opposition to commensurability, and insistence on diverse kinds of valuation, do not by themselves amount to opposition to market exchange, which is pervaded by choice among goods that participants value in diverse ways. (1997, 98)

In the same way, he agrees that money, rather than necessarily flattening goods and relations, is itself socially differentiated: "Social norms make for qualitative differences among human goods, and these qualitative differences are matched by ingenious mental operations involving qualitative differences among different 'kinds' of money" (1997, 41). While at first Sunstein seems to have responded to the nothing-but "law and economics" with a nothing-but culture alternative, he moves on to a much more sophisticated analysis of social relations.

More impatient than Sunstein is with uncritical adherence to hostile-worlds views, philosopher Martha Nussbaum sets out to debunk the wide-spread presupposition that "taking money or entering into contracts in connection with the use of one's sexual or reproductive capacities is genuinely bad" (1998, 695) (for a more general exposition of Nussbaum's ideas, see Nussbaum 1999). Nussbaum points out how much disdain for payment for bodily performance has proceeded from class prejudices. Using the case of prostitution to deconstruct sexual commodification more broadly, Nussbaum asks us to reassess rigorously "all our social views about money making and alleged commodification" (1998, 699).

Notice, she tells us, how most cultures mingle sexual relations and forms of payment, and establish differentiated continua of such relations: ranging from prostitution to marriage for money and including "going on an expensive date where it is evident that sexual favors are expected at the other end" (1998, 700). Nussbaum goes farther: she documents the wide range of paid occupations where we find women accepting money for "bodily services": from factory workers and domestic servants to nightclub singers, masseuses, and even the professor of philosophy, who "takes money for thinking and writing about what she thinks—about morality, emotion . . . all parts of a human being's intimate search for understanding of the world and self-understanding" (1998, 704).[20]

Yet despite sharing many features with these other forms of "bodily services," only prostitutes are stigmatized. Step by step Nussbaum dismantles standard explanations of what makes prostitution unique, such as its immorality or its support of gender hierarchies. Along the way, she provides persuasive philosophical argumentation against hostile worlds doctrines, in particular the assumption of money's incompatibility with intimacy. Not true, she argues, that a prostitute "alienates her sexuality just on the grounds that she provides sexual services to a client for a fee" (1998, 714). Accepting money in exchange for services, even intimate services, is not intrinsically degrading. After all, Nussbaum reminds us, musicians laboring under contract and salaried professors still produce honorable and spiritual works. In the same way, she insists, "there is no reason to think that a prostitute's acceptance of money for her services necessarily involves a baneful conversion of an intimate act into a commodity" (1998, 716). Nor does prostitution, despite hostile-worlds concerns, contaminate noncommercial sexual relations: different types of relationships can and have always coexisted.

Instead of debating the morality of commercial sex, insists Nussbaum, we should be concentrating on expanding women's limited labor opportunities by means of education, skills training, and creation of jobs. Criminalizing prostitution, Nussbaum argues, will not correct an unequal labor market but further limit poor women's employment alternatives. She does, however, draw the line at nonconsensual, coerced prostitution and child prostitution. Thus, short of that limit, Nussbaum provides a strong case against the hostile-worlds argument and for the equivalence of a wide variety of connections between payment and intimacy. That equivalence, however, fails to recognize sufficiently that in practice payment systems and social ties differentiate, and people attach great importance to those differentiations.

Legal scholars Linda Hirshman and Jane Larson propose a still more radical overhaul of hostile-worlds views. Although reading their alternative at first resembles a Posner-like nothing-but economistic perspective, on close analysis it puts us on quite a different, more political ground. Applying a feminist-sensitive bargaining theory to heterosexual relations, they advocate a new sexual order of what they call "hard bargains," in which "men and women can recognize the age-old political nature of their negotiations over sexual access as well as their more recent commitment to equality and begin to develop workable processes for resolving their differences and making a fair division of the goods of their sexual cooperation" (1998, 3). Dismissing the hostile-worlds paradigm, Hirshman and Larson insist that sexual bargaining goes on "despite the cultural association of male-female sex with unreasoning romance and passion" (1998, 27). Because heterosexual bargaining "takes place between naturally and socially unequal players," (1998, 267) they propose legal intervention to redress unequal bargaining outcomes. "Structured bargaining" is possible, they argue, precisely because "eroticism and emotions are [not] exempt from the ordinary rules of human behavior" (1998, 268).

More concretely, their policy proposals to achieve more equitable sexual bargains directly challenge notions of separate spheres. Instead, they distinguish four sexual regimes, each involving distinct relations between the parties and distinctive payment systems—except for rape, where they propose to criminalize the relationship entirely. The four are marriage (as seen from the viewpoint of adultery), concubinage (or in their terms, "fornication"), prostitution, and rape. Let us take them up each in turn.

When it comes to extramarital sex, Hirshman and Larson envision a radically transformed negotiation between spouses. Arguing that marriage should include "a nonnegotiable duty of sexual exclusivity" (1998, 285), they recommend civil compensation for the personal injury of adultery: either as a "bonus" when dividing marital property after divorce or death or by an even more revolutionary "tort action for money damages available during the ongoing marriage or after divorce" (1998, 285). They acknowledge that in the context of a "sharing model of marriage" (1998, 286) their proposed tort of adultery involving compensatory monetary transfers within legally intact marriages might appear incongruous. Yet they strongly justify their proposal as a much-needed legal strategy for redressing spouses' bargaining power.

In the case of nonmarital, long-term cohabitants, Hirshman and Larson's emphatic "concubinage proposal" (1998, 282) argues in favor of contractual obligations between unmarried sexual partners. Significantly, they recommend doing away with the legal fiction underlying the landmark *Marvin v. Marvin* palimony decision, which distinguishes meretricious or illicit (sexual) aspects of an unmarried couple's long-term relationship from their legitimate contractual agreements, such as contracts for domestic services or business partnerships.

This position would be quite a reversal, since courts have worked hard to construct such "severability" rules as a way of distinguishing legitimate marital ties from prostitution.[21] Arguing that "we see no reason why sex should be ruled out as motivation for an exchange between intimates" (1998, 280), Hirshman and Larson support nonmarital sexual bargains as "fair trades" (1998, 281). They do not, however, propose to abolish relational distinctions but instead seek to redraw the boundaries between relationships, matching types of entitlements to those relationships. Their proposed regulatory statute, for instance, applies to couples who "have been sexually involved for a specified duration of time" (1998, 280), not to short-term sexual partners. Therefore, as Hirshman and Larson explain, the differentiation between prostitutes and concubines "remains a morally meaningful distinction" (1998, 282). The regulation of concubinage, furthermore, offers couples choices "from a graduated series of relational obligations, with marriage as the most comprehensive" (1998, 285).

Meanwhile, prostitution, note Hirshman and Larson, appears to be the "purest of bargained-for sex" (1998, 6). Yet it is often a bad bargain involving unequal power, frequently bordering on coercion. That does not, however, make selling sex—especially adult consensual exchanges—a criminal activity. Instead of criminalizing prostitution, Hirshman and Larson propose the regulation of the sex business via existing labor laws, thereby redefining relationships between prostitutes, patrons, and pimps by assimilating them to a different, widely recognized relational category of employer-worker. Hirshman and Larson's clear-headed mapping of relational distinctions does not, however, lead them to blankly endorse all sexual relationships. In direct parallel to Nussbaum, when it comes to nonconsensual intercourse or, regardless of consent, sexual relations between adults and children, they recommend criminal penalties.

By legitimating new forms of monetary compensation for unmarried and married couples and by treating prostitution as labor rather than crime, *Hard Bargains* undercuts hostile-worlds views in fundamental ways. But regardless of their hard-nosed, economistic vocabulary, Hirshman and Larson are not forwarding a nothing-but market alternative. Like advocates of comparable worth in employment, they promote legal intervention to reorganize inequitable markets and to ban unacceptable contracts.

As critics of American law have formulated their opposition to hostile-worlds and nothing-but accounts, feminist economists have likewise taken up the intertwining of intimacy and monetary payments. While focusing on areas of intimacy and caring outside the sexual sphere, for instance, Julie Nelson claims that "either love or money" arguments "lead us to worry too much about the wrong issues, and not enough the right ones" (1998a, 1). Arguing that markets and money do not constitute separate and impersonal spheres, Nelson analyzes the child-care market. She portrays that market as thickly social and relational. Seldom do parents or caregivers, she tell us, "perceive the market as purely an impersonal exchange of money for services. . . . The parties involved engage in extensive personal contact, trust, and interpersonal interaction" (1998b, 1,470).

Paradoxically, hostile-worlds assumptions that see love and care as demeaned by monetization may in fact lead to economic discrimination against those allegedly intangible caring activities. As sociologist Paula England and economist Nancy Folbre point out, "the principle that money cannot buy love may have the unintended and perverse consequence of perpetuating low pay for face-to-face service work" (1999, 46). Noting that typically it is women who are expected to provide caring labor, we should suspect, they warn, "any argument that decent pay demeans a noble calling" (1999, 48).[22] Like their counterparts in law and philosophy, then, Nelson, England, and Folbre have all criticized the hostile-worlds doctrine as subverting women's power and the nothing-but doctrine as misrepresenting the actual social character of markets.

All these recent efforts reorient discussions of the intersections between intimacy and monetary payments in fundamental ways. They reject hostile-worlds dichotomies as well as nothing-but reductionisms. What's more, in one way or the other, each critic I have discussed recognizes the presence of differentiated social ties and corresponding variations in payment systems.

Thus they move closer to a differentiated ties model. The conclusion is more general. Intimacy takes many forms. So does its purchase.

WHAT NEXT?

This paper set out to answer the question of how people combine monetary transfers with intimate relationships. Focusing on sexually tinged relations, we have seen that the actual practice of American courts as well as the work of recent scholars converge in suggesting an answer that escapes from standard hostile-worlds and nothing-but paradigms. Not true, the differentiated ties view claims, that monetary transfers and intimate ties exist in separate spheres that, if they intersect, lead to contamination and degradation. Not true, this view insists as well, that intimate relations involving monetary transfers can be reduced to another form of market exchange, or the mere expression of cultural values, or a straightforward product of coercive power structures.

Instead, the view of differentiated ties claims that monetary transfers and intimate relations, including sexual ties, coexist in a wide variety of contexts and relationships, each relationship marked by a distinctive form of payment. More generally, this alternative approach argues that people pour unceasing effort into distinguishing qualitatively different social relationships—including their most intimate ties—from each other by means of well-marked symbols, rituals, and social practices. Rather like forms of clothing, styles of speech, choices of location, and kinds of meals, forms of payment mark the character and range of the social relationship people are currently enacting.

This argument sets a very large agenda for further inquiry. The inquiry must extend beyond erotically tinged relations into a considerably wider range of intimacy. In that vein, some dominant questions present themselves:

First, how can we identify, explain, and predict which relationships people differentiate within a particular population? For example, do critical distinctions exist between such settings as corporations, households, voluntary associations, religious groups? If so, how and why? To what extent, how, and why do arrays of differentiated ties vary from country to country and period to period?

Second, under what circumstances do people make especially vigorous, visible, and sustained efforts to use payment systems for differentiating relations? Is it true, for example, that people mark boundaries with particular energy when similar behavior occurs in morally dissimilar social relations? In these three cases, we saw courts and judges striving to distinguish situations in which behavior is similar—sexual intimacy—but relations very different. In such cases, legal categories and disputes become helpful guideposts.

Third, what forms of payment correspond to which relations, and why? To what extent are correspondences between forms of payment and types of relation subject to historical variability? For example, do payment systems change systematically (as they seem to) from arranged marriage to marriages contracted by the partners themselves? To what degree does a population's previous history, as crystallized in its current culture, constrain such correspondences? At the limit, do some cultures actually construct worlds in which monetary payment and intimate relations remain incompatible?

Fourth, to what extent, and why, do areas of law differ in their hospitality to direct allowance for social relations and social interaction? Is contract law, for instance, significantly more concerned with negotiated interaction than is criminal law? Do whole legal systems vary systematically in the extent to which they assume individually deliberated action or discursive interaction?

Fifth, when relevant law itself stresses individual action and responsibility, how do participants in the legal process and legal theorists solve the translation problem? How do they negotiate between observed interaction processes and the assignment of individual responsibility? How, for instance, do courts convert information about marital struggles into judgments about individual fault and responsibility? Do such conversions differ significantly from those that lay people make when observing social interactions but assigning individual credit or blame?

These questions are still rather abstract. Some concrete examples of inquiries that might flow from such questions follow:

- In the worlds of friendship, kinship, and patronage, to what extent do people trade off the amount and character of time given to a relationship with the amount and character of money devoted to that same relation?
- When wives begin to earn significantly more than their husbands, does that shift affect their bargaining over sexual relations?
- What happens to the definition, content, and monetary marking of gay or lesbian relations when partners gain legal recognition as married couples?
- As children's wage-earning activity rises or falls, do their relations to parents, including monetary transfers, change correspondingly?
- To what extent and how do governmental controls over inheritance and intergenerational transfers affect the quality of relations among parents, children, and siblings?
- How does the legal definition of a category of interpersonal relations as sexual harassment affect the patterning of similar social relations in workplaces and schools—as well as the relation of third parties to perpetrator and victim?

- Where it occurs, how, why, and to what extent does the commercialization of personal care (e.g., for elderly persons) transform the quality of relations among the parties?
- To what extent do electronic media facilitate the creation of new types of intimate social relations, and how?

Although researchers in the social sciences and legal studies have of course touched on these issues, repeatedly, they provide splendid opportunities for collaborative research. Legal theorists must continue to negotiate between available legal categories and the rights or obligations that vary from one kind of relationship to another. They must also keep attending to news from the many social scientists who are examining the dynamics of interpersonal ties. Meanwhile, social scientists must take on the dual task of mapping the co-variation of relationships and payments on the one hand and explaining that variation on the other. This paper underlines the urgency of that form of collaboration between social scientists and legal analysts.

NOTES

Viviana A. Zelizer, "The Purchase of Intimacy," *Law and Social Inquiry* 25 (Summer 2000): 817–48. Reprinted with permission.

1. The broadest distinctions people make separate *compensation* (direct exchange), *entitlement* (rightful claim to a share), and *gift* (one person's voluntary bestowal on another). Money as compensation implies an equal exchange of values, and a certain distance, contingency, bargaining, and accountability between the parties. Money as entitlement implies rights not contingent on the recipient's current performance. Money as gift implies intimacy and/or inequality plus a certain arbitrariness. Of course, finer and multiple distinctions appear within these three categories and at their boundaries. See Zelizer 1994, 1996, for further discussion of differentiations in relationships involving monetary transfers.

2. For treating, see also Peiss 1983, 1986. On Jewish courtship and treating, see Heinze 1990, 122–24. For dating, see Fass 1977; Bailey 1988; Modell 1989; Heinze 1990, 122–24; and for a general history of American courtship, Rothman 1984. For taxi-dance girls, see, e.g., Cressey 1932; Meckel 1995; Clement 1998. See also Clement on club hostesses and female vaudeville performers as new forms of commercial, heterosexual interaction after the 1920s. The literature on sexual payments between men is very thin. For preliminary indications, see Chauncey 1985, 1994; Reiss 1961. Distinctions between prostitution and other forms of sexual relations are not universal. For contrasting cultural configurations, including forms of payments, see, e.g., Day 1988; Bloch 1989, 166; Knodel et al. 1995, 1996.

3. See, e.g., Coles 1986, 176–77; Hoigard and Finstad 1992, 49; Day 1994; Hill 1993, chap. 8; Scambler and Scambler 1997, 129. For graphic description of prostitutes' negotiation over the category of sexual relationship and associated monetary

transfers, see Sanchez 1997. For the adjacent world of female dancers in strip clubs, see Frank 1998. On prostitution, see also Stinchcombe 1994.

4. See, e.g., Hochschild 1983; Di Leonardo 1987; DeVault 1991. On sex work, see, e.g., Overall 1992; Zatz 1997; Chapkis 1997. Scholars specializing in commercialized sex do of course distinguish between types of sex workers, such as erotic dancers, phone sex operators, escorts, strippers.

5. The lineage of this idea is of course ancient, running from Marx through Simmel to Habermas. For a review of relevant literature, see Zelizer 1994, chap. 1.

6. On the neglect of sexuality by organizational theorists, see Hearn and Parkin 1995.

7. For an argument against equating sexual activity with labor, see Barry 1995, 65–69.

8. For another example of a culturalist approach, see Laqueur 1990. For an excellent review of prostitution studies, including culturalist analyses, see Gilfoyle 1999. An influential culturalist account appears in Butler 1990, 1993.

9. For a comprehensive discussion of commensuration, see Espeland and Stevens 1998. For a historian's sweeping critique of cultural, economic, and political "imperialisms," see Sewell 1993.

10. For extended discussion of these processes, see Zelizer 1994, 1996.

11. On domestic labor, see, e.g., Siegel 1994; Williams 1994; Silbaugh 1996; Stanley 1988, 1998.

12. Examples of analysis concerning these various issues include Rouchell 1930; Lippman 1930; Brown 1934; Clark 1968; Staves 1982; Taylor 1983; Grossberg 1985; Graham 1993; Ziegler 1996; Hartog 1997. See, e.g., Hunter 1978 on legal distinctions in types of relationships between unmarried, sexually involved couples: i.e., putative wife, meretricious spouse, and faithful mistress arrangements. Relationships are also differentiated by spouses' racial categories. Pascoe (1998) shows how in civil miscegenation cases from Reconstruction to 1930, courts, by declaring all interracial relationships as illicit sexual ties, and therefore meretricious, deprived widows in interracial marriages of any testamentary rights. For comparative information on the legal treatment of concubines' testamentary rights in Germany, France, and Switzerland, see Muller-Freienfels 1968.

13. After an extensive search of law review articles and consultation with specialists in the field, I located perhaps one hundred cases that qualified from the United States since the late nineteenth century. From those I selected three exceptionally well-documented cases that illustrated the range of variation in cases conjoining contested payments and sexually tinged relations. I make no claim whatsoever of a representative sample of all such cases. These cases illustrate a number of other issues in connections between routine social life, social science, and the law. For example, they illustrate the long-term tendency of American law to treat women's sexuality as the property of males. This tendency makes more surprising the readiness of lawyers and courts to work out explicit matches between appropriate payments and sexual ties.

14. On this issue, see, e.g., Bittker 1983, 11–12, chap. 3; McDaniel et al. 1994, 149; Klein and Bankman 1994, 150–51. *United States v. Harris*, a criminal prosecution case, is of course an exception to the usual pursuit of such cases in civil courts.

15. On conflicting opinions concerning the legitimacy of compensation claims for past services by women deceived into fraudulent marriages, see McKintosh 1930; Havighurst 1932; Hunter 1978; Siegel 1994. For a discussion of changing legal treatment of cohabitation, see Dubler 1998.

16. Nonetheless, American courts generally resist singling out and legitimating contracts for sexual services alone, preferring strongly to evaluate sexual services in the context of other intimate ties. In nineteenth-century actions for loss of consortium—derived from husbands' common-law property rights in their wives' services and earnings—when a wife was injured by a third party, her husband could claim compensation for the loss of her services, society, and sexual relations. After late-nineteenth-century earnings statutes granted wives ownership of their own wages, courts began emphasizing noneconomic, sentimental damages to the marital relationship, yet continued to recognize a husband's claims to his wife's domestic labor. On changes in loss of consortium actions, see, e.g., Holbrook 1923; Lippman 1930; Prosser 1971. Only after 1950, with the influential decision in *Hitaffer v. Argonne*, 183 F.2d. 811 (1950), were actions for loss of consortium extended to women. Note that unlike tax and contract disputes, consortium cases involve third parties.

17. For a more general attempt to map relationships between formal, legal proceedings and routine social life, see Ewick and Silbey 1998; Lazarus-Black and Hirsch 1994. Comaroff and Roberts 1981, and Comaroff's 1980 work on Tswana marriage disputes provide compelling examples of similar translation problems between claimants and tribal dispute-settling agencies.

18. I am grateful to Susan Gal for guidance in these issues.

19. Similarly, Schulhofer, in his concern with establishing protections for sexual autonomy, dismisses economic reductionism as an explanatory model. He likewise moves away from a hostile-worlds view, but not completely. Recognizing that "we cannot automatically condemn every exchange of sex for money, regardless of context," Schulhofer still worries that "sexual relationships founded on economic motives seldom seem admirable, and we often regard them as degrading" (1998, 161). The challenge Schulhofer states, "is in knowing when, if ever, a person can *legitimately* link sexual intimacy with economic support."

20. For a male equivalent of bodily services, see Wacquant 1998 on boxing.

21. On how courts have moved away from the more severe "meretricious spouse" rules toward a more flexible contractual approach to cohabitation arrangements, see Hunter 1978. The controversial 1976 *Marvin v. Marvin* decision dramatized the new reach of the severability rule. Stating that "express agreements will be enforced unless they rest on an unlawful meretricious consideration," the court distinguished sexual services from domestic labor and the sacrifice of a career, allowing Michelle Marvin recovery for the latter. Ironically, by allowing recovery for domestic services, the court, as Hunter (1978, 1,092–94) points out, grants "meretricious partners" greater economic latitude than married couples, who cannot contract for domestic services.

22. In a directly parallel way, feminist legal scholars have argued that the resistance to monetary valuation of household services generally discriminates against women by devaluing their domestic labor. See especially Rose 1994; Siegel 1994;

Silbaugh 1996; Williams 1994 (on how what she calls "commodification anxiety" has shaped divorce settlements).

REFERENCES

Anderson, Elizabeth. 1993. *Value in Ethics and Economics*. Cambridge, Mass.: Harvard University Press.

Bailey, Beth. 1988. *From Front Porch to Back Seat: Courtship in Twentieth-Century America*. Baltimore, Md.: Johns Hopkins University Press.

Barry, Kathleen. 1995. *The Prostitution of Sexuality*. New York: New York University Press.

Becker, Gary S. 1996. *Accounting for Tastes*. Cambridge, Mass.: Harvard University Press.

Bittker, Boris I. 1983. *Fundamentals of Federal Income Taxation*. Boston: Warren, Gorham, and Lamont.

Bloch, Maurice. 1989. "The Symbolism of Money in Imerina." In *Money and the Morality of Exchange*, edited by Maurice Bloch and Jonathan Parry, 165–90. New York: Cambridge University Press.

Brown, Robert C. 1934. "The Action for Alienation of Affections." *University of Pennsylvania Law Review* 82 (March): 472–506.

Butler, Judith. 1990. *Gender Trouble*. New York: Routledge.

———. 1993. *Bodies That Matter*. New York: Routledge.

Chapkis, Wendy. 1997. *Live Sex Acts*. New York: Routledge.

Chauncey, George. 1985. "Christian Brotherhood or Sexual Perversion? Homosexual Identities and the Construction of Sexual Boundaries in the World War One Era." *Journal of Social History* 19 (Winter): 189–211.

———. 1994. *Gay New York*. New York: Basic Books.

Clark, Homer J., Jr. 1968. *The Law of Domestic Relations in the United States*. St. Paul, Minn.: West Publishing.

Clement, Elizabeth A. 1998. "Trick or Treat: Prostitution and Working-Class Women's Sexuality in New York City, 1900–1932." Ph.D. diss., University of Pennsylvania.

Coles, Robert. 1986. *The Moral Life of Children*. Boston: Atlantic Monthly Press.

Comaroff, J. L. 1980. "Bridewealth and the Control of Ambiguity in a Tswana Chiefdom." In *The Meaning of Marriage Payments*, edited by J. L. Comaroff, 161–96. London: Academic Press.

Comaroff, J. L., and Simon Roberts. 1981. *Rules and Processes*. Chicago: University of Chicago Press.

Cressey, Paul G. 1932. *The Taxi-Dance Hall*. Chicago: University of Chicago Press.

Darnton, Robert. 1994. "Sex for Thought." *New York Review of Books*, December 22.

Davis, Murray S. 1983. *Smut*. Chicago: University of Chicago Press.

Day, Sophie. 1988. Editorial review, "Prostitute Women and AIDS: Anthropology." *AIDS* 2:421–28.

———. 1994. "L'argent et l'esprit d'entreprise chez les prostituées à Londres." In the special issue, "Les usages de l'argent," edited by Maurice Bloch. *Terrain* 23:99–114.

DeVault, Marjorie L. 1991. *Feeding the Family*. Chicago: University of Chicago Press.

Di Leonardo, Micaela. 1987. "The Female World of Cards and Holidays: Women, Families, and the Work of Kinship." *Signs* 12 (Spring): 440–53.

Dubler, Ariela R. 1998. "Governing through Contract: Common Law Marriage in the Nineteenth Century." *Yale Law Journal* 107:1,885–1,920.

Edin, Kathryn, and Laura Lein. 1997. *Making Ends Meet: How Single Mothers Survive Welfare and Low-Wage Work*. New York: Russell Sage Foundation.

England, Paula, and Nancy Folbre. 1999. "The Cost of Caring." *Annals of the American Academy of Political and Social Science* 561 (January): 39–51.

Espeland, Wendy Nelson, and Mitchell L. Stevens. 1998. "Commensuration as a Social Process." *Annual Review of Sociology* 24:313–43.

Ewick, Patricia, and Susan S. Silbey. 1998. *The Common Place of Law: Stories from Everyday Life*. Chicago: University of Chicago Press.

Fass, Paula. 1977. *The Damned and the Beautiful*. New York: Oxford University Press.

Felstiner, William L. F., Richard L. Abel, and Austin Sarat. 1980–81. "The Emergence and Transformation of Disputes: Naming, Blaming, Claiming." *Law and Society Review* 15:631–54, 883–910.

Frank, Katherine. 1998. "The Production of Identity and the Negotiation of Intimacy in a 'Gentleman's Club.'" *Sexualities* 1:175–201.

Friedland, Roger. 1999. "When God Walks in History." *Tikkun* (May/June): 17–22.

Geertz, Clifford. 1973. "Deep Play: Notes on the Balinese Cockfight." In *The Interpretation of Cultures*, 412–53. New York: Basic Books.

Gilfoyle, Timothy J. 1999. Review essay, "Prostitutes in History: From Parables of Pornography to Metaphors of Modernity." *American Historical Review* (February): 117–41.

Graham, Laura P. 1993. "The Uniform Premarital Agreement Act and Modern Social Policy: The Enforceability of Premarital Agreements Regulating the Ongoing Marriage." *Wake Forest Law Review* 28:1,037–63.

Green, Leon. 1934. "Relational Interests." *Illinois Law Review* 29:460–90.

———. 1936. "Relational Interests." *Illinois Law Review* 31:35–57.

Grossberg, Michael. 1985. *Governing the Hearth: Law and the Family in Nineteenth-Century America*. Chapel Hill: University of North Carolina Press.

Hartog, Hendrik. 1997. "Lawyering, Husbands' Rights, and 'the Unwritten Law' in Nineteenth-Century America." *Journal of American History* 84 (June): 67–96.

Havighurst, Harold C. 1932. "Services in the Home—A Study of Contract Concepts in Domestic Relations." *Yale Law Journal* 41 (January): 386–406.

Hearn, Jeff, and Wendy Parkin. 1995. *"Sex" at "Work."* New York: St. Martin's Press.

Heinze, Andrew. 1990. *Adapting to Abundance*. New York: Columbia University Press.

Hill, Marilynn Wood. 1993. *Their Sisters' Keepers*. Berkeley and Los Angeles: University of California Press.

Hirsch, Fred. 1976. *Social Limits to Growth*. Cambridge, Mass.: Harvard University Press.

Hirshman, Linda R., and Jane E. Larson. 1998. *Hard Bargains: The Politics of Sex*. New York: Oxford University Press.

Hochschild, Arlie. 1983. *The Managed Heart*. Berkeley and Los Angeles: University of California Press.

Hoigard, Cecilie, and Liv Finstad. 1992. *Backstreets: Prostitution, Money, and Love*. Cambridge, Mass.: Polity Press.

Holbrook, Evans. 1923. "The Change in the Meaning of Consortium." *Michigan Law Review* 22:1–9.

Hunter, Howard O. 1978. "An Essay on Contract and Status: Race, Marriage, and the Meretricious Spouse." *Virginia Law Review* 64:1,039–97.

Klein, William A., and Joseph Bankman. 1994. *Federal Income Taxation*. 10th ed. Boston: Little, Brown.

Knodel, John, Mark Van Landingham, Chanpen Saengtienchai, and Anthony Pramualratana. 1995. "Friends, Wives, and Extramarital Sex in Thailand: A Qualitative Study of Peer and Spousal Influence on Thai Male Extramarital Sexual Behavior and Attitudes." Research Report no. 95-328 (March), Population Studies Center, University of Michigan.

———. 1996. "Thai Views of Sexuality and Sexual Behavior." *Health Transition Review* 6:179–201.

Kulick, Don. 1998. *Travesti*. Chicago: University of Chicago Press.

Laqueur, Thomas. 1990. *Making Sex: Body and Gender from the Greeks to Freud*. Cambridge, Mass.: Harvard University Press.

Lazarus-Black, Mindie, and Susan F. Hirsh. 1994. *Contested States: Law, Hegemony, and Resistance*. New York: Routledge.

Lessig, Lawrence. 1995. "The Regulation of Social Meaning." *University of Chicago Law Review* 62:943–1,045.

———. 1996. "Social Meaning and Social Norms." *University of Pennsylvania Law Review* 144:2,181–89.

———. 1998. "The New Chicago School." *Journal of Legal Studies* 27 (pt. 2): 661–91.

Lippman, Jacob. 1930. "The Breakdown of Consortium." *Columbia Law Review* 30:651–73.

McDaniel, Paul R., Hugh J. Ault, Martin J. McMahon Jr., and Daniel L. Simmons. 1994. *Federal Income Taxation: Cases and Materials*. Westbury, N.Y.: Foundation Press.

McKintosh, Andrew C. 1930. "Right of a Woman Who Lives with a Man on the Mistaken Belief That They Are Lawfully Married to Recover for Services." *Law Notes* 34 (July): 64–66.

Meckel, Mary V. 1995. *A Sociological Analysis of the California Taxi-Dancer*. Lewiston, N.Y.: Edwin Mellen Press.

Modell, John. 1989. *Into One's Own: From Youth to Adulthood in the United States, 1920–1975*. Berkeley and Los Angeles: University of California Press.

Muller-Freienfels, Wolfram. 1968. "Zur Rechtsprechung beim sog: 'Matressen-Testament.'" *Juristenzeitung* 19 (July): 441–49.

Nelson, Julie. 1998a. "For Love or Money—or Both?" Paper presented at the "Out of the Margin 2" Conference, Amsterdam, June 2–5.

———. 1998b. "One Sphere or Two?" In "Changing Forms of Payment," edited by Viviana A. Zelizer. Special issue of *American Behavioral Scientist* 41 (August): 1,467–71.

Nussbaum, Martha C. 1998. "Whether from Reason or Prejudice: Taking Money for Bodily Services." *Journal of Legal Studies* 27 (pt. 2): 693–724.

———. 1999. *Sex and Social Justice.* New York: Oxford University Press.

Overall, Christine. 1992. "What's Wrong with Prostitution? Evaluating Sex Work." *Signs* 17:705–24.

Pascoe, Peggy. 1998. "Race, Gender, and the Privileges of Property: On the Significance of Miscegenation Law in the U.S. West." In *Over the Edge: Mapping Western Experiences,* edited by Valerie Matsumoto and Blake Allmendinger, 215–30. Berkeley and Los Angeles: University of California Press.

Peiss, Kathy. 1983. "'Charity Girls' and City Pleasures: Historical Notes on Working-Class Sexuality, 1880–1920." In *Powers of Desire: The Politics of Sexuality,* edited by Ann Snitow, Christine Stansell, and Sharon Thompson, 74–87. New York: Monthly Review Press.

———. 1986. *Cheap Amusements.* Philadelphia: Temple University Press.

Posner, Richard A. [1992] 1997. *Sex and Reason.* Cambridge, Mass.: Harvard University Press.

Prosser, William L. 1971. *Law of Torts.* St. Paul, Minn.: West Publishing.

Radin, Margaret. 1996. *Contested Commodities.* Cambridge, Mass.: Harvard University Press.

Reiss, Albert J., Jr. 1961. "The Social Integration of Queers and Peers." *Social Problems* 9 (Fall): 102–19.

Rose, Carol. 1994. "Rhetoric and Romance: A Comment on *Spouses and Strangers.*" *Georgetown Law Journal* 82 (September): 2,409–21.

Rothman, Ellen K. 1984. *Hands and Hearts.* New York: Basic Books.

Rotman, Edgardo. 1995. "The Inherent Problems of Legal Translation: Theoretical Aspects." *Indiana International and Comparative Law Review* 6:1–10.

Rouchell, Harold M. 1930. "Life Insurance and the Concubine." *Loyola Law Journal* 11:161–69.

Sanchez, Lisa E. 1997. "Boundaries of Legitimacy: Sex, Violence, Citizenship, and Community in a Local Sexual Economy." *Law and Social Inquiry* 22 (Summer): 543–80.

Scambler, Graham, and Annette Scambler. 1997. *Rethinking Prostitution.* London: Routledge.

Schulhofer, Stephen J. 1998. *Unwanted Sex: The Culture of Intimidation and the Failure of Law.* Cambridge, Mass.: Harvard University Press.

Sewell, William H., Jr. 1993. "Toward a Post-materialist Rhetoric for Labor History." In *Rethinking Labor History,* edited by Leonard R. Berlanstein, 15–38. Urbana: University of Illinois Press.

Siegel, Reva B. 1994. "The Modernization of Marital Status Law: Adjudicating Wives' Rights to Earnings, 1860–1930." *Georgetown Law Journal* 82 (September): 2,127–2,211.

Silbaugh, Katharine. 1996. "Turning Labor into Love: Housework and the Law." *Northwestern University Law Review* 91:1–85.

Stanley, Amy Dru. 1988. "Conjugal Bonds and Wage Labor: Rights of Contract in the Age of Emancipation." *Journal of American History* 75 (September): 471–500.

———. 1998. *From Bondage to Contract: Wage Labor, Marriage, and the Market in the Age of Slave Emancipation.* New York: Cambridge University Press.

Staves, Susan. 1982. "Money for Honor: Damages for Criminal Conversation." *Studies in Eighteenth-Century Culture* 2:279–97.

Stinchcombe, Arthur L. 1994. "Prostitution, Kinship, and Illegitimate Work." *Contemporary Sociology* 23 (November): 856–59.

Sunstein, Cass. 1997. *Free Markets and Social Justice*. New York: Oxford University Press.

Taylor, Robert F. 1983. "Concubinage and Union Libre: A Historical Comparison of the Rights of Unwed Cohabitants in Wrongful Death Actions in France and Louisiana." *Georgia Journal of International and Comparative Law* 13:715–31.

Tushnet, Rebecca. 1998. "Rules of Engagement." *Yale Law Journal* 107:2,583–2,618.

VanderVelde, Lea. 1996. "The Legal Ways of Seduction." *Stanford Law Review* 48:817–901.

Wacquant, Loïc. 1998. "A Fleshpeddler at Work: Power, Pain, and Profit in the Prizefighting Economy." *Theory and Society* 27 (February): 1–42.

Walzer, Michael. 1983. *Spheres of Justice*. New York: Basic Books.

Williams, Joan. 1994. "Is Coverture Dead? Beyond a New Theory of Alimony." *Georgetown Law Journal* 82:2,227–90.

Woods, James D., with Jay H. Lucas. 1993. *The Corporate Closet*. New York: Free Press.

Zatz, Noah D. 1997. "Sex Work/Sex Act: Law, Labor, and Desire in Constructions of Prostitution." *Signs* 22 (Winter): 277–308.

Zeigler, Sara L. 1996. "Wifely Duties: Marriage, Labor, and the Common Law in Nineteenth-Century America." *Social Science History* 20 (Spring): 63–96.

Zelizer, Viviana A. 1994. *The Social Meaning of Money*. New York: Basic Books.

———. 1996. "Payments and Social Ties." *Sociological Forum* 11 (September): 481–95.

11

Kids and Commerce

Here are four vignettes of children's economic activities:

1. Studying children's vital labor contributions to their parents' Chinese take-away family businesses in Britain, Miri Song reports how children carefully differentiated "helping out" from formal employment. Parents' payments, for instance, were seldom treated as ordinary wages. As Anna, one of Song's respondents, recalled:

> We never asked for more. 'Cause it was seen as a bonus, 'cause we worked anyway. And it was just like a little token gesture to buy yourself a record or something nice to read. (Song 1999, 85)

2. Elizabeth Chin's ethnographic account of ten-year-old, poor and working-class black children's consumption practices in Newhallville, a neighborhood in New Haven, Connecticut, documents, among other patterns, children's contrasting relationships to shopkeepers in local neighborhood stores and downtown shops. Asia, one of Chin's young informants, tells her about her experience at Claire's, a popular jewelry shop in the downtown mall:

> "Last time I was in there the lady was laughing because I didn't have enough money. The other day I went in, and I bought all this stuff and the lady said, 'that will be forty dollars.' I pulled out a fifty-dollar bill and said, 'Here.'" Asia demonstrated how she slapped the bill down on the counter, and the look on her face was both self-satisfied and challenging. "I swear I was about to say 'keep the change' until my grandmother came up." (Chin 2001, 103)

3. Observing children's birthday-party practices among Parisian middle-class families, Régine Sirota found very young kids actively participating in gift selection. Until he was three, for instance, Adrien's mother chose his friends' birthday gifts, but then the pattern shifted:

> She [now] always shops with him, accepting his choices. These are often the result of earlier negotiations among peers during recess: thus, Tom (7 years old) arranged with his school pals to get what he wants: a stuffed Marsupilami, Batmans, a book about Knights of the Round-table that one of them already owns. (Sirota 1998, 458)

4. Bill Berkeley has been analyzing African political conflicts and covering them in major American media for two decades. He reports on a return to Liberia, where he earlier had been banned for his critical reporting. Here is one of the things he saw:

> On a Saturday morning in June 1992, the Liberian port of Buchanan sweltered in the dense tropical humidity of West Africa's rainy season. Four small boys ambled up a muddy and pothole-ridden sidewalk and entered a tea stall on the city's main street. They looked to be scarcely older than ten. Dressed in baggy jeans and grimy T-shirts not much taller than the loaded Soviet-era Kalashnikov assault rifles they cradled in their arms, the boys shuffled heavily in big brown military boots that on them resembled the outsized paws on a puppy. "How the day?" one of them muttered.
> A shudder ran down my spine. The bullets were bigger than his fingers. The boy brushed by the stool where I was sitting and approached the woman who owned the stall. He lifted his fingers to his mouth. The owner dutifully fetched some bananas and buttered some rolls. The boys shuffled out onto the street—no word of thanks, no suggestion of payment—savoring their breakfast as they walked. (Berkeley 2001, 21)

These vignettes open up the largely uncharted economic worlds of children. Masked by persistent assumptions of children's remoteness from processes of production, consumption, and distribution, children's economic practices have remained closeted, camouflaged by the supposedly exclusive dominance of play and learning over the market activity. The image of an impenetrable (and desirable) barrier between children and the economy has so taken hold that it has produced a stock character in recent American humor: the child who dresses up in adult economic garments. Remember how deftly Charles Schultz (1999), whose *Peanuts* portrayed a perfectly separate world of childhood, lampooned Lucy's setting herself up in business as a five-cent psychiatrist on the model of a child entrepreneur and a lemonade stand?

On the other side, the looming image of child labor as a corrupting force has also inhibited careful examination of children's economic activity. Long before Bill Berkeley's hardened child soldiers and anti-sweatshop campaigners' regimented child garment workers, the photographs of Jacob Riis warned Americans that premature economic involvement would make children old—and evil—before their time.

In the past decade or so, however, pioneering anthropologists, sociologists, education specialists, and psychologists have become impatient with prevailing beliefs and established paradigms. Using multiple methods of research, the new scholarship shows kids actively engaging in a broad range of economic relations. This article advances that program.

To be sure, people have long since studied some features of childhood economic activity. Investigations of early socialization, for instance, extensively document children's cognitive understandings of work and money. Other scholars have concerned themselves with the moral or developmental impact of economic activity on children's welfare: does paid labor help or hinder children's schooling? Will an allowance turn the child into a better consumer? Does consumption tarnish kids' moral worlds? Does poverty encourage consumerist youngsters to steal and to take up dangerous occupations so they can acquire media-hyped goods? Most of these queries are framed by an adult point of view, asking how children understand the adult economy, how they learn it, how they fit in, and how it affects them.

Adoption of an adult perspective has produced a framing of general questions about childhood that dominates recent research. Here are three persistent questions that appear in the adult-oriented literature:

- Are children basically adults-in-the-making or inhabitants of a distinct children's world?
- Does childhood pass through universal stages of development, or does it vary significantly by situation and category?
- Do children's practices, character, and experience depend primarily on relations to their family, relations to adults in general, or relations to their peers?

Of course, the proper answers to each of these questions combine some elements of both extremes. In any case, these same questions take on a different light when we shift our perspective to children's own experiences in the economy.

My book *Pricing the Priceless Child* (Zelizer 1985) emphasized adults' changing orientation to children in the United States between the 1870s and 1930s. That emphasis proved fruitful; it brought out adults' increasing valuation of children not for their economic contributions but for their distinctive personal characteristics. It did not reach very far, however, into children's own experiences of economic change. This article reverses the perspective by considering children as active economic agents, and adults as simply one category of persons with whom children carry on economic activities.

Despite demands such as Deborah Levison's (2000) for consideration of children as authentic economic agents, the recent upsurge of work on children in the economy has also generally incorporated an adult perspective. Students of childhood outside the world's wealthiest segments have, for example, begun to challenge the assumption that paid employment harms children, but even they ordinarily invoke local culture and household welfare rather than children's own experience in paid labor (see, for example, Nieuwenhuys 1996; Porter 1999; for an exception, see Woodhead 1999). Within wealthier segments, students of childhood have similarly stressed adult and household concerns; the rising cost of children and child care or the display value of children's consumption for their parents.

Nevertheless, an increasing minority of specialists in childhood have been calling for a deliberate shift of perspective from adults' observations or reactions to children's own economic lives. The vignettes with which I began represent an important revision in perspective.

Marketing specialists actually got there first, identifying children as savvy, active economic agents. As the authoritative researcher James McNeal reports, over the past two decades, marketing for children has gone from a laughing stock to a major industry. In fact, in some respects, academic scholars have not yet caught up with market researchers: there are vast stores of information on children still untapped in the files and publications of marketing experts. McNeal extensively documents the multiple business potential of a growing "kids market," as primary markets (spending their own money), influence markets (shaping their parents' expenditures), and future markets.

American children between the ages of four and twelve, reports McNeal, with an annual income of over $27 billion, spend $23 billion, and save what is left. Over $7 billion a year of children's own money goes for snacks and a similar amount for play items. They influence about $188 billion of their parent's spending each year (McNeal 1999, 29). Children's consumer power is not only an American phenomenon. In China's newly marketized economy, for instance, McNeal and his collaborators at China's Beijing University found that urban children control $6 billion per year in purchases, as well as influencing around 68 percent of their parents' consumption expenditures (McNeal 1999, 250, 259). That consumption notably includes Western-style snack food; in Asia, McDonald's and Kentucky Fried Chicken draw their principal customers from among children (Lozada 2000; Watson 1997).

Children, however, engage in a far wider range of economic activity than shopping (in this article "children" means fourteen years of age or younger). Despite the illusion of a historic shift of children from production to consumption, children have long engaged simultaneously in production, consumption, and distribution as well. What has changed is the character of their engagement in these three spheres. To see these changes clearly, we must examine children themselves at work.

Recent research provides new ideas and information about children's place in economic production, consumption, and distribution. It also helps identify three somewhat different sets of economic relations in which children regularly engage: with members (including adult members) of their own households, with children outside their households, and with agents of other organizations such as outside households, schools, stores, firms, churches, and voluntary associations. Contrary to cherished images of children as economic innocents, we discover children actively engaged in production, consumption, and distribution. We also discover that their economic activity varies significantly from one category of social relations to another.

Although it draws on fairly wide reading, this article makes no claims to survey the whole recent literature on childhood. That worthwhile effort would require, for example, much more attention to studies by psychologists and educational specialists than this article can offer. Nor do I survey either the history of children's economic activities or its worldwide variation.[1] Here I concentrate on analyses shedding light on variation in children's social relations as they carry on production, consumption, and distribution in different settings. I argue that:

- Once we examine social lives from children's own vantage points, we discover an extensive range of economic activity significantly differentiated by setting and social relation.
- On the whole, ethnographers have been more successful than other investigators in documenting that activity because they less often adopt adults' definitions of serious economic activity, rely less on individuals' conventionalized retrospective reports of activities, and more often observe negotiated social interaction as it occurs.
- Children develop extensive connections with adult-dominated spheres of production, consumption, and distribution but generally experience those encounters as unequal exercises of power.
- Despite adult efforts to contain them, they also establish segregated, partly autonomous spheres of production, consumption, and distribution on their own.
- It is therefore useful to adopt rough distinctions among three sets of social relations: with other household members, especially adults; with agents of organizations outside children's own households; with other children.
- In all these social relations, children negotiate understandings and practices with other participants, however unequally they do so.
- Such relations, understandings and practices vary systematically by broad social category, but we lack adequate information on how and why.
- Altogether, these observations suggest a promising agenda for new research on kids and commerce.

In keeping with the common assumption of the child as consumer rather than as producer or distributor, researchers have so far given much more attention to consumption practices. This article again reverses the perspective by stressing production and distribution before turning to a briefer sketch of consumption. In each of these sectors we find differentiation of children's economic activities depending on their predominant social relations. I focus here on three types of relations: with other household members; with agents of organizations outside the household; with other children.

CHILDREN AS PRODUCERS

Connecting with recent analyses of caring and household economies, let us adopt a broad definition of production. Production here means any effort that creates value (see Tilly and Tilly 1998). Such a definition obviously includes far more than the conventional paid employment and production for the market. In this framework, Miri Song's (1999) respondents are exceptionally active producers, fully collaborating in their parents' take-away shops. With some variation from family to family as well as by age and gender, she shows us children—often as young as seven or eight—in the evenings, after school, or during weekends, cooking, cleaning and taking customers' orders. At times, children were also involved in caring labor, translating, and mediating for their non-English-speaking parents (see also Orellana 2001; Valenzuela 1999).

These child workers carefully differentiated what they saw as their "helping out" from formal employment. As we heard earlier from Anna, bargaining with an employer-parent created distinct economic practices, turning compensation, for instance, into a perk or a bonus, rather than a standard wage. In fact, some children refused any payment at all. Laura, another of Song's respondents, explained:

> It's because being a family business, it's part of our lives, and you don't think, it doesn't feel like real work, you know? It felt awkward, the idea of receiving a wage. (Song 1999, 86)

In some cases, children, while uneasy about taking money for their labor, felt obliged to accept their parents' payments, more as filial recognition of parental provider status than as payment for work. Others, meanwhile, welcomed the money as tangible recognition of their household contributions. Paul told Song:

> Paying us was a nice way to do it; it meant that we weren't just putting out a hand and taking money from our parents. We were actually helping out as well. I felt sort of quite justified having taken it. (Song 1999, 86)

On the other hand, some children resented parents' payments as unwelcome bribes, forcing them into work they disliked. In all these cases, instead of passively accepting their parents' handouts or a standard wage, the children were bargaining out a distinctive set of meanings corresponding to their relationships with their parent-employer.

Similar bargaining occurs in households that do not run their own businesses. In an extraordinary and apparently neglected analysis of seven-year-olds' economic behavior in Nottingham, John and Elizabeth Newson document a wide range of household work for compensation among both middle-class and working-class families. Children, their mothers report, brought in the coal, dusted, helped in the garden, cleaned the car, washed pots, polished brass, cared for younger siblings, ran errands, vacuumed, fetched clothing, cleaned shoes, and even tickled their fathers' feet. Once again, parents and children bargained out compensation systems. A fireman's wife explains:

> Sometimes he'll go and help his Dad with the garden, but not a set rule; although I do sort of say that their pocket money—they are given it in return for running errands and washing pots and helping with the little ones. I mean, Saturday they have it, and they do two or three errands before they get their money—they get them done very quickly! (Newson and Newson 1976, 227; for other British cases and a New Zealand parallel, see Morrow 1994; Fleming 1997)

In the United States as well, children participate in a variety of productive domestic tasks, such as cleaning up their rooms, cooking, dusting, doing laundry, washing dishes, vacuuming, setting or clearing the table, cleaning the bathroom, sweeping floors, carrying out garbage, mowing the lawn, cleaning the yard, or caring for younger siblings and pets. A nine-year-old girl that Victoria Chapman classified as one of her "Chore Hounds" reported a very wide range of household tasks. Among other things, she helped her mother with grocery shopping:

> I push the carriage, I hold coupons that she uses, and usually the coupons that she does not use I hold and sometimes she'll tell me to go get something and I'll go get it. (Chapman 1994, 167)

Recent studies report that American children are spending increasing amounts of their time in such household chores (see, for example, Lee et al. 2000). Children's marketing specialist McNeal estimates that children in the United States perform 11 percent of total household work (1999, 71).

Likewise, Anne Solberg's study of eleven- and twelve-year-old Norwegian children's household work speculates that children, especially girls, may be more significant assistants to mothers than their fathers are (1994, 84). (This sort of substitution raises interesting questions about parallels between child-parent and spousal bargaining over household work; see, for example,

Brines 1994; Gerson 1993; Greenstein 2000; Hochschild 1989; Hochschild and Machung 1989; Lundberg and Pollak 1996).

In most cases, children expect some kind of domestic payment. Parents agree. McNeal itemizes five different sources of children's cash income. In the late 1990s, 16 percent of kids' income came from gifts from parents, 8 percent from others' gifts, 45 percent from allowances, 10 percent from work outside the home, and 21 percent from household work. Significantly, McNeal notes that children's compensation from household work rose to 21 percent from 15 percent in the mid-1980s (1999, 69, 71). However, since parents are not standard employers, negotiating suitable payment systems turns into a delicate and highly contested issue. At issue is not merely a wage bargain but a definition of proper relations between parents and their offspring.

Indeed, the nature of children's allowances has excited debate for over a century, with some experts and parents strongly advocating compensation for children's household work, and others insisting on a separation between work effort and allowances. In the latter cases, allowances qualify not as compensation but as a parent's discretionary gift or the child's entitlement. Nevertheless, whether compensation, gift, or entitlement, allowances are subject to continual bargaining between parents and children.

Negotiations occur over both allowances and other monetary transfers. Parents, for their own part, often impose a set of terms, deciding which chores to compensate with money or overseeing, and in some cases closely supervising, children's expenditure. In these transactions, however, children do not simply echo parents' preferences for household payments but work out their own moral views and strategies. Amy Nathan's *The Kids' Allowance Book*, based on interviews with 166 children between the ages of nine and fourteen from eleven schools around the United States, reports a variety of such rationales and strategies. Children, for instance, repeatedly praise regular allowances as welcome sources of discretionary income. Before getting an allowance, Katie explains: "If I wanted a pair of special sneakers, [my parents] might say it's too expensive and not a necessity. Now that I get an allowance, if they don't want to pay, I can pay for it myself" (Nathan 1998, 6).

Children divide, however, over whether or not allowances should compensate for their domestic chores, some children insisting that helping out is an expected, fair, and therefore free, household contribution. Others forcefully defend their often elaborate monetized exchanges. Listen, for instance, to Amanda:

On top of all the cleaning and garbage toting Amanda B. has to do for her allowance, she regularly does freebies like folding the clothes or setting the table. "If I'm sitting around and my mom asks me to do something, I'll say sure and won't ask to get paid," she says, "I do it to help out." But if she is saving up for something special, she'll hunt for a big job that needs doing, such as basement cleaning. Ugh! She'll ask if her mom will pay extra for it. That's when the freebies pay off. "Since I'm not always working just for money, when I ask if she'll pay me to do something extra, she usually does." (Nathan 1998, 15)

Children report numerous, often intricate, negotiating tips, ranging from how to choose chores (pick your own, "if your mom chooses, she might give you a chore you can't even bear the *thought* of doing"); getting a fair wage (find out what other kids earn); how to make sure parents pay on time ("I remind my dad on the day *before*, to make sure he has the right change for my allowance the next day"); how to get a raise ("no-nos" include whining, begging, asking for way too much, or not doing chores on time; among the "dos": "do lots of stuff to help out and be nice to your brother or sister [if you have one]," and "ask for a slightly *bigger* raise than you want so you can give in a little and still come out okay") (Nathan 1998, 55, 52, 20, 46).[2]

To understand this unexplored household economy fully, we need much more systematic information about actual bargaining between parents and children. Characteristically, and unfortunately, we know even less about children's production involving their peers, or with agents of organizations, including other households. When it comes to children working with peers, we draw on little more than sentimentalized visions of future self-made capitalists learning their skills on lemonade stands or sharing newspaper routes. Take *Rich Dad Poor Dad*, the runaway 1997 best-seller guide to financial success: its key inspirational anecdote shows us two nine-year-olds cashing in from their partnership renting comic books to other kids. They learned early "to have money work for us. . . . By starting our own business, the comic-book library, we were in control of our own finances, not dependent on an employer" (Kiyosaki and Lechter 1997, 52).

In such parables, we see only the above surface of what is surely a huge undersea continent. Only infrequently do researchers provide glimpses of what lies underneath. Consider, for instance, Elizabeth Chin's observations of how Tionna and Tiffany—two of her ten-year-old Newhallville informants—managed their cucumber stand, selling cucumbers one of them had grown in her backyard. Pricing their goods, Chin reports, settled into a delicate social bargain. They asked forty cents for the larger cucumbers, a quarter for smaller ones. Unsure of how much to ask for a larger cucumber,

> Tionna suggested sixty cents. Tiffany wondered if it should be seventy-five. Then, with authority, Tionna announced the price should be fifty cents because then they could split it easier and wouldn't have to wait for some change. . . . Tiffany's grandmother came by and bought a large cucumber, putting fifty, rather than forty, cents into the pot. The kids would occasionally count the money and divide it into two equal

piles, since they were planning to split the money equally. They ended up with each having about a dollar seventy-five. (Chin 2001, 72–73)

Multiple other forms of peer production remain invisible, catalogued as child play. Paul Webley describes the case of English children's marble economy, where he found some children "providing the capital (the marbles) while another provides his or her labour (playing the game). The winnings (earnings) are then divided between the two children" (1996, 156). Whole zones of children's activities, from building tree houses to collecting junk, involve more than play by producing value.

What about production for outside organizations, including other households? McNeal reports that children's income from work outside the home, unlike their increasing pay for household work, has remained fairly stable at around 10–13 percent for children under twelve. Children earn by babysitting; raking leaves; mowing lawns; watering plants; shoveling snow; cleaning garages; selling cookies, candies, or lottery tickets to raise funds for school activities or charities; washing cars; taking care of pets; as runners or lookouts for drug dealers; watching cars; or as baggers at supermarkets. More recently, some eleven- and twelve-year-olds have been making money with investments and savings (McNeal 1999, 72; see also Lewis 2001). Once we shift our attention outside households, it becomes clear how many of children's activities involve production, including volunteer work, and as Jens Qvortrup (1995) has forcefully argued, schoolwork.

Production outside households draws children into a new set of economic relationships with other adults/employers. Consider the case of the Norwegian *passepike*, or baby-walker, nine- to fifteen-year-old girls who for a fee take care of children up to the age of three for a couple of hours in the afternoon. Studying passepike in Bergen, Marianne Gullestad gives an account of their economic arrangements with employers. The fee, for instance, is established in relation to what the girls' friends get and what other mothers pay. Far more goes into this relationship, Gullestad observes, than purchasing the carer's time: mothers of smaller children often give passepike holiday gifts, birthday presents, and clothing. For their part, the girl carers offer gifts to their charges and regularly do more than their contract requires: "She comes in earlier or gladly changes and feeds the child before they go out. Or in addition . . . she may be a babysitter in the evening, may do the dishes, wash the floors, etc." (Gullestad 1992, 121). Close personal ties to the mother, suggests Gullestad, become part of the passepike's reward system (for related American practices; see Formanek-Brunell 1998).

As in productive relations with parents and with peers, we see children's productive ties with outside households and organizations varying significantly in content, but always involving creative input on the children's part. Over most of the world, relatively young children not only engage in the intermittent production relationships reviewed here but also take up full-time paid employment in agriculture, manufacturing, services, or even the military. To cover the full range of children's productive relationships would take me far beyond the scope of this article. The point should already be clear: like that of their elders, children's production takes place within negotiated sets of social relations and varies significantly as a function of those social relations' content and meaning.

CHILDREN AS DISTRIBUTORS

As with production, a quick survey of distribution shows children at work negotiating various ties within their households, with peers, and in relation to outside households and organizations. Let us again adopt a broad definition. Distribution here refers to all transfers of value, not just those in which quid-pro-quo exchange occurs (Davis 1992). From very early in their lives—perhaps later than when they begin consuming, but earlier than when we can meaningfully think of them as regular producers—children engage in economically significant transfers. Those transfers generally begin within children's own households, usually next turn to peers, but involve outside households and organizations from quite young ages.

Since distribution within households and with organizations is more obvious, let me concentrate on peers. Régine Sirota's observations of Parisian children's birthday parties show even very young kids actively engaged in their gift economy, starting with peer collusion in gift selection. Children negotiate not only with their parents but also with each other over the quality, value, and character of their gifts. Let me single out two observations from Sirota's rich ethnography: children's negotiation for their gifts and variation in gift giving by the kinds of ties among them. In their negotiations, children are working simultaneously to hammer out appropriate terms with their peers and with their parents who (at least for younger gift givers) subsidize purchases. The problem for children is that parents may not be willing to pay for the gift the child regards as most appropriate. For instance, Sirota reports one strong maternal gift rule, adjusting the gift's price to the strength of friendship ties: "For great buddies, great gifts, for lesser friends, lesser gifts" (Sirota 1998, 459).

As for the matching of gifts to children's networks, Sirota observed regular correspondence between the intensity of friendship ties and the personalization of gifts: closer friends are expected to pay careful attention to the other's taste. Sirota's respondents praise successful gift givers: "He pays real attention to what he offers" or "She always gives me something really pretty." Personalization turns even less popular objects, such as books, into prized gifts. Julien bought Barbara, partly with his own pocket money, Joffo's book *Agate et calots*, because "he had adored *Un sac de billes*, which he had just read, he was sure she would like it" (Sirota 1998, 461).

Children's gift transfers do not simply translate parental values or social position into material objects. On the contrary, children's own relations and understandings play a significant part in organizing the birthday gift economy. What is more, these are economically serious matters. Sirota calculates that the average household involved spends the French equivalent of $150 a year per child on birthday gift exchanges (the cost includes countergifts offered by the birthday celebrant to party guests). As they grow older, children themselves increasingly spend their own pocket money on such gifts, thereby acquiring greater control over the entire process. With appropriate adjustment for class and national culture, similar arrangements seem to be very widespread in Western countries.

Birthday gift transfers represent only one of children's multiple distribution systems, along with other holiday gifts, sales, trades, barter, treats, gambling, and sharing. Beyond their households, in schools, stores, summer camps, and other sites, children regularly engage in these sorts of economic transfers. Using a variety of monetary media, including cash, but also food, marbles, comic books, and Pokemon cards, they maintain a thriving distribution economy.

Schools provide a privileged location for observation of these processes. Notice what often goes on at lunchtime. During the half-hour allotted to Newhallville children, Elizabeth Chin saw them "trading portions of school lunch, homemade lunches, or cadging money to buy cookies" at a "fevered pitch that often rivals that found on the trading floor of the New York Stock Exchange" (Chin 2001, 77). As with birthday gift giving among Parisian children. New Haven's youngsters enacted their social networks in food trades, sales, and donations. Turning down a deal, therefore, implied social rejection. Chin reports how this worked:

> Kids very often refused to eat all or part of the lunch served; if they were willing to eat part of it (for instance the peanut butter and jelly on graham crackers) they would barter vigorously to get someone else's portion of that item and "Are you going to eat that?" was a phrase often repeated throughout lunchtime, in concert with "Can I have your milk?" or "Do you want your pizza?" The negotiation of relationships between children lay clear on the face of these interactions and I have seen children pointedly dump uneaten portions of their lunches—coveted by others at their table—into the garbage. As a gesture of rejection, such an action could hardly be more decisive. (Chin 2001, 78)

Studying first-grade African American girls' friendships, Kim Scott identifies racial patterns in such distribution systems. For instance, in the racially mixed American elementary school that Kim Scott calls Rose Mount, she repeatedly found white girls distributing gifts of candy, cookies, or quarters, while black girls (who in this school generally came from lower-income families) were typically recipients, not distributors. In other regards, however, distribution patterns strikingly resembled what Chin found in New Haven: girls offered food and money gifts first of all to their best friends, and then to less intimate or favored classmates. Scott notes that girls "she does not like" are given an excuse, such as, "I don't have that much . . . or a quick shake of the head no" (1999, 130). (For a linguistic analysis of six-year-old children's food trades, see Mishler 1979.)

But not all transfers of food are gifts. During her observations of African American eleven- and twelve-year-old boys in an impoverished urban school, Ann Ferguson registered their "thriving informal economy." Surprised to notice Jamar distributing apples, oranges, and bananas to kids outside his circle of friends, she discovered his apparent "sharing" was in fact a sale when his teacher threatened to report Jamar's unauthorized business to the principal (2000, 103).

Kids' commerce also takes place in the schoolroom. William Corsaro's comparison of American and Italian nursery schools shows us very young children defying school rules by bringing toys and other small objects—such as toy animals, matchbox cars, candy, or gum—to school, often concealed in their pockets. Children, reports Corsaro, "often would show his or her 'stashed loot' to a playmate and carefully share the forbidden object without catching the teachers' attention" (1997, 42). Barrie Thorne's classic study of elementary schoolchildren introduces the gendering of such clandestine distribution flows. She found kids stashing and trading small objects such as "'pencil pals' (rubbery creatures designed to stick on the end of pencils), rabbit feet, special erasers and silver paper" as well as more gendered goods, toy cars or trucks by boys, lip gloss, nail polish, or doll furniture by girls. These "secret exchanges," Thorne discovered, followed rigid gender lines, marking "circles of friendship that almost never included both girls and boys" (1993, 21; see also Feiring and Lewis 1989).

Thus, in lunchrooms, schoolrooms, and playgrounds, children fashion elaborate systems of distribution covering a wide variety of objects and representing both peer solidarities and their divisions. One could make the same demonstration for a variety of other encounters in which children interact. Researchers, for instance, have documented comic book trades in summer camps; bargaining by U.S. and Canadian kids over sports "chase" cards, Pokemon cards, and Beanie Babies; English children's marble swapping; and ritualized sharing among Israeli kids (see Cook 2001; Katriel 1987; Paris 2000; Webley 1996).

If we were to follow children's distribution practices into their household relations with parents, siblings, and other relatives, and their involvement in other organizations—such as gifts to charities, contributions to religious organizations, dues to scouts, transfers to savings banks, Internet allowance sites—the extent of systematic variation would become even clearer. Once we shake off adult prejudices, we discover extensively organized and differentiated children's distributional economies.

CHILDREN AS CONSUMERS

Because the consuming child has attracted greater media attention than the producer or distributor, we have more extensive documentation of children's consumption. Yet even that documentation misses the centrality of negotiated and differentiated social relations to youthful consumption activity. Marketers, for their part, mainly treat kids as a special category of individual purchasers. The growing social-scientific literature, in contrast, has stressed political and moral concerns: to what extent does consumption standardize, commodify, or repress children's experiences? Are children tools of capitalist interest? Does desire for expensive goods lead children into dangerous behavior? Meanwhile, social critics debate whether globalization and its commodities are wiping out authentic local cultures (see, for example, Buckingham 2000; Cook 2000; Cross 1997, 2000; Kline 1993, 1998; Kotlowitz 1999; Lozada 2000; Nightingale 1993; Pecora 1998; Seiter 1993; Steinberg and Kincheloe 1997).

Here, however, I follow the trail of children's social relations through consumption. Let us adopt the conventional understanding of consumption as acquisition of goods and services rather than their actual final disposition. Again it will help to employ a rough distinction among three categories of social relations: with agents of outside households and organizations, with other members of a child's own household, and with peers.

Earlier we saw Asia, one of Elizabeth Chin's New Haven informants, report her uneasy relationship to store clerks. Ferguson, meanwhile, showed us a youngster selling fruit in school. The anecdote means of course that other children were consuming the fruit. Surprisingly, the documentation of such consumption in organizations and other households is much more scattered than documentation concerning children's consumption within households, and with peers (for exceptions, see Cahill 1987; Cross 1997; Jacobson 1997; Miller 1997). Let me concentrate on households and deal fleetingly with peers.

Note Chin's findings on household consumption. To understand Newhallville's children's practices better, Chin supplemented her two-year participant observation in homes, schools, and neighborhoods with shopping trips. She gave twenty-three children $20 each to spend entirely at their discretion (some of the children brought along other children—siblings, relatives, or classmates). Here's what ten-year-old Shaquita bought with her money: two pairs of shoes at Payless—$6.99 denim mules for herself, and $9.99 for a pair of golden slip-ons as a birthday gift for her mother. She spent the remainder at Rite-Aid—$0.99 for a bag of bubble gum to share with her older sister and $2.09 for foam hair rollers to give her grandmother (Chin 2001, 126).

As with most of the other children, Shaquita's shopping spree did not turn into a wild, self-indulgent experience. Instead, Chin identified two notable features of child shoppers' purchases: practicality and generosity. They bought useful items for themselves, such as shoes, socks, underwear, or school notebooks, and picked gift goods for family members. Both types of purchases cemented children's position in the household. They also established or confirmed their social ties with family members.

Lest these New Haven children appear to be impossibly reasonable and altruistic, Chin reminds us of the mixture of meanings that flowed from their purchases: obligation to share with other members of poor families, acting out of responsibility within the household, as well as the pleasure of giving. Chin sums this up:

> The deep sense of mutual obligation, and even debt, between family members played a central role. [For kids] these obligations and debts were often not only sustaining and joyful but also painful, onerous, and highly charged. I sometimes suspected that the lesson imparted to children and imparted by them was at times a coercive generosity: share or else. (Chin 2001, 128)

Not all household relations of consumption, in any case, generate harmony and collaboration. In his study of Philadelphia's inner-city, poor, African American children—which also includes teenagers—Carl Nightingale reports acute rancor and conflict between parents and children in their negotiations over consumption. Parents exasperated by their kids' unreasonable and persistent demands for spending money are pitted against children disappointed by their parents' inability to provide them with material goods. Contest over how to spend limited family monies, including income tax refunds or welfare checks, Nightingale observes, severely strains household relations:

> All the kids whose families I knew well lived through similar incidents: yelling matches between Fahim and his mother on how she spent her welfare check, Theresa's disgust when she found out she was not going to get a dress because her mom's boyfriend had demanded some of the family's monthly money for crack, and Omar's decision to leave his mother's house altogether because "I hate her. She always be asking

y'all [the Kids' Club] for money. That's going to get around, and people'll be talking." Also he felt that she never had enough money for his school clothes. (Nightingale 1993, 159)

In the course of his fieldwork, Philippe Bourgois heard similar stories coming from "El Barrio," New York City's crack-ridden East Harlem. Ten-year-old Angel complained about his mother's boyfriend:

> [He] had broken open his piggy bank and taken the twenty dollars' worth of tips he had saved from working as a delivery boy at the supermarket on our block. He blamed his mother for having provoked her boyfriend into beating her and robbing the apartment when she invited another man to visit her in her bedroom. "I keep telling my mother to only have one boyfriend at a time, but she won't listen to me." (Bourgois 1995, 264)

Children's consumption within households takes place in a context of incessant negotiation, sometimes cooperative, other times full of conflict.

Among peers, consumption raises a different set of relational issues. We find unexpected evidence, for example, from recent studies of Chinese children. The success of China's one-child policy means that large numbers of the country's 90 million children under age fifteen have no siblings; in urban areas, single children are a majority. These "little emperors," as observers call them, have gained remarkable economic leverage within their households: young shoppers start spending money by age four. The social investment of Chinese parents in their children's futures increases that leverage (see Chee 2000; Davis and Sensenbrenner 2000).

Among other influences, the newly empowered child consumers have turned "trendy food" snacks, especially Western style, into highly desirable goods. Interviewing eight- to ten-year-old only children in Beijing, Bernadine Chee found the *xiaochi*, or snacks, marking children's network position. Thus, the affluent Shen Li, one of Chee's interviewees, despite the dishonor of having his father in prison, achieved peer inclusion with his food purchases. As Chee describes it:

> Shen Li often bought different foods to eat. . . . He would taste it, and if he did not like it, he would give it to his classmates. "Because I often give them something to eat," Shen Li explained, "they will also give something to me when they have it." (Chee 2000, 55)

Not that children democratically included every child in these distribution systems. In fact, Chee found they systematically excluded apparently rural children, who ate alone while others were sharing. However, as we learn from Gao Tianjun's experience, inclusion mattered greatly to individual children. Gao's father recalled one of their outings, when Gao unexpectedly asked him to buy the expensive Wall's ice cream. Considering their meager household income, the father was at first reluctant but, seeing his child's eagerness, he relented. He later discovered the reasons for Gao's insistence:

> His son explained that once when he was at school, his classmates had asked him, "Gao Tianjun, have you tried Wall's?" He had told the classmate that he had tried it. The classmates then asked him: "How did it taste?" He had replied that it tasted very good. Gao Tianjun's father remarked: "Actually, the child had never tried it before." (Chee 2000, 54)

Chee's observations show us children not simply enacting their parents' social position and category but creating networks of their own.

As with production and distribution, consumption demonstrates far more than individual acquisition. It reveals children as active, inventive, knowledgeable consumers. More important, it shows us dynamic, differentiated, social relations in action.

THE PRICELESS CHILD REVISITED

Does all this discovery of children's economic activities mean that the economically useless, emotionally priceless child was just a historical mirage? Far from it. To be sure, other parts of the world, with rampant paid and informal child labor, never had the luxury of establishing a priceless child. In the United States, however, household economies were indeed transformed between the 1870s and the 1930s in ways that revolutionized children's economic practices. Just as middle-class women withdrew from paid employment, children were put out of wage work. Increased attention and concern with the emotional value of children's lives led to a growing uneasiness with their practical contributions. Children's worlds, it seemed to most observers, were to exist outside market concerns, in classrooms, playrooms, playgrounds, or summer camps. Indeed, child labor laws pushed most children out of market employment while new principles of domestic economy redefined their household contributions as worthy lessons, not real work.

Pricing the Priceless Child (Zelizer 1985) traced this transformation by focusing on adults' changing evaluations of children and childhood. But there is more to the story that we can only capture by shifting our attention to children's experiences. When we do so, we discover that the creation of an ostensibly useless child never segregated children from economic life in general. Under changed symbolic and practical conditions, the priceless child remained a consumer, producer, and distributor. What's more, as we have seen repeatedly throughout this article, children engaged actively in bargaining, contesting, and transforming their own relations with the economy.

Rereading the book today suggests further questions. For instance, has the era of the priceless child ended? Focusing on the United States alone, if we consider the growing inequality of national income, the extent of child poverty, as well as the largely undocumented child labor of immigrant and migrant workers, we could argue that the priceless child is being wiped out among the poor and near-poor. The evidence is mixed. Despite strong evidence of child labor among some immigrant populations, observers of contemporary life, such as Carl Nightingale (1993) and Kathryn Edin and Laura Lein (1997), emphasize how even very poor parents make an effort to provide consumption goods to their children in order to match those of their peers.

In our middle and upper classes, meanwhile, the expensive, priceless child still reigns. Certainly the cost of raising a child continues to escalate, starting with increasingly high tuition for nursery schools and tutoring for entrance exams to private elementary schools. Parents also subsidize the growing consumer clout of their young children. For 60 percent of American children, McNeal reports, the no-strings-attached allowance constitutes the largest single source of income (1999, 69). Working parents as Arlie Hochschild found, engage in "time-deficit 'paybacks'" by buying their children gifts (1997, 216). It continues to be true, furthermore, that middle- and upper-class parents justify children's paid work not on the grounds of economic utility but its contribution to their moral upbringing.

What about my predictions of a contemporary, useful "housechild"? Here, as we saw earlier, studies suggest that as a majority of their mothers work, children are in fact starting to participate more actively in household economic activities. However, whether they are participating more in production, consumption, or distribution remains unclear. An important study of American three- to twelve-year-olds' time use in 1981 and 1997 indicates that among children of single parents, weekly household work increased from 42 minutes to 2 hours and 42 minutes (almost a fourfold rise) and shopping time from 1 hour 11 minutes to 1 hour and 57 minutes (a 65 percent rise). But in two-parent households average household work dropped from 4 hours and 11 minutes (far greater than the single-parent households) to 2 hours and 52 minutes (a bit more than the single-parent households). In those same two-parent households, meanwhile, shopping rose from 1 hour and 57 minutes to 3 hours and 8 minutes (Hofferth and Sandberg 2001, table 4). Judging from participation in shopping, American children's involvement in consumption is increasing not only in terms of dollar volume, but also in terms of time expended.

Evidence reviewed in this article, furthermore, suggests that when looked at more closely, a significant share of the 26 hours and 48 minutes American children spent at school in 1997, of the 12 hours and 12 minutes spent at play, and of the additional 8 hours and 53 minutes devoted to church, youth groups, sports, outdoors, hobbies, and art activities will turn out to consist of economically consequential production, consumption, or distribution. Adults may consider children priceless and economically useless, but they cannot deny children's substantial economic activity.

Thus, a new agenda for research on children's economic experiences emerges from the old.

CHILDREN, NEGOTIATION, AND ECONOMIC EXPERIENCE

Let us examine some possibilities for that new agenda. Here are some sample questions that follow from the literature that I have reviewed.

- How do children negotiate the amount, timing, and compensation for household tasks with their parents and with siblings?
- What sorts of issues become matters of dispute, and how is conflict settled?
- What changes in bargaining should we expect if the reported increase in children's domestic work continues?
- Do children in ethnic businesses have more leverage in their bargaining than children in other households?
- How does the bargaining change in households where children earn more than their parents, e.g., child models, actors, singers, or athletes?
- How do changes in these respects affect children's relations with other children and with outside organizations?
- How do children's earmarking practices vary: do children spend money from different sources (allowance, gift, wage, found money) for different kinds of goods?
- How do sources and uses of children's money vary internationally?
- Which other kids do children consult about their purchases: best friends, close friends, or acquaintances?
- How does their consultation vary by type of purchase (toys, computers, food, clothing) and by site of purchase (shopping mall, neighborhood store, Internet, catalog)?
- When are children likely to engage in theft, such as shoplifting? With whom and where? In supermarkets, shopping malls, neighborhood stores, school stores?
- How is trust established in children's school distribution networks? When and why do children give or accept loans of money or food?
- How, and when, do adult third parties—parents, teachers, clerks, shopping mall security guards, janitors, playground monitors, and employers—intervene in children's economic practices?

- How, and why, do all of these vary by age, class, gender, race, nationality, religion, and by household structure?
- What part do children's production, distribution, and consumption play in the national economies, and how does that part vary from one country to another?

Remember the terrible fourth vignette, the Liberian child soldiers and their gunpoint breakfast? It should remind us that the great bulk of recent research on children's economic lives concerns relatively protected capitalist enclaves. The full agenda for research on children's economic relations must reach outside those enclaves in three directions: toward the variable and unequal experiences of children within high-income capitalist countries; toward the enormous variety of children's circumstances in the lower-income regions where most of the world's kids actually live; toward the historical changes that are transforming children's economic relations in rich and poor countries alike.

NOTES

Viviana A. Zelizer, "Kids and Commerce," *Childhood* 4 (November 2002): 375–96. First published by SAGE/SOCIETY. Reprinted with permission.

1. For a convenient introduction to this literature, see Bandelj et al. 2001. For a review of the psychological literature, see Furnham and Argyle 1998, chap. 3; and Sonuga-Barke and Webley 1993.
2. For other kids' strategies, see also Consumer Reports for Kids, http://www.zillions.org (accessed July 25, 2001) and Kid's Money Web site, http://Kidsmoney.org (accessed July 25, 2001).

REFERENCES

Bandelj, Nina, Viviana A. Zelizer, and Ann Morning. 2001. *Material for the Study of Childhood.* Princeton, N.J.: Department of Sociology, Princeton University.

Berkeley, Bill. 2001. *The Graves Are Not Yet Full: Race, Tribe and Power in the Heart of Africa.* New York: Basic Books.

Bourgois, Philippe. 1995. *In Search of Respect.* New York: Cambridge University Press.

Brines, Julie. 1994. "Economic Dependency, Gender, and the Division of Labor at Home." *American Journal of Sociology* 100:652–88.

Buckingham, David. 2000. *After the Death of Childhood.* Cambridge: Polity Press.

Cahill, Spencer E. 1987. "Children and Civility: Ceremonial Deviance and the Acquisition of Ritual Competence." *Social Psychology Quarterly* 50:312–21.

Chapman, Victoria. 1994. "Working Hard or Hardly Working? An Examination of Children's Household Contributions in the 1990s." Ph.D. diss., Princeton University.

Chee, Bernadine W. L. 2000. "Eating Snacks and Biting Pressure: Only Children in Beijing." In *Feeding China's Little Emperors*, edited by Jun Jing, 48–70. Stanford, Calif.: Stanford University Press.

Chin, Elizabeth. 2001. *Purchasing Power: Black Kids and American Consumer Culture*. Minneapolis: University of Minnesota Press.

Cook, Daniel. 2000. "The Rise of 'The Toddler' as Subject and as Merchandising Category in the 1930s.'" In *New Forms of Consumption*, edited by Mark Gottdiener, 111–29. Boulder, Colo.: Rowman and Littlefield.

———. 2001. "Exchange Value as Pedagogy in Children's Leisure: Moral Panics in Children's Culture at Century's End." *Leisure Sciences* 23:81–98.

Corsaro, William A. 1997. *The Sociology of Childhood*. Thousand Oaks, Calif.: Pine Forge.

Cross, Gary. 1997. *Kids' Stuff: Toys and the Changing World of American Childhood*. Cambridge, Mass.: Harvard University Press.

———. 2000. *An All-Consuming Century: Why Commercialism Won in Modern America*. New York: Columbia University Press.

Davis, Deborah S., and Julia S. Sensenbrenner. 2000. "Commercializing Childhood: Parental Purchases for Shanghai's Only Child." In *The Consumer Revolution in Urban China*, edited by Deborah S. Davis, 54–79. Berkeley: University of California Press.

Davis, John. 1992. *Exchange*. Minneapolis: University of Minnesota Press.

Edin, Kathryn, and Laura Lein. 1997. *Making Ends Meet: How Single Mothers Survive Welfare and Low-Wage Work*. New York: Russell Sage Foundation.

Feiring, Candice, and Michael Lewis. 1989. "The Social Networks of Girls and Boys from Early Through Middle Childhood." In *Children's Social Networks and Social Supports*, edited by Deborah Belle, 119–50. New York: Wiley.

Ferguson, Ann. 2000. *Bad Boys: Public Schools in the Making of Black Masculinity*. Ann Arbor: University of Michigan Press.

Fleming, Robin. 1997. *The Common Purse: Income Sharing in New Zealand Families*. Auckland: Auckland University Press.

Formanek-Brunell, Miriam. 1998. "Truculent and Tractable: The Gendering of Babysitting in Postwar America." In *Delinquents and Debutantes: Twentieth-Century American Girls' Cultures*, edited by Sherrie A. Inness, 61–82. New York: New York University Press.

Furnham, Adrian, and Michael Argyle. 1998. *The Psychology of Money*. London: Routledge.

Gerson, Kathleen. 1993. *No Man's Land: Men's Changing Commitments to Family and Work*. New York: Basic Books.

Greenstein, Theodore N. 2000. "Economic Dependence, Gender, and the Division of Labor at Home: A Replication and Extension." *Journal of Marriage and the Family* 62:322–35.

Gullestad, Marianne. 1992. *The Art of Social Relations: Essays on Culture, Social Action and Everyday Life in Modern Norway*. Oslo: Scandinavian University Press.

Hochschild, Arlie Russell. 1989. "The Economy of Gratitude." In *The Sociology of Emotions: Original Essays and Research Papers*, edited by Thomas Hood, 95–111. Greenwich, Conn.: JAI Press.

———. 1997. *The Time Bind*. New York: Metropolitan Books.

Hochschild, Arlie Russell, and Ann Machung. 1989. *The Second Shift*. New York: Avon.

Hofferth, Sandra L., and Jack Sandberg. 2001. "Changes in American Children's Time, 1981–1997." In *Children at the Millennium: Where Have We Come From, Where Are We Going?*, edited by Timothy Owens and Sandra L. Hofferth 193–229. New York: Elsevier Science.

Jacobson, Lisa. 1997. "Raising Consumers: Children, Childrearing, and the American Mass Market, 1890–1940." Ph.D. diss., University of California at Los Angeles.

Katriel, Tamar. 1987. "'Bexibudim!' Ritualized Sharing among Israeli Children." *Language in Society* 16:305–20.

Kiyosaki, Robert T., and Sharon L. Lechter. 1997. *Rich Dad Poor Dad*. Scottsdale, Ariz.: Tech-Press.

Kline, Stephen. 1993. *Out of the Garden: Toys, TV, and Children's Culture in the Age of Marketing*. New York: Verso.

———. 1998. "Toys, Socialization, and the Commodification of Play." In *Getting and Spending*, edited by Susan Strasser, Charles McGovern, and Matthias Judt, 339–58. New York: Cambridge University Press.

Kotlowitz, Alex. 1999. "False Connections." In *Consuming Desires*, edited by Roger Rosenblatt, 65–72. Washington, D.C.: Island Press.

Lee, Yun-Suk, Barbara Schneider, and Linda J. Waite. 2000. "Determinants and Social and Educational Consequences of Children's Housework." Working paper no. 19, Alfred P. Sloan Center on Parents, Children, and Work. Chicago: University of Chicago Press.

Levison, Deborah. 2000. "Children as Economic Agents." *Feminist Economics* 6:125–34.

Lewis, Michael. 2001. "Jonathan Lebed's Extracurricular Activities." *New York Times Magazine*, February 25.

Lozada, Eriberto P., Jr. 2000. "Globalized Childhood? Kentucky Fried Chicken in Beijing." In *Feeding China's Little Emperors*, edited by Jun Jing, 114–34. Stanford, Calif.: Stanford University Press.

Lundberg, Shelley J., and Robert A. Pollak. 1996. "Bargaining and Distribution in Marriage." *Journal of Economic Perspectives* 10:139–58.

McNeal, James U. 1999. *The Kids Market*. Ithaca, N.Y.: Paramount.

Miller, Daniel. 1997. "How Infants Grow Mothers in North London." *Theory, Culture and Society* 14:67–87.

Mishler, Elliot G. 1979. "Wou' You Trade Cookies with the Popcorn? Talk of Trades among Six Years Olds." In *Language, Children and Society*, edited by Olga K. Garnica and Martha L. King, 221–36. New York: Pergamon Press.

Morrow, Virginia. 1994. "Responsible Children? Aspects of Children's Work and Employment outside School in Contemporary UK." In *Children's Childhoods: Observed and Experienced*, edited by Berry Mayall, 128–43. London: Falmer Press.

Nathan, Amy. 1998. *The Kids' Allowance Book*. New York: Walker.

Newson, John, and Elizabeth Newson. 1976. *Seven Years Old in the Home Environment*. New York: Wiley.

Nieuwenhuys, Olga. 1996. "The Paradox of Child Labor and Anthropology." *Annual Review of Anthropology* 25:237–51.

Nightingale, Carl H. 1993. *On the Edge*. New York: Basic Books.

Orellana, Marjorie Faulstich. 2001. "The Work Kids Do: Mexican and Central American Immigrant Children's Contributions to Households and Schools in California." *Harvard Educational Review* 71:366–89.

Paris, Leslie M. 2000. "Children's Nature: Summer Camps in New York State, 1919–1941." Ph.D. diss., University of Michigan.

Pecora, Norma Odom. 1998. *The Business of Children's Entertainment*. New York: Guilford Press.

Porter, Karen A. 1999. "An Anthropological Defense of Child Labor." *Chronicle of Higher Education* 46 (November 19): B11(1).

Qvortrup, Jens. 1995. "From Useful to Useful: The Historical Continuity of Children's Constructive Participation." *Sociological Studies of Children* 7: 49–76.

Schultz, Charles M. 1999. *Peanuts: A Golden Celebration,* edited by David Larkin. New York: HarperCollins.

Scott, Kim. 1999. "First-Grade African-American Girls' Play Patterns." Ph.D. diss., Rutgers University.

Seiter, Ellen. 1993. *Sold Separately: Parents and Children in Consumer Culture*. New Brunswick, N.J.: Rutgers University Press.

Sirota, Régine. 1998. 'Les copains d'abord: Les anniversaires de l'enfance, donner et recevoir." *Ethnologie Française* 28 (October–December): 457–71.

Solberg, Anne. 1994. *Negotiating Childhood*. Stockholm: Nordplan.

Song, Miri. 1999. *Helping Out: Children's Labor in Ethnic Businesses*. Philadelphia: Temple University Press.

Sonuga-Barke, Edmund, and Paul Webley. 1993. *Children's Saving: A Study in the Development of Economic Behaviour*. Hove, U.K. and Hillsdale, N.J.: Lawrence Erlbaum.

Steinberg, Shirley R., and Joe L. Kincheloe. 1997. *Kinderculture: The Cultural Construction of Childhood*. Boulder, Colo.: Westview Press.

Thorne, Barrie. 1993. *Gender Play*. New Brunswick, N.J.: Rutgers University Press.

Tilly, Chris, and Charles Tilly. 1998. *Work under Capitalism*. Boulder, Colo.: Westview Press.

Valenzuela, Abel, Jr. 1999. "Gender Roles and Settlement Activities among Children and Their Immigrant Families." *American Behavioral Scientist* 42:720–42.

Watson, James L., ed. 1997. *Golden Arches East: McDonald's in East Asia*. Stanford, Calif.: Stanford University Press.

Webley, Paul. 1996. "Playing the Market: The Autonomous Economic World of Children." In *Economic Socialization*, edited by Peter Lunt and Adrian Furnham, 149–61. Cheltenham: Elgar.

Woodhead, Martin. 1999. "Combatting Child Labour: Listen to What the Children Say." *Childhood* 6, no. 1: 27–49.

Zelizer, Viviana A. 1985. *Pricing the Priceless Child: The Changing Social Value of Children*. New York: Basic Books.

12

Intimacy in Economic Organizations

When Paul Wolfowitz took over as head of the World Bank, he faced a delicate problem: Shaha Ali Riza, the woman with whom he had been maintaining an intimate relationship, was a World Bank official. For her to remain in place would sound conflict-of-interest alarms, but he could not simply fire her. So, following the informal advice of the bank's ethics committee, Wolfowitz arranged his companion's transfer to the U.S. State Department. The problem was the terms of the transfer that Wolfowitz negotiated.

According to the World Bank Staff Association's expression of "concern, dismay and outrage," Riza's transfer involved several unacceptable features, namely, undue promotion, excessive pay raise, and unwarranted sharp annual pay increases.[1] The employees complained that Ms. Riza had received special treatment because of her relationship to Mr. Wolfowitz, thus violating the bank's orderly rules for promotion, transfer, and compensation. Four days after a special investigative World Bank committee concluded that he had "violated his contract by breaking ethical and governing rules in arranging the generous pay and promotion for Shaha Ali Riza," Wolfowitz resigned, effective June 30, 2007 (Weisman 2007).

Consider a very different story from MedAptus, a small Boston medical technology firm. When its marketing director, Jennifer Crowley, faced the tragedy of her seven-month-old baby Cian's imminent death from a rare pediatric cancer, project manager Andrea Berte Bellemare asked Dennis Mitchell, the company's chief executive, for permission to donate three of her leave days to Crowley. Mitchell not only agreed but also went further, creating a staff donation bank. As a result, Crowley received thirty-three additional leave days from her coworkers, which allowed her to keep her job and care for her child. "We felt so helpless," Mitchell reported, "It's really pulled the company closer together to be able to donate time" (Jackson 2006).

Intimacy in economic organizations: threat or boon? The Wolfowitz mishap portrays intimacy as a threat to organizational effectiveness, but the bank-leave story suggests that it is a boon. Two apparently contradictory principles come into play: disruption and solidarity. In the disruption view, intimacy disrupts organizational effort and therefore requires inhibition and damage control. In the solidarity view, on the contrary, intimacy builds solidarity and trust, thus enhancing organizational effectiveness. We might resolve the apparent contradiction by discovering that different kinds of intimacy have different effects on organizational life, that intimacy's effects do not depend on its sheer presence or intensity, and that they do depend on the location of intimate relations within an organization's interpersonal networks. I argue that all three are true. When it comes to the positive or negative impact of intimacy, the crucial fact is not the sheer presence of intimate relations but the type of relation and its location within the larger web of connections within the organization. My view contradicts both widespread organizational efforts to contain intimacy and the view of the ideal efficient organization as a zone of utter impersonality.

Intimacy consists of privileged access to another person's attention, information, and trust, all of which would damage the person if widely available to other people. Thus defined, intimate relations vary in breadth (from one narrow sort of attention to access that crosses a whole existence), in duration (from a fleeting rendezvous to a lifetime connection), and in intensity (from casual sharing to emotionally charged secrets). At one extreme—very broad, durable, and intense relationships—the case for disruption becomes compelling (Slater 1963). Short of that extreme, however, many different combinations appear to be compatible with organizational effectiveness, or even to enhance it.

This paper's main task is to survey and synthesize the scattered evidence for such a view. But before arriving at the evidence, we must clear some cluttered ground. Let us first look more closely at the disruption and solidarity views, noticing which sorts of intimacy and which features of organizational life advocates of those opposing views most often treat, and seeing in what ways they are plausible or implausible. Then we can move on to available evidence concerning intimacy's impact on economic organizations and from there to tentative conclusions. I will discipline an unruly subject by narrowing it in four ways:

- Fixing attention on formal economic organizations, thus leaving the informal economy, household production, and market transactions for treatment elsewhere.
- Restricting attention to relationships occurring *within* economic organizations, thus excluding questions about how outside intimate ties (e.g., close outside friendships with competitors, relationships with spouses, and notorious love affairs) affect organizational performance.
- Concentrating on just three varieties of intimacy—sexual relationship, friendship, and kinship, thus neglecting confidential relationships, management of organizational secrets, and formal mentoring or apprenticeship programs.
- Asking four main questions about such intimate ties: (1) How prevalent are intimate ties in economic organizations? (2) How

do organizations respond to such ties? (3) What are the overall impacts of intimate ties' prevalence, intensity, and organizational location on aggregate organizational effectiveness? (4) How does the presence of an intimate tie affect the organizational performance of the pair and their relations to third parties within the organization?

Sexual intimacy, friendship, and kinship sometimes do disrupt organizations. But they often coexist with organizational effectiveness, or even contribute to it. I single out these three forms of intimacy not because they are interchangeable or because they mark degrees on some scale of intensity but, on the contrary, because differences among them allow us to see more clearly how the presence of intimacy within economic organizations affects organizational performance. While lawsuits and scandals break into headlines much more often in cases of sexual intimacy, we will see that intimacy based on friendship and kinship can likewise have profound effects on how organizations perform.

Although they differ significantly in other regards, sexual intimacy, friendship, and kinship within economic organizations pose similar empirical, analytical, and policy problems for organizational analysts. Empirically, under what conditions do they proliferate, and to what extent does their presence coincide with disruption of organizational performance? Analytically, how extensively and in what ways does the existence of such intimate relations within organizations alter adjacent relations (e.g., with fellow workers or supervisors)? From a policy perspective, are these effects sufficiently large and deleterious to recommend blanket bans on intimacy—or at least its more intense forms—within economic organizations?

This said, the three sorts of intimacy vary in contrasting ways. Consider breadth and duration. Sexual relations range from fleeting and narrow—the one-night stand in which the parties hardly get to know each other—to broad and lasting. On the average, friendships last longer and cover a wider range of interactions. Kinship generally lasts even longer, but can run from quite narrow (the annual family reunion) to extremely broad (the shared household). The extent to which the three sorts of relations begin and remain within economic organizations also varies dramatically. As we will soon see, sexual relationships often start on the job. Friendships split between those generated in the workplace and those carried over from elsewhere. Kinship almost always precedes and overflows organizational membership. Eventually any fine analysis of intimacy's organizational impact must recognize these distinctions.

Let's turn now to the cases for disruption and solidarity. What are the organizational effects of intimacy according to these two different arguments?

THE THREAT OF INTIMIZATION

To move ahead analytically, we must look directly at the supposed organizational threat posed by the three forms of workplace intimacy discussed here: sexual relations, friendship, and kin ties.

In general, how do analysts and observers of economic life treat the intersection between intimacy and economic activity? Although earlier theorists had often allowed for the coexistence of solidarity and self-interest (Hirschman 1977), from the nineteenth century onward theorists of economic processes have adopted two closely related theories. We can call them the theories of separate spheres and of hostile worlds. Separate-spheres theories identify two distinct domains of social life that operate according to different principles: rationality, efficiency, and planning on one side; solidarity, sentiment, and impulse on the other. As Max Weber put it in his analysis of the erotic sphere: "[the lover] knows himself to be freed from the cold skeleton hands of rational orders, just as completely as from the banality of everyday routine" (Weber 1971, 347). In Weber's view, and many like it, intimacy generates and depends on warm sentiment, while efficiency requires rationality and, therefore, suppression of sentiment.

Pioneer organizational analyst Donald Roy says this about the standard view of workplace sex:

> Sex is considered not only functionally inappropriate for industrial activity but also out of place, in a literal sense, in regard to general layout and material furnishings of the typical factory. Industrial management may here and there show a diffuse sort of indulgence toward the pre-marital or extra-marital achievements of employees, but it is unlikely that benignity extends to approval of mating maneuvers on company time. (1974, 44)

Indeed, workplaces, as James Woods and Jay Lucas (1993, 33) have shown, are typically designed as asexual spheres where sexuality looms as "an external threat to an organization . . . something that must be regulated, prohibited, or otherwise held at the company gates." What Woods calls the "asexual imperative" goes beyond protecting vulnerable workers, typically women, from sexual harassment. It supports organizational prohibitions against the use of sexuality to determine matters of workers' hire, pay, promotion, or dismissal. One of the worst aspersions one can cast against a rising company official is that he or she slept the way to the top. Equally damning is the accusation of having put a lover on the company payroll.

In the separate-spheres account, a sharp divide exists between intimate social relations and economic transactions. Left to itself, goes the doctrine, each sphere works more or less automatically and well. Markets run themselves, and so do families and other intimate settings. But the two spheres remain alien to each other. Worse yet, contact between them produces moral contamination. Monetization of personal care, for example, corrupts that care into self-interested sale of services.

Thus emerges a view of the separate spheres as dangerously hostile worlds, properly segregated domains whose sanitary management requires well-maintained boundaries. The feared contamination cuts both ways. Generations of scholars and social critics have warned about the devastating effects of commodification on personal relations (for a critical overview see Zelizer 2005). Analysts of economic organizations, however, have implicitly adopted a precisely opposite doctrine: that a process we can call "intimization" undermines organizational performance. The dangers of intimization constitute the mirror image of commodification threats.

Here, the introduction of sentiment and interpersonal solidarity into rational transactions produces inefficiency, favoritism, cronyism, and other forms of corruption. Indeed, organizational analysts and managers often think of intimacy as inefficient noise or worse, as a threat to organizational efficiency and productivity. Only markets cleansed of sentiment, in this view, can generate true efficiency.

A survey of the relevant literature suggests that critiques of intimacy in organizations actually follow three somewhat different paths, but they end up in the same place. The first variant argues that intimate relations distract their participants from an organization's main goals and thus undermine organizational performance. A loving couple, in this view, are likely to make love on company time or even to appropriate crucial company resources for their private use. A pair of old friends, runs the same line of reasoning, may well service their friendship instead of following orders that reach them from their superiors. Collusion among workers, whether based on kinship, friendship, or sexual relations, can likewise subvert organizational programs. Call this the *distraction* thesis.

The second variant argues that matching of persons with jobs on the basis of intimate relations instead of appropriate human capital produces inferior work. Thus the boss's daughter who takes an important job presumably blocks better qualified candidates from the post. The common practice of letting present employees recruit fellow members of their immigration network to new vacancies in a firm presumably excludes more talented potential workers outside that migration network. In either case, intimacy causes suboptimal organizational performance. Call this the *human capital* thesis.

In a third variant, intimacy creates unfairness by disrupting organizational systems of reward, as when promotion and salary are determined by favoritism rather than merit. Finally, intimacy can undermine organizational life by becoming exploitative, as in sexual harassment. Call this the *disorder* thesis.

The distraction, human capital, and disorder theses are not simple fantasies. Sometimes each of these processes does undermine organizational effectiveness. World Bank employees were not fantasizing with their fear of organizational disorder. The question is how regularly and in what precise ways the presence of intimacy disrupts organizational effectiveness.

THE CASE OF SOLIDARITY

Despite the plausible fears that cronyism, nepotism, on-the-job romances, and favoritism disrupt organizational performance, one can also make the case that intimacy often enhances solidarity and thus actually promotes organizational performance. The case for solidarity builds on very different beliefs from separate spheres and hostile worlds. On the whole, goes the reasoning, a measure of intimacy within an organization fosters job satisfaction, enhances commitment of workers to the organization, facilitates communication among workers, and supports mutual aid in the performance of essential organizational tasks. We might call this view the *sociable satisfaction* theory (see Heimer 1992).

Savvy managers themselves implicitly recognize the case for solidarity. They bend the rules as they encounter circumstances in which mentoring, trust, friendship, shared secrets, and mutual aid actually contribute to organizational ends. More exactly, managers regularly choose among four different strategies for dealing with intimate relations on the job: ban, contain, regulate, and integrate.

At the extreme, sexual misconduct and nepotism codes simply *ban* certain relationships from organizations on the ground that in general they produce more trouble than they are worth. *Containment* works more subtly through such devices as permitting flirtation, gossip, gift exchanges, or mutual aid at office parties and coffee breaks but not on the job. *Regulation*, in contrast, directly recognizes the presence of an intimate relationship but subjects it to scrutiny by means of conflict-of-interest declarations and disclaimer contracts. Organizations also *integrate* intimate relations as they foster mentoring, reward secretaries who manage their bosses' personal affairs, or promote pairs known to work well together.

Managers who seek to contain, regulate, or integrate intimate relations within their organizations could draw support from a decades-old literature on human relations in industry back to F. J. Roethlisberger and William J. Dickson or George Homans. The literature certainly sees dangers that close friendships among workers promote resistance to management directives, but it also declares that workers draw much of their job satisfaction from relations with other workers, and that job satisfaction leads to superior performance by individuals and work groups. Although the classic industrial relations studies paid little attention to kinship and sexual relations, at least they raise the possibility that those forms of intimacy might contribute to solidarity and thereby to organizational performance.

More recently, a surprising array of literatures has confirmed this possibility. From disparate academic perspectives and often distinctive policy agendas, scholars—ranging from economic sociology to sexuality studies—coincide in identifying positive features of workplace intimacy.

Economic sociologists, for instance, have gestured in that direction by demonstrating the positive effects of certain kinds of personal ties for the overall effectiveness and efficiency of at least some kinds of economic organizations. Such analysts as Ronald Burt (2005, 2007); Asaf Darr (2006); Paul Ingram and Peter Roberts (2000); and Brian Uzzi and Ryon Lancaster (2004) have pinpointed the reliance of agents in presumably impersonal markets on ties of friendship among contractors and even putative competitors.[2]

Quite independently, organizational analysts have discovered the importance of some kinds of emotions to organizational performance, challenging the idea that rationality requires the suppression of feelings. They have insisted that such emotions as anger sometimes activate and enhance organizational effectiveness (Tiedens 2001; Sinaceur and Tiedens 2006). Dennis Mumby and Linda Putnam (1992), for example, introduced the concept of "bounded emotionality" to signal the contributions that emotions make to organizational effectiveness (see also Aldrich and Ruef 2006, 6, 121; Bandelj 2009; Hartel, Ashkanasy, and Zerbe 2005; Martin, Knopoff, and Beckman 1998; Steinberg and Figart 1999; Wharton and Erickson 1993; a classic of sociological work on this subject is Hochschild 1983). But so far no one has effectively connected the analysis of emotions within organizations to different kinds of relations among their members.

Some of the most provocative statements about workplace intimacy come from scholars in sociology and the law, many of them feminists. Some voice complaints about scholarly neglect of what they call "organization sexuality" (see, e.g., Brewis and Linstead 2000; Ely and Meyerson 2000; Hearn, Sheppard, Tancred-Sheriff, and Burrell 1989; Hearn and Parkin 1995), but others go much further. In a pioneer *Annual Review of Sociology* essay about sexuality in the workplace, Christine Williams, Patti Giuffre, and Kirsten Dellinger called for greater attention to consensual relationships, defined as those "reflecting positive and autonomous expressions of workers' sexual desire" (1999, 78). Acknowledging that some forms of workplace sexuality can be oppressive and exploitative, especially toward women, they insist that we should also recognize that sexuality may enhance "job satisfaction, self-esteem, and happiness" (91). Similarly, Kari Lerum argues that under certain conditions, "sexualized interactions can communicate and construct a sense of worker camaraderie" (2004, 772; see also Riach and Wilson 2007; Salzinger 2003).

Other scholars have emphasized the solidarity-generating place of non-sexual intimate relations. Specialists in work and occupations, for instance, draw attention to the crucial yet little-understood significance of coworker intimacy, ranging from close friendships and companionship to more tangible forms of social support (McGuire 2007; Pettinger 2005; for the special case of mentoring, see, e.g., Blake-Beard, Murrell, and Thomas 2006; Kram 1988; Laird 2006, 279–82, 328).

Meanwhile, legal experts voice impatience with what they see as the disruptive impact of intimization fears. Most emphatically, Vicki Schultz argues against what she calls the "sanitized workplace" where workers' sexuality is banished in order to prevent its potential deterioration into sexual harassment. Paradoxically, Schultz notes, by focusing on sexual oppression, organizations neglect the more crucial discriminatory impact of sex segregation and inequality that, in her view, breed harassment. Equally significant, Schultz worries that sexual sanitization blunts the "role of open expression in promoting employees' shared sense of solidarity, intimacy, and humanity" (2006, 103). Employers, Schultz insists, "should foster atmospheres of sexual tolerance and understanding and should recognize that sexual expression doesn't inherently undermine equality or organizational goals" (153).

Even when it comes to sexual harassment, for example, Schultz argues that "sexual harassment policies now provide an added incentive and an increased legitimacy for management to control and discipline relatively harmless sexual behavior without even inquiring into whether that behavior undermines gender equality on the job" (Schultz 2003, 2,065). Schultz concludes that instead of banning sexually tinged relations, organizations would serve their own purposes much better by concentrating on the reduction of gender inequality and segregation (for a different view, see Lee 2006; Williams 2006b).

Schultz is not alone. Equally concerned about the undermining of consensual workplace sexuality, legal scholar Sharon Rabin-Margalioth (2006, 251) calls for more studies of "how and to what extent intimate sexual relations affect productivity, organizational efficiency, [and] morale of coworkers." She furthermore takes on anti-nepotism policies, in particular no-spouse rules. Countering intimization fears that joint employment of spouses will create "organizational strife, favoritism, jealousy and tension among other co-workers" Rabin-Margalioth argues that anti-nepotism rules in fact have a discriminatory effect on women, who are more likely to be denied employment or fired as a result (2006, 245; see also Chandler et al. 2002; Wexler 1982).

The needed confrontation between disruption and solidarity views of intimacy has not yet occurred. Organizational analysts must stage the confrontation on both theoretical and empirical levels. How should we join the debate, and search for a synthesis?

How Intimacy Really Works

Despite their obvious contradictions, advocates of the cases for disruption and for solidarity have not joined a coherent debate, made a serious effort to synthesize their views, or organized a comprehensive research program concerning the impact of intimacy on organizational performance. As a cautious step toward those three goals, let me offer a selective review of empirical work bearing on four relevant questions:

1. How prevalent within economic organizations are intimate relations based on sexuality, kinship, and/or friendship?
2. How do organizational managers respond to the presence of different sorts of intimate ties?
3. How do the prevalence, intensity, and location of intimate ties within an organization affect the organization's overall performance?
4. How does the existence of an intimate tie affect the individual and joint job performance of the pair, and their relations to third parties within the organization?

Although my review will differentiate among sexual, kinship, and friendship ties, as well as intensities of intimacy where possible, in this survey it will be enough to draw tentative empirical conclusions from a highly disparate set of literatures. After the survey, I will offer a series of conjectures in hope of stimulating new work—both theoretical and empirical—on intimacy's impact within economic organizations.

How Prevalent Are Intimate Ties within Organizations?

Sexual, kinship, and friendship relations are all impressively prevalent in workplaces. In a controversial book, Deirdre McCloskey rightly observes:

> Markets and even the much-maligned corporations encourage friendships wider and deeper than the atomism of a full-blown socialist regime or the claustrophobic, murderous atmosphere of a "traditional" village. Modern capitalist life is love-saturated. (2006, 138)

With increasing entrance of women into the paid labor force, furthermore, increasing shares of love-saturated relationships cross gender lines. Although we lack a coherent literature documenting intimacy's prevalence and variety, a number of scattered but revealing studies provide valuable glimpses into workplace intimacies.

We get some early glimmers of workplace friendships, for instance, from Susan Porter Benson's study of department store saleswomen in the first decades of the twentieth century:

In one department, women contributed to the support of Aggie, a particularly destitute co-worker; they paid her insurance and sick-benefit premiums, bought extra food for her lunch, and helped her to stretch her meager clothing budget. But their actions went beyond self-help within the department to confront management on Aggie's behalf. When a manager halted their yearly collection to send Aggie on vacation and made them return the money, they ostentatiously collected it again outside the employee's entrance. They knew, however, that the only real solution to Aggie's problems was a higher salary, and their most impressive victory was in backing up her successful quest for a raise. (Benson, 1986, 247; see also Lamphere 1985; on nineteenth-century female textile workers, see Dublin 1979, 70–74)[3]

More recent evidence comes from Randy Hodson. Despite giving more attention to resistance than to mutual aid, Hodson has advanced our knowledge of coworkers' intimate ties by combing and cataloging more than a hundred ethnographies of workplace interaction. The ethnographies report such practices as gift giving in a chemical factory and mutual covering among sleeping car porters (Hodson 2001, 201). "Coworkers," concludes Hodson:

help provide meaning in work through the sharing of work life experiences and through friendships. Coworkers can also provide a basis for group solidarity and mutual support in the face of denials of dignity at work. (200)

Hodson identifies friendship and mutual aid as major compensations for physical hardship, tedious work routines, tyrannical managers, and even low wages. Without such close personal ties, we can infer, many workplaces, far from operating more efficiently, would actually collapse. Hodson reports a striking study of Washington, D.C., firefighters. A firefighter recalled:

It's hard to describe the closeness that you felt with the guys in the fire house. I don't think my wife has ever really understood it. I just used to love to come to work—especially on those long Saturdays when we'd have a big roast or a ham or something and sit around and talk or play cards. . . . Firemen then were a great bunch and a rough bunch. . . . They played hard and rough. But when the bells hit, nobody would do any more good for you than a fireman. It's a group of men with a unique brotherhood feeling—they'll never let you down. (223; see also Desmond 2007)

Gail McGuire's interviews with forty employees of a large, female-dominated financial services company about what she calls "intimate work" provide even more specific evidence about the prevalence and variety of workplace intimacy. Based on her respondents' reports of the types of social support they offered their network members, McGuire identified a broad range of assistance, including sharing, listening, counseling, caretaking, and nonwork services such as providing information about "managing finances, home improvements, church activities, real estate, weddings, weight loss, and pregnancy" (2007, 134).

Employees also reported offering coworkers help with a variety of tasks, including "residential moves, filing taxes, doing home improvements, babysitting, and giving help with transportation" (McGuire 2007, 134). Some provided straightforward material assistance, such as money or used furniture. Drawing on her evidence, McGuire argues for the significance of the workplace as "an important site for the development and expression of intimacy" (138; see also Williams 2006a, 82–83. On gift giving among coworkers, see Ruth 2004).

McGuire's findings echo Stephen Marks's 1994 attempt to gauge workplace intimacy. To do so, Marks analyzed 1986 General Social Survey data on close friendships among coworkers, plus Claude Fischer's 1982 Northern California Community Study. Based on his own analysis of these surveys, Marks concludes that "at workplaces, intimacy appears to be a rather pervasive phenomenon" (1994, 853). "For millions of American workers," Marks finds "close friendships are formed among coworkers, 'important matters' are discussed with them, and such discussions are associated with greater job satisfaction" (850; see also Sias and Cahill 1998).

Intimacy within corporations, of course, often goes beyond platonic friendships. As Roy colorfully reported:

> When the situation is one of men and women working side by side or sharing a task that calls for team work, Eros may infiltrate the production line to evoke attachments of various qualities and durations of affection, ranging from the protracted attentions of true love to ephemeral ardencies of the opportune moment. (1974, 46)

Likewise, Williams et al. point to a wide range of workplace sexual interactions, including "flirting with coworkers or clients (in person or via email); consuming pornography; sexual joking, bantering and touching; and coworker dating, sexual affairs, cohabitation and marriage" (1999, 75).

More concretely, the 2005 Society for Human Resource Management's (SHRM) survey of almost five hundred human resource professionals and four hundred employees, found that about 40 percent of employees had been involved in a workplace romance sometime in their careers (Parks 2006). Likewise, a 2007 Annual Office Romance Survey conducted by career publisher Vault among 575 employees in various industries around the United States confirms the importance of office romances: 47 percent of respondents reported having been involved in an office romance (Vault 2007; see also Lever et al. 2006).

One researcher estimates a current total of about 10 million workplace romantic relationships (Spragins 2004). Not surprisingly, self-help books now offer advice for workplace romance. The authors of a book called *Office Mate* advise that "the greatest pool of potential mates is not online, not in a bar, and not on a blind date. It's in the office" (Losee and Olen 2007, xvii). To what extent same-sex relationships originate in parallel ways remains uncertain in the present state of the literature (for fragmentary evidence, see Chauncey 1994; Schneider 1984; Woods and Lucas 1993; on gay men's workplace friendships, see Rumens 2008).

The Vault survey reveals a surge in an intriguing adjacent phenomenon of male-female nonsexual office "marriages." Twenty-three percent of employees reported a platonic office "husband" or "wife," with whom they "hang out" regularly, spending a great deal of time together, sharing breaks or lunch (Vault 2007; see also Prince 2005. On secretaries as their bosses' "office wife," see Kanter 1977, 89–91).

Available evidence, then, documents the widespread prevalence of intimate relations—both sexual and otherwise—within economic organizations. For this inquiry, that prevalence of intimacy has two strong implications. First, no valid theory of organizational interactions can assume that interpersonal relations are normally impersonal within firms and that intimate relations are ipso facto anomalous and risky. Second, no practical policy of banning or radically containing intimacy is likely to work within economic organizations.

Managers' Response to Workplace Intimacy

How, then, do managers actually react to the presence of intimacy within their organizations? Managers' practical responses to the perceived threat of intimization vary so widely as to baffle any confident detection of trends in actual organizational practices. The existing literature on workplaces from the 1990s onward so thoroughly mixes anecdotes, complaints, prescriptions, and reports on the prevalence and management control over intimate relations that we lack the essential evidence. Is there, as some suggest, a rising tide of prohibitions on sexual intimacy? What about kinship and friendship?

Such close students of the subject as legal scholar Vicki Schultz (2003, 2006) claim to see a substantial increase in workplace regulation of intimate relations, going well beyond sexual harassment. Schultz contends that managers are engaged in a "campaign of sexual sanitization" (2006, 103). "A new generation of managers and employees," asserts Schultz, "has internalized the age-old message that sex is out of place in the workplace and encoded it into new sexual harassment policies and programs" (2006, 137). Increased regulations range from "no-fraternization policies" prohibiting romantic involvement between supervisors and employees, even when consensual, to "date-and-tell" policies, where employees involved in such relationships must disclose their romance to management and be subject to monitoring, reprimand, or transfer. The 2005 SHRM survey of human resource professionals and employees found that among employers and employees it has not only "become generally accepted that romances between a supervisor and subordinate are off limits," but "organizations are also beginning to feel the need for employees to inform their supervisors of any relationships" (Parks 2006).

Managers' fear of intimate ties goes further. In 2005, the *National Law Journal* reported an increase in so-called cupid or love contracts for employees about to embark on a romantic relationship. To protect firms against sexual harassment suits, employment lawyers now recommend a signed, written arrangement between prospective lovers, which certifies that both partners understand that the relationship is consensual. Similarly, an article in the magazine of the prestigious Conference Board recommends a "personal relations policy" that includes a wide range of relatively intimate relations and goes beyond sexual relationships and mandates disclosure of close personal relationships as defined in the policy. Even though sexual involvement is perceived as posing the greatest threat to objectivity, close after-hours friendships are important to note as well:

> Research supports the suspicion that "old boy" buddies—and now "old girls," too—get more job perks than "lovers." That's why a policy should address potential conflicts with marital, extended-family, and close-friendship relationships as well as romantic ones. (Lever et al. 2006, 39; see also Sugarman 2003)

In a parallel move, since the 1980s, employers (especially in the public sector) have been increasingly imposing no-spouse and anti-nepotism rules. What is more, legal attempts to challenge nepotism rules, which prohibit couples from sharing a workplace have generally failed. Employers commonly justify bans on married couples by means of three claims: first, "the advancement of mutual interest" argument that marital solidarity might supersede employers' interests; second, a reverse "feuding" argument that couples' quarrels can seriously interfere both with their relationship and work environment; and third, a "breach of confidentiality" argument that married couples may improperly disclose secret information to each other (Wexler 1982; see also Podgers 1996). These three arguments incorporate the distraction, human capital, and disorder theses I distinguished earlier.

Let me not give the impression, however, that American firms generally adopt explicit anti-intimacy policies. In fact, the SHRM 2005 survey found that most companies do not have a policy designed to regulate office romances: over 70 percent of organizations reported they had no formal written or verbal policies. Those that did, had policies discouraging, but not prohibiting, workplace dating (Parks 2006).

The main thing we do know, then, is that both managers and management experts continue to flag the presence of different sorts of workplace intimacy and excessive familiarity as a significant management problem. As in the Wolfowitz case, these concerns often translate into organizational anti-intimacy rules, sets of defenses against contamination by intimacy. Along those lines, Tom Rath (2006), author of a best-selling survey of on-the-job friendships, reports that managers he talked to usually responded to the presence of workplace intimacy with caution, even fear.

Some countertrends deserve closer empirical attention. Such organizational innovations as self-managed work teams or quality circles, for example, presumably depend for their effectiveness on the fact that they promote friendship and thereby facilitate coordination of work efforts (McGuire 2007, 138). Similarly, the shift to horizontal organizational forms seems to provide efficiency gains partly because it draws on friendships that ease communication and cooperation across divisional lines (Flynn 2003; Kalev 2004; Ollilainen and Calasanti 2007; Vallas 2006; Smith 1997).

Still, not surprisingly, managers are less concerned with friendships than with sexual liaisons within organizations. Sexual liaisons are of course more likely to generate unfavorable publicity, lawsuits, and organizational crises than are the presence of kinship or friendship.[4] Sexual liaisons between supervisors and employees that go sour, furthermore, most likely generate a significant share of sexual harassment complaints. In fact, experts are increasingly concerned about adequate managerial response to dissolved workplace romances, which sometimes turn into sexual harassment (Pierce et al. 2004; Pierce and Aguinis 2005). The 2005 SHRM study found that concerns among human resource professionals about retaliation—meaning conflicts between coworkers after a breakup—grew from 12 percent in 2001 to 67 percent in 2005. With more women in the workforce, concern with exploitation and sexual predation (and fear of lawsuits stemming from them) grows more salient. For instance, a national survey of senior managers in 544 U.S. cities found overall favorable views on workplace friendships, but managers remained wary of office romances (Berman et al. 2002).

Note the irony: Human relations specialists and lawyers worry increasingly about the threat of on-the-job romance, every survey reports high levels of on-the-job romance, but only 30 percent of firms surveyed have policies banning or regulating on-the-job romance. The most likely conclusion is that experienced managers understand both that love will have its way at work and that writing regulations will not eliminate it. Nevertheless, it is not obvious either that these rules do drive intimacy from the workplace or that they actually serve organizational performance (see, e.g., Schultz 2003, 2006).

Intimacy's Impact on Organizational Performance

Surprisingly, more information is available on the overall impact of intimacy's presence in an organization than on my fourth question: its effects on intimate pairs' job performance and its third-party effects. Since the 1930s, industrial sociologists have stressed the positive impact of workplace solidarity on productivity. But that older literature generally neglected practices creating solidarity pairs in favor of practices fostering group identification (Hodson 2001, 51).

More recently, a number of studies report the prevalence and even management's promotion of job recruitment by current employees of friends and kin. Mutual recruitment often benefits the hiring organization by enhancing employee productivity (Castilla 2005; Fernandez et al. 2000; Grieco 1987). So far as one can tell, mutual hiring tends to integrate new hires more firmly into workplace networks and to give them greater access to personal attention.

In a fine example of a fast-paced call center, Fernandez et al. (2000) show that personal ties between current employees and potential employees often benefit the hiring organization by enhancing employee productivity. Castilla shows further that after mutually selective hiring, newcomers tend to produce more and display greater attachment to the firm than casual hires. He distinguishes between a "better match" account (in which referrals simply bring in new employees with more suitable qualifications for the job) and a "social enrichment" account (in which superior relations emerge between old and new employees), providing substantial evidence for social enrichment effects in the call center.

Castilla reports, for instance, that the staff was considering a "buddy" system of pairing old-timers with newcomers to reduce turnover and raise job satisfaction—very much a social enrichment strategy. "One trainer," says Castilla:

> highlighted the importance of having a friend on the job: "It really helps in making the job more comfortable." This trainer did not specifically say that the referrer might play an important role in this process. But when probed about the possibility that the referrer might be acting as an informal "buddy," she said this was "probably right." (2005, 1,273)

The work of Fernandez, Castilla, and others identifies crucial circumstances in which the presence of intimacy enhances organizational performance. Nevertheless, economic sociologists have not yet confronted intimate relations with sufficient directness or examined the supposed threat to organizational performance posed by such intimacy.

More generally, a surprising variety of studies document the positive effects of workplace intimate relationships on economic productivity. Consider these vignettes:

- Economist K. K. Fung provides a strong theoretical rationale for concluding that horizontal favor exchanges enhance organizational efficiency (Fung 1991).
- Business school professor Francis Flynn finds evidence that employees who exchanged favors were significantly more productive than their fellows (Flynn 2003).
- A large 2001 Gallup poll identifies a strong connection across firms between the proportion of workers who had best friends in the workplace, on one side, and firm profitability, productivity, safety, and customer loyalty, on the other (Ellingwood 2001).
- In 2007, a survey of senior executives and workers in the country's thousand largest firms finds widespread agreement that workers with coworkers who were "buddies" both on and off the job were more productive and committed contributors to firm performance ("Birds of a Feather" 2007).
- Legal scholar Sally Avelenda argues that spouses who share a workplace are more likely to stay on the job, to be recruitable together, to gain more satisfaction from working together, and to adopt more favorable attitudes toward the firm that hires them (Avelenda 1998, 704).
- A substantial literature on family firms indicates not only that on the average they create more worker-friendly environments than their nonfamily competitors but also that they enjoy greater organizational effectiveness (e.g., Anderson and Reeb 2003; Family Inc. 2003).

Family businesses offer an even more decisive empirical challenge to any notion of incompatibility between intimacy and economic effectiveness. Estimates of the share of all American businesses owned by families run in the vicinity of 90 percent and the share of all business income from such firms appears to be about 60 percent (Bellet et al. 2006; "Family Business Statistics" 2006).

What is more, such firms perform very well, perhaps even better than nonfamily firms (see, e.g., Anderson and Reeb 2003; for a historical and comparative perspective, see James 2006). They have lower turnover and often provide benefits such as child care, scholarships for employees' children, and profit-sharing, and are less likely to resort to layoffs. As expert John L. Ward comments: "Family firms see employees as a long-term resource. They just believe it's the right way to go" ("Family, Inc." 2003).

Not that family business relations operate just like nonfamily relations. A compensation handbook for family business points out a series of challenges that such businesses must face, for example, equity between family and non-family forms of compensation. The manual includes three striking examples of resolutions to this dilemma:

1. A family employed a diligent but handicapped son at full pay. The son made a meaningful contribution but less than the minimum expected of his peers. No one argued with or felt abused by this deviation from the company's compensation policy, probably because of the son's handicap, agreeable personality, and hard-work ethic.

2. A family bent experience requirements, giving a daughter who was a single mother a chance to learn a new position to which she brought aptitude but no experience or training. The family paid the daughter the full-position wage during the learning period of nearly a year. The company was rewarded with a loyal and capable performer who had permanent ties to the organization. The family was able to help a responsible member sustain a reasonable standard of living.

3. Two brothers, both of whom worked hard, agreed to earn the same amounts. Their abilities and contributions, however, were different. From the company's standpoint, the overpayment of one brother would not have been necessary except for the sibling relationship. However, the harmony and teamwork fostered by this accommodating relationship was a major benefit to the organization. Arguably, the organization would have been sold and dismantled if the brothers had not recognized the value of a situational overpayment in return for calm waters, productive efforts, and a focus on the company's important issues (Bieneman 2001, 52).

In all these cases, according to the manual, the integration of family relations into the organization enhanced organizational performance. These problems, moreover, are no more acute than those of compensation and incentives in nonfamily organizations.

Studies of new business ventures further support the crucial role of family ties. In a valuable survey article, Howard Aldrich and Jennifer Cliff make three observations about start-ups of American business: First, a significant proportion of new organizations are founded by two or more related individuals, including married couples or cohabiting partners. Second, the creation of new organizations is more likely to respond to alterations in family ties rather than simply the opening of economic options. Third, families play key roles in providing start-ups with financial resources, human resources, and physical resources such as space in the family household (2003, 577).

Available evidence on family firms makes three points of increasing importance for the place of intimacy in economic organizations. Most obviously and uncontroversially, the sheer prevalence and relative visibility of family firms establish the compatibility of intimate ties with a wide range of economic activity. More speculatively, descriptions of family firms suggest that they tend to substitute durable relations of solidarity for arm's length relations of short-term efficiency and thus gain their successes by somewhat different organizational means from firms that bar intimate relations. Third, we have at least a hint that family firms gain some of their durability from a simple fact: intimate ties generally operate on a longer time scale than impersonal ones and hence provide participants with extra capacity to ride out short-term failures and downturns in favor of long-term performance. In Albert Hirschman's terms, close kin faced with organizational decline tend to substitute voice and loyalty for exit (Hirschman 1970).

Intimacy's Effects on Internal Organizational Dynamics

Unfortunately, existing studies yield much less evidence on the organizational dynamics and interpersonal effects of intimate relations than on intimacy's overall impact. Those effects have two components: effects of intimacy on the pairs' work performance and the effects of intimacy on relations of the pair, singly or collectively, to third parties. In principle, we should be able to gauge intimacy's effect on organizational performance—negative or positive—simply by observing the job performance of intimate pairs as compared to the performance of nonintimate pairs in similar jobs. In practice, it is not so easy. Because of separate-spheres thinking, we only have scattered evidence of workplace intimate labors. We know little, for instance, of exactly how coworkers cover for each other's defects or absences, what sort of mentoring old-timers provide newcomers, how workers console each other for managers' injustices, what sorts of favors they exchange on the job, and how they support each other by such practices as taking up collections, trading work assignments, and pooling leaves.

Scattered anecdotes and complaints, to be sure, deplore the withdrawal of intimate couples from creative work and effective interaction with their fellow workers. Robert Quinn's (1977) study of the dynamics of organizational romance, for instance, identified many points in which romantic partners' work performance suffered, among them making costly mistakes as a result of distraction, covering mistakes of the partner, working less and worse, arriving late, leaving early, missing appointments, becoming inaccessible, showing favoritism, promoting the other. Nevertheless, Quinn also documents many ways in which on-the-job intimacy enhanced the performance of the pairs involved, such as improving coordination or lowering tensions.

In that positive vein, other more recent studies suggest that certain forms of intimacy frequently increase the general well-being of the workers involved in these ties. Marks's 1994 GSS-based study of workplace intimacy, for example, found an association between coworkers' friendship ties and greater job satisfaction (see also Hulbert 1991; for married couples, see Janning 2006). Similarly, in her account of "intimate work" McGuire notes that for some of her interviewees, "sharing facilitated good professional relationships

because it created trust and a general sense of good will between workers."
McGuire reports Larry's case:

> [He] described how sharing with one of his network members facili-
> tated trust between them, which made Larry feel comfortable having
> "off-line conversations" with him, or confidential discussions about
> work-related issues. (2007, 138; see also Bridge and Baxter 1992;
> Lively 2000)

More dramatically, relying on self-reports, Rath's *Vital Friends* trumpets
his finding that having a best friend on the job makes the worker seven
times as likely to be engaged in his or her job (2006, 53). Rath and others
furthermore find that having close friends on the job makes it less likely that
workers will leave. In a parallel way, Groysberg et al. report that the quality
of star performance among security analysts depends heavily on collaborative relations with colleagues, so much so that stars often undergo significant
losses of productivity when they make solo moves from one firm to the other
(Groysberg and Abrahams 2006; Groysberg and Lee 2008; Groysberg, Lee,
and Nanda 2008).

Despite the concern about romantic entanglements, office romances also
often enhance worker satisfaction and performance. Lisa Mainiero's review
of the literature on workplace romance identifies a number of studies that
"provide support for positive impacts on performance, job involvement and
enthusiasm of partners that engage in an office romance with a love motive"
(2005, 157).

Along the same lines, a British survey of 221 individuals in a wide variety
of organizations found that most of them reported having had intimate relations at the workplace. Most described the experience as positive:

> When closer and more positive relationships are formed, people report
> that they work better together, work harder to achieve their objectives
> and through such mutual respect and care, the organisation is also
> viewed in a more positive light. Equally, a substantial proportion of
> the survey respondents view physical intimacy in a positive light, either
> as parties directly involved or as third party onlookers. Overall, it is
> reported that work effectiveness increases as a result of the relationship.
> (Kakabadse and Kakabadse 2004, 111)

For instance, a male information technology director of financial services
made the following report:

> It just happened that we started working together here 10 years ago
> and the relationship just evolved. After two mergers we became the
> only two senior people from the old company. One of the key things
> that has been important for the development of our intimacy is the

extreme nature of the work-changing technology and the business. That required quite close relations and working together. . . . Consequently, the relationship gained high value for both of us, from information exchange to alliance to mutual support. Now, we have a very intimate relationship that perhaps some would not approve of, considering that she has a partner. (Kakabadse and Kakabadse 2004, 122)

Thus, couples who engage in intimate relations at work frequently report both personal satisfaction and enhanced work performance.

Intimacy affects not only the job performance of intimate pairs, but also individual and joint interactions of the pair with other workers within the organization. The threat to organizational performance comes from the possibility that members of intimate pairs will withhold needed communication and cooperation from third parties and will give each other unfair access to organizational resources and rewards. In fact, the stronger the correlation between intimacy and productivity, the greater the possibility of strong negative effects for those left out of the intimate relationship. The promise, in contrast, stems from the possibility that intimate pairs will collaborate more effectively with third parties, for example, but substituting for each other in cases of absence or illness. In truth, however, existing studies provide no more than glimmers of information on third-party effects (see, e.g., Foley and Powell 1999).

In his study of romantic entanglements among machine crew members, Roy contended that while in its early stages, "salutary effects on group morale and machine output may accompany the euphoria of a loving pair," soon the benefits soured, as "Eros and Vulcan draw apart." Eventually, Roy claimed, "the work group disintegrates, production collapses and blessings from the bossmen shrivel" (1974, 46).

With less flourish, others have noted that a couples' close ties sometimes disrupt the flow of communications, as fellow employees may fear a breach of confidentiality. Observing work relationships within the engineering division of a large U.S. high-tech corporation, Gideon Kunda noted the impact of overlapping relationships. One supervisor married to an engineer working in the same facility shared her concerns:

My husband works here too. We work on separate sides of the building and try not to see each other. I don't want to hear his voice. And I don't want any finger pointing. People might not trust you if they know you have a special relation. Some things you might not hear. I know my boss is sometimes concerned about information flow. I ride home with my husband. But some things I just wouldn't tell him. (1992, 169)

In a classic study, Rosabeth Moss Kanter showed how the relationship between a powerful boss and secretary affected relations—especially the boss's relationship—with the rest of the firm. Secretaries, Kanter found,

[c]ould make it easy or difficult to see a top executive. They could affect what managers read first, setting priorities for them without their knowing it. They could help or hurt someone's career by the ease with which they allowed that person access. (1977, 75)

Much of the published information on third-party effects, however, rests on anecdote and conjecture. James Dillard and Katherine Miller speculate for instance, that romantic couples "may be attempting to impress their partners by increasing their output" or to assuage management's fears about the impact of their relationship with increased performance (1988, 462).

However, there are wisps of evidence. In her interviews, McGuire found that coworkers' close ties

made it more likely that a work-related request would get done quickly, which was very important in this time-crunched organization. Lori described how she could call one of her network members, an administrative assistant who worked in a different area of the company, to help her with a Power Point presentation when she was "in a pinch." (McGuire 2007, 139)

IMPLICATIONS OF THE EVIDENCE

Available evidence on intimacy in organizations leaves many questions unanswered. It certainly establishes the widespread presence of intimate relations—sexual, friendship, or kinship—in economic organizations. That fact alone challenges any notion of intrinsic incompatibility between intimacy and organizational effectiveness. Separate-spheres and hostile-worlds interpretations of intimacy hinder our understanding of organizational processes.

When it comes to *how* intimate relations affect organizational processes, however, the evidence becomes more incomplete and complex. On the whole, existing studies suffer from several defects. They typically do the following:

- Consider only one type of intimacy at a time
- Concentrate not on everyday organizational intimacy but on extreme cases of nepotism, harassment, collusion, favoritism, and exploitation
- Assume that the sheer presence or absence of intimate relations, rather than the intersection of those relations with nonintimate relations, is the crucial phenomenon to analyze

The common view of intimacy as a general threat to organizational performance rests on two sorts of errors: analytical and empirical. The analytical errors fall into three parts: (1) fixation on the presence or absence of certain kinds of intimate relationships instead of considering how such intimate relationships impact on third parties within the organization, and thus on overall organizational performance; (2) failure to notice that some kinds of relationships within economic organizations actually contribute more to overall effectiveness if they involve a measure of intimacy; (3) uncritical acceptance of separate-spheres and hostile-worlds principles.

How can we avoid these errors? We must begin by recognizing a point that is obvious to organizational analysts: the overall performance of an organization is not the simple sum of individual performances but the outcome of interactions among its members. How the performance of worker A impinges on the performance of worker B, and how their joint performance impinges on the behavior of other workers determines the effect of the relationship between A and B on adjacent relationships, and thence on the organization as a whole.

To be sure, the impact of intimate work relations, including sexual interaction, varies from one kind of organization to another. As Christine Williams, Patti A. Giuffre, and Kirsten Dellinger say in their review of sexuality in the workplace:

> The same behavior in different organizational context can have different meanings and different consequences. Thus, while many service workers are paid to be sexy and to engage in sexual innuendo with customers, in other jobs, mere rumors of sexual behavior or desire can destroy a career. (1999, 90; see also Mano and Gabriel 2006)

What configurations should we take into account? To maintain intellectual discipline, we should begin with three-party relationships—triads—before moving on to more complex configurations. In the simplest case, we are asking how the presence of an intimate connection between A and B affects the connection between either or both of them and C. For example, we can ask how a close connection between a secretary and a boss affects the interaction between the boss and (a) his or her superiors, (b) his or her peers, or (c) his or her other subordinates. Or we can ask how close friendship between two workers on an assembly line affects the relations of each to (a) their common supervisor, (b) their helpers, and (c) other workers on the line.

In general, then, we need to distinguish among the following:

- Character and intensity of the intimate relation: breadth, duration, and intensity
- Relative rank equality or inequality of the organizational relationships involved: horizontal versus vertical
- Forms of collaboration built into those organizational relationships, for example, pooling of skills in complex tasks versus sharing of confidential information

So which configurations typically suffer or benefit from the presence of intimate relations? A whole research program awaits the question. Surprisingly and disappointingly, the concentration of organizational analysts on the sheer presence or absence of different varieties of intimate ties rather than their articulation with adjacent relationships has left us with few well-documented observations on third-party impacts: how fellow workers respond to a coworker's sexual predation, the extent to which the coincidence of intimacy with informational pooling affects a pair's interactions with superiors, coworkers, or subordinates, the conditions under which intimacy-based mutual learning enhances joint contributions to collective efforts, and so on. If my arguments hold up, investigators will identify a wide range of circumstances and relations in which kinship, friendship, or even sexual intimacy augment a pair's contribution to the effectiveness of larger collective efforts.

In the absence of solid evidence, let me risk seven conjectures that follow from the argument I have just made:

1. Sexual predation of subordinates by superiors almost always damages organizational performance because it introduces coercion and injustice directly into work relationships and excites fear, indignation, or both among adjacent workers.

2. Intimate relations often threaten organizations when they involve pairs of persons one of whom has access to a third party's valuable organizational secrets, as when an affair between an executive's confidential assistant and another employee tempts the pair to share and profit by those secrets.

3. Where pooling of confidential information facilitates coordinated effort, however, intimate relations perform better than strictly impersonal relations.

4. As generations of organizational sociologists have argued, friendships within work teams, on the average, reinforce commitment to performance by the work team and the organization as a whole.

5. Where the availability of personal information within a pair of coworkers prevents errors and/or promotes superior performance (e.g., an assistant who can compensate for a supervisor's bad day), a measure of intimacy enhances the pair's contribution to organizational effectiveness.

6. Where time-consuming mutual learning enhances collaboration because it establishes effective interpersonal routines and/or predictability, intimate relations improve organizational performance.

7. When pairs compensate for each other's failures, including sharing of tasks and compensation for absences, their joint contribution enhances organizational performance.

This does not mean, to be sure, that intimacy—even nonsexual intimacy—always enhances organizational performance. On the contrary, it means that the match between intimate relations and organizational configurations matters far more to organizational effectiveness than does the sheer presence or absence of one kind of intimacy or another. But it also means that flat bans of intimate relations are likely, on average, to damage organizational performance.

Hostile-worlds doctrines arise precisely because managers and organizational analysts are trying to work out good matches, but they are too blunt an instrument to do the job. It will not do to assume that all relationships within economic organizations will work better if they operate at arm's length. Nor, however, would organizations work well if any kind of intimacy occurred in any configuration. The analytic problem, then, is the identification of matches that enhance organizational performance without introducing unfairness and exploitation.

Separate-spheres and hostile-worlds doctrines will not do the job. Policies based on such assumptions regularly do the following:

- Distract from the main causes of unfairness and exploitation, which are sex segregation and inequality
- Provide a pretext for discriminating against unwanted workers
- Curtail opportunities for productive uses of interpersonal intimacy
- Discriminate against women, who are subject to anti-nepotism rules

The challenge consists of distinguishing configurations of relations, including intimacy, that (a) clearly damage individual welfare through discrimination, exploitation, or injustice; (b) clearly damage organizational performance in the aggregate; (c) coexist without damage; and (d) actually contribute to organizational performance. The goal is thus to rewrite rules so that they eliminate (a) and (b) but not (c) or (d).

Organizational analysts can make a major contribution to clarifying the policy issues by documenting, locating, and explaining the operation of intimate ties within economic organizations. The challenge is to trace configurations of relations, including intimate ties and their ramifications, though the rest of the organization rather than settling for the observation of intimate pairs alone. We need analyses that accomplish three things:

- Recognize—and even account for—the frequently positive effects of intimate solidarity within organizations on those organizations' overall performance
- Clarify how paired intimate solidarities affect third parties and larger networks
- Sort out which kinds of configurations, including intimate ties, commonly produce suboptimal performance, which actually contribute to organizational performance, and which have little impact one way or the other

I do not claim for a moment to have resolved these momentous questions. I make no claim to have posed general solutions for corruption, conflict of interest, and betrayal of trust. But I do claim that visions of a two-spheres world and of their mutual destruction will never allow us even to pose these questions properly. No one who sticks to separate-spheres and hostile-worlds reasoning will get very far with them. Once we understand the questions and recognize current theoretical obstacles to answering them, the investigation of intimacy within economic organizations poses a rich, challenging array of analytical problems whose proper resolutions will help scholars and policy-makers well outside the world of corporations.

Notes

Viviana A. Zelizer, "Intimacy in Economic Organizations," in *Economic Sociology of Work*, edited by Nina Bandelj, 23–55. Vol. 19 in *Research in the Sociology of Work* (Bingley, U.K.: Emerald, 2009). Reprinted with permission.

1. http://www.whistleblower.org/doc/2007/World%20Bank%20Staff%20 Association%20Email.pdf.
2. For a lucid and nuanced analysis of business friendships, see Ingram and Zou 2008.
3. In this instance, as in the MedAptus case discussed earlier, we find a category of intimacy based on in-group solidarity rather than an intimate pair.
4. On legal problems posed by friendship ties within organizations, see Leib 2007.

References

Aldrich, H. E., and J. E. Cliff. 2003. "The Pervasive Effects of Family on Entre-preneurship: Toward a Family Embeddedness Perspective." *Journal of Business Venturing* 18:573–96.

Aldrich, H. E., and M. Ruef. 2006. *Organizations Evolving.* 2nd ed. Thousand Oaks, Calif.: Sage Publications.

Anderson, R. C., and D. M. Reeb. 2003. "Founding-Family Ownership and Firm Performance: Evidence from S&P 500." *Journal of Finance* 58:1301–27.

Avelenda, S. M. 1998. "Love and Marriage in the American Workplace: Why No-Spouse Policies Don't Work." *University of Pennsylvania Journal of Labor and Employment Law* 691.

Bandelj, N. 2009. "Emotions in Economic Action and Interaction." *Theory and Society* 38:347–66.

Bellet, W., B. Dunn, R.K.Z. Heck, P. Parady, J. Powell, and N. B. Upton. 2006. *Family Business as a Field of Study.* Ithaca, N.Y.: Cornell University Family Business Research Institute—Bonfenbrenner Life Course Center. http://www.fambiz.com/Orgs/Cornell/articles/real/ifbpa.cfm (accessed March 12).

Benson, S. P. 1986. *Counter Cultures: Saleswomen, Managers, and Customers in American Department Stores, 1890–1940.* Urbana: University of Illinois Press.

Berman, E. M., J. P. West, and M. N. Richter Jr. 2002. "Workplace Relations: Friendship Patterns and Consequences (According to Managers)." *Public Administration Review* 62 (March/April): 217–30.

Bieneman, J. N. 2001. "The Family Compensation Picture Is Painted in Many Colors." In *The Family Business Compensation Handbook*, edited by B. Spector, 51–52. Philadelphia: Family Business Publishing.

"Birds of a Feather Flock Together . . . at Work." 2007. Accountemps, June 14. http://www.accountemps.com/portal/site/at-us/menuitem.b368a569778a 80c6cb42b21002f3dfa0/?vgnextoid = 39a73468151e6010VgnVCM100000e 2aafb0aRCRD (accessed July 12).

Blake-Beard, S., A. Murrell, and D. Thomas. 2006. *Unfinished Business: The Impact of Race on Understanding Mentoring Relationships*. Harvard Business School Working Paper no. 06-060.

Brewis, J., and S. Linstead. 2000. *Sex, Work and Sex Work: Eroticizing Organization*. London: Routledge.

Bridge, K., and L. A. Baxter. 1992. "Blended Relationships: Friends as Work Associates." *Western Journal of Communication* 56 (Summer): 200–225.

Burt, R. S. 2005. *Brokerage and Closure: An Introduction to Social Capital*. New York: Oxford University Press.

———. 2007. "Secondhand Brokerage: Evidence on the Importance of Local Structure for Managers, Bankers, and Analysts." *Academy of Management Journal* 50:119–48.

Castilla, E. J. 2005. "Social Networks and Employee Performance in a Call Center." *American Journal of Sociology* 110 (March): 1243–83.

Chandler, T. D., R. Gely, J. Howard, and R. Cheramie. 2002. "Spouses Need Not Apply: The Legality of Antinepotism and No-Spouse Rules." *San Diego Law Review* 39:31.

Chauncey, G. 1994. *Gay New York: Gender, Urban Culture, and the Making of the Gay Male World, 1890–1940*. New York: Basic Books.

Darr, A. 2006. *Selling Technology: The Changing Shape of Sales in an Information Economy*. Ithaca, N.Y.: Cornell University Press.

Desmond, M. 2007. *On the Fireline: Living and Dying with Wildland Firefighters*. Chicago: University of Chicago Press.

Dillard, J. P., and K. I. Miller. 1988. "Intimate Relationships in Task Environments." In *Handbook of Personal Relationships*, edited by S. W. Duck, 449–65. Hoboken, N.J.: Wiley.

Dublin, T. 1979. *Women at Work: The Transformation of Work and Community in Lowell, Massachusetts, 1826–1860*. New York: Columbia University Press.

Ellingwood, S. 2001. "The Collective Advantage." *Gallup Management Journal* (September). http://gmj.gallup.com/content/default.aspx?ci = 787&pg = 1 (accessed July 12).

Ely, R. J., and D. E. Meyerson. 2000. "Theories of Gender in Organizations: A New Approach to Organizational Analysis and Change." In *Research in Organizational Behavior*, edited by B. M. Staw and R. I. Sutton, 22:103–51. Stamford, Conn.: JAI.

"Family Business Statistics." 2006. American Management Services, http://www .amserv.com/familystatistics.html (accessed March 12).

"Family, Inc." 2003. Special report, *BusinessWeek* online. November 10. http://www.businessweek.com/magazine/content/03_45/b3857002.htm.

Fernandez, R. M., E. J. Castilla, and P. Moore. 2000. "Social Capital at Work: Networks and Employment at a Phone Center." *American Journal of Sociology* 105 (March): 1,288–1,356.

Flynn, F. J. 2003. "How Much Should I Give and How Often? The Effects of Generosity and Frequency of Favor Exchange on Social Status and Productivity." *Academy of Management Journal* 46:539–53.

Foley, S., and G. N. Powell. 1999. "Not All Is Fair in Love and Work: Coworkers' Preferences for and Responses to Managerial Interventions regarding Workplace Romances." *Journal of Organizational Behavior* 20:1043–56.

Fung, K. K. 1991. "One Good Turn Deserves Another: Exchange of Favors within Organizations." *Social Science Quarterly* 72 (September): 443–63.

Grieco, M. 1987. *Keeping It in the Family: Social Networks and Employment Chance.* London: Tavistock.

Groysberg, B., and R. Abrahams. 2006. "Lift Outs: How to Acquire a High-Functioning Team." *Harvard Business Review* 84 (December): 1–10.

Groysberg, B., and L. Lee. 2008. "The Effects of Colleague Quality on Top Performance: The Case of Security Analysts." *Journal of Organizational Behavior* 29 (November): 1123–44.

Groysberg, B., L. Lee, and A. Nanda. 2008. "Can They Take It with Them? The Portability of Star Knowledge Workers' Performance: Myth or Reality." *Management Science* 54 (July): 1213–30.

Hartel, C., N. M. Ashkanasy, and W. Zerbe. 2005. *Emotions in Organizational Behavior.* New York: Lawrence Erlbaum.

Hearn, J., and W. Parkin. 1995. *"Sex" at "Work": The Power and Paradox of Organization Sexuality.* New York: St. Martin's Press.

Hearn, J., D. L. Sheppard, P. Tancred-Sheriff, and G. Burrell, eds. 1989. *The Sexuality of Organization.* London: Sage Publications.

Heimer, C. 1992. "Doing Your Job and Helping Your Friends: Universalistic Norms about Obligations to Particular Others in Networks." In *Networks and Organizations: Structure, Form, and Action,* edited by N. Nohria and R. G. Eccles, 143–64. Boston: Harvard Business School Press.

Hirschman, A. O. 1970. *Exit, Voice, and Loyalty: Responses to Decline in Firms, Organizations, and States.* Cambridge, Mass.: Harvard University Press.

———. 1977. *The Passions and the Interests: Political Arguments for Capitalism before Its Triumph.* Princeton, N.J.: Princeton University Press.

Hochschild, A. R. 1983. *The Managed Heart: Commercialization of Human Feeling.* Berkeley: University of California Press.

Hodson, R. 2001. *Dignity at Work.* Cambridge: Cambridge University Press.

Hulbert, J. S. 1991. "Social Networks, Social Circles, and Job Satisfaction." *Work and Occupations* 18 (November): 415–30.

Ingram, P., and P. W. Roberts. 2000. "Friendships among Competitors in the Sydney Hotel Industry." *American Journal of Sociology* 106:387–423.

Ingram, P., and X. Zou. 2008. "Business Friendships." *Research in Organizational Behavior* 28:167–84.

Jackson, M. 2006. "In Bad Times, Workers Share Time Off." *Boston Globe,*

November 19. http://www.boston.com/jobs/news/articles/2006/11/19/in_bad_times_workers_share_time_off.

James, H. 2006. *Family Capitalism: Wendels, Haniels, Falcks, and the Continental European Model.* Cambridge, Mass.: Harvard University Press.

Janning, M. 2006. "Put Yourself in My Work Shoes: Variations in Work-Related Spousal Support for Professional Married Coworkers." *Journal of Family Issues* 27 (January): 85–109.

Kakabadse, A., and N. Kakabadse. 2004. *Intimacy: An International Survey of the Sex Lives of People at Work.* Houndmills, U.K.: Palgrave Macmillan.

Kalev, A. 2004. "Cracking the Glass Cages? Job Segregation, the Restructuring of Work and Managerial Diversity." Paper presented at the annual meeting of the American Sociological Association, San Francisco, August.

Kanter, R. M. 1977. *Men and Women of the Corporation.* New York: Basic Books.

Kram, K. E. 1988. *Mentoring at Work: Developmental Relationships in Organizational Life.* Lanham, Md.: University Press of America.

Kunda, G. 1992. *Engineering Culture: Control and Commitment in a High-Tech Corporation.* Philadelphia: Temple University Press.

Laird, P. W. 2006. *Pull: Networking and Success since Benjamin Franklin.* Cambridge, Mass.: Harvard University Press.

Lamphere, L. 1985. "Bringing the Family to Work: Women's Culture on the Shop Floor." *Feminist Studies* 11 (Autumn): 519–40.

Lee, R. K. 2006. "The Organization as a Gendered Entity: A Response to Professor Schultz's the Sanitized Workplace." *Columbia Journal of Gender and Law* 15:609.

Leib, E. J. 2007. "Friendship and the Law." *UCLA Review* 54:631.

Lerum, K. 2004. "Sexuality, Power, and Camaraderie in Service Work." *Gender and Society* 18:756–76.

Lever, J., G. Zellman, and S. J. Hirschfeld. 2006. "Office Romance: Are the Rules Changing?" *Across the Board* (March/April): 33–41.

Lively, K. J. 2000. "Reciprocal Emotion Management: Working Together to Maintain Stratification in Private Law Firms." *Work and Occupations* 27 (February): 32–63.

Losee, S., and Olen, H. 2007. *Office Mate.* Avon, Mass.: Adams Media.

Mainiero, L. A. 2005. "On the Ethics of Office Romance: Developing a Moral Compass for the Workplace." In *Supporting Women's Career Advancement: Challenges and Opportunities,* edited by R. J. Burke and M. C. Mattis, 151–73. Cheltenham, U.K.: Edward Elgar.

Mano, R., and Y. Gabriel. 2006. "Workplace Romances in Cold and Hot Organizational Climates: The Experience of Israel and Taiwan." *Human Relations* 59:7–35.

Marks, S. R. 1994. "Intimacy in the Public Realm: The Case of Co-workers." *Social Forces* 72 (March): 843–58.

Martin, J., K. Knopoff, and C. Beckman. 1998. "An Alternative to Bureaucratic Impersonality and Emotional Labor: Bounded Emotionality at the Body Shop." *Administrative Science Quarterly* 43 (June): 429–69.

McCloskey, D. N. 2006. *The Bourgeois Virtues: Ethics for an Age of Commerce.* Chicago: University of Chicago Press.

McGuire, G. M. 2007. "Intimate Work: A Typology of the Social Support That Workers Provide to Their Network Members." *Work and Occupations* 34 (May): 125–47.

Mumby, D. K., and L. L. Putnam. 1992. "The Politics of Emotion: A Feminist Reading of Bounded Rationality." *Academy of Management Review* 17 (July): 465–86.

Ollilainen, M., and Calasanti, T. 2007. "Metaphors at Work: Maintaining the Salience of Gender in Self-Managing Teams." *Gender and Society* 21 (February): 5–27.

Parks, M. 2006. "2006 Workplace Romance." Society for Human Resource Management, http://www.shrm.org/hrresources/surveys_published/2006%20Workplace%20Romance%20Poll%20Findings.pdf (accessed March 11, 2006).

Pettinger, L. 2005. "Friends, Relations and Colleagues: The Blurred Boundaries of the Workplace." In *A New Sociology of Work?*, edited by L. Pettinger et al., 39–55. Oxford: Blackwell.

Pierce, C. A., and H. Aguinis. 2005. "Legal Standards, Ethical Standards, and Responses to Social-Sexual Conduct at Work." *Journal of Organizational Behavior* 26:727–32.

Pierce, C. A., B. J. Broberg, J. R. McClure, and H. Aguinis. 2004. "Responding to Sexual Harassment Complaints: Effects of a Dissolved Workplace Romance on Decision-Making Standards." *Organizational Behavior and Human Decision Processes* 95:66–82.

Podgers, J. 1996. "Marriage Traps in the Workplace." *ABA Journal* (January): 46–48.

Prince, T. 2005. "Do You Have an Office Wife?" *GQ* Online, http://men.style.com/gq/features/landing?id = content_403.

Quinn, R. E. 1977. "Coping with Cupid: The Formation, Impact, and Management of Romantic Relationships in Organizations." *Administrative Science Quarterly* 22 (March): 30–45.

Rabin-Margalioth, S. 2006. "Love at Work." *Duke Journal of Gender Law and Policy* 13:237.

Rath, T. 2006. *Vital Friends*. New York: Gallup Press.

Riach, K., and F. Wilson. 2007. "Don't Screw the Crew: Exploring the Rules of Engagement in Organizational Romance." *British Journal of Management* 18:79–92.

Roy, D. 1974. "Sex in the Factory: Informal Heterosexual Relations between Supervisors and Work Groups." In *Deviant Behavior: Occupational and Organizational Bases*, edited by C. Bryant, 44–66. Chicago: Rand McNally.

Rumens, N. 2008. "Working at Intimacy: Gay Men's Workplace Friendships." *Gender, Work, and Organization* 15:9–30.

Ruth, J. A. 2004. "Gift Exchange Rituals in the Workplace: A Social Roles Interpretation." In *Contemporary Consumption Rituals: A Research Anthology*, edited by C. C. Otnes and T. M. Lowrey, 181–211. Mahwah, N.J.: Lawrence Erlbaum.

Salzinger, L. 2003. *Genders in Production: Making Workers in Mexico's Global Factories*. Berkeley: University of California Press.

Schneider, B. 1984. "The Office Affair: Myth and Reality for Heterosexual and Lesbian Women Workers." *Sociological Perspectives* 27 (October): 443–64.

Schultz, V. 2003. "The Sanitized Workplace." *Yale Law Journal* 112:2061.

———. 2006. "Understanding Sexual Harassment Law in Action: What Has Gone Wrong and What We Can Do about It." Ruth Bader Ginsburg Lecture. *Thomas Jefferson Law Review* 29:1.

Sias, P. M., and D. J. Cahill. 1998. "From Coworkers to Friends: The Development of Peer Friendships in the Workplace." *Western Journal of Communication* 62 (Summer): 273–99.

Sinaceur, M., and L. Z. Tiedens. 2006. "Get Mad and Get More Than Even: When and Why Anger Expression Is Effective in Negotiations." *Journal of Experimental Social Psychology* 42:314–22.

Slater, P. 1963. "On Social Regression." *American Sociological Review* 28:339–64.

Smith, V. 1997. "New Forms of Work Organization." *Annual Review of Sociology* 23:315–39.

Spragins, E. 2004. "Dangerous Liaisons: As Small Firms Relax Their Rules on Office Romances, Some Face Unexpected Consequences." *Fortune Small Business*, http://money.cnn.com/magazines/fsb/fsb_archive/2004/02/01/360633/index.htm.

Steinberg, R. J., and D. M. Figart. 1999. "Emotional Labor in the Service Economy." *Annals of the American Academy of Political and Social Science* 561 (January): 8–26.

Sugarman, S. 2003. "'Lifestyle' Discrimination in Employment." *Berkeley Journal of Employment and Labor Law* 24.

Tiedens, L. Z. 2001. "Anger and Advancement versus Sadness and Subjugation: The Effect of Negative Emotion Expressions on Social Status Conferral." *Journal of Personality and Social Psychology* 80:86–94.

Uzzi, B., and R. Lancaster. 2004. "Embeddedness and Price Formation in the Corporate Law Market." *American Sociological Review* 69:319–44.

Vallas, S. P. 2006. "Empowerment Redux: Structure, Agency, and the Remaking of Managerial Authority." *American Journal of Sociology* 111 (May): 1,677–1,717.

Vault. 2007. "Office Romance Survey." http://www.vault.com/nr/newsmain.jsp?nr_page = 3&ch_id = 420&article_id = 28739469.

Weber, M. 1971. "Religious Rejections of the World and Their Directions." In *From Max Weber: Essays in Sociology*, edited by H. H. Gerth and C. Wright Mills, 323–59. New York: Oxford University Press.

Weisman, S. R. 2007. "Wolfowitz Resigns, Ending Long Fight at World Bank." *New York Times*, May 18.

Wexler, J. G. 1982. "Husbands and Wives: The Uneasy Case for Antinepotism Rules." *Boston University Law Review* 62:75.

Wharton, A. S., and R. J. Erickson. 1993. "Managing Emotions on the Job and at Home: Understanding the Consequences of Multiple Emotional Roles." *Academy of Management Review* 18 (July): 457–86.

Williams, C. L. 2006a. *Inside Toyland: Working, Shopping, and Social Inequality.* Berkeley: University of California Press.

———. 2006b. "The Unintended Consequences of Feminist Legal Reform: Commentary on the Sanitized Workplace." *Thomas Jefferson Law Review* 29:101.

Williams, C. L., P. A. Giuffre, and K. Dellinger. 1999. "Sexuality in the Work-place: Organizational Control, Sexual Harassment, and the Pursuit of Pleasure." *Annual Review of Sociology* 25:73–93.

Woods, J. D., and J. H. Lucas. 1993. *The Corporate Closet.* New York: Free Press.

Zelizer, V. 2005. *The Purchase of Intimacy.* Princeton, N.J.: Princeton University Press.

PART FOUR

The Economy of Care

Searching for advice, a worried daughter posted her anxieties on a blog, asking:

> Can I get paid to take care of my mother who is elderly and needing full-time care? Up until recently, I had been working two full-time jobs but had to quit both jobs in order to care for my aging mother, who is disabled and unable to take care of herself since her release from the hospital. I am an only child, and not trying to make money off my mother's situation. . . . Do you or your readers know if I can get paid to provide care for my mother? (June 2008).[1]

Mary Ellen Geist, another concerned daughter, left a successful career as radio news anchor to assist her mother in caring for her father, disabled by dementia. According to a *New York Times* report on the "Daughter Track"—daughters who opt out of the workplace to attend their elderly parents—Geist's mother, in order to preserve the daughter's independence, paid her "a $22,000-a-year 'salary' so she has money in her pocket" (November 24, 2005).

Such are the poignant anecdotes of lives involved in the care of others. With the economy of care we enter a different arena of intimacy, one that has emerged in the past couple of decades as the focus of an extraordinary amount of attention by scholars as well as policymakers. With an aging population and with more women, the traditional caregivers, employed in wage work, the problems of adult and child care loom as an increasingly worrisome concern. Demand for careworkers is steep and growing. Who will provide the care for children, the elderly, the ill, the disabled? Who will pay for it? Most care is still managed by family members and friends. The collective economic value of such informal care is formidable, estimated at $375 billion in 2007.[2]

But informal care alone cannot solve what Arlie Hochschild has called our "care deficit." Unquestionably, over the past half-century or so a higher proportion of personal care has become commercialized. That trend shows no sign of reversing. Yet despite the critical importance of caregiving, people who provide care for a living receive outrageously low compensation, or none at all for their efforts. Of course, a minority of professional caregivers, such as physicians and dentists have organized their professions so that they mostly prosper from their work. Even when it comes to medical attention, however, unpaid family members and poorly paid household workers provide the bulk of the actual labor, with trivial compensation, compared to that of their professional cousins. With other forms of care such as feeding, clothing, babysitting, and emotional sustenance, the discrepancy grows even larger. People who deliver such caring services form a large, and largely unrecognized, category of unequal workers.

The economics of intimate care confront us with delicate, often troublesome quandaries: who has the right or obligation to give life-enhancing care? Who is entitled to receive care? What compensation, if any, does the provision of care justify? When should the state be responsible for paying? Given that most careworkers are women, does paying for care segregate female labor more firmly into traditional gender roles? Or does it properly and fairly recognize women's distinctive efforts?

Paying for care encounters the same difficulties and concerns that come up each time people try to think through the relationships between market activity and social obligations. For many, care should remain a free gift, untainted by economic concerns. Parents, spouses, friends, and providers of care, runs the argument, act out of duty and love that would dissolve if exposed to the acid of markets. What will happen, separate-spheres/hostile-worlds advocates worry, if paid care substitutes for informal assistance? Would the generalization of payment for such care destroy caring itself and the relationships within which it occurs? In any case, how can we possibly arrive at an appropriate financial evaluation of caretakers' contributions? Payment for care thus raises all the questions of possible corruption and disruption that so preoccupies critics of commercialization.

The chapters in this section propose a different approach to the care economy. Caring relationships, in this view, feature sustained and/or intense personal attention that enhances the welfare of its recipients. As with other forms of intimate connections, I argue that hostile-worlds concerns, while legitimate, fail to capture the realities of caring activity. Caring and economic considerations intersect all the time, from informal neighborly exchanges of babysitting to the high salaries of physicians. The challenge is not to ban economic transactions from care but to create appropriate and equitable economic arrangements for the various kinds of caring relations. Those relations are indeed distinctive and therefore require special forms of contracting, negotiation, and payment.

The search for new understandings of caring labor, which I developed in *The Purchase of Intimacy* (2005) and in multiple papers and presentations, drew me into a network of brilliant legal scholars, social scientists, philosophers, historians, and policymakers in the United States, France, and the United Kingdom. The economics of care, these experts argue, should not remain hidden behind sentimentalized blinders that not only obscure the suffering of the many invisible and underpaid caretakers but prevent superior care for those who need it. Hostile-worlds beliefs combined with the weak power position of people who provide care for pay creates a market that systematically undervalues personal care as measured against the contributions it makes to sustaining life and well-being.

By redefining caring labor, these care specialists intend to transform care-oriented social policies and legislation. British specialist Fiona Williams (2001), for instance, has ambitiously called for a "political ethic of care." Arlie Hochschild and others have focused their own efforts on the special case of female migrant careworkers (Ehrenreich and Hochschild 2002). Legal activists, meanwhile, are taking their concerns into court. Most prominently, Joan Williams has strongly endorsed and guided legal action as one crucial mechanism to end workplace discrimination against caregiving. She reports an increase in litigation as more employees file suits against unfair dismissals or penalties connected to their carework (Williams and Segal 2003).

Although carework remains predominantly a woman's job, men are also affected by the idea that intimacy and economic activity should not mix. No less than their female counterparts, employed men and women who visibly give priority to caring for their households run the risk of losing their jobs when they stay home to care for a sick child or an elderly parent. Recognizing the economic value of caring work, thus, will benefit both women and men.

This revisionist care economics strongly supports the view that caring efforts can simultaneously exist as a labor of love and yet receive adequate economic recognition. Why, these care experts ask, should low pay or no pay somehow guarantee the authenticity and efficacy of care? Discounting theories that pay "crowds out" nurses' intrinsic caring motivation by corrupting their vocational purity, economists Julie Nelson and Nancy Folbre (2006), for instance, note that "if high pay is given in such a way that nurses feel respected and rewarded for their care and professionalism, feelings of vocation can be reinforced and expanded." Some legal analysts go much farther in recognizing paid caretakers' emotional attachments. Pamela Laufer-Ukeles (2009), for instance, advocates that under certain circumstances caretakers' close involvement with children under their care should legally entitle them to child custody and visitation rights.

As this section's initial anecdotes suggest, paid kin care provides a crucial test of care's compatibility with economic compensation. While informal networks continue to provide most family care, state-sponsored programs around the world are starting to subsidize with varying forms of payment systems the home care provided by kin and friends for children, the elderly, and the ill. In the United States, to take just one case, the increasing challenges of caring for injured Iraq veterans raised the option of paid family caregiving. During the last session of Congress in 2008, families and veterans' groups persuaded lawmakers to introduce legislation that would allow families of soldiers with traumatic brain injuries to be paid for their caretaking after receiving some training. The following April, the Family Caregiver Program Act of 2009, proposing, among other changes, monthly caregiver stipends, was placed on the Senate Legislative Calendar.[3]

For other circumstances, some families formalize private agreements with care contracts drawn by lawyers specifying the terms of the arrangement. And in some cases, caretaking children are able to claim a tax credit for expenses involved in attending to their parents. Because they involve kin, hostile-worlds stalwarts decry such arrangements. In their view, payments pollute families' economic innocence by converting intimate ties into employer-employee relations. Yet existing studies suggest that compensated kin care, if certainly not a perfect solution, provides at least one honorable strategy that alleviates the often staggering burdens of care.[4]

Clearly, scholars of care economies face a rich and demanding research and policy agenda. Making carework visible constitutes a crucial first step. Florence Weber, a noted French specialist, has shown, for instance, how in France state policies subsidizing careworkers led not only to increased public recognition of family carework but more generally raised visibility of care as a "legitimate work activity" (Trabut and Weber 2009, 364). Beyond policy efforts, we need to better understand the everyday economics of care, because caring dilemmas are certain to increasingly filter into all of our lives. We still know little about how parents and their adult children reach agreements on sensitive economic arrangements. When, for instance, is care from parent or child defined as a favor, a gift, or a task deserving compensation? For which kind of service? And what constitutes acceptable forms of compensation? In some situations it could mean a greater inheritance share, a direct cash payment, or a special fund designated for particular expenses, such as a grandchild's college education.

Care regularly involves others beyond the family, thus introducing a new set of challenges. How do friends or neighbors enter the economics of care, and what sorts of payments emerge in those relationships? How are those transactions shaped by the class or ethnic identity of care providers and recipients? As we debunk notions that intimacy never contains economic transactions, we step up the need to specify the special contours of the multiple care transactions: how are they negotiated? Which are considered fair arrangements and which exploitative?

When it comes to paid care, beyond a broad agreement that carework is currently underpaid and undervalued, we must understand that the form and conditions of payment themselves matter. A daily payment in cash signifies a very different caregiver–care recipient relationship than a monthly check, or an insurance co-pay. A gift of clothing or other in-kind goods in lieu of or in addition to a cash salary immediately suggests another kind of tie. Although they matter in specific ways for intimate settings, taking notice of the form of payment is not a trivial sentimental consideration. We have extensive evidence of how much the form of compensation matters even to CEOs of large companies, who ordinarily receive a wide range of perquisites in addition to straight monetary payments. Take away the company car, the executive washroom, or the luxury travel, and you take away some of the CEO's distinction. The same principles apply to matches among careworkers and their compensation.

The "connected lives" perspective that I have been developing over the years argues that caring and economic considerations intersect all the time but only work well when people make the right matches between the two. Identifying good matches, moreover, is a first step toward a search for just, noncoercive sets of economic transactions for different types of caring relations.

The two essays in this section are efforts to define and better account for various forms of carework as well as to extend the analysis of the economics of care to other goods defined as outside markets. I prepared "Caring Everywhere" as a keynote talk for a remarkable interdisciplinary conference convened by historian Eileen Boris and sociologist Rhacel Parreñas in 2007 at the University of California at Santa Barbara (Parreñas and Boris 2010). The conference brought together scholars and policymakers to discuss multiple varieties of care and careworkers, including nurses, nannies, home health aides, prostitutes, hostesses, manicurists, and more. My article identifies a theoretical and empirical agenda for care investigators, starting with an attempt to specify the concepts of care, intimacy, and work. What exactly do we mean by intimate labors and carework? It then examines the variability of sites where care exists, both paid and unpaid. As already introduced by the essay on organizational intimacy in the previous section, it shows caring relations flourish outside as well as inside households.

The second chapter, "Risky Exchanges," was prepared for another innovative interdisciplinary workshop organized by law professor Michele Goodwin at Georgetown University Law Center in 2006 to discuss moral, economic, and legal issues surrounding baby markets (Goodwin 2010). My essay exports some lessons from the care economy to analyze the characteristics of what I call "risky exchanges"—other similarly sensitive markets involving human goods. This exploration returned me to some of the issues raised by the valuation of children's lives. How, I now ask, does the analysis of care economies help us to better understand baby markets and, more generally, the complex and often contentious economies of markets for human goods, such as blood, organs, eggs, sperm, genetic materials, and even the emerging market for mother's milk?

NOTES

1. "Can I Get Paid to Care for a Family Member?" Telling It like It Is, http://www.tellinitlikeitis.net/2008/06/can-i-get-paid-to-care-for-a-family-member-elderly-mother-or-father.html (accessed July 4, 2008).

2. "Valuing the Invaluable: The Economic Value of Family Caregiving, 2008 Update," AARP Public Policy Institute, http://assets.aarp.org/rgcenter/il/i13_caregiving.pdfhttp://assets.aarp.org/rgcenter/il/i13_caregiving.pdf (accessed August 29, 2009).

3. "S. 801: Caregiver and Veterans Health Services Act of 2009," Govtrack. us, http://www.govtrack.us/congress/bill.xpd?bill=s111-801 (accessed November 1, 2009).

4. Note, for instance, that Alan Krueger et al.'s (2008) innovative study of societal subjective well-being, based on time use and emotional experience, found that adult care ranked lowest among activities people report as enjoyable or contributing to their happiness—way lower than socializing and doing housework and even lower than receiving medical care.

References

Ehrenreich, Barbara, and Arlie Russell Hochschild. 2002. *Global Woman: Nannies, Maids, and Sex Workers in the New Economy.* New York: Metropolitan.

Goodwin, Michele, ed. 2010. *Baby Markets: Money and the New Politics Creating Families.* New York: Cambridge University Press.

Krueger, Alan B., Daniel Kahneman, David Schkade, Norbert Schwarz, and Arthur A. Stone. 2008. "National Time Accounting: The Currency of Life." Working paper, March 31. http://www.irs.princeton.edu/pubs/pdfs/523.pdf.

Laufer-Ukeles, Pamela. 2009. "Money, Caregiving and Kinship: Should Paid Caretakers Be Allowed to Obtain De Facto Parental Status?" *Missouri Law Review* 74:16.

Nelson, Julie, and Nancy Folbre. 2006. "Why a Well-Paid Nurse Is a Better Nurse." *Nursing Economics* 24 (May–June): 127–30.

Parreñas, Rhacel, and Eileen Boris, eds. 2010. *Intimate Labors: Culture, Technologies, and the Politics of Care.* Stanford, Calif.: Stanford University Press.

Trabut, Loïc, and Florence Weber. 2009. "How to Make Care Work Visible? The Case of Dependence Policies in France." In *Economic Sociology of Work*, edited by Nina Bandelj, 343–68. Vol. 19 in *Research in the Sociology of Work.* Bingley, U.K.: Emerald.

Williams, Fiona. 2001. "In and beyond New Labour: Toward a New Political Ethic of Care." *Critical Social Policy* 21:467–93.

Williams, Joan C., and Nancy Segal. 2003. "Beyond the Maternal Wall: Relief for Family Caregivers Who Are Discriminated against on the Job." *Harvard Women's Law Journal* 26:77.

13

Caring Everywhere

Here is how an Austrian woman reports her response to being paid by Caritas, a Roman Catholic charity, for taking care of her mother-in-law:

> You can only say that I simply felt as if I had been promoted. Society also saw it totally differently then. Suddenly it was, "Aha, you're doing a job." Although I didn't do anything differently from before, it was suddenly seen as self-evident. But if you then say that you're working for Caritas, people say to you, "Wow, you're working now." . . . As soon as you're in employment and can say to the doctor that you have your own health insurance, it appears you are a better type of person. From the point of view of society, this type of employment is very good for women. (Ungerson 2004)

This woman, who had earlier cared for her father-in-law outside the Caritas payment system, is one of the respondents interviewed in a remarkable cross-national study of "cash for care" schemes conducted by British researcher Clare Ungerson, Sue Yeandle, and four research teams in five European Union countries: Austria, France, Italy, the Netherlands and the United Kingdom (see also Ungerson and Yeandle 2007).

Why is this woman, as well as so many of us, surprised by the unexpected effects of paid kin care? Because, sadly, the prevalent commercialized view of the labor market has sharply truncated people's view of what counts as genuine work that deserves serious compensation. In the process, we have neglected the economic significance of nonmarket, nonfirm work. This neglect is particularly consequential when it comes to intimate labor.

As we will soon see, developing clear ideas about the actual operation of intimate labor will enhance our collective understanding of both intimacy and labor. It will also help sweep away erroneous notions about their intersection and thus provide valuable guidance for social criticism and public policy. I hope that my essay will stimulate discussion on these crucial issues. Let me start by clarifying what is meant by intimacy and labor.

We can think of relations as intimate to the extent that *interactions within them depend on particularized knowledge received, and attention provided by, at least one person—knowledge and attention that are not widely available to third parties.* The knowledge involved includes such elements as shared secrets, interpersonal rituals, bodily information, awareness of personal vulnerability, and shared memory of embarrassing situations. The attention involved includes such elements as terms of endearment, bodily services, private languages, emotional support, and correction of embarrassing defects.

Intimate social relations thus defined depend on various degrees of trust. Positively, trust means that the parties willingly share such knowledge and attention in the face of risky situations and their possible outcomes. Negatively, trust gives one person knowledge of, or attention to, the other, which if made widely available would damage the second person's social standing.

This broad definition of intimacy covers a range of personal relations, including parent-child, godparent-godchild, siblings, close friendships, and sexually tinged ties. It also extends to the varying degrees and types of intimacy involved in the relations psychiatrist-patient, lawyer-client, priest-parishioner, servant-employer, prostitute-customer, spy–object of espionage, bodyguard-tycoon, child-care worker–parent, boss-secretary, janitor-tenant, personal trainer–trainee, and hairdresser-customer. In all these social relationships at least one person is bestowing trust, and at least one person has access to information or attention that, if made widely available, would damage the other.

Intimate relations, then, come in many varieties. They vary in kind and degree: the amount and quality of information available to spouses certainly differ from that of child-care worker and parent, or priest-parishioner. The extent of trust likewise varies accordingly. Because we are dealing with a continuum, exactly where we set the limit between intimate and impersonal relations remains arbitrary. But it is important to see that in some respects even the janitor who knows what a household discards day after day gains access to information with some of the same properties as the information exchanged in more obviously intimate relations. In this article, I will therefore adopt a relatively expansive definition of intimacy.

We also need a relatively expansive definition of labor: not only paid market employment, but any effort that creates transferable use value, including the use value that economists commonly call human capital (see Tilly and Tilly 1998). Thus housework, child care, advice giving, and school attendance all count as labor to the extent that they do in fact augment the use values of their performers and/or recipients.

Intimacy and labor intersect in the main subject matter of this volume: intimate labor. Within intimate labor, we should distinguish four different sites for personal care: unpaid care in intimate settings, unpaid care in economic organizations, paid care in intimate settings, and paid care in economic organizations such as hospitals, day-care centers, and doctors' offices. These four sites differ significantly in the character and organization of intimate labor. I will emphasize widespread confusions that have arisen in thinking about differences among these four sites.

What do we mean by care? Caring relationships, in my view, feature sustained and/or intense personal attention that enhances the welfare of its recipients. Care thus counts as labor even if it provides pleasure to its givers and recipients. We might set the minimum for "sustained and/or intensive personal attention" at a manicure in a nail salon or a brief telephone counseling session on a mental health hotline. The maximum might then take the form of lifetime mother-daughter bonds or the devotion of a long-term personal servant.

This definition of care excludes two other areas of interpersonal relations: first, relatively impersonal provision of welfare-enhancing benefits, and second, intimacy that does not enhance well-being. Relatively impersonal forms of welfare enhancement include such attentions as a pharmacist's advice on the best over-the-counter cough remedy and a government's provision of unemployment compensation.

As for the second exclusion, we too often mistakenly equate intimacy with care. We thus ignore those intimate relationships where the parties remain indifferent to each other or even inflict damage on one another. Abusive sexual relations, for example, are certainly intimate, but not caring. Such relationships supply risky information to at least one party and thus entail trust of a sort, yet do not include caring attention. Intimacy and care do often complement each other, but they have no necessary connection.

Intimate labor is both puzzling and fascinating because so many people imagine that if a relation is intimate it cannot, and should not, involve labor. Where does this assumption come from? It draws from two powerful fallacies: we can call them "separate spheres" and "hostile worlds." Separate-spheres notions claim that the world divides into separate spheres of sentiment and of rationality; hostile-worlds beliefs say that contact between those separate worlds corrupts in both directions. Their mixing, goes the argument, introduces contaminating, self-interested calculation into the world of sentiment, but it also introduces nonrational action into a world in which efficiency should reign.

These pervasive assumptions blind us to the prevalence of, and variation among, intimate labors. More specifically, they prevent us from understanding and explaining crucial differences among four very different sites of intimate labor: unpaid intimate care in intimate settings, unpaid intimate care in economic organizations, paid care in economic organizations, and paid care in intimate settings. Because we have ample documentation for paid care in economic organizations, let me concentrate on the other three: unpaid care in intimate settings, unpaid care in economic organizations, and paid care in intimate settings. A separate-spheres perspective identifies the first—unpaid care in intimate settings—as natural. It sees the other two as anomalous, peripheral phenomena instead of recognizing their crucial significance.

Unpaid Care in Intimate Settings

Let us first consider unpaid care in intimate settings. As I said at length in my 2005 book *The Purchase of Intimacy*, intimate relations regularly coexist with economic transactions without being corrupted. Of course, not all intimate interactions consist of labor, yet a significant share of them do. For example, couples buy engagement rings; parents pay nannies or child-care workers to attend to their children; adoptive parents pay lawyers and agencies money to obtain babies; divorced spouses pay or receive alimony and child-support payments; and parents give their children allowances, subsidize their college educations, help them with their first mortgage, and offer them substantial bequests in their wills. Friends and relatives send gifts of money as wedding presents, and friends loan each other money. Immigrants dispatch hard-earned money as remittances to kinfolk back home. Indeed, people who maintain intimate relations with each other regularly pool money, make joint purchases, invest shared funds, organize inheritances, and negotiate divisions of household work. No loving household would last long without regular inputs of economic effort.

When it comes to unpaid intimate labor, consider the obvious examples of food preparation, child care, and health care. Even in a day of takeout and fast food, unpaid domestic preparation of food still counts as one of the major forms of labor in capitalist countries, not to mention the rest of the world. Child care likewise continues to absorb enormous amounts of value-enhancing effort across the world. Furthermore, despite the advances of scientific medicine, health care remains a major form of unpaid intimate labor.

In the case of health care, Geneviève Cresson's close study of French households (1995) underlines the extent to which household members—especially adult women—work to sustain each other's health. Far from serving as adjuncts to professional health-care specialists, the women in the forty households Cresson interviewed clearly provided the bulk of all health care their family members received. Furthermore, they made the decisions as to which specialists to consult and when. None of them received direct compensation for their health services. Indeed, most of them underestimated the frequency and extent of those services; even those who maintained health-care diaries at Cresson's request tended to omit the daily tasks they simply folded mentally into food preparation and child care.

Even when medical professionals provide instructions or medicine, family members regularly take part in supplying care. They assure hygiene, fetch drugs and other medical supplies, and learn medical technologies such as injections and monitoring of vital signs. Household members also manage sick persons' schedules and their transportation, as well as the special diets and other comforts appropriate for their condition. In Los Angeles, for instance, Cecilia Menjívar studied the health practices of Guatemalan immigrant women. The women relied heavily on their interpersonal networks to secure medical care for themselves and their family members. Through a variety of informal ties, the women gained knowledge and access to both American medicine and unofficial means of healing, such as herbs, rituals, and medicines regulated in the United States but available without prescription in the home country.

As a consequence, mothers involved themselves daily in the delivery of health care at home. Menjívar reports about Aida, one of the Guatemalan women she interviewed:

> Like almost all the women in this study, Aida feels fully responsible for her family's health needs. . . . She is always mindful of her family's health and is industrious in putting together whatever treatments she can find. There was a reminder to herself on the refrigerator door: *Darle las vitaminas a la beiby. Ponerle las pastillas en la lonchera a Luis.* (Give the vitamins to the baby. Put the pills in Luis's lunchbox). (Menjívar 2002, 452–53)

Indeed, over recent decades, the development of health management organizations and the aging of the American population have combined to place a growing burden of health care on households. In Canada, Pat and Hugh Armstrong's study of changes in the health-care system found that a shift to day surgery, shorter patient hospital stays, and deinstitutionalization resulted in a significant increase in women's unpaid domestic carework, including the management of such "complex care technologies . . . as catheters, intravenous tubes and oxygen masks [that] are sent home with the patients" (2005, 185). They also note that the women who do the work seldom define it as care, leading to an underestimation of the hours women spend doing this work (see also Bittman et al. 2004, 73–74).

In the legal arena, courts regularly treat care provided by one family member to another as ineligible for monetary compensation, even in cases of inheritance and divorce. When they do award compensation to household members, including nannies, maids, and dependent kin, furthermore, courts generally distinguish between services naturally provided by intimates to each other, which remain uncompensated, and services going sufficiently beyond natural obligation to deserve compensation at something like market rates. Separate-spheres doctrines thus persist in the law.

Nevertheless, American courts sometimes actually recognize that domestic health care merits financial compensation. In 1985, the Supreme Court of Minnesota took on Alice Ann Beecham's claim to a portion of her mother-in-law's $166,000 estate. The mother-in-law, Sara Edith Beecham, had cut Alice from her will in favor of her four grandchildren. Two years after marrying Edith's son, Alice had taken the elderly, sick woman into her home. For the last six and a half years of Edith's life, Alice cared for her full time, not only cooking and cleaning, but performing delicate nursing tasks. The court ruled that despite their family relation, Alice was entitled to a portion of the estate (*In re Estate of Beecham*, 378 N.W.2d. 800 [Minn. 1985]).

When Alice had first contested the will, the trial court had ruled in her favor, finding an implied contract to pay for her personal services. The court noted that Edith had shown no reciprocity for Alice's strenuous care, except for an occasional five- or ten-dollar "tip" for transportation expenses. An appeals court reversed that decision on the grounds that Alice's services, because they involved a family member in the absence of an oral or written contract, had to be gratuitous.

The Supreme Court, however, reinstated the initial decision to award Alice compensation, supporting the trial court's finding of an implied contract. Alice's "around the clock care" of Edith, the Minnesota Supreme Court concluded, went "beyond services usually and ordinarily gratuitously rendered to family members." Based on experts' estimates of Alice's home-care services' commercial value, the court set compensation at $32,000, toward the lower end of the estimated range. As we analysts of care should do, in this instance the courts recognized the great economic value of unpaid care in intimate settings.

Unpaid Care in Economic Organizations

While separate-spheres assumptions conceal everyday unpaid intimate labors, they also prevent us from observing and explaining unpaid intimate care in economic organizations, which separate-spheres doctrines treat as anomalous. Although on the average, relations within economic organizations involve less intimacy—less access and trust—than relations within intimate settings such as households, forms of intimacy such as close friendships and confidential relations do appear in economic organizations. Indeed, they commonly include provision of personal care: sustained and/or intensive attention that enhances personal well-being. (This section draws on Zelizer 2009.)

In theory, intimacy is not supposed to matter in formal organizations. Indeed, organizational analysts and managers tend to think of such care as inefficient noise or, worse, as a threat to organizational efficiency and productivity. Concerns about what we can call "intimization" lead to the construction of what legal scholar Vicki Schultz (2003) calls the "sanitized workplace."

Such close students of the subject as Schultz detect a substantial increase in workplace regulation of intimate relations, going well beyond legal requirements to prevent sexual harassment. These range from "no-fraternization" policies that prohibit romantic involvement between supervisors and employees, even when consensual, to "date-and-tell" policies, where employees involved in such relationships must disclose their romance to management and be subject to monitoring, reprimand, or transfer, as well as "cupid" or "love" contracts for employees about to embark on a romantic relationship. In a light-hearted report on couples waiting in a New York City marriage bureau, for example, the *New York Times* interviewed a man and woman who had just lost their jobs in a box-making factory, saying that "they were so in love that they were fired for being unproductive," thus confirming managers' wariness about intimacy in the workplace (Fernandez 2007).

And it is not just fear of sexual liaisons: the prestigious Conference Board recommends a "personal relations policy" that includes a wide range of relatively intimate relations, such as close after-hour friendships, noting that "'old boy' buddies—and now 'old girls,' too—get more job perks than 'lovers.' That's why a policy should address potential conflicts with marital, extended-family, and close-friendship relationships as well as romantic ones" (Lever et al. 2006, 39). In a parallel move, since the 1980s employers (especially in the public sector) have been increasingly imposing no-spouse and anti-nepotism rules. What is more, legal attempts to challenge nepotism rules that prohibit couples from sharing a workplace have generally failed.

Yet despite these determined efforts to ban workplace intimacy, actual observation suggests the constant presence of care among coworkers. Of course, because of separate-spheres thinking, we only have scattered evidence of workplace intimate labors. We know little, for instance, of exactly how coworkers cover for each other's defects or absences, what sort of mentoring old timers provide newcomers, how workers console each other for managers' injustices, what sorts of favors they exchange on the job, and how they support each other by such practices as taking up collections and pooling leaves (see Marks 1994; McGuire 2007).

We get some early glimmers of such caring practices from Susan Porter Benson's study of department store saleswomen in the first decades of the twentieth century:

> In one department, women contributed to the support of Aggie, a particularly destitute co-worker; they paid her insurance and sick-benefit premiums, bought extra food for her lunch, and helped her to stretch her meager clothing budget. But their actions went beyond self-help within the department to confront management on Aggie's behalf. When a manager halted their yearly collection to send Aggie on vacation and made them return the money, they ostentatiously collected it again outside the employees' entrance. They knew, however, that the only real solution to Aggie's problems was a higher salary, and their most impressive victory was in backing up her successful quest for a raise. (Benson 1986, 247)

Despite giving more attention to resistance than to mutual aid, Randy Hodson has advanced our knowledge of coworkers caring by combing and cataloguing more than a hundred ethnographies of workplace interaction.

The ethnographies report such caring practices as gift giving in a chemical factory and mutual covering among sleeping-car porters. "Coworkers," concludes Hodson, "help provide meaning in work through the sharing of work life experiences and through friendships. Coworkers can also provide a basis for group solidarity and mutual support in the face of denials of dignity at work" (2001, 201, 200). Hodson identifies caring friendship and mutual aid as major compensations for physical hardship, tedious work routines, tyrannical managers, and even low wages. Without caring, we can infer, many workplaces, far from operating more efficiently, would actually collapse. Hodson reports a striking study of Washington, D.C., firefighters. A firefighter recalled:

> It's hard to describe the closeness that you felt with the guys in the fire house. I don't think my wife has ever really understood it. I just used to love to come to work—especially on those long Saturdays when we'd have a big roast or a ham or something and sit around and talk or play cards. . . . Firemen then were a great bunch and a rough bunch. . . . They played hard and rough. But when the bells hit, nobody would do any more good for you than a fireman. It's a group of men with a unique brotherhood feeling—they'll never let you down. (2001, 223)

Over a wide range of workplaces, then, mutual caring turns out to be a crucial element of job satisfaction and solidarity.

We even have scattered evidence that intimacy enhances organizational performance. Since the 1930s, of course, industrial sociologists have stressed the positive impact of workplace solidarity on productivity. But that older literature generally neglected caring practices in favor of practices fostering group identification. More recently, a number of studies report the prevalence and even the management promotion of job recruitment by current employees of friends and kin. Mutual recruitment often benefits the hiring organization by enhancing employee productivity (Castilla 2005; Fernandez et al. 2000; Grieco 1987). So far as we can tell, mutual hiring tends to integrate new hires more firmly into workplace networks and to give them greater access to caring attention.

More generally, a surprising variety of studies documents the positive effects of workplace caring relationships on economic productivity. Consider these vignettes:

- Economist K. K. Fung (1991) provides a strong theoretical rationale for concluding that horizontal favor exchanges enhance organizational efficiency.
- Business school professor Francis Flynn (2003) finds evidence that workers who exchanged favors were significantly more productive than their fellows.

- A large 2001 Gallup poll identifies a strong connection across firms, between the proportion of workers who had best friends in the workplace, on one side, and firm profitability, productivity, safety, and customer loyalty, on the other (Ellingwood 2001).
- In 2007, a survey of senior executives and workers in the country's thousand largest firms finds widespread agreement that workers with coworkers who were "buddies" both on and off the job were more productive and committed contributors to firm performance ("Birds of a Feather" 2007).
- A substantial literature on family firms indicates not only that, on the average, they create more worker-friendly environments than their nonfamily competitors, but that they also enjoy greater organizational effectiveness (e.g., Anderson and Reeb 2003; "Family, Inc." 2003).

Conservatively, then, we can conclude that workplace caring deserves much greater and more systematic attention from students of care. More daringly, we can conclude that unpaid care within economic organizations should be a new frontier for analyses of care's enhancement of human welfare (see also Williams et al. 1999; Pettinger 2005).

Paid Care in Intimate Settings

As we have seen, unpaid care in intimate settings strikes most people as so natural as to be almost invisible. Unpaid care in economic organizations remains equally invisible, despite its near-universality, but for the opposite reason: because it does not fit the prevailing frame. Paid care in intimate settings, however, has raised a hue and cry because it defines a moral and political battleground: on one side, whether paid personal attention merits compensation comparable to that received in economic organizations; on the other side, whether payment for care generally degrades its quality.

If separate-spheres reasoning were not so widespread and powerful, either position would seem illogical. To the extent that paid care does enhance its recipients' welfare, beneficiaries and third parties should compensate it generously. One might think, furthermore, that care would be easy to gauge in monetary terms: simply compute the benefit gained by the recipient and third parties. But the separate-spheres notion that personal care occurs naturally as a free good blocks systematic reasoning and justifies gross inequities.

Indeed, the first American study focusing on the relative pay of carework documents a significant "wage penalty" for face-to-face service providers such as teachers, counselors, health-care aides, and child-care workers (England et al. 2002). Although both men and women involved in carework pay this penalty, women do so more often, as they are more likely to be involved in carework (see also Budig and England 2001; Correll et al. 2007).

The problem is not simply that people dumbly accept false beliefs. People who give and receive personal care in intimate settings are actually negotiating definitions of their social relations in a rapidly changing world. Everywhere and always intimates create forms of economic interchange that simultaneously accomplish shared tasks, reproduce their relations, and distinguish those relations from others with which they might become confused: are you my mother, my sister, my daughter, my nurse, my maid, or my best friend? Each has its own distinctive array of economic interchanges. In each case, people draw on available cultural models, and they use power and persuasion to negotiate unequal social relations. Paid care in intimate settings raises the fundamental question: who are we, and what do we owe each other?

Negotiation over appropriate interpersonal relations certainly goes on within households, but it also occurs over a much larger scale. In recent years, local, regional, and national governments have responded to changing household circumstances by intervening increasingly in compensation for care given within households. The United States has lagged behind other Western countries in public policies governing payment for household care.

In the United Kingdom, for instance, we find a legally established category of young carers (children under eighteen) who receive government subsidies for providing care to a household member. The 1995 Carer's Act acknowledged children's caring work by adding children under eighteen to the category of private, informal carers entitled to social services. Under specified conditions, local councils have the authority to make direct payments to the sixteen- and seventeen-year-olds who are providing care. Thus, British social policy compensates qualified child carers by awarding them direct access to social services as well as the possibility of monetary payments (Olsen 2000).[1]

In France, as Florence Weber (2003) has shown, the doctrine of "undue enrichment" provides another sort of compensation for household-based care. To the extent that they exceed ordinary filial duty, unpaid contributions of a child to the care of elderly parents during the parents' lifetime established the child's rightful claims for compensation from the parents' estate. In the Minnesota case discussed earlier, such a principle would have made it clear from the start that the dutiful but unpaid daughter-in-law deserved a share of her mother-in-law's estate.

We can return to Clare Ungerson and her collaborators for a systematic comparison of national policies. Ungerson's group studied paid care in five European countries. They make two valuable distinctions: (1) between systems in which the government regulates the working conditions closely and those in which it intervenes primarily by means of payment and (2) whether relatives can or cannot receive payment for the care they provide. For example, the highly regulated Dutch and Austrian systems qualify as "fully commodified," including payments to relatives. The evidence they collect suggests not only that such systems deliver care effectively but that caregivers and recipients express great satisfaction with the arrangement.

The Dutch scheme, for instance, compensated a daughter for the care she gave to her parents, elderly stroke victims, five mornings a week. The mother reported:

> Things are excellent the way they are now. And I am happy if she receives some money. I and my husband receive help and that is the main thing for us. I don't know how we would manage otherwise. And he will not have anyone else. He doesn't want a nurse, which is why our daughter does it. (Ungerson 2004, 197)

Thus, public policy can not only facilitate superior delivery of care but also help to redefine relations within kin groups. Not for a moment am I saying that all such schemes work fairly or well, that the more paid care the better, or that kin are always the best providers. On the contrary, we must return to the main point: that parties to care, including government agencies, for better of worse, are negotiating matches among the quality of care delivered, the social relations among the parties, and the compensation that caregivers receive.

I have deliberately avoided discussing paid care in economic organizations on the ground that we already know more about the varieties of care provided by medical professionals and other licensed caregivers than we do about caring elsewhere. Even there, however, we can gain a clearer understanding through recognition that in the delivery of care, professionals and their clients are likewise negotiating definitions of their social relations and forms of compensation to represent those definitions. In the cases of unpaid care within intimate settings, unpaid care within economic organizations, and paid care within intimate settings, we have plenty more to learn about how people create viable relations—and for that matter, how and why things go wrong in the delicate mingling of intimacy and labor. Our exploration has just begun.

NOTES

Viviana A. Zelizer. 2010. "Caring Everywhere." From *Intimate Labors: Cultures, Technologies, and the Politics of Care*, edited by Eileen Boris and Rhacel Salazar Parreñas. Stanford, Calif.: Stanford University Press. © 2010 by the Board of Trustees of the Leland Stanford Jr. University, all righs reserved. By permission of the publisher, www.sup.org.

1. See also the Carers (Recognition and Services) Act 1995, http://www.hmso
.gov.uk/acts/acts1995/Ukpga_19950012_en_1.htm (accessed July 12, 2007); personal communication, Chris Dearden, February 9, 2006.

References

Anderson, R. C., and D. M. Reeb. 2003. "Founding-Family Ownership and Firm
Performance: Evidence from S&P 500." *Journal of Finance* 58:1301–27.
Armstrong, Pat, and Hugh Armstrong. 2005. "Public and Private: Implications
for Care Work." In *A New Sociology of Work?*, edited by Lynne Pettinger et al.,
169–87. Oxford: Blackwell.
Benson, Susan Porter. 1986. *Counter Cultures: Saleswomen, Managers, and Custom-
ers in American Department Stores, 1890–1940*. Urbana: University of Illinois
Press.
"Birds of a Feather Flock Together . . . at Work." 2007. Accountemps, June 14.
http://www.accountemps.com/portal/site/at-us/menuitem.b368a569778
a80c6cb42b21002f3dfa0/?vgnextoid=39a73468151e6010VgnVCM
100000e2aafb0aRCRD (accessed July 12, 2007).
Bittman, Michael, Janet E. Fast, Kimberly Fisher, and Cathy Thomson. 2004.
"Making the Invisible Visible: The Life and Time(s) of Informal Caregivers."
In *Family Time: The Social Organization of Care*, edited by Nancy Folbre and
Michael Bittman, 69–89. London: Routledge.
Budig, Michelle J., and Paula England. 2001. "The Wage Penalty for Mother-
hood." *American Sociological Review* 66:204–25.
Castilla, Emilio J. 2005. "Social Networks and Employee Performance in a Call
Center." *American Journal of Sociology* 110:1243–83.
Correll, Shelley J., Stephen Benard, and In Paik. 2007. "Getting a Job: Is There a
Motherhood Penalty?" *American Journal of Sociology* 112:1297–1338.
Cresson, Geneviève. 1995. *Le travail domestique de santé*. Paris: L'Harmattan.
Ellingwood, Susan. 2001. "The Collective Advantage." *Gallup Management Jour-
nal* (September). http://gmj.gallup.com/content/default.aspx?ci=787&pg=1
(accessed July 12, 2007).
England, Paula, Michelle Budig, and Nancy Folbre. 2002. "Wages of Virtue: The
Relative Pay of Care Work." *Social Problems* 49:455–573.
"Family, Inc." 2003. Special report, BusinessWeek Online, November 10. http://
www.businessweek.com/magazine/content/03_45/b3857002.htm (accessed
July 10, 2007).
Fernandez, Manny. 2007. "Get Me to the Marriage Bureau on Time (45 Minutes
Early)." *New York Times*, July 10.
Fernandez, Roberto M., Emilio J. Castilla, and Paul Moore. 2000. "Social Capital
at Work: Networks and Employment at a Phone Center." *American Journal
of Sociology* 105: 1,288–1,356.
Flynn, Francis J. 2003. "How Much Should I Give and How Often? The Effects
of Generosity and Frequency of Favor Exchange on Social Status and Produc-
tivity." *Academy of Management Journal* 46:539–53.

Fung, K. K. 1991. "One Good Turn Deserves Another: Exchange of Favors within Organizations." *Social Science Quarterly* 72:443–63.

Grieco, Margaret. 1987. *Keeping It in the Family: Social Networks and Employment Chance*. London: Tavistock.

Hodson, Randy. 2001. *Dignity at Work*. New York: Cambridge University Press.

Lever, Janet, Gail Zellman, and Stephen J. Hirschfeld. 2006. "Office Romance: Are the Rules Changing?" *Across the Board* (March/April): 33–41.

Marks, Stephen R. 1994. "Intimacy in the Public Realm: The Case of Co-workers." *Social Forces* 72:843–58.

McGuire, Gail M. 2007. "Intimate Work: A Typology of Social Support That Workers Provide to Their Network Members." *Work and Occupations* 34: 125–47.

Menjívar, Cecilia. 2002. "The Ties That Heal: Guatemalan Immigrant Women's Networks and Medical Treatment." *International Migration Review* 36: 437–66.

Olsen, Richard. 2000. "Families under the Microscope: Parallels between the Young Carers Debate of the 1990s and the Transformation of Childhood in the Late Nineteenth Century." *Children and Society* 14:384–94.

Pettinger, Lynne. 2005. "Friends, Relations and Colleagues: The Blurred Boundaries of the Workplace." In *A New Sociology of Work?*, edited by Lynne Pettinger et al., 39–55. Oxford: Blackwell.

Schultz, Vicki. 2003. "The Sanitized Workplace." *Yale Law Journal* 112:2061.

Tilly, Chris, and Charles Tilly. 1998. *Work under Capitalism*. Boulder, Colo.: Westview.

Ungerson, Clare. 2004. "Whose Empowerment and Independence? A Cross-National Perspective on 'Cash for Care' Schemes." *Ageing and Society* 24:189–212.

Ungerson, Clare, and Sue Yeandle. 2007. *Cash for Care in Developed Welfare States*. New York: Palgrave Macmillan.

Weber, Florence. 2003. "Peut-on rémunérer l'aide familiale?" In *Charges de famille*, edited by Florence Weber, Séverine Gojard, and Agnès Gramain, 45–67. Paris: La Découverte.

Williams, Christine L., Patti A. Giuffre, and Kirsten Dellinger. 1999. "Sexuality in the Workplace: Organizational Control, Sexual Harassment, and the Pursuit of Pleasure." *Annual Review of Sociology* 25:73–93.

Zelizer, Viviana A. 2005. *The Purchase of Intimacy*. Princeton, N.J.: Princeton University Press.

———. 2009. "Intimacy in Economic Organizations." In *Economic Sociology of Work*, edited by Nina Bandelj, 23–55. Vol. 19 in *Research in the Sociology of Work*. Bingley, U.K.: Emerald.

14

Risky Exchanges

In October 2006, icon pop singer Madonna attracted international head-lines by adopting David Banda. David was a motherless one-year-old boy residing at the Home of Hope Orphan Care Centre in the isolated village of Mchinji, Malawi. The boy's father, reportedly unable to support his child, expressed great pleasure that the boy should escape local poverty and receive such great care. At the same time, Madonna pledged about $3 million to help orphans in Malawi. Meanwhile, Malawian advocacy groups objected to what they apparently saw as Madonna's impulse purchase. "It's not like sell-ing property," protested Eye of the Child, a child rights organization.[1]

The advocacy group sounded a familiar theme: some market transactions go beyond the boundary of decency. Similar objections arise with regard to the transfer of sperm, eggs, body parts, and even personal care. What do crit-ics worry about? Typically they voice two logically distinct objections; first, that some goods and services should never be sold, and second, that some market arrangements are inherently pernicious. These two concerns differ starkly. The first focuses on what is being exchanged, the second on the terms of the exchange.

This brief statement does no more than sketch a way of thinking about these issues. To clarify what is at stake, it stresses the analogy between ex-changes of personal care and exchanges of babies. Both of them involve the significant possibility that one party or another to the exchange will dam-age the other party through error, incompetence, or malfeasance (see Zelizer 2005, 14–18). Let us therefore call this class of transactions "risky exchanges." I will draw especially on my own work concerning baby markets and on a rapidly expanding literature concerning the economics of care.

I argue that in order to explain how commercial markets for these "risky exchanges" actually work we need to go beyond standard approaches to com-modification. Those approaches often rely on simplistic equations of market exchange with moral degradation. Instead, I argue that we need to identify and explain multiple ways of organizing commercial exchanges. Some mar-ket arrangements do indeed have pernicious consequences, but others offer benefits to all participants. Only by getting rid of prejudices can we start identifying good matches among objects of exchange, terms of exchange, and welfare of parties to exchange.

On the way to identifying such good matches, we must dispose of two ob-vious but misleading ways of justifying bans on risky exchanges: (1) that the objects of exchange deserve protection because of the strong emotions they involve, in contrast to other commodities; and (2) that they require special treatment simply because they are more important than other exchanges. Risky exchanges are not unique in arousing strong emotions: think of purchasing homes, life insurance policies, or engagement rings. Surely these and many other emotionally charged transfers pass through the market without disrupting or demeaning social life. Nor can we justify bans on body parts or babies because they are more important than other goods. Few people, after all, now suppose that payment for medical treatment to save lives somehow demeans the treatment.

Some more substantial obstacles to understanding also block our way to clear analysis of risky exchanges. Two opposite clusters of beliefs about markets in general stand in the way. On one side stand paired beliefs we can call separate spheres and hostile worlds: first, that social relations divide sharply into spheres of sentiment and solidarity on the one side and rational, self-interested calculation on the other; second, that any contact between these hostile worlds tends to produce mutual contamination: corruption of sentimental solidarity into narrow self-interest, or introduction of obfuscating sentiment into a sphere better served by efficient, means-end rationality.

Another version of the separate-spheres/hostile-worlds view identifies a continuum from total market immunity to complete commodification. For some sorts of exchanges, runs the argument, any monetary compensation pushes the transaction down a slippery slope toward corruption. "If a free-market baby industry were to come into being," Margaret Jane Radin postulates:

> how could any of us, even those who did not produce infants for sale, avoid measuring the dollar value of our children? How could our children avoid being preoccupied with measuring their own dollar value? This measurement makes our discourse about ourselves (when we are children) and about our children (when we are parents) like our discourse about cars. (Radin 1996, 138)

At the opposite extreme of separate-spheres/hostile-worlds beliefs we find an economistic, nothing-but belief: all social relations ultimately reduce to expressions of rational self-interest mediated by one sort of market or another. A generation of work in economics and sociology has undermined both extreme beliefs by documenting and analyzing the incessant interplay of economic activity with solidarity-sustaining interpersonal relations. As applied to markets for body parts such as blood and organs, Kieran Healy's book *Last Best Gifts* (2006) has shown that a number of different intersections between commercial transactions and personal connections actually transfer human goods without the widely feared mutual corruption of markets and human solidarity.

We can usefully approach risky exchanges by considering a class of exchanges for which opinions and practices divide even more widely than with regard to body parts and babies: the paid provision for personal care. Personal care qualifies as a valuable analogy because its commercial provision regularly elicits all the obfuscating beliefs:

- That the objects of exchange deserve special protection because of the strong emotions they arouse
- That they deserve special protection because they are more important than other exchanges
- That they belong intrinsically to mutually exclusive separate spheres
- That contact between the spheres corrupts them
- That, on the contrary, they are nothing but market commodities like anything else

When it comes to personal care, all of these widely held but fallacious principles obscure both the recognition and creation of good matches.

THE ECONOMICS OF CARE

With the aging of the population, and as more mothers are involved in the labor market, the problem of who cares for children, the ill, and the elderly has emerged as a serious policy concern. Over the past century or so, unquestionably, a higher proportion of personal care has become commercialized. That trend shows no sign of reversing. Nevertheless, the bulk of interpersonal care in Western countries still occurs outside the market. That raises two important questions: first, under what conditions does market-based care provide adequate support for both the recipients and the providers of care? Second, to what degree is the quality of care given via the market and outside the market fundamentally different?

Critics, advocates, care providers, and recipients of care disagree vociferously about these questions. Separate-spheres, hostile-worlds, and nothing-but ideas often arise in those disagreements. One side, at the extreme, declares that genuine care requires insulation from the market, while the other insists that care should be a commercial service just like the rest. In fact, personal care ranges from relations whose ample compensation no one disputes to others whose commercialization people often abhor. Consider this range of caregivers:

- mothers
- grandmothers
- siblings
- children
- other relatives
- baby-sitters
- servants
- day-care workers

- home aides
- teachers
- nurses
- psychotherapists
- physicians
- pharmacists

By and large, nobody objects to financial compensation for the professionals on this list. These days, no one raises objections to paying physicians and nurses for their professional care of either babies or body parts. On the contrary, almost everyone seeks expensive medical attention for an ailing infant or a defective kidney. Nor does it seem strange to pay pharmacists for their crucial contributions to personal care.

Clearly, payment for care as such does not offend fundamental principles. Yet many people insist that financial compensation for care threatens interpersonal relations either because the prospect of material benefit corrupts those relations or because the quality of unpaid care is intrinsically superior to that of paid care. In order to sort out beneficial from pernicious versions of compensation for care, we must look at the social arrangements by which such risky exchanges occur.

Including markets for care in the debate clarifies the issues, precisely because critics of existing arrangements for care have often voiced both of the classic objections: that some goods and services should never be sold and that some market arrangements are inherently pernicious. Applied to care of babies, for example, we hear both the claim that mother-child relations are too sacred, delicate, or consequential for delegation to paid helpers and the further claim that rich parents have no right to hire vulnerable immigrants as baby tenders at starvation wages because it cheats the babies of proper care while exploiting their caretakers.

From both perspectives, many people have worried that payment for personal care degrades it, by rationalizing and marketizing what should be based on altruism and affection. Yet accumulating evidence indicates that effective care and financial compensation are perfectly compatible. For example, pointing to the child-care market as thickly social and relational, Julie Nelson notes that parents or caregivers seldom define that market "as purely an impersonal exchange of money for services. . . . [T]he parties involved engage in extensive personal contact, trust, and interpersonal interaction." "The specter of the all-corrupting market," she argues, "denies that people— such as many child-care providers—can do work they love, among people they love, and get paid at the same time." Paid care, Nelson insists, should not be treated as "relationally second rate" (1998, 1470).

What's more, experimental programs make it feasible, equitable, and personally acceptable to compensate family members for care they would otherwise have to provide without payment at great cost to household welfare.

A study of the California system, funded at UCLA by the U.S. Department of Health and Human Services, concluded that family members actually provided higher quality service than unrelated workers (Doty et al. 1999). Specifically, the study found that clients employing family careworkers "reported a greater sense of security, having more choice about how their aides performed various tasks, a stronger preference for directing their aides, and a closer rapport with their aides."

Other experimental public programs have tried paying poor women for the care of their own sick or disabled children, thus formalizing them as paid providers of care. Consider Tasha's case, as reported in a study of strategies used by welfare-reliant mothers caring for children with chronic health conditions or disabilities after the welfare reforms of the early 1990s. Tasha, a forty-five-year-old, unmarried African-American living in Cleveland with her two children, had first dropped out of Ohio State University to care for her sick father. She then became primary caregiver for her daughter, who had a severe seizure disorder. Pushed out of welfare, she managed to get hired by an agency that paid her a low hourly wage without medical benefits for thirty hours of weekly carework. The meager salary helped redefine Tasha's social standing:

> I feel good, good you know because like I said, I feel fortunate that I can still do things at home. I went to look at some living room furniture the other day and the guy said: "Are you employed?" And I said: "Yes, I'm employed." You know my social security number, you know, you check it out. So, that kinda thing, it makes you, it makes you feel good. . . . You know, you're in a different status [when] you're not considered unemployed. (London et al. 2002, 109)

In this case, the entry of paid care into the household by no means undermined its moral economy; quite the contrary.

Persistent hostile-worlds assumptions portraying love and care as demeaned by monetization may in fact underpin unjust policies and lead to economic discrimination against those allegedly intangible caring activities; for example, lack of economic security for unpaid caregiving, low pay for caregivers such as nannies and home health aides, and resistance to compensating relatives for carework.

Consider the painful impact on the mothers of chronically ill children of the 1996 U.S. welfare reform that introduced stringent work requirements for recipients. A comprehensive study found these women caught in a terrifying dilemma: if they worked, their sick children did not get proper care, but if they stopped working to care for their children, the mothers lost their welfare benefits. To compound the difficulties, few American child-care facilities are prepared to receive such children. A dozen concerned medical organizations proposed a solution: change welfare policy to make the care of sick children count as work, thus permitting mothers to meet the work requirement. But their proposal was turned down. Instead, the Bush administration called for increases in work requirements (Chavkin 2006; "Doctors Speak Out" n.d.).

What practical implications does this approach imply? Our search should be directed toward just, noncoercive sets of economic transactions for different types of caring relations. The goal is not therefore to cleanse intimacy from economic concerns: the challenge is to create fair mixtures. We should stop agonizing over whether or not money corrupts but instead analyze what combinations of economic activity and caring relations produce happier, more just, and more productive lives. It is not the mingling that should concern us but how the mingling works. If we get the causal connections wrong, we will obscure the origins of injustice, damage, and danger.

Baby Markets

The same principle applies to baby markets. As in the case of personal care, widespread misunderstandings about baby markets block us from seeing variations in the organization of commercial exchanges involving babies. As a result, we fail to distinguish between pernicious markets and monetary arrangements that actually enhance the welfare of children and their families.

Recall the two objections to risky exchanges: first, that some goods and services should never be sold, and second, that some market arrangements are inherently pernicious. Both apply to baby markets. Think first about babies as commodities. Separate-spheres and hostile-worlds purists—as we saw with the uproar over Madonna's baby adoption—insist on an impermeable division between babies and market transactions: we should never mix babies with monetary interests. The exchange of children should be regulated by altruism, not profit.

Economistic nothing-but enthusiasts, on the other hand, hail a baby market as an efficient solution to imbalances between demand and supply of babies. Most famously, Elizabeth Landes and Richard Posner argued in 1978 for the outright legalization of baby selling as the best solution to the baby shortage. But Landes and Posner fail to say what concrete organization of the baby market would simultaneously promote efficiency, welfare, and active participation of their "producers" and "consumers."

Ironically, despite their conflicting agendas, moral objectors and market enthusiasts similarly overlook the remarkable variety of existing baby market arrangements. When it comes to the second common objection about inherently pernicious market arrangements, the most common concern about baby markets is the creation of an impersonal competition for personal attributes. Here the critics have two valid points: first, the terms of exchange are absolutely crucial for the pernicious or beneficial effects of baby markets, and second, no baby market will be beneficial if it does not take into account the prevailing understandings of childhood in their context.

PRICELESS BABIES

For me, current discussions of payments for infants call up a strong sense of déjà vu. Variation and change in markets for babies have preoccupied me for years. My book *Pricing the Priceless Child*, for example, documented the long history and versatility of commercial exchanges involving babies in the United States between the 1870s and 1930s (Zelizer 1985). Most important, the history illustrates that seemingly predetermined separate-spheres domains are in fact cultural and social constructs. Those constructs, in turn, shape the organization and legitimacy of economic practices.

The changing U.S. baby market was intimately tied to the profound cultural transformation in children's economic and sentimental value at the turn of the twentieth century; specifically, the emergence of the economically worthless but emotionally priceless child. While in the nineteenth century the market value of children was culturally acceptable, the new, twentieth-century normative ideal of the child as an exclusively emotional and affective asset made any instrumental or fiscal consideration offensive. In an increasingly commercialized world, children were assigned a separate, noncommercial space, *extracommercium*. The economic and sentimental values of children were thereby declared to be radically incompatible.

The creation of this "priceless" child deeply affected the exchange value of children. Nineteenth-century foster families took in useful children, expecting them to help out with farm chores and household tasks. It was considered a fair bargain. Not surprisingly, the premium went to children (preferably boys) older than ten—those old enough to be useful. In this context, babies were "unmarketable" and hard to place, except in foundling asylums or commercial baby farms.

After the 1920s, adoptive parents were only interested in (and willing to wait several years for) a blue-eyed baby or a cute two-year-old, curly-haired girl. While nineteenth-century mothers who could not afford to raise their illegitimate child were forced to pay to get rid of the baby, by the 1930s, unwanted babies were selling for $1,000 or more. As a result, the value of a priceless child became increasingly monetized and commercialized. Ironically, the new market price for babies was set exclusively by their noneconomic, sentimental appeal.

As demand for adoptable children grew, it became a seller's market, and a wide range of commercial arrangements emerged, some of which persist today. They include black-market baby sales, with cash payments for the mother and profit for the broker; gray markets, where placements are arranged without profit by parents, friends, relatives, doctors, and lawyers (although professional fees for legal and medical services are part of the arrangement); "gratitude donations" from adoptive parents to child-placement agencies; adoption fees; and board payments to foster parents.

Babies Today

My own analysis of American baby markets stops around 1950. Fortunately, Debora Spar (2006) has provided a fine survey of recent developments in the same field. She documents extensive, varied payment arrangements in contemporary baby markets. Spar concludes:

> Parents acquire children all the time, and we generally regard it as a fine thing to do. What differs, of course, is the mode of acquisition in the baby business; it is the entry of commerce into what many regard as an entirely noncommercial affair. This argument, though, does not carry any kind of natural weight. If we think that markets are good and children are good, then it's not obvious why mixing the two is inherently vile. Instead, we can just as easily turn this argument on its head, examining how market mechanisms might help to produce a socially desirable outcome. (2006, 196)

Here Spar directly parallels my own conclusions about earlier markets. Similar principles apply to adjacent baby markets, ranging from surrogacy fees paid to women for "made-to-order" babies to the multiple payments involved in the growing global market of international adoptions. In addition to an application fee, home study fee, and program fee, agencies assisting foreign adoptions include fees to the agency's local representative, driver, and interpreter, sometimes plus a required donation to a local orphanage (Spar 2006, 182; Dorow 2006, 81).

At the edge of baby markets appear paid exchanges for eggs and sperm. Rene Almeling (2007) has beautifully documented these two paired but gender-differentiated markets. She makes three keen observations: first, that beyond the expected biological distinctions, these transactions differ significantly for men and women donors; second, that agencies, recipients, and donors mark those distinctions with differential recruitment, advertising, and compensation arrangements; and third, in a paradoxical reversal of the standard gendered wage gap that penalizes women, Almeling finds that in the reproductive market, women are better paid than men.

As Almeling notes, the organizational structure of both egg and sperm markets are similar: in both cases commercial agencies rely on advertising and careful screening to match paying customers with paid donors. The two are also complex markets: the bulk of prospective donors on each side turn out to be ineligible. What's more, both markets require extensive adaptation by the donors; for example, egg donation involves invasive and risky medical procedures.

Despite such similarities, Almeling shows that sperm and egg markets operate differently, as agencies, donors, and recipients negotiate distinct and varied definitions of their relationships to each other. While sperm donation is often categorized as an ordinary job, involving legitimate financial incentives, egg agencies emphasize donors' altruistic motivations, minimizing women's desire for monetary gain. Agencies extol the caring dimensions of providing eggs to childless clients to the point of sometimes rejecting donors who appear overly greedy. Egg donation is further personalized by providing donors' photographs and by matching specific donors to recipients, thus reducing the anonymity of the transactions.

Payment systems mark these distinctions: men's compensation is typically standardized, so that donors receive similar payment per usable sample. They do not get paid for substandard samples. Women, on the other hand, get paid regardless of the number of eggs produced. And their compensation is negotiated at the time when the agency matches donor to recipient: pay varies depending on such factors as experience (first-time donors get less), education (higher education gets more), and in some cases race (often minorities get more because of recruitment shortages). Pay also hinges on the donor's physical appearance and to some extent on the agency's perceptions of a donor's caring motivations. Significantly, gifts reaffirm the personalized quality of the egg donor–recipient connection. Grateful egg recipients, Almeling reports, often send their donor flowers, jewelry, or "gift" money. Sometimes the giftlike quality of the transactions is formalized: one of the egg agencies Almeling studied defines the donor's fee as a nontaxable gift.

Thus, in egg and sperm markets young men and women are involved in selling their reproductive materials, yet these "risky exchanges" do not result in identical rationalized markets. What is fascinating in Almeling's account is how similar commercial arrangements produce different outcomes. They do so precisely because they incorporate different kinds of interpersonal relations, in this case strongly marked by gender. Far from becoming standardized exchanges, each market depends on different kinds of relationships among donors, recipients, and agencies.

As elsewhere, we cannot understand markets for sperm and eggs without taking into account the meanings assigned by participants in the exchange. These differential meanings, Almeling argues, produce the unexpected economic advantages of egg donors. Despite the difficult process of extracting eggs, the supply of donors, she shows, outstrips the supply of sperm donors. Why, then, are egg donors better paid and more highly valued? Both high pay and the simultaneous definition of a giftlike exchange, Almeling argues, result from "cultural norms of caring motherhood." Here gender trumps supply and demand.

Of course, one could read Almeling's account of egg and sperm markets as confirming nothing-but economistic accounts. The altruistic rhetoric could be nothing more than camouflage for a maximizing exchange no different than the purchase of any other consumption good. That would be a mistake. Most of the time, donors, recipients, and commercial agencies are organizing the market to reflect the particular meanings and characteristics of the social relations established by exchange of reproductive goods. Indeed, Martha Ertman (2003), critic of current limits on baby markets, argues that the market for artificial insemination provides a model for more equitable access to parenthood by same-sex and single parents.

For separate-spheres/hostile-worlds advocates, all such risky exchanges threaten the sacredness of children. To be sure, in many cases babies and parents do suffer from these market arrangements: there are dangers of exploiting poor women, and there is rampant inequality in the kinds of children that are produced or acquired. But much of the time, participants in these exchanges work out a morally acceptable set of conditions for the exchange, which involves severe restrictions as to who gets what, when, for what.

These multiple baby markets also refute the nothing-but arguments that hold out the possibility of an impersonal rational market that extends into the world of baby exchanges. Both hostile-worlds and nothing-but arguments miss the creation of morally contingent relational markets. The involvement of money does not necessarily convert all exchanges into ordinary sales. Take the surrogacy payment: it can be a venal and dehumanizing payoff, but it can also symbolize acceptable remuneration.

Risky Assumptions

Analysts of these sorts of risky exchanges often rely on strong, if largely implicit, assumptions about human nature and politics:

- That people in general—givers and recipients of care alike—operate uniformly on self-interest
- That both governmental and market interventions in the provision of care simultaneously attack legitimate interests and corrupt valued interpersonal relations
- That existing political alignments therefore forbid—and should forbid—thoroughgoing governmental and market transformations of current arrangements for exchanges involving babies and care

Given accumulating evidence of widespread human preferences for fair arrangements that produce secure collective goods, all those assumptions deserve scrutiny and debate.

In particular, critics of risky exchanges worry about the effects of market solutions. They warn against three classes of perverse effects from market interventions:

1. Exploitation of the poor
2. Decline in altruism
3. Negative impact on other social relations

All three do sometimes occur in markets. But the question is: do all kinds of market arrangements entail these negative outcomes?

My general answer runs as follows. *Markets vary enormously in the extent to which and the way in which they actually produce such perverse effects.* Let me make the case briefly in three major points:

1. Widespread but false beliefs about the universal properties of markets make it seem that the perverse effects themselves are likewise universal.
2. The feasibility of alterations in market arrangements does indeed depend on connections between the internal organization of markets and existing configurations of power and culture.
3. A variety of markets analogous to those of babies and care demonstrates the possibility of benign market effects.

Of course—to take up my second main point—the extent to which various market arrangements actually produce efficient, equitable, and politically viable outcomes depends heavily on connections between internal market structures and existing configurations of power and culture. Within economics and sociology, institutional analysts have been insisting on this formulation for two decades or so.

In general, institutional analysts have drawn from this observation not a conservative pessimism based on the immutability of politics, culture, and human nature but a cautious belief that all three change in response to shifting circumstances, including deliberate policy interventions. In the case of transfers of body parts, as Healy (2006) shows, various organizational structures involving different mixtures of economic and moral incentives sometimes produce relatively efficient and equitable connections between supply and demand.

In defense of my third point—that a variety of markets, analogous in some respects to those of babies and the provision of care, demonstrates the possibility of benign market effects—consider just two analogies: life insurance and monetary compensation for disaster such as 9/11. Life insurance initially raised the same sorts of moral objections as payments for babies or care, as a violation of the sacredness and integrity of human life. In fact, people called life insurance "blood money." But eventually, Americans and Westerners more generally, came to accept it as a prudent provision for welfare, one so important that it should be universal and backed by government

regulation. Although one might offer the 2005 Katrina disaster as a coun-
terexample, the 9/11 Victim Compensation Fund overcame objections to the
financial evaluation of lost lives by instituting public and equitable rules for
compensation of loss.

Does this mean that market solutions unfailingly deliver equity, efficiency,
and political viability? On the contrary, it means that inventing market-
based systems for equitable, efficient, and politically viable transfers of delicate assets requires all the craft that social planners can summon up. Remember the two classic objections to risky exchanges: that some goods and
services should never be sold and that some market arrangements are inherently pernicious. Fixation on the first—the sale of sacred objects—blocks
serious consideration of the second.

A similar lesson applies to compensation for replacement of organs and
to exchanges of blood. As Healy claims about these markets in his superb
study,

> [w]hile we should worry about exploitation in the exchange of hu-
> man goods, it is a mistake to think that commodification as such is
> the reason exploitation happens. Commodified exchanges may well
> be exploitative, but market exchange does not automatically make it
> so. Both gift and market systems depend on their specific institutional
> realization for their effects. The choice is not between morally worth-
> while gift giving and morally suspect markets. (2006, 124)

Considering the highly exploitative gray market for kidneys and corneas,
Healy notes that the problem is not created by the individuals who contract
to sell their own organs. Instead, "it is the wider social context in which they
find themselves—their dominated class position, long-term disadvantage,
and poor life chances—that puts them in a situation that invites their exploitation by 'transplant tourists'" (2006, 124). The question is not contamination but fairness.

Once people stop worrying so much about mixing "sacred" goods and
services with economic activity, they can start working toward the right
mixes: what sorts of economic arrangements for babies and care provision
produce happier, more just, and more productive lives? Of course, those that
worry about commodification and the intrusion of economics into certain
goods and services are trying to protect us. Yet, oddly, they often hurt us. The
myth of separate spheres often ends up justifying bad economic conditions,
as when moralists devalue paid care and when prohibitions create black
markets for babies. That is precisely why the law, government, and public
policy should take full account of how such markets actually work.

Brazilian economist Ricardo Abramovay makes the general point:

> If the economy is part of our intimacy and if our intimacy contains
> crucial economic dimensions, that means that money or the market

cannot be taken as clear and distinct categories whose objective meaning is to necessarily take us away from who we are and from our most
authentic human relations. Therefore, influencing the organization of
markets, shaping them in ways that were not part of the initial objectives of their protagonists is currently a decisive means for social
change. (Abramovay 2007)

Speaking specifically of baby markets, Spar similarly presses for reorganiza-
tion, not elimination:

First, we need to fix the market itself, providing the baby business with
the commercial attributes it currently lacks: a semblance of property
rights, some common definitions, and a framework that applies across
its disparate parts. Second, we need to embed this market in an appropriate political and regulatory context, to impose the rules that
will enable the market to produce the goods we want—happy, healthy
children—without encouraging the obvious risks. (Spar 2006, 197)

When it comes to markets for babies and care, we need better law and public policy. Instead of worrying about market-based corruption, designers of
public policy in these areas should be promoting just, attractive, and life-
enhancing economic arrangements. Clear analysis of how existing economic
arrangements actually operate provides a significant first step toward that
goal.

Notes

Viviana A. Zelizer, "Risky Exchanges," in *Baby Markets: Money and the New
Politics of Creating Families*, edited by Michele Goodwin (New York: Cambridge
University Press, 2010), 267–77. Reprinted with permission. I have adapted a few
paragraphs from Zelizer (2005).

1. "Madonna Adoption Bid Challenged," BBC News, October 13, 2006. http://
news.bbc.co.uk/go/em/fr/-/1/hi/entertainment/6048674.stm (accessed March 11,
2007).

References

Abramovay, Ricardo. 2007. "A economia na intimidade e a intimidade na eco-
nomia." *Valor Econômico*, February 23.
Almeling, Rene. 2007. "Selling Genes, Selling Gender: Egg Agencies, Sperm
Banks, and the Medical Market in Genetic Material." *American Sociological
Review* 72 (June): 319–40.

Chavkin, Wendy. 2006. "Mothers of Ill Children." Letter, *New York Review of Books* 53:76–77.

"Doctors Speak Out about Welfare Reform." N.d. Finding Common Ground. http://www.findingcommonground.hs.columbia.edu/speakout.pdf (accessed April 1, 2006).

Dorow, Sara K. 2006. *Transnational Adoption: A Cultural Economy of Race, Gender, and Kinship.* New York: New York University Press.

Doty, Pamela, A. E. Benjamin, Ruth E. Matthias, and Todd M. Franke. 1999. "In-Home Supportive Services for the Elderly and Disabled: A Comparison of Client-Directed and Professional Management Models of Service Delivery." U.S. Department of Health and Human Services and the University of California, Los Angeles. http://aspe.hhs.gov/daltcp/reports/ihss.htm (accessed March 11, 2007).

Ertman, Martha M. 2003. "What's Wrong with a Parenthood Market? A New and Improved Theory of Commodification." *North Carolina Law Review* 82:1.

Healy, Kieran. 2006. *Last Best Gifts.* Chicago: University of Chicago Press.

Landes, Elizabeth M., and Richard A. Posner. 1978. "The Economics of the Baby Shortage." *Journal of Legal Studies* 3232.

London, Andrew S., Ellen K. Scott, and Vicki Hunter. 2002. "Children and Chronic Health Conditions: Welfare Reform and Health-Related Carework." In *Childcare and Inequality: Rethinking Carework for Children and Youth*, edited by Francesca M. Cancian, Demie Kurz, Andrew S. London, Rebecca Reviere, and Mary C. Tuominen, 99–112. New York: Routledge.

Nelson, Julie A. 1998. "One Sphere or Two?" In "Changing Forms of Payment," special issue, edited by Viviana A. Zelizer, of *American Behavioral Scientist* 41:1,467–71.

Radin, Margaret Jane. 1996. *Contested Commodities.* Cambridge, Mass.: Harvard University Press.

Spar, Debora. 2006. *The Baby Business: How Money, Science, and Politics Drive the Commerce of Conception.* Cambridge, Mass.: Harvard Business School Press.

Zelizer, Viviana A. 1985. *Pricing the Priceless Child: The Changing Social Value of Children.* New York: Basic Books.

———. 2005. *The Purchase of Intimacy.* Princeton, N.J.: Princeton University Press.

PART FIVE

Circuits of Commerce

- Why do immigrants, often at the expense of their own needs, set as a budgetary priority sending large chunks of their hard-earned money to relatives in their country of origin?
- When legal tender works so well to bridge across commodities, transactions, and people, and at time when the euro links ever-wider spaces, why in the world do people go to great lengths to create local monetary systems, with their own rules, membership, trading, and value?
- Why is it that in organizations such as the military or prisons, which in theory provide all members' needs for survival, very active economies exist, exchanging legitimate goods and contraband despite top-down attempts to stamp them out?
- Given the fact that corporations set up hierarchies with clear rewards and mobility, how is it that cliques of people promoting each other's welfare and economic program arise and contend for power?
- When households exchange services such as babysitting, they often invent elaborate bookkeeping systems and rules of exchange. How and why does that happen?

These sorts of questions inspired the two chapters in this section and set up a research agenda intended to provide some answers to the puzzles they raise.

Thus, while earlier sections reflect on past research, this one takes on future investigations. I ask when, why, and how people create such economic arrangements. To be sure, I am not the first to notice these practices, but perhaps precisely because they are familiar, students of economic processes have not yet done the hard work of reflecting on the practices' common properties. Standard thinking about economic structures does not fully capture what is going on with the multiple, often surprising ways in which people organize their economic lives. Many of these economic connections do not function quite like markets or as firms or networks, at least in the conventional understanding of those concepts. And yet we see them sprouting in all sorts of locations. Sometimes we may dismiss them or not even notice them, precisely because they do not fit neatly within established frameworks.

I call these economic arrangements circuits of commerce. Like a firm, a clique, or a household, an economic circuit is a distinctive and widespread form of economic interaction that recurs across an enormous variety of circumstances. How do we recognize a circuit? By the following characteristics:

(a) distinctive social relations among specific individuals; (b) shared economic activities carried on by means of those social relations; (c) creation of common accounting systems for evaluating economic exchanges, for example, special forms of monies; (d) shared understandings concerning the meaning of transactions within the circuit, including their moral valuation; and (e) a boundary separating members of the circuit from nonmembers, with some control over transactions crossing the boundary. Circuits embody and emphasize the centrality of negotiated meanings and social relations in the very economic transactions that analysts have often thought of as impersonal and detached from rich social life. In that way, circuits represent a further effort of constructing the vision of connected lives I report in the earlier sections of this book, where we find complex and variable coexistence between people's social ties and their economic transactions. Studying circuits also contributes to the search for better understandings of the multiplicity and earmarking of money and other media, discussed in an earlier section.

As for the genealogy of the term *circuits of commerce*, Randall Collins (2000) first coined the phrase "Zelizer circuits" drawing from my book *The Social Meaning of Money* (1994) to illustrate the microfoundations of our economic lives. Even before Collins's insightful formulation, I had been intrigued by the creative integration of consumer goods and monies into particularized circuits of exchange as a counter to uniform top-down templates (Zelizer 1999). But the intuition that I later formalized was that a structure combining its own economic activities, media, accounting systems, interpersonal relations, boundaries, and meanings reappears in a wide variety of social circumstances and cannot simply be reduced to firms, markets, or networks. I named that structure a circuit of commerce.

After I began teaching graduate and undergraduate courses in economic sociology during the late 1990s, I became increasingly impatient with two of the field's features: first, its almost exclusive focus on firms and production markets, and second, the implicit supposition that we had fully grasped the basic structures of the economy—hierarchies, markets, and networks. The first practice resulted in the marginalization of such sites as households, informal economies, or gift networks. The second tendency suppressed the possibility that other basic structures exist and perform consequential economic work.

As the twenty-first century jolts us away from standard economic prescriptions and assumptions, it becomes urgent to recognize the multiplicity of economic arrangements and explain how they work, whether it be the vigorous Internet peer production, microcredit arrangements, barter groups, local currency systems, gift-exchange communities, investment clubs, corporate work teams, mutual aid associations, garage sales, and more.

Some of these arrangements qualify as circuits of commerce. Circuits thus expand the repertoire of economic structures deserving close attention.

Where do we find circuits? As my initial queries suggest, we observe them in a wide range of contexts and social circumstances. Their parameters vary from relatively short-lived or fixed term (but never instantaneous) to long term, from intimate to impersonal, from equal to unequal, from small to large, and across several other dimensions. Although circuits of commerce may emerge in spatially segregated domains, such as communes or prisons, they typically cut across multiple social sites, coordinating only certain activities and social ties within each of them.

Take for instance the kind of care economies discussed in the last section. Here care providers and recipients frequently establish complex circuits, exchanging babysitting, cooking, health care, companionship, and other services. They often create their own media to mark a particular set of social relations and transactions. Consider the case of flourishing babysitting co-ops that rely on poker chips, movie tickets, Monopoly money, or special scrip as their accounting media.

Paid child-care providers sometimes create their own circuits. Armenta (2009) reports the emergence of a bounded, close set of relations among Latina nannies caring for children in a West Los Angeles park. Connected by their common language and cultural understandings, the women exchanged favors as they assisted each other with the care of children and also shared food in a weekly potluck or Thanksgiving dinner. In addition, they occasionally raised money for each other. While including the Latino park staff in their circuit, the nannies firmly excluded their non-Latina "gringas" (female employers). Within such playgrounds, as well as in school classrooms and lunchrooms, children themselves often become circuit-creators, constructing elaborate webs of exchange for such commodities as lunches, cookies, marbles, or cards, as well as money (see, e.g., Thorne 1993; Scott 2003).

Think about the very different world of art markets. Based on his interviews with art dealers in Amsterdam and New York, Olav Velthuis (2005) extensively documents the creation of distinct relational circuits among art collectors, dealers, and artists. In many cases, Velthuis shows, those differentiated art circuits, most notably the traditional and avant-garde, mark and sustain their distinct understandings about art and moral worth not simply by the quality of the art displayed, but with different pricing strategies and business practices. Countering standard views of price as strictly determined by supply and demand, Velthuis thus discovers that diverse pricing strategies (which he labels honorable prices, superstar prices, and prudent prices) serve, along with special marketing and business practices, as meaningful boundary-markers that demarcate art circuits.

Does this mean that circuits only appear at the outskirts of capitalist organizations, in the allegedly "softer" economies of women, children, and art specialists? Anyone who has worked in large organizations will recognize that circuits also emerge within corporate and other formal structures.

Firms themselves create social circuits by organizing differentiated systems of payments and mobility; sociologists have often called attention to these systems as internal labor markets. Or consider autonomous work groups, where group members not only define the work to be done and the division of labor but also share resources such as time off and bonuses. Those systems in their turn generate bounded sets of social relations—circuits in my use of the word.

Corporations usually mark such internal circuits formally by means of distinctive media, transfers, and interpersonal ties. At the grossest level, modes of payment themselves differentiate circuits: hourly, weekly, monthly, or annual wages; payment in cash, kind, or check; presence or absence of distinctive perquisites (see, e.g., Dalton 1959; Morrill 1995). As Calvin Morrill's (1995) study of corporate managers vividly reveals, some corporate circuits are faction-defined, and others separate major "cultures" within firms. In French factories, Michel Anteby (2003) discovered circuits of clandestine production and distribution. He shows that the production of what workers call "perruque"—objects fashioned for personal use with factory materials and machines—plays a significant part in the moral economies of those factories. Circuits form even in the electronically mediated worlds of contemporary global finance. Karin Knorr Cetina and Urs Bruegger (2002) have identified the formation of circuitlike connections among global financial traders, as traders engage in repeated transactions involving not only currencies but information.

Lest we sentimentalize circuits, Alice Goffman, drawing from her remarkable observations of a group of poor, African American young men who live at the margin of the law in Philadelphia, points to certain circuits paradoxically maintained by betrayal and deceit rather than trust and solidarity. Within such circuits, for instance, it happens that "some people get others arrested simply to extort money from them, which they request in exchange for not showing up as a witness at the ensuing trial" (2009, 349n8 and personal communication). To be sure, Morrill's managers similarly support their corporate-based circuit boundaries through conflict and extensive backbiting.

Does all of economic life take place in circuits? Certainly not. Many economic transactions do not constitute circuits. Consider for instance bank-to-bank electronic transfers or all the customers of a particular bank. In neither case do we find bounded sets of people connected by particular combinations of media, transactions, relations, and meaning systems. Although bank customers may appear to approximate a circuit, they lack the ongoing interaction that would make their activities open to negotiation, contestation, and reshaping. Nor do dyads count as circuits. That means that, although they involve personal ties, most of our everyday purchases do not take place within circuits. If, for example, you establish a close personal connection with the supermarket cashier you see each week, that link does not by itself create a circuit. Unlike dyads, circuits involve multiple actors creating and maintaining distinctive forms of economic activity.

When do circuits emerge? Properly answering that question ranks high in my future research agenda. People seem to have invented circuits over and over when they have faced significant collective problems of trust in the absence of central authorities that could enforce agreements. Problems of trust become more serious when people are carrying on consequential long-term collective activities such as long-distance trade, child rearing, family formation, or the provision of credit for commercial enterprises, and when the costs of defection and misbehavior for long-term collective welfare rise.

Historically, most people have implicitly solved such problems by restricting trust to those others with whom they maintain frequent close interaction: household members, coreligionists, and kin. But when relations become more intermittent or contingent, people have often elaborated those relations into commercial circuits. Even there, to be sure, circuits seem to have operated more effectively when the participants already shared some prior ties of kinship, proximity, ethnicity, religion, or common economic activity. No doubt the dependence of circuits on mutual monitoring accounts for that apparent regularity.[1]

Although I concentrate on economic circuits, similar structures emerge outside of economic life. Charles Tilly, for instance, noticed parallels with political circuits, as "not simply networks of connection among political activists but the full combination of boundaries, controls, political transactions, media, and meaningful ties." Social movements, Tilly writes, "build on, create, and transform political circuits" (2004, 103).

In what ways is thinking about circuits an improvement on thinking about networks? After all, network analysts have developed an impressive set of tools for deciphering economic connections. Network specialists, however, have largely focused on relatively stable patterns and configurations of social relations. They have not explored the variable content of transactions or their meanings nor the dynamic, incessantly negotiated interactions they involve. As I searched for ways to better understand precisely these features, I was drawn to the concept of circuits. A French scholar vividly characterized my effort as inserting "*le coeur dans les networks*." But circuits, however, are not simply constituted by adding and mixing culture into networks.

Instead, circuits (in this case, circuits of commerce) define a special social structure. Every circuit certainly includes a network—that is, particular ties and relations—and a boundary. But it also contains distinctive cultural materials, particular forms of economic transactions and media, as well as crucial relational work involved in the constant negotiation and maintenance of relations. Circuits therefore are not simply a culturally sensitive version of networks. Thinking about circuits raises questions about meanings and relational work that remain invisible to strictly network analysts.

Of course, all new ideas have genealogies. Circuits echo earlier scholars' efforts to account for variable forms of connectedness among sets of economic practices, persons, and objects, such as anthropologists' explorations of exchange spheres, Max Weber's spheres, Pierre Bourdieu's fields, Bruno Latour and Michel Callon's actor-network theory, Florence Weber's "*scènes sociales*," and more. But circuits, unlike some of these earlier, broader theoretical schemes, introduce a distinct agenda for theorizing and researching certain types of economic phenomena.

Thinking about circuits engaged me in dynamic conversations, especially with younger scholars in the United States, but also in Argentina, Brazil, France, Italy, and the United Kingdom. These innovative researchers share a concern for developing a more culturally and relationally sensitive lens for understanding the specific economic phenomena they study. As they investigate such wide-ranging sites as informal economies, local money initiatives, art markets, venture capitalists, bankers, and fair-commerce entrepreneurs, these students of economic processes discover that the circuit framework helps them explain patterns that cannot be sufficiently accounted for by standard concepts.

The task of explaining circuits, however, has only just begun. Many crucial questions remain, such as when and how do circuits form? Why and when do they change and disappear? How do people mark boundaries among circuits? When, for instance, do they create new bounded monies or other media? Do people invent special vocabularies to portray their circuit transactions and media? How much inequality is consistent with circuits? What happens when circuits compete for members' allegiance? Do circuits serve to legitimate or challenge categorical forms of inequality such as gender or race? And how do states respond to localized circuits?

The chapters in this section represent two stages in my investigation of some of these questions, which kept bubbling even as I worked on *The Purchase of Intimacy*. My first formal discussion of circuits took place at an American Sociological Association annual meeting session in 2000, organized by Wendy Espeland and Mitchell Stevens. That same year, I also published my first statement about circuits in the ASA economic sociology section newsletter. Since then I have presented my ideas to multiple audiences in the United States, France, the Netherlands, and Italy. Meanwhile, I also published six statements on the topic, including one in French and two translations into Italian and Spanish.

The first essay, "Circuits within Capitalism," represents one of my initial excursions into the topic. It was prepared for a conference on the economic sociology of capitalism organized by Victor Nee and Richard Swedberg at Cornell University during the fateful September 2001 and later published in the volume that came out of that meeting. It focuses on the cases of local monies and caring circuits. Written five years later, the second chapter in this section, "Circuits in Economic Life," reports more recent developments in my elaboration of circuits, concentrating on migrant remittances. It appeared in the *European Economic Sociology Newsletter*, then edited by Nina Bandelj, my student and expert scholar of economic processes. Both articles further the attempt to understand and explain how people organize their economic lives from the ground up.

NOTE

1. For a valuable discussion of variable forms of economic governance, including informal mechanisms, see Dixit 2009.

REFERENCES

Anteby, Michel. 2003. "La 'perruque' en usine: Approche d'une pratique marginale, illégale et fuyante." *Sociologie du Travail* 45:453–71.

Armenta, Amada. 2009. "Creating Community: Latina Nannies in a West Los Angeles Park." *Qualitative Sociology* 32:279–92.

Collins, Randall. 2000. "Situational Stratification: A Micro-Macro Theory of Inequality." *Sociological Theory* 18:17–43.

Dalton, Melville. 1959. *Men Who Manage: Fusions of Feeling and Theory in Administration*. New York: Wiley.

Dixit, Avinash. 2009. "Governance Institutions and Economic Activity." *American Economic Review* 99 (March): 5–24.

Goffman, Alice. 2009. "On the Run: Wanted Men in a Philadelphia Ghetto." *American Sociological Review* 74:339–57.

Knorr Cetina, Karin, and Urs Bruegger. 2002. "Global Microstructures: The Virtual Societies of Financial Markets." *American Journal of Sociology* 107: 905–50.

Morrill, Calvin. 1995. *The Executive Way*. Chicago: University of Chicago Press.

Scott, Kimberly A. 2003. "In Girls, Out Girls, and Always Black: African-American Girls' Friendships." *Sociological Studies of Children and Youth* 9:179–207.

Thorne, Barrie. 1993. *Gender Play*. New Brunswick, N.J.: Rutgers University Press.

Tilly, Charles. 2004. "Social Movements Enter the Twenty-First Century." In Charles Tilly, *Social Movements, 1768–2004*, 95–122. Boulder, Colo.: Paradigm.

Velthuis, Olav. 2005. *Talking Prices*. Princeton, N.J.: Princeton University Press.

Zelizer, Viviana. 1999. "Multiple Markets, Multiple Cultures." In *Diversity and Its Discontents: Cultural Conflict and Common Ground in Contemporary American Society*, edited by Neil Smelser and Jeffrey Alexander, 193–212. Princeton, N.J.: Princeton University Press.

15

Circuits within Capitalism

In recent years, economic prophets have frequently warned us against global commodification and the loss of moral-emotional fiber it brings. From Robert Kuttner's *Everything for Sale* (1997), Robert Lane's *The Loss of Happiness in Market Democracies* (2000), to Jeremy Rifkin's *The Age of Access: The New Culture of Hypercapitalism Where All of Life Is a Paid-For Experience* (2000), social critics fret incessantly over what Rifkin calls the "clash of culture and commerce." "When most relationships become commercial relationships," Rifkin worries, "what is left for relationships of a noncommercial nature . . . when one's life becomes little more than an ongoing series of commercial transactions held together by contracts and financial instruments, what happens to the kinds of traditional reciprocal relationships that are born of affection, love, and devotion?" (2000, 112). Rifkin's implied answer: nothing is left but cold, instrumental rationality. Jean Bethke Elshtain agrees: while "it used to be that some things, whole areas of life, were not up for grabs as part of the world of buying and selling," today, she laments, "nothing is holy, sacred, or off-limits in a world in which everything is for sale" (2000, 47).

Worries about the incompatibility, incommensurability, or contradiction between intimate and impersonal relations follow a long-standing tradition. Since the nineteenth century social analysts have repeatedly assumed that the social world organizes around competing, incompatible principles: *Gemeinschaft* and *Gesellschaft*, ascription and achievement, sentiment and rationality, solidarity and self-interest. Their mixing, goes the theory, contaminates both; invasion of the sentimental world by instrumental rationality desiccates that world, while introduction of sentiment into rational transactions produces inefficiency, favoritism, cronyism, and other forms of corruption.

The theory gained force with reactions to nineteenth-century industrial capitalism. We can usefully follow Chris and Charles Tilly in defining capitalism as "the system of production in which holders of capital, backed by law and state power, make the crucial decisions concerning the character and allocation of work" (1998, 24). Although markets for commodities, labor, land, and capital itself thrive under a wide variety of economic systems, capitalism stands out from the rest in the extent to which holders of capital shape those markets by means of their investments, transfers, and organizational interventions. For advocates of the system, it benefits from the tight interaction of capitalist rationality with the rationality of markets. For critics of the system, that is precisely the problem: capitalism serves capital all too well, while neglecting or exploiting other worthy contributors to collective welfare.

Although earlier theorists had often allowed for the coexistence of solidarity and self-interest, both advocates and critics of industrial capitalism therefore adopted a sweeping, risky assumption: that capitalist rationality was driving solidarity, sentiment, and intimacy from markets, firms, and national economies (Hirschman 1977; Tilly 1984). Whether they deplored capitalism's advance, celebrated it, or treated it as a necessary evil, they commonly agreed on an idea of contamination: sentiment within the economic sphere generates favoritism and inefficiency, while rationality within the sentimental sphere destroys solidarity. Thus strong segregation of the spheres served both of them.

The theory of separate spheres had a perverse consequence. It provided a justification for giving lesser economic rewards, or none at all, to efforts supporting solidarity, sentiment, and intimacy. Parents, spouses, friends, and providers of care, ran the argument, acted out of duty and love that would dissolve if exposed to the acid of markets. Public policy, the argument continued, should actually reinforce the barrier between the two spheres by such devices as assuring male breadwinners of sufficient wages to support their (nonworking) families, banning the underpaid work of women and children, encouraging charity for the worthy unemployed, and (more daringly) paying family allowances from public funds.

The theory reappeared in camouflage as organizational analysts noticed new forms of capitalism emerging after World War II. Where firms, markets, friendships, families, governments, and associations had seemed to be differentiating ever more sharply as capitalism advanced, now new organizational forms called forth such terms as *flexible production, hybrid firm,* and *network forms.* As Paul DiMaggio puts it,

> For all their diversity, the firms to which researchers called attention shared several notable features: greater suppleness than their more traditionally bureaucratic counterparts, a greater willingness to trust employees and business partners, a preference for long-term "relational contracting" over short-term market exchange for many transactions, a commitment to ongoing technological improvement—and an apparent renunciation of central features of Weber's model [of bureaucratization]. (DiMaggio 2001, 19)

Given dichotomous theories of sentiment and rationality, the new organizational forms raised an acute puzzle: would such new ways of doing business eventually suffer inefficiency, cronyism, and corruption precisely because they breached boundaries between *Gemeinschaft* and *Gesellschaft?* For the most part, analysts of economic change clung to the idea of incompatible separate spheres.

Economic sociologists and other professional students of economic processes have commonly incorporated more sophisticated versions of the same doctrine into their analyses of globalization, commodification, and rationalization. They have thought that market expansion inexorably eroded intimate social ties and narrowed the number of settings in which intimacy could prosper, while increasing contrasts between such settings and the cold world of economic rationality. They have therefore often joined social critics in supposing that twenty-first-century globalization will undercut caring activity, deplete the richness of social life, and thus threaten social solidarity.

The twenty-first century may well bring terrifying changes in social life, but they will not occur because commodification in itself generally destroys intimacy. This essay challenges the widespread assumption that markets ipso facto undercut solidarity-sustaining personal relations. It offers an alternative to the conventional account of interplay between market transactions and personal relations. The analysis brings together seven elements:

- A sustained critique of radical dichotomies between intimate and impersonal social ties
- Identification of commercial circuits as bridging structures that facilitate the coexistence of intimate and impersonal social ties
- Reminders that anthropologists have frequently encountered commercial circuits in supposedly noncapitalist social settings
- After a quick glance at capitalist firms, a review of two areas of economic activity commonly thought to demonstrate (and suffer from) the incompatibility of intimate and impersonal social ties—local monetary systems and caring labor—for evidence of stable coexistence between commercial transactions and interpersonal intimacy
- Identification of parallels in the formation and operation of commercial circuits within those two areas
- Arguments that in each area those circuits facilitate the coexistence of commercial transactions and interpersonal intimacy but also generate exclusion and inequality in relation to outsiders
- Proposals for further inquiry into relations between commercial circuits (which form widely outside of capitalism) and capitalism as such

Interweaving these themes, I take up in the following order the general critique, the presentation of circuits, the anthropological literature, circuits of local money, caring connections, proposals, and conclusions.

How Analysts Go Wrong

Explicitly or implicitly, most analysts of intimate social relations join ordinary people in assuming that the entry of instrumental means such as monetization and cost accounting into the worlds of caring, friendship, sexuality, and parent-child relations depletes them of their richness, hence that zones of intimacy only thrive if people erect effective barriers around them. Thus emerges a view of *hostile worlds:* of properly segregated domains whose sanitary management requires well-maintained boundaries.

Uncomfortable with such dualisms and eager to forward single-principle accounts of social life, opponents of hostile-worlds views have now and then countered with reductionist *nothing-but* arguments: the ostensibly separate world of intimate social relations, they argue, is nothing but a special case of some general principle. Nothing-but advocates divide among three principles: nothing but economic rationality, nothing but culture, and nothing but politics. Thus for economic reductionists, caring, friendship, sexuality, and parent-child relations become special cases of advantage-seeking individual choice under conditions of constraint—in short, of economic rationality. For cultural reductionists, such phenomena become expressions of distinct beliefs. Others insist on the political, coercive, and exploitative bases of the same phenomena.

Neither hostile-worlds formulations nor nothing-but reductions deal adequately with the intersection of intimate social ties and ordering institutions such as money, markets, bureaucracies, and specialized associations. Careful observers of such institutions always report the presence, and often the wild profusion, of intimate ties in their midst.

In order to describe and explain what actually goes on in these regards, we must move beyond hostile-worlds and nothing-but ideas. Let me propose an alternative third way: the analysis of *bridges*. We can bridge the analytical gap between intimacy and impersonality by recognizing the existence of differentiated ties that cut across particular social settings. In all sorts of settings, from predominantly intimate to predominantly impersonal, people differentiate strongly among various kinds of interpersonal relations, marking them with distinctive names, symbols, practices, and media of exchange. Ties themselves do vary from intimate to impersonal and from durable to fleeting. But almost all social settings contain mixtures of ties that differ in these regards.

Interpersonal ties typically connect people within the setting to different arrays of others both within and outside the setting. Such differentiated ties often ramify into what Randall Collins (2000, 2004) calls "Zelizer circuits." Each distinctive social circuit incorporates somewhat different understandings, practices, information, obligations, rights, symbols, and media of exchange. I call these *circuits of commerce* in an old sense of the word, where commerce meant conversation, interchange, intercourse, and mutual shaping. They range from the most intimate to quite impersonal social transactions.[1]

By definition, every circuit involves a network, a bounded set of relations among social sites. *Circuit*, however, is neither simply a fancy new name for *network* nor a sanitized version of *community*. Two features distinguish circuits from networks as usually conceived. First, they consist of dynamic, meaningful, incessantly negotiated interactions among the sites—be those sites individuals, households, organizations, or other social entities. Second, in addition to dynamic relations, they include distinctive media (for example, legal tender or localized tokens) and an array of organized, differentiated transfers (for example, gifts or compensation) between sites. Commercial circuits also differ from communities as conceived of in the *Gemeinschaft-Gesellschaft* tradition. They do not consist of spatially and socially segregated rounds of life; although circuits sometimes exist *within* encompassing communities, they ordinarily cut across multiple social settings, coordinating only certain kinds of activities and social relations within each setting.

More specifically, any commercial circuit includes four elements:

- It has a well-defined boundary with some control over transactions crossing the boundary.
- A distinctive set of transfers of goods, services, or claims upon them occurs within its interpersonal ties.
- Those transfers employ distinctive media.
- Ties among participants have shared meaning.

In combination, these four elements imply the presence of an institutional structure that reinforces credit, trust, and reciprocity within its perimeter but organizes exclusion and inequality in relation to outsiders.

Social relations vary in the extent to which they convey information and attention that is (or is not) widely available to third parties. I call *impersonal* those relations conveying only widely available information and attention; *intimate,* those that convey information and attention not widely available to third parties. Since media and transfers always attach to specific sets of meaningful social relations and since to choose a medium is also to commit oneself to a corresponding set of transfers and relations, hostile-worlds doctrines express wariness of conflicting commitments between impersonal and intimate relations to the same or closely connected persons.

Earmarking practices and creation of circuits reduce that risk, especially because (almost by definition) intimate relations generate circuits of smaller scope—particularized information and attention depend heavily on shared local knowledge and do not easily sustain uniform institutions like those that underlie standardized, large-scale exchange systems. The fragility of disciplined sects that do impose intimacy and their reliance on extensive institutional controls indicate that the point is not tautological; intimate circuits only work on the large scale under exceptional institutional conditions. Hence the interest of trade diasporas, migrant remittances, underground sects, rotating credit associations, and credit in the absence of authoritative central institutions.

Circuits, then, do not comprise communities in the sense of closed-off, all-encompassing social relations. Circuits do not differentiate whole social settings or organizations. In fact, the same people participate in different circuits simultaneously. Contrary to the views of such social critics as Michael Walzer (1983), that is why there are no specific "spheres" that can be contaminated by money. Despite the ideologies of their proponents, as we shall see, local monies do not form closed communities; the same people who participate in local currency systems ordinarily use nationally sanctioned legal tender for a wide variety of transactions outside those systems.

Nevertheless, circuits do not exhaust all cross-cutting social structures. Legally established categories such as Social Security recipient or registered Republican do not in themselves constitute circuits. Nor do organizations, neighborhoods, kinship groups, religious congregations, or networks defined by diffusion of certain objects or information (e.g., disease or rumor)—*unless* they also create bounded sets of media and transfers. The pressing theoretical and empirical tasks are therefore (1) to specify the mechanisms and processes that generate bounded media and transfers and (2) to describe and explain how and why those mechanisms and processes operate differently across the range from impersonal to intimate transactions.

How does thinking about circuits improve on straightforward thinking about networks? If you only have a set of relations that are not bounded and have no distinctive content, no circuit exists. Every circuit includes a boundary, distinctive cultural materials, and particular forms of transfer and media. It of course also includes a network—particular ties and relations. But thinking about circuits raises questions that remain invisible to strict network analysis.

ANTHROPOLOGISTS CONFRONT CIRCUITS

Without using the term *circuits*, anthropologists have frequently noticed the phenomenon. Nearly half a century ago, Paul Bohannan (1955, 1959) discerned what he called spheres of exchange among the Tiv. Each sphere, according to Bohannan, specialized in a restricted set of commodities that people could not exchange across spheres. In this analysis, modern money supplanted such spheres by making a medium of universal exchange available. Subsequent anthropologists followed Bohannan's error in supposing that restricted spheres of exchange disappeared with the onset of modern society or the integration of nonliterate people into the metropolitan world.

Frederick Pryor (1977) formalized the idea, identifying "exchange spheres" as social arrangements in which valuables of one delimited set cannot be exchanged for valuables of another such set without the breaking of a prohibition or one of the parties' losing prestige if the transaction becomes widely known. For Pryor an "exchange circuit" is the special case of an exchange sphere in which goods within the set cannot be traded symmetrically—for example, one can get B for A, C for B, and A for C, but not A for B, B for C, or C for A. Pryor actually recognizes that money in complex societies shares some characteristics of exchange spheres and circuits, by excluding certain goods and services, but fails to pursue that insight into the contemporary world (see also Barth 1967).

Recent ethnography has moved one step beyond Pryor, noting how the integration of previously distinct economies has refuted the widespread expectation that state-backed currencies would obliterate those economies' differentiated monetary spheres. For Melanesia, David Akin and Joel Robbins remark:

> Widespread social scientific expectations that global capitalist expansion would quickly overwhelm traditional Melanesian economies have been confounded by the latter's dynamism and resilience. Indeed, many local systems of exchange appear to have flourished rather than withered from linkage with the world economy, and state currencies and imported goods mingle within formal exchange systems fundamental to social reproduction. Far from the advent of money having consigned indigenous currencies to irrelevance, the two instruments of exchange are clearly in dialogue throughout Melanesia. (1999, 1; see also Crump 1981; Parry and Bloch 1989; Guyer 1995)

Thus, anthropologists have recognized most elements of commercial circuits in nonliterate as well as in developing social settings, and even occasionally in advanced capitalist countries (see Bloch 1994). They have not, however, assembled those elements into a working model or traced their variations within contemporary capitalist economies. Similarly, economists are increasingly paying attention to the phenomenon that Jérôme Blanc calls "parallel monies." Pointing to the vibrant presence of multiple monies in contemporary economies—ranging among foreign currencies circulating alongside national legal tender, merchandise coupons, school vouchers, local currencies, and commodities such as cigarettes used as media of exchange—Blanc contends that such parallel currencies

> are not a residual and archaic phenomenon, which would imply their disappearance with the increasing rationalization of money in westernizing societies; it concerns as well, and especially so, developed and financially stable economies. As witnessed by the emergence of a vast number of parallel monies in the last quarter of the 20th century, we

cannot conclude that social modernity will destroy these instruments. (2000, 321)

Still, neither anthropologists nor economists have specified the social processes through which people create, sustain, and change distinctive configurations of media, transfers, and social relations.

We can gain theoretically and empirically by picking up where the anthropologists and economists have left off. Many apparently disparate social phenomena incorporate circuits of commerce. Sensitized by the concept, we can detect interesting parallels among the worlds of professional boxers, the art trade, sales of electronic components, financial traders, favor-trading networks maintained by Russian households, French amateur gardeners, American garment manufacturers, Australian hotel managers, rotating credit associations, direct sales organizations, migrants' use of remittances, ties among venture capitalists, and concentration camps (see, e.g., Wacquant 1998, 2000; Velthuis 2003; Darr 2003; Knorr Cetina and Bruegger 2002; Ledeneva 1998; Weber 1998; Uzzi 1997; Ingram and Roberts 2000; Biggart 1989, 2001; Durand et al. 1996; Indergaard 2002; Narotzky and Moreno 2002).

Circuits of commerce, then, clearly play significant parts in economic transactions. Economists, sociologists, and anthropologists who have seen them in operation have commonly treated them as imperfect markets, as institutional contexts for market transactions, or as nonmarket systems of exchange, but not as distinctive social structures with dynamics of their own. Nevertheless, close observers of capitalist corporations have regularly detected circuits operating *within* those presumably rationalized hierarchies—not only internal labor markets and patron-client networks with their own distinctive media and understandings, but also faction-defined circuits, gender-segregated circuits, and circuits separating major "cultures" within the firm (see, e.g., Anteby 2003; Dalton 1959; Kanter 1977; Morrill 1995; Tilly 1998).

Instead of following such important but relatively well-documented instances of corporate circuits, let us examine their operation in two spheres that people have usually considered to be extraeconomic: local currencies and the provision of personal care.

LOCAL CURRENCIES

An intriguing instance of circuit building comes from a recent proliferating movement in Europe and the Americas: the local money movement. In a partial reconstitution of the multiple monetary circuits that existed before governments imposed national legal tenders, many communities around the world have over the past two decades been creating their own distinctive currencies. During the nineteenth century, American stores, businesses, and other organizations often produced their own currency, mostly as a way to counter the scarcity of small change. Even company towns, labor exchanges, churches, and brothels sometimes issued their own monies. Similarly, during the U.S. Depression of the 1930s, many schemes of barter and scrip grew up in economically hard-pressed areas (for a more general review of labor exchanges dating from the Depression, see Diehl [1930–35] 1937).

Creating a medium to mark a circuit, then, is not a new strategy. Plenty of current practices include one version or another of specialized media. Discount coupons in grocery chains, frequent-flier miles on airlines, and credit purchasing within local communities involve formation of distinctive circuits. Food stamps likewise establish their own configurations of media, transfers, and interpersonal ties. Or consider the case of affinity credit cards, issued by a given community or organization and having proceeds earmarked for that group. Local currencies, however, are uniquely situated within distinct spatial territories. The recent deliberate creation of local monies simply dramatizes the significant place of interpersonal circuits in the organization of ostensibly impersonal economic life. Unlike their predecessors, however, many of the new local currencies come out of a broader movement seeking to escape what participants commonly regard as the corrupting effects of national and global economies.

From the Australian *green dollar* and the French *grain de sel* to the Italian *misthòs*, the German *Talent*, the Mexican *Tlaloc*, the Argentine *créditos*, the Japanese *ecomoney*, or the *SEED* of Mendocino, California, local currencies mark geographically circumscribed circuits of commerce (see Helleiner 1999, 2000; Powell 2002; Rizzo 1999; Schroeder 2002; Servet 1999; *Trends in Japan* 2001). These currencies belong to well-organized local groups that go by names such as local exchange and trading schemes (LETS), *systèmes d'échange local* (SEL), *banca del tempo* (BDT), *sistema di reciprocità indiretta* (SRI), *club del trueque, Tauschring*, and HOURS.

In the year 2000, an obviously incomplete listing by the Schumacher Society, specialists in promoting local currencies, included thirty-three such groups in the United States alone.[2] Observers of Germany, France, and Italy report some three hundred such circuits in each country, including such currencies as grain de sel (Ariège), Piaf (Paris), Cocagne (Toulouse), or Talent (Germany) (see, e.g., Laacher 1999; Pierret 1999). In the United States, along with the Mendocino SEED, we find such fetching currency names as Kansas City's Barter Buck, Prescott, Arizona's High Desert Dollar, New Orleans's Mo Money, and Berkeley's BREAD. Although some enthusiasts for these local arrangements imagine they are doing away with money entirely, in fact they are creating new forms of money devoted to distinctive circuits.

Discussions of local money often mention, and sometimes confuse, four rather different phenomena: pegged currencies, time exchanges, commodity-based systems, and barter. *Pegged currencies* establish a distinct local medium whose value corresponds to that of legal tender. *Time exchanges* take their value from hours of effort contributed by their members. *Commodity-based systems* involve coupons, vouchers, and credits that are ultimately redeemable only in certain earmarked goods or services. *Barter* includes direct exchange of goods and services for each other without intervention of a currency. Although combinations of all four systems appear here and there, the overwhelming majority of deliberately organized local monetary systems fall in the range of the first two, from pegged currencies to time exchanges.

To see the actual working of local currency circuits, I will focus on one example of each of those two types; first, pegged systems and then, time exchanges. In neither case is the local currency convertible into national legal tender. In local exchange and trading schemes (LETS) members transfer goods and services using a locally circumscribed medium, usually pegged to a national currency. At least two major variants of LETS exist. Some create tokens to represent their currency, while others rely on telephone-linked or computer-based central accounts without physical tokens. How do LETS work? Participants generally pay an entrance fee and subscribe to a service listing available goods and services provided by members of a circuit. Buyers and sellers contact each other and negotiate a price; their transaction is then recorded by the local LETS office.

These local monetary systems range from half a dozen members to several thousand. Observers report a total of some twenty thousand LETS members in England and thirty thousand in France, a figure suggesting an average of about one hundred members per circuit (C. Williams 1996; Laacher 1999). In his excellent survey of local currencies, Jérôme Blanc estimates 250,000 members of LETS across the world at the beginning of the year 2000 (Blanc 2000, 243). The systems vary with respect to each of the elements of circuits identified earlier: a well-defined boundary with some control over transactions crossing the boundary; a distinctive set of transfers of goods, services, or claims upon them occurring within the ties; distinctive media; and ties among participants having some shared meaning. The hundreds of French SEL, for example, vary in the networks on which they build; local memberships range among engineers, ecological enthusiasts, city people who have fled to the country, and low-income populations. In the French town of Pont-de-Montvert, of the local SEL's 130 members, 15 are children who exchange toys, books, and musical instruments (Servet 1999, 45).

Although no one has looked comparatively at the composition of local monetary systems in detail, available descriptions leave the impression that they tend to be socially homogeneous and, on balance, relatively high in status. Internal differences in participation by age and gender (see, e.g., Raddon 2003) do not significantly qualify that impression. All such systems restrict participation in some regards. In Germany some *Tauschring* circuits restrict their membership to the elderly, the handicapped, foreigners, or women.

Others expand their circuit to include whole communities or firms (Pierret 1999). Even those, however, remain radically delimited as compared to the scope of legal tender.

Accordingly, local trading systems also specialize in different arrays of goods and services. In France, for example, exchanges in urban SEL concentrate on transportation, administrative service, education, bodily care, and counseling (Laacher 1999). In rural areas, on the other hand, participants are more likely to trade in food products, clothing, construction, and machine repair. As a French commentator observes, "Courses in analytic philosophy offered in Ariège are less likely to find takers than food or transportation. In Paris, a laying hen or farm tools would most likely be less in demand than administrative services computing" (Laacher 1998, 251).

Significantly, many SEL circuits ban transfers of certain goods and services as morally, ecologically, or politically off-limits. Banned commodities may include firearms, animals, goods manufactured by third-world exploitation, and in one case a member's book on "how to get rich quick" (Bayon 1999, 73–74). Denis Bayon, an investigator at the University of Lyon, reports:

> One of the SEL made an interesting specification concerning "massages." An internal document distinguishes erotic massages (growing out of members' personal relations), therapeutic massages (that require the intervention of qualified professionals, eligible for social security reimbursement and exchanges in national currency) and massages designed for general well-being and relaxation. (1999: 73–74)

The first two kinds of massage, according to Bayon, are forbidden, the third acceptable. More generally, this circuit favors treatment by means of alternative medicines.

At first, the list of exchanges at the Ferrara BDT in Italy seems enormous: it ranges across *lavori e servizi vari* (for example, animal sitting, assistance with school papers, making ice cream, proofreading, company for the elderly, reading aloud); *consulenze* (for example, assistance with computers, social activities, organizing a library); and *lezioni* (for example, lessons in martial arts, dance, German, tai chi, photography).[3] Nevertheless, the list concentrates very heavily on small and personal services, excluding a wide range of consumer goods and commercially available services.

When it comes to pricing goods and services they exchange, local trading systems commonly reject existing market prices for their own negotiated tariffs. Often the local price reflects the circuit's greater evaluation of services that, in the members' estimation, the national market undervalues. What is more, apparently equivalent goods and services fetch different prices depending on the parties' evaluation of the relationship. In a report from the Centre Walras, Etienne Perrot notes: "The personality of the *provider* and the affective dimension of SEL relationships lead the 'client' to pay a friend's price (*prix d'ami*) independent from strict economic calculation" (1999, 386). Similarly, Bayon observes:

> We do not set against each other the hours of babysitting, or the hours of reading stories to children. . . . It's Jean-Paul my neighbor who watched my child yesterday, it's Hélène who came to read "scary stories" to my young children, etc. At the core of SELs . . . we find chains of exchange and solidarity mixing and interweaving with each other as invisible threads designing the common good. It's Jacques who tells Françoise he needs someone to help him with housework, or precisely Françoise knows Pierre who was helped by Luc, etc. It's people who join in to share chores. (1999, 80–81)

As a result, Bayon continues,

> The structure of "prices" in SEL currency would make an ordinary economist scream. The "same" (but it is not precisely the same) hour of ironing earns here 50 grains, there, 60 grains, here 40 grains, etc. An oversize new pair of shoes bought by mistake will be offered here for 100 grains, there 150 grains. (1999, 81)

By the same token, SEL members, according to Bayon, reject prices that seem morally excessive to them, regardless of the amount that the good or service would bring in national currency outside the circuit (see also Raddon 2003).

Even the best-managed SEL, however, eventually discover that they cannot insulate their circuits entirely from the rest of the world. In 1998, in a landmark lawsuit in France, for instance, external labor unions tried to control SEL exchanges of goods and services that the unions themselves had an exclusive right to produce.[4] In the deliberations, the courts retranslated SEL's own units of currency into the national equivalent and interpreted them in terms of market value. Thus, SEL circuits' boundaries become something each SEL must not simply draw but also defend.

Time exchanges attempt to reinforce those boundaries by insulating themselves more firmly from national currencies. While pegged systems have become much more common in Europe and Canada, time-based systems prevail in the United States. Ithaca, New York's HOURS, the community currency pioneer, is the best known of the more than thirty American local monetary circuits. Each prints its own, fully legal, local currency. The U.S. government, however, regulates the physical dimension of notes—smaller than dollar bills—and requires their issue in denominations valued at a minimum of $1.

Since the currency's creation in 1991, over seven thousand Ithaca HOURS have been issued. Each HOUR, which must be spent in local transactions, is valued at $10. The organization estimates that through multiplier effects the $70,000 equivalent has added several million dollars to the local economy. HOURS have gained strong local legitimacy: grants of Ithaca HOURS have been awarded to thirty-five community organizations, political candidates solicit HOURS, the town's Chamber of Commerce accepts them, the Department of Social Services distributes HOURS to its clients, while the local credit union offers HOUR-denominated accounts.[5] During the summer of 2000, in what it hailed as "the world's largest local currency loan," the Ithaca HOUR system issued three thousand HOURS ($30,000) to the Alternatives Federal Credit Union; the loan covered 5 percent of contract work involved in building the credit union's new headquarters (*HOUR Town*, Summer 2000). Like their European counterparts, American authorities take Ithaca HOURS seriously enough to impose income and sales tax on transactions taking place within the system.[6]

To join Ithaca HOURS, participants pay a small fee in exchange for their first two HOURS; the goods or services they offer, as well as those they request, are then printed in the bimonthly *HOUR Town* newspaper.[7] Three categories of HOURS members participate in the Ithaca circuit: individuals with listings in the group directory, employees of participating businesses who collect part of their wages in HOURS, and other HOURS supporters. In Ithaca and elsewhere, HOURS exchanges range across auto repair, carpentry, counseling, errand running, editing, grant writing, Internet training, notarizing, trucking, weddings, and yoga. Generally, price-setting reflects hours of work, but it is still subject to bargaining over the relative value of different kinds of labor.

Concretely, this system produces extensive rounds of life for some participants. Elson, a retired Ithaca craftsman who earns HOURS doing heating and air-conditioning consulting, reports:

> My wife and I spend HOURS at the Farmer's Market, where we browse and chat with old friends. We dine at restaurants, buy apples for mother's homemade apple pie and applesauce. I had my hearing aid repaired and get periodic massages for my failing back. Also I was very pleased last winter to hire two girls with HOURS to shovel heavy snow. They used the HOURS for rent. (Glover n.d.)

Other time-exchange circuits place greater restrictions on relations and transfers. Kansas City's Barter Bucks, for instance, are earned by city volunteers as payment for one day's work on a farm and are then spent back in the city to buy produce from the farmer at the Farmer's Market. In Toronto, Dollars are awarded as grants to community organizations, while the group's "Spirit at Work" project fosters caring services by offering honoraria or Toronto Dollars gift certificates to needy volunteers.

IDEOLOGIES IN LOCAL CURRENCIES

Zealots among local currency advocates commonly reject compromises built in by systems like Ithaca HOURS or LETS that permit variable valuation of members' times. Purists insist on strong insulation from anything that resembles a commercial market and on strict equivalents of hourly inputs. They often justify this strictness with an appeal to moral values of equality and community. Consider the notable case of Time Dollars, a system of chits used to regulate exchange of services such as elderly care, tutoring, phone companionship, housecleaning, or reading to the blind. A central coordinator keeps a record of time spent and received: exchange rates are fixed. Unlike the negotiated HOURS pricing system, here all hours of service have identical value.[8] And, in contrast to the expansiveness of Ithaca HOURS, Time Dollars organizers deliberately restrict the range of services and the participants within their circuit.

One of its earliest and most successful projects, Brooklyn's Member to Member Elderplan is a social HMO that allows seniors to pay 25 percent of their premiums in Time Dollars, earned by providing social support for other seniors. For each hour they serve, members get a credit that they "bank" in Elderplan's computer, to be spent when they need help. Services exchanged include shopping, transportation, bereavement counseling, or telephone visiting among housebound members (Binker 2000; Rowe n.d.). Meanwhile, in Suffolk County, Long Island, welfare mothers earn enough Time Dollars to make a down payment toward a computer by bringing their children to the public library for computer lessons, and in Washington, D.C., teenagers earn Time Dollars by serving on youth juries sentencing first-time juvenile offenders (Cahn 2001).

These systems have a remarkable feature: instead of simply facilitating short-term exchanges, they allow people to accumulate credits over a long period, against a day of need. As a result, beyond their immediate payoff, Time Dollar systems require greater guarantees of continuity in availability of services than other sorts of local monies. Authorities recognize the difference of Time Dollars transactions by refraining from taxing them.

Indeed, one subset of currency systems concentrates on the transfers of caring personal services among people with strong commitments to each other. Time Dollars and some of the LETS circuits have already shown these principles in operation; they often restrict the range of services that members may exchange, setting an ethical standard for those services. What is more, they commonly assure that restriction by limiting membership as well. Advocates of Time Dollars, in fact, often call them the "currency of caring."

A distinctive time-exchange variant appears in New York City's Womanshare, a women-only group restricted to one hundred members exchanging their skills; members receive "credits" from the Womanshare "bank" to be spent on other members' services. Devoted to "honor what is traditionally called 'women's work'—work that has been denigrated in our culture,"[9] participants, as the *New York Times* describes it, "have planted one another's gardens, cooked for the weddings of one another's daughters, seen one another through illnesses and grief, vacationed together, counseled one another on changing careers or wardrobes" (Kaufman 1993).

In both systems—pegged currencies and time exchanges—the very creation and coordination of local monies establishes distinctive circuits of interpersonal relations. To manage their currencies, for instance, participants regularly create standards, institutions, and practices, such as local meetings to decide the issue of new notes, newsletters, Web sites, catalogues of available goods and services, monthly potluck dinners, and trading fairs. In Ithaca, the organizers of Ithaca HOURS have created a formal organization that elects officers and holds regular public meetings. An instructional Hometown Money Starter Kit and video, produced by the Ithaca HOURS inventor, Paul Glover, has sold briskly to over six hundred communities, instructing other local money organizers on step-by-step how-to's of creating currencies.

Participants often reinforce their community by incorporating locally meaningful symbols into their monetary tokens. Ithaca HOURS, for example, feature native flowers, waterfalls, crafts, and farms, while LETS networks, which do not rely on physically distinct monies, use symbolically charged names. In Britain, for instance, Greenwich uses "anchors," Canterbury "tales," and Totnes "acorns" (Helleiner 2000, 46–47). Here, as elsewhere, the choice of a medium actually involves commitment to a particular network of social relations, localized symbol system, and set of transfers.

What *meanings* do organizers of local currencies attribute to ties among members? In fact, competing positions have arisen within the local currency movement. Time Dollars creator Edgar Cahn (2001) claims moral and political superiority for the strict hour system, as compared with others, in these terms:

> LETS is expressly a currency designed to create an *alternative* economy, one that seeks to offer much that the global market economy offers but on a more decent, human, sustainable basis. . . . Time Dollars . . . are designed to rebuild a fundamentally different economy, the economy of home, family, neighborhood and community. . . . Home, family, and neighborhood are not an alternative economy. They are the CORE Economy.

With Cahn's position at one ideological extreme, local monetary circuits also vary greatly in the meaning that they attribute to relations within them. While some of their advocates mean them to protect local commercial interests, others insist that local monies build community ties, forging social along with monetary bonds. Local currencies often serve as potent ideological symbols of what Nigel Thrift and Andrew Leyshon (1999) see as alternative moral economies, countering global financial markets. At times, organizers' ideologies dip into the wells of communitarian cooperativism and even anarchist thinking. In the latter vein, savor the tone of a French pronouncement:

> The resurgence of parallel or alternative experiences goes beyond its microscopic dimensions representing the health of civil society. . . . Social cleavage is the chasm into which the state, having forsaken its duties as guardian of the public interest, will now collapse. By rejecting its role as an actor, the state reveals its failure and its self-contradiction. Civil society had made the state responsible, but its ethical treason and its political withdrawal are now on the way to forcing it to give up its function, without glory or honor. (Latour 1999, 383)

As this declaration suggests, communitarian advocates of local currencies easily slip over into radical libertarianism, a program for the dismantling of governmental controls in behalf of individual freedom.[10]

Others take on a missionary tone. For example, Argentina's Club de Trueque makes the following announcement:

> Our system has extended to Spain (the Basque Country), Uruguay, Brazil, Bolivia and now Ecuador and Colombia. The web page has also allowed us to advise faraway countries, such as Russia and Finland. . . . We are not building barriers to protect our domestic economies, but the foundations and walls for the great cathedral our millennium demands. (Primavera 1999; see also DeMeulenaere 2000; Guerriero 1996)

Such ideological and moral resolutions result in a paradox: while local money practices directly challenge hostile-worlds ideas, their ideologies often reinforce those very same ideas by postulating a frontier between the impure external world of legal tender and the purity of local money. Indeed, the effort of Manchester LETS organizers to integrate their exchanges extensively into the national economy outrages other British LETS organizers. Critics of the Manchester plan, Keith Hart reports, prefer "sealing off a more wholesome kind of circuit from the contamination of capitalism" (1999, 283).

Although most enthusiasts for local currency are practical activists rather than high-flying social critics and theorists, the movement has attracted attention from critics and theorists (e.g., C. Williams 1996; Lee 1996; Thorne 1996; Neary and Taylor 1998; Hart 1999; Thrift and Leyshon 1999; Boyle 2000; Helleiner 2000, 2003). In their *Beyond Employment*, for example, Claus Offe and Rolf Heinze lay out a program of reform clearly influenced by the local money movement. Their Cooperation Circle program has the following components:

- It centers on exchange of services among households.
- It employs a principle of equivalence represented by media deliberately insulated from legal tender.
- The accounting system depends on time expended, with the implication that every member's time is equivalent.
- The currency and the membership network form as a function of potential service exchanges.
- They exclude services that are widely available in markets mediated by legal tender.
- They are designed to operate in milieux—especially urban milieux—where participants do not all know each other, and where trust-maintaining institutions must be built into the design.
- They depend on "supportive, promotional initiatives by provincial or municipal authorities or other sponsors" (Offe and Heinze 1992, 52–55).

In short, Offe and Heinze are specifying boundaries, transfers, media, and ties among participants.

As local currency systems create their particular forms of commercial circuits, we can expect more social thinkers to treat them as promising alternatives to the prevailing organization of work and exchange. That worries practitioners such as Paul Glover, Ithaca HOURS founder. The self-regarding academic, he predicts,

> is going to dissect this like a living cadaver. . . . Part of my aggravation with the academics is that they pile on this as a phenomenon, a novelty, something they can study, write papers about, pass the papers back and forth to each other, getting comfortable salaries. And I'm out here up to my neck in it day to day, translating what I learn into actual programmes. (Boyle 2000, 114; see also Savdié and Cohen-Mitchell 1997)

Glover is certainly right to think that local monies are attracting widespread attention among scholars. But scholars and activists can benefit each other: activists gain by knowing where their particular practices fit into the range of possible practices, while scholars gain from drawing on the practical experience of activists.

As we might reasonably expect, it turns out that local currencies overlap with the second sort of circuit I examine, the circuit of intimacy.

CARING CONNECTIONS

What about intimate circuits of commerce? Monetized intimate ties loom as the ultimate nightmare for hostile-worlds analysts and the strongest challenge for nothing-but reductionists. Many observers assume that when money enters relations between spouses, parents and children, or caregivers and care recipients, intimacy inevitably vanishes. Nothing-but opponents, on the other hand, typically argue that monetized intimate relations reduce to another indistinguishable market exchange, exercise in coercion, or expression of general cultural values. Thus they deny effectively any special features of intimacy as such.

Let us think of relations as intimate to the extent that transactions within them depend on particularized knowledge and attention deployed by at least one person, knowledge and attention that are not widely available to third parties. Intimacy thus defined connects not only family members but also friends, sexual partners, healer-patient pairs, and many servant-employer pairs as well. Although hostile-worlds doctrines lead to the expectation that commercial transactions will corrupt such relations and eventually transform them into impersonal mutual exploitation, close studies of such relations invariably yield a contrary conclusion: across a wide range of intimate relations, people manage to integrate monetary transfers into larger webs of mutual obligations without destroying the social ties involved. As Carol Heimer puts it, "universalistic norms generate responsibilities to particular others as named nodes in a functioning network" (1992, 145; see also Zelizer 2000a). People do so precisely by constructing differentiated circuits of commerce.

As examination of local currencies has already shown us, the existence of differentiated circuits challenges two cherished and oddly complementary myths: of the universal, unifying, all-pervasive market on one side, and of incompatibility between rationality and intimacy on the other. Instead of either one, we discover multiple partly independent circuits, each one incorporating a distinctive system of valuation into its bounded media, transfers, and social relations.

My survey of local currencies has only hinted at two further features of commercial circuits that observers regularly misconstrue through failure to recognize those circuits' existence. The first is their production and maintenance of inequality through what Charles Tilly (1998) calls "opportunity hoarding"; the second is fortification of differences among circuits through legal distinctions cast in other terms but corresponding precisely to the boundaries of their media, transfers, and social relations. Just as we see French labor unions seeking the aid of courts in declaring local labor exchanges "clandestine labor," we find generations of male American workers using legal means to contest any claim of equality for women's work, caring or otherwise. In effect, legal distinctions back the opportunity hoarding of those who already maintain and benefit from advantaged circuits. Feminists and advocates of rewards for caring labor—who overlap, but sometimes disagree furiously with each other—have sensed the existence of circuit-based inequality without quite recognizing what it was or how it worked.

Consider the debate over paid care, which has emerged as a crucial issue on the national political agenda. With the aging of the baby-boom generation, and as most mothers in the United States participate in paid work, the care of children, the elderly, and the sick is being seriously reconsidered. Would the generalization of payment for such care destroy caring itself? Would its subjection to calculation in terms of legal tender rationalize away its essential intimacy?

Increasingly impatient with standard hostile-world and nothing-but an-swers, feminist analysts—sociologists, economists, philosophers, and legal scholars—are rethinking the economics of intimacy generally, and of care in particular. Some argue that care should acquire full market value, while oth-ers defend new conceptions of rewards for caring, and still others carry out empirical studies that document what actually takes place in paid systems of care. In the process they are discovering how interpersonal circuits of inti-macy shape monetary media.

Take for instance Deborah Stone's study of home-care workers in New England, which documents two points of great importance for my argu-ment: a highly bureaucratized monetary payment system for intimate per-sonal care does not by any means produce a cold, dehumanized relationship between caregiver and recipient. Caregivers actually manipulate the payment system to make sure they can provide care appropriate to the relationship. Although they do not usually create new currencies, they actually redefine the media of payment.

Deeply concerned with the effects of turning care into a profit-making business, Stone investigated how changes in Medicare and managed-care fi-nancing restructured caring practices. Interviewing home-care workers, she discovered a payment system that compensated caregivers exclusively for patients' bodily care, not for conversation or other forms of personal atten-tion or assistance. She also discovered, however, that home-care workers did not transform themselves into unfeeling bureaucratic agents. They remained, Stone reports, "keenly aware that home health care is very intimate and very personal" (1999, 64).

The care providers she interviewed included nurses, physical therapists, occupational therapists, and home-care aides. Almost without exception, they reported visiting clients on their days off, often bringing some grocer-ies or helping out in other ways. The agency's warnings against becoming emotionally attached to their clients, aides and nurses told Stone, were un-realistic: "If you're human," or "if you have any human compassion, you just do" (1999, 66). To circumvent an inadequate payment system, home-care workers define their additional assistance as friendship or neighborliness. Or they simply manipulate the rules, for instance, by treating other than the officially approved problems and sometimes even attending to a patient's spouse's health. To be sure, as Stone remarks, inadequate payment structures exploit paid caregivers' concerns for patients. Her interviews conclusively demonstrate, however, that monetary payment systems do not obliterate car-ing relations.

In short, Stone is observing the creation of interpersonal caregiving circuits with their own representations of values, symbols, and practices (see also, e.g., Hondagneu-Sotelo 2001; Menjívar 2002; M. Nelson 2002; Salazar Parreñas 2001; Ungerson 1997; Uttal 2002). Caregiving circuits are not unique. Similar circuits involving their own monetary practices arise in networks of kinship, friendship, and neighborhood, not to mention within households.

The Politics of Care

While analysts such as Stone document and explain caring circuits, others have focused on the politics and morality of caring labor. They raise pointed questions about the equity and propriety surrounding the reward and recognition of care as a critical contribution to social well-being. A significant part of the debate focuses on the economics of care: proper compensation for paid careworkers; adequate provision for care of children, the sick, and the elderly; and economic security for unpaid caregivers.

As the normative questions gain focus, the debate encounters the same difficulties that come up each time people try to think through the relationships between market activity and social obligations. What will happen, they worry, if paid care substitutes for informal assistance? Will recognizing the economic contributions of housewives turn households into impersonal minimarkets? How can we possibly arrive at an appropriate financial evaluation of caretakers' contributions? Will subsidies to housewives increase the ghetto barriers separating them from other workers?

Rejecting both nothing-but and hostile-worlds formulations, a group of imaginative thinkers are moving toward a contrasting approach very much in the spirit of bridging. They identify multiple forms of connection between interpersonal relations and different spheres of economic life. In the process, they are building a new economics of care. Consider for instance, the challenge laid down by economists Nancy Folbre and Julie Nelson:

> An a priori judgment that markets must improve caregiving by increasing efficiency puts the brakes on intelligent research, rather than encourages it. Likewise, an a priori judgment that markets must severely degrade caring work by replacing motivations of altruism with self-interest is also a research stopper.

Instead, they insist, "the increasing intertwining of 'love' and 'money' brings us the necessity—and the opportunity—for innovative research and action" (Folbre and Nelson 2000, 123–24).

What's more, advocates of bridges note that hostile-worlds assumptions portraying love and care as demeaned by monetization may in fact lead to economic discrimination against those allegedly intangible caring activities. As Paula England and Nancy Folbre point out, "the principle that money cannot buy love may have the unintended and perverse consequence of perpetuating low pay for face-to-face service work" (1999, 46).

Books by Joan Williams, Ann Crittenden, and Nancy Folbre advance this line of thought. Williams's *Unbending Gender* boldly sets out to transform outdated and unjust American gender arrangements. Invoking the tradition of Latin American feminists, legal theorist Williams intends "to spark a movement within feminist theory that is theoretically sophisticated, yet committed to talking in language capable of reaching audiences outside of academics" (2000, 243).

Williams's diagnosis is forthright: our inherited system of domesticity, she argues, binds us to a deeply flawed organization of market work and household labor. On the one hand, an ideal-worker norm demands full-time workplace involvement, leaving little space for child bearing or child rearing. Occupational excellence and caregiving are thereby inexorably pitted against each other. On the other hand, and as a direct result of traditional ideal-worker norms and practices, our system of caregiving routinely marginalizes caregivers—typically women—making them economically vulnerable. Williams focuses on the liabilities of mothering. Our economy, she asserts, "is divided into mothers and others" (2000, 2). Yet mothers are not the only victims of current domesticity structures: so are men obliged to perform as ideal-workers and children raised in flawed caring arrangements. When their mothers are economically marginalized, children are also more likely to be poor.

There is a way out. *Unbending Gender* works as a manual in what Williams calls "reconstructive feminism." Its goal is to restructure current family and work arrangements that routinely marginalize caregivers, instituting a norm of parental care to replace mother care. Its three-step method consists of (1) eliminating the ideal (male) worker norm in market work; (2) eliminating it also in family entitlements; and (3) introducing a new gender discourse. Williams offers us more than passionate rhetoric: she provides a set of specific policies to restructure both work and family, most notably legal action. She makes a sustained, knowledgeable case for treating the lower rewards given to the kinds of work women do as a violation of equal rights. She also points out the blatant and perhaps legally remediable differences between women's market and nonmarket work, between men's and women's sides of divorce settlements, and between evaluations of men's and women's contributions to household wealth. In all these cases, a sentimentalized conception of women's caring labor justifies discrimination.

Determined to undo such prejudicial sentimentality, Williams puts forth remedial policies to achieve just compensation for women. For instance, her joint property proposal would recognize family work as economically valuable, justifying income sharing by spouses after divorce. It would thereby undermine courts and legislatures' assumption that "men's claims give rise to entitlements while women's claims are treated as charity" (2000, 131).

At times, Williams's hard-nosed critique of hostile worlds edges toward nothing-but economists' reductionism. Nevertheless, she is careful to distinguish her income-sharing proposals from others that rely on what she sees as "strained analogies to commercial partnership law" (2000, 126). In so doing, she begins to recognize differentiation of social ties among such settings as families, firms, markets, and organizations. At the same time, however, she wants a reading of the law in which such relations cast legal shadows that are financially equivalent. In short, Williams rejects both hostile-worlds and nothing-but arguments in favor of building bridges by legal means. She does not quite say that her analysis gains plausibility from its implicit identification of distinctive caring circuits with their own media, transfers, and social relations. Explicit recognition of caring circuits would actually advance Williams's program by specifying the new institutional forms whose legal standing she seeks to fortify.

CRITTENDEN'S CRITIQUE

In *The Price of Motherhood* (2001), investigative journalist Ann Crittenden deploys a line of argument overlapping with that of Joan Williams. The result is a compelling exposé of current misunderstandings on the subject of caring. In fifteen crisp chapters, sprinkled with pointed vignettes, Crittenden dissects the current U.S. domestic economy, unmasking its relentless marginalization of careworkers generally, mothers in particular.

Her catalogue of unjust treatment ranges across the following:

- The "mommy tax" exacted by workplaces discriminating against workers who adapt their working schedules to care for their children
- Divorce courts that disregard the economic contributions of caregivers
- Child-support arrangements that shift the bulk of child-raising costs to divorced and single mothers
- A Social Security system that protects only paid labor
- Unemployment and workmen's compensation policies that exclude mothers
- Internal domestic economies that perpetuate mothers' financial dependency on husbands

True, Crittenden agrees, women's recent progress in the labor market has indeed been remarkable, but that success stops short when it comes to mothers. Despite media images of career-driven working mothers, and the relative increase in father-care, mothers, insists Crittenden, continue to provide the bulk of child care. Like Williams, Crittenden punctures the illusory goal of achieving women's full-time labor market participation while retaining their second unpaid job as primary housekeeper and child-carer.

Crittenden writes after more than five years of research, wide-ranging reading of the relevant literature, plus hundreds of interviews with mothers and fathers in the United States and Europe, as well as with leading experts—including Joan Williams and Nancy Folbre themselves. Crittenden concludes that fairness can only be achieved by redefining caregiving as work, thereby putting a stop to our collective "free riding on women's labor" (2001, 9). It's time to break down, she contends, the "artificial distinction" between wage earners and providers of unpaid care (2001, 263).

Inspired by the more enlightened European model, Crittenden concludes with a wide-ranging blueprint for change: "adding care to our pantheon of national values, along with liberty, justice and the pursuit of happiness through the pursuit of money" (2001, 259). Her proposals include workplace reforms (e.g., parental one year's paid leave); government policies (e.g., equalizing Social Security for spouses); new marital financial arrangements (e.g., after a child is born or adopted, both parents' income becomes the joint property of the new family unit); and increased community support. Adopting even a few such measures, Crittenden reasons, would transfer significant income to women. "Female caregivers," she repeatedly reminds us, "have been the world's cheap labor for too long" (2001, 274). Once again, Crittenden's analysis would gain strength from recognition that she is simultaneously discovering the existence of distinctive care circuits and advocating their fortification by legal and economic means.

FOLBRE CARES

Economist Nancy Folbre adds important new notes to the discussion. In *The Invisible Heart* (2001), she embraces both Williams's and Crittenden's challenges to our current economics of caring. Like Williams and Crittenden, she implicitly recognizes the distinctive character of care circuits, takes them as models for economic reform, and advocates injecting new resources into them. Unlike Williams and Crittenden, however, Folbre calls for fundamental revisions of the economy, the state, and kinship in order to accomplish their shared goals. Along with Julie Nelson and other colleagues, Folbre has pioneered the feminist critique of standard economic models.

For too long, Folbre argues, our confidence in the self-regulating powers of the invisible hand to coordinate market transactions has concealed the crucial economic and moral significance of the invisible heart. True, econo-mists from Adam Smith with his theory of moral sentiments onward have recognized the crucial place of honesty and trust as underpinnings of market transactions. They saw, as Folbre puts it, how the "invisible handshake" helps the invisible hand. They failed, however, to examine the equally fundamental invisible heart: those "feelings of affection, respect and care for others that reinforce honesty and trust" (2001, xiv).

Indifference to caring labor was possible, Folbre explains, as long as pa-triarchal arrangements kept women involved in attending to children, the elderly, and the sick. Not any more: since competitive labor markets upset traditional separate-spheres worlds by opening up better paid employment for women, the caring problem has become an urgent economic, social, and political concern.

Yet caring remains marginalized, exacting an economic and emotional "care penalty" from its providers. One of Folbre's few flickers of ambivalence appears in her treatment of markets for care. She worries about two possible consequences of the market's extension: first, that inferior care providers will enter the market and, second, that the market will form in such a way as to undervalue proper care. On the other hand, she wants proper compensation for caring labor, recognizing that payment does not necessarily erode love. Folbre dismisses conventional economic reasoning that poorly paid caring jobs assure properly altruistic motivations. Perhaps a better formulation of her argument would have been to say that every market transaction has a moral penumbra and that beneficial market transactions must have the right penumbra. In my terms, she is emphasizing the distinctive systems of valua-tion built into caring circuits.

Even more emphatically than Williams and Crittenden, Folbre challenges two common feminist lines of argument. The first is that full integration of women into markets will in itself produce equity and efficiency. The second, rather different, challenge denies that recognizing the special contributions of caretakers and their empirical association with women will undermine demands for gender justice and equality. Folbre is certainly not yearning for a return to romantic visions of traditional families, where "Big Daddy was usually in control" (2001, 20). Nor is raw, selfish individualism the only answer. The alternative? A social feminist agenda fashioned to "distribute responsibilities for care more equally and reward caring more generously" (2001, 18).

Folbre relies on a folksy, breezy tone to deliver a set of profoundly insur-rectionary proposals. If carried out, her agenda amounts to a social revolu-tion. Its three key elements are market socialism, participatory democracy, and shared care. More concretely, Folbre includes reformed ownership, a highly progressive income tax, an expanded welfare state, restructuring capi-tal mobility, revamping definitions of kinship to strengthen caring obligations to children and the elderly, and expanding recognition of caring ties to include friends.

To accomplish such change, Folbre notes, we need to revise economic theory fundamentally, incorporating the economic value of nonmarket work:

> [W]e can't continue to visualize the economy as a man's world of cars and trucks and steel, things that can be easily counted and weighed. The economy now encompasses many and varied activities that once took place within families, activities whose quality is defined by personal contact, responsiveness to individual needs, respect, and affection. (2001, 79)

Williams and Folbre are marvelously complementary. While Williams confronts the legal apparatus that maintains inequality and inhibits care, Folbre addresses the economic theories, practices, and institutions that do the same. Williams makes proposals in sympathy with Folbre but tells us specifically how to carry out change: identifying features of existing laws that produce inequality and suggesting remedies based on existing laws.

Williams, Crittenden, and Folbre join efforts in breaking down the traditional hostile-worlds dichotomies that erroneously split economic transactions and intimate personal relations into separate spheres. To bring caring labor out of its economically marginal ghetto, they forcefully establish its fundamental economic significance and its variable economic content. The three authors mostly stay away from alternative economic, cultural, or political reductionisms, working their way to a fuller understanding of multiple, variable interactions between intimate ties and economic transactions. Only after we recognize that caring labor has always involved economic transfers can we construct democratic, compassionate caring economies.

Awareness of care's economic contribution leads quickly to a further discovery: that caregivers create and operate distinctive circuits of commerce, with their own bounded media, transfers, and meaningful social relations. The new economic feminist agenda rests on a half-articulated recognition that existing circuits of care organize around distinctive media, transfers, and social relations without somehow suffering the disabilities feared by hostile-worlds theorists. Economic feminists call, in essence, not only for recognizing those circuits as distinctive but also for supplying them with greater resources, legal standing, and respect than they have previously enjoyed.

PROPOSAL AND CONCLUSIONS

This chapter has by no means developed a full theory of circuits, much less explained their variability across local monies and caring connections. It has elaborated on an important but poorly recognized phenomenon: formation of differentiated ties crossing organizational or household boundaries, involving organizational and household members in distinct circuits of commerce. It has not provided a coherent, comprehensive answer to the larger question it raises: how do new forms of differentiation and integration, such as commercial circuits, arise and change? The analysis merely suggests that culturally embedded, problem-solving people devise solutions to pressing new social challenges by inventing novel commercial circuits.

Nevertheless, concrete observation of these commercial circuits raises some more general questions and conjectures concerning their relationship to capitalism as an economic system. Without quite articulating the concept, after all, anthropologists and historians have long since documented the activity of commercial circuits in a wide variety of economic systems, including not only nonindustrial economies but also those of state socialism. What, if anything, distinguishes the operation of commercial circuits under capitalism? Let me propose three ideas for further investigation:

First, precisely because capital-dominated markets serve the interests of capital, they fail to solve a wide range of problems that matter greatly to concrete economic actors: creating solidarity, providing security, maintaining self-esteem, caring for dependents, and more. Solutions to those problems require economic resources: labor, land, and capital. People create or adapt commercial circuits at exactly those intersections between capitalist markets and pressing problems.

Second, capitalists and their political allies commonly act to contain or suppress those commercial circuits that threaten their own power to control markets and the disposition of capital, for example, by subordinating local monies to legal tender and by driving unlicensed but paid providers of care underground. Since capitalists and their political allies also employ commercial circuits to solve their own problems, however, they never suppress circuits entirely.

Third, participants in commercial circuits regularly invoke hostile-worlds doctrines as they distinguish those circuits from other social relations and defend the circuits' boundaries against complicating interference from other social relations, including those of wide-ranging capitalist markets. They thereby hide from themselves and others the extensive economic activity and the mingling of economic with intimate transactions that occur incessantly within commercial circuits.

Obviously, my investigations of local monies and caring relations do not provide nearly enough evidence to validate these conjectures. But proliferation of the two sorts of circuits under capitalism does suggest that the people involved are, among other things, solving problems posed by capitalism itself.

Local monies and caring connections obviously differ in their settings and contents. We should resist, however, the ever-present temptation to array them along a standard continuum from genuine, general, impersonal markets at one end to nonmarket intimacy at the other. To do so would reconstruct the very *Gesellschaft-Gemeinschaft* dichotomies a clear recognition of circuits helps us escape. In all three types of circuits—corporate, monetary, caring—mentioned in this chapter, we find intense interpersonal ties commingling with regularized media and transfers. In all three, for that matter, we find ties that vary greatly in their intensity, scope, and durability. Differences among the three types of circuits depend not on overall extent of rationalization or solidarity but on variable configurations of media, transfers, interpersonal ties, and shared meanings attached to their intersection.

How then should we generalize the cases of local monies and caring connections? Here is a rapid summary.

- Neither hostile-worlds nor nothing-but accounts adequately describe, much less explain, the interplay of monetary transfers and social ties, whether relatively impersonal or very intimate.
- Analysts of that interplay clearly need theoretical bridges—ways of explaining the mostly peaceful coexistence of impersonality and intimacy within the same social settings.
- Both intimate and impersonal transactions work through differentiated ties, which participants mark off from each other through well-established practices, understandings, and representations.
- Such differentiated ties compound into distinctive circuits, each incorporating somewhat different understandings, practices, information, obligations, rights, symbols, idioms, and media of exchange.
- Far from determining the nature of interpersonal relationships, media of exchange (including legal tenders) incorporated into such circuits take on particular connections with the understandings, practices, information, obligations, rights, symbols, and idioms embedded in those circuits.
- Indeed, participants in such circuits characteristically reshape exchange media to mark distinctions among different kinds of social relations.

These are the means by which people bridge the apparently unbridgeable gap between social solidarity and commercialized transactions.

NOTES

Viviana A. Zelizer, "Circuits within Capitalism," in *The Economic Sociology of Capitalism*, edited by Victor Nee and Richard Swedberg, 289–322 (Princeton, N.J.: Princeton University Press, 2005). Reprinted with permission. I have adapted a few passages each from Zelizer 2000a, 2000b, 2001, and 2002a, plus substantial portions of Zelizer 2002b and 2004.

1. For a clear statement of the assertion that such circuits emerge from small-scale social interactions, see Collins 2000. In fact, as we shall see, they can also form through borrowing of organizational models across social settings.

2. E. F. Schumacher Society, "Local Currency Groups," June 2001, http://www.schumachersociety.org/cur_grps.html (accessed June 25, 2001).

3. Banca del Tempo di Ferrara, "La lista di ispirazione," February 1999, http://www.comune.fe.it/bancadeltempo/listaispir.htm (accessed June 25, 2001).

4. The appeals court finally decided to support the exemption, recognizing that the SEL members involved in the dispute were not guilty of "clandestine labor"; see Laacher 1999.

5. http://www.schumachersociety.org/cur_grps.html.

6. On the legal aspects of local currencies, see Solomon 1996.

7. Ithaca Hours Local Currency Home Page, June 2001, http://www.ithacahours.org (accessed June 25, 2001). In 2001, to manage the growing volume of participants and transactions, organizers began issuing a yearly HOUR Directory.

8. For a contrasting way of negotiating time's monetary value, see Yakura 2001.

9. Womanshare: A Cooperative Skill Bank, "Statement of Principles," 1999, http://www.angelfire.com/ar2/womanshare/principl.html (accessed June 25, 2001).

10. For an illuminating discussion of local currencies as a political movement challenging neoliberal ideologies by changing consumption patterns, see Helleiner 2000.

References

Akin, David, and Joel Robbins, eds. 1999. *Money and Modernity: State and Local Currencies in Melanesia*. Pittsburgh: University of Pittsburgh Press.

Anteby, Michel. 2003. "The 'Moralities' of Poaching: Manufacturing Personal Artifacts on Factory Floors." *Ethnography* 4:217–39.

Barth, Fredrik. 1967. "Economic Spheres in Darfur." In *Themes in Economic Anthropology*, edited by Raymond Firth, 149–74. London: Tavistock.

Bayon, Denis. 1999. *Les S.E.L., systèmes d'échanges locaux, pour un vrai débat*. Levallois-Perret: Yves Michel.

Biggart, Nicole Woolsey. 1989. *Charismatic Capitalism: Direct Selling Organizations in America*. Chicago: University of Chicago Press.

———. 2001. "Banking on Each Other: The Situational Logic of Rotating Savings and Credit Associations." *Advances in Qualitative Organization Research* 3:129–53.

Binker, Mary Jo. 2000. "Volunteers Use Time Dollars to Help Others." Timedollar Institute, January 21. http://www.timedollar.org/Articles/Articles2000/Points_of_light.htm (accessed June 25, 2001).

Blanc, Jérôme. 2000. *Les monnaies parallèles*. Paris: L'Harmattan.

Bloch, Maurice. 1994. "Les usages de l'argent." *Terrain* 23:5–10.

Bohannan, Paul. 1955. "Some Principles of Exchange and Investment among the Tiv." *American Anthropologist* 57:60–70.

———. 1959. "The Impact of Money on an African Subsistence Economy." *Journal of Economic History* 19:491–503.

Boyle, David. 2000. *Funny Money: In Search of Alternative Cash*. London: Flamingo.

Cahn, Edgar S. 2001. "On LETS and Time Dollars." *International Journal of Community Currency Research* 5. http://www.geog.le.ac.uk/ijccr/5no2.html.

Collins, Randall. 2000. "Situational Stratification: A Micro-Macro Level of Inequality." *Sociological Theory* 18:17–43.

———. 2004. *Interaction Ritual Chains*. Princeton, N.J.: Princeton University Press.

Crittenden, Ann. 2001. *The Price of Motherhood: Why the Most Important Job in the World Is Still the Least Valued*. New York: Metropolitan Books.

Crump, Thomas. 1981. *The Phenomenon of Money*. London: Routledge and Kegan Paul.

Dalton, Melville. 1959. *Men Who Manage: Fusions of Feeling and Theory in Administration*. New York: Wiley.

Darr, Asaf. 2003. "Gifting Practices and Interorganizational Relations: Constructing Obligation Networks in the Electronics Sector." *Sociological Forum* 18:31–51.

DeMeulenaere, Stephen. 2000. "Reinventing the Market: Alternative Currencies and Community Development in Argentina." *International Journal of Community Currency Research* 4. http://www.geog.le.ac.uk/ijccr/4no3.html.

Diehl, Karl. [1930–35] 1937. "Labor Exchange Banks." In *Encyclopaedia of the Social Sciences*, edited by Edwin R. A. Seligman, 7:737–44. New York: Macmillan.

DiMaggio, Paul. 2001. "Introduction: Making Sense of the Contemporary Firm and Prefiguring Its Future." In *The Twenty-First-Century Firm: Changing Economic Organization in International Perspective*, edited by Paul DiMaggio, 3–30. Princeton, N.J.: Princeton University Press.

Durand, Jorge, Emilio A. Parrado, and Douglas S. Massey. 1996. "Migradollars and Development: A Reconsideration of the Mexican Case." *International Migration Review* 30:423–44.

Elshtain, Jean Bethke. 2000. *Who Are We?* Grand Rapids, Mich.: William B. Eerdmans.

England, Paula, and Nancy Folbre. 1999. "The Cost of Caring." In *Emotional Labor in the Service Economy*, edited by Ronnie J. Steinberg and Deborah M. Figart. Special issue, *Annals of the American Academy of Political and Social Science* 561:39–51.

Folbre, Nancy. 2001. *The Invisible Heart: Economics and Family Values*. New York: New Press.

Folbre, Nancy, and Julie A. Nelson. 2000 "For Love or Money—or Both?" *Journal of Economic Perspectives* 14 (Fall): 123–40.

Glover, Paul. n.d. *Hometown Money: How to Enrich Your Community with Local Currency*. Ithaca, N.Y.: Ithaca Money.

Guerriero, Leila. 1996. "Siglo XXI: La vuelta al trueque." *Revista la Nación*, November 3, 44–49.

Guyer, Jane I., ed. 1995. *Money Matters: Instability, Values, and Social Payments in the Modern History of West African Communities*. Portsmouth, N.H.: Heinemann.

Hart, Keith. 1999. *The Memory Bank: Money in an Unequal World*. London: Profile Books.

Heimer, Carol A. 1992. "Doing Your Job and Helping Your Friends: Universalistic Norms about Obligations to Particular Others in Networks." In *Networks and Organizations: Structure, Form, and Action*, edited by Nitin Nohria and Robert C. Eccles, 143–64. Boston: Harvard Business School Press.

Helleiner, Eric. 1999. "Conclusions—The Future of National Currencies." In *Nation-States and Money: The Past, Present and Future of National Currencies*, edited by Emily Gilbert and Eric Helleiner, 215–29. London: Routledge.

———. 2000. "Think Globally, Transact Locally: Green Political Economy and the Local Currency Movement." *Global Society* 14:35–51.

———. 2003. *The Making of National Money: Territorial Currencies in Historical Perspective*. Ithaca, N.Y.: Cornell University Press.

Hirschman, Albert O. 1977. *The Passions and the Interests: Political Arguments for Capitalism before Its Triumph*. Princeton, N.J.: Princeton University Press.

Hondagneu-Sotelo, Pierrette. 2001. *Doméstica: Immigrant Workers Cleaning and Caring in the Shadows of Affluence*. Berkeley: University of California Press.

Indergaard, Michael. 2002. "The Bullriders of Silicon Alley: New Media Circuits of Innovation, Speculation, and Urban Development." In *Understanding the City: Contemporary and Future Perspectives*, edited by John Eade and Christopher Mele, 339–62. Malden, Mass.: Blackwell.

Ingram, Paul, and Peter W. Roberts. 2000. "Friendships among Competitors in the Sydney Hotel Industry." *American Journal of Sociology* 106:387–423.

Kanter, Rosabeth Moss. 1977. *Men and Women of the Corporation*. New York: Basic Books.

Kaufman, Michael T. 1993. "Trading Therapy for Art to Forge a Community." *New York Times*, May 19.

Knorr Cetina, Karin D., and Urs Bruegger. 2002. "Global Microstructures: The Virtual Societies of Financial Markets." *American Journal of Sociology* 107:905–50.

Kuttner, Robert. 1997. *Everything for Sale: The Virtues and Limitations of Markets*. New York: Knopf.

Laacher, Smaïn. 1998. "Economie informelle officielle et monnaie franche: L'exemple des systèmes d'échange locaux." *Ethnologie Française* 28:247–56.

———. 1999. "Nouvelles formes de sociabilités ou les limites d'une utopie politique: L'exemple des systèmes d'échange locale (SEL)." *International Journal of Community Currency Research* 3. http://www.geog.le.ac.uk/ijccr/3no2.html.

Lane, Robert E. 2000. *The Loss of Happiness in Market Democracies*. New Haven, Conn.: Yale University Press.

Latour, Germain. 1999. "Crépuscule de l'état ou l'économie au péril de la république." In *Exclusion et liens financiers*, edited by Jean-Michel Servet, 380–83. Paris: Economica.

Ledeneva, Alena V. 1998. *Russia's Economy of Favours: Blat, Networking and Informal Exchange*. Cambridge: Cambridge University Press.

Lee, Roger. 1996. "Moral Money? LETS and the Social Construction of Local Economic Geographies in Southern England." *Environment and Planning* A28:1,377–94.

Menjívar, Cecilia. 2002. "The Ties That Heal: Guatemalan Immigrant Women's Networks and Medical Treatment." *International Migration Review* 36:437–66.

Morrill, Calvin. 1995. *The Executive Way: Conflict Management in Corporations.* Chicago: University of Chicago Press.

Narotzky, Susana, and Paz Moreno. 2002. "Reciprocity's Dark Side: Negative Reciprocity, Morality, and Social Reproduction." *Anthropological Theory* 2: 281–305.

Neary, Michael, and Graham Taylor. 1998. *Money and the Human Condition.* New York: St. Martin's Press.

Nelson, Julie A. 1999. "Of Markets and Martyrs: Is It OK to Pay Well for Care?" *Feminist Economics* 5:43–59.

Nelson, Margaret K. 2002. "Single Mothers and Social Support: The Commitment to, and Retreat from, Reciprocity." In *Families at Work: Expanding the Boundaries,* edited by Naomi Gerstel, Dan Clawson, and Robert Zussman, 225–50. Nashville, Tenn.: Vanderbilt University Press.

Offe, Claus, and Rolf G. Heinze. 1992. *Beyond Employment: Time, Work, and the Informal Economy.* Cambridge: Polity Press.

Parreñas, Rhacel Salazar. 2001. *Servants of Globalization: Women, Migration, and Domestic Work.* Stanford, Calif.: Stanford University Press.

Parry, Jonathan, and Maurice Bloch, eds. 1989. *Money and the Morality of Exchange.* New York: Cambridge University Press.

Perrot, Etienne. 1999. "La compensation des dettes de SEL." In *Exclusion et liens financiers,* edited by Jean-Michel Servet, 384–91. Paris: Economica.

Pierret, Dorothée. 1999. "Cercles d'échanges, cercles verteux de la solidarité: Le cas de l'Allemagne." *International Journal of Community Currency Research* 3. http://www.geog.le.ac.uk/ijccr/3no2.html.

Powell, Jeff. 2002. "Petty Capitalism, Perfecting Capitalism or Post-Capitalism? Lessons from the Argentinian Barter Network," working paper 357. The Hague: Institution of Social Studies.

Primavera, Heloisa. 1999. "Como formar un primer club de trueque pensando en la economía global." http://www3.plala.or.jp/mig/howto-es.html.

Pryor, Frederick L. 1977. *The Origins of the Economy: Comparative Study of Distribution in Primitive and Peasant Economies.* New York: Academic Press.

Raddon, Mary-Beth. 2003. *Community and Money: Caring, Gift-Giving, and Women in a Social Economy.* Montreal: Black Rose Books.

Rifkin, Jeremy. 2000. *The Age of Access: The New Culture of Hypercapitalism Where All of Life Is a Paid-For Experience.* New York: Tarcher/Putnam.

Rizzo, Pantaleo. 1999. "Réciprocité indirecte et symétrie: L'émergence d'une nouvelle forme de solidarité." In *Exclusion et liens financiers,* edited by Jean-Michel Servet, 401–8. Paris: Economica.

Rowe, Jonathan. n.d. "Life-Enhancing Social Networks for the Elderly." Timedollar Institute, January 2001. http://www.timedollar.org/Applications/Elderly_article.htm (accessed June 25, 2001).

Savdié, Tony, and Tim Cohen-Mitchell. 1997. *Local Currencies in Community Development.* Amherst, Mass.: Center for International Education.

Schroeder, Rolf F. H. 2002. "Talente Tauschring Hannover (TTH): Experiences of a German LETS and the Relevance of Theoretical Reflections." *International Journal of Community Currency Research* 6. http://www.geog.le.ac.uk/ijccr/vol4-6/6toc.htm (accessed July 25, 2003).

Servet, Jean-Michel, ed. 1999. *Une économie sans argent: Les systèmes d'échange local.* Paris: Seuil.

Solomon, Lewis D. 1996. *Rethinking Our Centralized Monetary System: The Case for a System of Local Currencies.* Westport, Conn.: Praeger.

Stone, Deborah. 1999. "Care and Trembling." *American Prospect* 43:61–67.

Thorne, Lorraine. 1996. "Local Exchange Trading Systems in the United Kingdom: A Case of Re-embedding?" *Environment and Planning* A 28(8):1,361–76.

Thrift, Nigel, and Andrew Leyshon. 1999. "Moral Geographies of Money." In *Nation-States and Money: The Past, Present and Future of National Currencies,* edited by Emily Gilbert and Eric Helleiner, 159–81. London: Routledge.

Tilly, Charles. 1984. *Big Structures, Large Processes: Huge Comparisons.* New York: Russell Sage.

———. 1998. *Durable Inequality.* Berkeley: University of California Press.

Tilly, Chris, and Charles Tilly. 1998. *Work under Capitalism.* Boulder, Colo.: Westview.

Trends in Japan. 2001. "Yen Rivals: The Rising Popularity of Local Currencies." Trends in Japan, January 15. http://www.jinjapan.org/trends00/honbun/tj010115.html (accessed July 25, 2003).

Ungerson, Clare. 1997. "Social Politics and the Commodification of Care." *Social Politics* 4:362–81.

Uttal, Lynet. 2002. "Using Kin for Childcare: Embedment in the Socioeconomic Networks of Extended Families." In *Families at Work: Expanding the Boundaries,* edited by Naomi Gerstel, Dan Clawson, and Robert Zussman, 162–80. Nashville, Tenn.: Vanderbilt University Press.

Uzzi, Brian. 1997. "Social Structure and Competition in Interfirm Networks: The Paradox of Embeddedness." *Administrative Science Quarterly* 42:35–67.

Velthuis, Olav. 2003. "Symbolic Meaning of Prices: Constructing the Value of Contemporary Art in Amsterdam and New York Galleries." *Theory and Society* 32:181–215.

Wacquant, Loïc. 1998. "A Fleshpeddler at Work: Power, Pain, and Profit in the Prize Fighting Economy." *Theory and Society* 27:1–42.

———. 2000. *Corps et âme.* Marseilles: Agone.

Walzer, Michael. 1983. *Spheres of Justice: A Defense of Pluralism and Equality.* New York: Basic Books.

Weber, Florence. 1998. *L'honneur des jardiniers.* Paris: Belin.

Williams, Colin C. 1996. "The New Barter Economy: An Appraisal of Local Exchange and Trading Systems (LETS)." *Journal of Public Policy* 16:85–101.

Williams, Joan. 2000. *Unbending Gender: Why Family and Work Conflict and What to Do about It.* New York: Oxford University Press.

Yakura, Elaine K. 2001. "Billables: The Valorization of Time in Consulting." *American Behavioral Scientist* 44:1,076–95.

Zelizer, Viviana. 2000a. "The Purchase of Intimacy." *Law and Social Inquiry* 25: 817–48.

———. 2000b. "How and Why Do We Care about Circuits?" *Accounts* (newsletter of the Economic Sociology Section of the American Sociology Association) 1:3–5.

———. 2001. "Transactions intimes." *Genèses* 42:121–44.

———. 2002a. "Intimate Transactions." In *The New Economic Sociology: Developments in an Emerging Field*, edited by Mauro F. Guillen, Randall Collins, Paula England, and Marshall Meyer, 274–300. New York: Russell Sage.

———. 2002b. "How Care Counts." *Contemporary Sociology* 31:115–19.

———. 2004. "Circuits of Commerce." In *Self, Social Structure, and Beliefs: Explorations in Sociology*, edited by Jeffrey Alexander, Gary T. Marx, and Christine Williams, 122–44. Berkeley: University of California Press.

Znoj, Heinzpeter. 1998. "Hot Money and War Debts: Transactional Regimes in Southwestern Sumatra." *Comparative Studies in Society and History* 40: 193–222.

16

Circuits in Economic Life

Let me explain why economic sociologists should find circuits interesting. I began work on economic circuits about six years ago, but then left the topic aside while writing *The Purchase of Intimacy*. That book did not deal with circuits explicitly, but it did raise the more general questions for which circuits provide a possible answer: through what configurations of interpersonal relations do people carry on valued economic activities, and how do they work?

Not that I have a neat logico-deductive theory of circuits to propose in answer to that question. Within economic sociology, scholars adopt remarkably contrasting styles of work. Some follow a theoretical agenda deliberately from one analysis to the next, advancing the agenda step by step with new arguments and data. Others immerse themselves in a body of observations and evidence, writing up what they see, then gradually clarifying the main points they want to get across. Still others sit in the middle of intellectual fields with a dozen projects buzzing, some of them empirical analyses, some of them critical syntheses, and some of them combinations of the two.

For my part, I find I can only work effectively by first identifying a phenomenon that people do not understand well, then plunging into cases that embody the phenomenon, moving back and forth repeatedly between cases and arguments, only arriving at provisional syntheses through long struggles to reconcile evidence and theory. That is no doubt why most of my work organizes around books, with my articles usually taking shape as offshoots of book projects. What's more, one book project typically leads to the next: writing a book makes me acutely aware of relevant problems I have not solved, and that would be worth solving.

That certainly happened with *The Purchase of Intimacy*. The book examines the interaction of many varieties of intimate relations with many kinds of economic activity, asking how people make them work together despite the frequent fear that each will corrupt the other. As I worked on the book, I saw two things ever more clearly: first, that treating only two-person relations one set at a time missed the large impact of third parties on the forms and qualities of intimacy as well as the character and significance of the economic activity involved; second, that conventional concepts of economic sociology, such as network, hierarchy, market, household, and firm, did not accurately capture the cross-cutting complexity of the social interactions I was examining. That realization brought me back to circuits.

Given this style of thought, I cannot present a neat account of circuits here, much less tell you exactly how I will refine and verify such a theory. Instead, I want to identify the social arrangements I call circuits of commerce, say how they matter to economic life, tell you where to look for them, enumerate some questions we should be asking about them, and sketch an approach to investigating them. Naturally, I will build on cases.

Earlier papers describe three circuitlike phenomena: local monies, caring connections, and clusters within corporations (Zelizer 2000, 2002, 2004, 2005). Instead of elaborating on those three, I begin with two other economic phenomena that are widespread, consequential, multiply invented, and puzzling: migrants' remittance networks and rotating savings and credit associations.

I start with migrants' remittances. How are they widespread, consequential, multiply invented, and puzzling? Remittances consist of money and other resources acquired by migrants at their destinations and sent back to their home communities as support for persons and activities. Remittances most often go to family members who have stayed behind or returned but sometimes also support more distant connections, such as neighbors, priests, and politicians.[1]

They are certainly widespread and consequential. According to the World Bank's latest *Global Economic Prospects*, remittances to developing countries have now passed both development aid and foreign direct investment as sources of international income. Including informal and unrecorded transmissions, World Bank estimates place the total for 2005 at around $250 billion. Remittances appear to have significantly reduced domestic poverty in such low-income countries as Uganda, Bangladesh, Ghana, and Guatemala. Finally, a significant share of all remittances to developing countries—most likely a third or more—flow not from rich countries like the United States, but from poorer countries, for example Russia, to even poorer countries elsewhere (World Bank 2006). Remittances, in short, are having a major macroeconomic impact on the world's lower-income regions—which is, of course, precisely why the World Bank has now taken an interest in them.

It is not just money. Migrants also send back food, clothing, appliances, and other sorts of gifts. In addition, recipients regularly reciprocate by sending food, medicine, and other goods, as well as by helping with the emigrants' responsibilities at the place of origin. Consider the remarkable remittance networks described by Rhacel Parreñas for Filipino families. Mothers as far away as Taiwan, Israel, and Hong Kong not only remit significant portions of their earnings but also maintain regular connections to their families with repeated telephone calls, letters, voice recordings, instant messages, photographs, and visits. What's more, Parreñas discovered, emigrant women closely monitor their households' spending, typically through agreements with their eldest daughters, who act as their mothers' proxies.

The daughter in the Philippines co-manages with her mother a shared bank account, disbursing funds as her mother stipulates. Nineteen-year-old Barbara Latoza, for example, lives with her twelve- and fifteen-year-old brothers while her mother works in Taiwan and sends back monthly remittances from there. She explained to Parreñas:

> I am the one who gets the money from the bank. After that, sometimes my mother calls and tells me how to spend it. She budgets it so that we could afford the household expenses and my tuition. Before I go to withdraw the money, she will call me and tell me what to do with it. (2005, 326)

Filipino mothers are not unique. Across the world and with many cultural variations, migrants create similar systems of mutual control at long distance and over long periods of time. How do they do it? It will not suffice to say simply that absence makes the heart grow fonder. Nor is sending remittance money simply like sending a charitable check for a good cause. These are negotiated, two-way exchanges that build on residues of the past and expectations for the future. Remittance senders and recipients are therefore involved in close social control and coordination. Given our usual cynical assumptions that people who have access to desirable resources will ride free, defect, and cheat in the absence of severe threats and close monitoring, how do these social arrangements maintain themselves?

Rotating savings and credit associations raise parallel puzzles. Once again, across the world and with many cultural variations, people without access to formal banks or credit organize themselves into small, informal saving and lending groups. Whether the money comes from outside lenders or from the members' own savings, such arrangements give substantial sums to one member while other members wait their turns. For instance, most of the migrant Filipino domestic workers interviewed by Parreñas in Los Angeles and Rome had at one time or another belonged to a rotating credit association. Such arrangements often take the name ROSCA, an acronym for Rotating Savings and Credit Association. Worldwide, they appear to draw in women much more frequently than men, probably because men have greater access to conventional forms of capital and credit. Ivan Light describes these thriving financial systems in *The Handbook of Economic Sociology*:

> ROSCA is the generic name for a popular financial system found in many countries of Asia, Latin America, and Africa. Members of a ROSCA, usually numbering 10 to 30, come together monthly or weekly to make a contribution to a common fund, which is lent in turn to each member until all members have received the fund. At that point, the club is disbanded, and a new one formed, usually with substantial continuity of membership. Early recipients of ROSCA funds

are borrowers, who may pay interest to the fund; later recipients are savers, who may receive interest. (2005, 658; see also Biggart 2001)

According to Light, most ROSCAs convey $10,000 or less, but in some cases large amounts of money, sometimes millions of dollars are involved. The money is used to start up businesses, for saving, and for spending. The wonder here is that such collective arrangements frequently work with little default and considerable return for all participants.

Microcredit borrowing groups raise similar puzzles. Phenomenally successful around the world, microcredits also exist in the United States. While some microcreditors lend to individuals, in the case of microcredit borrowing groups, creditors loan small sums of money to a group of borrowers who are unable to get credit from banks. Borrowers often have no preexisting ties but come together for this specific venture. If one member defaults on the loan, the entire group commonly loses its credit. As Denise Anthony remarks, "Given the high-risk characteristics of most borrowers, group failure is surprisingly rare" (2005, 501).

What explains these puzzles? As currently instituted, theories of markets, hierarchies, and networks do not provide an adequate description of these structures, much less a satisfying explanation for their persistence and effectiveness. I see all these economic arrangements, remittances, ROSCAs, and microcredits as instances of a more general but poorly recognized set of economic structures. I call those structures commercial circuits or circuits of commerce in an old sense of the word, where *commerce* meant conversation, interchange, intercourse, and mutual shaping.

How do we recognize a circuit? Is it just a fancy name for networks? No, it has network properties but much more than that. As conventionally understood in economic sociology, neither markets, hierarchies, networks, nor their combinations in firms and organizations come close to identifying the special features of commercial circuits. Nor do circuits qualify as all-embracing communities in the usual sociological sense of the term. Circuits bear greater resemblances to common pool systems as described by Elinor Ostrom (1990) and trust networks as analyzed by Charles Tilly (2005). But neither of those helpful analogies captures the dynamics of circuits. Using the label "Zelizer circuits," Randall Collins asserts:

> Micro-translating economic class shows, not a hierarchical totem-pole of classes neatly stacked up one above another, but overlapping transactional circuits of vastly different scope and content. Because these circuits differ so much in the particularity or anonymity of connections, in the kind of monitoring that is done and in orientation toward economic manipulation or consumption, individuals' experiences of economic relations put them in different subjective worlds, even if these are invisible from a distance. (2004, 268)

In his essay on circuits of commerce for the newly published *International Encyclopedia of Economic Sociology*, Olav Velthuis declares that the concept of circuits "draws attention to the fact that exchange is invariably conducted in particularized social and cultural settings" (2005a, 57). Although the concept has by no means swept the field, scholars on both sides of the Atlantic have started to use the idea of circuits in studies covering the broad range among art markets (Velthuis 2005b), French factory workers (Anteby 2003), Cuzco market women (Seligmann 2004), Brazilian folk religion (Baptista 2005), New York Senegalese migrants (Sagna 2004), Argentine barter networks (Ortiz 2004), U.S. microcredit borrowing groups (Anthony 2003), Silicon Alley and Philadelphia venture capitalists (Indergaard 2002; Mote 2004). Like me, other researchers have sensed that a distinctive form of economic interaction is at work. Circuits of commerce obviously need further investigation.

To identify a circuit, look for the following elements:

- A distinctive set of social relations among specific individuals
- Shared economic activities carried on by means of those social relations
- Common accounting systems for evaluation of economic exchanges, for example, special forms of monies
- Shared meanings that people attach to their economic activities
- A well-defined boundary separating members of the circuit from nonmembers, with some control over transactions crossing the boundary

It is tempting to add a sixth stipulation to the ideal type: mutual awareness of the participants. But that criterion will be difficult to apply. In any case, the "shared meaning" stipulation suffices to distinguish commercial circuits from, say, the set of persons connected by circulation of a particular dollar bill or all the people who cash frequent-flier miles with a given airline.

These circuit characteristics obviously appear in remittance networks and rotating credit arrangements. Both systems qualify unquestionably as commercial circuits. Thinking of remittance circuits, let me briefly take up the five elements one by one, as described by Parreñas:

- What set of distinctive social relations are involved here? Clearly, in the Filipino case we find remittances connecting mothers to their eldest daughters in special ways, but also establishing diverse relations among the mother and her other children, members of the extended household, as well as fathers. Each of these has a somewhat different relationship to the remittance stream: migrant mothers, for instance, rarely delegate financial management responsi-

bilities to husbands or their sons, but they do often remit money
directly to a son designated for his personal use.

- Shared economic activities? Remittances serve the households' current consumption—spent for food, furniture, and other household goods but also for celebratory gifts, such as birthdays or holidays, as well as down payments for homes and savings for the future.
- Accounting system? This is most dramatically represented by the joint bank account, co-managed with the eldest daughter, but more generally built into a household budget; the participants' explicit naming of these complex transactions as "remittances" underlines their special status as an accounting system.
- Remittances convey powerful shared meanings? For Filipino migrant mothers, Parreñas finds, the monies symbolize and enact their caring connections to the family back home. The monies partly define "good" migrant mothering.
- Boundaries separating members of the circuit from those outside? In the Filipino case, kin relations establish those boundaries. In other cases boundary-setting poses greater challenges, as they may include more distant kin, neighbors, friends, children's caretakers, clergy, and even local officials.

Much more generally, notice two remarkable features of such remittance circuits. First, these relations do not simply constitute a fixed table of organization with its prescribed roles: participants are constantly negotiating, contesting, and reshaping their relationships to each other. The process is often contentious, as people struggle not only over who has the right to receive remittances, but over quantities and uses. Parreñas reports, for instance, other members of the extended family's annoyance with migrant mothers for subverting kin authority by sending monies to the eldest daughter and not to them.

Remitters often engage in interventions already familiar from the study of a wide range of monetary practices: earmarking. In this case, earmarking consists not merely of sending an amount of money but also marking that amount for a particular destination, often by endowing it with a specialized name and form. Yen Le Espiritu, who like Parreñas, has looked closely at the remittance experience of Filipino migrants and their families, finds migrants sending money specifically "to help an ailing parent, to finance a sibling's college education, to alleviate an emergency situation, to purchase property, or to provide extra spending money for family members during holidays" (Espiritu 2003, 90). In Rome, Jennifer Jeremillo told Parreñas about her allocation of remittance monies:

> I send 500,000 lira [U.S. $333]. I have to pay for the domestic helper, and then I have a regular allowance for my kids, and then the rest is

for my mother. . . . [M]y parents are using the money to renovate and expand the house. (Parreñas 2001, 112)

Those who remit also earmark their own funds as they run their daily lives: they negotiate what portion of the earnings they will spend on themselves and how much to send back home. Interviewing Hispanic migrants to Miami and Los Angeles in 2002, a Pew Hispanic Center study found not only that almost all respondents reported sending remittances to support families back home but that most gave remittances priority over their bills and expenses in the United States. "Before anything," Mexican emigrant respondent Marisela remarked, "I send them the money because they count on it. Then afterwards I pay the bills, my rent, but the first thing I do is send it" (Suro et al. 2002, 7).

Negotiations over remittances, however, do not always run smoothly. Espiritu describes, for instance, Ruby Cruz's recollection of her parents' bitter disputes over remittances sent to the Philippines:

My dad's always proving himself to his relatives back home. So whenever they ask him for money, he just gives it to them. That makes my mom really, really mad because she worked two jobs so that my brother and me wouldn't have to work when we are in college. But now that money is gone. (Espiritu 2003, 93)

Turning to a second crucial feature of remittances, we see them exerting collective control over the circuit's members. Obviously the forms of negotiation I have just been discussing produce collective control over participants and their relations with each other. In the case of Filipino mothers' collaborations with their eldest daughters, Parreñas shows how the arrangement assured the mothers' control over how her earnings were spent, thus protecting that money from abuse by fathers or other kin. In this instance, the mother and daughter become crucial partners in a very effective and more general system of control.

In such social arrangements, those who fail to meet their obligations first feel sanctions and then exclusion. In both migration remittance systems and rotating credit arrangements participants regularly warn, shame, sanction, and finally expel defaulters or foot-dragging members; they become pariahs (see, e.g., Philpott 1968). In many such systems, the boundary between faithful remitters and defaulters divides upstanding family members from dishonorable exiles, but it also separates households that regularly receive support of their migrant members from less fortunate households at the origin.

Beyond definition and description, what general properties will we find in circuits? For further investigation, I propose these features:

- Circuits have special properties that constrain members' economic behavior.
- They lend coherence to economic activity that neither purely individual interest nor general market principles can explain.
- Intuitively, but sometimes even consciously, participants make significant efforts to create, maintain, and enter such configurations.
- Circuits create an institutional structure that reinforces credit, trust, and reciprocity within its perimeter but organizes exclusion and inequality in relation to outsiders.

In my earlier papers on circuits, I described local monetary systems, relations involving the provision of personal care, and (much more briefly) circuits within corporations. In addition to more work on these varieties of commercial circuits, we could certainly look at relatively obvious, sharply bounded cases such as communes, prisons, company towns, asylums, concentration camps, military units, trade diasporas, religious cults, and isolated communities. For a greater challenge, we should turn to the informal economy, including sex work, street vendors, garage sales, and commerce in contraband. Commercial circuits on college campuses have not attracted the attention they deserve. All of them raise important further questions, including the following:

- The conditions under which, and the processes by which, circuits (rather than, say, firms or thin and loosely bounded networks) form and take up significant economic activities
- How they maintain themselves over time, change, and disappear
- How boundaries work, both in controlling members' behavior and in signaling differences between insiders and outsiders
- How the extent and character of inequality within circuits affect their operation—and therefore whether circuits disintegrate beyond some threshold of inequality
- To what extent and in what ways members become aware of their membership in circuits, give it a name, or otherwise represent that membership, and build that awareness into their mutual influence

These questions define a promising research frontier. Economic sociologists have already produced voluminous research on organizations, networks, and dyadic economic relations. They have not so far conducted much substantial work on circuits. Even if commercial circuits turn out to be more complex and variable than my simple sketch indicates, clearly they occupy a space—theoretical and empirical—adjacent to organizations, networks, and dyadic economic relations. Commercial circuits deserve more sustained analytical attention than they have received so far.

Notes

Viviana A. Zelizer, "Circuits in Economic Life," *European Economic Sociology Newsletter* 1 (November 2006): 30–35. Reprinted with permission.

1. For an extensive bibliography on remittances, see Zelizer and Tilly 2006.

References

Anteby, Michel. 2003. "Factory 'Homers': Understanding a Highly Elusive, Marginal, and Illegal Practice." *Sociologie du Travail* 45:453–71.

Anthony, Denise. 2003. "Social Capital in the Creation of Financial Capital: Social Control in Micro-Credit Borrowing Groups." Paper presented at the American Sociological Association annual meetings, Atlanta, August.

———. 2005. "Cooperation in Microcredit Borrowing Groups: Identity, Sanctions, and Reciprocity in the Production of Collective Goods." *American Sociological Review* 70:496–515.

Baptista, José Renato de Carvalho. 2005. "No candomblé nada é de graça . . . : Estudo preliminar sobre a ambiguidade nas trocas no contexto religioso do Candomble." *Rever Revista de Estudos da Religiao* 1:68–94.

Biggart, Nicole Woolsey. 2001. "Banking on Each Other: The Situational Logic of Rotating Savings and Credit Associations." *Advances in Qualitative Organization Research* 3:129–53.

Collins, Randall. 2004. *Interaction Ritual Chains*. Princeton, N.J.: Princeton University Press.

Espiritu, Yen Le. 2003: *Home Bound: Filipino American Lives across Cultures, Communities, and Countries*. Berkeley: University of California Press.

Indergaard, Michael. 2002. "The Bullriders of Silicon Alley: New Media Circuits of Innovation, Speculation, and Urban Development." In *Understanding the City: Contemporary and Future Perspectives*, edited by John Eade and Christopher Mele, 339–62. Oxford: Blackwell.

Light, Ivan. 2005. "The Ethnic Economy." In *The Handbook of Economic Sociology*, edited by Neil J. Smelser and Richard Swedberg, 650–77. New York: Russell Sage Foundation; Princeton, N.J.: Princeton University Press.

Mote, Jonathan. 2004. "Sometimes Connect: Circuits and the Culture of Social Networks." Paper presented at the 2004 annual meeting of the American Sociological Association, San Francisco, August.

Ortiz, Jacqueline. 2004. "Networks, Circuits, and Hierarchies: The Argentine Global Barter Market, 1995–2003." Paper presented at the meetings of the Society for the Advancement of Socio-Economics, Washington, D.C., July 8–11.

Ostrom, Elinor. 1990. *Governing the Commons: The Evolution of Institutions for Collective Action*. Cambridge: Cambridge University Press.

Parreñas, Rhacel Salazar. 2001. *Servants of Globalization*. Stanford, Calif.: Stanford University Press.

———. 2005. "Long Distance Intimacy: Class, Gender and Intergenerational Relations between Mothers and Children in Filipino Transnational Families." *Global Networks* 5:317–36.

Philpott, Stuart B. 1968. "Remittance Obligations, Social Networks and Choice among Montserratian Migrants in Britain." *Man*, n.s., 3:465–76.

Sagna, Lamine. 2004. "Migration, Money, and Religion: Confronting Zelizer's Circuits within New York's Senegalese Community." Paper presented at the Center for Migration and Development, Princeton University, March 30.

Seligmann, Linda J. 2004. *Peruvian Street Lives: Culture, Power, and Economy among Market Women of Cuzco*. Urbana: University of Illinois Press.

Suro, Robert, Sergio Bendixen, B. Lindsay Lowell, and Dulce C. Benavides. 2002. "Billions in Motion: Latino Immigrants, Remittances and Banking." Washington, D.C.: Pew Hispanic Center and the Multilateral Investment Fund. http://www.iadb.org/mif/v2/files/nov22b.pdf (accessed October 13, 2005).

Tilly, Charles. 2005. *Trust and Rule*. Cambridge: Cambridge University Press.

Velthuis, Olav. 2005a. "Circuits of Commerce." In *International Encyclopedia of Economic Sociology*, edited by Jens Beckert and Milan Zafirovski, 57–58. Oxford: Routledge.

———. 2005b. *Talking Prices: Symbolic Meanings of Prices on the Market for Contemporary Art*. Princeton, N.J.: Princeton University Press.

World Bank. 2006. *Global Economic Prospects 2006: Economic Implications of Remittances and Migration*. Washington, D.C.: World Bank.

Zelizer, Viviana. 2000. "How and Why Do We Care about Circuits?" *Accounts* (newsletter of the Economic Sociology Section of the American Sociological Association) 1 (Fall): 3–5.

———. 2002. "La construction des circuits de commerce: Notes sur l'importance des circuits personnels et impersonnels." In *Exclusion et liens financiers: Rapport du Centre Walras*, edited by Jean-Michel Servet and Isabelle Guérin, 425–29. Paris: Economica.

———. 2004. "Circuits of Commerce." In *Self, Social Structure, and Beliefs: Explorations in Sociology*, edited by Jeffrey C. Alexander, Gary T. Marx, and Christine Williams, 122–44. Berkeley: University of California Press.

———. 2005. "Circuits within Capitalism." In *The Economic Sociology of Capitalism*, edited by Victor Nee and Richard Swedberg, 289–322. Princeton, N.J.: Princeton University Press.

Zelizer, Viviana, and Charles Tilly. 2006. "Relations and Categories." In *The Psychology of Learning and Motivation*, edited by Arthur Markman and Brian Ross, 1–31. San Diego: Elsevier.

PART SIX

Appraising Economic Lives: Critiques and Syntheses

During 1990–91, I participated in an exciting and pioneering seminar on economic sociology sponsored by the Russell Sage Foundation. Of the sixteen members regularly attending the seminar, I was the only woman. At the time, this was not unusual. Two decades later, the gender composition of the field has certainly changed, but only moderately. True, young women scholars are publishing exceptional work, teaching economic sociology, and also taking up leadership positions within the field's organizations. Yet consider the following: among the thirty-four economic sociologists identified by Richard Swedberg in 1997 as "key people" in the field, only four were women. Ten years later, in an equivalent list of thirty-one "key authors" compiled by French scholars Bernard Convert and Johan Heilbron (2007) we find five women. Or take the forty-five authors in the 1994 first edition of Neil Smelser and Richard Swedberg's foundational text, *The Handbook of Economic Sociology*. Nine were women. By its second edition in 2005, the ratio had not changed substantially: of forty-three authors, eleven were women (Smelser and Swedberg 1994, 2005; see also Zelizer 2000; England and Folbre 2005).

Somehow, until 1998, when I found myself for the first time introducing the field to graduate students, I had never stopped to analyze its gender demographics or the consequences for what we were studying at the time. In fact, beyond gender awareness, teaching economic sociology drew me into closer observation and critique of the field. Not only as a token woman but also a cultural and historical specialist interested in such topics as households, childhood, consumption, and morality, I had at times wondered whether the work I was doing, so distant from mainstream concern with firms and corporations, counted as economic sociology at all. That changed as the field matured. New generations of energetic young scholars benefited from the excellence of past research but went beyond familiar canons, opening up novel vistas for the study of economic activity.

Stimulating conversations with colleagues and students about the field's transformations inspired me to write some twenty papers and notes published between 1992 and 2008 dealing with various features of economic sociology. The four essays in this final section report a few of those reflections.

While in no way attempting to offer yet another detailed assessment of the field, let me provide some background for the chapters, briefly placing them within current developments.

The first couple of articles offer overviews of economic sociology while the other two turn to specific issues that have only recently gained visibility within the field. Almost twenty years separate the first two essays, "Beyond the Polemics on the Market" and "Pasts and Futures of Economic Sociology." Their arguments necessarily reflect some of the changes that took place during that time. The first paper was prepared for a seminal interdisciplinary conference on the study of economy and society coorganized by a sociologist, Roger Friedland, and an anthropologist, A. F. Robertson, in the spring of 1988 (Friedland and Robertson 1990). I presented the second paper at an American Sociological Association annual meeting session organized by Nicole Woolsey Biggart in 2005 to discuss new directions in economic sociology (Biggart 2007). The large, enthusiastic audience of mostly young scholars attending the event certified the field's vibrancy.

In the late 1980s, as I wrote "Beyond the Polemics on the Market," the "new" economic sociology was gaining coherence and strength. Arthur Stinchcombe, for example, had published his *Economic Sociology* in 1983, and two years later Mark Granovetter published his pathbreaking article on embeddedness. My essay, written during a year as a Russell Sage Foundation fellow, grew out of impatience with the constant cross-disciplinary rehashing of standard rebukes against conventional market models. It was time, I felt, to move forward by dropping tired polemics and instead formulating alternative explanations of markets and more broadly, economic activity. I proposed a "multiple markets" model geared toward empirical analyses of types and patterns of social structural and cultural market variation.

By 2005, when I wrote the second overview paper, much had changed. The field now bubbled with an exciting spectrum of alternative explanations for economic activity. Instead of slumping into middle-age complacency, the no-longer-so-new "new" economic sociology thrived with novel ideas and approaches. "Pasts and Futures" highlights some of those advances—including an update on the social study of money. The publication of two influential editions of *The Handbook of Economic Sociology* plus the field's first encyclopedia (Beckert 2005) in addition to two major specialized newsletters and, since 2001, a thriving section within the American Sociological Association further attest to an international surge in the field's productivity and institutionalization during those years.

The second set of chapters concentrates on consumption and ethics. Previously marginalized, both topics are now gradually finding their place within economic sociology's intellectual agenda. Prepared for *The Handbook of Economic Sociology*'s 2005 edition, "Culture and Consumption" reviews and critiques the study of consumption. Having earlier investigated historical and contemporary features of consumer processes, I gladly accepted the invitation from the *Handbook*'s editors to contribute to their volume. In the United States, the study of consumption continued to be curiously exiled from economic sociology's core as a somewhat fuzzy field of cultural activity, a world of symbols and meanings separate from the sturdier zone of production and distribution. The task remained mostly the turf of British social scientists engaged in multiple analyses of consumption, albeit with a significant culturalist bent. My essay challenges consumption's ungrounded segregation into culture's expressive domain. Drawing from empirical studies on households, ethnic-racial communities, and retail settings, I propose a relational approach that studies the place of consumption in the formation, maintenance, and transformation of interpersonal relations. Considering the social as well as the political significance of consumption, its further inclusion in serious conversations by economic sociologists should be encouraged and welcomed. Indeed, in recent years, specialists in consumption and economic sociologists have begun building those necessary bridges.

The last chapter in this section, "Ethics in the Economy," was prepared at the request of Jens Beckert for a special journal issue on economic sociology and ethics that he edited. I had long been intrigued by the impact of ethical concerns on economic activity. Starting with the life insurance industry's struggles to confront what many saw as their ethically dubious marketing of life, issues of ethics and morality repeatedly emerged in my various projects. Certainly, ethical quandaries loomed large when I examined the world of consumption: does relentless materialistic pursuit of consumer goods deplete personal values? Can ethical consumption exist—and if so, when and how? Do marketers surrender ethical principles in their pursuit of consumers? For this article, I eventually settled on an analysis of business codes of ethics as a limited but strategic window into a variety of broader concerns. Codes reveal, for instance, which ethical issues become hotly contested within organizations and how they vary across organizations and over time.

More generally, however, sustained investigation of economic ethics has long remained hampered by hostile-worlds views that situate ethics in a separate domain from hard-nosed rationality. Ethics and morality, from this perspective, should be left to philosophers' speculations. The underlying assumption, moreover, is that if ethics and economic activity do come into contact, the latter would necessarily drive out ineffectual ethical concerns.

In a welcome reversal, a determined set of visionary young scholars galvanized around issues of morals and markets has begun bridging the worlds of ethics and economics. Their explorations range from exchanges of blood and organs (Healy 2006) to corporate responsibility (Bartley 2005), and include systematic treatment of business ethics (Abend 2008). Some are even returning with fresh insights to moral issues raised by the life insurance industry (Chan 2009; Quinn 2008). Albeit from a decisively political stance, French students of economic life set an important precedent for such attempts with their longer-standing concerns with ethical economies.

Beyond specific targets and topics, however, these efforts matter greatly by providing crucial alternatives to standard tropes concerning effects of commodification on social life. Rather than seeing the market as inevitably obliterating morality, they show how markets themselves are constituted by varying moralities. As Marion Fourcade and Kieran Healy elegantly argue in their influential essay "Moral Views of Market Society," this new literature opens up "the black box of morality," providing insights into the construction of markets' moral categories (2007, 305). Markets themselves thus become moralizing entities, as people implement and broadcast moral schemes via various types of economic transactions.

To be sure, the flourishing of twenty-first-century economic sociology is not restricted to its incorporation of consumption or morality. Those two arenas, however, provide revealing windows into broader normative and political concerns raised by what to some observers appears as an overly benign or unduly optimistic vision of economic lives. Indeed, in speaking to audiences in the United States and elsewhere, as well as in reviews of my work, I often confront a set of challenging questions. By debunking absolute notions of pernicious, amoral markets, including consumer markets, or by insisting on the social meanings of money, am I, some worry, providing convenient apologies for hard-nosed free-market advocates? Likewise, by promoting a view of connected lives with its intertwining of economic transactions and personal ties, are we not dangerously underestimating devastating extensions in commodification? What kind of superior policy implications, if any, can we draw from a connected-lives approach?

Consider, for instance, Louis Edgar Esparza and Pablo Lapegna's concern about what they see as the connected-lives approach's normative "plasticity." Their insightful critique of *The Purchase of Intimacy* comes with a lovely history. First drafted for a Stony Brook University graduate economic sociology seminar led by Michael Schwartz, the paper then became part of an "authors-meet-critics" session exceptionally organized by the Stony Brook graduate student team for the Eastern Sociological Society 2006 meetings. In their critique (which along with two other papers appeared in *Sociological Forum* 2007), Esparza and Lapegna contend that, once we move beyond relatively benign mixtures of intimacy and economic activity at the microlevel, a connected-lives approach could justify damaging neoliberal market intrusions into our private lives. They invoke Karl Polanyi's *The Great Transformation* for evidence that "the intermingling of economic transactions and intimate relationships could destroy the ties of solidarity in the latter by amplifying the scope of the former" (Esparza and Lapegna 2007, 611).

Philippe Steiner, a leading French economic sociologist, agrees. In an overall sympathetic essay comparing my work with Polanyi's, Steiner chides me for insufficiently confronting what he calls the "Polanyian fear" of increased commodification (2009, 103). So too, Nancy Folbre, in her perceptive commentary on *The Purchase of Intimacy*, returns to Polanyi's concern with negative consequences of disembedded markets, including fraud and exploitation. "Even if instrumental reasoning is not literally toxic to affective connections," she reasons, "it may reduce their relative importance" (2007, 7).

Are these critics right to worry? Only in part. I certainly never set out to promote a particular political agenda. As this book reveals, in *The Purchase of Intimacy* and elsewhere, I have instead pursued the more modest aim of explaining how people integrate economic activity into the wider range of their social relations, and with what consequences for those social relations. Yet the normative and policy implications of my arguments undoubtedly suggest a fundamental break from well-established prescriptions targeting markets and money's increasing dominance as key sources for contemporary social and moral ills. It challenges the unquestioned premise that once you mediate transactions with markets you will necessarily have uniform, powerful, and negative effects.

Let's be clear: a connected-lives perspective certainly does not deny markets' or money's advance or their potential for harm. Unmistakably, over the past few centuries an increasing range of goods and services entered the market, affecting producers and consumers unequally. True also that injustice and oppression often result from capitalists' pursuit of their narrow advantage, and yes, many a combination of intimacy with economic activity produces unfairness, exploitation, and unhappiness.

Reformers often respond to these inequities with a hostile-worlds conclusion: markets corrupt. Their serious error consists of uncritical allegiance to an ideology built on flawed causal reasoning. Whenever "the" market or money crosses the line into personal or—worse still—intimate territory, the ideology claims, the effects are uniformly devastating. Such absolutism dangerously ignores social realities, shutting out serious debate about the variable social and moral impact of different kinds of markets and monetary transactions. When and why, we should ask, do certain economic arrangements produce injustice and which enhance welfare?

Paradoxically, despite good intentions, adherence to hostile-worlds ideology—much like devotion to free-market ideology—sometimes ends up justifying unfair economic conditions, such as inadequate compensation for those involved in carework or other types of intimate labor.[1] Indeed, for the first time in my career, I was drawn into policy-oriented discussions by feminist scholars concerned with the often perverse effects on women's welfare of sentimentalized concerns over market intrusion. As Folbre herself writes, "the exclusion of non-market work from the definition of 'the economy' had distributional consequences that marked the influence of collective interests: it weakened women's claims on the income of other family members and the larger income of the polity" (2009, 263).

By promoting clearer descriptions and explanations, a connected-lives approach to the intersection of economic activity and personal relations, including intimacy, prods scholars, lawmakers, and policy experts to identify normatively superior combinations. The scope of the perspective goes well beyond feminist concerns. As Polanyi-expert Fred Block astutely observes, "If one expands the political point beyond women, one ends up at a Polanyian point—that winning certain rights and protections through politics and law can make market relations a sphere of choice rather than coercion. Polanyi does not want an end to the labor market; he wants employees to have certain rights and protections that would allow them to avoid exploitation and oppression at work" (2009, personal communication).

In a lucid review of *The Purchase of Intimacy*, legal scholar Martha Ertman (2009) offers specific evidence from yet another controversial domain, the market for genetic materials. Ertman systematically lays out how the book's argument could be translated into judicial decision making for that field. Here the debate centers on the relative property rights of patients who provide genetic materials for research and medical treatment versus those of the biotechnology companies or research universities that utilize such materials. Ertman points out the contradictions in decisions made by judges and legislators who, invoking hostile-worlds arguments, reject patients' property claims to their own body tissues as unseemly marketization, while they allow biotechnology companies or other institutions to profit by granting them the very property rights that they deny to the persons providing those genetic materials. She recommends a more nuanced legal approach that would instead recognize patients' rights to their own bodies, including bodily products, not only as a more just but an ethically superior option, thus linking "dignity and markets." If applied properly, Ertman contends, a connected-lives framework could increase fairness in court decisions that address genetic materials and, more broadly, in cases involving other kinds of contested commodification.

The four essays in this section attempt to further such delicate and often controversial discussions and proposals for how to properly organize economic lives.

NOTE

1. For an outstanding related discussion of public/private ideological dichotomies' political and social effects, see Gal and Kligman 2000.

REFERENCES

Abend, Gabriel. 2008. "A Genealogy of Business Ethics." Ph.D. diss., Northwestern University.

Bartley, Tim. 2005. "Corporate Accountability and the Privatization of Labor Standards: Struggles over Codes of Conduct in the Apparel Industry." *Research in Political Sociology* 14:211–44.

Beckert, Jens, ed. 2005. *International Encyclopedia of Economic Sociology*. Oxford: Routledge.

Biggart, Nicole Woolsey, ed. 2007. Special issue, "Coming and Going in Economic Sociology." *American Behavioral Scientist* 50 (April).

Chan, Cheris. 2009. "Creating a Market in the Presence of Cultural Resistance: The Case of Life Insurance." *Theory and Society* 38:271–305.

Convert, Bernard, and Johan Heilbron. 2007. "Where Did the New Economic Sociology Come From?" *Theory and Society* 36 (March): 31–54.

England, Paula, and Nancy Folbre. 2005. "Gender and Economic Sociology." In *The Handbook of Economic Sociology*, edited by Neil Smelser and Richard Swedberg, 2nd ed., 627–49. New York: Russell Sage Foundation; Princeton, N.J.: Princeton University Press.

Ertman, Martha M. 2009. "For Both Love and Money: Viviana Zelizer's *The Purchase of Intimacy*." *Law and Social Inquiry* 34 (Fall): 1017–37.

Esparza, Louis Edgar, and Pablo Lapegna. 2007. "The Limits of the Connected Lives Theory." *Sociological Forum* 22:606–11.

Folbre, Nancy. 2007. "Care Worries." *Accounts* (newsletter of the Economic Sociology Section of the American Sociological Association) (Spring): 6–8.

———. 2009. *Greed, Lust, and Gender: A History of Economic Ideas*. New York: Oxford University Press.

Fourcade, Marion, and Kieran Healy. 2007. "Moral Views of Market Society." *Annual Review of Sociology* 33:285–311.

Friedland, Roger, and A. J. Robertson, eds. 1990. *Beyond the Marketplace: Rethinking Economy and Society*. New York: Aldine de Gruyter.

Gal, Susan, and Gail Kligman. 2000. *The Politics of Gender after Socialism*. Princeton, N.J.: Princeton University Press.

Granovetter, Mark. 1985. "Economic Action and Social Structure: A Theory of Embeddedness." *American Journal of Sociology* 91:481–510.

Healy, Kieran. 2006. *Last Best Gifts*. Chicago: University of Chicago Press.

Quinn, Sarah. 2008. "The Transformation of Morals in Markets: Death, Benefits, and the Exchange of Life Insurance Policies." *American Journal of Sociology* 114 (November): 738–80.

Smelser, Neil, and Richard Swedberg, eds. 1994. *The Handbook of Economic Sociology*. New York: Russell Sage Foundation; Princeton, N.J.: Princeton University Press.

———. 2005. *The Handbook of Economic Sociology*. 2nd ed. New York: Russell Sage Foundation; Princeton, N.J.: Princeton University Press.

Steiner, Philippe. 2009. "Who Is Right about the Modern Economy: Polanyi, Zelizer, or Both?" *Theory and Society* 38:97–100.
Stinchcombe, A. L. 1983. *Economic Sociology*. New York: Academic Press.
Swedberg, Richard. 1997. "New Economic Sociology: What Has Been Accomplished, What Is Ahead?" *Acta Sociologica* 40:161–82.
Zelizer, Viviana A. 2000. "A Gendered Division of Labor." *European Economic Sociology Newsletter* 1 (June): 2–5.

17

Beyond the Polemics on the Market

Establishing a Theoretical and Empirical Agenda

The market is no longer a safe place to theorize. Its long-standing neutrality is being increasingly violated by scholars from various disciplines who refuse to treat the market as a purely economic institution. Among others, White (1981) asks "Where Do Markets Come From?"; Granovetter (1985) explores the social "embeddedness" of economic life; Barber (1977) demystifies the "absolutization" of the market; Agnew (1986) traces the emergence of a market culture in Britain and America; and in *The Rise of Market Culture*, Reddy (1984) boldly argues that the market is nothing but a cultural construction. And while most economists remain hostile or simply indifferent to this reassessment of the market, others become its outspoken collaborators. For instance, Lester Thurow (1983) in *Dangerous Currents*, his harsh critique of conventional economic theory, decries the "absurd" notion that "economic events never have social consequences and that social events never have economic implications." *Homo economicus* himself has been demoted to the status of a "rational fool" by Sen (1977), another "heathen" economist.

In the process, the market is recapturing portions of its history, its culture, and its social context. To be sure, this is not a sudden intellectual revolution, nor are the current critics of the market absolute pioneers. Durkheim and Weber set the agenda at the turn of the century, by empirically disputing a dominant economic ideology that was largely indifferent to the importance of noneconomic variables. In his *Protestant Ethic*, Weber traced the independent impact of religious ideas, values, and attitudes on economic activities. Durkheim's writings demonstrated that the market could not be conceptualized as simple self-interest but involved the "institution" of the contract. This "noncontractual element" regulated types of socially approved contracts as well as the expected behavior of the contracting parties, aside from their self-interest. Reacting against nineteenth-century utilitarian models, Durkheim and Weber stressed the role of nonutilitarian, nonmaterial social forces. Theirs was a pathbreaking attempt to integrate the economic and noneconomic dimensions of social life.

But, as Parsons and Smelser recognized half a century later in *Economy and Society* (1956), the potential synthesis of economic and sociological approaches had never materialized. Nor did *Economy and Society* make great inroads with economists. In an excellent essay, Holton points out that while the book was reviewed in economic periodicals, "the general reception given to it was a highly critical and skeptical one" (1986, 95). Thus, although in 1955, Wilbert Moore had detected an "upsurge" in "social economics" (1955, 2), by 1963 Smelser acknowledged that economic sociology was stagnating or developing only in "shreds and patches" (1963, 2).[1] A decade later, Boulding observed that still "one of the most interesting of unasked questions of intellectual history" was how economics remained "an abstract discipline void almost of any cultural context" (1973, 47). Or any historical past, for that matter. As Barber (1977) discovered in his overview of economic theorists, economists remain remarkably silent when it comes to documenting the market as a social institution. Even Schumpeter's voluminous *History of Economic Analysis*, notes Barber, includes no section on "the market."

Interdisciplinary efforts by economists and sociologists in the 1970s were similarly frustrating to the advancement of economic sociology. Consider, for instance, an international seminar on sociological economics held in Paris in 1977, where sociologists and economists met to discuss a possible "bridge" between the two disciplines. There was little doubt about the disciplinary bearings of that intellectual bridge. For socioeconomics was never concerned with theory integration but only with bold theory expansion—testing "the explanatory power of the economic approach" (Lévy-Garboua 1979, 1) in traditionally sociological domains. Microeconomists thus developed novel theories of fertility, racial discrimination, crime, education, marriage, and divorce without any fundamental alteration of the economic model. Characteristically, the lead paper by Gary Becker at the Paris conference explicitly dismissed noneconomic factors such as values and social norms as "ad hoc and useless explanations of behavior" (Lévy-Garboua, 1979, 18).

Economists, as one of their own recently confessed, are "imperialists by nature. We view the rational choice model as the uniquely correct way to explain and interpret human behavior and we apply it without apology to questions once thought to be the exclusive province of other disciplines. Equally, we are disinclined to view facts and theories from other disciplines as relevant for economic behavior" (Frank 1987a, 1,307).[2] But "economist-bashing" is not enough to understand the relative dormancy of economic sociology. Sociologists are not blameless intellectual victims. As Granovetter has perceptively noted, sociologists have "implicitly accepted the presumption that 'market processes' are not suitable objects of sociological study because social relations play only a frictional and disruptive role, not a central one, in modern societies" (1985, 504). Thus sociologists have surrendered the market to economists, or else (as with Homans and Blau) they have further bolstered the dominance of a market model by adopting economic analytical tools for their own research.

Since the mid-1970s, however, there have been signs of change. In a shift that Swedberg et al. identify as the start of a "new economic sociology" (1987,

206), a number of sociologists breached established disciplinary "turf" to study the social structuring of economic phenomena, ranging from labor markets to financial markets, contracts, and banking. (For an overview of these studies, see Swedberg 1987.) In the late 1980s, the time seems right for an even more aggressive sociological "invasion" of the market. In fact, novel and exciting critiques of conventional market models are being conducted not only by sociologists but also by anthropologists, social historians, political scientists, economic psychologists, philosophers, legal theorists, and by economists themselves. (See, for example, McCloskey 1985; Solow 1985; Buchanan 1985; Gudeman 1986; Goode 1986; Etzioni 1987; Lea et al. 1987; Radin 1987.) Even the vocabulary changes to treat the cultural and social significance of the market, as scholars discuss "market culture," "the morality of spending," the "social life of things," or "the culture of consumption."

Research and academic institutions are responding to the growing concern for a systematic understanding of the interplay between the economy and noneconomic factors in the modern world. For instance, an interdisciplinary Center for Economy and Society was recently organized at the University of California at Santa Barbara. In New York, the Russell Sage Foundation sponsors a program in behavioral economics, which focused initially on decision making but is now moving toward the study of more socially embedded economic processes. And at Boston University, the Institute for the Study of Economic Culture supports research on the interrelation of economics and culture.

This new effort to disturb the alleged moral and social neutrality of the market goes beyond cataloging complaints. For the theoretical case against conventional economic models has been made. Almost any scholar interested in the field can quickly enumerate the mistaken assumptions of purely macro- or microeconomic models, namely: (1) that modern markets are autonomous, self-subsistent institutions, undisturbed by extraeconomic cultural and social factors; (2) modern markets are not only "free" but powerful determinants of social institutions and cultural values; (3) noneconomic factors are thus dependent on the market and irrelevant as explanatory factors; (4) individual behavior is best explained by the ahistorical rational choice model.

Turning this tired theoretical polemic into a working dialogue will contribute to the specification of theoretical and empirical guidelines for a better understanding of the interplay between the market and noneconomic factors in modern society. We must explore the best ways to "complicate" economic life, as Hirschman (1986) recommends. What do we mean precisely by the interrelationship between economic and noneconomic factors? Which noneconomic factors do we single out, and how? What kinds of empirical research can better demonstrate the independent impact of cultural or social forces? How do we analyze the historical, cultural, and social variability of markets?

This paper will examine some of the recent interdisciplinary attempts to develop theoretical alternatives to purely economic models of the market. The very definition of the market is at stake. In contrast to the neoclassical assumption of the market as a universal and exclusive form of economic arrangement, market revisionists define the market as one among many different possible social arrangements, such as barter or gift exchange, that involve economic processes (see Polanyi 1957; Barber 1977). The market is thus one institutionalized type of social relations involving consumption, production, and exchange. Its essence is the rational calculation of costs and benefits and the regulation of exchange by the price mechanism.

Critiques of the economic market model take three quite different general orientations:

1. The "boundless market" model: an ideological critique of the power of the market that centers on the destructive social, moral, and cultural effects of commoditization.
2. The "subordinate market" model: a more fundamental rejection of the accepted instrumentalist paradigm of markets by demonstrating the ongoing cultural, structural, and historical constraints of the supposedly autonomous market. This model offers two alternative conceptions of the market:
   (a) The cultural alternative: the market as a set of meanings.
   (b) The social-structural alternative: the market as a set of social relations.
3. The "multiple markets" model: the market as the interaction of cultural, structural, and economic factors.

I will argue that the "multiple markets" model represents the most useful alternative to the neoclassical paradigm of the market. As an interactive model, it precludes not only economic absolutism but also cultural determinism or social-structural reductionism in the analysis of economic processes. Thus, although it shares some of the underlying theoretical assumptions of the "subordinate market" model, the "multiple markets" approach rejects one-dimensional idealist or instrumental interpretations. It is thus conceptually equipped to develop a fuller sociological alternative to the economic model of the market. The market is analyzed as one category of social relations that involves consumption, production, and exchange under a variety of cultural and structural settings. The theoretical and empirical "puzzle" thus turns on determining the social and cultural variation of these "multiple markets."

The concept of "multiple markets" also provides a positive point of theoretical departure for economic sociology. It shifts away from the useful but ultimately negative task of "correcting" the economic model by bringing out the noneconomic elements of economic life. This "add-on" corrective technique in fact allows economics to define the terms of the discourse. The result is not just a matter of rhetorical advantage, but this approach perpetuates a conceptual flaw. Economic processes should not be set in opposition to extraeconomic cultural and social forces but understood as one special category of social relations, much as is kinship or religion. Thus economic phenomena, although partly autonomous, are interdependent with a system of meanings and structures of social relations.

The paper will first discuss some underlying assumptions of the three general critiques of the market model and then turn to the analysis of specific studies that reflect alternative conceptions of the market. My goal is to delineate major *types* of responses rather than to present an exhaustive review of the literature. Nor is my selection a perfectly representative sample of all recent work. It is, however, a useful sample to illustrate major theoretical alternatives.

TESTING THE LIMITS OF THE MARKET

Each of the three alternative conceptions of the market involves a set of distinct fundamental assumptions. For instance, the moral revisionism of the "boundless market" model is based on the following five premises:

1. Acceptance of the dominance of the market in modern society.
2. A dichotomization between the market as an amoral cash nexus and sacred, social, and personal noninstrumental values.
3. The market as an ever-expanding and destructive force that, by penetrating all areas of life, makes the market/nonmarket dichotomy dangerously precarious. Once market exchange enters, self-interest displaces all noninstrumental social ties.
4. The intrusion of the market into personal, social, and moral areas of life leads to their degradation or dissolution.
5. The only "protection" of noneconomic values is made possible by (a) an "insulation" process: the existence of normative constraints that preserve certain items outside the cash nexus or (b) external legal and institutional constraints or prohibitions that deliberately restrict the market.

The "subordinate market" model and the "multiple markets" model share a different set of assumptions:

1. There is an interpenetration rather than a dependence of noneconomic factors with the market.
2. The dichotomization assumed by (2) above thus breaks down. The market is not an amoral self-subsistent institution but a cultural

and social construct. The market has (a) its own set of values and norms and (b) is interdependent with other institutions and values.

3. The constraints of market power are not limited to the exceptional protective devices described in (5) above, which exclude certain items from the cash nexus. "Market imperialism" (Walzer 1983, 120) is routinely dethroned by cultural and social influences. In fact, no market transaction can be "protected" from extraeconomic influences.

4. Market exchange is therefore not homogenous and ahistorical, but variable. As Barber points out: "As a result of these interdependencies with, or constraints from, both values and other institutional structures, economic exchange can be patterned in different ways" (1977, 23).

The "multiple markets" model, however, differs in a fundamental way from the "subordinate market" conception. As an interactive model, it not only rejects the option of a "boundless" market unrestrained by culture and social structure but also the notion of a "subordinate" market determined by either culture or social structure. Although, to be sure, cultural and social structural analysts recognize in an ad hoc manner the existence of alternative explanatory factors, the central argument is frequently reductionist.

Let us now examine specific applications of these three models and determine to what extent these analyses offer successful alternatives to the purely economic model of the market.

The "Boundless Market": A Moral Critique

The "self-destruction" thesis of market society, as Hirschman calls it (1986, 109), carries with it the intellectual imprint of nineteenth- and early twentieth-century fears. Marx was deeply concerned over the dehumanizing effects of a greedy "cash nexus." A corrupt "fraternization of impossibilities" was created in bourgeois society when personal values became purchasable: "Since money, as the existing and active concept of value, confounds and exchanges all things, it is . . . the confounding and compounding of all natural and human qualities" ([1844] 1964, 169). And Simmel, in his *Philosophy of Money*, suggests a radical contradiction between a monetary economy and personal values, which initially obstructs the expansion of the market into certain areas of exchange. But, argues Simmel, this "protection" of human values is precarious and is constantly threatened by the invasion of the cash nexus: "The more money dominates interests and sets people and things into motion, the more objects are produced for the sake of money and are valued in terms of money, the less can the value of distinction be realized in men and in objects." Inevitably, concludes Simmel, pricing will "trivialize" or destroy value. For instance, in prostitution, marriage for money, or bribery, where the market directly intersects with personal values, monetization leads to a "terrible degradation" of those values ([1900] 1978, 365–66, 380, 390–92, 407). The sale of nonmarketable commodities is thus the ultimate conquest by the market in the modern world.

A number of contemporary social observers have recaptured this sense of moral gloom and social vulnerability. To them, the late twentieth-century market is more powerful and potentially damaging than ever before. Consider one of the more prominent and influential spokesmen for the "boundless market" model: Richard Titmuss. In *The Gift Relationship*, his path-breaking, cross-national comparison of voluntary and commercial systems of providing human blood for transfusions, Titmuss assails the laws of the marketplace with specific empirical evidence. His book argues that commercial systems of distributing blood are not only less efficient than voluntary blood donation, but, more important, they are morally dangerous to the social order. Transform blood into a commercial commodity, insists Titmuss, and soon it will become "morally acceptable for a myriad of other human activities and relationships also to exchange for dollars and pounds" (1971, 198). In the process, "the possessive egoism of the marketplace" would displace social and moral considerations (1971, 13). Rejecting market exchange, Titmuss argues that only reciprocal or gift forms of exchange are suitable for certain items or activities: blood transfusions, organ transplants, foster care, and participation in medical experimentation, among others.

Similar concerns with what he diagnoses as the "depleting moral legacy" of the modern market are expressed by political economist Fred Hirsch. The market, argues Hirsch in his compelling monograph *Social Limits to Growth*, weakens the moral and social foundations of modern society. Traditional forms of social responsibility and cooperation cannot resist "the opposing mainstream of the market ethos" (1978, 143). As he explores the social threat posed by the "commodity bias" of both capitalist and socialist markets, Hirsch identifies a "commercialization effect," which diminishes the quality of a product or activity by supplying it commercially. It does matter, argues Hirsch, whether we buy a product or activity or we exchange it without calculation or profit. For instance, a "consumerist approach" to sexual unions—ranging from prostitution to marriage contracts—corrodes all romance and trust: "Orgasm as a consumer's right rather rules it out as an ethereal experience" (1978, 101).

Thus Titmuss and Hirsch dramatize the moral dangers of a boundless market by suggesting that, if left unchecked, a sort of institutional "instinct" drives the market to breach any restraining boundary and therefore pollute any object or relationship. The outcome is a generalized social decline of altruism and mutual obligation. In an intriguing essay, Kopytoff, an anthropologist, explains it as "a drive inherent in every exchange system toward optimum commoditization—the drive to extend the fundamentally seductive idea of exchange to as many items as the existing exchange technology will comfortably allow" (1986, 72).

Within this mode of analysis, the only recognized limit to the inexorable "drive to commoditization" (Kopytoff 1986, 72) is the normative or legal preservation of selected items or activities outside the cash nexus, as with blood in Titmuss's case. For Kopytoff, this "singularization" of certain objects or relations is a fundamental cultural counterdrive to the "onrush of commoditization" (1986, 73). The "singularization" drive is theoretically close to what Walzer identifies as "blocked exchanges" (1983, 97). The market, recognizes Walzer, can easily become "a sphere without boundaries, an unzoned city—for money is insidious, and market relations are expansive" (1983, 119). To restrict this potential "market imperialism," we "block" certain values from "wrongful" monetary exchange. We "fix" the boundaries of the market by a selective cultural censorship of the use of money. But this "protection" against the market, admits Walzer, is only a cultural Band-Aid: black-markets, for instance, however illegitimate, signal the breakdown of "blocked exchanges."

Moral critics of the "boundless market" thus raise nightmarish visions of a fully commoditized world. But do they provide any alternative to the established instrumental model of modern markets? Often movingly and sometimes accurately, these moral critics warn about the dehumanizing effects of marketing social ties, but, ironically, their outrage does not essentially challenge established views of the market. Titmuss and Hirsch, much like conventional economists, in fact accept the unlimited reach of the market, ignoring its cultural and social structural constraints. From their perspective, the market may be "blocked" or obstructed but is ultimately able to "escape" cultural or social restrictions. Thus the model of a powerful, autonomous instrumental market persists. There is no theoretical argument that fundamentally questions its limits.

THE "SUBORDINATE MARKET":
TOWARD A SOCIOLOGICAL INTERPRETATION

A different set of critics find the accepted paradigm of a boundless market empirically incorrect and theoretically implausible. So they dwell less on the expansion of the cash nexus and more on its limits. As the puzzle changes, so do the questions. It is no longer how do we stop the market? but how do we account for the illusion of market dominance? And rather than identifying the moral constraints of an amoral market, the focus shifts to the morality of the marketplace. Which values shape the market? How do social ties and interaction transform economic transactions? What are some of the historical and cultural variations of market exchange?

The preliminary answers to these queries present two alternative models with which to understand the market: (1) the cultural alternative that explores the market as a constructed set of meanings and (2) the social-structural alternative that defines the market as a network of social relations.

The Cultural Alternative

Here we find the new cultural biographers of the market, breaking through the ahistorical utilitarian facade of economic interpretation. For too long, complains Agnew, the history of the market has been conceived "as a calculable rather than an interpretable phenomenon" (1986, 1). We must understand, argues Wuthnow, "the morality of the marketplace" (1987, 81). The culturally indifferent, timeless market is thus treated as a culturally meaningful and historically variable system of economic exchange. Interestingly, those few economists engaged in professional "whistle-blowing" join the cultural critics of the market. Dissatisfied with the explanatory limitations of the economic model, they grasp, in an ad hoc way, at cultural factors. For instance, in his essay "Toward the Development of a Cultural Economics," Boulding explicitly lobbied for the study of "the complex cultural reality" that underlies the "abstractions of demand and supply" (1973, 47). Or consider Sen's use of the concept of "commitment" in his compelling critique of the rational choice model. Commitment is vaguely defined as "being closely connected with one's morals . . . covering a variety of influences from religious to political" (1977, 329). Hirschman's (1986) argument "against parsimony" in economic discourse is a more specific plea to include values in the explanation of behavior.

How is culture to be injected into the market? First, by understanding the market as a normative structure. What kinds of values underlie market exchange? How do they emerge? How do market values affect social life? Economic rationality in the marketplace, for instance, is a normative prescription. Second, the cultural "life" of market exchange is shaped by extra-economic values that modify the utilitarian orientation of the market.

Let us consider three types of strategies to bring culture into the market.

TAUSSIG AND AGNEW: MARKET CULTURE AS A SET OF COMMODIFIED MEANINGS

Taussig's analysis of Bolivian tin miners in *The Devil and Commodity Fetishism in South America* (1986) and Agnew's (1986) intriguing study of the market and the theater in Britain and America from 1550 to 1750 use different historical settings to examine the formation of a market culture, or as Taussig dubs it, "a commoditized apprehension of reality" (1986, 10). What does market culture mean in this analysis? For Agnew it consists of "the fundamental structures of meaning and feeling [that were] framed around the characteristic problems and prospects of an expansive market system" (1986, 1). Market culture emerges as a response to a market economy: to render "intelligible, acceptable, and controllable the socially and culturally subversive implications of the 'free' market" (1986, 5). But if the market is no longer amoral, its culture remains ultimately immoral—a collaborator in the commodification of the modern world. As Taussig puts it, "The advance of market organization not only tears asunder feudal ties and strips the peasantry of its means of production but also tears asunder a way of seeing." In the process, "the perception of the socially constituted self gives way to the atomized perception of the isolated maximizing individual" (1986, 121).

SAHLINS AND REDDY: THE MARKET AS CULTURAL CAMOUFLAGE

Here market culture moves to theoretical center stage. Culture is not an adaptation to a utilitarian world, argues Sahlins, but instead it is "culture which constitutes utility" (1976, viii). In *Culture and Practical Reason*, Sahlins pierces through the bourgeois "illusion" of a world run by material rationality by exposing the cultural basis of rationality (1976, 210). Ironically, utilitarianism is such a convincing cultural script that participants of the modern world accept it as a concrete reality: "the basic symbolic character of the process goes on entirely behind the backs of the participants—and usually of the economists as well" (1976, 213). How is the meaningful backbone of capitalist society so successfully concealed? In part, suggests Sahlins, because "the illusion has a material basis" (1976, 210). Capitalism is a symbolic process, but its symbolism is indeed primarily economic. Whereas in primitive society, kinship relations are the dominant site for symbolic production, in bourgeois society, "material production is the dominant locus of symbolic production" (1976, 212).

Reddy is an even bolder cultural revisionist than Sahlins. *The Rise of Market Culture: The Textile Trade and French Society, 1750–1900*, uses the development of the French textile industry as a text to rewrite the history of the market as a grand cultural hoax. On the first page Reddy sets the record straight: "In contrast to what we normally hear, market society did not come into being in Europe in the nineteenth century." Instead, argues Reddy, nineteenth-century society created a powerfully persuasive market culture that deluded people into believing that markets existed when they did not and that defined social relationships "exclusively in terms of commodities and exchanges when they continued to involve so much more" (1984, 3). Traditional critics of the market add to the mirage by assuming the reality of a market society. Polanyi's (1944) classic critique of the nineteenth-century self-subsistent market, for instance, traces the eventual failure of that economic system but never disputes its initial success.

For Reddy, Polanyi is documenting the vanishing of a mirage. The market system never succeeded because it could not overcome the countervailing power of extraeconomic factors—emotional, political, familial, and technical. Yet, argues Reddy, we remained entrapped by a market culture that camouflages the historical persistence of a nonutilitarian moral economy. (For a very different perspective on the "triumph" of economic ideology, see Dumont 1977.)

Summing up, cultural critics modify the utilitarian understanding of the market by treating its previously invisible culture. Yet, paradoxically, in some respects they remain traditionalists. Market culture emerges from their analysis but is stigmatized by the same ideological censure reserved for the amoral market. In this cultural paradigm, the market may appear as a meaningful system, but its system of meanings is still corrosive and destructive of social life.

Let us now consider a third set of cultural studies that pose a still more direct challenge to the utilitarian model of the market.

MATERIAL CULTURE: THE MARKET AS A CULTURAL RESOURCE

The recent takeover of consumption from economists by anthropologists, sociologists, and social historians has turned the study of consumer goods into an intriguing test case of the power of cultural analysis. As new questions are being asked about modern consumer society, the unfolding answers directly challenge the utilitarian, individualistic understanding of commodities. Researchers are no longer satisfied with determining what people buy, how much they buy, or the utility of their purchases. Instead they turn to the symbolic meaning of those purchased goods, asking "why people want goods" (Douglas and Isherwood 1979, 15). The intent, as Appadurai says in his introduction to *The Social Life of Things*, a collection of essays on the cultural context of commodity exchange, is to "demystify the demand side of economic life" (1986, 58). Consumption, argues Appadurai, should be approached as "eminently social, relational, and active rather than private, atomic, or passive" (1986, 31).

To be sure, this social analysis of consumption was pioneered by Veblen ([1899] 1953) almost a century ago. But Veblen's analysis was more a social critique of consumerism than a cultural analysis of goods. Parsons and Smelser's *Economy and Society* (1956) moved toward a sociology of consumption, yet their analysis did not prompt a development of the field. In fact, as Holton points out, the theoretical "discovery" of consumption as a symbolic process "represents one of the most under-appreciated elements of Parsonian economic sociology" (1986, 58).

Sahlins's *Culture and Practical Reason* and Douglas and Isherwood's *The World of Goods* were turning points in the study of material culture. Boldly appropriating consumption as an anthropological intellectual "good," both books show the fallacy of a purely economic atomistic model. Consumption, as defined by Douglas and Isherwood, became "the very arena in which culture is fought over and licked into shape" (1979, 57). Sahlins's wonderful analysis of American choices of food and clothing serves as very concrete evidence of "the reproduction of culture in a system of objects" (1976, 178). What we choose as food or what we discard as inedible, what we wear and when we wear it, become, from this perspective, a "veritable map . . . of the cultural universe" (1976, 179). For if the capitalist economy is a "cultural system," capitalist commodities are tangible evidence of cultural classifications (see also Fox and Lears 1983).

But the recent literature on consumption goes beyond establishing the symbolic meaning of consumer goods. More fundamentally still, it turns the uncritical ideological assumption that a modern market economy will necessarily commoditize all nonmaterial values into an arguable empirical question: What precisely is the impact of consumer goods on cultural values? What is the relationship between what we believe and what we buy? As Schudson contends in his study of advertising, "Goods themselves are not (only) the enemies of culture and not (only) the debasement of culture and not (only) something foisted unwillingly upon defenseless consumers" (1984, 160). He suggests a distinction between materialistic values and "a materials-intensive way of life, which may use goods as means to other ends" (1984, 143).

In *Material Culture and Mass Consumption*, Daniel Miller puts forth an even more radical revisionist argument, turning consumption into a tool for cultural survival rather than cultural surrender. For too long, Miller contends, we have accepted "blanket assumptions concerning the negative consequences of the growth of material culture" (1987, 3). We have mistakenly concluded that an emphasis on goods "is itself inevitably inimical to the development of communal and egalitarian social relations of a positive nature." Instead, argues Miller, consumption has the potential "to produce an inalienable culture" (1987, 17). It can promote rather than corrode "social cohesion and normative order" (1987, 197).

Is Miller's argument simply a contemporary revival of the eighteenth-century "*doux-commerce*" thesis described by Hirschman, where commerce was promoted as "a powerful moralizing agent," the economic ticket to a "good society"? (1986, 109). Not really, for Miller is turning the effects of material consumption—whether positive or negative—into a researchable puzzle rather than a necessary conclusion, seeking to specify which conditions "appear to promote, as opposed to those which appear to prevent, the development of the positive forms of consumption as a process" (1987, 18). There are, argues Miller, "myriad strategies" of consumption that have developed "to overcome the alienatory consequences of mass consumer culture"

(1987, 209; see also Csikszentmihalyi and Rochberg-Halton 1981; Campbell 1987; McCracken 1988).

Some of the empirical analysis is being provided by social historians who document the making of a consumer culture. Horowitz's *The Morality of Spending* is, for instance, a fascinating account of changing attitudes toward consumption in the United States between 1870 and 1940. Although primarily an intellectual history of the moral response toward consumption by prominent nineteenth- and early twentieth-century social critics and social scientists, the book also provides compelling insights into an unfolding consumer culture. We see a society struggling to construct proper rules for spending money. Traditional primary sources are used in novel ways. Budget studies, for instance, turn out to be not just quantifiable indexes of a particular standard of living but interpretable sources for understanding the meaning of a particular way of life.

Thus household budget studies, which mushroomed between 1875 and the late 1930s, were, as Horowitz discovered, not simply economic statements but "morality plays," dramatizing the moral significance of consumption and drawing cultural boundaries between legitimate and illegitimate expenses. Recent studies of immigrant groups also document the meaningful appropriation of consumption (see, e.g., Ewen 1985; Peiss 1986). Reversing the traditional understanding of consumption as homogenizing and destroying immigrant culture, the recent literature looks at the ways groups use goods to add meaning to their lives.

THE CULTURAL ALTERNATIVE: SUMMING UP

By declaring the market cultural "territory," studies of market culture and material culture raise a theoretical alternative to the purely instrumental understanding of the modern market. These studies show that (1) the market is a cultural and not just an economic structure; (2) commoditization does not destroy subjectivity, but rather values shape material life; (3) consumption, as a particular case of economic behavior, is not just a cultural process but a cultural resource, providing new meanings to an industrial society.

But if the cultural alternative breaks out of the accepted instrumental paradigm, it falls into a different theoretical trap by overly subjectivizing the reality of the market. The market is indeed a cultural construct, but it is not only that. Reducing the market to an abstract set of meanings excludes the material, institutional, and social reality of economic life. Yet while some writers do acknowledge the interaction of cultural meanings with social-structural factors, the focus is on the independent impact of meaning.[3] The cultural approach thus needs a better connection to class systems, family structure, gender, age, and other such structural factors. As Preteceille and Terrail argue in a contemporary Marxist study of consumption, "However interesting one may find the ideas of culturalists . . . who declare themselves to be dealing exclusively and directly with the daily practice outside the sphere of production, the values invested in it and their symbolic logic, these propositions will never cover the whole reality" (1985, 71). (For an insightful analysis of fashion that does include both cultural and social-structural factors, see Barber 1952.)

The more tolerant approach to consumption also runs the risk of replacing traditional ideological censure with a revisionist ideological complacency, minimizing the power of market forces and dominant groups to constrain social and individual life and to restrict the construction of meaning with the rigors of economic necessity. As Preteceille and Terrail warn, "Consumption is certainly not an innocent affair" (1985, 68).

Finally, the cultural alternative is begging for a more coherent understanding of market culture. What do we mean by market culture? Is it a set of ideas or is it values, or norms, or ideology?

While cultural critics treat the market as a system of meanings, a different set of analysts disregard meaning in their theoretical revamping of the economic model. Let us now turn to the structural critique of the market.

The Social-Structural Alternative

Sociologists of the 1980s, contends Granovetter, "are much more interested in social structure, flows of information and influence, networks of social relations, and the exercise of power" than in cultural values (1981, 37). Indeed, while anthropologists and social historians build a cultural analysis of markets, the sociology of economic life has put meaning aside to focus on the social structure of market processes. A sociological approach, whether presented by social network analysts (Granovetter 1985; Burt 1983; White 1981) or in the macrolevel comparative argument developed by Stinchcombe (1983), puts forth a primarily rationalistic, structural interpretation of economic life. Culture lingers on as a relic of a dangerous Parsonian past, interfering, suggests Granovetter, with current attempts to establish a dialogue between economists and sociologists. Economists are put off by the mistaken vision of a sociological world composed of "actors so constrained by their values and ideas about what is proper that they move through life like automatons" (Granovetter 1981, 37).

Thus Granovetter's important argument on the "embeddedness" of economic action is restricted to the constraints of networks of social relations. Similarly, White defines markets as social structures, "tangible cliques of producers observing each other" (1981, 543). Where does culture fit into this perspective? Only exceptionally, argues Granovetter, in cases that clearly defy economic rationality, such as tipping. Otherwise, appeals to "generalized morality" risk "calling on a generalized and automatic response." The assumption of rational action oriented to a variety of goals remains a more useful explanation of behavior than the "automatic application of 'cultural' rules" (Granovetter 1985, 489, 506).

To be sure, the social-structural approach contributes important information to the understanding of economic life. And it adds an indispensible structural grounding to the overly culturalist models of the market. After all, we do not live in a purely invented world, and structural analysis specifies some of the nonnormative constraints of cultural designs. Granovetter's own sociological analysis of income differences (1981) is a splendid example of how sociology can contribute to the understanding of a specific market process. But it need not be at the expense of the cultural dimension.

The "Multiple Markets" Model: An Interactive Alternative

Cultural and social-structural critiques offer powerful corrections to the instrumental model of the market but still have not developed a convincing alternative model. The next step is to plot a theoretical middle course between cultural and social-structural absolutism designed to capture the complex interplay between economic, cultural, and social-structural factors. It is, to be sure, simpler to propose such a theoretical agenda than to specify precisely how an interactive model should be constructed. In concrete, empirical cases, how do we demonstrate the complex interaction between economic and noneconomic factors? A sociological model should, for instance, identify types and patterns of social-structural and cultural variation in "multiple markets."

That has been the goal of my own research: working toward a "multiple markets" model through a series of empirical case studies—first on life insurance, then the market for children, and now a study of "special monies." In *Morals and Markets: The Development of Life Insurance in the United States* (1983), I worked out this problem in a very preliminary way by documenting the effects of noneconomic factors in the development of a major American economic institution. I chose life insurance because it forcefully represents the intersection of monetary interests with sacred concerns. How did life insurance entrepreneurs successfully establish monetary equivalences for life and death? The history of insuring life is therefore also a case study of the noneconomic aspects of economic behavior.

Morals and Markets stressed the cultural response to life insurance, examining changing attitudes to the monetary evaluation of human life as well as the effect of changing cultural definitions of risk and gambling on the development of life insurance. But it also included the effect of structural factors, exploring, for instance, the strains of shifting from a gift-type system of social exchange in assisting the bereaved to an impersonal market system. Life insurance revolutionized not just the meaning of death but also its management. Friends, neighbors, and relatives, who had relieved the economic misery of the eighteenth-century widow, were replaced by a profit-making bureaucracy.

Pricing the Priceless Child: The Changing Social Value of Children (1985) built on *Morals and Markets* but examined more directly the interaction between economic and noneconomic factors, specifically between the market or price (defined as economic worth) and personal and moral values. The book traces the social construction of the economically "useless" but emotionally "priceless" child in the United States between 1870 and 1930. It examines three major institutions directly involved with the economic and sentimental valuation of child life: children's insurance, compensation for wrongful death of children, and adoption and the sale of children. The book shows that the changing relationship between the economic and sentimental value of children resulted in a unique pattern of valuation of child life. While economic criteria determined both the "surrender" value of children at death and their "exchange" value in the nineteenth century, the price of the twentieth-century child had to be set exclusively by its sentimental worth. Children's insurance policies, compensation awards, and the sale price of an adoptive child became unusual types of markets, regulated in part by noneconomic criteria.

As with *Morals and Markets, Pricing the Priceless Child* looks at the effect of cultural factors redefining the value of children in the United States, but it is not exclusively a cultural analysis. Attention is also given to how social-structural factors, such as class and family structure, interact with both the price and value of children. Beyond the analysis of how noneconomic factors constrain, limit, and shape different markets, both books challenge the assumptions of the "boundless market" model about the inevitable social effects of a market economy. The cases of life insurance and the pricing of children show that the process of rationalization and commodification of the world has its limits, as the market is transformed by social, moral, and sacred values.

My current study, *The Social Meaning of Money*, represents a third stage in this research program: a theoretical and empirical analysis of the social functions of money. Classic interpretations of the development of the modern world portray money as a key instrument in the rationalization of social life. Money, as the most material representation of the market, is defined as the ultimate objectifier, homogenizing all qualitative distinctions into an abstract quantity.

In keeping with the idea of a "multiple markets" model, I propose a model of "special monies" that counters the utilitarian model of "market money" by introducing different fundamental assumptions in the understanding of money. First, while money does serve as a key rational tool of the modern economic market, it also exists outside the sphere of the market, profoundly shaped by cultural and social-structural factors. Second, while the economic model assumes that all monies are the same in the modern world, the "special monies" model assumes that there is a plurality of different kinds of monies, each "special money" shaped by a particular set of cultural and structural factors and thus qualitatively distinct. "Market money" does not escape these extraeconomic influences but is in fact one type of a "special money" subject to particular social and cultural influences. Using historical data from the United States from the 1870s through the 1930s, I examine qualitative distinctions between four different types of "special monies": domestic money, gift money, institutional money, and sacred money. Different cultural and social settings introduce special forms of controls, restrictions, and distinctions in the uses, users, allocation, regulation, sources, and meanings of money.

For too long, the study of economic life has been monopolized by economists. But theoretical polemics alone are not enough to take it away from them. Shifting paradigms involves the creation of alternative explanations based on painstaking empirical research. It has been my argument in this paper that the current alternatives to the economic model are overly dichotomized into cultural or social-structural arguments. We should therefore aim toward an interactive theoretical model that will explore and explain the complex historical, cultural, and social-structural variability of economic life.

Notes

Viviana A. Zelizer, "Beyond the Polemics on the Market: Establishing a Theoretical and Empirical Agenda," *Sociological Forum* 3 (Fall 1988): 614–34. Reprinted with permission.

1. For an excellent historical account of the slow development of economic sociology, see Swedberg 1987.

2. Frank himself is an imaginative, unorthodox economist critical of the "narrow rationalist view" (1987b, 21) that ignores the role of emotions in motivating behavior. Yet, while recognizing the empirical importance of nonrational factors, Frank incorporates emotions into a utilitarian theoretical framework. His concept of "shrewdly irrational" behavior suggests that in certain situations moral sentiments are not entirely irrational but in fact a more efficient strategy to achieve material success than rational, self-interested calculation. The "new institutional economics" also departs from neoclassical economics by its empirical concern with social institutions. But, as Granovetter (1985, 505) points out, this new perspective remains theoretically loyal to economics by arguing that institutions emerge and persist as efficient solutions to economic problems.

3. On the limitations of "culturalist" reductionism more generally, see Alexander 1987, 302–9.

References

Agnew, Jean-Christophe. 1986. *Worlds Apart: The Market and the Theater in Anglo-American Thought, 1550–1750*. Cambridge: Cambridge University Press.

Alexander, Jeffrey C. 1987. *Twenty Lectures: Sociological Theory since World War II*. New York: Columbia University Press.

Appadurai, Arjun. 1986. "Introduction: Commodities and the Politics of Value." In *The Social Life of Things: Commodities in Cultural Perspective*, edited by Arjun Appadurai, 3–63. Cambridge: Cambridge University Press.

Barber, Bernard. 1952. "Fashion in Women's Clothes and the American Social System." *Social Forces* 31:124–31.

———. 1977. "The Absolutization of the Market: Some Notes on How We Got from There to Here." In *Markets and Morals*, edited by G. Dworkin, G. Bermant, and P. Brown, 15–31. Washington, D.C.: Hemisphere.

Boulding, Kenneth E. 1973. "Toward the Development of a Cultural Economics." In *The Idea of Culture in the Social Sciences*, edited by Louis Schneider and Charles Bonjean, 47–64. Cambridge: Cambridge University Press.

Buchanan, Allen. 1985. *Ethics, Efficiency, and the Market*. Totowa, N.J.: Rowman and Allanheld.

Burt, Ronald. 1983. *Corporate Profits and Cooptation*. New York: Academic Press.

Campbell, Colin. 1987. *The Romantic Ethic and the Spirit of Modern Consumerism*. Oxford: Basil Blackwell.

Csikszentmihalyi, Mihaly, and Eugene Rochberg-Halton. 1981. *The Meaning of Things*. Cambridge: Cambridge University Press.

Douglas, Mary, and Baron Isherwood. 1979. *The World of Goods*. New York: Norton.

Dumont, Louis. 1977. *From Mandeville to Marx: The Genesis and Triumph of Economic Ideology*. Chicago: University of Chicago Press.

Etzioni, Amitai. 1987. "How Rational We?" *Sociological Forum* 2:1–20.

Ewen, Elizabeth. 1985. *Immigrant Women in the Land of Dollars: Life and Culture on the Lower East Side, 1890–1925*. New York: Monthly Review Press.

Fox, Richard, and T. J. Jackson Lears, eds. 1983. *The Culture of Consumption: Critical Essays in American History, 1880–1980*. New York: Pantheon Books.

Frank, Robert H. 1987a. Book review. *Journal of Economic Literature* 25:1,307–8.

———. 1987b. "Shrewdly Irrational." *Sociological Forum* 2:21–41.

Goode, William J. 1986. "Individual Choice and the Social Order." In *The Social Fabric*, edited by James F. Short Jr., 39–62. Beverly Hills, Calif.: Sage.

Granovetter, Mark. 1981. "Toward a Sociological Theory of Income Differences." In *Sociological Perspectives on Labor Markets*, edited by Ivar Berg, 11–47. New York: Academic Press.

———. 1985. "Economic Action and Social Structure: The Problem of Embeddedness." *American Journal of Sociology* 91:481–510.

Gudeman, Stephen. 1986. *Economics as Culture*. London: Routledge and Kegan Paul.

Hirsch, Fred. 1978. *Social Limits to Growth*. Cambridge, Mass.: Harvard University Press.

Hirschman, Albert. 1986. *Rival Views of Market Society*. New York: Viking.

Holton, Robert J. 1986. "Talcott Parsons and the Theory of Economy and Society." In *Talcott Parsons on Economy and Society*, edited by Robert J. Holton and Bryan S. Turner, 27–105. London: Routledge and Kegan Paul.

Horowitz, Daniel. 1985. *The Morality of Spending*. Baltimore: Johns Hopkins University Press.

Kopytoff, Igor. 1986. "The Cultural Biography of Things: Commoditization as Process." In *The Social Life of Things: Commodities in Cultural Perspective*, edited by Arjun Appadurai, 64–91. Cambridge: Cambridge University Press.

Lea, Stephen E. G., Roger Tarpy, and Paul Webley. 1987. *The Individual in the Economy*. New York: Cambridge University Press.

Lévy-Garboua, Louis, ed. 1979. *Sociological Economics*. London: Sage.

Marx, Karl. [1844] 1964. *The Economic and Philosophic Manuscripts of 1844*. New York: International Publishers.

McCloskey, Donald. 1985. *The Rhetoric of Economics*. Madison: University of Wisconsin Press.

McCracken, Grant. 1988. *Culture and Consumption*. Bloomington: Indiana University Press.

Miller, Daniel. 1987. *Material Culture and Mass Consumption*. New York: Basil Blackwell.

Moore, Wilbert E. 1955. *Economy and Society*. New York: Doubleday.

Parsons, Talcott, and Neil J. Smelser. 1956. *Economy and Society*. New York: Free Press.

Peiss, Kathy. 1986. *Cheap Amusements: Working Women and Leisure in Turn-of-the-Century New York*. Philadelphia: Temple University Press.

Polanyi, Karl. 1944. *The Great Transformation*. Boston: Beacon Press.

———. 1957. "The Economy as Instituted Process." In *Trade and Market in the Early Empires*, edited by Karl Polanyi, Conrad M. Arensberg, and Harry W. Pearson. New York: Free Press.

Preteceille, Edmond, and Jean-Pierre Terrail. 1985. *Capitalism: Consumption and Needs*. New York: Basil Blackwell.

Radin, Margaret. 1987. "Market Inalienability." *Harvard Law Review* 100:1849.

Reddy, William M. 1984. *The Rise of Market Culture: The Textile Trade and French Society, 1750–1900*. Cambridge: Cambridge University Press.

Sahlins, Marshall. 1976. *Culture and Practical Reason*. Chicago: University of Chicago Press.

Schudson, Michael. 1984. *Advertising: The Uneasy Persuasion*. New York: Basic Books.

Sen, Amartya. 1977. "Rational Fools: A Critique of the Behavioral Foundations of Economic Theory." *Philosophy and Public Affairs* 6:317–44.

Simmel, Georg. [1900] 1978. *The Philosophy of Money*. Translated by Tom Bottomore and David Frisby. London: Routledge and Kegan Paul.

Smelser, Neil J. 1963. *The Sociology of Economic Life*. Englewood Cliffs, N.J.: Prentice-Hall.

Solow, Robert M. 1985. "Economic History and Economics." *American Economic Review* 75:328–31.

Stinchcombe, Arthur L. 1983. *Economic Sociology*. New York: Academic Press.

Swedberg, Richard. 1987. "Economic Sociology: Past and Present." *Current Sociology* 35:1–221.

Swedberg, Richard, Ulf Himmelstrand, and Göran Brulin. 1987. "The Paradigm of Economic Sociology." *Theory and Society* 16:169–213.

Taussig, Michael T. 1986. *The Devil and Commodity Fetishism in South America*. Chapel Hill: University of North Carolina Press.

Thurow, Lester. 1983. *Dangerous Currents*. New York: Random House.

Titmuss, Richard M. 1971. *The Gift Relationship*. New York: Vintage Press.

Veblen, Thorstein. [1899] 1953. *The Theory of the Leisure Class*. New York: New American Library.

Walzer, Michael. 1983. *Spheres of Justice*. New York: Basic Books.

White, Harrison C. 1981. "Where Do Markets Come From?" *American Journal of Sociology* 87:517–47.

Wuthnow, Robert. 1987. *Meaning and Moral Order*. Berkeley: University of California Press.

Zelizer, Viviana A. 1983. *Morals and Markets: The Development of Life Insurance in the United States*. New Brunswick, N.J.: Transaction.

———. 1985. *Pricing the Priceless Child: The Changing Social Value of Children*. New York: Basic Books.

18

Pasts and Futures of Economic Sociology

Economic sociology has gone through astonishing changes in the past twenty-five years. From a simultaneous critique of, and complement to, neoclassical economics, it has become a rich, self-sustaining field. It has begun to generate or incorporate serious alternatives to neoclassical economics. These changes have deeply affected my own attitude toward, and relationship to, economic sociology.

In fact, a funny thing happened to me on the way to economic sociology. For my entire career, I have worked on different economic processes, with books on how life insurance became acceptable, on the valuation of children, on interpersonal monetary practices, and more recently on the economy of intimate social relations, as well as shorter forays into such eminently economic topics as consumption and children's work. For years, no one, including me, called what I was doing economic sociology.

In a peculiar sense, they were right. The economic sociology that was growing up twenty to twenty-five years ago clung closely to mainstream economics, either extending its main ideas to ostensibly more sociological subjects, or identifying social contexts that constrained economic activity—still mostly assumed to behave according to precepts of neoclassical economics. It dealt almost exclusively with firms and markets, those favorite subjects of economists. It concentrated on what we can call extension and context accounts.

Extension theorists applied relatively standard economic models to apparently noneconomic processes, like religious congregations, household behavior, or professional sports teams. Context analysts looked at standard economic phenomena, such as labor markets, commodity markets, or corporations, showing how social organization as context shaped the options of economic actors. Advocates of context spoke of the "embeddedness" of economic phenomena in social processes and often referred to interpersonal networks as they did so. This context approach made the implicit assumption that economists had gotten some phenomenon, such as bargaining or price setting, right. What was missing, according to the economic sociologists? Economists, argued context theorists, had neglected the cultural and social context that mattered, such as previously existing connections among potential economic partners.

Over the past ten to fifteen years, I have been as surprised as anyone else to see myself become part of the economic sociology establishment, which is why you see me joining this symposium. What happened? Part of it is that I learned more about the variety of work going on in economic sociology and took a greater part in that increasingly energetic conversation. Three changes in my relation to the field made a big difference:

1. To my surprise, intellectual organizers of the field such as Richard Swedberg, Harrison White, and Neil Smelser started pointing to my work as an example of a new current within the field.
2. I found myself teaching economic sociology to expanding circles of graduate and undergraduate students alike.
3. The first two changes forced me to confront major premises of mainline economic sociology more directly than in the days when I thought of myself primarily as a student of American history and culture.

Instead of firms and markets alone, it seemed to me that all forms of production, consumption, distribution, and transfers of assets deserved attention from economic sociologists, including me.

This article therefore necessarily mixes an intellectual autobiography with a critical survey of past, present, and future changes in a fast-moving field. I begin with a summary of long-term shifts in the study of economic processes at large. Next comes a closer look at newly prominent emphases within economic sociology and a discussion of how those emphases undermine previously dominant presumptions concerning intersections between economic life and interpersonal relations. I illustrate these points extensively by means of recent analyses, including my own, of money. The article closes with a quick survey of other trends within the field.

ECONOMIC PROCESSES REASSESSED

Economic sociology does not stand alone in its challenge to standard understandings of economic processes. Whereas big changes did occur within the field, similar transformations took place elsewhere. Three of those changes deserve special attention. First of all, change occurred within economics itself. Such currents as behavioral economics, feminist economics, organizational economics, institutional economics, household dynamics, and, more recently, neuroeconomics, mounted their own critiques of neoclassical models. These new forms of economics all started to create alternative accounts of economic processes, including the range of interpersonal relations on which I had been concentrating for many years. Something so simple as the introduction of game theory into household bargaining models, for example, substituted a set of interactions among players for the single, preference-bound choices of earlier models.

Second, outside economics, critics of law and economics, organization theorists, students of inequality, and critical feminists contributed to our thinking about how economic and social processes actually work. They, too, insisted on power, bargaining, and interpersonal transactions.

Third, at the edge of economics and sociology, a number of new, hybrid disciplines emerged to propose their own versions of economic processes. They included socioeconomics, communitarian economics, the French *économie solidaire et sociale*, and world-systems analysis.

At the same time, economic sociologists not only grew in number and confidence but also moved increasingly away from extension and context accounts toward the formulation of truly alternative, socially based description and explanation of economic activity. (An impressively energetic parallel surge has occurred within French social science.)[1] This alternative analysis attempted to identify social processes and social relations at the very heart of economic activity, including the previously sacred and unexplored territory of markets themselves. Many of these analysts rallied to Harrison White's declaration that markets were deeply social creations rather than autonomous arenas on which social processes merely impinged.

Indeed, during his later years Pierre Bourdieu was moving in the same direction. In the 2000 version of his *Structures sociales de l'économie*, he declared, "Attempts to 'correct' the errors or omissions of a paradigm without challenging the paradigm itself . . . remind me of Tycho Brahe's heroic efforts to save Ptolemy's geocentric model from the Copernican revolution" (Bourdieu 2000, 12n1).

In general, sociological seekers after an alternative economic sociology criticized the idea of embeddedness, which implied that social processes supplied the economy's shell, but the shell's real contents consisted of economics's rational exchange systems. Just as institutional economists, shocked by the failure of markets alone to transform postsocialist economies, were beginning to portray economic activities as social processes, economic sociologists were venturing into the cores of firms, markets, organizations, and financial institutions.

Through these changes, I found that my own concentration on meaningful interpersonal aspects of economic activity no longer stood at the periphery of what was going on. Now, from the inside, I can see more clearly that the process of expansion continues. As one sign, browse the table of contents in Neil Smelser and Richard Swedberg's second edition of their *Handbook of Economic Sociology* (2005). It prominently features new institutionalism, emotions, behavioral economics, and law—all subjects absent from the first edition's table of contents only eleven years earlier.

Even more is going on in and around economic sociology. New topics and emphases include the following:

- *Multiple markets*: From an earlier almost exclusive focus on production, economic sociologists are now expanding their analysis into other markets, especially financial markets, consumption markets, markets for personal care, and what they loosely call the informal economy.
- *Culture of firms*: Economic sociologists are finally shedding their structural armor and studying how the meaningful content of social ties shapes transactions and alignments within firms.
- *The production and reproduction of inequality, notably gender inequality*: Economic sociologists increasingly challenge status attainment models that account for inequalities as results of encounters between biased market selection and attributes of individuals.
- *Households as intense sites of economic activity*: Here economic sociologists, along with their allies in economics and anthropology, not only identify extensive, consequential production, consumption, distribution, and transfers of assets but also interaction patterns that defy representation as short-term spot markets.

My recent work shows the influence of all these innovations, especially analyses of multiple markets and of households. My 2005 book, *The Purchase of Intimacy*, for example, looked hard at how both everyday practices and American law manage the intersection of intimate interpersonal relations and economic activity (Zelizer 2005b). In couples, households, and provision of personal care, the book shows, participants work hard to find appropriate matches between relations and economic transactions. Showing how those matching processes worked engaged me inevitably in criticism of widespread misconceptions concerning the interactions of personal relations and economic activity (Zelizer 2005a).

Most important, from my perspective, is the attack on a common presumption among economists and sociologists alike: what I call the twinned stories of separate spheres and hostile worlds. With separate spheres, we have the assumption that there are distinct arenas for rational economic activity and for personal relations, one a sphere of calculation and efficiency, the other a sphere of sentiment and solidarity. The companion doctrine of hostile worlds declares that contamination and disorder result from close contact between the spheres. Economic rationality corrupts intimacy, and intimate relations hinder efficiency.

Challenging this false boundary matters. Why? Because the boundary perpetuates damaging divisions between ostensibly "real," consequential market activity and peripheral, trivial, economies. More specifically, the dichotomy between serious economic phenomena, such as firms, corporations, or financial markets, and supposedly inconsequential, sentimental economies, such as households, microcredits, local money communities, immigrant ROSCAs (rotating savings and credit associations), pawning, gifts, or remittances. The real economy, in this mythology, consists only of market-mediated transactions, just as "real" money consists of a single, homogeneous, fungible legal tender.

What is wrong with this view? Among other failings, it ignores that collectively such supposedly minor transactions are not trivial. They have large macroeconomic consequences, for example, in generating large flows of remittances from rich countries to poor countries, and in transmitting wealth from one generation to the next. As intergenerational transmission of wealth illustrates, furthermore, intimate transactions also create or sustain large-scale inequalities by class, race, ethnicity, and even gender. More generally, the separate-spheres/hostile-worlds doctrine perpetuates the context-oriented belief that economic activities follow their own laws, for which social relations simply supply constraints.

Uncomfortable with such dualisms and eager to put forward single-principle accounts of social life, opponents of hostile-worlds views have now and then countered with reductionist "nothing-but" arguments: the ostensibly separate world of personal relations, they argue, is nothing but a special case of some general principle. Nothing-but advocates divide among three principles: nothing but economic rationality, nothing but culture, and nothing but politics. Thus, for economic reductionists, personal relations of caring, friendship, sexuality, or parent-child ties become special cases of advantage-seeking individual choice under conditions of constraint—in short, of economic rationality. For cultural reductionists, such phenomena become expressions of distinct beliefs. Others insist on the political, coercive, and exploitative bases of the same phenomena.

Even those economic sociologists who avoid nothing-but reductionism, unfortunately, continue to adopt an attenuated variety of the separate-spheres/hostile-worlds conception, for example, by distinguishing more and less marketlike transactions rather than recognizing that every market depends on continuously negotiated, meaningful, interpersonal relations. Nevertheless, in general, economic sociology is moving away from extension, context, and separate-spheres/hostile-worlds reasoning toward a more fully social conception of economic activity.

THE CASE OF MONEY

We can see these changes clearly in the sociological study of money. Marx, Weber, Simmel, Simiand, and Mauss all made influential statements about money. But for much of the twentieth century, the study of money became the monopoly of economists, with other social scientists regarding money as a sort of economic intrusion—often dangerous—into social life (see, e.g., Habermas 1989). The prevailing economic view absolutized a market conception of money as operating in its own morally neutral sphere with autonomous laws, independently from social relations. Even Talcott Parsons's analysis of money as a symbolic language restricted money's symbolism to the economic domain (1967, 358). Indeed, in 1979, Randall Collins complained that sociologists ignored money "as if it were not sociological enough" (190).

Since the 1980s, however, North American, British, and European scholars have restarted the social interpretation of money. They have asked a set of questions that echo the questions posed about economic processes more generally. Is money indeed an abstract phenomenon with autonomous laws? Does social life provide context for monetary transactions? How does that context constrain money? How vulnerable are social relations to the allegedly corrupting impact of money? Or is money itself constituted by social ties and therefore a social process and product? Is there a single money or multiple monies?

Many recent analysts have contributed to that debate.[2] Significantly, whereas the first edition of Smelser and Swedberg's *Handbook of Economic Sociology* included a single essay on "Money, Banking, and Financial Markets," the 2005 edition split the topic in two: banking and financial markets in one chapter, money and credit in another.

These developments shaped my own work. My 1994 book, *The Social Meaning of Money*, challenged classical theories that treated money exclusively as an impersonal, neutral medium of economic exchange suitable for the rationalized market-driven contemporary world. It also challenged the more ominous prediction that money inevitably undermined meaningful social ties, reducing interpersonal connections to instrumental calculation. To do so, *The Social Meaning of Money* followed changes in U.S. social practices with the expansion of monetary transactions.

Focusing on the period roughly between 1870s and 1930s, the book explored these processes in a variety of settings: households, the gift economy, and welfare transactions. It showed that monetization did indeed present Americans with new challenges. But it also documented that instead of turning away from money or letting their social relations wither in the headlong pursuit of money, Americans actually incorporated money into their construction of new social ties and transformed money's meaning as they did so. More specifically, as money entered the household, gift exchanges, and charitable donations, individuals and organizations invented an extensive array of currencies, ranging from housekeeping allowances, pin money, and spending money to money gifts, gift certificates, remittances, tips, mother's pensions, and food stamps.

How do people actually implement the multiple distinctions the book described? Here is one recurrent pattern across all the book's materials.

In each case people employ a set of practices we can call earmarking: treatments of money that signal the nature of the relationship between the parties to a particular kind of transaction.

Techniques of earmarking include three main varieties:

1. Establishing social practices that sort otherwise identical media into distinct categories. Depending on how it is used, when, and, most important, for what type of social relation, the same physically indistinguishable medium (e.g., dollar or a euro) can serve as a wage, a bonus, a tip, a gift, an allowance, charity, or a remittance. Each calls for a different set of routines representing its character.
2. Creation of segmented media in the form of tokens, coupons, scrip, chits, food stamps, affinity credit cards, local currencies, money orders, vouchers, or gift certificates, which are appropriate for restricted sets of relations and transfers, and in many cases are not legal tender within the larger economy.
3. Transformation of selected objects into monetary media, as with cigarettes, postage stamps, subway tokens, poker chips, or baseball cards.

This is where I left the problem in 1994. Although it received respectful reviews, my book had less impact than I had hoped on general discussions of monetary processes. That happened in part because the book concentrated on small-scale social relations and avoided polemics with theorists except for objections to different versions of the "money corrupts" doctrine.

But there is a more fundamental reason for why it took a long time for the book to have an impact. In their preface to the French edition of *The Social Meaning of Money*, Jérôme Bourdieu and Johan Heilbron astutely noted that superficial reading of the book runs the risk of reinforcing the propensity to think of sociological analysis, especially its culturalist versions, as placing economic phenomena in a second dimension and concentrating on marginal phenomena, providing exotic sidelights that fail to touch the real things of the genuine economy (Bourdieu and Heilbron 2005, 14). Heilbron and Bourdieu are right. More than I realized as I wrote the book, it is easy for careless or hostile readers to dismiss the book as irrelevant to their concerns on two grounds: that it focuses on marginal monetary phenomena, not "real" money, and that it is an essentially culturalist explanation, rich in trimmings but not in serious substance.

One can see why this impression occurs: the book does concentrate on small-scale processes rather than macromonetary transformations. It studies family, gift, and welfare economies, and it explores monetary meanings. Given the long-standing propensity to divide the economic world between, on one side, the serious, "real" markets of corporations and finance dealing

with "real" money and, on the other side, allegedly minor, marginal economies with their "quasi" imperfect monies, the book does not seem to take on
crucial economic sites. If you believe that the real economy consists only of
market-mediated transactions and the serious business of money takes place
only within corporations or finance, it is easier to consider the materials of
the book as irrelevant.

Finally, for understandable reasons, I set the book out against standard
views of commodification: of money as a rationalizing force that transformed
social relations wherever it went. Intent on showing the failure of such arguments, I did not highlight sufficiently what was distinctive about the alternative I proposed. As a result, I let some readers read the book's main message
thus: "Money is more cultural than traditional thinkers allowed." However,
as Bourdieu and Heilbron (2005) pointed out, such conclusions are wrong.
They are wrong on several grounds:

First, the central insight of the book is not that money is cultural. Its most
distinctive contribution is attaching monetary practices to social relations,
and that is something that is simply not on the screen of most social-science
analyses of money.

Second, and more specifically, the book argues that people regularly differentiate forms of monetary transfers in correspondence with their definitions of the sort of relationship that exists between them. They adopt symbols, rituals, practices, accounting systems, and physically distinguishable
forms of money to mark distinct social relations.

Third, people work hard to maintain such distinctions: They care greatly
about differentiating monies because payment systems are a powerful way
in which they mark apart different social ties. Each of these ties has a different quality, and each one therefore calls for different forms and rituals of
payment.

It happens that relations, in my conception, are not the thin, flat relations of network analysis but the rich relations of ethnography. Ethnography
reveals a great deal of negotiation of meaning and the actual production of
cultural meaning. This is not a trivial feature of money. As Bourdieu and
Heilbron (2005) said, that is how money works. Relational work and earmarking are general, crucial features of money. In this view, culture is not an
abstract entity. People create culture relationally. The earmarking of money
raises just that issue; earmarking is a relational practice. People do not just
adopt categories from the surrounding culture. They negotiate their social
lives, earmarking monies for different sets of relations.

These days, I would state the book's main themes more polemically. Here,
for example, is an obvious point I took for granted but did not dramatize
sufficiently: monetary phenomena consist of and depend on social practices.
We cannot simply treat money as the volume and flow of transactions within
accounting systems and such tokens of those systems as banknotes, coins,

and credits. By treating consumption, distribution, and transfers of assets as market-mediated processes, analysts abstract away the concrete social relations and practices that constitute and drive consumption, distribution, and transfers of assets.

CONTROVERSIES AND CONVERGENCES

Several years after its publication, *The Social Meaning of Money*'s concentration on personal ties and practices therefore set me on a collision course with other theorists. Critics such as Ben Fine and Costas Lapavitsas (2000) and Geoffrey Ingham (2001) insisted on the generalizing, power-backed process of money (see also Lapavitsas 2005). They even raised doubts that the transactions I was analyzing were truly monetary.

For example, Fine and Lapavitsas found disturbing my emphasis on heterogeneity, in particular my apparent disregard for money's "homogenizing influence." They conceded that "it is the dual nature of money that must always be emphasized—universal and homogenized money creates scope for expressing relations that are socially and culturally specific" (2000, 372). Yet money's socially bound variations, within Fine and Lapavitsas's framework, struggle feebly against its universalizing tendencies. "The broader aspects and meaning of social relations that are expressed through money," Fine and Lapavitsas told us, "find themselves trapped within the featurelessness of universal exchangeability" (367). Thus, Fine and Lapavitsas insist both on a universal money and on the causal priority of money's utter fungibility. "There is one money," they asserted, "even though it assumes different forms" (377).

Although certainly aware of the social dimensions of money, such critics cling to a safer contextual approach, which concedes the significance of social constraints on money but ignores its relational basis. As a result, this view perpetuates the separate-spheres model of economic and social life. The "one" money is the real thing; other monies, within this model, remain "quasi" approximations.

In the current debate, economic sociologists are making a serious effort to go beyond both critiques of economic analysis as well as contextual interpretations, studying instead the actual social processes that constitute money. As Bruce Carruthers (2005) has recently pointed out, that trend has already gone far both in the analysis of money and of its twin, credit. In the process, current studies are replacing the classical view of modern money as a single, homogeneous, liquid medium for economic exchange with a continuum involving a wide variety of monetary media.

Consider Nigel Dodd's (2005) able mapping of money's plurality. Dodd challenged the outdated dichotomy between "real money" and what he called "emaciated monies" and others often label as "quasi-monies." As he introduced money's variation, Dodd proposed an admirable research agenda: explaining differences among kinds of monies, as well as identifying the "different causal trajectories . . . involved in the emergence of new forms of money (2005:572)."

Dodd's analysis of variation in the forms of money helps construct better answers to what he identified as a significant contemporary paradox—the simultaneous increase in homogenization of state-issued currency and diversification of monies. More specifically, he used his analytical tools to identify what he sees as the euro's "hybrid" nature. He rightly portrayed the euro as a striking instance of a recurrent process in which homogenization of currency stimulates diversification of money—diversification, that is, through the multiplication of both noncurrency monetary media and units of account. Dodd's approach thus shares in the healthy trend within economic sociology, as scholars increasingly liberate themselves from an earlier obsession with providing critique or context to conventional economic analysis.

Yet even Dodd fails to recognize the incorporation of social relations into monetary transactions and of monetary transactions into social relations. Such reluctant integration of money's social elements is not trivial. It led Dodd to omit two crucial, partly independent, elements in his analysis: money's relational differentiation and monetary practices. People regularly match forms of monetary transfers to the sort of relationship that obtains between the parties. As for practices, they rely on symbols, rituals, accounting systems, and varying monetary tokens to mark distinctive social ties.

Which media or unit of account people adopt, when, and how depends on the type of social relations involved. Parent-child, priest-congregant, welfare official–aid recipient, legislator-constituent, courting couple—all these relations sometimes involve monetary transactions, but each calls for a very different combination of media and units of account. As they calculate who owes what favors, services, tributes, and gifts to whom at both ends of a migration stream, participants in the complex relations of a remittance system often employ currencies of the sending and receiving countries as their media, but they typically create their own hybrid units of account.

We must therefore take Dodd's analysis a step further. All monies are actually dual; they serve both general and local circuits. Indeed, this duality applies to all economic transactions. Seen from the top, economic transactions connect with broad national symbolic meanings and institutions. Seen from the bottom, however, economic transactions are highly differentiated, personalized, and local, meaningful to particular relations. No contradiction therefore exists between uniformity and diversity; they are simply two different aspects of the same transaction. Just as people speak English in a recognizably grammatical way at the same time that they pour individual and personal content into their conversations, economic actors simultaneously adopt universalizing modes and particularizing markers.

Some recent analysts have gone at this first point in a somewhat different way by saying that money depends on accounting systems. I agree, but with a qualification. Accounting systems are not just top-down mechanisms of banks or states. People create and negotiate their own accounting systems on a smaller scale. They incorporate and shape social practices.

Traditional analysts are also wrong to dismiss households and other nonmarket-mediated economies and their monetary worlds as peripheral to the real economy. They are wrong because households, kinship groups, friendship networks, neighborhoods, and ostensibly noneconomic organizations such as churches and voluntary associations play significant parts in a wide range of economic activity. Take the obvious example of migrant remittance systems. They loom very large in the national economies of such countries as Turkey and Mexico, but—to the despair of many development economists—work chiefly through ties of kinship, friendship, and neighborhood rather than banks and other formal economic institutions.

Why did I choose to focus on families, welfare, and gifts? These are areas where, according to the traditional dichotomy between the market and personal relations, either money should not have entered at all or rationalization should have wrought the largest changes, homogenizing core personal and social relations and commodifying sentiment in family, friendship, charity, death. My research shows instead that it is very hard work to suppress the active creative power of supposedly vulnerable social relations.

WHITHER ECONOMIC SOCIOLOGY?

Not all informed observers, to be sure, share my enthusiasm for current trends in economic sociology. Reviewing major compilations in the field, Rob Faulkner and Eric Cheney (2003) and Jesper Sørensen (2003) have offered precisely opposite criticisms of the field: Faulkner and Cheney declared that economic sociologists have excluded major fields of analysis, such as crime and the "dark side" of capitalism, that earlier sociologists handled quite effectively. Sørensen countered that the organizers of the field have become so inclusive they risk diluting the field's intellectual content.

Each, as it happens, had a point. In their zeal to get institutional processes right, economic sociologists have spent little energy questioning the very existence of the institutions they study. And the expansion of subject matter I have been celebrating has reduced the field's theoretical coherence as compared with the time when it operated chiefly as a close complement to mainstream economic theory. Yet we have grounds for thinking that new, more critical versions of economic sociology will emerge and that new syntheses are in the making.

In my part of the field, in any case, I see students of economic processes taking three important, promising, if partly contradictory steps.

Step 1, as I suggested before, consists of abandoning separate-spheres and hostile-worlds arguments in favor of analyses following differentiated social ties with their distinctive accounting systems, media, economic transactions, meanings, and boundaries.

Step 2 involves questioning the attenuated version I likewise mentioned earlier, the idea that all spheres have economic activity but some are more marketlike—more rational, more governed by impersonal efficiency than others, a condition that organizational analysts often describe as arm's-length transactions.

A very interesting third step partly contradicts the first two. As typified by Michel Callon (1998) and Donald MacKenzie and Yuvai Millo (2003), we encounter the idea that economics has grown up around corporations and markets but by its very development has reshaped those corporations and markets in its own image. If theories actually shape relations and practices in that way, some areas of social life could, after all, become more "marketish" than others, through the performativity of theories applied to those areas.

If so, a new version of step 2 could conceivably apply. If constructivists are right, it may be that some areas constructed by economic theory lend themselves to superior explanation by economic theory as compared with other areas, such as households. In that case, economic sociologists would have to think seriously about fashioning theories that would simultaneously shape and explain other arenas of production, consumption, distribution, and asset transfers than the beloved capitalist firms and markets of the old economic sociology.

I am not declaring that performativity fills the future of economic sociology. I am saying instead that the presence of such intriguing ideas in a field that once clung closely to mainstream economics marks economic sociology as a vital, even visionary, academic enterprise.

Notes

Viviana A. Zelizer, "Pasts and Futures of Economic Sociology," *American Behavioral Scientist* 50 (April 2007): 1,056–69. First published by SAGE/SOCIETY. Reprinted with permission.

1. See, for example, "L'argent en famille" 2005; Boltanski and Chiapello 1999; Caillé 1994; Convert and Heilbron 2004; Cusin and Benamouzing 2004; De La Pradelle 1996; Gislain and Steiner 1995; Guérin 2003; Hassoun 2005; Saint-Jean and Steiner 2005; Sciardet 2003; Servet 1999; Servet and Guérin 2002; Steiner 1999, 2003; Wacquant 2002; Weber et al. 2003; Weber 2005.
2. See, for example, Aglietta and Orléan 2002; Akin and Robbins 1999; Baker 1987; Blanc 2000; Bloch 1994; Carruthers 2005; Carruthers and Espeland 1998;

Cohen 2003; Dodd 1994, 2005; Fishman and Messina 2006; Gilbert 2005; Guyer 1995; Helleiner 2003; Ingham 2004; Keister 2002; Leyshon and Thrift 1997; Mizruchi and Brewster Stearns 1994; Pahl 1989; Parry and Bloch 1989; Raineau 2004; Singh 1995; Woodruff 1999.

REFERENCES

Aglietta, M., and A. Orléan. 2002. *La monnaie: Entre violence et confiance.* Paris: Odile Jacob.

Akin, D., and J. Robbins, eds. 1999. *Money and Modernity: State and Local Currencies in Melanesia.* Pittsburgh: University of Pittsburgh Press.

"L'argent en famille." 2005. *Terrain* 45 (September). Paris: Maison des Sciences de l'Homme.

Baker, W. 1987. "What Is Money? A Social Structural Interpretation." In *Intercorporate Relations,* edited by M. S. Mizruchi and M. Schwartz, 109–44. Cambridge: Cambridge University Press.

Blanc, J. 2000. *Les monnaies parallèles.* Paris: L'Harmattan.

Bloch, M. 1994. "Les usages de l'argent." *Terrain* 23:5–10.

Boltanski, L., and E. Chiapello. 1999. *Le nouvel esprit du capitalisme.* Paris: Gallimard.

Bourdieu, J., and J. Heilbron. 2005. "Préface à l'édition française." In Viviana A. Zelizer, *La signification sociale de l'argent,* 11–19. Paris: Seuil, collection Liber.

Bourdieu, P. 2000. *Les structures sociales de l'économie.* Paris: Seuil.

Caillé, A. 1994. *Don, intérêt et désintéressement.* Paris: La Découverte.

Callon, M. 1998. "The Embeddedness of Economic Markets in Economics." In *The Laws of the Markets,* edited by M. Callon, 1–57. Oxford: Blackwell.

Carruthers, B. G. 2005. "The Sociology of Money and Credit." In *The Handbook of Economic Sociology,* edited by N. Smelser and R. Swedberg, 2nd ed., 355–78. New York: Russell Sage Foundation; Princeton, N.J.: Princeton University Press.

Carruthers, B. G., and W. Espeland. 1998. "Money, Meaning and Morality." *American Behavioral Scientist* 41:1,384–1,408.

Cohen, B. J. 2003. *The Future of Money.* Princeton, N.J.: Princeton University Press.

Collins, R. 1979. Review of *The Bankers,* by Martin Meyer. *American Journal of Sociology* 85:190–94.

Convert, B., and J. Heilbron. 2004. "Genèse de la sociologie économique américaine." In *Pour une histoire des sciences sociales: Hommage à Pierre Bourdieu,* edited by J. Heilbron, R. Lenoir, and G. Sapiro, 223–41. Paris: Fayard.

Cusin, F., and D. Benamouzing. 2004. *Economie et sociologie.* Paris: Quadrige/PUF.

De La Pradelle, M. 1996. *Les vendredis de Carpentras.* Paris: Fayard.

Dodd, N. 1994. *The Sociology of Money.* New York: Continuum.

———. 2005. "Reinventing Monies in Europe." *Economy and Society* 34: 558–83.

Faulkner, R. R., and E. Cheney. 2003. Review of *The New Economic Sociology: Developments in an Emerging Field*, edited by M. F. Guillén, R. Collins, P. England, and M. Meyer. *Contemporary Sociology* 32:445–47.

Fine, B., and C. Lapavitsas. 2000. "Markets and Money in Social Theory: What Role for Economics?" *Economy and Society* 29:357–82.

Fishman, R. M., and A. M. Messina, eds. 2006. *The Year of the Euro: The Cultural, Social, and Political Import of Europe's Common Currency*. Chicago: University of Notre Dame Press.

Fourcade, M. 2007. "Theories of Markets and Theories of Society." *American Behavioral Scientist* 50(8): 1015–34.

Gilbert, E. 2005. "Common Cents: Situating Money in Time and Place." *Economy and Society* 34:357–88.

Gislain, J.-J., and P. Steiner. 1995. *La sociologie économique 1890–1920*. Paris: Presses Universitaires de France.

Guérin, I. 2003. *Femmes et économie solidaire*. Paris: La Découverte.

Guyer, J. I., ed. 1995. *Money Matters*. Portsmouth, N.H.: Heinemann.

Habermas, J. 1989. *The Theory of Communicative Action*, vol. 2. Boston: Beacon.

Hassoun, J.-P., ed. 2005. Special issue, "Négoces dans la ville." *Ethnologie française* 35.

Helleiner, E. 2003. *The Making of National Money: Territorial Currencies in Historical Perspective*. Ithaca, N.Y.: Cornell University Press.

Ingham, G. 2001. "Fundamentals of a Theory of Money: Untangling Fine, Lapavitsas and Zelizer." *Economy and Society* 30:304–23.

———. 2004. *The Nature of Money*. Cambridge: Polity.

Keister, L. 2002. "Financial Markets, Money, and Banking." *Annual Review of Sociology* 28:39–61.

Lapavitsas, C. 2005. "The Social Relations of Money as Universal Equivalent: A Response to Ingham." *Economy and Society* 34:389–403.

Leyshon, A., and N. Thrift. 1997. *Money Space: Geographies of Monetary Transformation*. London: Routledge.

MacKenzie, D., and Y. Millo. 2003. "Constructing a Market, Performing Theory: The Historical Sociology of a Financial Derivatives Exchange." *American Journal of Sociology* 109:107–45.

Mizruchi, M. S., and L. Brewster Stearns. 1994. "Money, Banking, and Financial Markets." In *The Handbook of Economic Sociology*, edited by N. Smelser and R. Swedberg, 313–41. Princeton, N.J.: Princeton University Press; New York: Russell Sage Foundation.

Pahl, J. 1989. *Money and Marriage*. London: Palgrave Macmillan.

Parry, J., and M. Bloch, eds. 1989. *Money and the Morality of Exchange*. New York: Cambridge University Press.

Parsons, T. 1967. *On the Concept of Influence: Sociological Theory and Modern Society*. New York: Free Press.

Raineau, L. 2004. *L'utopie de la monnaie immatérielle*. Paris: PUF.

Saint-Jean, I. T., and P. H. Steiner, eds. 2005. Special issue, "Sociologies économiques." *L'Année Sociologique* 55.

Sciardet, H. 2003. *Les marchands de l'aube: Ethnographie et théorie du commerce aux Puces de Saint-Ouen*. Paris: Economica.

Servet, J.-M., ed. 1999. *Une économie sans argent: Les systèmes d'échange local*. Paris: Editions du Seuil.

Servet, J.-M., and I. Guérin, eds. 2002. *Exclusion et liens financiers*. Paris: Economica.

Singh, S. 1995. *Marriage Money: The Social Shaping of Money in Marriage and Banking*. St. Leonards, Australia: Allen and Unwin.

Smelser, N., and R. Swedberg, eds. 2005. *The Handbook of Economic Sociology*. 2nd ed. Princeton, N.J.: Princeton University Press; New York: Russell Sage Foundation.

Sørensen, J. B. 2003. Review of *The New Economic Sociology: Developments in an Emerging Field*, edited by M. F. Guillén, R. Collins, P. England, and M. Meyer. *Administrative Science Quarterly* 48:534–37.

Steiner, P. 1999. *La sociologie économique*. Paris: La Découverte.

———. 2003. "Gift of Blood and Organs: The Market and 'Fictitious' Commodities." *Revue Française de Sociologie* 44(Suppl.): 147–62.

Wacquant, L. 2002. *Corps et âme*. Paris: Agone.

Weber, F. 2005. *Le sang, le nom, le quotidien: Une sociologie de la parenté pratique*. Paris: Aux lieux d'être.

Weber, F., S. G. Gojard, and A. Gramain. 2003. *Charges de famille*. Paris: La Découverte.

Woodruff, D. 1999. *Money Unmade: Barter and the Fate of Russian Capitalism*. Ithaca, N.Y.: Cornell University Press.

Zelizer, V. 1994. *The Social Meaning of Money*. New York: Basic Books.

———. 2005a. "Missing Monies: Comment on Nigel Dodd, 'Reinventing Monies in Europe.'" *Economy and Society* 34:585–88.

———. 2005b. *The Purchase of Intimacy*. Princeton, N.J.: Princeton University Press.

Culture and Consumption

Strange as it may now seem, during the 1960s many American planners argued that shopping malls could provide solutions to suburban sprawl and urban anomie. Designer and developer Victor Gruen led the chorus, building some of the country's largest and best-publicized suburban shopping centers. Moreover, he wrote eloquently about their virtues. Speaking especially of the Northland and Eastland centers his company built in the Detroit metropolitan area, Gruen crowed that they had created a new, intense kind of community:

> I remember the surprised faces of my clients when we drove out to a shopping center on a Sunday and found the parking area full. The courts and malls, the lanes and promenades were filled with milling crowds dressed in their Sunday best, engaging in an activity that was believed to be long forgotten: family groups strolling leisurely, their youngsters in go-carts and dogs on the leash; relaxed and admiring the flowers and trees, sculptures and murals, fountains and ponds, and, incidentally, using the opportunity for window-shopping. To the joy of the merchants, this last resulted in strong business activity on the following weekdays. (1964, 203)

Gruen went on to boast that civic organizations, churches, hobby clubs, political rallies, art exhibitions, and theaters thrived in the new environment, even that "[n]ational minority groups arranged for special musical and folk dancing evenings" (1964, 203). Good planning, he concluded, could integrate retail activity with active social life.

A third of a century down the suburban road, political scientist turned prophet Robert Putnam offered a grimmer judgment of the shopping mall. "Rather than at the grocery store or five-and-dime on Main Street, where faces were familiar," lamented Putnam,

> [t]oday's suburbanites shop in large, impersonal malls. Although malls constitute America's most distinctive contemporary public space, they are carefully designed for one primary, private purpose—to direct consumers to buy. Despite the aspirations of some developers, mall culture is not about overcoming isolation and connecting with others, but about privately surfing from store to store—in the presence of others, but not in their company. The suburban shopping experience does

not consist of interaction with people embedded in a common social network. (2000, 211)

The very innovations that Gruen thought were renewing lost community, according to Putnam, actually destroyed it. Increasingly, consumption privatized and isolated Americans instead of providing occasions and means of sociability.

In a sophisticated and closely documented account, Lizabeth Cohen (2003) reports what actually went on within America's transformed consumer marketplaces. Shopping centers did offer their customers a whole range of community activities, including charity fairs, Weight Watchers meetings, and concerts. Moreover, looked at closely, shopping turns out to have often been a joint family activity; women, who were the principal shoppers, frequently took their children and their husbands along with them. Spurred by anxious merchants, however, shopping malls became much more exclusive than city streets. Legal restrictions limited the range of political activities permitted and the kinds of people who could enter the malls. Finally, the malls catered to strongly segmented populations.

> When developers and store owners set out to make the shopping center a more perfect downtown, they aimed to exclude from this public space unwanted urban groups such as vagrants, prostitutes, racial minorities, and poor people. Market segmentation became the guiding principle of this mix of commercial and civic activity, as the shopping center sought perhaps contradictorily to legitimize itself as a true community center and to define that community in exclusionary socioeconomic and racial terms. (Cohen 1996, 1,059)

Neither all-embracing communities nor habitats of the Lonely Crowd, shopping centers represented America as a whole: both connected and segmented, differentiated by gender, ethnicity, race, and class, mingling commercial and sociable activity, entangling consumption in the strands of meaningful social relations (see also Zukin 2003).

In principle, one might think that production, distribution, and consumption would occupy well-defined, tightly integrated, and roughly equal spaces in the work of economic sociologists. Within sociology, however, a rough division of labor has arisen: economic sociologists examine production and distribution with no more than occasional gestures toward consumption, while specialists in culture, gender, family, inequality, and other fields lavish attention on consumption almost without regard to the questions—or answers—posed by economic sociologists. Meanwhile (as the work of historian Lizabeth Cohen suggests), nonsociologists have been making major contributions to the study of consumption that have not regularly come to economic sociologists' attention.

The *Handbook*'s editors assigned me the analysis of interactions between culture and consumption, not the treatment of consumption as a whole. A full survey of consumption would require a close look at the interdependence among production, distribution, and consumption—for example, how producers promote the purchase and use of newly designed goods and services. It would also entail consideration of macroeconomic interactions among prices, supply, and demand of consumer goods and services. Instead, my analysis stresses the participation of consumers in economic life. In compensation for that narrowing of its focus, it takes an exceptionally broad view of consumption.

Although this chapter concentrates on intersections of culture and consumption, the unfortunate existing division of labor between students of culture and specialists in economic processes warns precisely against the dangers of considering the two as separate spheres that only occasionally bump into each other. Reification of the boundary between culture and consumption encourages three incorrect and equally reductionist positions: (1) consumption is "really" rational maximizing behavior that acquires a carapace of culture after the fact; (2) consumption is essentially expressive behavior that does not conform at all to economic rationality; (3) consumption divides between a hard-nosed region of rational maximizing behavior and a soft-hearted region of cultural expression. In fact, all consumption (like all economic life) builds on culture in the sense of shared understandings and their representations. The secret to understanding consumption lies in careful observation of how culture, social relations, and economic processes interact.

With that aim in mind, let us take up in turn

1. Recent investigations of consumption outside of sociology
2. Sociological studies of consumption, outside the claimed territory of economic sociology
3. Consequent challenges to economic sociology

Following those three points, the chapter reviews three different sites of consumption—households, ethnic-racial communities, and retail settings—where extensive research has recently occurred, with an eye to better integration between economic sociology and empirical studies of consumption.

Consumption Outside of Sociology

One might have thought that consumption would preoccupy economists, since it is the point where individual lives most obviously integrate into the economy at large. Through much of the twentieth century economists did study consumption in the aggregate. Economists long collaborated with sociologists in surveys of consumer expenditures and behavior, a line of work that significantly influenced market research. Elihu Katz and Paul Lazarsfeld (1955), for example, applied the analysis of personal influence to both political and consumption behavior. Furthermore, a few economists braved the trend by giving the social determination of preferences a central place in their analysis; in a review of the topic, Juliet Schor (1998, 9) singles out Thorstein Veblen, James Duesenberry, John Kenneth Galbraith, Fred Hirsch, Tibor Scitovsky, Richard Easterlin, Amartya Sen, Clair Brown, and Robert Frank as leaders in the economic analysis of consumption (for a detailed review of consumption economics, see Frenzen, Hirsch, and Zerrillo 1994).

Nevertheless, economists have concentrated mostly on production and distribution, commonly throwing up their hands when it came to integrating change and variation in consumer preferences directly into economic analysis. As Gary Becker himself says:

> The economist's normal approach to analyzing consumption and leisure choices assumes that individuals maximize utility with preferences that depend at any moment only on the goods and services they consume at that time. These preferences are assumed to be independent of both past and future consumption, and of the behavior of everyone else. This approach has proved to be a valuable simplification for addressing many economic questions, but a large number of choices in all societies depend very much on past experiences and social forces. (1996, 3–4)

Becker endogenizes preferences by retaining economics's cherished assumption of individual rational maximizing but incorporating two new aspects of human capital: *personal capital*, involving past consumption and other experiences that shape present and future preferences; and *social capital*, involving other people's past actions that shape the same preferences. Thus Becker clings to the economist's individual perspective but explicitly builds in experiential and social influences on the individual. Other economists seek to repair the conventional account of consumption by replacing abstract definitions of rational maximization with decision-making principles based on findings from psychologically sophisticated observations and experiments (see, e.g., Thaler 1991, 1999; Aversi et al. 1999). Both these "behavioral economists" and Becker-style neoclassical economists, then, sense that conventional economic accounts of consumption leave much unexplained. Similarly, psychologists in the lineage of Herbert Simon, Amos Tversky, and Daniel Kahneman have mounted influential critiques of neoclassical economics's behavioral assumptions (see, e.g., Kahneman and Tversky 1982). But they have not yet shifted the attention of most economists away from production and distribution.

Consumption has attracted much more attention outside economics. Indeed, for the past quarter-century anthropologists, historians, cultural psychologists, marketing analysts, and cultural studies specialists have revolutionized traditional understandings of consumption. Rescuing consumption from the grip of social critics, budget experts, marketers, and scholars began asking, "Why do people want goods?" The so-called cultural turn swept away standard utilitarian and individualistic accounts of consumption as maximization. It also challenged deeply entrenched moralistic concerns about the corrupting effects of consumption by reframing the purchase and use of goods and services as meaningful practices. Similarly, students of gender countered the totalization of consumption typical of earlier social history and social criticism. Where generations of home economists had tried to assimilate kitchen and nursery into the world of industrial efficiency, many feminists sought to identify distinctive cultural traits of women's worlds, notably including the world of female consumption.

Specialists in gender played a crucial part in renewing consumption studies. They made a double contribution. First, they emphasized distinctions between the consumption patterns of women and men rather than taking consumption as a homogeneous expression of class or nationality. Second, they often challenged understandings of consumption as mass behavior by stressing the creativity and empowerment of female consumers. They did so by carefully investigating diverse facets of consumption's gendered practices, including interactions between saleswomen and customers in American department stores (Benson 1986), middle-class women shoplifters (Abelson 1989), women's sale and use of cosmetics (Peiss 1998, 2002), immigrant housewives' expenditures (Ewen 1985), women shopping in London's West End (Rappaport 2000), Old Regime France seamstresses (Crowston 2001), and the American doll industry (Formanek-Brunell 1993). (See also Andrews and Talbot 2000; de Grazia and Furlough 1996; Horowitz and Mohun 1998; Scanlon 2000; and for male consumers Swiencicki 1999.)

Meanwhile, anthropologists provided noneconomic or even antieconomic models of consumption. Marshall Sahlins's *Culture and Practical Reason* (1976) along with Mary Douglas and Baron Isherwood's *The World of Goods* (1979) set the tone for the new consumption studies, boldly appropriating consumption into the domain of shared meanings. Two complementary trends occurred in anthropology, history, cultural studies, and a few corners of sociology: a shift of focus away from production and producers to consumption and consumers, as well as an increasing concentration on consumption as expressive behavior—the site of mentalities, identities, and culture.

In her contribution to a three-volume set that Craig Clunas called "a major monument in a turn toward the history of consumption and away from the history of production" (1999, 1,497), Lorna Weatherill reports a characteristic study of probate inventories from late seventeenth- and early eighteenth-century England. Sampling from eight localities, including the London area, Weatherill reconstructs a wide range of household goods, showing variation by locality, occupation, social rank, and gender. She interprets the array of furniture, looking glasses, pictures, books, clocks, silver, and cooking utensils as expressing the special worldview of seventeenth- and eighteenth-century ordinary people. For instance, detailed inventories of cooking gear, Weatherill suggests, underline the centrality of food to daily life at that time. More generally, Weatherill declares that "material goods themselves contain implicit meanings and are therefore indicative of attitudes. Through understanding the nonmaterial attributes of goods it is possible to move to the meaning of ownership in social and other terms" (1993, 211).

Scholars of consumption range widely, from studying economic institutions such as department stores, to analyses of commercialized leisure, taste formation, food consumption, media advertising, and household budgets (see, e.g., M. Miller 1981; Rosenzweig 1983; Tiersten 2001; Mintz 1996; Lears 1994; D. Horowitz 1985). Out of this variety of studies emerged a continuing conversation on the culture of consumption.[1]

In the 1990s, dissenting voices joined that conversation. Concerned that the "cultural turn" had gone too far, detouring its practitioners from other crucial aspects of consumption processes, scholars urged new agendas. "Today's burgeoning cottage industry of study devoted to 'consumer culture,' " noted historians Victoria de Grazia and Lizabeth Cohen, "draws its impulse . . . chiefly [from] the problem of postmodernity and the fluid social and personal identities it appears to have instated" (1999, 1). Missing, according to de Grazia and Cohen, was the political economy of inequality and consumption, namely, its link to class relations and class power.[2] Missing as well, complained other specialists, were links between consumption and the production of goods (see, e.g., Crowston 2001; Green 1997).

In *A Consumers' Republic: The Politics of Mass Consumption in Postwar America* (2003) Lizabeth Cohen pushes forward the revised historical agenda, directly examining the political economy of American consumption in the period following the Second World War. Consumption, in her reading, is not merely expressive behavior but a site, cause, and effect of major changes in American experience. In Cohen's view, the government-backed promotion of consumption during the 1930s as a cushion and antidote for economic crisis sowed the ground both for governmental intervention in wartime consumption and for postwar policies centered on consumption as foundation of a "consumer's republic" (for a contrary view of consumption, see Cross 2000).

Cohen's analysis demonstrates furthermore the heavy involvement of women and African Americans in the politics of consumption. For example, Cohen reports:

Throughout the North, and less visibly in the South, the ten years between the war and the Montgomery Bus Boycott of 1955 saw an explosion in black challenges to exclusion from public accommodations, many of them sites of consumption and leisure, given that much of public life transpired in commercial venues by the postwar era. By the time of Montgomery and the lunch-counter sit-ins and boycotts of the early 1960s—usually credited with launching the modern civil rights movement through disciplined consumer action—and the passage of the federal Civil Rights Act of 1964 barring discrimination in public accommodations nationwide, politicized black consumers had already spent years agitating at the grassroots for, literally, a place at the table. That attacking segregation in public places became the focus of many local civil rights struggles after the war, particularly in the North, testified to the widespread appeal of the inclusive ideals of the Consumers' Republic. (2003, 166–67)

Thus, consumption reaches far beyond expressive behavior into the very constitution of American public politics (see also Frank 1994; Glickman 1997; Jacobs 1997).

At a smaller scale, but with no less effectiveness, anthropologist Daniel Miller has been likewise investigating the place of consumption in the constitution and maintenance of significant interpersonal relations. Miller (1987) has led the way in challenging the view of consumption as a form of subjugation and exploitation, emphasizing instead the creativity of consumers. In *A Theory of Shopping*, Miller proposes a relational approach to consumption. Closely observing shopping practices of seventy-six households on and around Jay Road, a North London street, Miller found consumers, as he provocatively sums it up, "making love in supermarkets." Far from being "an expression of individual subjectivity and identity," shopping, Miller argues, serves as "an expression of kinship and other relationships" (1998, 35).

As Miller remarks, shopping can "best be understood as being about relationships and not about individuals" (2001, 41; see also D. Miller et al. 1998). Activities Miller includes are housewives' selection of goods that will enhance their influence over the comportment of other household members, courting couples representing the current state of their relationship, and parents boosting the position of children within their peer groups. In a direct challenge to individualistic accounts of consumption, Miller provides evidence that sociability and purchasing of goods support each other, while isolation promotes withdrawal from consumption (1998, 34; 1995, 24).

Sociologists clearly have much to learn about consumption from scholars outside their discipline; in particular, historians and anthropologists have been proceeding quite independently to uncover the social implications and involvement of consumption behavior.

SOCIOLOGICAL STUDIES OF CONSUMPTION

Beginning with nineteenth-century concerns about the condition of the poor, from the first days of their discipline sociologists have dealt with consumption. They have, however, alternated between treatment of consumption as a process bearing heavily on the quality of life, and other interpretations of consumption as an expression of social position. Thorstein Veblen ([1899] 1953); Georg Simmel ([1904] 1957); Robert and Helen Lynd (1929); Paul Lazarsfeld (1957); David Riesman (1964); and David Caplowitz (1967) wrote important works in one vein or another (for an early effort linking studies of social stratification and consumption, see Barber 1957; for a programmatic statement not much followed, see Smelser 1963, 92–98; for a recent review, see Swedberg 2003, 241–58).

In recent decades, perhaps the most influential synthesis came from sociologist Pierre Bourdieu. Bourdieu combined an ambitious theoretical program with a remarkable range of concrete studies of consumption practices, including photography ([1965] 1990) and housing markets (2000). Most notably, Bourdieu's *Distinction* (1984) introduced the ideas of cultural and social capital into the analysis of consumption. Instead of treating consumption as a straightforward reflection of class culture, Bourdieu represented occupants of different positions within fields of inequality as actively deploying their capital to enhance their own positions.

British sociologists, likewise responding to earlier class analyses, used consumption studies to examine patterns of inequality and cultural change within their own country. In these studies two currents emerged—one, a post-Marxist effort to shift the focus of economic studies from production to consumption as a material experience, and the other, a more postmodern effort to treat consumption as an expression of consciousness and culture (see Campbell 1995; Slater 1997; for an attempt to link consumption, production, and distribution, see du Gay 1996).

Within North American sociology we find extensive consumption studies, but they remain remarkably fragmented, with various sociological specialists taking them up as part of other inquiries (see, e.g., Gottdiener 2000). Various dimensions of consumption have become mainly the province of specialists in family, class, gender, childhood, ethnicity, race, religion, community, the arts, and popular culture. Such talented analysts as Daniel Cook (2000); David Halle (1993); Gary Alan Fine (1996); Chandra Mukerji (1983); Michael Schudson (1984); Robert Wuthnow (1996); and Sharon Zukin (1991) have taken up topics varying from the creation of the "toddler" as a merchandising category, the purchase of art, the culture of restaurant work, circulation of mass consumer goods (pictorial prints, maps, and calicoes) in fifteenth- and sixteenth-century western Europe, to the impact of advertising, how

Americans talk about their purchases, and Disney World as a "fantasy landscape." Meanwhile, George Ritzer (1996) has single-handedly initiated a somewhat separate analysis of what he calls "McDonaldization," pursuing the thesis that the spread of standardized fast-food franchises creates uniform practices and understandings at a world scale (for qualifications, see Ritzer and Ovadia 2000; Ritzer 2003a, 2003b).

Thus, while there is a fair amount of consumption research in sociology, it remains segmented both within sociology and in terms of connections with consumption studies outside of sociology. For example, within the American Sociological Association, as of 2004, separate formal clusters existed for consumption, economic sociology, and the sociology of culture, drawing on vastly different constituencies and with little communication among the three (Cook 1999; see also Ritzer 2000).

Launched in 2001, the *Journal of Consumer Culture* (George Ritzer and Don Slater, editors) promised to bring together multidisciplinary European and North American work but not to bridge all other gaps. The prospectus for the new journal stressed a two-pronged program: first, the study of consumption as mediation and reproduction of culture and social structure, including that of class; second, consumer culture as a special feature of modernity and therefore a privileged prism for its examination (Ritzer and Slater 2001).

What of economic sociology itself?

How Consumption Studies Challenge Economic Sociology

Economic sociology's most prominent reader, *The Sociology of Economic Life*, with twenty-two selections of what its two editors, Mark Granovetter and Richard Swedberg, define as "the most interesting work done in modern economic sociology" (2001, 19), barely touches on consumption. The closest instances are a famous article by Clifford Geertz (no economic sociologist) on bazaars and an essay by Paul Hirsch on fads and fashions, which looks primarily at their production. Indeed, economic sociology grew up concentrating on production and distribution, rather than consumption.

The implicit intellectual strategy of economic sociology reinforced this emphasis. Three somewhat different approaches have characterized the field; we might call them extension, context, and alternative. They vary with respect to economics in two regards: their proximity to standard economic explanations and their proximity to conventional economic subject matters (for elaboration of this argument, see Zelizer 2001, 2002b).

Extension theorists apply relatively standard economic models to social phenomena economists themselves have not treated widely or effectively, for example, household behavior, sporting competition, religious recruitment, and compliance with states. A *context* approach identifies features of social organization that work as facilitators or constraints on economic action. This position is intent on revamping economists' portrayals of individual and collective decision making, for example, by specifying conditions other than short-term gain that influence decisions. Advocates of context often speak of the "embeddedness" of economic phenomena in social processes, and often refer to interpersonal networks when they do so (see, e.g., Granovetter 1985; Granovetter and Soong 1986). Followers of this approach have focused on firms and different kinds of markets.

In the *alternative* perspective, sociologists propose competing accounts of economic transactions. Rather than expanding the economic approach or complementing it, one prominent view argues that in all areas of economic life people are creating, maintaining, symbolizing, and transforming meaningful social relations (see, e.g., Tilly and Tilly 1998; White 2002). As a result, the subject matter certainly includes firms and markets but also ranges over households, immigrant networks, informal economies, welfare transfers, or organ donations.

The first two orientations largely follow economists' own stress on production and distribution. The third deals more extensively with consumption but without working out a consistent, comprehensive line of explanation.

A further barrier to the systematic study of consumption results from a common misunderstanding that cuts across the three different variants of economic sociology. Analysts of economic processes share a powerful view of a world split into two diametrically opposed spheres: a zone of markets and rationality, another of sentiment and meaning. In this *hostile-worlds* framework, production and distribution belong to the "real" economy, while consumption remains segregated into culture's expressive domain. Any contact between the two, in this view, produces contamination of one by the other: penetration of the cultural realm by the rationality of production and distribution taints its expressive and affectionate character, while the diffusion of sentiment into the world of economic rationality generates inefficiency, cronyism, and confusion.

Thus the hostile-worlds doctrine hinders analysis of interplay between the social relations of consumption and the processes of production and distribution. Some analysts have resolved this dualism by turning to *nothing-but* reductionist alternatives: consumption becomes nothing but a special case of economic rationality, a form of cultural expression, or an exercise of power. Thus, French sociologist Jean Baudrillard offers an extreme version of cultural reductionism:

Consumer behavior, which appears to be focused and directed at the object and at pleasure, in fact responds to quite different objectives: the metaphoric or displaced expression of desire, and the production of a code of social values through the use of differentiating signs. That which is determinant is not the function of individual interest within a corpus of objects, but rather the specifically social functions of exchange, communication and distribution of values within a corpus of signs. (1999, 47; see also Bauman 1998, 79–85)

Neither hostile-worlds tropes nor nothing-but simplifications will help us understand how consumption actually works. We need a different approach we might call "crossroads": identifying multiple forms of connections between complex social processes and their economic components.

Reaching such an intersection, we find two major forms of analysis dealing with consumption without crippling limitations. The first has a long pedigree in sociology. In the tradition of Veblen, it treats consumption as positional effort—establishment of social location, boundaries, and hierarchies through the display of goods and services. For example, Diana Crane casts a keen eye on class differences in clothing among nineteenth-century French men:

Workers behaved as if they considered some types of fashionable items, such as gloves, canes, top hats and bowlers, as inappropriate for their own use. The reluctance to use these items cannot be explained by their expense. Workers' incomes were rising throughout the period. . . . Instead, the explanation may lie in the fact that these items required a greater understanding of standards of middle-class etiquette than other items. In this sense, these sartorial signs were effective in distinguishing between those who knew the "rules" and were able to follow them and those who did not. (2000, 62)

The second approach treats consumption as relational work—the creation, maintenance, negotiation, and alteration of interpersonal connections through acquisition and use of goods and services. Thus when Elizabeth Chin (2001) worked with ten-year-old, low-income black children in New Haven, Connecticut, she found that the children's purchases recurrently served to affirm relations with other members of their households.

Economic sociologists have recently built social relations firmly into the analysis of connections among Australian hotel managers, negotiations among New York City apparel manufacturers, purchases of consumer durables, consumption struggles in Chilean workers' households, and rotating savings and credit associations (see Ingram and Roberts 2000; Uzzi 1997; DiMaggio and Louch 1998; Stillerman 2004; Biggart 2001; for more general treatments of culture, social relations, and consumption, see DiMaggio 1990, 1994).

Summing up that trend, Nicole Woolsey Biggart and Richard Castanias (2001, 491–92) enumerate five characteristics of interplay between economic transactions and social relations:

1. Social relations should not be conflated with irrationality.

2. Social relations can facilitate exchange, not only act as an impediment or friction.
3. Social relations can manage the risks associated with exchange.
4. Actors can appropriate others' social relations for their own exploitation and gain.
5. While social relations may result from exchange, social relations may be prior to economic activity and be the very reason that the transaction takes place between given parties.

This welcome trend has not gone far enough. We must probe further into the negotiation of meaning, the transformation of relations in the course of economic interaction, and the social process of valuation itself. To do so, we need a junction between research being done outside economic sociology and the work within the field. Our agenda, however, should not be to glue everything together but to obtain a new theory of consumption organized around meaningful, negotiated social relations. Historical evidence, ethnographic accounts, and marketing studies all can help us clarify how precisely social relations operate in consumption.

That agenda will become more concrete as I examine three major sites of consumption: households, ethnic-racial communities, and retail settings. In each case, I scrutinize consumption relations from three different angles: within the site, across the site's boundaries, and with respect to variation and change in those sites. In each case, the argument will have a negative and a positive side. Negatively, it will reject the notions that consumption is a peripheral economic process, that it resides in a separate world of sentiment, or that it consists primarily in the acquisition rather than the use of goods and services. Positively, it will show the centrality of continuously negotiated and meaningful interpersonal relations in a wide range of consumption processes. Because consumption of services often involves activation or creation of interpersonal relations by definition, the following discussion will concentrate on the less obvious side: acquisition and use of goods.

HOUSEHOLDS AS SITES OF CONSUMPTION

In the case of the household, analysts long assumed it would remain, in Christopher Lasch's (1977) terms, a "haven in a heartless world," protecting its members from the harshness of markets. Instead, we find households to be central sites of production, distribution, and consumption. Researchers have amply established, furthermore, the complex internal diversity within household units and the incessant interplay between households and extra-household economic activities.

Marjorie DeVault's (1991) analysis of feeding work traces the profoundly social character of households' most fundamental economic activities. The largely invisible, unpaid labor of planning, shopping, and preparing meals involves constant, often contested, negotiations of family relationships. Drawing from her interviews of a diverse set of thirty households in the Chicago area, DeVault reports women—who do most of the feeding work within households—striving to match meals with expected definitions of husband-wife or mother-child relationships. For example, appropriate meals for husbands involved enactment of deference to a man's preoccupations and responsibilities outside the household. Meals, DeVault demonstrates, involved more than nutrition or economy: they routinely symbolized appropriately gendered ties.

Food acquisition and preparation, however, inform a whole set of social relations beyond gender. DeVault provides a telling example of how Janice, a nurse living with her husband and two adult children, manages simultaneously to preserve both family cohesion and independence:

> Meals are often family events, prepared and eaten at home together. Janice or the children decide on the spur of the moment whether or not to cook, and "whoever is home sits down and eats it." Janice's shopping is what makes this kind of independence possible: "What I do is provide enough food in the house for anybody who wants to eat. And then whoever is home, makes that meal, if they want it." (1991, 63)

Each of her respondents, DeVault observes, "[t]hrough day-to-day activities . . . produces a version of 'family' in a particular local setting: adjusting, filling in, and repairing social relations to produce—quite literally—this form of household life" (1991, 91; for parallel observations on gay and lesbian households, see Carrington 1999).

To be sure, as DeVault shows, not all household relations of consumption generate harmony and collaboration. Consider another well-documented study. In his account of Philadelphia's inner-city, poor, African American children, Carl Nightingale reports acute rancor and conflict between parents and children in their negotiations over consumption. Parents exasperated by their kids' unreasonable and persistent demands for spending money are pitted against children disappointed by their parents' inability to provide them with material goods. Contests over how to spend limited family monies, including income tax refunds or welfare checks, Nightingale observes, severely strain household relations:

> All the kids whose families I knew well lived through similar incidents: yelling matches between Fahim and his mother on how she spent her welfare check, Theresa's disgust when she found out she was not going to get a dress because her mom's boyfriend had demanded some of the family's monthly money for crack, and Omar's decision to leave his mother's house altogether because "I hate her. She always be asking y'all [the Kids' Club] for money. That's going to get around, and

people'll be talking." Also he felt that she never had enough money for his school clothes. (1993, 159; see also Bourgois 1995)

Thus, consumption within households takes place in a context of incessant negotiation, sometimes cooperative, other times full of conflict.

As DeVault's and Nightingale's studies illustrate, negotiations over consumption within the household regularly involve the parties in economic relations that cross the household's boundaries. Consider the purchase of a home, a household's most significant investment. In their detailed investigation of how French households acquire their homes, Pierre Bourdieu's (2000) research team observed interactions and bargaining sessions between sellers and potential buyers in home shows, recorded conversations between sellers and buyers, and interviewed salespeople, merchandisers, and builders (for changes in the Chinese housing market, see Davis 2002).

Based on those observations, Bourdieu stresses the following points:

- The purchase of a home engages interactions not only between nominal buyer and seller, but among multiple parties: other household members, friends, credit agencies, and builders.
- In addition to these parties, the state always plays a crucial part as guarantor, and sometimes as a direct participant in the transaction.
- For household members, the purchase of a home represents simultaneously a deep financial commitment, a statement concerning the household's social position, the creation of space for household activities, and a series of commitments concerning futures of the households' members. As Bourdieu summarizes: a home is a "consumer good, which, because of its high cost, represents one of the most difficult economic decisions and one of the most consequential in the entire domestic life-cycle" (2000, 33).
- When it comes to buyer-seller negotiations, bargaining involves elements of manipulation along with personalization.
- A triple negotiation takes place over the purchase of a house: identification of the suitable home, establishment of credit, and working out a story of what the house will do for the buyer.

The path that led to a particular seller often passed through the buyer's friends and neighbors.

Bourdieu concludes that the housing market, while profoundly structured by established political interests, legal limitations, financial constraints, and its deep symbolic charge is, nevertheless, far from being a static, prescribed set of exchanges. Buyers and sellers' negotiations create unanticipated, often surprising outcomes. Bourdieu observes that a sale takes place

only through a series of interactions, all of them unforeseen and aleatory—for example a couple who might have passed by, gone to another stand, or left saying they would return, actually find themselves signing a commitment. . . . Far from simply expressing the logic of the economic relation, the interaction actually creates that relation; it is always uncertain and its development is full of suspense and surprise. (2000, 210)

When Paul DiMaggio and Hugh Louch (1998) undertook their own investigation of how Americans acquired consumer durables, including homes, their findings pointed in the same direction as Bourdieu's. Analyzing a general survey of the American population, they looked closely at reports of recent major purchases. As they examined preexisting, noncommercial ties between buyers and sellers in consumer transactions involving the purchase of cars, homes, as well as legal and home repair services, DiMaggio and Louch found a remarkably high incidence of what they call within-network exchanges. Contrary to the notion of an impersonal market, a substantial number of such transactions took place not between strangers but among kin, friends, or acquaintances. Noting that this pattern applies primarily to risky, one-shot transactions involving high uncertainty about quality and performance, DiMaggio and Louch conclude that consumers will be more likely to rely on such noncommercial ties when they are unsure about the outcome.

These close-up studies by DeVault, Bourdieu, and DiMaggio and Louch give us a keen sense of the importance of interpersonal ties in household consumption. They naturally provide little information, however, about larger-scale change and variation in the character of those ties. For that kind of information we must turn to another style of research. Following the trails blazed by Susan Gal and Gail Kligman (2000), Caroline Humphrey (1995), Alena Ledeneva (1998), and Katherine Verdery, Daphne Berdahl (1999) has used her sustained ethnography of Kella, an East German border village, to pursue a double comparison—between East and West Germany under separate regimes, and in East Germany before and after unification.

Among other things, Berdahl shows that interpersonal and interhousehold networks played a critical part in mutual aid under East Germany's socialist regime. Household consumption was at the very center of those exchanges. In conditions of great scarcity, as they obtained food products, clothing, and other household goods, Kella villagers depended less on available cash than on their personal connections. As one woman explained to Berdahl: "Money actually did help you: it helped maintain the connections! But the connections were most important" (1999, 120). In this informal economy, Berdahl reports, "networks of friendships, acquaintances, and associates were created and maintained through gift exchange, bribes, and barter trade" (118). The type of transfer, furthermore, differed by the nature of the relationship (see Rose-Ackerman 1998; Zelizer 1998). While gifts and barter took place among friends, kin, and acquaintances, bribes were reserved for more distant connections:

Slipping the local grocery clerk an extra twenty marks or a western chocolate bar meant that she would probably set aside a few bananas or green peppers under the counter whenever a shipment of these or other coveted fruits and vegetables came in. A homemade wurst could guarantee being bumped to the top of the waiting list of the driving school. (Berdahl 1999, 119)

After the fall of the Wall, Berdahl suggests, consumption practices and relations were transformed. In the new market economy, as money became a greater mediator of personal relationships, informal networks lost much of their importance in providing access to consumer goods. However, consumption did not lose its importance. The character and quantity of goods and services—especially visibly expensive ones—consumed by a household, Berdahl argues, became an even greater point of distinction among households.

The very richness of Berdahl's ethnography raises the question of whether networks have actually shriveled or instead, changed in character, as seems more likely. In any case, Berdahl's close observation provides a model for the examination of variation and change in household consumption.

Consumption in Ethnic and Racial Communities

In history and the social sciences a great deal of attention has gone into ethnic production, especially in the form of sweatshops, labor market segregation, and the informal economy. Ethnic consumption has received somewhat less attention. Any discussion of consumption in ethnic and racial communities, however, plays out against two general debates—one about the relative merits of assimilation versus multiculturalism, the second concerning bases of ethnic and racial inequality (for convenience, the remainder of this discussion will use *ethnic communities* to signal both race and national origin). More specific debates surrounding ethnic consumption pivot on the following issues: Does consumption trump ethnic solidarities by homogenizing tastes, or is consumption a means for asserting ethnic identities? Are all ethnic groups equally competent consumers, or do some ethnic populations require education? Does consumer culture oppress and exploit relatively impoverished, powerless ethnic groups, or can consumption subvert domination?

To some extent market researchers avoid these moral and political questions; they commonly seek to explain or influence the purchases by members of different demographic categories (see, e.g., Turow 1997; Schreiber 2001; Venkatesh 1995; Weiss 1988; for similar processes among gay and lesbian consumers, see Badgett 2001). In history and the social sciences, however, the discussion of consumption in ethnic communities rarely proceeds without these pressing issues in the background. Thus, energy and imagination pour into a wide range of analyses concerning consumption in ethnic communities. As with households, this overview will move from internal consumption practices to relations between ethnic communities and other sites, then close with change and variation among ethnic communities.

What is distinctive about ethnic communities? They have two special characteristics: first, their reinforcement through residential, labor market, and linguistic segregation and, second, the frequent feeding of major segments of their population by extensive migration streams. Segregation not only sharpens the boundaries between insiders and outsiders, but also intensifies communication within the boundaries and establishes populations that share a common fate. Shared migration streams produce their own characteristic clusters of social relations, their own cultural practices, and their own lines of communication to fellow migrants elsewhere as well as to their place of origin. As Charles Tilly puts it: "networks migrate; categories stay put; and networks create new categories" (1990, 84).

All of these traits have strong implications for the culture of consumption. Let us concentrate on four salient ways in which this works within ethnic communities: first, members of the community (for example, first-generation migrants) often maintain their community's internal representation through consumption goods and practices; second, consumption marks distinctions within the ethnic community, for example young/old, male/female, rich/poor, religious/nonreligious; third, households use ethnic forms of consumption to maintain their position within the community; fourth, some members of the ethnic community—ethnic entrepreneurs—specialize in retailing ethnic merchandise representing their community.

Ewa Morawska's classic study of eastern European immigrants and their descendants in Johnstown, Pennsylvania, shows us all four sorts of processes at work. Johnstown's Slovaks, Magyars, Croatians, Serbs, Slovenes, Poles, Ukrainians, and Rusyns had members who attempted to maintain group identity and solidarity through consumption, marked their internal differences through consumption, employed ethnic involvements to meet their consumption needs, and hosted entrepreneurs who made their businesses the interfaces among production, distribution, and consumption. In hard times, the third process provided the means of survival. As Morawska puts it, Johnstown's ethnic communities used their connections to seek or preserve the good life:

> These options included the search, through kinship and ethnic networks, for a better job: if possible, better-skilled, as there appeared in the mills more of the mechanized tasks; if not, then more remunerative, either within the same or another Bethlehem department or with a different local manufacturer. They included, too, overtime work and moonlighting at night and during weekends. They also involved

increasing the total family income by entering into the labor market all employable members of the household, keeping boarders, renting out part of a newly purchased house, reducing household expenditures through extensive reliance on home production of food from gardens and domestic animals, on women's abilities to prepare and preserve food and to sew and weave, and on men's old-country skills in carpentry, masonry, and other household repairs. (1985, 185–86)

Thus consumption did not merely reproduce, amuse, and satisfy members of Johnstown's ethnic communities; it helped them organize their social lives.

Of course, the four consumption processes often intersect. For instance, Kathy Peiss's study of the cosmetic industry in the United States provides clear indications of African American entrepreneurship, gender distinctions within the African American community, as well as showing the significance of the beauty culture for maintaining black solidarity. Peiss reports how, between the 1890s and 1920s, black women, along with immigrant and working-class women, pioneered the cosmetic industry. Successful African American female entrepreneurs, such as Madam C. J. Walker and Annie Turnbo Malone, Peiss notes, "embedded the beauty trade in the daily life of black communities linked by kin, neighbors, churches, and schools" (1998, 90). Indeed, the beauty business both depended on and reinforced customers' social connections:

Word of hair growers and shampoos made by African-American women spread rapidly. Women convinced each other to try these new products, buying boxes of glossine and hair grower for relatives and friends, practicing the art of hairdressing on each other. Like many women, Elizabeth Clark placed an order with Madam Walker "not for my self" but "for a friend of mine." For these businesses, word of mouth was the finest form of advertising. (1998, 90)

The women's connections went well beyond mutual grooming. Some cosmetic entrepreneurs in fact involved themselves, their agents, and their customers in public politics. Madam Walker, for instance, not only supported her agents' participation in African American community affairs but encouraged their political activism. Walker herself, Peiss notes, backed the politically militant National Equal Rights League and the International League of Darker Peoples. As Peiss observes: "commercial beauty culture was something much more than an isolated act of consumption or vanity. In the hands of African American women entrepreneurs, it became an economic and aesthetic form that spoke to black women's collective experiences and aspirations" (1998, 95).

Consumption also builds connections between ethnic communities and the rest of the world. In fact, ethnic entrepreneurs often specialize in mediating between their communities and producers, distributors, or consumers outside. While doing a splendid job of portraying the internal consumption practices of Mexican immigrants in early-twentieth-century Los Angeles, George Sánchez (1993) also shows such entrepreneurs at work.

Examining the lively Mexican music industry during the 1920s, Sánchez reports ethnic middlemen's crucial role in linking promising local musicians with American recording industries (for a pioneering statement on how cultural industries operate, see Hirsch 1972). For instance, Mauricio Calderón, a noted entrepreneur and owner of the music store Repertorio Musical Mexicana,

> recruited talented musicians by advertising in the Spanish-language press, and kept an ear out for the latest musical trends among the city's performers and audiences. Not only did Calderón make money by serving as go-between between American companies and the Mexican artists, but he also held a monopoly on the area-wide distribution of these recordings through his store. (Sánchez 1993, 182)

Within the community, Calderón likewise merchandised Mexican music; for example, by giving records away with purchases of a Victrola, or by playing corridas—one of the most popular musical styles—from a loudspeaker in front of his store: "a small group of men regularly stood in front of the store, listening intently and enjoying the music" (Sánchez 1993, 182).

But that was not all. Mexican-American brokers sustained a flow of musicians into Los Angeles from Mexico; they supplied music for Mexican street festivals, weddings, and other ethnic celebrations. They also exported Mexican music to Anglo festivities, as a reminder of the city's Spanish past. Pedro González, later a renowned musician, recalled playing at events sponsored by city officials and the fire department.

What is more, between the 1920s and 1930s, Spanish-language radio became a major link among entrepreneurs, Mexican immigrants, and the Anglo world. For example, Calderón and other Chicano middlemen, reports Sánchez, "profited handsomely as they negotiated with stations, paying them a flat rate during cheap broadcasting time, which they then sold to businesses advertisements" (Sánchez 1993, 183). Mexican immigrants tuned into the radio shows during early morning hours as they prepared for work, enjoying the music but also receiving crucial job information.

Behind all this cultural activity lay the work of Mexican-American entrepreneurs, who

> served as conduits between the Mexican immigrant population and the corporate world. These individuals were often the first to recognize cultural changes and spending patterns among the immigrant population. Individuals such as Mauricio Calderón and Pedro J. González

were able to promote Mexican music in entirely new forms in Los Angeles because they had daily contact with ordinary members of the Los Angeles Mexican community. Although they found tangible financial rewards in their efforts, they also served an important role in redefining Mexican culture in an American urban environment. (Sánchez 1993, 187)

Thus, ethnic entrepreneurship fed on swelling migration of Mexicans to Los Angeles, strengthening ties between Mexican and Californian cultures (for a variety of ethnic entrepreneurs and marketers, see Lamont and Molnár 2001; Nightingale 1993; Pérez Firmat 1994; Portes and Stepick 1993; Weems 1994).

Immigrant remittances similarly strengthen ties between places of origin and destination (Roberts and Morris 2003). Remittances show us, furthermore, that not all ethnic entrepreneurs stay fixed within their communities (on transnationalism, see Portes 2001; Portes, Haller, and Guarnizo 2002). Sarah Mahler's study of undocumented Salvadoran immigrants in Long Island clarifies their reliance on personal couriers for conveying goods and cash to and from their homeland (1995, 142–44). Personal couriers take their place among a variety of media for transmitting back and forth between El Salvador and Long Island: the U.S. Postal Service, Western Union–style specialized remittance organizations, and local multipurpose agencies. They carry not only money but gifts of food and clothing, including "Corn Flakes, CD players, soccer shoes . . . brand-new jeans and T-shirts" and even love notes for distant sweethearts" (Moreno 2001, B1).

Goods and services flow in both directions. Salvadoran residents supply their migrant relatives with local medicines and food: "they might bring a box stuffed with mom's grilled chicken to a lonely son or a fresh pot of mango spread to a granddaughter" (Moreno 2001, B1). Some migrants, Mahler reports, "waited weeks to receive salves or pills from home instead of seeking costly medical care and prescription drugs here" (1995, 143).

The Salvadoran remitters face a double relational problem of exchanging resources with distant family members and establishing reliable ties with the intermediaries. The *viajeros* (couriers) establish personal relations with both senders and receivers, thus building the trustworthiness (*confianza*) of the connection. Couriers, observes Mahler, "seal their transactions with handshakes, not receipts" (1995, 143). In earlier conditions of civil war, Salvadoran couriers filled in where official transactions had no power to operate.

In the Salvadoran case, senders and recipients are connected by intermediaries. In other cases, donors actually deliver money, goods, and services themselves. For example, any flight from New York City to Central America or the Caribbean—most dramatically on holidays—carries numerous migrants who are returning to their place of origin with household goods and other gifts. On their return trip, travelers usually have lighter baggage but have stocked up on their favorite homeland products.

Peggy Levitt describes how this transnational economy operates. In her close observation of ties between Miraflores, a Dominican Republic town, and the Boston neighborhood of Jamaica Plains where many of their relatives migrated, Levitt notes that

> fashion, food, and forms of speech, as well as appliances and home decorating styles, attest to these strong connections. In Miraflores, villagers often dress in T-shirts emblazoned with the names of businesses in Massachusetts, although they do not know what these words or logos mean. They proudly serve their visitors coffee with Cremora and juice made from Tang. (2001a, 2)

Nonmigrant Dominicans, in turn, often provide migrants with child care, supervise their local affairs, and treat them as "royal guests" during visits. Forty-year-old Cecilia, with three siblings in Boston, "wants to give something back to her brothers and sisters, but she is exhausted when they leave" (Levitt 2001a, 90). Levitt points out that narrowly economic interchange is only part of the remittance flow; she calls attention to what she calls "social remittances," the transfer of "ideas, behaviors, identities, and social capital that flow from host- to sending-country communities" (54). Social and material remittances, however, do not constitute separate streams; in both cases people are fashioning and refashioning meaningful social relations, in some cases with consumer goods, in others with belief systems, social practices, or network connections. (On how remittance systems connect to bargaining within households, see Curran and Saguy 2001; Grasmuck and Pessar 1991.)

Collectively, remittances are consequential transfers, with large macroeconomic impact. For instance, in 1994, almost 40 percent of Miraflores's households reported that between 75 and 100 percent of their income came from remittances. Nearly 60 percent of those households reported receiving some monthly income from migrant relatives (Levitt 2001b, 200). Official estimates of national totals surely understate their true value. Nevertheless, for the Dominican Republic as a whole, the 1996 count was $1.14 billion, while for Mexico, the official figure was $2 billion (Waller Meyers 1998; see also de la Garza and Lowell 2002; Pew Hispanic Center 2003).

Finally, while participants and observers of remittance systems often deplore the fact that a good deal of expenditure goes into consumer display rather than productive investment, Durand, Parrado, and Massey (1996) demonstrate that in fact consumption creates large demand for both local and national producers. Even what they call "migradollars" earned by immigrants, and spent for food, drink, music, or fireworks in apparently "wasteful" local Mexican festivities, spur regional production and income. Durand,

Parrado, and Massey estimate that, at the national level, the $2 billion migra-dollars generate $6.5 billion additional production in Mexico.

Holiday celebrations, in fact, provide an entrée to the comparative analysis of ethnic consumption. Consider this selection from the mid-nineteenth century's vast assortment of local civic holidays reported by Leigh Schmidt: New York City's republican Evacuation Day, Irish Catholics' St. Patrick's Day, Scots' St. Andrew's Day, patrician Knickerbockers' St. Nicholas's Day, New Englander's Pilgrim Day, Charlestown's Bunker Hill Day. "Ethnic particularity, eclecticism, and localism," Schmidt notes, "seemed to impede national observances at every turn" (1995, 33–34). Yet, by the end of the century national holiday traditions had been installed, largely propelled by the expansion of a consumerist economy and culture. Merchants, recognizing the commercial potential of holiday celebrations, displayed, promoted, and in the process nationalized both holiday observances and material symbols, such as the mass-produced greeting cards, Valentine cupids and hearts, Santa Clauses, or chocolate Easter bunnies. "The consumer culture," Schmidt concludes, "more than folk tradition, local custom, or religious community, increasingly provided the common forms and materials for American celebrations" (297).

Yet, as with other consumer goods, people and groups, even as they shared in the increasingly nationalized, standardized, consumer-oriented celebrations, found ways to simultaneously particularize their holidays. Mary Waters (1990) has shown that contemporary Americans attach themselves to symbolic ethnicity by means of holiday celebrations, foods, and other representations of their origins. This process was already well under way a half-century ago. By the 1920s, for instance, American Jews revitalized the languishing holiday of Chanukah into what Jenna Joselit (1994, 229) calls a "functional equivalent" to Christmas, shopping for and exchanging gifts (see also Heinze 1990). Even the Christmas Club savings concept was adapted to Chanukah: "Save for Chanukah" ads by the East River Savings Institution appeared in Yiddish newspapers. Although printed in Yiddish, the ads pictured a young couple standing next to a Christmas tree (Joselit 1994, 234, and personal communication). Once again, merchandisers picked up the cue, creating specialized products and connections for the Chanukah market. Toy manufacturers, for instance, produced

> Jewish-oriented novelties that ran the gamut from pinwheels and board games . . . to cookie cutters shaped like a Jewish star and oversized dreidels like the four-foot-tall "Maccabee." A creation of the Dra-Dell Corporation of Bergen, New Jersey, this object "expresses a true holiday spirit in the home . . . and is a fine addition to the Chanukah atmosphere." . . . [T]hese objects reflected the needs of a new community of Jewish consumers: children. (Joselit 1994, 80–81)

Christmas also changed. In earlier U.S. history, as Karal Ann Marling (2000, 256–76) points out, one of the most remarkable developments was the integration of African Americans into public representations of Christmas. By the 1960s, however, African Americans fashioned their own December holiday of Kwanzaa, drawing not only from Christmas but also from African harvest festivals, Chanukah, and New Year's Eve. Elizabeth Pleck sums up the holiday's origins:

> Kwanzaa was a nationalist—specifically, black nationalist—holiday and had a specific creator [Ron (Maudana) Karenga], who designed it as a celebration of the African harvest, with the intention that American blacks, in exile from their African homeland, would continue traditions and celebrate their African heritage. (2000, 6)

Although Kwanzaa was intended to counter the commercial orientation of dominant holidays, by the early 1980s it had incorporated consumerism in its practice, with the production of videos and books, Kwanzaa greeting cards and wrapping paper, cookbooks, along with Afrocentric clothes, artwork, jewelry, and music (Schmidt 1995, 300–301; Austin 2004). Recent Indian immigrants likewise construct dual holiday celebrations; one study reports Indian immigrant families celebrating Thanksgiving with turkey and stuffing combined with curries and other Indian foods (Mehta and Belk 1991, 407). Armenian families, meanwhile, serve their Thanksgiving turkey with rice pilaf, boreog, and stuffed vine leaves (Bakalian 1993, 366: see also Gabaccia 1998; Halter 2000; Light and Gold 2000).

Clearly, across ethnic communities, culture, social relations, and consumption vary and change together in dramatic fashion.

RETAIL SETTINGS FOR CONSUMPTION

Nor does culture disappear from retail settings. On the contrary, a surprising degree of cultural work goes on within and among retail establishments—places where consumers purchase goods and services. In fact, people engage in three somewhat different types of relational activity in such settings. They acquire goods and services for other people, engage in sociable interactions with fellow customers and retail personnel, and display group memberships and differences from other people by means of their purchases.

My earlier discussion of shopping malls, however, indicated that observers have often interpreted the expansion of retail trade as promoting commodification, thereby destroying earlier forms of meaningful social connections. Bidding up Robert Putnam, social critic Jeremy Rifkin, for instance, declares shopping malls' "central mission" to be "the commodification of lived experiences in the form of the purchase of goods and entertainment" (2000, 155).

Commodification, in this account, substitutes impersonal rationality for the rich, sentimental connections of earlier ages.

Yet, as we have already seen, people construct and refashion meaningful social relations across a wide variety of commercial settings. To be sure, major changes in retailing did occur from the nineteenth to the twenty-first centuries: a larger proportion of all goods and services arrive through commercial transactions, the scale and geographic concentration of retail establishments has increased, and the direct sale and delivery of goods and services to households has declined (Cowan 1983). Households, therefore, found themselves much more heavily engaged in external shopping than had once been true. At first glance, moreover, a series of innovations in retailing, for example, the one-price system, self-service, and the substitution of credit cards for local account books, seemed to replace personalized connections with impersonal routines. In fact, within the retail setting, each of these altered the terms of social interaction but without eliminating personal contact between merchant and customer. The effects of these multiple changes in retail practice, then, were never to obliterate meaningful social relations but to alter their character and geography significantly.

Paralleling the previous discussions, this section will examine retail settings in three steps: first, relations within retail establishments; then, relations across boundaries; and, finally, change and variation.

For culturally informed social relations within retail settings, consider restaurants. In their study of food consumption outside the home in England during the 1990s, Alan Warde and Lydia Martens discovered that, paradoxically, "eating out is more convivial than eating at home" (2000, 108; see also Illouz 1997, chap. 4). Using interviews and a survey, they found that most of their 1,001 respondents ate out with family members. Other frequent dining companions were friends and romantic partners. In fact only 2 percent reported being alone the last time they had eaten out. However, eating out did make some difference, since the effort of preparing the meal did not fall on women, as characteristically happens in households. Eating outside the home thus provides the opportunity for a more equal exchange around the table.

What is more, eating out might even generate greater sociability than dining at home. As one respondent, Trisha, put it:

I think it's easier, when you're sat over a meal, to talk about things. Probably if you're sat with a take-away you tend to be glued to the telly, whereas rather if you're just sat together over a meal you do tend to have a better conversation really because you haven't as many distractions and things like that, it's quite nice. You know, it's socialising involved especially with your boyfriend. (Warde and Martens 2000, 205)

Yet one might think that any sort of social interaction vanishes in the world of fast foods. After all, Edward Hopper's emblematic painting of a diner, *Nighthawks*, shows each customer and a counterman staring silently into private spaces. In the modern equivalent of the diner, the fast-food palace, however, Robin Leidner (1993) observes a steady flow of social interaction between customers and serving personnel. McDonald's, of course, represents the paradigm of an impersonal, routinized consumer world. Indeed, George Ritzer (1996) has made McDonald's the central symbol of economic standardization in the world of consumption. Drawing on her fieldwork at a McDonald's franchise near Chicago, Leidner reports extensive organizational scripting of work routines, ranging from food preparation to worker-consumer interaction. The Six Steps of Window Service, for instance, closely guide workers' behavior: "(1) greet the customer, (2) take the order, (3) assemble the order, (4) present the order, (5) receive payment, and (6) thank the customer and ask for repeat business" (Leidner 1993, 68). More significantly, as Leidner shows, the rules standardized "attitudes and demeanors as well as words and actions" (73).

However, anyone who enjoys ballroom dancing, tennis, or chess knows that routinized interaction need not be impersonal. There are two fallacies to avoid: first, the notion that standardization of interpersonal relations necessarily destroys human contact; and second, the contrary view that all social interaction is intrinsically satisfying. As Leidner discovered: "despite the specificity of the script and the brevity of most encounters with customers, the service interactions were not all alike and were not necessarily devoid of personal involvement" (1993, 136). Workers enjoyed their albeit brief conversations or jokes with customers, occasionally providing some customers with extra services.

Regular customers, meanwhile, often established ongoing ties with workers. As Matthew told Leidner:

> What I like [is that] when you work window you get to know every customer that come in here every day. You get to remember their faces, you get to know what they want . . . and all they have to [do is] just show their faces, and you just grab the tray and set up everything they need, 'cause they get everything the same every day. (Leidner 1993, 141)

Personalized interactions, however, were not all cordial. Partly because of the low status of their jobs, workers were sometimes subjected to customers' "rude, sarcastic, and insulting remarks" (Leidner 1993, 132). In such cases, the interactive script broke down: the worker "might withhold smiles, risk a show of impatience or irritation with a customer, or refuse to suggest additional purchases or to encourage return business" (135; for similar interactions in New York's Harlem, see Newman 1999). Furthermore, some workers actually welcomed the protection provided by routinized interactions. The point is that whether friendly, hostile, or strictly limited, the participants were engaging in negotiated, meaningful social interactions (for discussions of conflicts between blacks and shopkeepers, see Austin 1994; Lee 2002).

The custom of thinking about retail settings as self-contained locations makes the thought of cross-cutting ties hard to manage at first. However, if we consider a retail setting to be any location in which people purchase goods and services, this immediately calls to mind, among others, supermarkets, shopping malls, department stores, country stores, video stores, garage sales, street fairs, junk shops, pawnshops, thrift shops, restaurants, coffee shops, airport shops, bookstores, newsstands, fashion outlets, automobile dealerships, art galleries, movies, theaters, and mom-and-pop stores. In all of these retail sites, relations of both consumers and merchants to such groups as neighbors, friends, households, police, protesters, looters, gangs, credit agencies, labor unions, courts, and so on, play a significant part in their operations.

Rather than focusing on the more obvious cases of department stores or supermarkets, let us take two challenging sites: pawnshops and direct-selling organizations. In both cases, we observe the intersection of an active retail setting with webs of social relations that extend far beyond that site.

The pawnshop is a remarkable device, a sort of bank that lends cash against the security of saleable objects. Pawnbrokers must develop great skills in judging other people and establishing trustworthy relations with them. With the expansion of wage labor and purchased commodities during the nineteenth century, the pawnshop became a crucial institution in working-class communities across the Western world. In the United States, Lendol Calder notes, "a wide variety of people found their way into pawnshops, including salesmen and travelers with emergency needs for cash, and petty shopkeepers in need of a quick loan to pay off creditors" (1999, 43). Commonly pawned objects ranged from items of clothing and jewelry, to musical instruments, bedding, guns, household furniture, and more exceptionally coffins, false teeth, and even automobiles (44).

Among the wide range of customers, households often balanced short-run fluctuations in their budgets by pawning or redeeming household objects. In her account of housewives' economic strategies among the London poor between 1870 and 1918, Ellen Ross reports women's extensive reliance on pawnshops to make ends meet: "COS [Charity Organisation Society] caseworkers investigating the assets of households applying for aid were invariably shown bundles of pawn tickets by the women with whom they spoke. . . . Lent, stolen, or honestly obtained pledge tickets were transferred and traded in complex patterns among groups of women" (1993, 82; see also Tebbutt 1983).

Women developed specialized bargaining skills, knowing which shops gave better value to their pledges—so much so that thieves regularly relied on women to serve as their intermediaries with pawnbrokers. While recounting his long life to Raphael Samuel during the 1970s, retired East London petty criminal, cabinetmaker, and furniture merchant Arthur Harding recalled a time before World War I:

> There was a woman in nearly every street of the East End of London who got a living taking neighbours' things to the pawn shop. The pawn-shop broker would lend her more than he would an ordinary customer on the goods because he knew that she would get 'em out again on Saturday—he trusted her. He didn't want to be lumbered up with a shop-load of stuff that wasn't going to be redeemed. He'd sooner do business with her, than a person who fetched a load of stuff in there and didn't intend to redeem 'em. (Samuel 1981, 90)

Indeed, women fashioned particularized relations with pawnbrokers' clerks. Ross reports a son describing his mother's negotiating skills:

> One went into a cubicle where the gent behind the counter usually knew his customers. "How much?" were his first words. "Ten shillings," says Mum. "Seven," said the gent behind the counter. "Oh Christ," says Mum. "Don't be like that, Sid." "All right," says Sid, "I'll make it eight bob, but don't forget it's the last time I take this lot in." (1993, 83)

Pawnshops still thrive in Western cities today. With sharpening income inequality and partial deregulation of banking, America's pawnshops, after a decline between 1930 and 1970, have multiplied since the 1980s. From a low of 4,849 in 1985, they climbed to 14,000 over the next fifteen years (Manning 2000, 203). That number produced the highest per capita concentration of pawnshops in American history (Caskey 1994, 1). According to John Caskey, the customers of today's American pawnshops have low or moderate incomes and are drawn especially from the African American and Hispanic populations. Typical jobs include "an enlisted person in the military, a nonunion factory worker, a nurse's aid, a retail sales clerk, or a general helper in an automobile service station." Caskey reports that loans usually cover such expenses as paying for rent or a vacation, fixing a car, or buying Christmas presents, food, alcohol, illegal drugs, lottery tickets, or gasoline (69–70). Loan customers usually lack access to credit cards and routine banking. Pawnshops thus serve as their alternative banks.

On the average, direct selling involves a somewhat more prosperous segment of the population; across the world, a wide variety of customers purchase goods not directly from stores, but from friends, neighbors, and kin who bring the goods to their homes. Sometimes, rather than individual door-to-door sales, direct selling involves the creation of special social settings within homes. As Nicole Woolsey Biggart says in her classic study, direct-selling organizations counter the idea that efficiency depends on bureaucratized impersonality:

Executives in the direct selling industry understand, just as do the leaders of many social movements, the power of preexisting social relations and networks in recruiting distributors and channeling their actions. . . . In direct selling social bonds are not an encumbrance but an instrument for soliciting and controlling a sales force and for appealing to customers. (1989, 167; see also Frenzen and Davis 1990)

Following up on Biggart's leads, British scholar Alison Clarke's (1999) analysis of Tupperware illustrates the particular intersection of retail trade with households. In the 1950s, Earl Tupper, inventor of the now emblematic airtight plastic containers, withdrew his products from retail outlets, launching the "Tupperware party" marketing strategy. Dealers went to a volunteer "hostess" home, first demonstrating, and then selling, their products to a gathering of friends and neighbors. For her efforts, the hostess received a Tupperware gift product contingent on the amount of sales. At the party, dealers recruited future hostesses, encouraging them as well to join up as commission-paid dealers. In the process, homes became intensely social retail outlets, as well as recruiting grounds for commercial operations. Tupper's marketing strategy worked. By 1997, according to Clarke, worldwide net sales were of $1.2 billion, and about 118 million people had attended a Tupperware demonstration (2).

Direct-selling organizations changed over time and varied significantly in their organizational strategies. Biggart stresses three axes of change and variation: first, the gender of salespeople, which differentiated the kinds of networks they activated; second, the degree of orientation within the organization to a single charismatic leader (e.g., Mary Kay Ash for Mary Kay cosmetics); finally, the extent of bureaucratization and differentiation, for example, the degree to which successful salespeople became full-time managers and recruiters.

Let us think of change and variation in retail settings at an international scale. Global fast-food chains and electronic commerce provide two current settings in which many observers have thought that uniformity and impersonality were locked into place. Despite Leidner's demonstration of intensive social interaction within U.S. fast-food outlets, a number of critics have interpreted the worldwide spread of McDonald's and other chains as the imposition of uniform impersonal forms of consumption on alien cultures. Political theorist Benjamin Barber, for instance, goes so far as to portray a cosmic struggle between Jihad and McWorld, pitting the forces of religious and ethnic fragmentation against the inexorable economic homogenization of the world. Using fast food as a symbol of a much broader world conquest, Barber declares,

Music, video, theater, books, and theme parks—the new churches of a commercial civilization in which malls are the public squares and suburbs the neighborless neighborhoods—are all constructed as image exports creating a common world taste around common logos, advertising slogans, stars, songs, brand names, jingles, and trademarks. (1995, 17)

Looked at closely, however, despite common top-down designs, fast-food restaurants turn out to vary dramatically in actual social process from one locality to another. An international team of anthropologists has studied consumer behavior in McDonald's outlets across five East Asian cities. Although they certainly see an impact on local cuisine and practices, they do not observe the homogenization that many critics have feared. On the contrary, they identify a process of "localization," integrating McDonald's into different cultural settings (for various types of localization, see also Appadurai 1990; Barron 1997; Caldwell 2004; Cohen 1990; Fantasia 1995; Goody 1998; Howes 1996; Kuisel 1993; Lozada 2000; Patillo-McCoy 1999; Peiss 2002; Stephenson 1989; Warde 2000; Yan 2000). Summing up, James Watson says,

> East Asian consumers have quietly, and in some cases stubbornly, transformed their neighborhood McDonald's into local institutions. . . . In Beijing, Seoul, and Taipei, for instance, McDonald's restaurants are treated as leisure centers, where people can retreat from the stresses of urban life. In Hong Kong, middle school students often sit in McDonald's for hours, studying, gossiping, and picking over snacks; for them, the restaurants are the equivalent of youth clubs. (1997, 6–7)

If fast food does not stamp out local culture, what about electronic commerce? After all, at first glance electronically mediated consumption appears to reduce social interaction to its barest minimum. At any particular site, all an observer sees is a shopper and a computer interacting.

However, as in all the previous cases of culture and consumption, we find people creating, confirming, and transforming their social relations as they consume (on social relations in electronic communication, see DiMaggio et al. 2001; Miller and Slater 2000; Wellman and Haythornthwaite 2002). Take the case of Lands' End—the leading online apparel retail site. Malcolm Gladwell found customer-service representatives routinely engaged in online chats with customers. In one instance, an East Coast woman he calls Carol was trying to decide on what color to pick for an attaché case:

> Darcia [the rep] was partial to the dark olive. . . . Carol was convinced, but she wanted the case monogrammed and there were eleven monogramming styles on the Web-site page. "Can I have a personal suggestion?" she wrote. "Sure," Darcia typed back. "Who is the case for?" "A conservative psychiatrist," Carol replied. Darcia suggested block initials, in black. Carol agreed, and sent the order in herself on the Internet. "All right," Darcia said, as she ended the chat. "She feels better." The exchange had taken twenty-three minutes. (Gladwell 1999, 5–6)

"It's a mistake," concludes Gladwell, "to think that E-commerce will entirely automate the retail process. It just turns reps from order-takers into sales advisers." Indeed, Bill Bass, head of Lands' End e-commerce, told Gladwell: "One of the big fallacies when the Internet came along was that you could get these huge savings by eliminating customer-service costs . . . [but] people still have questions, and what you are getting are much higher-level questions. Like, 'Can you help me come up with a gift?' And they take longer" (1999, 6).

Electronic commerce does not merely present opportunities for sociability. Like other forms of consumption, it also presents problems of trust. When people purchase expensive or potentially harmful goods and services on line, they regularly seek reassurance through three social strategies that apply broadly across the whole range of consumption: by repeated interaction with the supplier; by identifying reliable suppliers through mutual ties to third parties; and by creation or consultation of monitoring agencies. All three rely on or create more trustworthy cultural knowledge, thus converting uncertainty into manageable risk.

Looking at the giant electronic emporium eBay, Peter Kollock finds that despite vast numbers of transactions and no central guarantees of quality or delivery, the default rate for trades is minimal. According to a 1997 eBay report, for instance, only twenty-seven out of 2 million auctions that took place between May and August 1997 appeared to be fraudulent. Users prevent fraud by a series of practical procedures: first, they establish a verifiable identity for each buyer and seller; second, they post summaries of reports from previous trading partners concerning the reliability of each trader; third, groups of users create Web sites posting advice (including information about frequent traders) for the pursuit of trustworthy exchanges; and fourth, some participants station themselves as paid or voluntary advisers for less experienced traders. As Kollock sums up: "at least for the core users, this is not a market of atomized price-takers" (1999, 118). It is a connected web of consumers creating a distinctive set of cultural links and producing trust by recognizable social strategies.

Similar findings emerge from Laura Sartori's (2002) large Italian study of Internet users from 1998 to 2001 (on electronic commerce in Australia see Singh 1999; in England, Pahl 1999). The study as a whole included a household survey, an online questionnaire, focus groups, and in-depth interviews. Sartori sees electronic consumption as actually increasing the autonomy and effectiveness of consumers because it makes substantial amounts of confirmatory (or, for that matter, negative) evidence concerning products and traders available at very low cost. More significantly for my purposes, Sartori identifies significant variations in the ways people gather information for their purchases.

Scrutinizing online shopping, Sartori reports that persons acquiring goods and services electronically most often first entered the process with the help of others they already knew, relied on their existing networks to reduce uncertainties in their purchases, but formed new social ties electronically in the process. Thus, Sartori's respondents repeatedly emphasized the signifi- cance of kin, friends, and colleagues' opinions when shopping online. As one thirty-three-year-old woman explained:

> I am not quite sure on what I base my decision. Surely on the advice of people at work or of friends. We often discuss it with friends. It always happens, even when I'm looking for the most stupid thing. (2002, 139)

But respondents also regularly consulted their new virtual connections in chat, newsgroups, or discussion forums. A twenty-five-year-old man reported:

> It's quite normal to exchange information about products or sites, or else ask advice to someone online. It's even easier to check a site directly since if one is in chat it means you are connected. Sometimes they ask me: "I'm looking for something, can you help me?" For instance it's happened with cell phones. Someone who's looking for a new cell phone and asks who knows a site. Then someone gives a name, some- one else a different one, and that way the conversation begins. (2002, 138)

However, as Sartori says, the two sources of information are not mutually exclusive; in fact, online acquaintances sometimes become friends. Sartori, therefore, makes a negative and a positive contribution to my general discus- sion. Negatively, her findings deny the flattening of culture by electronic media. Positively, Sartori shows us once again how creatively people adapt their social relations to different media and forms of consumption.

CONCLUSIONS

Although cultural variation plays a significant part in consumption, it is a common mistake to suppose that consumption forms a warm cultural is- land in a frigid economic sea. Shared understandings and their represen- tations—the components of culture—undergird all of economic life, from e-commerce to sweatshops. Another common error portrays consumption as centering on acquisition of goods and services rather than on their uses. A much clearer understanding of consumption practices comes from recogniz- ing how meaningful social relations pervade economic processes, including production, acquisition, and use of goods and services. Combined, the two mistakes lead to a third pervasive error: treatment of consumption as primar- ily expressive behavior, whether it expresses social position, local culture, or individual idiosyncrasy. Consumption, like production and distribution, actually does crucial social work, not only sustaining human lives and social institutions but also shaping interpersonal relations.

These recurrent misunderstandings of consumption directly parallel confusions about money. Scholars, social critics, and ordinary people often assume that monetizing goods, services, and social relations strips away their culturally grounded personal meanings: paid personal care, for example, necessarily lacks the intimacy and power of unpaid care. Closely observed, however, intimate social relations turn out to incorporate monetary flows quite productively over a wide range of circumstances. The confusion results from overestimating the capacity of media—money, goods, or services—to control human behavior and thereby underestimating the capacity of human beings to bend media into means of pursuing their own social lives.

Similarly, social critics frequently warn against two different versions of consumerism: first, acquisition of standardized goods and services that crush individuality, spontaneity, and local culture, and second, a headlong rush to accumulate that leaves no time, energy, or imagination to enjoy what you already have. Some mass-produced goods do drive higher-priced, more varied, and superior goods out of markets. Some goods and services (hard drugs provide obvious examples) damage their consumers. Some people do engage in conspicuous consumption to the detriment of their welfare. But our most careful studies of consumption—inside and outside sociology—challenge the idea that consumers in general are increasingly leading impoverished lives as a consequence of growth in consumption.

Once again, confusion stems from assuming the existence of two hostile worlds: a world of rationality, efficiency, and impersonality on one side; a world of self-expression, cultural richness, and intimacy on the other—with contact between the two worlds inevitably corrupting both of them. Nor will any of the available nothing-buts—nothing but economic calculation, nothing but culture, nothing but power—resolve the dilemma. We have no choice but to pave crossroads connecting continuously negotiated, meaning-drenched social relations with the whole range of economic processes.

NOTES

Viviana A. Zelizer, "Culture and Consumption," in *The Handbook of Economic Sociology*, edited by Neil Smelser and Richard Swedberg, 2nd ed., 331–54. Princeton, N.J.: Princeton University Press; New York: Russell Sage Foundation, 2005. Reprinted with permission. I have adapted a few passages from Zelizer 1999, 2001, and 2002a, and 2002b.

1. Landmark essays in consumer culture include Appadurai 1986; Brewer and Porter 1993; Bronner 1989; Fox and Lears 1983; McKendrick et al. 1982. For an

excellent bibliographic essay on the history of consumption, see Glickman 1999; for a critical review, see Agnew 2003.

2. For observations of interactions between organized politics and consumption in Great Britain, see Hilton 2002.

References

Abelson, Elaine S. 1989. *When Ladies Go a-Thieving: Middle-Class Shoplifters in the Victorian Department Store*. Oxford: Oxford University Press.

Agnew, Jean-Christophe. 2003. "The Give-and-Take of Consumer Culture." In *Commodifying Everything*, edited by Susan Strasser, 11–39. New York: Routledge.

Andrews, Maggie, and Mary M. Talbot, eds. 2000. *All the World and Her Husband*. London: Cassell.

Appadurai, Arjun, ed. 1986. *The Social Life of Things*. Cambridge: Cambridge University Press.

———. 1990. "Disjuncture and Difference in the Global Cultural Economy." *Public Culture* 2:1–24.

Austin, Regina. 1994. "'A Nation of Thieves': Securing Black People's Right to Shop and to Sell in White America." *Utah Law Review* 147–77.

———. 2004. "Kwanzaa and the Commercialization of Black Culture." *Black Renaissance/Renaissance Noir,* September 22.

Aversi, Roberta, Giovanni Dosi, Giorgio Fagiolo, Mara Meacci, and Claudia Olivetti. 1999. "Demand Dynamics with Socially Evolving Preferences." *Industrial and Corporate Change* 8:353–408.

Badgett, M. V. Lee. 2001. *Money, Myths, and Change: The Economic Lives of Lesbians and Gay Men*. Chicago: University of Chicago Press.

Bakalian, Anny. 1993. *Armenian-Americans: From Being to Feeling Armenian*. New Brunswick, N.J.: Transaction.

Barber, Benjamin. 1995. *Jihad vs. McWorld*. New York: Times Books.

Barber, Bernard. 1957. *Social Stratification*. New York: Harcourt, Brace and World.

Barron, Hal S. 1997. *Mixed Harvest: The Second Great Transformation in the Rural North, 1870–1930*. Chapel Hill: University of North Carolina Press.

Baudrillard, Jean. 1999. "Consumer Society." In *Consumer Society in American History: A Reader*, edited by Lawrence B. Glickman, 33–56. Ithaca, N.Y.: Cornell University Press.

Bauman, Zygmunt. 1998. *Globalization: The Human Consequences*. Cambridge: Polity Press.

Becker, Gary. 1996. *Accounting for Tastes*. Cambridge: Harvard University Press.

Benson, Susan Porter. 1986. *Counter Cultures: Saleswomen, Managers, and Customers in American Department Stores, 1890–1940*. Urbana: University of Illinois Press.

Berdahl, Daphne. 1999. *Where the World Ended: Reunification and Identity in the German Borderland*. Berkeley and Los Angeles: University of California Press.

Biggart, Nicole Woolsey. 1989. *Charismatic Capitalism*. Chicago: University of Chicago Press.

———. 2001. "Banking on Each Other: The Situational Logic of Rotating Savings and Credit Associations." *Advances in Qualitative Organization Research* 3:129–53.

Biggart, Nicole Woolsey, and Richard P. Castanias. 2001. "Collateralized Social Relations: The Social in Economic Calculation." *American Journal of Economics and Sociology* 60:471–500.

Bourdieu, Pierre. [1965] 1990. *Photography: A Middle-Brow Art*. Cambridge: Polity Press.

———. 1984. *Distinction: A Social Critique of the Judgement of Taste*. Translated by Richard Nice. Cambridge, Mass.: Harvard University Press.

———. 2000. *Les structures sociales de l'économie*. Paris: Seuil.

Bourgois, Philippe. 1995. *In Search of Respect*. Cambridge: Cambridge University Press.

Brewer, John, and Roy Porter, eds. 1993. *Consumption and the World of Goods*. London: Routledge.

Bronner, Simon J., ed. 1989. *Consuming Visions: Accumulation and Display in America, 1880–1920*. New York: W. W. Norton.

Calder, Lendol. 1999. *Financing the American Dream: A Cultural History of Consumer Credit*. Princeton, N.J.: Princeton University Press.

Caldwell, Melissa L. 2004. "Domesticating the French Fry! McDonald's and Consumerism in Russia." *Journal of Consumer Culture* 4:5–26.

Campbell, Colin. 1995. "The Sociology of Consumption." In *Acknowledging Consumption*, edited by Daniel Miller, 96–126. London: Routledge.

Caplowitz, David. 1967. *The Poor Pay More*. New York: Free Press.

Carrington, Christopher. 1999. *No Place Like Home: Relationships and Family Life among Lesbians and Gay Men*. Chicago: University of Chicago Press.

Caskey, John P. 1994. *Fringe Banking: Check-Cashing Outlets, Pawnshops, and the Poor*. New York: Russell Sage Foundation.

Chin, Elizabeth. 2001. *Purchasing Power: Black Kids and American Consumer Culture*. Minneapolis: University of Minnesota Press.

Clarke, Alison J. 1999. *Tupperware: The Promise of Plastic in 1950s America*. Washington, D.C.: Smithsonian Institution Press.

Clunas, Craig. 1999. "Modernity Global and Local: Consumption and the Rise of the West." *American Historical Review* 104:1,497–1,511.

Cohen, Lizabeth. 1990. *Making a New Deal: Industrial Workers in Chicago, 1919–1939*. Cambridge: Cambridge University Press.

———. 1996. "From Town Center to Shopping Center: The Reconfiguration of Community Marketplaces in Postwar America." *American Historical Review* 101:1,050–81.

———. 2003. *A Consumers' Republic: The Politics of Mass Consumption in Postwar America*. New York: Alfred A. Knopf.

Cook, Daniel Thomas. 1999. "Consumers, Commodities, and Consumption." http://www.asanet.org/sections/consumers.htm (accessed September 2001).

———. 2000. "The Rise of 'The Toddler' as Subject and as Merchandising Category in the 1930s." In *New Forms of Consumption*, edited by Mark Gottdiener, 111–29. Lanham, Md.: Rowman and Littlefield.

Cowan, Ruth Schwartz. 1983. *More Work for Mother*. New York: Basic Books.

Crane, Diana. 2000. *Fashion and Its Social Agendas*. Chicago: University of Chicago Press.

Cross, Gary. 2000. *An All-Consuming Century: Why Commercialism Won in America*. New York: Columbia University Press.

Crowston, Clare Haru. 2001. *Fabricating Women: The Seamstresses of Old Regime France, 1675–1791*. Durham, N.C.: Duke University Press.

Curran, Sara R., and Abigail Cope Saguy. 2001. "Migration and Cultural Change: A Role for Gender and Social Networks?" *Journal for International Women's Studies* 2:54–77.

Davis, Deborah S. 2002. "When a House Becomes His Home." In *Popular China: Unofficial Culture in a Globalizing Society*, edited by Perry Link, Richard P. Madsen, and Paul G. Pickowicz, 231–50. Lanham, Md.: Rowman and Littlefield.

de Grazia, Victoria, and Lizabeth Cohen, eds. 1999. "Class and Consumption." Special issue of *International Labor and Working-Class History* 55 (Spring).

de Grazia, Victoria, and Ellen Furlough, eds. 1996. *The Sex of Things: Gender and Consumption in Historical Perspective*. Berkeley and Los Angeles: University of California Press.

de la Garza, Rodolfo O., and Briant Lindsay Lowell, eds. 2002. *Sending Money Home: Hispanic Remittances and Community Development*. Lanham, Md.: Rowman and Littlefield.

DeVault, Marjorie L. 1991. *Feeding the Family*. Chicago: University of Chicago Press.

DiMaggio, Paul. 1990. "Cultural Aspects of Economic Action and Organization." In *Beyond the Marketplace*, edited by Roger Friedland and A. F. Robertson, 113–36. New York: Aldine.

———. 1994. "Culture and Economy." In *The Handbook of Economic Sociology*, edited by Neil J. Smelser and Richard Swedberg, 27–57. New York: Russell Sage Foundation; Princeton, N.J.: Princeton University Press.

DiMaggio, Paul, Eszter Hargittai, W. Russell Neuman, and John P. Robinson. 2001. "Social Implications of the Internet." *Annual Review of Sociology* 27:307–36.

DiMaggio, Paul, and Hugh Louch. 1998. "Socially Embedded Consumer Transactions: For What Kinds of Purchases Do People Use Networks Most?" *American Sociological Review* 63:619–37.

Douglas, Mary, and Baron Isherwood. 1979. *The World of Goods*. Cambridge: Cambridge University Press.

duGay, Paul. 1996. *Consumption and Identity at Work*. London: Sage.

Durand, Jorge, Emilio A. Parrado, and Douglas S. Massey. 1996. "Migradollars and Development: A Reconsideration of the Mexican Case." *International Migration Review* 30:423–44.

Ewen, Elizabeth. 1985. *Immigrant Women in the Land of Dollars: Life and Culture on the Lower East Side, 1890–1925*. New York: Monthly Review Press.

Fantasia, Rick. 1995. "Fast Food in France." *Theory and Society* 24:201–43.

Fine, Gary Alan. 1996. *Kitchens: The Culture of Restaurant Work*. Berkeley and Los Angeles: University of California Press.

Formanek-Brunell, Miriam. 1993. *Made to Play House: Dolls and the Commercialization of American Girlhood, 1830–1930.* New Haven, Conn.: Yale University Press.

Fox, Richard Wightman, and T. J. Jackson Lears, eds. 1983. *The Culture of Consumption.* New York: Pantheon.

Frank, Dana. 1994. *Purchasing Power: Consumer Organizing, Gender, and the Seattle Labor Movement, 1919–1929.* Cambridge: Cambridge University Press.

Frenzen, Jonathan K., and Harry L. Davis. 1990. "Purchasing Behavior in Embedded Markets." *Journal of Consumer Research* 17:1–12.

Frenzen, Jonathan K., Paul M. Hirsch, and Philip C. Zerrillo. 1994. "Consumption, Preferences, and Changing Lifestyles." In *The Handbook of Economic Sociology*, edited by Neil J. Smelser and Richard Swedberg, 403–25. New York: Russell Sage Foundation; Princeton, N.J.: Princeton University Press.

Gabaccia, Donna R. 1998. *We Are What We Eat: Ethnic Food and the Making of Americans.* Cambridge, Mass.: Harvard University Press.

Gal, Susan, and Gail Kligman. 2000. *The Politics of Gender after Socialism.* Princeton, N.J.: Princeton University Press.

Gladwell, Malcolm. 1999. "Clicks and Mortar." *New Yorker*, December 6. http://www.gladwell.com (accessed February 15, 2002).

Glickman, B. Lawrence. 1997. *A Living Wage: American Workers and the Making of Consumer Society.* Ithaca, N.Y.: Cornell University Press.

———, ed. 1999. *Consumer Society in American History: A Reader.* Ithaca, N.Y.: Cornell University Press.

Goody, Jack. 1998. *Food and Love: A Cultural History of East and West.* London: Verso.

Gottdiener, Mark, ed. 2000. *New Forms of Consumption.* Lanham, Md.: Rowman and Littlefield.

Granovetter, Mark. 1985. "Economic Action and Social Structure: The Problem of Embeddedness." *American Journal of Sociology* 91:481–510.

Granovetter, Mark, and Roland Soong. 1986. "Threshold Models of Interpersonal Effects in Consumer Demand." *Journal of Economic Behavior and Organization* 7:83–99.

Granovetter, Mark, and Richard Swedberg, eds. 2001. *The Sociology of Economic Life.* 2d ed. Boulder, Colo.: Westview Press.

Grasmuck, Sherri, and Patricia R. Pessar. 1991. *Between Two Islands: Dominican International Migration.* Berkeley and Los Angeles: University of California Press.

Green, Nancy L. 1997. *Ready-to-Wear and Ready-to-Work: A Century of Industry and Immigrants in Paris and New York.* Durham, N.C.: Duke University Press.

Gruen, Victor. 1964. *The Heart of Our Cities: The Urban Crisis: Diagnosis and Cure.* New York: Simon and Schuster.

Halle, David. 1993. *Inside Culture: Art and Class in the American Home.* Chicago: University of Chicago Press.

Halter, Marilyn. 2000. *Shopping for Identity: The Marketing of Ethnicity.* New York: Schocken Books.

Heinze, Andrew R. 1990. *Adapting to Abundance.* New York: Columbia University Press.

Hilton, Matthew. 2002. "The Fable of the Sheep: Or, Private Virtues, Public Vices; The Consumer Revolution of the Twentieth Century." *Past and Present* 176:222–56.

Hirsch, Paul. 1972. "Processing Fads and Fashions: An Organization-Set Analysis of Cultural Industry Systems." *American Journal of Sociology* 77:639–59.

Horowitz, Daniel. 1985. *The Morality of Spending.* Baltimore: Johns Hopkins University Press.

Horowitz, Roger, and Arwen Mohun, eds. 1998. *His and Hers: Gender, Consumption, and Technology.* Charlottesville: University Press of Virginia.

Howes, David, ed. 1996. *Cross-Cultural Consumption: Global Markets, Local Realties.* London: Routledge.

Humphrey, Caroline. 1995. "Creating a Culture of Disillusionment: Consumption in Moscow, a Chronicle of Changing Times." In *Worlds Apart: Modernity through the Prism of the Local,* edited by Daniel Miller, 43–68. London: Routledge.

Illouz, Eva. 1997. *Consuming the Romantic Utopia.* Berkeley and Los Angeles: University of California Press.

Ingram, Paul, and Peter W. Roberts. 2000. "Friendships among Competitors in the Sydney Hotel Industry." *American Journal of Sociology* 106:387–423.

Jacobs, Meg. 1997. "'How about Some Meat?': The Office of Price Administration, Consumption Politics, and State Building from the Bottom Up, 1941–1946." *Journal of American History* 84:910–41.

Joselit, Jenna Weissman. 1994. *The Wonders of America.* New York: Hill and Wang.

Kahneman, Daniel, and Amos Tversky. 1982. "The Psychology of Preferences." *Scientific American* 246:160–73.

Katz, Elihu, and Paul F. Lazarsfeld. 1955. *Personal Influence.* New York: Free Press.

Kollock, Peter. 1999. "The Production of Trust in Online Markets." In vol. 16 of *Advances in Group Processes,* edited by Edward J. Lawler, Michael W. Macy, Shane R. Thyne, and Henry A. Walker, 99–123. Greenwich, Conn.: JAI Press.

Kuisel, Richard. 1993. *Seducing the French: The Dilemma of Americanization.* Berkeley and Los Angeles: University of California Press.

Lamont, Michèle, and Virág Molnár. 2001. "How Blacks Use Consumption to Shape Their Collective Identity: Evidence from Marketing Specialists." *Journal of Consumer Culture* 1:31–45.

Lasch, Christopher. 1977. *Haven in a Heartless World: The Family Besieged.* New York: Basic Books.

Lazarsfeld, Paul. 1957. "Sociological Reflections on Business: Consumers and Managers." In *Social Science Research on Business: Product and Potential,* edited by Robert A. Dahl, Mason Haire, and Paul F. Lazarsfeld, 99–156. New York: Columbia University Press.

Lears, Jackson. 1994. *Fables of Abundance: A Cultural History of Advertising in America.* New York: Basic Books.

Ledeneva, Alena V. 1998. *Russia's Economy of Favours: Blat, Networking, and Informal Exchange.* Cambridge: Cambridge University Press.

Lee, Jennifer. 2002. "From Civil Relations to Racial Conflict: Merchant-Customer Interactions in Urban America." *American Sociological Review* 67:77–98.

Leidner, Robin. 1993. *Fast Food, Fast Talk: Service Work and the Routinization of Everyday Life*. Berkeley and Los Angeles: University of California Press.

Levitt, Peggy. 2001a. *The Transnational Villagers*. Berkeley and Los Angeles: University of California Press.

————. 2001b. "Transnational Migration: Taking Stock and Future Directions." *Global Networks* 1:195–216.

Light, Ivan, and Steve J. Gold. 2000. *Ethnic Economies*. San Diego: Academic Press.

Lozada, Eriberto P., Jr. 2000. "Globalized Childhood? Kentucky Fried Chicken in Beijing." In *Feeding China's Little Emperors*, edited by Jun Jing, 114–34. Stanford, Calif.: Stanford University Press.

Lynd, Robert S., and Helen M. Lynd. 1929. *Middletown: A Study in American Culture*. New York: Harcourt, Brace and World.

Mahler, Sarah J. 1995. *American Dreaming: Immigrant Life on the Margins*. Princeton, N.J.: Princeton University Press.

Manning, Robert D. 2000. *Credit Card Nation*. New York: Basic Books.

Marling, Karal Ann. 2000. *Merry Christmas!* Cambridge, Mass.: Harvard University Press.

McKendrick, Neil, John Brewer, and J. H. Plumb. 1982. *The Birth of a Consumer Society: The Commercialization of Eighteenth-Century England*. Bloomington: Indiana University Press.

Mehta, Raj, and Russell W. Belk. 1991. "Artifacts, Identity, and Transition: Favorite Possessions of Indians and Indian Immigrants to the United States." *Journal of Consumer Research* 17:398–411.

Miller, Daniel. 1987. *Material Culture and Mass Consumption*. Oxford: Blackwell.

————. 1995. "Consumption as the Vanguard of History: A Polemic by Way of an Introduction." In *Acknowledging Consumption*, edited by Daniel Miller, 1–57. London: Routledge.

————. 1998. *A Theory of Shopping*. Ithaca, N.Y.: Cornell University Press.

————. 2001. *The Dialectics of Shopping*. Chicago: University of Chicago Press.

Miller, Daniel, Peter Jackson, Nigel Thrift, Beverley Holbrook, and Michael Rowlands. 1998. *Shopping, Place, and Identity*. London: Routledge.

Miller, Daniel, and Don Slater. 2000. *The Internet: An Ethnographic Approach*. Oxford: Berg.

Miller, Michael B. 1981. *The Bon Marché: Bourgeois Culture and the Department Store, 1869–1920*. Princeton, N.J.: Princeton University Press.

Mintz, Sidney W. 1996. *Tasting Food, Tasting Freedom: Excursions into Eating, Culture, and the Past*. Boston: Beacon Press.

Morawska, Ewa. 1985. *For Bread with Butter: The Life-Worlds of East Central Europeans in Johnstown, Pennsylvania, 1890–1940*. Cambridge: Cambridge University Press.

Moreno, Sylvia. 2001. "A Courier with Connections." *Washington Post*, March 26.

Mukerji, Chandra. 1983. *From Graven Images: Patterns of Modern Materialism*. New York: Columbia University Press.

Newman, Katherine S. 1999. *No Shame in My Game: The Working Poor in the Inner City*. New York: Alfred A. Knopf and Russell Sage Foundation.

Nightingale, Carl H. 1993. *On the Edge*. New York: Basic Books.

Pahl, Jan. 1999. *Invisible Money: Family Finances in the Electronic Economy*. Bristol: Policy Press.

Patillo-McCoy, Mary. 1999. *Black Picket Fences: Privilege and Peril among the Black Middle Class*. Chicago: University of Chicago Press.

Peiss, Kathy. 1998. *Hope in a Jar: The Making of America's Beauty Culture*. New York: Metropolitan Books.

———. 2002. "Educating the Eye of the Beholder—American Cosmetics Abroad." *Daedalus* 131(4): 101–9.

Pérez Firmat, Gustavo. 1994. *Life on the Hyphen: The Cuban-American Way*. Austin: University of Texas Press.

Pew Hispanic Center and the Multilateral Investment Fund. 2003. *Billions in Motion: Latino Immigrants, Remittances, and Banking*. http://www.pewhispanic.org/site/docs/pdf/billions_in_motion.pdf (accessed September 26, 2003).

Pleck, Elizabeth H. 2000. *Celebrating the Family: Ethnicity, Consumer Culture, and Family Rituals*. Cambridge, Mass.: Harvard University Press.

Portes, Alejandro. 2001. "Introduction: The Debates and Significance of Immigrant Transnationalism." *Global Networks* 1:181–94.

Portes, Alejandro, William J. Haller, and Luis Eduardo Guarnizo. 2002. "Transnational Entrepreneurs: An Alternative Form of Immigrant Economic Adaptation." *American Sociological Review* 67:278–98.

Portes, Alejandro, and Alex Stepick. 1993. *City on the Edge: The Transformation of Miami*. Berkeley and Los Angeles: University of California Press.

Putnam, Robert D. 2000. *Bowling Alone: The Collapse and Revival of American Community*. New York: Simon and Schuster.

Rappaport, Erika Diane. 2000. *Shopping for Pleasure: Women in the Making of London's West End*. Princeton, N.J.: Princeton University Press.

Riesman, David. 1964. *Abundance for What? And Other Essays*. Garden City, N.Y.: Doubleday.

Rifkin, Jeremy. 2000. *The Age of Access*. New York: Jeremy P. Tarcher/Putnam.

Ritzer, George. 1996. *The McDonaldization of Society*. Thousand Oaks, Calif.: Pine Forge Press.

———. 2000. "A Sub-field in Search of Discovery." *Footnotes*, February 6.

———. 2003a. *The Globalization of Nothing*. Thousand Oaks, Calif.: Pine Forge Press.

———. 2003b. "Islands of the Living Dead: The Social Geography of McDonaldization." *American Behavioral Scientist* 47:119–36.

Ritzer, George, and Seth Ovadia. 2000. "The Process of McDonaldization Is Not Uniform, nor Are Its Settings, Consumers, or the Consumption of Its Goods and Services." In *New Forms of Consumption*, edited by Mark Gottdiener, 33–49. Lanham, Md.: Rowman and Littlefield.

Ritzer, George, and Don Slater. 2001. Editorial. *Journal of Consumer Culture* 1: 5–7.

Roberts, Kenneth D., and Michael D. S. Morris. 2003. "Fortune, Risk, and Remittances: An Application of Option Theory to Participation in Village-Based Migration Networks." *International Migration Review* 37:1,252–81.

Rose-Ackerman, Susan. 1998. "Bribes and Gifts." In *Economics, Values, and Organization*, edited by Avner Ben-Ner and Louis Putterman, 296–328. Cambridge: Cambridge University Press.

Rosenzweig, Roy. 1983. *"Eight Hours for What We Will": Workers and Leisure in an Industrial City, 1870–1920*. Cambridge: Cambridge University Press.

Ross, Ellen. 1993. *Love and Toil: Motherhood in Outcast London, 1870–1918*. Oxford: Oxford University Press.

Sahlins, Marshall. 1976. *Culture and Practical Reason*. Chicago: University of Chicago Press.

Samuel, Raphael. 1981. *East End Underworld: Chapters in the Life of Arthur Harding*. London: Routledge and Kegan Paul.

Sánchez, George J. 1993. *Becoming Mexican American: Ethnicity, Culture, and Identity in Chicano Los Angeles, 1900–1945*. Oxford: Oxford University Press.

Sartori, Laura. 2002. "Consumo e vita quotidiana nell'era di Internet." Ph.D. diss., University of Trento.

Scanlon, Jennifer, ed. 2000. *The Gender and Consumer Culture Reader*. New York: New York University Press.

Schmidt, Leigh Eric. 1995. *Consumer Rites: The Buying and Selling of American Holidays*. Princeton, N.J.: Princeton University Press.

Schor, Juliet B. 1998. *The Overspent American*. New York: Basic Books.

Schreiber, Alfred L. 2001. *Multicultural Marketing*. Chicago: NTC Business Books.

Schudson, Michael. 1984. *Advertising, the Uneasy Persuasion*. New York: Basic Books.

Simmel, Georg. [1904] 1957. "Fashion." *American Journal of Sociology* 62:541–58.

Singh, Supriya. 1999. "Electronic Money: Understanding Its Use to Increase the Effectiveness of Policy." *Telecommunications Policy* 23:753–73.

Slater, Don. 1997. *Consumer Culture and Modernity*. Cambridge: Polity Press.

Smelser, Neil J. 1963. *The Sociology of Economic Life*. Englewood Cliffs, N.J.: Prentice-Hall.

Stephenson, Peter H. 1989. "Going to McDonald's in Leiden: Reflections on the Concept of Self and Society in the Netherlands." *Ethos* 17:226–47.

Stillerman, Joel. 2004. "Gender, Class, and Generational Contexts for Consumption in Contemporary Chile." *Journal of Consumer Culture* 4:51–78.

Swedberg, Richard. 2003. *Principles of Economic Sociology*. Princeton, N.J.: Princeton University Press.

Swiencicki, Mark A. 1999. "Consuming Brotherhood: Men's Culture, Style, and Recreation as Consumer Culture, 1880–1930." In *Consumer Society in American History: A Reader*, edited by Lawrence B. Glickman, 207–40. Ithaca, N.Y.: Cornell University Press.

Tebbutt, Melanie. 1983. *Making Ends Meet: Pawnbroking and Working-Class Credit*. New York: St. Martin's Press.

Thaler, Richard H. 1991. *Quasi Rational Economics*. New York: Russell Sage Foundation.

———. 1999. "Mental Accounting Matters." *Journal of Behavioral Decision Making* 12:183–206.

Tiersten, Lisa. 2001. *Marianne in the Market: Envisioning Consumer Society in Fin-de-Siècle France*. Berkeley and Los Angeles: University of California Press.

Tilly, Charles. 1990. "Transplanted Networks." In *Immigration Reconsidered: History, Sociology, and Politics*, edited by Virginia Yans-McLaughlin, 79–95. Oxford: Oxford University Press.

Tilly, Chris, and Charles Tilly. 1998. *Work under Capitalism*. Boulder, Colo.: Westview.

Turow, Joseph. 1997. *Breaking Up America: Advertisers and the New Media World*. Chicago: University of Chicago Press.

Uzzi, Brian. 1997. "Social Structure and Competition in Interfirm Networks: The Paradox of Embeddedness." *Administrative Science Quarterly* 42:35–67.

Veblen, Thorstein. [1899] 1953. *The Theory of the Leisure Class*. New York: New American Library.

Venkatesh, Alladi. 1995. "Ethnoconsumerism: A New Paradigm to Study Cultural and Cross-Cultural Consumer Behavior." In *Marketing in a Multicultural World*, edited by Janeen Arnold Costa and Gary J. Bamossy, 26–67. Thousand Oaks, Calif.: Sage.

Waller Meyers, Deborah. 1998. "Migrant Remittances to Latin America: Reviewing the Literature." Working paper, Tomás Rivera Policy Institute, May. http://www.thedialogue.org/publications/meyers.html (accessed February 5, 2002).

Warde, Alan. 2000. "Eating Globally: Cultural Flows and the Spread of Ethnic Restaurants." In *The Ends of Globalization*, edited by Don Kalb, Marco van der Land, Richard Staring, Bart van Steenbergen, and Nico Wilterdink, 299–316. Lanham, Md.: Rowman and Littlefield.

Warde, Alan, and Lydia Martens. 2000. *Eating Out: Social Differentiation, Consumption, and Pleasure*. Cambridge: Cambridge University Press.

Waters, Mary. 1990. *Ethnic Options*. Berkeley and Los Angeles: University of California Press.

Watson, James L., ed. 1997. *Golden Arches East: McDonald's in East Asia*. Stanford, Calif.: Stanford University Press.

Weatherill, Lorna. 1993. "The Meaning of Consumer Behavior in Late Seventeenth- and Early Eighteenth-Century England." In *Consumption and the World of Goods*, edited by John Brewer and Roy Porter, 206–27. London: Routledge.

Weems, Robert E., Jr. 1994. "The Revolution Will Be Marketed: American Corporations and Black Consumers during the 1960s." *Radical History Review* 59:94–107.

Weiss, Michael J. 1988. *The Clustering of America*. New York: Harper and Row.

Wellman, Barry, and Caroline Haythornthwaite, eds. 2002. *The Internet in Everyday Life*. Oxford: Blackwell.

White, Harrison C. 2002. *Markets from Networks: Socioeconomic Models of Production*. Princeton, N.J.: Princeton University Press.

Wuthnow, Robert. 1996. *Poor Richard's Principle*. Princeton, N.J.: Princeton University Press.

Yan, Yunxiang. 2000. "Of Hamburger and Social Space: Consuming McDonald's in Beijing." In *The Consumer Revolution in Urban China*, edited by Deborah S. Davis, 201–25. Berkeley and Los Angeles: University of California Press.

Zelizer, Viviana A. 1998. "How Do We Know Whether a Monetary Transaction Is a Gift, an Entitlement, or a Payment?" In *Economics, Values, and Organiza-*

tion, edited by Avner Ben-Ner and Louis Putterman, 329–33. Cambridge: Cambridge University Press.

———. 1999. "Multiple Markets, Multiple Cultures." In *Diversity and Its Discontents: Cultural Conflict and Common Ground in Contemporary American Society*, edited by Neil J. Smelser and Jeffrey Alexander, 193–212. Princeton, N.J.: Princeton University Press.

———. 2001. "Economic Sociology." In vol. 6 of *International Encyclopedia of the Social and Behavioral Sciences*, edited by Neil J. Smelser and Paul B. Baltes, 4,128–31. Amsterdam: Elsevier.

———. 2002a. "Kids and Commerce." *Childhood* 4:375–96.

———. 2002b. "Enter Culture." In *The New Economic Sociology: Developments in an Emerging Field*, edited by Mauro F. Guillén, Randall Collins, Paula England, and Marshall Meyer, 101–25. New York: Russell Sage Foundation.

Zukin, Sharon. 1991. *Landscapes of Power: From Detroit to Disney World*. Berkeley and Los Angeles: University of California Press.

———. 2003. *Point of Purchase: How Shopping Changed American Culture*. London: Routledge.

Ethics in the Economy

In 2003, an ailing Boeing corporation brought back from retirement former president Harry Stonecipher to turn the company around. Amid a flurry of reforms, the now CEO Stonecipher installed a code of company ethics to publicize the firm's new self-discipline. Only two years later, however, he fell afoul of his own reforms. One provision of the new ethics code stipulated that "employees will not engage in conduct or activity that may raise questions as to the company's honesty, impartiality, or reputation or otherwise cause embarrassment to the company."[1]

As newspapers around the United States reported, Stonecipher did embarrass Boeing. He carried on an affair with a divorced female executive. After an anonymous informant within the company disclosed evidence of the relationship, including some steamy e-mails, to the heads of the company's legal and ethical departments, Boeing's board of directors decided that the sixty-eight-year-old Stonecipher, long married and with grown children, had to go. Stonecipher had violated the very code of ethics the company had put in place on his arrival in office. As he said later: "We set—hell, I set—a higher standard here. I violated my own standards. I used poor judgment."[2] The collapse of Enron and other twenty-first-century business scandals have kept violations of ethical codes in headlines.

Ethics and economic activity seem to be uneasy companions. If economic activity centers on the maximization of efficiency in production, consumption, distribution, and transfers of assets, what place can it allow for ethical concerns? Institutional economics offers a useful reply: among the institutions that stabilize economies, lower transaction costs, and assure commitments, formally enacted rules of good behavior play a significant part.

This paper pursues that insight by identifying a series of intersections between ethics and economic activity. Despite the frequency with which CEOs speak of ethics and business schools teach courses on the subject, researchers have so far produced no more than scattered findings on how ethical questions actually arise within economic life, how economic actors respond to them, and what effects those responses have on economic performances. The paper therefore concentrates on identifying salient research questions and then closes with concrete suggestions concerning the sort of inquiries that would produce better answers than are now available.

What do we mean by ethical questions? The *Oxford English Dictionary* defines ethics as "the science of morals: the department of study concerned with the principles of human duty." In economic activity, then, ethics concerns the proper way of conducting production, consumption, distribution, and transfer of assets. For instance, ethical questions assume such varied forms as, Is it right to pay women for their eggs? Is it wrong for a supervisor to make sexual advances to an employee? May a CEO legitimately issue public reports exaggerating a firm's economic performance? Is it appropriate for company executives to use company jets for personal trips? More generally, is it feasible to set rules that eliminate conflicts of interest between a person's corporate responsibility and private interests? May a lawyer appropriately use confidential information from a client to make profitable investments? May a psychiatrist who learns about a patient's embezzlement on the job appropriately withhold that information from an employer or the police?

These are everyday questions in economic life. Within business circles people have had a field day with issues of ethics. In his introduction to a 2006–7 annual collection on business ethics, John E. Richardson declares:

> Recent events have brought ethics to the forefront as a topic of discussion throughout our nation. And, undoubtedly, the area of society that is getting the closest scrutiny regarding its ethical practices is the business sector. As corporate America struggles to find its ethical identity in a business environment that grows increasingly complex, managers are confronted with some poignant questions that have definite ethical ramifications. Does a company have any obligation to help solve social problems such as poverty, pollution, and urban decay? What ethical responsibilities should a multinational corporation assume in foreign countries? What obligation does a manufacturer have to the consumer with respect to product defects and safety? (Richardson 2007, iv)

Economic ethics have also preoccupied moral philosophers and feminist thinkers (e.g., Anderson 1993; Buchanan 1985; Gilligan 1982; Held 2005; Larson and Freeman 1997; Tronto 1993). Even some economists and economic sociologists have joined the discussion of morality and economic behavior (e.g., Frank 2003; Hausman and McPherson 1993; McCloskey 2006; Sen 1987; Swedberg 2005). Questions of moral and immoral action arise recurrently in some branches of economic sociology, for example, the study of professions, of crime, of inheritance, of consumption, the economics of care, and the commodification of human goods, such as organs, blood, and eggs. A flourishing literature documents the "dark side of organizations," the prevalence of corruption, and the recurrent temptation to subvert organizational ends in pursuit of parochial interests (e.g., Ashforth and Anand 2003; Baker and Faulkner 2004; Palmer and Maher 2006; Vaughan 1999).

Confronted with questions of this sort, both economists and economic sociologists often return to comforting dichotomies between the separate spheres of proper economic activity and proper normative behavior. On one side is a self-contained world of hard-nosed rationality; on the other, another self-contained world of sentiment and obligation. Mix the two, goes the reasoning, and both of them suffer (Zelizer 2005). As a consequence, economic analysts find it easier to ban ethical and normative questions from their own agendas as work for philosophers, theologians, and advocates.

Thomas Piper of Harvard Business School, a pioneer in the development of ethics courses for MBAs, reports that he met considerable resistance from both sides. Quantitative economists voiced "real doubts about whether this was just philanthropy and foolishness." Meanwhile, ethicists were "troubled when economics was introduced into the conversation" (Rosenberg 2006, 49). Economist Julie Nelson explains:

> A particular belief about commerce and its relation to ethics is implicit in many contemporary discussions, both academic and popular. This is the belief that money, profits, markets, and corporations are parts of an "economic machine." This machine operates in an automatic fashion, following inexorable and amoral "laws." While the machine organizes provisioning for our bodies, it is itself soulless and inhuman. Ethical questions, on the other hand, concern the appropriate respect and care for other creatures that we—as living, social, and soulful beings—should demonstrate. Since machines are incapable of morality, thinking about economies as machines puts commerce firmly outside the ethical realm. (2006, 1–2)

Economic analysts' banning of ethics oddly parallels the tendency of ethical critics to deal with unethical behavior by strict prohibition.

My own first book, in fact, took up closely related issues. *Morals and Markets* examined the transformation of life insurance from a stigmatized violation of ethical principles into a prudent and morally laudable economic investment in the future. In its early phases, critics of life insurance decried its insertion of crass commercialism and narrow self-interest into a zone of sacred commitments. They questioned: "Has a man the right to make the continuance of his life the basis of a bargain? Is it not turning a very solemn thing into a mere commercial transaction?" (*Our Mutual Friend* 1867, as cited in Zelizer 1979, 45–46). Insurance agents, in this view, were selling an unethical product and thereby undermining public morality. Only by invoking an alternative morality did advocates of life insurance succeed in making it first acceptable, and then even ethically desirable.

The early response to life insurance brings out a recurrent feature of ethical disputes at large. Critics of unethical behavior do not merely seek to stigmatize it or to make it less attractive. They regularly propose to ban specific elements: render them illegal, make them conditions for expulsion from an organization, and organize attacks on perpetrators. Any economic sociologist who studies environmental pollution, automobile safety, or other presumed threats to human well-being regularly encounters calls for outright bans on this menace or that.

Economics and economic sociology, however, have no coherent body of description and explanation concerning ethical principles and their application. As Paul DiMaggio remarked when I told him my intention to write this paper: "Yes, economic ethics is all about eliminating personal influence from organizations, while economic sociology is all about finding personal influence in organizations." Max Weber lost to Schumpeter and Hayek. On the whole, views of the economy as an autonomous, distinctive sphere of human activity organized around rationality and efficiency have impeded the serious consideration of morality's place in economic life.

This preliminary survey does not take up every question of morality that comes up in economic activity. Instead, it closes in on one crucial junction between morality and economic life: the formation and operation of formal ethical codes within different sorts of economic activity. The paper identifies a series of questions about ethical codes that deserve serious theoretical and empirical attention from economic sociologists and illustrates the interest of those questions by referring to a variety of existing empirical analyses. By "formal ethical codes" I mean a codified set of rules for moral behavior applying to a specific population. In codes, according to Charles Tilly, "reasons given for actions cite their conformity to specialized sets of categories, procedures for ordering evidence, and rules of interpretation. Together, categories, procedures, and rules make up codes" (2006, 102). They include ethical codes labeled as such but also implementation in the form of grievance procedures and do-don't statements of principle.

One further narrowing of this subject matters. Here I concentrate on codes adopted by economic organizations, including professional organizations such as medical societies. That narrowing ignores powerful codes enacted by legislatures and governmental agencies, not to mention codes promulgated by religious bodies, advocacy groups, and clusters of intellectuals. Such codes, as we will see, sometimes put pressure on economic organizations. To treat them all in detail here, however, would hinder the work of systematizing the place of ethics in economic activity.

Ethical codes in economic organizations, then, apply categories, procedures, and rules to some specific group of actors. For example, corporate codes of ethics typically identify categories of contested behavior and of persons at risk from those behaviors, procedures for identifying and handling violations, and rules for implementing these principles within the corporation. Stonecipher suffered the penalties prescribed by just such a code. Five questions call for attention:

1. What are the distinctive properties of ethical codes?
2. How do they arise?

3. How do they produce their effects?
4. What produces violations?
5. How do codes and responses affect economic activity?

These are both empirical and analytical questions. The paper takes up each in turn.

DISTINCTIVE PROPERTIES OF CODES

An impressive proportion of economic organizations adopt formal ethical codes. In their survey of one thousand major U.S. corporations, Gary Weaver, Linda Klebe Treviño, and Philip Cochran found that 98 percent claimed to address ethical issues in some formal document, 78 percent explicitly cited codes of ethics, 51 percent had telephone lines for reporting ethical concerns, and 30 percent had offices for dealing with ethics and legal compliance. Nearly two-thirds of these offices were created in the 1990s (Weaver et al. 1999). Indeed, in a 2005 *Business Ethics* article, James Hyatt, a freelance business writer, notes:

> A lot of companies are singing the compliance blues these days, as they struggle to cope with the complexities of Sarbanes-Oxley legislation, passed in 2002 in the wake of financial scandals. . . . Corporations are rushing to learn ethics virtually overnight, and as they do so, a vast new industry of consultants and suppliers has emerged. The ethics industry has been born." (Hyatt 2005)

Hyatt cites the rush to ethics by Goldman Sachs, Citigroup, and The New York Times Company, among many others. In fact, world standards are already emerging for corporate ethical codes. A Harvard Business School research team has created a so-called Global Business Standards Codex synthesizing the ethical principles and rules that recur in the most prestigious and influential codes (Paine et al. 2005). From those codes the team distills eight recurrent principles: fiduciary, property, reliability, transparency, dignity, fairness, citizenship, and responsiveness. Looked at more closely, the codes involved synthesize Tilly's categories, procedures, and rules. Codes are in vogue.

Codes may conform to general moral principles such as "do no harm." But they often go beyond general principles by specifying (a) categories of persons, activities, and sites of activity to which they apply; (b) procedures for identifying instances of those categories; and (c) rules distinguishing between required and banned activities in those circumstances. They sometimes also specify (d) penalties for banned activities. Ethical codes governing sexual behavior within a corporation, for example, typically state to whom, what, and where they apply (do offsite liaisons matter?); who should report a violation and how (does every employee who learns of an illicit affair have an obligation to report it, and if so to whom?); exactly what counts as a violation (does recurrent flirting without further sexual relations transgress the code?); and what penalties transgressors should receive (does a violation lead to automatic firing?).

In addition to sexual behavior, ethical codes often govern other forms of intimacy. FedEx's extensive "Code of Business Conduct and Ethics" of 2003, for example, illustrates its principles with this Q&A:

> Question: I believe that I did not receive a promotion because my manager knows that I am attempting to become pregnant. I heard my manager say that when a woman becomes pregnant, it inevitably interferes with job performance. Is there anything I can do?
> Answer: Yes. All employment-related decisions at FedEx (e.g., promotion, remuneration, training, etc.) must be based on job-related criteria, skills, and performance. You should use the complaint processes within your operating company or report the situation to our human resources representative or to your company's legal department. A report could also be made using the FedEx Alert Line."[3]

As compared with the rules of thumb and matters of degree that most people adopt when facing everyday moral questions, codes describe sharp boundaries between acceptable and unacceptable behavior. In its 1989 company handbook, the giant retailer Wal-Mart, for example, forbade married employees (whether separated or not) from dating other employees of the firm. When a romantic couple fell under the ban and lost their Wal-Mart jobs, they sued. In a 1995 landmark case a New York court upheld the company's ban.[4] Later, however, Wal-Mart dropped that provision, restricting its prohibition to relationships between supervisors and employees (Sugarman 2003). The pertinent section of its 2005 "Statement of Ethics" reads: "You may not date or become romantically involved with another Associate if you can influence that Associate's terms and conditions of employment or if that Associate can influence the terms and conditions of your employment."[5] Such regulations do not necessarily work well outside the United States. In 2005, for example, workers' representatives from Wal-Mart's ninety-one German stores successfully blocked in court the installation of a ban on interoffice dating.[6]

In 1998, *Business Week* reported a remarkable variant on codes governing office romance: the so-called cupid contract. "A few months back," reported the magazine:

> Garry G. Mathiason, senior partner with Littler, Mendelson, Fastiff, Tichy & Mathiason, the nation's largest employment law firm, got a

call from a very sheepish general counsel for a major company. The president of the company, the counsel said, "is planning to have a consensual affair with one of his employees," but before he does, "he wants to draft a written agreement" stating that the affair is voluntary—to reduce the chance that the woman might file a sexual-harassment suit if they broke up. "You won't believe it," Mathiason assured the nervous counsel. "But we've already drafted a standard form" for just such cases. (Symonds et al. 1998)

Legal scholar Vicki Schultz (2003) identifies such regulations as attempts to create a "sanitized workplace." According to Schultz, codes and compacts of this sort not only stifle creative collaboration within economic organizations but, even more dangerously, they also distract the same organizations from more profound sources of gender inequality. Whether or not they produce such deleterious effects, codes regularly mark sharp boundaries that employees' behavior must not transgress.

Ethical codes, furthermore, often attach penalties for infractions that bear little relationship to the economic organization's loss from the infraction. The Johnson and Johnson corporation pioneered ethical codes as early as the 1940s. Researcher Michael Lindsay reports an interview with former Johnson and Johnson CEO Ralph Larsen, who made a striking comparison. As a young executive in the early 1960s, Larsen had made an egregious ordering error that cost the company $25,000, a very large sum for the time. The executive recalls his fear that his mistake would cost him his job.

Instead, Larsen recalled: "My boss called me in, and he said, you learn anything? He asked me what happened. And I say, yeah. He said, get out of here. That was the end of it." About the same time, another Johnson and Johnson employee who walked out of the plant with two bottles of baby shampoo lost his job immediately: "Never saw him again. He was fired immediately. These were things, you know coming off the line in the thousands" (Lindsay 2006). The ethical boundary was sharp and the penalty immediate.

How Do Ethical Codes Arise?

Three rather different circumstances promote the formation of ethical codes: external pressure, emulation, and internal crisis. First, external authorities sometimes insist on enacting internal codes as they enforce conformity to tax codes, professional standards, or licensing of specialized services. Second, prestigious organizations provide models of internal regulation that other organizations adopt readily as ways of demonstrating their own effectiveness and/or membership in an elite circle. Third, internal crises often generate new rules, and sometimes whole codes—especially if the crisis produces a moral debate within the organization or a scandal that tarnishes the organization's public reputation (March et al. 2000). Family businesses appear to be somewhat less vulnerable to such pressures; at least they less frequently install formal codes of ethics (Adams et al. 1996).

Crises have been generating codes for a long time. Paul Starr points out that the relatively weak nineteenth-century American Medical Association adopted its code of ethics in response to a deep crisis: loss of protection against standard medicine's rivals when a competition-loving New York State repealed its licensing statutes in 1844. In this crisis, according to Starr:

> The orthodox profession could no longer look to the state for protection against what it viewed as the degradation of its standards. This was the impetus for the AMA's adoption of a code of professional ethics, with its concern for excluding sectarian and untrained practitioners. (Starr 1982, 91)

Among other things, the new code barred patient stealing, free advice to affluent friends, and public airing of disagreements concerning the proper treatment of a given patient (Starr 1982, 94; Rothman 2002, 110). In short, the crisis caused orthodox physicians to close ranks in defense of a threatened monopoly.

Ethical codes have a long history in American business and professions (Abbott 1983). As early as the 1920s, Edgar L. Heermance published a compilation of codes of ethics, and the American Academy of Political and Social Science produced a special issue on the subject (Heermance 1924; "The Ethics" 1922). When external pressures or internal crises built up, firms regularly defended themselves by enacting codes.

After the Watergate and the Securities and Exchange Commission scandals of the 1970s, for example, many American corporations installed top-down ethical codes in which chief executives instructed their underlings on behavior that would avoid corporate disgrace. In an analysis of 119 conduct codes promulgated during the period, Donald Cressey and Charles Moore identified two spurs to production of new codes: defensive responses to the scandals themselves, and direct SEC pressure to eliminate false books as a device for concealing corporate misconduct (Cressey and Moore 1983, 56–57).

Top executives were not alone, however, in promoting ethical codes. In a comprehensive analysis of sexual harassment grievance procedures and antiharassment training from 1977 to 1997, Frank Dobbin and Erin Kelly (2007) show that personnel managers pushed the adoption of such practices over considerable resistance from company lawyers and substantial doubt that the practices reduced legal liability. The personnel experts—now relabeled human resources management specialists—defended their turf against lawyers who had been taking over concerns with civil rights, employment discrimination, and related matters. In short, external pressures combine with internal struggles to generate more extensive and explicit ethical codes.

How Do Ethical Codes Produce their Effects?

We must distinguish between two kinds of effects: display effects and enforcement effects. Enactment of a code almost always involves an element of display, advertising to people inside and outside the organization's vigilance, uprightness, and/or membership in an organizational elite. Many a code adopted for display suitably impresses the naive but leaves knowledgeable insiders smirking.

Enforcement effects concern direct influence over behavior within the organization. Leaving aside perverse effects such as sabotage and simple dissimulation, genuine enforcement effects for ethical codes operate through four clusters of causes:

(1) Most obviously but not necessarily most effectively, rewards for good behavior and penalties for bad behavior, if actually delivered, deter banned activities through threat, promise, or simple elimination of bad actors from the organization. Thus the dramatic firing of a cashier who dips his fingers into the till sends a signal to everyone else who handles the organization's money.

(2) As analysts of principal-agent relations regularly point out, selection eliminates candidates for ethically sensitive positions who lack credentials, previous records of reliability, or attributes employers associate with propensities for ethical uprightness. Potential cashiers generally undergo much more extensive screening for likely moral responsibility, say, than computer programmers do.

(3) Socialization also makes a difference. Assimilation into an organization where everyone evinces horror—or fright—at the very idea of falsifying accounts reinforces the reluctance of new members to cheat in that way, almost regardless of the likelihood of detection and punishment for falsifying accounts. As little effect as pious exhortations from CEOs are likely to have, daily teaching from fellow workers increases the effectiveness of ethical codes.

(4) More subtly, ethical behavior becomes part of the mutual expectations of organization members who are engaged in relations of reciprocity: my not breaking the rules increases the chances that in the future I will refrain from undercutting you as well as decreasing the likelihood that I will pull you down through guilt by association. Thus multiple developers of the same software come to owe each other protection of the software's secrets from outside competitors.

To be sure, each of the four enforcement effects remains vulnerable to collusion by code violators within the organization: joint concealment of violations from sanctioning agents, recruitment of confederates, socialization into code-violating subcultures, and mutual protection among violators. Yet when organizations' ethical codes do work, they do so through some combination of sanctions, selection, socialization, and mutual investment in interpersonal relations.

Visible sanctions get plenty of attention from corporate managers. In his 2005 best seller, *Winning*, famous manager Jack Welch speaks about "a culture of integrity":

> In such cultures, there can be no head fakes or winks. People who break the rules do not leave the company for "personal reasons" or to "spend more time with their families." They are hanged—publicly—and the reasons are made painfully clear to everyone.
>
> Perhaps the lawyers will warn you against saying too much. But if you've got the facts right, you should be comfortable laying out who broke the rules and how. There are enormous organizational benefits from making examples of people who have violated your policies. (2005, 151)

Similarly, online giant Google has issued an elaborate code of conduct that includes many a thou shalt and thou shalt not, but warns unambiguously that violations will receive punishment. In the code's 2004 version, fair employment practices; bans on harassment and discrimination; warnings against drugs, alcohol use, weapons use, and violence; exclusion of cats from company premises; controls over conflicts of interest; preservation of confidential information; maintaining accurate records; protecting company property; and obeying the law all find their way into the Google code. At the end, nevertheless, comes the sting:

> If you know of a situation or incident that you feel may violate this Code, please report it to your manager or to Human Resources. Your report will be reviewed and any Googler found to have violated any of the terms of this code will be subject to disciplinary action that may include termination of employment. We'll also take any appropriate steps to prevent any further violations.[7]

In code after code, the bottom line ends with dismissal. But curtailment of privileges, demotion, or even turnover for outside prosecution may also occur to wayward employees.

What happens, however, when malfeasance occurs at an organization's top? At times, whistle-blowers or conscientious professionals illustrate the combined effects of socialization and mutual investment. Robert Jackall identifies a fascinating variation on this theme: a British-trained chartered public accountant in a large American firm discovered that the company's top officers were bribing officials of foreign countries and fudging internal accounts, including pension funds, to their own financial advantage. After he had complained, Brady, the accountant, returned from a hospital stay to discover that the company had demoted and transferred him. Brady reported the problem to an influential friend within the corporation, who took the affair to the chair of the corporate board's audit committee. The company immediately fired the friend and escorted him from the building with armed guards (Jackall 1988, 108). Clearly, enforcement effects only work within limits set by the current structure of corporate power (see Morrill et al. 1997).

WHAT PRODUCES VIOLATIONS OF ETHICAL CODES?

Even well-articulated ethical codes suffer violations. Failure of the main code-enforcing factors—sanctions, selection, socialization, and mutual investment in interpersonal relations—makes violations possible but does not cause them directly.

What does? Broadly speaking, we can distinguish among (a) individual advantage, (b) interpersonal loyalty, and (c) unauthorized collective enterprises. In the presence of an ethical code, almost every organizational member has incentives to cheat at least now and then, if only to save effort. Those incentives become substantial when the member's organizational position puts resources or information at the member's disposition that, if used in violation of the code, would bring significant rewards outside the organization. But even in the absence of material rewards, abuse of job-related perquisites sometimes becomes the means of acquiring prestige, wielding influence, or receiving sexual favors.

Interpersonal loyalty figures in violations of ethical codes when the code requires reporting of unethical behavior, but mutual commitments within pairs or small clusters of coworkers inhibit that very reporting, because the likely damage to the violator would break bonds of loyalty. Whistle-blowers regularly face charges of disloyalty and self-aggrandizement.

Within economic organizations, workers often create unauthorized collective enterprises: organized factions and patron-client chains, systems of collaboration and job-trading, betting pools, gossip circuits, and more. Many of them do the organization no harm, and some even serve the organization by enhancing commitment or solving production problems (Granovetter 2007). To the extent that such enterprises develop their own internal solidarities and raisons d'être, chances nevertheless increase that they will have three kinds of effects on organizational life: generating violations of ethical codes in pursuit of the collective enterprise, enabling participants to screen their collective activities from organizational monitoring, and inhibiting individual participants from reporting infractions to higher authorities. Powerful organizational subcultures form in the shadows.

Michel Anteby uses his detailed observations of a French aerospace factory to illustrate the general practice he calls *poaching*, "the use of company machines or material on company time to create artifacts for employees' personal use" (Anteby 2003, 218). In the plant Anteby studied, workers regularly made parts for their own vehicles, barbecues, and domestic appliances. Strictly forbidden by the plant codes, these widespread practices depended on extensive collaborative enterprises. Bosses who learned about them, furthermore, often had little choice but to tolerate their subordinates' departure from the rules. In fact, as Anteby documents in detail, such unauthorized collective enterprises recur in a wide range of manufacturing. Those workers who actually receive punishment for this sort of violation typically have operated outside the conspiracy, or have somehow fallen out with its participants.

Managers themselves sometimes collude in their subordinates' evasion of well-defined ethical codes. Prohibitions on the exchange of gifts with outside contractors and officials typically raise dilemmas for sales personnel, so much so that corporate codes often exclude occasional exchanges of meals, entertainment, and symbolic objects from the ban on gifts. The Toys "R" Us 2003 ethics code, for example, declares:

> The Company generally prohibits the acceptance from suppliers or customers of the Company of any gifts or gratuities, whether in the form of money, merchandise, services, meals, entertainment, travel or any other form. If permitted by applicable law, a gift may be accepted by an associate from a supplier or a customer if the gift is (i) a perishable item (for example, food) that has little or no resale value, (ii) any other non-cash gift valued at less than $50 provided the gifts are not received on a regular or frequent basis, (iii) a meal or entertainment that is permitted by this paragraph, or (iv) approved by an Ombudsperson on the basis that acceptance of the particular gift serves a legitimate, business-related purpose.[8]

Calvin Morrill tells the tale of a major toy company dealing with suppliers in Southeast Asia. During a business trip, two prominent company officials accepted the supplier's gifts—Rolex watches for themselves, jade jewelry for their wives—on the belief that the gifts reinforced their company's ties to the supplier. The senior vice president to whom they reported objected vigorously to this violation of the company code, ordering the officials to return the gifts. Nevertheless, the vice president recognized the dilemma. He and the officials made the following arrangement: the vice president himself would travel to Asia for clarifying talks with the suppliers, and until then the two men would accept no further gifts. Nor did anyone report the violation to the company's ethics committee (Morrill 1995, 199). Thus, every code allows for nuances, exceptions, and minor subversions.

How do Codes and Responses to them Affect Economic Activity?

Even more so than in the case of the earlier questions, any prudent answer to this question runs like this: let us do a lot more systematic research, and then decide. So far, we have no systematic body of research and theory that allows us to pinpoint effects of organizations' ethical codes and organization members' responses to them. The closest we come is the recently superabundant discussion of corporate social responsibility (see, e.g., Bartley 2005). But even in that area, a comprehensive survey published in 2003 concludes that the widespread consensus on the positive effects of responsibility initiatives may result from an illusion (Margolis and Walsh 2003). Back to the drawing board! Throwing prudence to the winds, however, we can at least draw out the implications of my earlier arguments. If ethical codes, for example, substitute sharp yes-no boundaries for continua from unacceptable to meritorious behavior, we should expect two complementary effects to occur: concentration of organizational efforts at monitoring, control, and conformity itself precisely along that boundary, and displacement of dubious behavior into gray areas left gray by that concentration on the boundary. Thus we should find money-handlers punctilious about the transactions singled out by the code but ready to compromise or obfuscate when it comes to other transactions.

The sources of ethical codes should also make a difference. External pressure should, in principle, produce quasi-conspiracies in which an organization's members (or at least its chief monitors) create collective performances that will satisfy external agencies without necessarily rectifying abuses in the areas under scrutiny. Emulation of prestigious organizations should produce an even greater fixation on labels and procedures, and even less internal monitoring of the code's effects. Internal crisis, in contrast, most likely produces more extensive efforts to construct explanations of what went wrong, greater elaborations of prohibitions and penalties based on those explanations (however valid), broader internal monitoring, and serious impacts on employee behavior.

As for how codes produce their effects, the distinction between display effects and enforcement effects again clarifies the question. To the extent that displays respond to pressure from powerful external agencies, we can expect them to shift the organization's visible performances in the directions demanded by those agencies. To the extent that the displays serve the purposes of advertising, executive self-esteem, or organizational self-image, however, we should expect relatively superficial effects on actual organizational performance as represented either by interactions among internal segments or by aggregate output in the form of efficiency, productivity, profitability, or quality of goods and services produced.

When it comes to enforcement effects, we enter a likely zone of fascinating but controversial results. Do clearly announced rewards and punishments for coded behavior, selection, deliberate socialization, or the integration of codes into interpersonal relations affect overall performance differently? For future investigation, I suggest the following hypotheses:

(1) The four sorts of enforcement effects fall into an ascending order of cost to managers, with selection generally easier to perform, new rewards and penalties relatively cheap to put into place (at least initially), interpersonal relations costly to penetrate, and socialization in between.

(2) The extent of organizational transformation that results from the four enforcement effects falls in precisely the opposite order, with penetration of interpersonal relations far more transformative than socialization, selection, and, especially, generally applied rewards and punishments.

(3) Nevertheless, as before, the institution of ethical codes generally concentrates attention along the boundaries identified explicitly in the codes and shifts dubious behavior toward unspecified gray areas.

(4) Codes always become instruments of internal power struggles, and therefore vary greatly in their overall effects, depending on internal structures of, and struggles over, power.

These risky hypotheses follow more or less directly from my earlier arguments. That is, of course, no guarantee that they are correct. They call out for systematic research.

I also proposed earlier that violations of codes spring from three sources: individual advantage, interpersonal loyalty, and unauthorized collective enterprises. If so, we should discover distinctly different effects of ethical codes depending on which of the three prevails. We could reasonably expect codes entailing specific rewards and punishments for specific forms of behavior to shift individual advantage visibly and rapidly. Interpersonal loyalty is likely to resist the application of codes more tenaciously but to be vulnerable to public disclosure.

Unauthorized collective enterprises offer the most interesting challenge both to codes and to analysts. Surely we would first have to know how much workers have invested in the enterprise: a betting pool disappears more easily than an internal system of job collaboration. But in general we should suppose that unauthorized collective enterprises lend their participants the capacity to preserve the enterprise while altering visible signs and behaviors enough to simulate conformity with publicly announced ethical codes.

ECONOMIC SOCIOLOGY AND ETHICS: FUTURE AGENDA

For the purposes of this paper, I have narrowed the scope of ethics radically. Codes are crucial, but they do not exhaust the topic. Three agendas follow: first, we need to examine the relationship between general ethical contexts and the specific forms of code that organizations adopt. We might reasonably expect, for example, that national ethical traditions shape contrasting approaches to both the construction and the contents of formal ethical codes (see, e.g., Langlois and Schlegelmilch 1990).

Second, we can appropriately ask how differently more general ethical principles such as "do no harm," "render good for good," and "act fairly" operate as compared with the boundary defining codes that I have reviewed here. It could well be, for example, that general principles of this kind have stronger effects on organizational behavior than explicit codes to the extent that the principles involved belong to the cultural context and cover a wider range of behavior than economic activity within organizations.

Beyond those two relatively manageable agendas for economic sociology looms a much larger set of questions that many economic sociologists might prefer to avoid. Critics of capitalism often complain that the system itself incorporates unethical principles, such as exploitation, profit-maximization, and neglect of the vulnerable. Advocates of what the French call *économie solidaire* and *commerce equitable*, for example, do not merely propose building greater solidarity into existing economic relations but claim that such arrangements as microcredits, cooperatives, and alternative currencies (*monnaies sociales*) implement superior ethical principles (see, e.g., Blanc 2006; Le Velly 2006; Mertz 2005; Servet and Guérin 2002).

Similarly, advocates of corporate responsibility, social democracy, welfare capitalism, and radical environmentalism claim superiority for their own ethical principles. Whether or not economic sociologists subscribe to such programs, they ought to consider whether capitalism and its alternatives spring from competing ethical principles, and if so, how.

NOTES

Viviana A. Zelizer, "Ethics in the Economy," *Journal for Business, Economics and Ethics* (*Zeitschrift für Wirtschafts- und Unternehmensethik*) 1 (2007): 8–23. Reprinted with permission.

1. "Ethical Business Conduct Guidelines," 5. Boeing, http://www.boeing.com/companyoffices/aboutus/ethics/ethics_booklet.pdf (accessed July 19, 2006).

2. http://www.globalethics.org/newsline/members/issue.tmpl?articleid=03140519022148 (accessed July 18, 2006).

3. FedEx, "Code of Business Conduct and Ethics," 4, http://fdx.client.shareholder.com/downloads/code.pdf (accessed July 18, 2006).

4. *State v. Wal-Mart Stores, Inc.* 621 N.Y.S. 2d. 158 (N.Y.A.D. 3 Dept. Jan 05, 1995).

5. http://media.corporate-innet/media_files/IROL/11/112761/corpgov/Ethics%20_Current.pdf (accessed July 18, 2006), 16.

6. http://www.germany.info/relaunch/info/publications/week/2005/050617/economy1.html (accessed July 18, 2006). That court action was only one sign of Wal-Mart's incompatibility with German corporate culture. In 2006, the big firm pulled out of Germany.

7. http://investor.google.com/conduct.html (accessed July 18, 2006), 11.

8. http://media.corporate-innet/media_files/irol/12/120622/Corp%20Gov/Code_of_Ethics_031504.pdf (accessed July 19, 2006), 5.

References

Abbott, A. 1983. "Professional Ethics." *American Journal of Sociology* 88 (March): 855–85.

Adams, J. S., A. Taschian, and T. Shore. 1996. "Ethics in Family and Non-family Owned Firms: An Exploratory Study." *Family Business Review* 9:157–70.

Anderson, E. 1993. *Value in Ethics and Economics.* Cambridge, Mass.: Harvard University Press.

Anteby, M. 2003. "The 'Moralities' of Poaching: Manufacturing Personal Artifacts on the Factory Floor." *Ethnography* 4:217–39.

Ashforth, B. E., and V. Anand. 2003. "The Normalization of Corruption in Organizations." *Research in Organizational Behavior* 25:1–52.

Baker, W. E., and R. R. Faulkner. 2004. "Social Networks and Loss of Capital." *Social Networks* 26:91–111.

Bartley, T. 2005. "Corporate Accountability and the Privatization of Labor Standards: Struggles over Codes of Conduct in the Apparel Industry." *Research in Political Sociology* 14:211–44.

Blanc, J. ed. 2006. "Exclusion et liens financiers: Monnaies sociales." In *Rapport 2005–2006*, 535–38. Paris: Economica.

Buchanan, A. 1985. *Ethics, Efficiency, and the Market.* Totowa, N.J.: Rowman and Allanheld.

Cressey, D. R., and C. A. Moore. 1983. "Managerial Values and Corporate Codes of Ethics." *California Management Review* 25:53–77.

Dobbin, F., and E. Kelly. 2007. "How to Stop Harassment: Professional Construction of Legal Compliance in Organizations." *American Journal of Sociology* 112 (January): 1,203–43.

"The Ethics of the Professions and of Business." 1922. *Annals of the American Academy of Political and Social Science*. Vol. 101, entire issue.

Frank, R. H. 2003. *What Price the Moral High Ground? Ethical Dilemmas in Competitive Environments*. Princeton, N.J.: Princeton University Press.

Gilligan, C. 1982. *In a Different Voice: Psychological Theory and Women's Development*. Cambridge, Mass.: Harvard University Press.

Granovetter, M. 2007. "The Social Construction of Corruption." In *On Capitalism*, edited by V. Nee and R. Swedberg. Stanford, Calif.: Stanford University Press.

Hausman, D. M., and M. S. McPherson. 1993. "Taking Ethics Seriously: Economics and Contemporary Moral Philosophy." *Journal of Economic Literature* 31 (June): 671–731.

Heermance, E. L. 1924. *Codes of Ethics*. Burlington, Vt.: Free Press.

Held, V. 2005. *The Ethics of Care: Personal, Political, and Global*. New York: Oxford University Press.

Hyatt, J. C. 2005. "Birth of the Ethics Industry." *Business Ethics* (Summer): http://www.business-ethics.com/current_issue/summer_2005_birth.html.

Jackall, R. 1988. *Moral Mazes: The World of Corporate Managers*. New York: Oxford University Press.

Langlois, C. C., and B. B. Schlegelmilch. 1990. "Do Corporate Codes of Ethics Reflect National Character? Evidence from Europe and the United States." *Journal of International Business Studies* 21:519–39.

Larson, A. L., and R. E. Freeman, eds. 1997. *Women's Studies and Business Ethics: Toward a New Conversation*. New York: Oxford University Press.

Le Velly, R. 2006. "Le commerce equitable: Des échanges marchands contre et dans le marché." *Revue Française de Sociologie* 47:319–40.

Lindsay, M. 2006. Personal communication. Interview conducted by D. Michael Lindsay, Princeton University, with Ralph Larsen, former CEO of Johnson and Johnson, June 23, 2004, at Larsen's residence in Wycoff, N.J.

March, J. G., M. Schulz, and X. Zhou. 2000. *The Dynamics of Rules: Change in Written Organizational Codes*. Stanford, Calif.: Stanford University Press.

Margolis, J. D., and J. P. Walsh. 2003. "Misery Loves Companies: Rethinking Social Initiatives by Business." *Administrative Science Quarterly* 48:268–305.

McCloskey, D. 2006. *The Bourgeois Virtues: Ethics for an Age of Commerce*. Chicago: University of Chicago Press.

Mertz, F., ed. 2005. *Ethique et commerce: Réalités et illusions*. Paris: Harmattan.

Morrill, C. 1995. *The Executive Way: Conflict Management in Corporations*. Chicago: University of Chicago Press.

Morrill, C., E. Snyderman, and E. J. Dawson. 1997. "It's Not What You Do, but Who You Are: Informal Social Control, Social Status, and Normative Seriousness in Organizations." *Sociological Forum* 12:519–43.

Nelson, J. A. 2006. *Economics for Humans*. Chicago: University of Chicago Press.

Paine, L., R. Deshpande, J. D. Margolis, and K. E. Bettcher. 2005. "Up to Code: Does Your Company's Conduct Meet World-Class Standards?" *Harvard Business Review* (December): 122–33.

Palmer, D., and M. W. Maher. 2006. "Developing the Process Model of Collective Corruption." *Journal of Management Inquiry* 15 (December): 1–8.

Richardson, J. E., ed. 2007. *Business Ethics*. 18th ed. Dubuque, Iowa: McGraw-Hill Contemporary Learning Series.

Rosenberg, J. S. 2006. "An Education in Ethics: Teaching Business Students Life Lessons in Leadership." *Harvard Business Magazine* 109(1) (September–October): 42–49, 102–3.

Rothman, D. J. 2002. "Money and Medicine: What Should Physicians Earn, and Be Paid?" In *The Economist as a Public Intellectual*, edited by I. L. Horowitz and E. Ginzberg, 107–20. New Brunswick, N.J.: Transaction.

Schultz, V. 2003. "The Sanitized Workplace." *Yale Law Journal* 112:2061.

Sen, A. 1987. *On Ethics and Economics*. Oxford: Blackwell.

Servet, J. M., and I. Guérin, eds. 2002. *Exclusion et liens financiers: Rapport du Centre Walras*. Paris: Economica.

Starr, P. 1982. *The Social Transformation of American Medicine*. New York: Basic Books.

Sugarman, S. D. 2003. " 'Lifestyle' Discrimination in Employment." *Berkeley Journal of Employment and Labor Law* 24:377.

Swedberg, R. 2005. "Capitalism and Ethics: How Conflicts-of-Interest Legislation Can Be Used to Handle Moral Dilemmas in the Economy." *International Social Science Journal* 57:481–92.

Symonds, W. C., S. Hamm, and G. De George. 1998. "Sex on the Job." *Business Week*, http://www.businessweek.com/1998/07/b3565063.htm (accessed July 18, 2006).

Tilly, C. 2006. *Why?* Princeton, N.J.: Princeton University Press.

Tronto, J. C. 1993. *Moral Boundaries: A Political Argument for an Ethic of Care*. New York: Routledge.

Vaughan, D. 1999. "The Dark Side of Organizations: Mistake, Misconduct, and Disaster." *Annual Review of Sociology* 25:271–305.

Weaver, G. R., L. K. Treviño, and P. L. Cochran. 1999. "Corporate Ethics Practices in the Mid-1990's: An Empirical Study of the Fortune 1000." *Journal of Business Ethics* 18:283–94.

Welch, J. 2005. *Winning*. New York: HarperCollins.

Zelizer, V. A. 1979. *Morals and Markets: The Development of Life Insurance in the United States*. New York: Columbia University Press.

———. 2005. *The Purchase of Intimacy*, Princeton, N.J.: Princeton University Press.

Published Works of Viviana A. Zelizer on Economic Sociology

BOOKS

1979. *Morals and Markets: The Development of Life Insurance in the United States.* New York: Columbia University Press. Paperback edition, New Brunswick, N.J.: Transaction Books, 1983. Japanese edition, Tokyo: Chikura Shobo, 1994.

1985. *Pricing the Priceless Child: The Changing Social Value of Children.* New York: Basic Books. Paperback edition, Basic Books, 1987. Revised paperback edition, Princeton, N.J.: Princeton University Press, 1994. Chinese edition, Shanghai: Shanghai People's Publishing House, 2009.

1994. *The Social Meaning of Money.* New York: Basic Books. Paperback editions, Basic Books, 1995; Princeton, N.J.: Princeton University Press, 1997. Chinese edition, Hsin-Tien City, Taiwan: Cheng Chung Book Co., 2004. French edition, Paris: Editions du Seuil, 2005. Russian edition, Moscow: Higher School of Economics, 2004. Spanish edition, Buenos Aires, Argentina: Fondo de Cultura Económica, forthcoming.

2005. *The Purchase of Intimacy.* Princeton, N.J.: Princeton University Press. Paperback edition, Princeton University Press, 2007. Chinese edition, Shanghai: Shanghai People's Publishing House, 2009. Korean edition, Seoul: Eco-Livre, forthcoming. Spanish edition, Buenos Aires, Argentina: Fondo de Cultura Económica, 2009.

2009. *Vite economiche.* Bologna: Il Mulino, 2009.

SELECTED ARTICLES

1978. "Human Values and the Market: The Case of Life Insurance and Death in 19th Century America." *American Journal of Sociology* 84 (November): 591–610.

1981. "The Price and Value of Children: The Case of Children's Insurance in the United States." *American Journal of Sociology* 86 (March): 1,036–56. German translation, "Preis und Wert von Kindern: Die Kinderversicherung." In *Macht der Unschuld: Das Kind als Chiffre*, edited by Doris Bühler-Niederberger, 123–48. Wiesbaden: VS Verlag für Sozialwissenschaften, 2005.

1986. "Pricing Life: A Historical and Sociological Perspective." In *Risk and Reason*, edited by Per Oftedal and Anton Brogger, 59–70. New York: Alan R. Liss.

1988. "Beyond the Polemics on the Market: Establishing a Theoretical and Empirical Agenda." *Sociological Forum* 3 (Fall): 614–34.

————. "From Baby Farms to Baby M." *Society* 25 (March/April): 23–28.

1989. "The Social Meaning of Money: 'Special Monies.'" *American Journal of Sociology* 95 (September): 342–77. Portuguese translation, "O significado social do dinheiro: 'Dinheiros especiais.'" In *A nova sociologia económica*, edited by Rafael Marques and João Peixoto, 125–65. Oreiras, Portugal: Celta.

1992. "Money." In the *Encyclopedia of Sociology*, edited by Edgard F. Borgatta and Marie L. Borgatta, 1,304–10. New York: Macmillan. (2nd ed., 2000, 1,888–94.)

————. "Repenser le marché." *Actes de la Recherche en Sciences Sociales* 94 (September): 3–26.

1993. "Making Multiple Monies." In *Explorations in Economic Sociology*, edited by Richard Swedberg, 193–212. New York: Russell Sage Foundation.

1994. "The Creation of Domestic Currencies." *American Economic Review Papers and Proceedings* 84 (May): 138–42.

1996. "Payments and Social Ties." *Sociological Forum* 11 (September): 481–95.

1997. "The Many Enchantments of Money." In *Sociological Visions*, edited by Kai Erickson, 83–93. New York: Rowman and Littlefield.

1998. "How Do We Know Whether a Monetary Transaction Is a Gift, an Entitlement, or a Payment?" In *Economics, Values, and Organization*, edited by Avner Ben-Ner and Louis Putterman, 329–33. New York: Cambridge University Press.

————. "How People Talk about Money." Special issue, "Changing Forms of Payment," edited by Viviana A. Zelizer. *American Behavioral Scientist* 41 (August): 1,373–83.

————. "The Proliferation of Social Currencies." In *The Laws of the Markets*, edited by Michel Callon, 58–68. Oxford: Blackwell.

————. "Social Context and Monetary Transfers." In *Il denaro nella cultura moderna*, edited by Carlo Mongardini, 139–47. Rome: Bulzoni.

1999. "Multiple Markets, Multiple Cultures." In *Diversity and Its Discontents: Cultural Conflict and Common Ground in Contemporary American Society*, edited by Neil Smelser and Jeffrey Alexander, 193–212. Princeton, N.J.: Princeton University Press. German translation, "Die Farben des Geldes, Vielfalt der Märkte, Vielfalt der Kulturen." Special issue, "The Power of Money." *Berliner Journal für Soziologie* 10 (2000): 315–32.

————. "Official Standardization vs. Social Differentiation in Americans' Uses of Money." In *Nation-States and Money: The Past, Present and Future of National Currencies*, edited by Emily Gilbert and Eric Helleiner, 82–96. London: Routledge.

2000. "Fine Tuning the Zelizer View." *Economy and Society* 29 (August): 383–89.

————. "From Child Labor to Child Work: Changing Cultural Conceptions of Children's Economic Roles, 1870s–1930s." In *Ideas, Ideologies, and Social Movements: The U.S. Experience since 1800*, edited by Stuart Bruchey and Peter Coclanis, 90–101. Columbia: University of South Carolina Press.

————. "Monetization and Social Life." *Etnofoor* 13:5–15.

————. "The Purchase of Intimacy." *Law and Social Inquiry* 25 (Summer): 817–48.

2001. "Economic Sociology." In *International Encyclopedia of the Social and Behavioral Sciences*, edited by Neil J. Smelser and Paul B. Baltes, 6:4,128–31. Amsterdam: Elsevier.

———. "Sociology of Money." In *International Encyclopedia of the Social and Behavioral Sciences*, edited by Neil J. Smelser and Paul B. Baltes, 15:9,991–94. Amsterdam: Elsevier.

2002. "La construction des circuits de commerce: Notes sur l'importance des circuits personnels et impersonnels." In *Exclusion et liens financiers: Rapport du Centre Walras*, edited by Jean-Michel Servet and Isabelle Guérin, 425–29. Paris: Economica.

———. "Enter Culture." In *The New Economic Sociology: Developments in an Emerging Field*, edited by Mauro F. Guillén, Randall Collins, Paula England, and Marshall Meyer, 101–25. New York: Russell Sage Foundation. French translation, "Place à la culture." Special issue, "Sociologie économique: Quoi de neuf?" *Interventions Economiques* 33 (April 2006): http://www.teluq.uquebec .ca/pls/inteco/rie.entree?vno_revue=1.

———. "How Care Counts." *Contemporary Sociology* 31 (March): 115–19.

———. "Intimate Transactions." In *The New Economic Sociology: Developments in an Emerging Field*, edited by Mauro F. Guillén, Randall Collins, Paula England, and Marshall Meyer, 274–300. New York: Russell Sage Foundation. French translation, "Transactions intimes." *Genèses* 42 (March 2001): 121–44.

———. "Kids and Commerce." *Childhood* 4 (November): 375–96.

2004. "Circuits of Commerce." In *Self, Social Structure, and Beliefs: Explorations in Sociology*, edited by Jeffrey C. Alexander, Gary T. Marx, and Christine Williams, 122–44. Berkeley: University of California Press.

2005. "Argent, circuits, relations intimes." *Enfances, Familles, Générations* (Spring). http://www.erudit.org/revue/efg/2005/v/n2/index.html.

———. "Circuits within Capitalism." In *The Economic Sociology of Capitalism*, edited by Victor Nee and Richard Swedberg, 289–322. Princeton, N.J.: Princeton University Press.

———. "Culture and Consumption." In *The Handbook of Economic Sociology*, edited by Neil Smelser and Richard Swedberg, 2nd ed., 331–54. Princeton, N.J.: Princeton University Press; New York: Russell Sage Foundation.

———. "Intimate Truths." *Guardian*, September 24. Reprinted in *Ha'aretz*, September 29.

———. "Intimité et économie." *Terrain* 45 (September): 13–28.

———. "Missing Monies." *Economy and Society* 34 (November): 584–88.

———. "The Priceless Child Revisited." In *Studies in Modern Childhood: Society, Agency and Culture*, edited by Jens Qvortrup, 184–200. London: Palgrave.

———. "To Commodify or Not to Commodify: That Is *Not* the Question." With Joan Williams. In *Rethinking Commodification: Cases and Readings in Law and Culture*, edited by Martha Ertman and Joan Williams, 362–82. New York: New York University Press.

2006. "Children, 'Good Matches,' and Policies for Care." Research note, Working Group on Childhood and Migration, May. http://globalchild.rutgers.edu/ index.htm.

———. "Do Markets Poison Intimacy?" *Contexts* 5 (Spring): 33–38.

———. "Money, Power, and Sex." *Yale Journal of Law and Feminism* 18:303ff.

———. "La sociología del dinero." In *Diccionario de sociología*, edited by Salvador Giner, Emilio Lamo de Espinosa, and Cristóbal Torres. 2d ed. Madrid: Alianza Editorial.

———. With Charles Tilly. "Relations and Categories." In *The Psychology of Learning and Motivation*, vol. 47, edited by Brian Ross and Arthur Markman, 1–31. San Diego: Elsevier.

2007. "Monétisation et vie sociale." Special issue, "Philosophies de l'argent," edited by Jean-Ives Trépos. *Portique* 19:43–58. French translation of "Monetization and Social Life." *Etnofoor* 13 (2000): 5–15.

———. "Pasts and Futures of Economic Sociology." Special issue, "Coming and Going in Economic Sociology," edited by Nicole Woolsey Biggart. *American Behavioral Scientist* 50 (April): 1,056–69.

———. "The Purchase of Criticism." *Sociological Forum* 22 (December): 612–17.

———. "Reflections on Intimacy." *Accounts* (newsletter of the Economic Sociology Section of the American Sociological Association) (Spring): 10–12.

2008. "Dinero, circuitos, relaciones íntimas." *Sociedad y Economía* 14 (June): 11–33. Spanish translation of "Argent, circuits, relations intimes." *Enfances, Familles, Générations* (Spring 2005).

———. "L'économie du care." *Revue Française de Socio-Economie* 2:13–25.

———. "Ethics in the Economy." *Accounts* (newsletter of the Economic Sociology Section of the American Sociological Association) (Summer): 2–12. Revised version of paper published in *Journal for Business, Economics and Ethics* (*Zeitschrift für Wirtschafts- und Unternehmensethik*) 1 (2007): 8–23.

———. "Pagos y lazos sociales." *Crítica en desarrollo: Revista Latinoamericana de Ciencias Sociales* 2:43–61. Spanish translation of "Payments and Social Ties." *Sociological Forum* 11 (September 1996): 481–95.

———. "The Real Economy." *Qualitative Sociology* 31 (June): 189–93.

———. "La rémuneration des services d'aide à la personne." *Retraites et sociétés* 53 (January): 14–19.

2009. "Dinheiro, poder e sexo." *Cadernos Pagu 32* (June): 135–57. Portuguese translation of "Money, Power, and Sex." *Yale Journal of Law and Feminism* 18 (2006): 303ff.

———. "Dualidades perigosas." *Mana: Studies in Social Anthropology* 15 (April): 241–60.

———. "Intimacy in Economic Organizations." In *Economic Sociology of Work*, edited by Nina Bandelj, 23–55. Vol. 19 of *Research in the Sociology of Work*. Bingley, U.K.: Emerald.

2010. "Risky Exchanges." In *Baby Markets: Money and the New Politics of Creating Families*, edited by Michele Goodwin. New York: Cambridge University Press.

———. "Caring Everywhere." In *Intimate Labors: Cultures, Technologies, and the Politics of Care*, edited by Rhacel Parreñas and Eileen Boris. Stanford, Calif.: Stanford University Press.

———. "Culture and Uncertainty." In *Robert K. Merton: Sociological Theory and the Sociology of Science*, edited by Craig Calhoun. New York: Columbia University Press.

———. "Moralizing Consumption." *Journal of Consumer Culture*.

Selected Interviews

2006. "Le commerce de l'intimité." By Xavier de la Vega. *Sciences Humaines* (December): 40–41.

—. "Viviana Zelizer: L'argent social." By Florence Weber. *Genèses* 65 (December): 126–37.

2007. "Interview: Viviana Zelizer Answers Ten Questions about Economic Sociology." *European Economic Sociology Newsletter* 8 (July): 41–45.

—. "Viviana Zelizer on Money and Intimacy." *EconTalk*, February 26. http://www.econtalk.org/archives/2007/02/viviana_zelizer.html.

2009. "Los intelectuales." *Nación*, May 27. http://www.lanacion.com.ar/nota.asp?nota_id=1132610.

—. "Rethinking Markets, Monies, and Organizations: An Interview with Viviana A. Zelizer." By David Franz. *Hedgehog Review* 11 (Summer): 66–75.